New Voices in Native American Literary Criticism

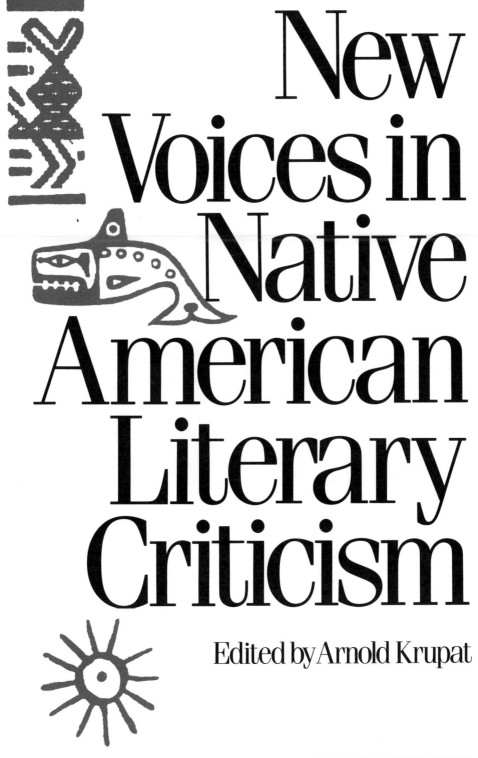

New Voices in Native American Literary Criticism

Edited by Arnold Krupat

SMITHSONIAN INSTITUTION PRESS
Washington and London

© 1993 by the Smithsonian Institution
All rights reserved

Copy Editors: Gregory McNamee and Jessica Alma Ryan
Production Editor: Duke Johns
Designer: Janice Wheeler

Library of Congress Cataloging-in-Publication Data
New voices in native American literary criticism / edited by Arnold Krupat.
    p. cm.
  Includes bibliographical references and index.
  ISBN 1-56098-201-2 (alk. paper : cloth).—ISBN 1-56098-226-8
(alk. paper : pbk.)
   1. Indian literature—History and criticism. 2. American
literature—Indian authors—History and criticism. I. Krupat,
Arnold.
PM155.N48   1993
897—dc20   92-18673

British Library Cataloguing-in-Publication Data is available

Manufactured in the United States of America
00 99 98 97 96 95 94 93   5 4 3 2 1

∞ The paper in this publication meets the minimum requirements of the American National
Standard for Permanence of Paper for Printed Library Materials Z39.48-1984

The cloth design, fish, and sun figures on the cover and title page are taken from various
Smithsonian Institution Bureau of American Ethnology bulletins. The cloth design is a pattern
used by the Cayapa Indians of Ecuador.

FOR BRIAN SWANN AND PETER WHITELEY

CONTENTS

PART 2: AUTHORS AND ISSUES

CONTRIBUTORS

CRISCA BIERWERT has worked with Lushootseed and Halkomelem Salish people of Washington state and British Columbia for fifteen years. Her academic research focuses on the politics and semiotics of arts including visual aesthetics, land use, and oral and written literatures. She is the editor of a forthcoming volume of Lushootseed Texts. Her work in Salish communities has included community education, curriculum development, writing, and resource rights advocacy. Holding a Ph.D. from the University of Washington, she now teaches anthropology at the University of Michigan.

KIMBERLY M. BLAESER is an assistant professor in the English and Comparative Literature Department at the University of Wisconsin-Milwaukee. A mixed-blood of Ojibway and German ancestry from the White Earth Reservation in Minnesota, she teaches twentieth-century American literature, including courses in Native American literature and American nature writing. Her publications include personal essays, poems, reviews, and scholarly articles, as well as the book *Gerald Vizenor: Writing in the Oral Tradition* (University of Oklahoma Press, 1993).

ALANNA KATHLEEN BROWN is an associate professor of English at Montana State University. She received her doctorate from the University of California at Santa Barbara in 1974. Since teaching *Cogewea, the Half-Blood* in 1983, she has focused primary critical attention on understanding the life and works of Mourning Dove. Long-term projects include a publication of *Okanogan Sweathouse,* Mourning Dove's original, unedited collection of Salish tales; a literary biography on Mourning Dove for *The Western Writers Series;* and a book-length manuscript on the friendship and collaboration between L. V. McWhorter and Mourning Dove.

KATHLEEN A. DANKER is assistant professor of English at South Dakota State University in Brookings, South Dakota. She met Felix White, Sr., while she was employed as a VISTA (NOVA) worker in curriculum development on the Nebraska Winnebago Reservation from 1971 to 1972. In 1978, they published a volume of Winnebago stories for Winnebago youth entitled *The Hollow of Echoes* through the Nebraska curriculum Development Center of the University of Nebraska at Lincoln. Currently she is working on a volume of transcriptions and translations of Mr. White's oral Trickster narratives.

JAY COURTNEY FIKES completed his doctorate in anthropology at the University of Michigan in 1984 and since then has taught courses in cultural anthropology, policy research, and social science research methods at the United States International University, Marmara University in Istanbul, and New Mexico Highlands University. His new book, *Carlos Castaneda, Academic Opportunism, and the Psychedelic Sixties,* should stimulate debate about authenticity in studies of Native American religions. He is currently researching and writing about Huichol rituals as a postdoctoral fellow at the Smithsonian Institution. He does pro bono work for the Native American Church of North America.

BRIGITTE GEORGI-FINDLAY is an assistant professor of American literature at the John F. Kennedy Institute for North American Studies, Free University of Berlin, Germany. She received an M.A. in 1981 and a Ph.D. in 1985 from the University of Heidelberg and is the author of two books, *The Indian in American Literature* and *Tradition and Modernism in Contemporary Native American Literature,* both published in German. She is currently conducting research on women's frontier writings and the rhetoric of American westward expansion.

RIDIE WILSON GHEZZI received her doctorate from the Department of Folklore and Folklife at the University of Pennsylvania in 1990. Her area of concentration is Native American language and culture, with particular interest in Native American literature. Dr. Ghezzi is currently undertaking a Master of Science degree in library and information studies at Drexel University in Philadelphia.

WILLARD GINGERICH is dean of the Graduate School of Arts and Sciences at St. John's University, Jamaica, N.Y. His publications include essays on Chicano and Native American writers and on critical frameworks—William Empson, Heidegger, and oral formulaic and archetypal theory—for the reading of Aztec literature. His translations of the Quetzalcoatl narrative from the *Anales de Cuauhtitlán* and of the *Leyenda de los soles* manuscript appear in Markmans's *Myths of the Spirit*.

JANET WALL HENDRICKS carried out fieldwork among the Shuar of southeastern Ecuador in 1982–84 and in 1987. Her research interests include lowland South American Indians, life histories, indigenous political movements, and discourse-centered studies of culture. Her publications include essays in *American Ethnologist, Semiotica*, and *Journal of Folklore Research*.

WOLFGANG HOCHBRUCK currently holds a position as professor of American studies at the University of Osnabrück, Germany. He has published on American and Canadian literature, Native American studies, and American political rhetoric.

GEOFFREY KIMBALL is a postdoctoral fellow in the Department of Anthropology, Tulane University, New Orleans. He has published *Koasati Grammar* and *Koasati Dictionary*, which was written with the support of the National Science Foundation. In addition he has published articles in the *International Journal of American Linguistics* and elsewhere. Currently, with support from the National Endowment for the Humanities, Kimball is working on a project to edit and translate a collection of Koasati traditional narratives.

MIGUEL LEÓN-PORTILLA is a distinguished scholar of the ancient and modern cultures of Mesoamerica. A professor emeritus at the Institute for Historical Research at the National Autonomous University of Mexico, he is the author of many books, among them *The Broken Spears* and *Aztec Thought and Culture*. He is now Mexico's ambassador to UNESCO in Paris.

KATHERINE MCNAMARA was schooled in the history of ideas at Marywood College and Cornell University, and received a *bourse* from the French government for her research on Marcel Mauss and his theory of magic. In 1976 she left Paris for Alaska. For four years she lived on the frontier and in an Athabaskan village, working as an itinerant poet in the schools. She returned in 1983, remained for several more years, and made her last trip to the North in 1989. She lives now in New York, and is the author of the forthcoming *Narrow Road to the Deep North*, a memoir.

DAVID L. MOORE is now completing a dissertation on contemporary Native American literature at the University of Washington. He taught English at Salish Kootenai College on the Flathead Reservation in Montana through most of the 1980s, after spending much of the previous decade teaching in South Dakota and there studying Indian history, literature, and the Lakota language. He is particularly interested in the pedagogical uses of postcolonial theories of ethnicity for Indian students.

BERNADETTE RIGAL-CELLARD is *maître de conférences* in American Studies at Bordeaux University. She received her Ph.D. in American religions from the University of California at Santa Barbara, and has written various articles on contemporary American religious movements. The study of Native American religions shifted her emphasis, and for the past seven years she has focused on Native American literature with a research group on multiculturalism in America at Bordeaux University. Her publications in European journals include articles on Welch, Vizenor, Momaday, and P. G. Allen, focusing on the modes of adaptation and representation of traditional myths.

CELESTE RIVER received her master of interdisciplinary studies degree in journalism, religious studies, and Native American studies from the University of Montana. She is a recipient of the William Lang Award from the Montana Historical Society for her thesis "A Mountain in His Memory," about Frank Bird Linderman's role in the creation of the Rocky Boy Indian Reservation; and the Matthew Hansen Endowment to initiate research on Linderman's literary works. She is a member of the Montana Committee for the Humanities Speakers Bureau and on the committee's list of independent scholars.

HANS-ULRICH SANNER was born in 1958 in Mannheim, Germany. He received his doctorate in historical ethnology from Frankfurt University in 1993, served an internship at the Arizona State Museum in 1988, and conducted fieldwork on the Hopi Reservation at various times from 1989 to 1991. His dissertation was on Hopi ritual clowning.

GREG SARRIS is an American Indian of mixed-blood heritage, Kashaya Pomo/Coast Miwok and Filipino on his father's side, and Jewish and German on his mother's. Currently, he is an assistant professor of English at the University of California at Los Angeles. Forthcoming books include *Keeping Slug Woman Alive* and *Prayer Basket: Hearing the Stories of Mabel McKay.*

JANA SEQUOYA, of mixed Chickasaw descent, is a graduate student in Stanford's modern thought and literature program. Her writings include contributions to *American Indian Quarterly,* and *Global Literacy,* edited by Henry Louis Gates, Jr., and K. Anthony Appiah. Her essays, "Scene through the rear-view mirror," and "Anamorphosis" appear in *Standards,* edited by Carméla Jaremillo. She is currently at work on "Representations of Identity in the Discourse of 'Indianness' " for David Palumbo-Lui's forthcoming book, *Revising the Ethnic Canon.*

PERRY SHEARWOOD has studied at McGill, Concordia, and the University of London Institute of Education. He has taught English in Canada's Eastern Arctic, the People's Republic of China, and Nicaragua, as well as in Toronto and Montreal. Currently he is working on his doctoral thesis, tentatively entitled "Literacy and Social Identity in the Eastern Arctic," at the Ontario Institute for Studies in Education in Toronto.

CLIFFORD E. TRAFZER is professor and chair of ethnic studies at the University of California, Riverside, where he is also director of Native American studies. He has written and edited several scholarly books and articles, including *Renegade Tribe: The Palouse Indians and the Invasion of the Inland Pacific Northwest* and *Mourning Dove's Stories,* both with Richard D. Scheuerman. He is currently completing *Death Stalks the Yakima: A Social-Cultural History of Death on the Yakima Reservation, 1888–1962* and *Earth Song, Sky Spirit: An Anthology of Native American Writers.* Trafzer is a mixed-blood Wyandot and member of the California Native American Heritage Commission.

WILLIAM WILLARD received his Ph.D. in cultural anthropology from the University of Arizona. He is currently a professor at Washington State University, Faculty of Native American Studies, Department of Comparative American Cultures. An associate editor of *Wicazo Sa Review,* a Native American studies journal, Dr. Willard is the editor of a special issue of the journal entitled "American Indian Transformation of Religion."

SHAMOON ZAMIR teaches in the Department of English at the University of York, England. He is currently working on studies of W. E. B. Du Bois and late-nineteenth century American intellectual traditions and of Ishmael Reed and the American literary and cultural scene since the 1960s. He has previously taught at Sarah Lawrence College and at the University of Chicago.

INTRODUCTION

Arnold Krupat

I n 1987, in an introduction to a collection of critical essays on Native American literatures we coedited, Brian Swann and I wrote that "eclecticism" in Native American studies may well have "outlived its usefulness" and that "critical anthologies" coming after our own thoroughly eclectic volume might indeed find it useful to adopt "distinctively Marxist, feminist, structuralist, and post-structuralist" (4) perspectives—or, indeed, as we should have added, specifically Native perspectives. I now find myself in the position of editing, and, just here, writing an introduction to yet another eclectic volume of essays. This does not so much represent a change of mind (I speak now, of course, only for myself)[1] as it does a change of situation.

I mean by this only to note that, as the reader well may be aware, this volume is the first of a projected series of studies in Native American literatures, as it is a volume that appears, more by accident than by design, just after the close of the fateful year 1992, a year when the indigenous people of this hemisphere couldn't help but bitterly note or actively protest the fact that five hundred years ago they "discovered" Cristoforo Columbo, that somewhat confused Italian sailor for Spain, bouncing around these parts. The most aggressive nation-state to be founded on Columbus's confusion, the present-day United States, was and is Protestant, capitalist, individualist, and violent, and in the current "post"-ages announced by Daniel Bell, Francis Fukayama, and others (e.g., we are presumably postideological and posthistorical, as well as postmodern, poststructuralist, and the like) only a little more willing to recognize and positively respond to the other and different now than it was then, whenever the "then"—1492, 1620, 1783, 1830, 1890, 1973—may have been. In view of some of the recent fuss over the "threats" that multi-culturalism and "political correctness" supposedly present to the "American way of life"; in view of a headline such as "Plan to Emphasize Minority Cultures Ignites a Debate" (*New York Times,* June 21, 1991); or the outrage in the halls of Congress over the Smith-sonian Institution's 1991 exhibition on the American West, we are obviously not, in main-stream America, entirely "post"-narrow-minded or "post"-self-righteously attached to our mythical best-case scenarios.

These remarks are intended to help the reader understand something of the back-ground for choosing the focus of this first volume of the Smithsonian series. If, as we were quite certain, Native American verbal expression—literature—is as alive and im-portant today, five hundred years after Columbus's incursion, as it ever was, it would probably have engaged the attention of a whole new generation of students. Thus the decision was made (by Swann and me) and ratified (by Daniel Goodwin of the Smithson-ian Institution Press and by our editorial board) to put together what we are calling a "new voices" collection of essays.

This decision, however, meant that whatever I might have thought about the matter before, no single thematic or perspectival orientation and no single discursive mode could be asserted; the studies the volume would present would simply take up whatever subjects our "new voices" found of interest, and they would treat those subjects in whatever fashion seemed most attractive. Thus it is that I find myself again editing and introducing a volume that is quite eclectic, a volume that is not consistent or unified in subject matter, method, perspective, or mode of discourse—for all that academic modes of discourse predominate. (I'll speak to that issue just below.)

I've said above that the "new voices" concept initially imagined a new genera-tion of students of Native literary expression—younger scholars, people at early stages of their researches and careers, and so forth. While this is largely true of the contributors to this volume, it is by no means exclusively true. Among our contributors are people who entered the field late; those who, although they had been working for years, had held back from publishing, had published in small journals or with small presses—people whose names, for a variety of reasons, are likely to be "new" to the majority of readers, rather less familiar, at any rate, than the names of Hymes, Tedlock, and Ramsey; Evers, Allen, and Kroeber, for example. New as the names may be (and, by the time this volume appears, some of the names may *not* be so "new"), it remains to be seen the degree to which the newness of the work involves more nearly a break with what has come before, or, rather, a development, a carrying forward of what has come before.

Most of the work in this book is academic work. I want to say a few words about that here, words that in some measure are apologetic, as they are also quite unapologetic for I remain optimistic in regard to the possibilities of academic work in the field of Native American studies (as in other fields). Some measure of this optimism rests on my view that since the 1960s, a good deal (by no means all) of academic work on Indian literatures, whether by anthropologists, linguists, or literary critics has been undertaken with a commitment to undo the imperial legacy of Western knowledge-gathering.

This means initially—epistemologically and discursively—that some academics have begun to explore what I have recently tried to define as an "ethnocritical" perspective. They—we—have come to see ourselves as—in the currently (1991) fashionable phrase—"border intellectuals," persons who have chosen to situate themselves at the "frontiers" of knowledge, where the "frontier" is not conceived as marking the extent to which colonization by Western "science" has "progressed," but rather as simply the point where two cultures meet. That meeting, if it is indeed a meeting rather than yet another occasion of conquest, must involve an attempt to mediate different, sometimes radically different, ways of understanding the world and "having" knowledge—as it must then attempt to mediate very different ways of speaking or writing about this "knowledge."

In some important advice to academics (and others), Hopi Tribal Council chairman Vernon Masayesva has said, "Research needs to be based on the reality of our [Hopi] existence as we experience it, not just from the narrow and limited view American universities carried over from the German research tradition" (quoted in Whiteley). This seems to me irresistible advice. The question is, What would it mean to follow it? One way *not* to follow it, I believe (and have argued elsewhere)[2] is to assign (with whatever good intentions) Native American experiential reality to some totalized category of the "biological," as Calvin Martin has done, Indian biologicality then being neatly set off against an equivalently and quite erroneously totalized Western anthropologicality. Nonetheless, it may well be the case that any "research" that wishes *to base itself* "on the reality" of Native experience as privileged, must then adopt what was once called the "emic" perspective, or, more recently, the "native's point of view" (Geertz).

This is because what the West has defined as "scientific" knowledge, and claimed, moreover, as *not* merely the universalization of its local (German/American, what-have-you) perspective but as cross-culturally "*true*" in at least "probabilistic" if not absolute fashion for all peoples, all times, all places, requires a movement beyond any and all "realities" as experienced. To attain scientific knowledge, the Western, presumptively "scientific"/critical worker must "verb-ify," or "meta-ize," in Hartwig Issernhagen's terms,[3] working on a level that is abstracted and distanced from the subject/object of concern and his/her/its lived-everyday experience. But it is just this abstracting and distancing that makes such "knowledge" suspect at best or entirely inimical to those whose lives or works it is supposed to illuminate, most particularly when, as in the case of Native Americans, it encounters constructions of the categories of "knowledge" that are hardly consonant with those of "science."

I believe it is the case that in recent years some academic researchers have wanted very much to take seriously, even, indeed, to base their research upon not only Native experience but Native constructions of the category of knowledge. Still, as I have said, the question remains: How to do so? It is an urgent question, inasmuch as a good number of us are quite clear that we do not wish any longer to "domesticate the savage mind" (in Jack Goody's phrase), or (in Eric Cheyfitz's sense) to engage in imperial acts of translation that simply override indigenous experiential and conceptual understandings.[4] But if, nonetheless, we are still unwilling to abandon some (increasingly modest, increasingly qualified) commitment to the scientific perspective as more than just (I repeat) the Western worldview universalized, we encounter problems that cannot simply be undone by good intentions. And, for now, such a perspective, while it must of course take into account "the reality" of Hopi and Native American "existence" as Native people "experience it," still cannot, I think, base its explanations/interpretations on that experiential reality. Like criticism in relation to the text, so "science" (and scientific "research") in relation to experience tries to articulate what the text and the experience do not know and cannot say. Inevitably it uses a language that is not "real" in the sense of being true to anyone's experience, but useful, if it is indeed science or criticism in the best sense, not only to American universities and German traditions but to Hopis and others as well.

For all the persistence of the epistemological difficulties I have remarked—the problems of theory—there is, at least, a discursive move that can be made, a gesture on the level of praxis, that is not really so difficult at all. If we choose to go on "verb-ifying" and "meta-izing," we can also commit ourselves to doing so in a manner that is less rarefied, less militantly distant from "ordinary language." I am far from urging a turn to "simple" and "plain" speech; rather, I am urging a turn away from some of the imperializing and exclusivist jargon (I've written a good deal of it myself) that has marked "high" criticism in recent years. It's not that I think that if only we write more clearly we will automatically think through more clearly; obviously if we could think more clearly we might also write more clearly. But this is a version of the paradox raised by Leon Trotsky (in *Literature and Revolution*) when he pointed out that we will never have a fully adequate theory until it is supported by some concrete social praxis—but we need theory, in whatever form, in order solidly to found praxis. In urging that we revise the language we use as a matter of practical intent and possibility, I am hardly assuming that a solution to the theoretical question will automatically reveal or dis-cover itself; I am simply suggesting that we do what we can, for all that what we can is short of what we would.

Vernon Masayesva—let me return to his talk—affirms that "the inclusive agenda would involve mutual study, not just one person or group objectively studying the other" (quoted in Whiteley); this "agenda," again, seems consistent with much of what I have tried to define as the "agenda" of ethnocriticism,[5] and I have, in my own work, been optimistic about its prospects. But I would not want to be sentimental or stupid: the extent, that is, to which an ethnocriticism—a critical discourse constructed on *both* Western and indigenous understandings and "realities"—is anything more than merely a high-minded hope remains to be seen.

Hopis have detailed stories about how they got to the places they have for long inhabited; Western scientists have, in the past century at least, offered counter-narratives involving passages over a land bridge across the Bering Straits. In this volume, Clifford Trafzer tells of the "first *history of the Americas*" (my emphasis) in a manner that challenges the Western meaning of history, based upon a strong distinction between history and *myth*—the term Trafzer rejects as appropriate to Native origin stories. If one chooses an oppositional mode of proceeding, e.g., *either* the Hopis *or* the Western scientists are "right," *either* the Native elders *or* the Western historians are "right," it is hard, given our present state of understandings, to know what to do. Indeed, there may be some bottom-line projects where one does, in fact, have to choose sides in some bald and uncompromising fashion. But, in point of actual, factual, everyday practice, one rarely is in this position. For it is usually quite possible to reformulate the research questions or projects in view so that Hopi narrative can work in relation to "scientific" archaeological research; so that the elders' stories of an ecosystem in which animals and humans related differently than they do today can inform "historical" accounts of cultural development.

I have placed Trafzer's essay in the third section of this book, a section in which it and the studies that accompany it can be read as making certain initiatory gestures in the direction of some kind of ethnocritical work, most particularly—I shift from theoretical to more nearly practical ground—work in which the cognitive and the social meet. If we cannot theoretically reconcile the meaning of "science" with experiential realities, that is to say, we can at least practically begin to work with the fact that one cannot decently attend to the "meaning and function" of song or story without also attending to the situation of the singer or storyteller, her or his existence not just as an "artist," an informant, or a culture-bearer, but as a person enmeshed in the usual day-to-day social needs and relations—needs and relations that for Native Americans are both like and unlike those of other Americans. Thus it is that at least some students of Native American literatures, in common with most of those who study the cultural expression of other marginalized or subordinated groups in America, increasingly have shown acute concern for the usefulness of their work not only to their colleagues, but as well to those about whom they speak. How to make it useful is not clear—especially to those like myself whose teaching is addressed to mostly non-Native students, and whose writing is almost surely attended to by mostly non-Native persons. Vernon Masayesva again is instructive in laying out a sense of Indian needs, when he says,

> The key to our survival as Indian people is not just preserving our cultural ways, but in devising ways to effectively interact with the dominant society, and other cultures with which we coexist. . . . The university has a major responsibility in sharing its academic tools with us. . . . However . . . any university-sponsored project . . . will surely fail if consultation with Indian tribes is not part of the planning process from the project's inception. (quoted in Whiteley)

Whatever the results of such "consultation," it is nonetheless clear, that, as Whiteley cogently notes, we must no longer claim "the exalted ground of 'pure research'" and thereby disavow "the political situation that underpins [our] work, i.e., the state of political dominance and subordination between [our] society of origin and those of [our] subjects" (quoted in Whiteley).

For all that I have spoken of a developing sense of modesty and responsibility among academics in the field of Native American literatures, I can't help but recall that my own generation's modesty was strictly a function of one's newness to academia; professional modesty was something, it seemed, only for the neophyte. I hope things are different now, but I recall vividly the way in which we at Columbia University, where I took my degrees, and others elsewhere, from stories I have heard, were forced to participate, at doctoral orals or dissertation defenses, in rituals of abasement. If one could be sufficiently humiliated so that she or he would abandon all hope of entering the charmed circle of doctors and professors, all the better. (Or so, at least, it seemed.)

Native American cultures, of course, have their initiatory rites as well, and these are, like those of the Western academy, oriented toward conformity and control. But, if I am not mistaken, severity on the part of the Native elders was and is not self-protective and potentially exclusionary. Each new batch of initiates, however "raw" or unworthy, must nonetheless be initiated; there is little question of discouraging them to the point where they will simply go away.

I say these things in order to specify to the reader that this volume, unless I badly delude myself, is something of a testament to the possibility of cooperation and collaboration between the old and the new even in academic publishing—between the series editors and the editorial and editorial advisory boards in our garb of authority, and the contributors of whatever age and level of publication, whether located within or outside the academy.

First, members of our boards were asked to provide names of people who might offer something for this volume. Then prospective contributors were contacted and invited to submit an outline or sketch of what they would like to do. Next a fair amount of correspondence between myself and the contributors took place in the way of clarifying the work in process. As essays came in, I first read them and then sent them to one or more members of the editorial advisory board, occasionally, where their specific expertise was required, to persons not on our board. While it must be the contributors' views that weigh here, it is my sense that all the submissions received careful readings all along the line and a good deal of constructive criticism. To a degree beyond anything I could have predicted, many of the contributors entered into lively correspondence with advisory board members and with each other, establishing relationships that I hope will prove fruitful and lasting.

It was important to me that the book come into being in such a way, and my model for "such a way" was rather more nearly a Native American one—for instance, centralizing the values of cooperation and community—than strictly an academic one, for all that the West, too, has its models of generous inclusivity. While I had no desire to conform to nor any fear of failing to conform to what has recently been called—usually scornfully—"political correctness" in the makeup of this book I am nonetheless very pleased that it contains work by as many women as men and by Native as well as non-Native scholars. It also contains work by academics and those outside the academy, poets, and "organic intellectuals," by people working in Canada, England, France, Germany, and Mexico, as well as in the United States.

A word, now, as to the structure of this volume. As I have had occasion to note elsewhere, anthologies are a particularly vulnerable genre of text: they are always open to the charge of omissions and either lack of or faulty organization. This volume is no less vulnerable than any of its kind, and I hope to do no more here than to make explicit the thinking behind my organizational decisions. As I noted above, prospective contributors were asked only to write on the subjects they found most congenial, and I made no attempt either to secure essays on specific authors or topics or to exclude specific authors or topics. (Nor did I accept only essays that accorded with my own views: I think every piece in this book offers something important, but this is not to say that every piece in this book reflects my own views.) Once I had essays in hand, the three-part structure I've proposed, "Performances and Texts," "Authors and Issues," and "Ethnocritiques" (a parallel term to "ethnocriticism" as sketched above), seemed a useful—admittedly not an inevitable—way to organize them. (A four-part, or "Indian," pattern-number structure would have been nice, but, then, it didn't seem to happen.) As any reader can remark, there are essays in each of the sections that might well or almost as well (or better?) have found place in another section. For all that this is true, let me state briefly what I intended by the titles I have given these section headings, and thus at least implicitly explain why each contribution is placed as it is.

Native American literatures were and are today performative and oral; *that* seemed a fact to affirm from the start. Their study, however, has required textualization: thus, "performances and texts"—with attention to individual Ojibwe, Koasati, and Shuar storytellers as their narratives appear on the page. With attention, too, to Inuit writing, Hopi clowning, Huichol funeral oration, and to the written compositions of contemporary poets reviving an ancient language (Nahuatl). Although it has lengthened this book considerably, it seemed important to include Native language texts where possible. As it happens, this section contains work that runs from South America, Mexico, and the American Southwest and Southeast, northward to Chippewa (Ojibwe) country, and up into the Canadian Arctic. I am particularly grateful to Miguel León-Portilla for his introduction to the contemporary poetry in Nahuatl, and to Willard Gingerich for his fine translations not only of the poems but also of Dr. León-Portilla's Spanish.

The essays in the second section, "Authors and Issues," receive their placement as a result of attention to the written work of some named author (Vizenor, Silko, Mourning Dove, Todd Downing, Sarah Winnemucca Hopkins)—or, in Linderman's case, editor—which attention, in all of the contributions, necessitates discussion of some "issue," whether the constitution of the category "Native American Literature(s)" (Hochbruck), "Native American women's writing" (Georgi-Findlay), the place of the editor (River, Brown), "post-colonial praxis" (Moore), or the concept of "a national sacrifice area" (Zamir). In William Willard's study, it is the "issue" that more nearly determines the "authors," rather than the other way around, Willard's shrewd determination to anthropologize anthropology leading him to a great many named authors who have, in one form or another, sought to represent the Southwest. Although, as it happens, there is no study of Erdrich, Momaday, or Welch—to mention some of the most visible contemporary Native authors—it is particularly interesting that we have two studies of Mourning Dove, an author we are just beginning to know, and two of very different aspects of Gerald Vizenor's work. We also have in this section two views of Leslie Marmon Silko, who receives still further attention in Part III. It is fascinating to me that Jana Sequoya, working in California, and Shamoon Zamir, working for the most part in London and York, each independently invented the phrase a "contest of stories" to come at aspects of Silko's work, Sequoya using it for her title, Zamir for the first section of his text.

This third section, "Ethnocritiques," is named, as I have already said, to invoke the border or dialogical perspectives and procedures, my own term for which is *ethnocriticism*. In a recently published book, I have tried to define ethnocriticism as that form of critical practice consistent with multiculturalism on the pedagogical level and cosmopolitanism on the sociopolitical level. The essays I have tended to see as examples of ethnocriticism, or ethnocritiques, are, in my reading, texts that cross the borders between Western and non-Western—here, to be sure, Indian—modes of knowing and articulating, mediating between anthropological and indigenous modes of self-construction and storytelling (Sequoya), imagining occluded or repressed alternative narratives (Sarris), and, in the last three essays, presenting the work of indigenous "organic intellectuals," in the Gramscian term. In rather different ways, Danker, McNamara, and Bierwert—a professor of English, a poet, and an anthropologist—convey their excitement and sense of the enormous contemporary importance of the stories of Felix White, Sr., Peter Kalifornsky, and Martin Sampson. Either or all of these essays, of course, might well have found place in Part 1, "Performances and Texts," dealing as they do with—well, to be sure, performances and texts. So, too, might they have been located in Part 2, "Authors and Issues," for in their own cultures, White, Kalifornsky, and Sampson approximate to the status and function in the West of named authors—presenting issues of importance to their respective cultures. That I have chosen to see these essays more nearly as ethnocritiques is only to emphasize the dimension of cross-cultural encounter.

I have indicated my feeling that this book has been a collective and collaborative endeavor marked by generosity and a strong sense of community. At the risk of repetition—no sin, to be sure, in oral presentation—I want, here, specifically to thank the members of the editorial and editorial advisory boards of the Smithsonian series for their detailed attention to the materials sent them, and for their general advice and support.

Several of our editorial advisors read a number of essays and offered commentary and constructive criticism with a promptness and good humor that are deserving of special notice. Thanks are also due Charles Briggs, Peter Roe, and Peter Whiteley for their evaluations of essays our boards could not consider. Their labors testify to a deep commitment to and concern for the subjects at issue. I am also most grateful to my undergraduate research assistant, Jessica Buckley, whose help was invaluable. The dedication of this book indicates gratitude for things above and beyond the call of any reasonable duty. Swann and Whiteley, in more ways than they know, are very much in this book.

NOTES

1. Swann has gone on to edit a volume focused specifically on translation.

2. See the introduction to my book *The Voice in the Margin* (Berkeley: University of California Press, 1989).

3. In a talk at the Netherlands American Studies Association Conference, Middleburgh, Holland, June, 1991.

4. See Goody's *The Domestication of the Savage Mind* (Cambridge: Cambridge University Press, 1977) and Cheyfitz's *The Poetics of Imperialism* (New York: Oxford University Press, 1991).

5. See my *Ethnocriticism: Ethnography, History, Literature* (Berkeley: University of California Press, 1992).

PART 1

Performances and Texts

KOASATI NARRATOR AND NARRATIVE

Geoffrey Kimball

K oasati is an American Indian language of the Muskogean family, now spoken in southwestern Louisiana and eastern Texas. Although there are probably no more than five hundred speakers, these comprise the vast majority of the tribe, and the language is spoken by people of all ages and is still being learned by children. The Koasati tradition of oral literature, however, is not as well preserved as the language. In 1910 John R. Swanton collected nearly fifty narratives from two speakers in a very short period; it has taken the writer fourteen years to collect a similar number from a dozen speakers. The social situations in which traditional narratives were told rarely occur now. In former times, and up until the late 1950s, traditional narratives were told by older men and women of a household as entertainment for household members, at night, or during bad weather, or whenever stories were requested of them. At present the greater integration of the Koasati with their non-Indian neighbors, and ubiquitous television ownership, have reduced the opportunities for the telling of traditional narrative. Furthermore, because traditional narratives on the whole contain fantastic elements, younger people have been taught to disdain them, due to a general prejudice of common American culture against fantasy (see Le Guin, 1974:39–46). Adults who grew up listening to these narratives may be well acquainted with them, but still be unable to tell them. The telling of stories in Koasati is considered by them to be a talent, and persons who feel that they do not have the talent are unwilling to relate them. Furthermore, for Koasati narratives to be recorded in permanent form, a skilled storyteller also has to be willing to tell stories to non-Indians, which is not always the case. In 1910 John R. Swanton was able to collect narratives from Jackson Langley (1870–1947) and Selin Williams (1841–1917), both apparently fine storytellers. At present, Bel Abbey (b. 1916), who is considered by other Koasati-speaking people as one of the best present-day storytellers, is so willing. [The author notes with regret Bel Abbey's death in 1992, after this essay had been written.] Another fine modern storyteller is Martha John (b. 1908); however, the tales that she knows best come from another Koasati tradition than the one typified by Langley, Williams, and Abbey, and are otherwise unknown.

THE NATURE OF KOASATI TRADITIONAL NARRATIVE AND ROLE OF THE NARRATOR

A notable feature of Koasati traditional narratives is the fact that a specific tale is different each time it is told by a single speaker; the differences are even greater between two versions of the same tale told by different narrators. This is due to three factors: the way that Koasati culture defines the form of traditional narrative, the role of the narrator in performing the narrative, and the audience to which the narrative is told.

The form of a traditional narrative is left open. For any particular tale, all that is required is that certain events be related in a certain order. Depending on the situation in which the narrative is related, the narrator can expand or contract the narrative, or embroider those elements which she or he finds interesting or attractive.

Traditional narratives, being an oral form of art, do not exist per se except in the mind of the narrator. Given the lack of an obligatory structure in narrative, aside from the basic plot, it is the responsibility of the narrator to give it form and shape. The native conception of narratives gives free range to the creativity of the narrator by requiring only the skeleton of a narrative to remain the same from narration to narration.

A good Koasati traditional narrative consists of an ordered series of events explaining the origin of some natural feature, illustrating a basic philosophical tenet of Koasati culture, or both. For example, *Corn Woman* at one time tells how corn came into being and teaches the virtue of hospitality; *The Thunderer and the Man* teaches the value of accepting supernatural help, and explains the origin of the dung beetle; and *The Peregrine Falcon and the Great Horned Owl* teaches about confronting and overcoming the evil in one's own nature.

Narratives also vary depending on the audience. Most notable is the fact that narratives are edited by speakers when told to non-Indians. To the Koasati it seems that non-Indians are excessively prudish; therefore, when telling a traditional narrative to an unfamiliar non-Indian, scenes pertaining to sex or excretion are edited out, or whole stories are not told. Once a non-Indian shows that he is not offended by such matters, these scenes are not omitted. These same stories can be told to Indian women and girls without giving offense; they find them as amusing as all other Indians do.

Constraints of time also cause editing of a narrative. Generally this situation occurs when a non-Indian is recording a traditional narrative by dictation. In such a case scenes are compressed, and stylistic elaboration is allowed to fall by the wayside. It is unclear under what conditions shortened tales were told aboriginally; it is possible that such abbreviated narratives were told when an adult, busy working, was asked by a child for a story, and the teller did not have the time to elaborate.

NARRATIVE STRUCTURE

A Koasati narrative is composed of lines, which are generally equivalent to a sentence; in this work lines will be numbered. The term line is here used, rather than verse, as in other studies of American Indian oral literature (such as Hymes 1987), because at this point in the study of Koasati literature, it is not clear what the equivalent of a verse is. The use of anticipatory switch-reference, which has a tendency to bind large sections of a narrative into a seamless fabric, makes it debatable how one is to go about separating items out of that fabric. The use of quoted speech also makes for difficulty. The linguistic device used in Koasati to mark quoted speech is SUBJECT *ónkak*, QUOTE *ká:han;* however, a phrase such as *cokfík ónkak, "X" káhhan* is always translated as "Rabbit said 'X,'" even though the Koasati device consists of two verb phrases. In this paper phrases such as *cokfík ónkak, "X" káhhan* is translated as two separate lines: "Rabbit spoke, 'X' he said." Nonetheless, the possibility exists that these phrases are in reality single lines. Intonational features (which are poorly marked in Swanton's material) offer some aid; generally a line, which consists of from one to four words, begins with a slight rise of pitch and ends with a slight fall. However, morphological criteria occasionally conflict with intonational criteria; in these cases the former criteria are used in distinguishing a line.

As for the Koasati sentence, it is not always equivalent to a single English sentence, but rather a series of sentences, for in addition to sentences marked with a phrase terminal marker (the linguistic correspondent to the English orthographic period), there are sentences that terminate in a switch-reference suffix, which indicates the coreferentiality of the subject of the following phrase or sentence. A line is determined by linguistic and semantic criteria. A line generally terminates in the switch-reference suffix *-n,* or a phrase terminal marker. The appearance of a sentence-initial conjunction is an indication of the beginning of a line. And quoted speech, as indicated above, always begins a new line.

Although as a rule it is easy to determine what elements form a line, variation has been permitted in the treatment of sentence initial conjunctions (such as *má:mo:sin* and *má:min*). These conjunctions, which are grammatically independent verbs, are treated as separate lines when they directly precede quoted speech, as a segment of a longer line in all other cases. The use of sentence-initial conjunctions is stylistically governed, for they have sensitive differences in meaning. For example, *mó:tohon* merely indicates that the following action is later in time than the preceding, while *má:mo:sin* indicates in addition that the following action occurs as a result of the preceding.

Lines can also consist of two or more sub-lines, which here are labeled with lower case letters. Sub-lines are phrases which combine to form a line. They have the stylistic function of highlighting important sections of a narrative. The narrator marks important sections by a combination of four or five sub-lines, and uses combinations of six to eight sub-lines to indicate the climactic or the most important action of a narrative.

Narrative can be divided into larger groups, here called scenes. A scene consists of a number of lines which are semantically bound together. The number of scenes in a narrative appears not to be fixed; however, for a narrative to consist of four, eight, or twelve scenes seems to be very common. The fact that these numbers are multiples of four, the Koasati ritual number, may not be due to chance. Narratives with more than eight scenes seem to have larger-scale structures. Such narratives often can be divided into halves, the first half of which initiates the action of the story, and the second half completes the action of the story. Furthermore, it is possible to associate the scenes in pairs; thus, in eight-scene narratives, such as Langley's version of *The Theft of Fire* and Abbey's version of *The Bungling Host,* scenes I and II form a pair, and are joined with III and IV to form the first half of the narrative, and scenes V and VI are paired and joined with VII and VIII to form the concluding half. The analysis of Koasati narratives has its theoretical base in the work of William Bright, Dell Hymes, and Dennis Tedlock; a discussion can be found in Kimball 1989. The use of the hearsay evidential suffix *-mpa-*, usually in the string *-toho:limpa-*, is a linguistic usage that is unique to traditional narrative. It commonly occurs in every scene of a narrative at least once, and obligatorily in the first and last scenes; however, it is not uncommon for one scene, or several scenes in a row, to lack it. When it is used, it occurs on the last verb of a sentence, but it is not obligatory on every such verb.

It should be noted that the basic structure of a traditional narrative is dictated by the nature of the language, not by the nature of the genre. Any common narrative can be divided into scenes and lines like a traditional narrative; differences between the two are ones of content and stylistics, not structure.

QUALITY OF A NARRATIVE

Can the quality of a narrative be judged? Is it possible for the author to set forth Koasati criteria for narrative quality? This could allow a narrative to be judged not merely by

Western standards. By reading a large number of narratives aloud to a Koasati audience, as well as playing taped narratives, and by listening to the comments of native speakers on the quality of various narrations, the writer has recognized a number of native stylistic and semantic standards. Stylistic standards include the use of parallelism, in which the statement of an action is partially restated in a following phrase; the use of quoted speech occasionally to carry the narrative burden of the tale; the use of long lines to highlight important semantic content in the narrative, and clarity of language, in which the narrator uses language in order to express the narrative forthrightly. The semantic standard, on the other hand, is relatively simple: the behavior of characters in a narrative should be logical, given their natures and the circumstances in which they are found. Stylistic faults include an overreliance on parallelism, allowing the pause word *ná:hon* (the meaning of which falls between English *er* and *well*) to stand as the main element of a line or sub-line, and the failure to follow the above listed standards: lack of quoted speech, lack of long lines at an appropriate place, lack of clarity, and behavioral inconsistency of characters.

At the present there is no information available on determining narrative quality in other Southeastern Indian languages. There has been no study of traditional narrative in other Muskogean language. Published texts from other Southeastern languages, such as Tunica, Biloxi, Atakapa, Chitimacha, Natchez, and Yuchi come from situations of language moribundity or death, where there is insufficient variation in the material available to make stylistic comparisons possible. This being the case, it is impossible at present to tell how Koasati narrative fits into the areal pattern.

THE NARRATORS AND THEIR RELATIONS TO THE NARRATIVES

The two Koasati traditional narratives (*The Theft of Fire* and *The Bungling Host*), the comparison of which forms the basis of this paper, were related by three of the best storytellers of this century. Because the personality and the basic nature of the narrator has such a strong influence on the form of a narrative, the following biographical sketches are provided.

Jackson Langley

Jackson Langley, whose Koasati name was Satowáyhki, was born in 1870 and was forty years old in 1910 when he provided a series of Koasati traditional narratives to John R. Swanton. His mother, Selin Williams (1841–1917), also provided a number of traditional narratives to Swanton in the same year.

Langley was a complex person, and is still well remembered by older persons. At the time he provided Swanton with the narratives from which *The Theft of Fire* and *The Bungling Host* have been taken his life had been relatively stable. He was of a prominent family (his paternal aunt was married to the chief, John Abbey); he was happily married to Sinnie Polyte (Sihó:ki), his third son and sixth child had just been born, and all the children were flourishing.

Older people report that a notable feature of his personality was an excessive (by Koasati standards) interest in sex. While being satisfied with one wife at a time, he was extremely uxorious, in the sense of being excessively devoted to his wife; furthermore he was excessively proud of the number of children he fathered (fifteen by his two Koasati wives). In addition, he is recalled as being very much a patriarchal figure, which is deviant in the matrilineal and traditionally sex role-free culture of the Koasati.

He converted to Christianity in adulthood, and became one of the founding members of St. Luke's Congregational Church. However, his personal religious views were syncretic, and he saw no conflict in supporting traditional dances, ceremonies, and ritual ball games. He was well regarded by his family; his grandchildren remember him with particular affection.

These features of Langley's personality are the ones that are germane to the interpretation of the narratives that he provided; nonetheless, it is of interest to sketch the remainder of his life. The Koasati chief died in 1910, and within two years Langley was elected chief, with all the responsibilities and prerogatives of that office. However, in 1919 he suffered a stunning personal blow when his wife and his newborn son both died during the influenza epidemic that decimated the tribe. The depth of his emotions can be attested to by the headstones (the only ones erected before the war) he set up for them in St. Luke's Cemetery, laboriously inscribed by his own hand.

After his wife's death, it is said that his interest in women led to his undoing, for he fell in love with a Tunica Indian, Alice Pocoto, who had come with other Tunica on their regular prewar visits to the Koasati community. She did not wish to remain with the Koasati, but returned to her tribe's lands near Marksville, Louisiana. Langley abandoned his responsibilities as chief to follow her and marry her. The Koasati, unhappy at his desertion, replaced him as chief with the son of the former chief. Langley's marriage to Alice Pocoto did not last, and he returned to the Koasati after a few years, fully expecting to take up where he left off. When he was not permitted to do so, he grew embittered, and this embitterment colored the rest of his life. In accordance with the traditional levirate he married his late wife's niece (his late wife's sisters already being married), and fathered a new family. He did more linguistic work with Swanton in 1930, and was Mary R. Haas's consultant when she did her fieldwork on Koasati in 1936. He retained his forceful personality, and remained the patriarch of his large family until his death in 1947.

Bel Abbey

Bel Abbey (born 1916) was in his late sixties and early seventies when he provided the writer with the traditional narratives *The Theft of Fire* and *The Bungling Host*. Although in the paternal line he belonged to the family from which chiefs were elected, he was not recognized as belonging to that family because his father had been born from a traditional Indian marriage and not the new, legally registered one. On the other hand, his mother's family was notable, containing traditional doctors and ritual specialists.

Abbey was in the first generation to be Christian from childhood, but he absorbed much of traditional Koasati culture from his mother, his maternal uncles, and grand-parents, who were only superficially Christianized. He received little Western education, primarily a few years at the Congregational church school; he learned to write English only while in the Army during World War II. Nonetheless, he learned a great deal from his relatives, especially in regard to traditional hunting, fishing, and gathering activities, and he bent his natural curiosity and keen sense of observation to learning about the natural world. He was married to Nora Williams (1920–84) for nearly forty-five years, and since her death has remained content with his role as widower. He had three daughters (the sex of child most highly valued by the Koasati), and a number of grandchildren and now great-grandchildren. He worries about their commitment to being Indian, and their preservation of their ancestral tongue, and he occasionally gathers them together to express his views on these subject to them.

Three features that deeply color Abbey's personality are a solid pragmatism, a respect for truth, and a skepticism for things that cannot be tested by the senses. Thus, though he enjoys traditional narrative, he is highly suspicious about its veracity. When telling any kind of traditional narrative, he always gives a warning introduction to the effect that what he is relating is something that he heard, and the truth of which he cannot attest.

Selin Williams

Selin Williams, the narrator of one version of *The Bungling Host*, was the mother of Jackson Langley. She is, except for her name, almost completely forgotten by the present-day Indians, so only a bare biographical sketch of her can be made. She was born in 1841. The names of her father and mother are unknown, although she may be the grand-daughter of the legendary Koasati Williams, who was supposed to have been born of a union between an Indian man and a white woman, perhaps in the late 1790s.

In the 1860s, she married a Koasati Indian named Joe Henderson, who adopted the surname Langley from an Acadian in Louisiana, and was the forefather of all the Koasati with the surname Langley. Her husband's sister's husband was the then-chief John Abbey, and she may have been of a chiefly lineage; her brother was the last known traditional weatherworker.

When she worked with John R. Swanton in 1910, she had five living children, ranging in age from twenty-five to forty, and seventeen grandchildren. She had the large family prized by the Indians, and her son was the tribal chief. Thus, it can be assumed that her social position was high. Only one photograph survives of her (Swanton 1946, plate 27); it shows a slender, tired- and old-looking woman, with the sunken cheeks of one who has lost her teeth.

The only clue to her personality can be found in the stories that she related to John R. Swanton. That she was not reticent about sexual matters can be inferred from several stories, in one of which Rabbit tells Great-One-Who-Eats-Human-Beings who is trying to kill him:

Cállin ónkalaho:š,	It will make a noise as I die,
ná:sok tokóhka mók,	something also will pop,
cállin ónkalaho:š,	it will make a noise as I die,
cahiłihcík ónkalaho:š.	my testicles will make a noise.

Other such stories are *The Origin of Crow*, in which two boys create Crow by rubbing a bowstring across the anus of their dead father, who had tried to kill them, and *Deer Women*, in which a man has sexual intercourse with a doe.

Selin Williams seemed to be fascinated by Rabbit the Trickster; her best tales are the ones concerned with Rabbit playing tricks on various animals and humans. She also seemed to like the idea of the Trickster tricked, and included two different tales on that theme. She was apparently very traditional, which is not unexpected in a person raised away from contact with non-Indians in the nineteenth century. Several of her tales contain supernatural beings associated with the colors blue and red; these were apparently ritual colors. Furthermore, she was familiar with the Koasati version of the ancient game of chunkey, which is now unknown to all Indians, even the eldest.

One can thus discern, albeit dimly, the outlines of her personality. She was traditional, frank, and humorous; it is notable that frankness and humor also can be discerned in the personality of her son, Jackson Langley. Although in many ways he was traditional, his view of the relationships of men and women was one which his mother in all likelihood did not share.

THE NARRATIVES

The following are parallel English texts of the narratives. These were translated by the writer from the original language. Each narrative is divided into scenes, and the texts are aligned so that parallel scenes begin at the same location. Lines and sub-lines are numbered and lettered. These refer to the corresponding Koasati texts in the appendix, and are used for identification in the analyses of the narratives which follow them. It should also be noted that of the pairs of texts, the narrative located in the left-hand column is the one that is considered better according to native standards.

I. The Theft of Fire

The Theft of Fire

by Jackson Langley

Scene I: The World Without Fire

1 It is said that fire did not exist here.
2a Later,
 b [people found out that] fire existed
   only on the other side of the ocean.
3a Right away,
 b   the people here wanted fire from them,
 c   but the others did not want to give it to
   them.
4a Then,
 b   they lived without fire.

Scene II: The Quest for Fire Is Proposed

5a Later on,
 b   Rabbit spoke,
6   "As for me, I can run with those people's
   fire," he said.
7a Thereupon,
 b   a person whose daughters were many
   spoke,
8   "To whomever goes and brings back fire I
   shall give one of the women," he said.
9   Rabbit spoke,
10   "But just one of the women is not enough for
   me," he said.

Scene III: The First Questers Fail

11   Then,
12   "I," said Great One Who Eats Human
   Beings, so it is reported.

The Theft of Fire

by Bel Abbey

Scene I: The World Without Fire

It is said that among people dwelling   1
 here fire used not to exist.
It is said that people continued on   2
 without fire existing.
This being so,   3a
 I do not know the way that they lived,   b
  but they lived without fire.   c
Now,   4a
 it was the case that the people living on   b
 the other side of the ocean had fire.
And the people continued to want it from   5
 them; so it is said.
When they continued to cook things with   6a
 fire and eat them,
  the people here also wanted it from   b
  them like that,
   but they continued on without it,   c
   so it is said.
They lived without fire.   7

Scene II: The Quest for Fire Is Proposed

Thereupon,   8a
"If someone were to go,   b
 if someone were to go and run with   c
 those people's fire,
  or if someone were to ask for it   d
  from them and return with it,
   bringing it, would that we would   e
   live so!" they said, speaking
   to each other.

Scene III: The First Questers Fail

Thereupon,   9
"I can bring it," someone said,   10
Having said "I can bring it,"   11a

13 "I can bring it," he said.

14 The person spoke,

15 "Well, as for you, go off, go and look for it and bring it!" he said.

16a Great-One-Who-Eats-Human-Beings wanted women,

b and he went first, so it is said.

17 And at that he went and dived into the sea, so it is said.

18 He disappeared into the water.

19a Then,

b he did not come back and was gone.

when one went, it is said that all the time he was unable to do it,   b

it is said that all the time he did not return,   c

even though he was unable to do it, there were others.   d

Scene IV: Rabbit Is Sent on the Quest

20 Rabbit spoke,

21 "No one has come back," he said, so it is reported.

22a "I alone am the one.

b I can come back," he said, so it is reported.

23 The person also sent for him.

24a Then,

b Rabbit spoke,

25a "Well, if I bring fire,

b I shall have sexual intercourse with all of the young women individually," he said, so it is reported.

26a Then,

b the person spoke,

27 "Let it be so!" he said.

Scene IV: Rabbit Is Sent on the Quest

This being so,   12

"I am the one, I can bring it," said Rabbit.   13

Thereupon,   14

"I am the one, I can bring it," he said.   15

"Well, if it is the case that you going about   16a
bring it,

if it is the case that you bring fire,   b

whatsoever you want we will give to you," they said.   c

Then,   17

"As for me, nice women,   18a

women are attractive to me,   b

I want nice women," Rabbit said, so it is reported.   c

Rabbit will want their women perhaps, or maybe not.   19

Thereupon,   20

"Well, whomsoever you want we will obtain for you,   21a

if you go and look for fire from them and bring it," they said.   b

"I can bring it. I am the one," he said,   22a
and it is said that he went.   b

Scene V: Rabbit Crosses the Ocean and Steals Fire

28a Thereupon,

b Rabbit went quickly, so it is said.

29a He went, and arrived over there to the ocean,

b he took off his shirt and threw it off,

c and sitting on a rotting log,

Scene V: Rabbit Crosses the Ocean and Steals Fire

He forded the ocean.   23

Looking for fire,   24a

over there they all had fire.   b

He asked for fire from people,   25a

they had fire all the time,   b

all the time they had fire.   c

d   it is said that he went off sailing.

30a Then,

b   he forded the ocean, so it is said.

31   He went about there, so it is said.

32a And later,

b   he wanted fire from people,

c   and they did not give it to him,

d   and taking it from them,

e   he ran with it from them, so it is said.

33a At that,

b   it is said that they chased after him.

34a Then,

b   he carried it,

c   through the whole forest he ran with it,

d   and he really carried it,

e   and having arrived over at the ocean

f   he went and stood with it.

Scene VI: Rabbit Swims the Ocean with Fire

35a And then,

b   pine resin on the back of his head,

c   having rubbed it full of pine,

d   he stood there,

e   and when the people who were chasing him arrived,

f   he dived into the water with the fire.

36a He held it up in his hand,

b   He went in the water with the fire.

37a Nevertheless,

b   when he became tired,

c   it is said that he struck the back of his head with the fire,

d   set it on fire, and went in the water with it.

38   In such a way, it is said, did he carry it in the water and go in the water with it.

Thereupon,   26a

he tried to go and steal fire from them,   b

he continued to try to run with it from them.   c

After he tried to run with it from them,   27a

he carried it about burning,   b

he carried it,   c

when they said "How is it that you can go back?"   d

he carried it saying nothing.   e

Then,   28a

it is said that they chased him.   b

They chased him,   29

And he continued carrying the fire.   30

So it is said.   31

Scene VI: Rabbit Swims the Ocean with Fire

When he took it and carried it,   32a

he dived with it into the ocean, so it is said.   b

This being so,   33a

he lifted it up, and went with it in the water,   b

a long time he brought it swimming,   c

when he brought it swimming,   d

because he brought it in such a manner,   e

it is said that he became tired out.   f

Having become tired out from it,   34a

if he dropped the fire into the water,   b

it would be extinguished.   c

If he dropped it in the water,   35a

and it went out,   b

he did not know how ever he might   c

bring it;   d

he had completely tired legs and was unable to do more,

because he had been swimming.   e

Thereupon,   36a

he did not know how it might be good,   b

but there was a thought,   c

his head was sufficiently sticky with resin,   d

he would not be short of breath,   e
and he spread the fire onto   f
  the back of his head,
   he spread it onto his head,   g
    and took it, bringing it   h
     swimming,
      it is said that he forded   i
       the ocean and brought it.
But he forded the ocean once.   37

Scene VII: Rabbit Receives His Reward

39a	Then,
b	he brought it to that person.
40a	Right then,
b	he gave him the young women and spoke,
41	"Now indeed these are your women," he said, so it is reported.
42a	Thereupon,
b	Rabbit was in a state of extreme happiness.
43a	And then,
b	night having fallen,
c	when they were about to lie down,
d	Rabbit spoke,
44	"In the middle is where I shall be lying!" he said.
45a	Then,
b	the young women having finished speaking to one another,
c	made the bed for Rabbit.
d	"Now!" they said, and he lay down.

Scene VIII: Rabbit Receives His Comeuppance

46a	When that had taken place,
b	the young women spoke to one another.
c	"Rabbit having lain down,
d	we are to continue to laugh and to speak to him,
e	and when Rabbit is lying down and sufficiently happy,
f	we are to play with him, and grab him together, and go out,
g	and arriving outside,
h	we shall strip off his shirt,
i	beat him, and dispose of him," they said, so it is reported.

Scene VII: Rabbit Receives His Reward

Then it was at that time,	38a
he brought it and they all were extremely happy.	b
He brought fire and they were extremely happy.	39
So it is said.	40
"Now, please tell us whomsoever you want!	41a
Perhaps you might take one. Please tell us whatever you want!	b
	c
"As for me, I do not merely want women.	42a
Women who are so nice,	b
ones who have a nice appearance will please me."	c

47a Then,
  b   when they lay down,
  c   they played with Rabbit, so it is said.
48a Thereupon,
  b   it is said that Rabbit was lying in the middle
          sufficiently happy.
49a He was just lying so,
  b   and they grabbed him together playing with
          him,
  c   having taken him outside,
  d   now they were in the process of trying
              to throw him,
  e   and when Rabbit, excessively
                frightened, jumped,
  f   they were holding on to him so
                  tightly,
  g   that he slipped out of the skin of
                    his back,
  h   ran off and disappeared, so it
                      is said.

[Epilogue]	**Epilogue**	
50 [Then he went about.	Thereupon,	43a
51a Then he met Great-One-Who-Eats-Human Beings,	that one arrived and asked of them,	b
	and it is said that they provided him with them.	c
b and they spoke to one another.		
52 Right then Great-One-Who-Eats-Human Beings spoke,	"Women who are nice," he said.	44
53 "Why do you have no shirt on your back?" he said, so it is reported.	Then,	45a
	that rabbit brought fire,	b
54 He said it,	he asked for nice women, and they provided them for him,	c
55 and Rabbit spoke,		
56a "It is the case that I am working," he said, so it is reported.	and those people who dwelth there were very happy, so they say,	d
b It is the case that my women are many.	because he brought fire.	e
c I am very happy," he said, so it is reported.		
57 But it is said that Great-One-Who-Eats Human-Beings did not believe him.		

Analysis and Comparison

The Langley Version

This narrative was dictated to John R. Swanton in 1910. The Koasati language text was not published, but a translation based on its interlinear glosses was published by Swanton

(1929:203–204). Of these two versions of the narrative Jackson Langley's is of better quality than Bel Abbey's. Abbey himself was not pleased with the quality of his own version; it was not one of the stories that he really liked, and so he rarely told it.

In 1936 Langley gave Mary R. Haas a truncated version of this narrative, one from which he had ruthlessly deleted every reference to sex. Because sexual matters are freely discussed only among Indians themselves or in sexually segregated groups with non-Indians, Langley felt free to include the sexual element only with an adult male non-Indian audience (Swanton), and produced an edited version for an adult female non-Indian audience (Haas).

Line 10

This line provokes laughter among listeners, for it reflects the role of Rabbit as one who openly violates the norms of society. Although the exchange of women for fire is part of the plot skeleton of this narrative, Langley's version emphasizes Rabbit's sexual voracity, in contrast to Abbey's version, which subordinates it to other elements.

Line 25

Rabbit's statement is considered quite shocking, and the language is blunt. The use of the verb *apoló:kan,* "to have sexual intercourse with someone (singular object)," with a plural object (*tayyí imaníhtaha óhyan,* "all the young women") implies that he will have sexual intercourse in sequence with the women, leaving one and going on to the next. That this element is completely lacking in Abbey's version indicates that it is one of Langley's creative additions to the tale. It is unlikely that Abbey bowdlerized his version of the tale, for he did not edit other tales he told that had risqué content. On the other hand Langley did bowdlerize the version of this tale that he told to Mary R. Haas in 1936.

Line 28

The combination of the four sub-lines is an indication that this is an important point in the narrative. Rabbit sailed over the ocean on a rotten log; however, he returned by swimming. His swimming over the ocean is one of the climactic points in Langley's version, and the only climactic point in Abbey's version. The statement that Rabbit threw off his shirt implies that he transformed himself from his human form into his animal form; in this version the same transformation occurs at the second climax. The use of a rotten log as Rabbit's vessel is a good descriptive element; it is based on the observation that rabbits in nature, when hunted by dogs during the spring floods, will leap onto a rotten log floating by (rotten logs being hollow, and thus better-floating) and thus escape the hunters.

Lines 32–34

The increasing lengths of the lines as this scene draws to a close indicates the importance of what is told here to the plot of the story. The land across the ocean is sketched by the mention of the forest that reaches down to the ocean; dramatic tension is heightened by Rabbit, reaching the ocean with fire, stopping, even though others are in pursuit of him.

Line 34 contains a very finely wrought parallel structure: *he carried it* of line 34b is parallelled by *he ran with it* in 34c, repeated again as *he really carried it* in 34d, and parallelled by *he went and stood with it* in 34f. The *forest* in line 34c is balanced by the *ocean* in 34e.

Lines 35–38

This scene also is marked as important by the lengths of the lines. The most important part of the scene is that in which Rabbit rubs the back of his head with pine resin, although at the time the reason he does so is not stated. The reason for his action becomes clear in the second half of the scene, in which Rabbit, having grown tired holding the fire up above the water with his hand, strikes it to the back of his head, where the ignited pine resin will keep it burning until he returns to the other side of the ocean.

Line 44

Rabbit's statement here is another expression of his hypersexuality. Again, Langley seems to dwell on this feature of Rabbit's personality with interest, although the next scene will prove that Langley's interest is not unaffected by traditional mores.

Lines 46–49

The very long lengths of lines 46 and 49 indicate that to Langley this was the main climax of the tale. As far as it can be determined, it is entirely of his creation; not even a hint of this scene can be found in Abbey's version, which maintains all the other plot elements. Within this scene Rabbit receives his comeuppance for his hubris, in this case his hubris being of a sexual nature: that all the women would want him just as much as he wanted them. Hubris, in Koasati *ilakasamotilká,* is considered by the Koasati to be a vice, and the comeuppance of a character with hubris is the main topic of those traditional narratives told with frequency at the present. Also, the punishment for hubris is kept in character with the kind of offence. The revolt of the women, who heretofore have been reified as goods to be given to Rabbit for his services, is much more typical of Koasati culture than Langley's patriarchal fantasies. The older Indians report that in the 1930s a woman whose husband took a secondary wife was so incensed that she beat the living daylights out of him.

In this scene Langley almost revels in the tables' being turned on Rabbit; a violent reassertion of the norms of his culture in contrast to the patriarchal situation given in the previous scenes of the tale. The scene is quite descriptive; however, the sexual goings-on are hinted at rather than made explicit. The part at the end in which Rabbit slips out of his skin, that is, transforms himself from human to animal, is very well handled. Listeners find this scene very funny, the humor lying in the deflation of Rabbit's sexual hubris.

Lines 50–57

This epilogue is the weakest part of Langley's version; listeners preferred to have the tale end with the last line of the eighth scene. The epilogue violates the semantic standard for a well-formed tale by reintroducing Great-One-Who-Eats-Human-Beings, who dived into the ocean and disappeared (or drowned) in lines 17–19. The only connection with the rest of the tale is the lack of a shirt (or skin) on Rabbit's back, having been stripped from him by the women. The only possible reason that Langley added this epilogue to the narrative was to show that Rabbit never learns from experience, that he is still full of hubris. Like the typical braggart and liar, as soon as he leaves the scene of his humiliation, Rabbit returns to his old self.

The Abbey Version

I recorded this text in March 1989. Bel Abbey had to be cajoled into giving it because he was not happy with his proficiency with it, as it was not one of the tales that he was in the habit of narrating. In his prologue to the narrative (not given here), in addition to the usual caveats about the truthfulness of the tale, he attributes his version to Jefferson Abbey (1865–1951), his paternal grandfather, and tells about how he heard the tale from him. This is the only traditional narrative collected from any speaker in which an attribution is made to a specific person. Furthermore, Abbey calls this narrative an "old story," which means that he felt it was a tale that was typically told very long ago. Although Abbey's version has some scenes that are longer than Langley's, length is not necessarily a criterion for quality. From experience, the writer has found that dictated narratives are shorter and can be less complex than the same narrative given by the same speaker on tape; and it should be noted that all of Jackson Langley's narratives were made by dictation, and Abbey's were made on tape.

Line 3

This line is one of the typical asides that Abbey gives while telling a traditional narrative. It is not sufficient for him that the situation be told; he feels obliged to contemplate the implications of the situation. For him, life without fire is unimaginable, and he says so. To insert asides, however, is a stylistic fault, although one that is received by listeners in a good-humored fashion.

Lines 9–11

This scene is vague in comparison with Langley's version of the same scene. It is linguistically marked by the number of sub-lines as an important scene, for the lack of success in obtaining fire sets up the situation in which Rabbit is able to go. For Langley, this is not an important consideration.

Lines 18–19

Only here in the fourth scene does Abbey introduce the exchange of women for fire, as opposed to Langley, who introduced it in the very first scene. Furthermore, Abbey qualifies Rabbit's desire in line 19 by saying that Rabbit might perhaps not want the women. The reason for this may well be that for him Rabbit cannot shift from human to animal shape, but is permanently in animal form.

Lines 23–31

This scene is very weak in comparison to Langley's version. It lacks Langley's descriptiveness and dramatic tension. Furthermore, there is a logical inconsistency in that in line 25 Rabbit asks for fire and in line 26 he steals it. One is perhaps to assume that the response to the request was negative; however, Langley's version makes their unwillingness to share clear. Finally the fact that line 31 is made up entirely of a form of the pause form *ná:hon* is a stylistic fault.

Lines 32–37

In Abbey's version this is the climax of the tale, where Rabbit, swimming across the ocean, must somehow keep the fire burning even though he is unable to hold it above his head while swimming. For Abbey, the struggle of Rabbit to complete his task is the most interesting part of the tale, and so here he has lavished his creative talents in embroidering its fabric. In lines 35 and 36 it is clear that he identifies with Rabbit, and he allows the listeners to see into Rabbit's mind as he considers what is to be done. It is stylistically rare in any kind of Koasati narrative, literary or non-literary, for the listener to be given a clue into the thought of a character, unless the character is the person narrating, as in a non-literary narrative. It is rather more typical to require the listener to make his or her own judgment about the nature of a character by the character's actions and words. While Abbey's style here is attractive to the Western reader, long used to access to a character's thoughts in literary works, it is unusual to the Koasati listener.

Lines 38–42

At this point the versions of Abbey and Langley diverge the most. In this scene, Abbey simply relates that Rabbit received a few good-looking women, and then goes directly to the epilogue. Clearly for him all of the tale subsequent to Rabbit's successful crossing of the ocean is not of much importance. This is in contrast to Langley, where the seventh scene is used to set the stage for the eighth scene and Rabbit's humiliation, which for him is the most important scene in the narrative. Abbey's version lacks any hint that there should be an eighth scene; this strongly implies that the eighth scene is entirely Langley's creation. Abbey repeats the stylistic flaw of making a line out of the pause form in line 40.

Line 45

Abbey uses the combination of five sub-lines to highlight a quick restatement of the plot of the narrative: Rabbit brought fire, he was given women, and everyone was happy to have fire.

II. The Bungling Host

| **The Bungling Host** | **The Bungling Host** |
| by Bel Abbey | by Selin Williams |

| **Scene I: Bear Invites Rabbit to Dinner** | **Scene I: Bear Invites Rabbit to Dinner** |

1a Now, Bear used to dwell somewhere,	Bear and Rabbit were friends with each 1
b and he and Rabbit used to visit each other,	other, so it is said.
so it is said.	Then, 2a
2 Thereupon,	Bear spoke, b
3 "Visit me later!" he said,	"Go and visit me later," he said and went. 3
4 "Visit me later!" he said to Rabbit.	
5 Thereupon,	
6 "I was about to visit you," said Rabbit to	
Bear.	

| **Scene II: Bear Feeds Rabbit with Himself** | **Scene II: Bear Feeds Rabbit with Himself** |

7a Thereupon,	Rabbit went and arrived over there, 4
b he went over there to visit him,	And Bear, having sliced himself up the 5a
c and after the two of them were sitting,	middle,
d he had nothing to give to him to eat;	took out some fat, b
e "What *am* I going to feed him?" he	and fried it, and it is said that c
thought,	Rabbit ate it.
f and then he knew.	
8a Well, because Bear was fat,	
b he pulled out his stomach,	
c and picking up a knife,	
d and cutting off a piece,	
e cooked it,	
f and fed Rabbit with it, so it is said.	
9a Thereupon,	
b Rabbit really sat and watched, so it is said.	

| **Scene III: Rabbit Invites Bear to Dinner** | **Scene III: Rabbit Invites Bear to Dinner** |

10a Thereupon,	Thereupon, 6a
b having merely just visited him, he	Rabbit spoke, b
returned home.	"You too go over to my place later!" 7

11 "You too go over to my place later!" he said.

12 "You too go over to my place later!" he said,

13 And Bear went to visit Rabbit, so it is said.

14a Well, he went over to visit Rabbit,

b and after he sat down. . . .

15a Now, Bear's house was the inside of a hollow tree,

b the two of them sat dwelling in the hollow tree,

c and after the two of them dwelt there,

d he went over to Rabbit's dwelling place.

16a Rabbit dwelt within a little grass dwelling;

b within that was his dwelling, so it is said.

17 Over there the two of them sat.

he said.

Scene IV: Rabbit Injures Himself Imitating Bear

18 Rabbit spoke,

19a "Please sit down! I shall cook!" he said,

b and after the two of them stayed there,

20a He himself did what he had seen,

b he picked up a knife and cut out a piece,

c he cut his stomach, so it is said.

21a Now he himself being scrawny and lean,

b he injured himself cutting himself,

c "Help me! Help me! I need help!" he said.

22 Bear ran over.

23 "What is it?"

24 "I am injured. It is the case that I have cut myself," he said.

25 Thereupon,

26a "I intend to look for a doctor, then," Bear said,

b and it is said that he ran out.

27a The other lay on the ground,

b he had cut his stomach.

Scene IV: Rabbit Injures Himself Imitating Bear

Bear having arrived over there to visit him, 8

Rabbit sliced himself up the middle, 9a

and there was nothing there. b

Bear having sliced himself up the middle 10
again fried it and they ate.

Afterwards, 11a

Rabbit was about to die. b

Scene V: Bear Encounters Vulture

28a Thereupon,

b after he had run a ways,

c he caught sight of him sitting on a branch,

Scene V: Vulture Is Encountered

He was laying on the ground, 12

And they went around looking for 13
a doctor,

d   he caught sight of Vulture sitting on a
       branch,

e   he asked questions of him, so it is said.

29   Thereupon,

30   After he said, "I need help."

31   "What is it that you want?"

32   "I am looking for a doctor."

33   "Why do you want to look for help?"

34a "It is the case that my friend Rabbit is
       injured," he said.

b   "It is the case that Rabbit is injured,

c   it is the case that he has suffered a
         knife wound," he said.

35a "If you tell me about it, I will perhaps help
       him,

b   and it is the case that I will doctor him,"
       he said.

And they sent for Vulture.   14

Scene: VI: Vulture "Doctors" Rabbit

36   After they arrived over there,

37   Thereupon,

38   "Where is he lying?" he said.

39   "He lies over here," he said.

40   Thereupon,

41a "What are you doing?

b   What do you want?" he said.

42a "Fence in his house perhaps!

b   Would that it be encircled!" he said.

43a "Look for palmetto leaves,

b   Fence it all in and make a house encircling
         it!"

44a "Enough now!

b   Go out!

c   He will follow you upon my doctoring
         him," he said.

45a Thereupon, well,

b   Vulture made Rabbit cry out, so it is said.

46a When Rabbit cried out,

b   Bear said, "Why is he making a sound?"

47   "It is nothing. He does not want the
       medicine from me," he said.

48   Thereupon,

49   "Why is it that he doesn't want it?" he said.

50a "It is the case that he doesn't want me to
       give him my medicine,

Scene VI: Vulture "Doctors" Rabbit

Vulture spoke,   15

"You all are to close me up in his house   16a
   with him,

   and there are to be no cracks,   b

      no one can look at me,   c

         only so can I doctor him," he said. d

They closed him up with him.   17

And then, for a time, Rabbit cried out, and 18
   then it ceased.

   "Why is it?" they said.   19

"It is nothing! He is really afraid of the   20
   medicine," he said.

Then,   21

"Open ye the door for me!" he said.   22

They opened it for him,   23a

   and he flew over there and perched on a   b
   branch.

b   and he made noise," he said.

51   Thereupon,

52   "What else do you need?" he said.

53   Then,

54a "Nothing.

b   I am about to finish doctoring him.

c   But now he is good.

d   Now it is the case that he is good," he
         said,

e   And flying up went and perched on
         a tree branch.

Scene VII: Bear Assaults Vulture

55a Thereupon,

b   after Bear went in and saw it,

c   that he had eaten Rabbit all up,

d   that he had eaten up his flesh,

e   that he had thrown down nothing but
         bones,

f   Bear became extremely angry,

g   he took out the knife that he carried,

h   and he threw it overhand at Vulture.

56a After he threw it at him,

b   it went through his beak,

c   it pierced his beak,

d   it went through his beak, and he took it,

e   he took the knife and threw it away,
             so it is said.

Scene VIII: The Result of Bear's Action

57a He would have killed him,

b   he missed,

c   and it is said that he pierced his beak.

58a Thereupon,

b   he was pierce-beaked,

c   it is the case that Bear pierced it on him;

d   it seems he carried it as his possession
         unceasingly,

e   it is said that they carried it all the time.

59   Just like that, any kind of bird is
         pierce-beaked.

60   Just so it is said that they are pierced.

61   Just so much [is what I know of this].

62   *Finis!*

Scene VII: Vulture Is Assaulted

They went and saw Rabbit,   24

And it is said that he had laid down   25
   nothing but bones.

Thereupon,   26a
   they loathed vulture and shot at him,   b

They shot and hit and made it pass   27
   through only his beak.

Vulture spoke,   28

"Oh! I will like a nose-ring," he said,   29

Analysis and Comparison

The Abbey Version

This was the first Koasati text obtained by the writer, in the fall of 1977. As it was a narrative that was readily volunteered, as opposed to *The Theft of Fire,* which the writer had to request of the storyteller, it is one that he knew well, liked, and enjoyed telling. This is reflected throughout the narrative by the expert use of stylistic devices, such as parallelism, description, and quoted speech. Furthermore, in the seventh scene (lines 36–54), irony is used in the repeated duplicitous speech of Vulture. It contrasts strongly with Selin Williams's version, which is sketchy, poorly developed, and replete with stylistic faults.

Dell Hymes suggests that only scenes I through IV should be entitled *The Bungling Host,* and that scenes V through VIII should be entitled *The Sham Doctor,* based on the widespread nature of the latter theme among the North American Indians.

Lines 3–6
This is a good example of the use of stylistic parallelism, with line 3 giving a statement, line 4 a repetition with addition, and line 5 a restatement.

Lines 7–8
The use of five sub-lines to compose each of these lines indicates that this scene is an important part of the narrative. Again, as in *The Theft of Fire,* Abbey identifies himself with a character, in this case Bear, and reveals to the listeners how Bear reasoned what to feed Rabbit. Line 8, containing a vivid description of Bear's actions, is stylistically good, according to native criteria.

Lines 15–16
These lines are an interpolation of material that Abbey felt was germane to the narrative. They describe in turn Bear's home and Rabbit's home, both of which are the naturalistic dens of real bears or rabbits. The description provides the listener with a vivid location in which the action takes place.

Lines 19–21
The actions of Rabbit here result from hubris, in this case his belief that he can do anything that anyone else can do. Bear has the magic power to provide food from his own flesh without injuring himself, but Rabbit does not, and in imitating Bear does injure himself.

Lines 30–35

These lines are a good example of dialogue carrying the narrative of a tale. Generally, when speech is quoted, the quoted speech is introduced by the verb *ónkak* and followed by the verb *ká:han*, "to say," which carries person, tense, and aspectual information. However, in literary narrative, frequently *ónkak* and its subject are deleted, and here *ká:han* and its associated elements are also deleted so that the speech of each character follows the other, almost as if one were overhearing natural conversation.

In earlier years, when Koasati mythology still formed a coherent system, it seems that Vulture was considered to be the doctor among the various theriomorphic characters. In a story provided to Swanton by Selin Williams (1841–1917) Vulture acts as a true doctor, not the sham doctor that he is in this narrative.

Lines 41–44

Encircling the place where Rabbit is lying with a woven fence of palmetto leaves may reflect the practice of traditional Indian doctors, who were very possessive of their medicines, songs, and rituals. The secrecy of the doctor being expected, the listener does not realize that Vulture is having Rabbit hidden away for a more sinister reason.

Lines 45–50

There is a double meaning to the words that Vulture uses. Bear understands that Rabbit is crying out because he does not like the taste of the medicine that Vulture is giving him. Vulture very cynically refers to his true actions, which are tearing Rabbit apart and eating him, as "his medicine."

Line 54

Marked by its length as an important segment of the scene, Vulture's words again have double meanings. To Bear (and the listener), when Vulture says that Rabbit is good, he understands that Rabbit is now healthy again. In fact, Vulture is cynically mocking Bear, for he means that Rabbit is tasty.

Line 55

This is marked as the climax of the narrative, when Bear realizes how he has been tricked by Vulture, and as a result his friend Rabbit has been killed. Lines c–e are a good example of the use of parallelism to increase dramatic tension.

Line 56

This, the subsidiary climax of the scene, shows the result of Bear's action. Rather than killing Vulture with as he intended by throwing his knife, he only pierced Vulture's beak. It is then left unstated that Vulture escaped with his life.

Lines 57–62

This final scene in its first line sums up the intentions of Bear, and what his actions actually caused, then goes on to state that magically, because Bear pierced Vulture's beak, the beaks of all birds are pierced in the same way. In the end this take has cautioned the listener against hubris like Rabbit's, blind trust, like Bear's, and explained a feature of the natural world.

The Williams Version

This narrative has the distinction of being the first Koasati text to be published, albeit only in part (Swanton 1924:47–48). It was published in translation by Swanton in 1929 (210–211), based on his interlinear glosses. Stylistically, it is one of the weaker stories Selin Williams told, and clearly it was not of much interest to her. The fact that the Abbey version of 1977 is so far superior to Williams's 1910 version is a strong indication that storytellers were not expected to be able to recite the whole corpus of Koasati traditional narrative, but rather specialize in those narratives in which they had a special interest. Selin Williams's best narratives, which are very well told, are unique to her repertoire and are not found elsewhere. In the same way, the well-told traditional narratives in the repertoire of Martha John, one of the best living women storytellers, are unique to her, and are also not found elsewhere. The mixture of quality in narrative recorded nearly eighty years apart, with both good-quality and poor-quality narrative being found at both times, indicates that a dying literary tradition does not necessarily become impoverished over time.

Line 5

The bald statement of what Bear did should be compared to Abbey's elaboration of his scene.

Lines 9–11

There is in these lines a major stylistic flaw. The flaw consists of inconsistent behavior of the characters. After Rabbit cuts himself, rather than Bear running immediately for aid, as in Abbey's version, Bear feeds Rabbit and himself with his own flesh, and then it is mentioned that Rabbit is about to die. Dell Hymes suggests that this flaw is due to interference from a tradition in which the guest, the original benevolent host, feeds the other after the other has failed.

Lines 12–13

This scene, completely bare of any stylistic elaboration contains a further flaw, an inconsistency in the number of characters. Until this point, the only characters are Bear and Rabbit; after this point Bear is replaced by an indefinite "they." This is extremely poor style, according to native standards, and can only be explained by the fact that Williams was not interested enough in the tale to bother to tell it well. Swanton seems to have tried to milk Williams of every story that she had ever heard; in such a case it is only natural that there would be some stories on which she did not feel like exerting herself.

Line 16

This is the only line which Williams bothered to elaborate. For her the deceit of Vulture was the climactic element in the story. This coincides with her interest in the psychology of the Trickster, which is so evident in many of her other narratives.

Lines 24–29

While lines 26 and 27 of this scene consist of two well-structured parallel lines, the ending of the narrative, lines 28 and 29, is extremely weak. Vulture is described as pleased with what happened to him, thus negating the effects of the anger of the others against him for his treachery. Williams's version entirely lacks the explanation that the piercing of Vulture's beak was the origin of the piercing of all birds' beaks, even though the tale, insofar as it goes, sets up the situation where this can be explained.

CONCLUSION

Koasati traditional narrative is an extremely interesting genre, due not only to its linguistic and cultural content but also for what it shows about how a culture can encourage creativity in verbal art. The fact that little is absolutely required of a storyteller beyond the plot skeleton means that he or she can exercise whatever amount of creativity he or she desires, and still produce an acceptable narrative. Furthermore, this way of structuring narratives permits the personality of the narrator to be incorporated into the narrative, so that it bears his or her personal stamp.

The traditional verbal art of the Indians of the southeastern United States is little known, and so it is unclear if Koasati narrative fits into an areal pattern, or whether it has unique features. It may be possible in the future with more work on the viable southeastern Indian languages to discern whether the structuring of traditional narrative reflects the historic interrelationships of the speakers of these languages.

APPENDIX: KOASATI TEXTS

The Koasati texts of the narratives of Jackson Langley and Selin Williams have been retranscribed by the writer from Swanton's 1910 manuscript into the orthography of Kimball 1991. The Koasati texts of Bel Abbey's narratives were transcribed by the writer directly from magnetic recording tape. Abbey's prologues to the narratives are not included, and certain slips of the tongue have been edited out of the texts.

I. The Theft of Fire

Jackson Langley's version	Bel Abbey's version
Scene I: The World Without Fire	**Scene I: The World Without Fire**

1	Yá:li tikbák íksotoho:limpatš.	Yá:lip í:safa tikbák iksóhcotoho:limpáhcok.	1
2a	Mó:tohon,		
b	okicobá tałón má:lon ná:hoto:š tikbák.	Tikbák íkson ohi:sáhcotoho:limpak.	2
3a	Máhmin,	Kámmik,	3a
b	yá:lik tikbá̧ ohimbánnatik,	kámmit í:sato casobáykotik,	b
c	ínká:hi̧ bánkoto:š.	tikbá-íkson í:san.	c
4a	Má:min,	Ma:fó:kap,	4a
b	í:sato:s tikbá-íkson.	okí tałá í:sap tikbák inna:hóhcok óhmin.	b
		Imbànnak í:satoho:limpáhcok.	5
		Tikbá ná:si libá:tlit í:pat í:sa:fó:kon,	6a
		yá:li mók kámmit imbànnok	b
		í:sayok imíksotoho:limpáhcok.	c
		Tikbák imíkson í:san.	7

Scene II: The Quest for Fire Is Proposed	**Scene II: The Quest for Fire Is Proposed**

5a	Mó:tohon,	Má:mo:sin,	8a
b	cokfík ónkak,	naksók áłła:k,	b
6	"Anók ómmi:k, tikbá astiwwalí:kalik" ká:hato:š.	tikbá osta:tiwwalí:kat	c
7a	Má:mo:sin,	ohta:timasílhat stí:la:p,	d
b	á:ti ocotaykihák hasaykáhcok cokkó:tohok ónkak,	"Stí:lan ístílka:p mo:lihalpí:s!" káhhok ittinna:łí:kan.	e
8	"Naksók tikbá ostí:lan tayyihá caffá:kan ínkala:š" káhhan.		
9	Cokfí:kok ónkak,		
10	"Mántik tayyihá caffá:ka:sip stamalpísko:š," ká:hato:š.		

Scene III: The First Questers Fail	**Scene III: The First Questers Fail**

11	Má:min,	Má:mo:sin,	9
12	"Anók," ká:hatoho:limpatš a:ti:pacobák.	"Anáp stí:lalo̧," káhhan,	10
13	"Stí:lalíhc," káhhan.	"Anáp stí:lalo̧," káhhok,	11a
14	Á:ti:kok ónkak,	áłła:p sánkonánnatoho:limpáhcok,	b
15	"Mó:li:p, isnók áłłok ohwíhlit stí:lš!" káhhan.	stíklonánnatoho:limpáhcok,	c
		sánkotikap anáhkan.	d

16a A:ti:pacobá:kok tayyihá bánnak,

 b bikkón ałí:yatoho:limpatš.

17 Má:mik okicobá ohto:cofóttoho:limpatš.

18 O:nakáłto:š.

19a Má:mik,

 b íklot nakáłłan.

Scene IV: Rabbit Is Sent on the Quest

20 Cokfí:kok ónkak,

21 "A:ti ná:sok łóykat íklot," ká:toho:limpatš.

22a "Aná:łok ómmo:š.

 b łóykat í:lahalpí:sak," káhhan.

23 A:ti:kok mán mattóhnoto:š.

24a Má:min,

 b cokfí:kok ónkak,

25a "Mó:li:p, tikbá stí:lali:p,

 b tayyí imaníhtaha óhyan apołó:kallaho:š,"

   ká:toho:limpatš.

26a Má:min,

 b á:tik ónkak,

27 "Mámmitikš!" káhhan.

Scene IV: Rabbit Is Sent on the Quest

Kámmin, 12

"Anók ónkǫ, stí:lalíhc," 13

 ká:hatoho:limpáhcok cokfík.

Má:mo:sin, 14

"Anók ónkǫ, stí:lalíhc," káhhan. 15

"Mó:li:p, ascí:yok stisláhcok ómmi:p, 16a

 tikbá stisláhcómmi:p, b

 ná:son cibanná cįhílkalahǫ," c

 hoká:n.

Má:min, 17

"Anáp tayyihák ká:no:s, 18a

 tayyihák scaká:no:t, b

  tayyihák ká:non cabàn," c

  ká:hatoho:limpáhcok cokfík.

Cokfík intayyihą́ bànnalahomáhco mók 19

ínkotot ómmǫ.

Má:mo:sin, 20

"Mó:li:p, naksón cibànnat 21a

 ohcinfáyhíllahǫ,

  tikbá ohhowíhlit stisláhcok ómmi:p," b

 hoká:n.

"Stí:lalíhc, anók ónkǫ," káhhok, 22a

 ałí:yatoho:limpak. b

Scene V: Rabbit Crosses the Ocean and Steals Fire

28a Má:mo:sin,

 b cokfí:kok yawophilkón ałíytoho:limpatš.

29a Ałí:yak, okifón ó:łat,

 b holikfá síhlit apíslok,

 c ittó tóspon pa:cokkóhlok,

 d sto:wałíytoho:limpatš.

30a Má:mik,

 b o:łopóttoho:limpatš.

31 Á:yatoho:limpatš.

32a Mó:tohon,

 b tikbán a:timbánnan,

 c ohįhíkkon,

Scene V: Rabbit Crosses the Ocean and Steals Fire

O:łopótlitǫ. 23

Tikbá wíhlá:hik, 24a

 kołá o:wá:tatohok tikbá. b

Tikbá a:timásilha:p, 25a

 tikbá ohí:sanánnan, b

 í:sanannatohon. c

Má:mo:sin, 26a

 tikbá i:tinkoybóhlih bànnak, b

 astiwwalí:kah bànnak á:tatoho:limpak. c

Stiwwalí:kah bánnak á:tat ómmá:tok, 27a

 hiłi:líhcok stá:yan, b

 stá:yan, c

d	astimíhsok,	"Sammí:cik ó:łak óncí?" hoká:p,	d
e	astiwwalí:katoho:limpatš.	na:łihíkkot stá:yan.	e
33a	Má:min,	Má:min,	28a
b	hołóhtoho:limpatš.	hołóhtoho:limpáhcok.	b
34a	Má:min,	Hołóhlin,	29
b	stá:yat	Tikbá stá:yat ałí:yatok.	30
c	óhya ittohayó swalí:kat,	Ná:hotoho:limpak,	31
d	stá:ya:sin,		
e	okicobafón óhłok,		
f	oshaccá:lik.		

Scene VI: Rabbit Swims the Ocean with Fire

Scene VI: Rabbit Swims the Ocean with Fire

35a	Mó:tohon,	Stí:sit stá:yato:p	32a
b	coyyí nihán isbakkí obá:li,	masto:cofótlitoho:limpáhcok	b
c	coyyí mashamóhlit anóhlok,	okicobafá.	
d	haccá:tohon,	Kámmik,	33a
e	á:tik łóhli:k ilá:ci:fó:kon,	slakáwwit sto:cowíhlok,	b
f	sto:cofóttoho:limpatš.	stilokmáylok stontíhcoto::,	c
36a	Ilbí abón swáylit,	stilokmáylit stónti:fó:k,	d
b	tikbá stó:wałí:yato:š.	ibi:caslascon stóntiskan,	e
37a	Má:máhpok,	lóhkat anó:katoho:limpáhcok.	f
b	lóhkat anó:kak,	Stonalóhkat anóhkok.	34a
c	isbakkí obá:lin tikbá masbatáplit	tikbá:kok sto:wapí:li:p,	b
d	hiłi:lí:cit sto:wałí:toho:limpatš.	illabóská:hiska:s.	c
38	Kámmit sto:wá:yat o:łopóttoho:limpatš.	Sto:wapí:li:p,	35a
		illabóskan	b
		sammǐ::cit stóntá:hik sobáykot,	c
		obaklóhkat anóhkok sánkon,	d
		ilokmaylíhco:liskan.	e
		Má:mo:sok,	36a
		sǎ:mmit ka:ná:hin sobáykotik,	b
		akostinnicilkók ómmi:p,	c
		isbakkí ákba stalpíscok,	d
		onafáykolahokko:p,	e
		kobalifá maslapa:líhcok,	f
		bakkifá maslapa:líhcok,	g
		ilokmáylik stóntik í:sitohok,	h
		sto:łopótlit	i
		stí:latoho:limpáhcok.	
		Sto:łopótli mántik acaffá:kan.	37

Scene VII: Rabbit Receives His Reward

Scene VII: Rabbit Receives His Reward

39a	Má:mok,	Má:mo:tohok,	38a
b	á:tifa:kon stí:lato:š.	stí:lan stohayókpahónka:sik.	b

40a Máhmin,

b   tayyihá imaníhta ínkak ónkak,

41   "Hiná:p yók cintayyí mó:š," ká:toho:limpatš.

42a Má:mo:sin,

b   cokfí:kok ayókpat ayókpat á:tatoho:limpatš.

43a Mó:tohok,

b   tamóhkan,

c   bálká:hi:fó:kon,

d   cokfík ónkak,

44   "Hotahón tàmmilaho:š anók,"

     ká:toho:limpatš.

45a Má:min,

b   tayyihák ittimmánkak anóskok

c   cokfí ohimpátlin,

d   "Híc!" hoká:n, ballá:kato:š.

Tikbá stí:lan stayókpahónka:sik.   39

Ná:hotoho:limpak,   40

"Hiná:p, naksón cibannáhcon iska:tók!   41a

   Íscá:hik ómmǫ. Ná:son cibannáhcon   b

   iska:tók!"

"Anók hotayyihá cabánkáhp.   42a

   Hotayyihák naksámmit káhnot,   b

    káhnot stimaho:báhcok   c

    scaka:nolahok."

Scene VIII: Rabbit Receives His Comeuppance

46a Ma:fó:kon,

b tayyihák ittimmánkak,

c   "Cokfík balláhkan,

d   inna:łí:kat afá:kat stistílkan,

e   cokfík ayókpahalpí:sat tàmmi:fó:kon,

f   shompá:nit ittȷhalátkok ittaskáhhílkok,

g   acón stonłá,

h   holikfá ȷsíhlok,

i   łómmit apí:hílá:š," hoká:toho:limpatš.

47a Mó:tohok,

b bálka:fó:kon, cokfí:kon shompántoho:limpatš.

48a Má:mo:sin,

b   cokfí:kok hotahán támmit

    ayókpahalpístoho:limpatš.

49a Akkámmit tàmmo:sin,

b   ittȷhalátkok shompá:nit,

c   acón stałá:cok,

d   himá:k sbakóhlá:hih bànnok stí:sa:sin,

e   cokfí:kok yawópkat yawópkok cofótli:k,

f   hohalátkahónka:sin,

g   atabifá afakcón socáffok,

h   walí:kak nakáłtoho:limpatš.

[Epilogue]

50a [Mó:tohok,

b   á:yatoho:š.

51a Mó:tohon,

b   a:ti:pacobók afánkan,

Epilogue

Má:mo:sok,   43a

   máp í:lan a:timasílhan,   b

   ohȷfáyltoho:limpáhcok.   c

"Tayyihák kahnóhco:lin," ká:n.   44

c   ittinna:łí:katoho:š.

52a Máhmin,

b   a:ti:pacobák ónkak,

53   "Naksámmin cįholikfák cipa:íksó?"
     ka:toho:limpatš.

54   Ká:han,

55   Cokfík ónkak,

56a "Iltóhnolik ó:š," ká:toho:limpatš.

b   Tayyihák ǧhasaykáhcok ómmo:š.

c   Acayókpat acayókpš," ká:toho:limpatš.

57   Mántik a:ti:pacobák iyyínkotoho:limpatš.]

Má:mo:sin,   45a

 má cokfík tikbá stí:lan,   b

 tayyihá káhnǫ asílhan ohįfáylin,   d

 stayókpá:hostoho:limpáhcok akkó   d
 í:sak,

  tikbá stí:laskan.   e

II. The Bungling Host

Bel Abbey's version

Scene I: Bear Invites Rabbit to Dinner

1a   Nitáp a:táhcotohok,

b   cokfík ittimbiní:litoho:limpáhcok.

2   Má:mo:sin,

3   "Ambiní:lįh!" ka:háhcotohon,

4   "Ambiní:lįh!" ka:háhcotohon cokfį́.

5   Má:mo:sin,

6   "Cimbiní:lilá:hiton," káhcok cokfík nitá.

Scene II: Bear Feeds Rabbit with Himself

7a   Má:mo:sin,

b   imbiní:lá:hik ó:łan,

c   cikkí:kat ómmá:ton,

d   ná:son ínkat í:pat í:pá:hik imíksoton,

e   "Ná:son ínkat í:palahá'wá?" á:lok,

f   sobbáylok á:tatohok.

8a   Ná:hok, niták nì:háhco:liskan,

b   ikfí:kon mathalátkok,

c   aksalí matíhsok,

d   matkoyóffok,

e   illibá:łok,

f   ínkat í:patoho:limpáhcok cokfį́.

9a   Má:mo:sin,

b   cokfík hi:cat cokkŏ::toho:limpáhcok.

Scene III: Rabbit Invites Bear to Dinner

10   Má:mó:sok, imbiní:láhpok łóykaton.

11   "Isnok amó:łąh!" ká:haton,

Selin Williams's version

Scene I: Bear Invites Rabbit to Dinner

Nitón cokfón ittimóklatoho:limpatš.   1

Máhmin,   2a

 niták ónkak,   b

"Ohtambiní:li:š," ká:hok ałí:yatohon.   3

Scene II: Bear Feeds Rabbit with Himself

Cokfí:kok ałí:yak óhłan,   4

Nitá:kok ilipitáffok,   5a

 nihá matpíhlok,   b

 sawwí:cin í:patoho:limpatš.   c

Scene III: Rabbit Invites Bear to Dinner

Ma:mó:sin,   6a

 cokfí:kok ónkak,   b

12 "Isnok amó:łąh!" ká:haton,

13 Niták ałí:yatoho:limpáhcok imbiní:lit cokfí.

14a Ná:hon, cokfík imó:łan,

b cokkó:t ómmá:tok.

15a Akkáp nitá imí:sap ittó:bihayot ómmi:k,

b ittó:bihayo cikkí:kat áswat,

c áswat ómmá:ton

d cokfí imó:łaton.

16a Cokfík pahí scokkó:lo:sihayó cokkó:tohon,

b má á:tahayotoho:limpáhcok.

17 Má:fon cikkí:katohon.

"Isnok amo:łá:š," ká:haton.　　7

Scene IV: Rabbit Injures Himself Imitating Bear

18 Cokfík ónkak,

19a "Cokkó:citík! Libátlili má!" káhhan,

b áswat ómmá:ton.

20a Ibisnók akkammí:cit hí:ca:fó:k,

b aksalí matí:sit matacakoyóffitohon,

c ikfí koyóffitoho:limpáhcok.

21a Ibisnáp sówwit solotkáhcotoho:litá:łok,

b ilikoyóffit ilįho:páhcok,

c "Amawíc! Amawíc! Amawicilkón cabàn!" káhhan.

22 Niták walí:katon,

23 "Naksámmik?"

24 "Anok ąhó:p. Ilikoyóffilíhcónka:s" káhhan.

25 Má:mo:sin,

26a "Alikcón wíhlilą, mó:li:p," káhhok,

b achalí:kok walí:katoho:limpáhcok niták.

27a Ittatámmin,

b koyóffok ikfį.

Scene IV: Rabbit Injures Himself Imitating Bear

Nitá:kok imbiní:lik óhłan,　　8

Cokfí:kok ilipitáftohon,　　9a

Ná:sok íksotohon,　　b

Nitaká:lok ilipitáffok sawwí:cin ohí:pato:š.　　10

Ma:fó:kap,　　11a

cokfí:kok íllá:himá:š.　　b

Scene V: Bear Encounters Vulture

28a Má:mo:sin,

b walí:kat ómma:tok,

c pa:cokkó:tohon híhcokš,

d saykík pa:cokkó:tohon híhcok,

e imasilhá:citoho:limpak.

29 Má:mo:sin,

30 "Amawicilkón cabàn," ká:hat ómmá:ton,

31 "Ná:son cibànnok ómmi:k?"

32 "Alikcón wíhlili:s."

33 "Naksán awicilkán hí:cáhik cibá?ná?"

34a "Cokfík amoklák įho:páhcon ónkah," káhhan,

Scene V: Vulture Is Encountered

Tàmmin,　　12

Alikcón howíhlik yomáhtohok,　　13

Saykón hotóhnon.　　14

b   "Cokfík i̯ho:páhcon ónkan,
c   koyofkáhcon ónkan," káhhan. ·
35a "Stammą́híska:p, cimawí:cillahomá:mik,
b   imalíkcillaho katík óm," káhhan.

Scene VI: Vulture "Doctors" Rabbit

36   Ołá:cit ómmá:ton,
37   Má:mosin,
38   "Naksofón tá?mí?" káhhan.
39   "Yin tàm," káhhan.
40   Má:mo:sin,
41a "Ná:son sammi:císká?
b   Ná:son cibá?ná?" káhhan.
42a "Imí:sa stimaholihtá:cimá:mik,
b   stimatanahlí:ci:p mo:lihalpí:s," káhhan.
43a "Tá:la hísson wíhlok,
b   óhya stimaholihtá:cit isá:cit
     stimatanatlíhcok!"
44a "Mǫ́ hiná:p!
b   Achalí:k!
c   Acicákkik imalíkcilá:híhcon óm,"
     káhhan.
45a Má:mo:sin, ná:hok,
b   saykí:kok cokfí yahlí:citoho:limpáhcok.
46a Cokfí yahlí:ci:fó:kon,
b   niták, "Sámmin ónká?" ká:toho:limpak.
47   "Ínko:š. Ahissí ambánkon ónk," káhhan.
48   Má:mo:sin,
49   "Sámmin bánkon ó?mí?" káhhan.
50a "Ahissí ínkalá:hik ambánkon ónkan,
b   naksá:kak," káhhan.
51   Má:mo:sin,
52   "Ná:son cibá?ná mán?" káhhan.
53   Má:min,
54a "Ínkǫ.
b   Imalíkcit fáylilá:hin óm.
c   Ka:nóhco:liyon hiná:p.
d   Hiná:p̣ ka:nóhco:lin ónk," ká:hok,
e   wáykat abá itto insá:wa
     ohpa:cokkó:lin.

Scene VII: Bear Assaults Vulture

55a Má:mosin,
b   niták cokhalí:kat hí:cat ómmá:ton,

Scene VI: Vulture "Doctors" Rabbit

Saykik ónkak,	15
"I:san staconokbáhhácin,	16a
sakíklon,	b
á:tok caikhí:con,	c
má:łon alíkcilíhco:š," káhhan.	d
Stonokbáhto:š.	17
Máhmin, ihǫ́:cap cokfí:kok yáhkat	18
nakáłłan.	
"Sámmin," hoká:n.	19
"Mánko:š! Ahissí immałátlihónkš,"	20
ká:to:š.	
Mó:tohok,	21
"Okhicá antiwaphó:š!" káhhan.	22
Ohintiwáplin,	23a
wáykat má:fon ohpa:cokkó:lin.	b

Scene VII: Vulture Is Assaulted

Cokfí:kon ohhohí:catohon,	24
Cofkoninánnan ballá:toho:limpatš.	25

c   cokfí óhya í:pat anó:lok,

d   nipón í:pat anó:lok,

e   cokfoninánnan cikkí:tohon,

f   niták noksí:pahónka:sik,

g   aksalí ilasá:citohok íhsok,

h   sbakóhlit saykí pilahón.

56a Sbakóhlit ómma:tok,

b   ibisá:ni matacasáhlin,

c   ibisá:ni įłobóffin,

d   ibisá:ni matacasáhlin í:sit,

e   aksalį́ í:sit matapí:litoho:limpáhcok.

Má:mo:sin,   26a

saykí:kon ohįhó:pak mathohóccaton,   b

Ibisá:ni má:łon łá:hit   27

ohintalałopotlí:cok.

Saykík ónkak,   28

"Ó:! Ibisá:ni ataká:kon stankano:cá:š,"   29

ká:toho:limpatš.

Scene VIII: The Result of Bear's Action

57a Í:bilahotok,

b   immáttok,

c   ibisá:ni łobóffitoho:limpáhcok.

58a Má:mo:sin,

b   ibisá:ni łobófkak,

c   niták įłobóffit ómmin,

d   ímmot stá:yat stonafáyt ómmok,

e   ímmot syomáhlinánnampáhcok.

59 Kámmisk, fó:sik naksántik ibisá:ni łobófka.

60 Kámmin įłobófkat ommimpáhcok.

61 Ká:mo:s.

62 Tafhiyám!

REFERENCES

Haas, Mary R. n.d.*a*. Koasati texts. Manuscript.

———. n.d.*b*. Koasati-English Vocabulary. Manuscript.

Hymes, Dell. 1987. "Tonkawa Poetics: John Rush Buffalo's 'Coyote and Eagle's Daughter'." In *Native American Discourse: Poetics and Rhetoric,* edited by Joel Sherzer and Anthony C. Woodbury, 17–61. Cambridge: Cambridge University Press.

Kimball, Geoffrey. 1989. "Peregrine Falcon and Great Horned Owl: Ego and Shadow in a Koasati Tale." *Southwest Journal of Linguistics* 9:45–74.

———. 1991. *Koasati Grammar.* Lincoln: University of Nebraska Press.

LeGuin, Ursula K. 1974. "Why Are Americans Afraid of Dragons?" In *The Language of the Night,* 39–46. New York: G. P. Putnam's Sons.

Swanton, John R. 1910. Koasati Texts, Second Series. American Anthropological Archives. Manuscript no. 1818. Washington, D.C.

———. 1924. "The Muskhogean Connection of the Natchez Language." *International Journal of American Linguistics* 3:46–75.

———. 1929. *Myths and Tales of the Southeastern Indians*. Bureau of American Ethnology Bulletin no. 88. Washington, D.C.

———. 1930. Koasati Linguistic Material from Jackson Langley. American Anthropological Archives. Manuscript no. 4153. Washington, D.C.

TRADITION AND INNOVATION
IN OJIBWE STORYTELLING

Mrs. Marie Syrette's "The Orphans and Mashos"

Ridie Wilson Ghezzi

In the period of intense collecting of Native American texts at the turn of the century, the anthropologist William Jones made a contribution by transcribing narratives collected from Ojibwe storytellers in the region north of Lake Superior. Mrs. Marie Syrette's narration of "The Orphans and Mashos" represents a single performance within a long tradition of verbal art in Ojibwe culture. Her story is one of many Ojibwe narratives collected and transcribed by Jones, a student of Franz Boas, between 1903 and 1905. After Jones's death, these texts underwent further editing by the anthropologist Truman Michelson, again under Boas's direction, for publication by the American Ethnological Society. Mrs. Syrette was living in Fort William, Ontario, at the time of her narrative work with Jones, although she grew up at Lake Nipigon, near Lake Superior. Her Ojibwe name was Kaagigepinaasikwaa, "Forever-Bird-Woman." Unfortunately, this small amount of information is all that is available from Jones's field notes.

This article is concerned with a narration by one storyteller within the tradition of Ojibwe taletelling. In Mrs. Syrette's telling of "The Orphans and Mashos" there are aspects of her narrative that are *individual,* innovative on a personal level, and those that are *collective,* coming out of the traditions of her culture and tribe. The combination of her personal style and the traditional forms of Ojibwe storytelling interweaves to create her special art. These individual and collective elements are manifest in both the structure and the content of a text, and play a significant role in the analysis of this and any traditional narrative.

There are certain hazards and complications that exist when studying a text transcribed almost a century ago. There are the hazards of transcription itself: how representative is the transcription of the actual performance? There were no tape recorders or video cameras to record the event, only Jones's pad and pencil. As he did not record any notes on surroundings, participants, gestures, pauses, and so forth, any knowledge of the context has disappeared. There are complications involved in the translation process. William Jones collected and translated the present text, but he died before the final translation was completed. Michelson's editing is careful, yet he mentions in the introduction to the collection that the typed copy of Jones's field notes was prepared by someone "who had no knowledge of Ojibwa" and revised and occasionally retranslated by Michelson, all after a ten-year lapse. Fortunately, Jones's interest was in the stories themselves, "not to find out how well a story could be told" (xi) and the form of the story that Jones recorded represents the first dictation, not necessarily a "better" rendition.

Before presenting "The Orphans and Mashos" in both the Ojibwe original and the English translation, I think it is important to discuss certain aspects of presentation and the decisions made in regard to form. As mentioned briefly above, Mrs. Syrette's tale is one of 124 Ojibwe narratives collected and transcribed by the anthropologist William Jones from 1903 to 1905, only years before his sudden death in 1909. Franz Boas requested that the Ojibwe manuscript be turned over to him for the purpose of reporting on its condition. Boas then obtained the cooperation of the American Ethnological Society, and the editorial work was then assigned to Truman Michelson for completion. Little is known about Jones's informants, including Mrs. Syrette. Even in the manuscripts of his field notes Jones provides no more information about these than is available in the introduction to his text collection.

In addition to realigning Mrs. Syrette's tale from paragraphs of sentences to groups of lines, I have attempted to clarify the text by replacing archaic and awkward forms of speech found in the original with more modern vocabulary. In conjunction with this effort, I have occasionally changed the word order of sentences to provide a more readable structure. These changes have not affected meaning within the narrative. To the contrary, they have frequently provided clarification.

While great care was taken by Jones to preserve the original word order of the Ojibwe text, great liberties were taken in the retention or omission of initial markers. The retention of initial markers and their consistent translation are paramount to understanding the patterns and structures of these texts. These markers are frequently the key to the rhetorical conception of the text itself, yet their presence in the translation is not consistent. The frequent repetition of these markers appears to have been regarded more as a hindrance than as a window into the internal workings of the narrative.

These changes in texts occurred not only in Jones's work but also in that of many of the fieldworkers who translated texts in his day. The markers' function was not recognized, and exact repetition was considered a violation of desirable style. Hence their occurrence in English was misleading as to the rhetorical relations of the original in three ways: markers were sometimes left untranslated; when translated, the English translation would vary according to the context ("and," "then," "so," and the like); these same words might be supplied in English where they did not occur in the original. All of these changes take one further from the original text.

I have chosen to present the text in a linear form, loosely based on the structure of dramatic poetry. There is strong evidence from within the texts themselves that a consistent prose rendering, as this tale was originally transcribed by Jones, may conceal important internal patterns and rhythms. The rearrangement of a prose form into lines and groups of lines, even with no further analysis, initiates the recognition of patterns in the text and highlights naturally existing relationships between form and content.

The realignment of Mrs. Syrette's text is primarily based on divisions made according to predication. Divisions into lines are also made by the presence of quoted speech and by the locutives surrounding that speech ("he thought," "he said," and so on). These divisions are especially significant in the present text, for Mrs. Syrette uses these descriptives frequently in moments of heightened intensity.

In working with texts collected and transcribed at a much earlier date, with no access to the performance context, one must rely on the relationships between words and grammatical features, such as particles, to disclose the inner workings of a text. By using a linear form, similar to Dell Hymes's "measured verse" (1981), patterns are more easily recognized and compared. Originally oral, these narratives were in neither a prose nor a verse form, so the statement that one form of presentation is more correct than another is superfluous. Many of the divisions and features within the text are so real that they jump off the page at you. Their presence would be obvious in whatever form the narrative was presented. Other possible divisions, however, are not as clear and the decisions made are sometimes arbitrary but educated ones rather than indicated explicitly by the text itself.

In the case of recent fieldwork where more of the context can be documented, presentation on the page becomes significant primarily for the indication of changes in performance style and, as in the present study, recognition of patterns within the text. Whether the narrator saw these patterns in his or her own mind as the tale was performed is impossible to know for sure. There is certainly evidence in the research that these patterns are significant and recurrent within the literary traditions of many Native American groups (see Bahr 1975; Bright 1979; Hymes 1981; McClendon 1982; Tedlock 1978, 1983; Woodbury 1985).

There is now much significant discussion about the presentation of prose and poetic forms on the page. Many scholars believe that in the literature with which they work there probably exists a relationship between the two forms. The presence of one does not necessarily cancel out the other. Instead, there may be sections of a narrative that can be appropriately represented in prose form and others whose rhythm warrants a poetic line (see especially Bright 1980 and Glassie 1982). In Mrs. Syrette's narrative, for instance, I have wondered about the possibility of the presence of both prose and poetic structures. Her narrative is filled with long, descriptive passages, with sentences much longer than those of other Ojibwe storytellers I have studied from the same period. At moments of heightened intensity, however, her lines become truncated, staccato-like. The long sentences disappear. I am not sure of the significance of these patterns, but these findings resemble patterns that Henry Glassie has found in Irish English, and indicate a need for further study in this area.

Mrs. Syrette's narrative of "The Orphans and Mashos" is actually a story in two sections. The first part, presented here, is a version of the traditional "rolling head" tale, represented in the oral traditions of many Native American cultures as well as in the Grimms' *Kinder- und Hausmärchen* (see Thompson 1929:163 ff, and Bierhorst 1985:214). "The Orphans and Mashos" story relates separate adventures of two little orphaned brothers. The first tells of the orphaned boys as they escape from their "dead" mother who pursues them. The second, not discussed here, tells of the older of the two boys and Mashos, the old man who first tricks the elder boy into leaving his baby brother on a deserted island, then unsuccessfully tries several times to kill the older boy as he sees him growing into a strong young man in his village.

The first adventure relates how the boys become orphans and begin their travels. When the boys' mother is discovered to be a *manito,* a transformed being of great power, their father kills her and sends the boys away in fear of the mother's revenge on them. On their father's instructions, they run in the direction of their grandmothers' villages. The two grandmothers give them, first, an awl and comb and then some flint and punk. As their mother's skeleton chases them, they throw the grandmothers' gifts behind them, one at a time, thereby creating large mountains that stand in her way. They reach a river where the Horned Grebe takes them safely across. The Horned Grebe agrees to carry the mother across as well when she reaches the river, but warns her not to step on his back. In her haste to reach the other side she ignores the Horned Grebe's warning, steps on his back, and falls into the river and drowns.

As can be seen, the outline of the tale gives no indication of the richness of this story and Mrs. Syrette's own artistry. As Mrs. Syrette tells it, the story of "The Orphans and Mashos" is full of pathos and drama. When the father has to send the boys away, the listener feels the weight of the cradleboard upon the little boy's back. One senses the terror and horror as the small boys are chased by their own mother, who is now only a skeleton and wants to kill them. Mrs. Syrette has the ability as a storyteller to draw the listener into her tale through her careful use of repetition and parallel action.

In both content and structure, collective and individual ingredients inform Mrs. Syrette's text. In regard to structure, specific elements found in all Ojibwe texts also recur in this and other texts narrated by Mrs. Syrette. The most indicative of these collective forms is the consistent use of initial markers, most significantly *ninguting* (translated here as "now presently") and *miidac* (translated as "now then").

The discourse marker *ninguting* is the most prominent and consistent of all the structural markers identifying points of transition within an Ojibwe narrative. It is a significant marker in all of the Ojibwe texts I have studied and is used consistently to mark major sections of a narrative. The linguist Richard Rhodes, who has undertaken important research in Ojibwe discourse, regards its basic function as one of a major transitional marker (Rhodes 1979). While Rhodes states that *ninguting* appears as the first word in the first sentence of an episode (107), it is clear from my own study of Ojibwe narratives that its presence is more complicated than may have been originally assumed. While almost always linked to the beginning of a new episode, and always appearing as the first word in a sentence, it is clear that this marker only occasionally occurs in the first sentence of an episode. More frequently, *ninguting* appears in a non-initial position, at the beginning of a text as well as in subsequent episodes within a narrative. In Ojibwe texts I have studied the sentence containing *ninguting* is preceded by a line of "going along," a line indicating the passage of time or another line whose content marks a shift in emphasis. *Ninguting* occasionally occurs more than once at the beginning of an episode, repeating two or three times within the same section of a text. Clearly there is room for more study of the variety of positions available to *ninguting,* but it is indisputable that this marker consistently highlights primary divisions within Ojibwe narratives.

Mrs. Syrette's use of *ninguting* follows the general pattern of its use found in the majority of Ojibwe narratives. In the first episode, she repeats *ninguting* three times at the beginning of the narrative, a common repetition in other Ojibwe texts. From the content of the narrative, it is clear that the three occurrences of this marker belong together and are not indications of new major sections.

Of all the markers appearing in the Ojibwe storytelling tradition, the most pervasive is the marked *miidac* ("and then"). Richard Rhodes states that "the function of *dash* [I would include the particle *mii* which is consistently attached to it] seems to be to indicate a subset of the most prominent sentences expressing both thematic and background information as the outline or synopsis of a text" (106). My findings agree with his conclusions, although I would add that the actual use of *miidac* varies greatly by narrator. When it is not used frequently, either a variety of other markers take its place, none given greater weight than the others, or few markers are used at all. When *miidac* does appear frequently, however, its presence is of major consequence within the text, and it can be used with great force in moments of heightened intensity. No other marker appears to have this individualistic role in Ojibwe narratives. *Miidac* is a perfect example of the interplay between collective and individual elements within a narrative.

As an individual within a collective tradition, Mrs. Syrette's own use of this initial marker indicates her skill at manipulating traditional forms for her own creative intentions. In "The Orphans and Mashos" *miidac* dominates the narrative, marking 108 of the 136 verses. Its appearance is consistent but much less frequent in other Ojibwe texts studied. Not only does *miidac* appear consistently throughout her text, but its use becomes even more consistent during incidents of heightened drama, initiating every line of what are usually shortened staccato-like sentences. This is most clearly evident through lines 218–289 and again through lines 331–468, as the mother chases the boys. Nearly every line of the text at this point is marked by *miidac*. The drama becomes even more heightened as *miidac* and its derivatives ("and," "then") are coupled with *miinawa* ("again"), adding to the urgency and fast pace of these scenes:

> And again then she was in pursuit of her children.
> And then again did the children hear their mother,
>   faintly they heard the sound of her voice coming
>   closer.
>
> Again as before it came saying:
>   "Bring him to me!
>   I want to suckle your little brother!"
>
> And then again the boy wept aloud,
>   all the harder did he begin to run.
> And then again he bumped his heels.
> Then again they heard their mother,
>   ever nearer kept coming the sound of her voice.
>   (ll. 256–266)

There are situations within Mrs. Syrette's tale where the marker *miidac* is not present. These occur throughout the text, usually one line here, one line there. In lines 148–168, however, eight verses are delivered with only one instance of *miidac* occurring. Within these eight verses the boys' father burns the mother/manito after he has caught her at the snake tree. Three times the woman pleads with the man not to burn her, and three times the man does not speak. This section stands out as it is surrounded by sections containing consistent repetition of *miidac* initiating verses. The presence of the repetition of threes, as opposed to the two/four pattern more common to Ojibwe narrative, has proven significant in foregrounding scenes of heightened intensity. The lack of the use of *miidac* here marks this section different in some way, just as in certain situations where speech may be expected, silence becomes marked.

Another discourse marker that plays an important collective role in Ojibwe narrative is *giiwe* ("they say"). Richard Rhodes labels this type of marker part of the "interactive phenomena" of a text or "how the speaker is using the text to interact with the hearer" (103). In addition to this role, *giiwe* also functions as a way of distancing the narrator from the events occurring within the text, due either to its sacred mythological content or, in more contemporary narrative, to the storyteller's desire not to be held responsible for the information being relayed in the story.

This type of reported speech was originally explained to me by an Ojibwe informant in Minnesota. *Giiwe* allows the narrator to tell a story about anything or anybody, without being held responsible for the material as "truth," only what the narrator has heard rumored as true. *Giiwe* infers that the information is secondhand; "it is rumored that" as my informant put it. Craig Mishler discusses the use of "they say," a form common to the narratives of many Native American groups, and its possible significance in traditional discourse (Mishler 1981). There is also a growing corpus of literature concerned with the phenomenon of "reported speech" in discourse (see Banfield 1973; Bauman 1983; Hymes 1987; Silverstein 1985; Urban 1984).

While the marker *giiwe* can certainly be considered a collective marker in the sense that many Ojibwe narrators use this form in their storytelling repertoire, there are some storytellers who never employ this marker within their texts. Mrs. Syrette repeats *giiwe* five times in the first fifty lines alone, then includes the marker nine times more through line 250. She stops using the marker at this point. She seems to use the marker most significantly in setting the stage at the beginning of the story, in a traditional means of distancing herself from what will follow. It appears that not only is there an individual choice in how one uses this traditional marker, it is also part of an individual's choice whether or not to use it at all.

Another structural aspect of Ojibwe narrative, indeed of all traditional Native American literature, is repetition, and again there are both collective and individual variations on its use. Repetition can occur as the direct recurrence of verbal elements used for intense effect within a text, such as described above in regard to Mrs. Syrette's use of *miidac*. In "The Orphans and Mashos" there is also frequent repetition of "he thought" and "he said" at the beginning and ends of lines, particularly in the long, discursive passages (see, e.g., ll. 90–117, and especially ll. 408–460). The consistent repetition of these two markers of reported speech are extensions of Mrs. Syrette's use of *miidac*. That is, they provide constant rhythmic breaks in the dialogue where initial particles do not occur.

Repetition may also refer to the recurrence of entire ideas or events in a pattern or to the summation of preceding episodes of the narrative, which often occur as epilogues. In Mrs. Syrette's narrative, the orphaned boys visit their two grandmothers, one who gives them an awl and comb with directions and interdictions, another who gives them flint and punk with more directions and interdictions. Certain events occur when the boys meet the Horned Grebe, and the episode is repeated with different results when their mother's skeleton reaches the Horned Grebe.

It is clear from the above discussion that there are structural elements in traditional Ojibwe literature that occur on a collective level; that is, certain formal aspects that come out of the cultural tradition and inform all texts within that tradition. Within that collective information, individual innovation occurs as well; a narrator manipulates the collective structure to his or her own creative ends.

This process occurs not only at the structural but also at the content level. The story of "The Orphans and Mashos" contains many traditional elements of Ojibwe culture and worldview that give the narrative meaning from an Ojibwe point of view. Through her own skill and artistic style, however, Mrs. Syrette takes this collective skeleton and creates a horror story comparable in its effect to any Hitchcock tale.

Ojibwe narratives are the tradition bearers of Ojibwe culture; they represent all that is traditionally significant and sacred to the Ojibwe people, manifested in a thickly metaphorical and allegorical form. While the allusions in these stories are significant reaffirmations of traditional beliefs to the Ojibwe listener, "for one who is not a Woodland Indian, even a casual reading of these tales makes one aware of being taken into another world, a world in which the contour of things, their inter-relations and transformations, are ordered but unfamiliar" (Overholt and Callicott 1982:23).

The Ojibwe are an Algonquin-speaking group whose original homeland was primarily around the northern shore of Lake Huron and the eastern end of Lake Superior. There is no single Ojibwe "tribe" in the sense of a single sociopolitical entity due mainly to the strong effects of the French fur trade, which stimulated migrations of various groups from their earlier homeland. By as early as 1800, there were four identifiable segments of Ojibwe. The most northern of the groups migrated west through the territory north of Lake Superior. This group is commonly referred to as the Saulteaux (due to their former residence at Sault Ste. Marie) or as the Northern Ojibwe. The Northern Ojibwe consisted primarily of small, isolated hunting bands, carrying on the traditional patterns of hunting life. They would come together as a band in the summer months and separate during the harsh winters into family groups on traditional hunting grounds. This is the area where the anthropologist A. Irving Hallowell undertook his study of Ojibwe worldview and culture, and it is significant that even in the early mid-twentieth century, when Hallowell undertook his fieldwork, the Northern Ojibwe were still relatively isolated, leading a considerably more traditional life than more southerly bands.

The group known as the Southwestern Ojibwe traveled through the Upper Peninsula of Michigan westward into Wisconsin and Minnesota, displacing the Sioux tribes already living there. These groups were also hunters and gatherers and were heavily involved in the fur trade. The Southeastern Ojibwe inhabited portions of the Lower Peninsula of Michigan and adjoining areas in Ontario. Their primary means of subsistence were hunting, fishing, and some horticulture. The Bungee, or Plains Ojibwe, moved westward, integrating themselves into the bison-hunting economy of the Plains.

William Jones did his fieldwork west and north of Lake Superior. Mrs. Syrette's narrative therefore comes from the northern portion of Southwestern Ojibwe territory. There are some important cultural differences between the four groups; for example, the villages were more permanent and significant in the southern groups than in the northern, where nomadic systems of hunting and trapping territories played a larger role in the sociopolitical picture. These differences, however, are overshadowed by a broader, a historically deeper linguistic and cultural matrix that connects the four groups.

The most important element of Ojibwe culture that has a pervasive effect on all traditional Ojibwe narratives, including Mrs. Syrette's, is the relationship between humans, the *anicinaabek,* and what Irving Hallowell calls the other-than-human class of beings, the *pawaaginaak* or the *manitok* (Hallowell 1960). There are numerous *manitok* with different types of relationships to different individuals. The most powerful *manitok* were the Four Winds, the Underwater Manito, Thunderbirds, Windigo, and Nanabush. There were, however, many more minor *manitok* who also played important roles in the daily lives of the Ojibwe, most particularly in the other-than-humans' ability to affect hunting success and in the influence they maintained in the social relationships between people.

The significance of Hallowell's term other-than-human lies in the *manitok* being perceived, not as supernatural beings, but as absolutely natural forces of their own kind. The role of the *manitok* is directly related to the Ojibwe's concepts of animate and inanimate. According to Hallowell, objects normally considered inanimate may acquire an animate personality due to historical events, those occurring in the narratives, that forever change the way an object is perceived. This fluidity of animism and inanimism can be clarified by understanding the Ojibwe concepts of power and metamorphosis, all central ideas in traditional Ojibwe narrative.

The concepts of power and metamorphosis appear throughout Ojibwe narratives and are closely linked to one another. Other-than-human beings occupy the top rank in the hierarchy of animate beings. Human beings do not differ from them in kind, only in power. The realization of power comes in a being's or object's ability to transform itself into another shape. It is taken for granted that a manito can assume a variety of forms, since their powers are the greatest (thus explaining the mother/skeleton's ability to suggest sexual offers). For human beings, however, while the potential for metamorphosis exists, any outward manifestation is inextricably associated with unusual power for good or evil (see Hallowell 1960, Vecsey 1983, and Overholt and Callicott 1982).

These collective cultural concepts pervade "The Orphans and Mashos." What may seem to be magical elements within the story from a Western European narrative point of view are in fact possible natural occurrences from the traditional Ojibwe viewpoint. The metamorphosis of the boys' mother into the snakes' lover is a reasonable possibility. Her skeleton chasing them, calling out to the two boys certifies her manito status and her great power. Throughout the story, the traditional relationship between humans and those of other-than-human status is consistently illustrated and reinforced.

In addition to the collective elements of Ojibwe culture represented in Mrs. Syrette's narrative, there are other factors that connect this tale to the Western European narrative tradition. Most interesting is the presence of a traditional tale motif found in European tales in a variety of forms. In "The Orphans and Mashos" the two boys are given four magic objects by their grandmothers to aid them in their escape from their mother/skeleton. One grandmother gives them a comb and an awl, while the second grandmother gives them flint and punk. They are to throw the objects behind them when they think the manito is near, but each grandmother warns them not to look behind. They obey her warning, a mountain of each item appears as they hurl the objects, and they are finally saved from the manito's danger.

An almost identical series of events occur in the Grimm story of the "Water Nixie," when two children escape from the well witch who has captured them by throwing first a comb then a mirror behind them from which mountains of combs and glass appear.

In the Motif Index, this element is identified as D672, "Obstacle Flight," and is documented in note 205 in folklorist Stith Thompson's *Tales of the North American Indians* (1929). Its similarity to the Ojibwe tale is striking despite the difference in context (see also Thompson 1919 for further discussion of this phenomenon). As mentioned above, the motif of the "rolling head" is also common in both Native American and Western European tales, again indexed by Thompson as Motif R261 and documented in note 238 (Thompson 1929).

What makes Mrs. Syrette's story unique is the individual innovation she brings to this traditional tale. In regard to content, the aspect of her tale that makes it most specifically her own is her intense connection to the children and their plight. There is little biographical information on Mrs. Syrette, and it is impossible to know if she had children and grandchildren. Her response to these two little boys, however, and her subtle use of language to portray their vulnerability indicate her great artistic abilities. Several times she refers to the smaller brother as "your tiny little brother" (lines 8, 95, and 103). Mrs. Syrette also indicates the smallness of even the older brother by the size of the cradleboard upon his back:

> And then they say he took up the cradleboard on which was
> > tied his little son.
> > He lifted it upon the back of his son who was older.
> And with that cradleboard the boy almost touched the ground.
> > > (ll. 119–121)

> And then he started to run;
> > he was not able to run very well,
> > > then he would hit his heels with the cradleboard.
> > > (11. 225–227)

When Mrs. Syrette's narrative is compared to a similar story by another storyteller in Jones's collection, her involvement with the children and her ability to articulate that involvement become even more evident. In Waasagunackank's text, "The Rolling Skull," the story line is basically the same, but there is a lack of descriptive elaboration, especially in regard to the children and their flight from their mother (Jones 1917:405–413).

The difference in elaboration is also evident in the two narrators' respective involvement with the father in the story. In "The Orphans and Mashos," the boys' father simply "goes away" after he has killed the mother, a departure that takes all of five lines (ll. 169–173). Mrs. Syrette then returns to the children: "And then again the children are taken up in the story" (line 174). In "The Rolling Skull," the father tells the boys that if they see a red glow in the sky at evening time, then he has been killed. Waasagunackank even includes a song that the father tells his sons to sing about him as they go along. As the boys continue, they see the sky redden and know that their father has been slain. Waasagunackank's entire text is only 212 lines, which makes the allowance of forty-three lines in which to narrate the plight of the father even more significant. As is clear here and everywhere else in her narration, Mrs. Syrette's primary interest is with the children. Once the mother is killed, Mrs. Syrette is eager to continue with the plight of the two little boys.

Again, in comparing these two versions of the same tale it is clear that what makes Mrs. Syrette's narrative more than twice as long as "The Rolling Skull" are the long descriptive lines that occur in both the narrative and discursive sections of her story. Through her descriptive use of language, she is able to paint a picture of terror and urgency that pervades sections of the tale. She successfully contrasts these longer lines with the shorter ones found in the highly dramatic sections of the text (see, for example, ll. 218–289).

Looking at the whole picture of a text is imperative to understanding that text. As has been illustrated above, any work of art coming out of a particular tradition is constructed of both collective and individual elements that are interwoven to create the complete performance. These collective and individual aspects pervade the structure and the content of a narrative. The strength of Mrs. Syrette's narrative of "The Orphans and Mashos" lies not only in the tradition of storytelling that exists in Ojibwe culture, but also in what she brings to the basic story from her own experience and her own artistry as a teller of tales.

In order to treat Native American literature with the seriousness that it is due, one has to take into account not just the text but, when possible, the individual artist behind the text as well. There are those who have always been committed to this idea: Dell Hymes and his work with texts by Louis Simpson, Hiram Smith, and others (Hymes 1976, 1980a, 1980b, 1981, 1983, 1984); Barre Toelken and the stories told by Yellowman (Toelken 1969, 1981). More often, however, Native American texts have been dealt with as separate entities with no relationship to the creative mind behind them. There are differences in the narrative traditions between tribes, but there are also differences between the creative acts of individuals within a tribal group.

The Orphans and Mashos I

Narrated by Mrs. Marie Syrette

Ningutinga giiwe aniicinaabä aiindaa wiidigämaaganan,   1
    gayä niijiwan kiiwä uniidcaanisiwaan.
        Päjik aa'pidci agaaciiwan.
Miidec giiwe aiindaawag.
    Inini ändasogijiik andawäncigä;   5
        awädec i'kwä kayä wiin manisä tciibaa'kwä
            gayä.
Iniw dec uniidcaanisiwaa madciniij kwiiwisänsag.
    Miidec awä zäzii'kizit kwiiwisäns känawänimaat
        uciimäyänsan ugiin manisänit
            tanama'kamigizinitsagu gayä.

Ningudingdac giiw*e* aiindaawaat,   10
    awäinini kayä wiin ändasogiiji'k maadcaat
                        papaandowändcigät.
Awinini patagwicing umi'kawaan,
    wiiwan pitcinag wiimanisät kayä
        wiitciibaa'kwät.
Abinodciiyag gayä aa'pitci niciiwunaatisiwag.   15

Niiguting dac giiw*e* awinini maaminonändam,
    inändank:
    "Amantcisa äjiwäbatogwän?",
                inändam.
Miigu tasing äjimi'kawät,   20
    iiniw wiiwan pitciinag maadci'taanit
                        tciibaa'kwänit.
Kaawiin kägo i'kitosii inini.

Miidec giiw*e* änändank:
    "Taga niingagagwätcimaa ningwisis zäzii'kisit
                aaniin äjiwäba'k ändaawaat."
Miidac kägät äjigagwädcimaat ogwisisänsan kiimotc: 25
    "Ningwisis,"
        udinaan,
            "Ambäsanonaa wiindamawicin,
                aaniin äna'kamigisit kiiga?
    "Pitciinag kimaadci'taad tägwicinaanin.   30
    "Kayä giin keciimäyäns kayä ijinaagusi mawit
                        panä."

Kwiiwizänsidac kaawiin kägo wiikitusi.
    Gäga'piidac ainini aaiindacimaat,
        udigon:
    "Aaniic kigawiindamonsa,   35
        aanawi kaawiin kägo
                kiiwiwiindamosiinunninaaban;
        "Kigawiindamonidacigu,
            ä'piitci kaskändamaan a'panä,
            niciimäyäns mawit kaakabägiiji'k,"
                udinaan osan.   40
    "Miigu' kaanimaadcaayanini kigicäp naanaage,
        kayä wiin ninganaan miiga'yä wiin ujii'tad
                zazägaawat wäwäni gayä pinaa'kwäu."
        "Miidec äjimaadcaat kayä wiin,
            miidec kägaa kiigäsi'kawaa pitagwicing.
        "Piiaantcikwanayät,   45
            kayädec pinunaat niciimäyänsan,"
                udinaan osan.

Ininidec i'kito:
   "Miiwe waa'ki'kändamaan,"
                i'kito.   50

Miidac awinini giiwe weyaabaninig kaaijia'kamowaat
              iiniw wiiwan.
   Kägät awinini weyaabaninig kigijäp maadcaa'kaazo.
Päcudac ä'kudäbaaabandank wiigiwaam,
   kiiayaa ki'kaazut.
Kiinändank: 55
   "Ningawaabamawa taga kädaiindigwän."

Miidec kägät äjimaadcaat.
Kumaa'pi cayigwa kägät pimisägamon wiiwan.
   Aa'taa aaniina äjiunit!
   Aa'pidci zazägaawawan.   60
Panä iwiti kwaya'k änijaanit manisä'kanang.
Kaawiindec wäwäni ugiigi'känimaasin iiniw wiiwan
                  äna'kamigizininigwän.

Miidec miinawaa giiwe weyaabaninig tiibicko kaa'todank,
   kiijaat iwiti kaanijipickwaabamaa'pan pitciinaago.
Miidec kiimi'kawaat päjik gistcimi'tigon pada'kizunit   65
   aa'pitci miskwaa'kuskiigaasonidcin.

Miidec,
   "Mii ganabatc omaa äijaat,"
             inändam.
   Aa'pitci gayägi'tamonini mi'kana omi'kanaani.   70
Miidac änändank:
   "Miimaa päcu tcikaasoyaan,"
             inändam.
Miidac kägät cayiigwa miinawaa pinaagusiwan wiiwan.
Aa'ta miidac kägät minounit!   75
Cayiigwa piiaya imaa mi'tigon pata'kizunit.
Miidac awi'kwa äjipa'kitä'kowaat iiniw mi'tigon,
   pä'kic i'kitut:
      "Ninaapämitug!
         Nintagwicin minawaa aabinding."   80
               i'kito.
Apanä giiwe pasaagitotäwaat kinäbigok.
   Wayiibagu ukiiaangwäckaagon,
      wiiumwigut.

Miidac awinini kiiwabamaat wiiwan ändodaminit.   85
   Kiianimaadcaa wäwiip;
      kiiniaapamiskaat.
         kiijaat ändaawaat.

Miidac kiiwiindamaawaat uniidcaanisa,
 kiinaat: 90
  "Ningiiwabamaa kiigiwaa ändodank.
  "Miidac kiigiicänimak tcinisak.
  "Kiindac ningwisis,"
      udinaan,
   "Kiciimäyäns kiigamaadciinaa,   95
    kiigapimomaa,"
      udinaan.
  "Niindac omaa ningatayaa piinic
     tcipitagwicing kiigiwaa,"
      udinaan.
  "Aiyaangwaamisin ningwisis,"   100
      udinaan;
   "wii'pimaatisiyu'k wiipimaadci,
   kayä kiciimäyäns.
  "Miiwe gwaya'k kädacaiyäg',
      udinaan,   105
   "Gwaya'k niingaabiianung,
   "miídac iwiti tcianiwaabamatwaa
      ko'komisag',
    udinaan iiniw
     ugwisisänsan.
  "Miidec äninaan,
   kiigano'pinacaogowaa;   110
    po'tc aw kigiwaa.
  "Kägu dac baa'pic aabanaabi'kägun!",
      udinaan.
  "Kägu gayä kipitcipato'kägun!"
      udinaan.   115
  "Pitcinag kayä iwiti ko'kumesag
     kiigagigii'kimigog,"
      udinaan.

Miidec kiiwe äjodaa'pienaang iw ta'kinaagan
   ta'kupisunit ägaaciinit ugwisisänsän.
 Umbiwanät iiniw zäzaa'kisit ugwisisan.   120
'Iwidec ta'kinaagan kägaa umaci'kizidon iwe ta'kinaagan
     aw kwiiwisäns.
Miidec äjimaadcaanit,
 "Kicii'kaan,
  ningwisis!
   "Änigu'k pimusän,"
    udinaan ainini.   125
 "Mii niin omaa dciayaayaan."

Miidec kägät aw inini kiia'taat.
 Kiiuci'taat,
  niibiwa misan ugiikiickanan.

Miidac kaagiicii'taat   130
   kaaicipindigät.
      Kiiuci'taat wiinisaat wiiwan.
Cayiigwa gägät udaminisudawaan.
Miidec äjiacunawaat tcipipiindigänit.
   Pitcinagidacigu paaumbinang iw skwaandäm,   135
     miiäcipimwaat,
        mayaadac udäining udininawaan.

Miidac ägut:
   "Aaniic kiinaa totaman?"
     Inini kaawiin kägo i'kitosii.   140
     Qwidac i'kwä miimaa tcigaskutä piipangicing.

Miidac awinini äjiwi'kutaabaanaat,
   nawatc naawuckutä.
Miidac äjiki'tcipotawät,
Miidac äjisa'kawaat;   145
   mägwaadac tanaa'kisunit
     kana wabamaat iiniw wiiwan.

Udigon:
   "Aaniic wiin wändcitotawiyan?
   "Kitinigaak kiniidcaansinaanig kiiuciiatwaa."   150
Inini kaawiin kägo i'kitosii;
   aaniic ogiiwabamaan kaaicitigänit wiiwan,
   aa'pitcidac ugiinickiigon.
Awidec i'kwä ga'kina kägo i'kito
   käundci cawänimigut unaabäman.   155
Ininidac kaawin kanagä aabiding aganonaasiin;
   miigä'tagu ki'tciano'kiit wiiaangwaa'kiswaat.

Miigu' pangi aniaa'towäg,
   miigu' minawaa kanonigut,
     piinic igu maawit awi'kwa.   160
Aanukaagiisumaat iiniw unaabäman.
   Aanic kaawiin ucawänimigusiin.
Miidec kiiw*e* awinini aa'pitci aiyä'kusit podawät
             kabädibi'k,
   wiinipaat gayä.
Miigu tibicko ä'pitwäwidaminit wiiwan.   165
   Miiminawaa äki'tcipotawät.
Tciigayaiidac kiiw*e* weyaabaninig miicigwa
          tcaagaa'kiswaat;
   kayä kaawiin keyaabi onondawaasiin.

Miidec kägät kätciänigu'k podawaat.
Miidac giiw*e* wabaninig tcaagaa'kiswaat.   170
Miidec kaaijiningwank iw udickutäm.

Miidec kayä wiin kaaicimaadcaat,
   na'paatcigu kayä wiin kiicimaadcaat.
Miidec miinawaa abinotciiyag äjitibaadcimindwaa.
Mägwaa kiiw*e*gu ninguting anipapimosät anaagucig,   175
   kwiiwisäns pimomaat uciimäyänsan,
     aapitci aiyä'kusi.
Niigaanninaabit,
   owabandaan kwayu'k äjaat wiigiwaamäns
                   pada'kitänig.

Miidec änijinaazi'kang.   180
Pitcinaag giiw*e* päcu äniayaat,
   awiya onondawaan kiigitonit,
    i'kitunit:
      "Niiyaa!
        Nocis,   185
          kigiikitimaagisim,"
         utiguwaan.

Mii giiw*e*gu äjiki'tcimawit aw kwiiwisäns,
   a gayä pämomint ta'kinaaganing.
"Pindigän!"   190
   ugogowaan o'komisiwaan.

Miidac kägät äjipiindigäwät.
   Kiiacamigowaat,
    kiinibäigowaat kayä.
Wayaabanimigidac kiiw*e* udigowaann o'komisiwaan: 195
   "'A'aw, ambä anickaan!
    Kiigamaadcaam minawaa,"
        udigowaan.
Miidac giiw*e* äcimiinigut o'kumisan migos pinaa'kwaan
              kayä.
Miidac ägut: 200
   "Pitcinaag kiigapiminijagowaa aw kigiwaa.
    Aiyaanngwamisin,
     nojis.
   "Mii o' wändcimiininaan tciiaabadci'toyan kiicpin,
    piminijaonäg,   205
      päcudec tanänimat;
        mii tciaabagitoyan kitodaanaaming.
   "Kiigapagiton migos,"
           udigon.
   "Kägu dac inaabi'kän.   210
"Miigu' minawaa kätodaman iwä päji'k,"
        udigon.
   "Miidac tcitäutisat minawaa päji'k kokumis."

Miidac äji umbiwanäigut uciimäyänsan.
Miidac äjimaadcaat kaaickwaautcimigowaat o'kumisiwaan.
"Miidac maatcaag änigu'k!"

                    udigowaan.

Miidec kägä't äjimaadcaawaagubanän.
Ningutingidac giiw*e* anipapimiba'tot,
    caiigwa awiya onondawaan udodaanaaming, igut: 220
        "Miimaa ayaan!
           niiwiinonaa kiciimä!"
Miidac giiw*e* aw kwiiwisäns mi'kwändank kaaigut osan
                  kayä o'komisan.
Miidac äjiki'tcisägisit.

Miidec äjimaadciiba'tod;   225
    kaawiin aa'pitci ogaskitosiin tcipimipa'tot,
        mii äjipaa'piitaaguskank ta'kinaagan
                udondanaang.

Miidec minawaa nondawaat ogiin igut:
    "Miimaa ayaan!
        "Niiwiinonaa kiciimä!"   230
Nawatcidac kistcimawiwag nondawaawaat ugiwaan,
    kayädac wiipisiskitawaasigwa.
Minawaa dac naasaab udigon ugiin:
    "Miimaa ayaan, kitinin!
    "Niiwiinonaa kuca kiciimä, kitinin.   235
        "Kitinikaa kuca!"
          udigon.

Miidac kägä't änigu'k pimiba'tod,
    äckam a'pitci päcu' tannwäwitamon.
Miidac äjiaa'pagitod migos.   240
Miidac kitciwadciw äjiayaamagat;
    miziwä migosiwan.
Miidac kiinaawii'tawaawaat ugiwaan.

Miidac awä tciibai migosing kiinaanaapisänig u'kanan.
Miidac giiw*e* ädank migos: 245
    "Tawiskawicin,
        nino'pinanaag niniitcaanisag!"
    Kaawiindac kanagä upisikitaagusiin.
Miidac minawaa änaat:
    "'Aaw!"   250
          änaat,
    "Mäckut kiigawiiwin",
          udinaan.
Kaawiindac kanagä wiitäbwä'taagusiin.

Wii'kaadac kiikackiu imaa kii'paaciitciskang 'iw
             migosiwadciw.   255

Minawaadac mii kiino'pinacawaat uniidcaanisa.
Miidac miinawaa iigiw abinodciyag nondawaawaat
                    ugiiwaan,
   agaawa pitäpitaagusinit.
Minawaa naasaab pi'kitunit:
    "Piic!   260
      Niiwiinonaa kiciimä!"

Miidac minawaa aw kwiiwisäns äjiki'tcimawit,
   nawatc ki'tcimaadciiba'tod;
Miidacigu minawaa äjipa'pitaakutuntanäcing.
Mii minawaa nondawaawaat ugiiwaan,   265
   nawatc päcu' piidanwäwitaminit.

Miidac minawaa maadciiba'tot.
Mii minawaa nnondawat ugiin.
   Aa'pidci päcu' pidanwäwitaminit igut:
     "Piic kiciimä!   270
      Niwiinonaa!"

Miidac nawatc maadciiba'tod.
Miidac miinawaa äjiaapagitod udaanaang pinaa'kwaan,
Miidac pinaa'kwaaniwadciw äjipimatinaanig
                  udutaanaaming.
Miidac äjiki'tcimaadciiba'tod;   275
   kumaa'pi minawaa unondawaawaan,
     agaawa täbi'tagusinit.
Kaawiin miinawaa wiiba kackiusi awi'kwä.

Miigu minawaa naasaab ädank iw wadci'w,
   kaawiindac upisi'kitaagusiin;   280
     wii'kaadec kackiu.
Miidac minawaa noswäwämaat.
Miidac inät:
"Piic kiciimä!
   Niwiinonaa kiciimä!"   285
Miidac aabinding ä'ta giitäbi'waawaat.

Miidac awä kwiiwisäns änigu'k äjipimosät,
   aa'pidci ayä'kusit;
     kayä aa'pidci cigwa tibikatinig.

Ningutingidac cigwa anitätakanaabit,   290
   owabandaan wiigiwaamäns;
     o'kumisan ändaanit minawaa bäjik.
   Aa'pidci ocawänimigon.

Miidac ägut:
 "Kitimaagisi,   295
  nojis.
"Piindigän!"
   udigon.
Miidac kaaijiacamigowaat,
 kiinibäigowaat kayaa.   300
Weyabaninig dac minawaa udigon o'kumisan:
 "Ambä,
  nojis,
   unickaan!
 "Ambä,   305
  minawaa cayiigwa kiigamaadcaa."

Miidac minawaa äjimiinigut o'kumisan,
 kätacwiinit,
  piwaanagon saka'taaganan kayä.
Miidac äjiumbiiwanäigut uciimäyan.   310
Miidac ägut:
"Keyaabi kiigapiminicaogowaa aw kigiwaa.
 "Awidac,
  nojis,
   saka'taagan maaninaan mii aw skwatc
    käda'paginat;   315
 "Miidac tcidämadaabiiyan kistciziibi.
Miicimaa tciwabamat kistciusi'kaasi
   tcipabaagumut imaa siibing.
 "Miidac aw käganonat kiigatinaa:
  'Nimicomis,
   skumaanaa aacawaaocicinaam,   320
    manido nimpiminicagonaan','"
   udigon okumisan.
 "Mii kädinat",
  udinaan.

 "Kiipaacidäman dac iw ziibii,   325
  miiw kaawiin minawaa käyaabi
    kiigapiminicaogusiiwaa.
 "Wäwäni,
  nojis,
   pisindawicin äjikagii'kiminaan,"
    udinaan.   330
Miidec äjimaadcaat kwiwiisäns minawaa.
Ninigutingdac minawaa anipapimiba'tod,
 cayiigwa minawaa awiiya onondawaan udodaanaaming
   piimamaazinaawi'tagusinit.
Pa'kic pipiipaaginit,

igut: 335
    "Miim aayaan!
        Niiwiinonaa kiciimä!"
Miidac kägä't kistci änigu'k maadciipa'tod aw
                  kwiiwisäns;
  ki'tcimawit kayä,
    ki'känimaat ugiin no'pinacagut;   340
Kayädac mi'kwändank kiinisimint ugiwaan,
  kayädac kusaawaat.
Minawaa onondawaan.
  Nawatc päcu' piidwäwitaminit,
    iguwaat: 345
      "Piic kiciima!
        nimiininaa kiciiwä!"
      udigowaan.

Miidac änigu'k maadciipa'tod.
Minawaa onondawaan,   350
  aa'pidci päcu pidanwäwitaminit.
Naasaap igut:
  "Piic kiciimä!
    niwiinonaa kiciimä!"

Miidac aw kwiiwisäns gägä't ki'tcisägisit.   355
  Kägaa udonändaan kaaigut okumisan,
    undci wägunän ni'tam kätapagi'tod.
Wii'kaadac omi'kwändaan.
  Aa'pidci päcu odaanaang udinänimaan päminicaogut.
Miidac aa'paginaat piiwaanagon,   360
Miidac zäsi'ka kiipimadinaag wadci'w—piiwaannago
                wadci'w.
Miidac minawaa äniwäg kiia'pänimut waasa tcitagwicing.

A'widac i'kwä äjicoskupisut piiwaanagunk.
  Miigu aanugitaa'kiiwät näyaap,
    minawaa aajäyaaposut.   365
Miidac minawaa ädank:
  "Maanu, pimusäicin!
    Mäckut kiigawiwim,"
      uditaan.
Miidac wii'kaa pitciinag kiikackiut.   370
Miidacigu iwiti kaaundapozut.
Miidac miinawaa kimaadcinicawaad uniitcaanisa.
Miidac ninguting minawaa kwiiwisäns anipapimiba'tod.
Cayiigwa minawaa awiya pi'täbi'tagusiwan
             udodaanaamiwaang,
  iguwaat tibicko udaanaang kaaini'tamowaat: 375
    "Piic kiciimä!
      Niiwiininaaaa kiciimä!"

Miidac aw kwiiwisäns nawatc ki'tci änigu'k pimiba'tod.
Minawaa unondawaan:
   "Piic kiciimä!   380
      niiwiinonaa kiciimä!"

Nawatc päcu pitanwäwitaminit.
   Iiniwidac kayä pämomaat uciimäyänsan,
     wiingä kii'kimowan.

Miidac miinawaa onondawaan,   385
   aa'pidci päcu pidanwäwitaminit:
     "Piic kiciimä!
       Niiwiinonaa kicimä!"
Mägwaa dac tanwäwitaminit
   ugiiaa'paginaan iiniw skwaatc saga'taaganan,   390
     kii'kitut:
       "Miiawä skwaatc,
         no'kumis,
           kaamijiyan.
       "Sa'kan!"   395
Miidac kägä't ki'tciwadci'w ickutä pijicik,
   täta'kamayaiiupi'kwanaawang.
Miidac maadcaawaat minawaa änigu'k.
Miidac 'aw kwiiwisäns nondawaat ugiin
                  madwäki'tcimawinit.
   Awantcicidac maadcaa,   400
     kayä wiin ki'tcimawit.

Minawaa onondawaan,
   agaawa täbi'tagusini madwägistcinaniinawadämunit.
Miidac kayä wiinawaa aa'pidci naniinawadämuwag.

Miidac kiiwä awi'kwä äjikiiwitaaskang iw ckutä piinic   405
          kiiuditank umi'kanaani uniitcaanisa.
   Iigi'widac abinotciiyag kiimadaapiiwag ziipi.
Miidac kägät äjiwabatamowaat o'kumisiwaan
                  kaaiguwaa'pan.

Miidac kägä't äjikanonaat kwiiwisäns iiniw
                uzi'kaasiwan:
   "Skumaanaa,
     nimicomis,   410
       aajawaocicinaan!
   "Manido nimpiminicaogonaan,"
        udinaan.
Miidac kägäa't ägut kaaigut o'kumisan.
   "Kiicpinsa wii'todaman,   415
     kädininaan kigataajawaonininim,"
        udigowaan.

"Äye,"
    udinaan.
"Kiinä'tagu kigataajawaonin,   420
kaawiin wiin kiciimä,"
    udigon.

Miidac änaat:
"Kaawiin wiin iw kitaatäbwätosinon.
    Aa'pidci nisaagiaa niciimäyäns,"   425
    udinaan.
"'Awisa!"
    udigon;
kiini'tamisa kiigataajawaonin."
Miidac änat: 430
"Aaniic käicikacki'toyaan tciumbomak niciimä
                kiicpin pagitomak?"
    udinaan.
"Aa, kiigakackiton,"
    udinaan.
"Pagitom!"   435
    udigon.
Miidac kägä't waicipagitomaat,
Miidac "Tapangicin",
    inändam.
Mi minawaa äjinogit.   440
"Pagitom!",
    udigon umicomisan.
"Kawiin tapangicinzii,"
    udigon.
Miidac kägä't käga'pi kaaijipagitomaat wäwäni.   445
"Aawidac kiini'tam kigataajonin,"
    udigon.

Miidac aw zäzii'kisit kwiiwisäns
                kaaijiki'tciaanzanaamut.
Pä'kic inaat umicomisan:
"Nimicomis!   450
Mano niciimäyäns ni'tam aajawaoc!"
    udinaan.
Miidac kägä't äjitäbwä'taagut omicomisan.
Owabamigonsa aa'pidci saagiaat uciimäyan,
    kayä aiyaangwaamisit tciwaniaasig.   455
Miidac ägut:
"'Aaw!
"Posi',
    kägu dac wiin taangawiganäckawici'kän!"
    udinaan.   460
Miidac äjiaajawaonaat kiiasaat agaaming.

Miidac kayä wiin pitciinag kiiaajawaonint.
Miidac taabicko agaaming kiiyaawaat.
Miidac kiigut omicomisan:
    "Miiciumbom kiciimä",   465
        udigon.
Miidac nawatc kiiwäni'panisit kii'umbomaat
                              uciimäyänsan,
    pii'tcidac kaaijisanagisit wiipagitomaat ni'tam.

Miidac minawaa kaaijimaadcaawaat.
Ninguding idac minawaa i'kwä kayä wiin pitagwicinogopan
               imaa zibing.   470

Miidac kayä ticicko aajiwabamaat iiniw uzi'kaasiwan,
        inaat:
    "Skumaana,
        aajowaocin,
            niciim!"   475
            udinaan.
"Awaspina!"

"Awaw!",
    udinaan.
        Ninitcaanisag niwiino'pinanaag,"   480
            udinaan.
"Awaspina!
    Kaawiin!"
            udigon.

"'Aaw,   485
    udinaan.
        "Mäskut kiigapaapotcikana'kawaa
                    nindapisku'kä,"
            udinaan.
"Awaas kaawiin,"
            udinaan.   490

"'Aaw,
    wäwiiptaan!"
"'A'aasa'!"
        udinaan,
            "Kägudac paacitauci'kän,"   495
            udinaan.

Miidac kägä't ijiaajawaonigut.
Miidac päcu tcigabaat inändam ai'kwä:
    "Mii dcitäbikwaackuniyaan,"
        inändam.   500
Miidec äjipaacitawaat iiniw usa'kaasiwan pä'kic
                   anikwaackunit.

Miidac äjipangicing awi'kwä naanaawayaiiki'tcigaming.
Miidac imaa ickwaayatcimint awi'kwä.

Part II, Series I, No. 3, 45–63.

The Orphans and Mashos I

Narrated by Mrs. Marie Syrette

(introduction)

Now presently they say there lived a man and his wife,
 and two they say was the number of their children.
  One was very small.
And then they say that they continued along.
 The man, as often as the days came round, hunted
    for game,   5
  and the woman gathered firewood and cooked
    the meals.
And those two children were boys.
 And then the boy that was older had the care of
    his tiny brother
  while his mother went to gather firewood and
    while she was busy at her work.

Now presently they say while they were living at home, 10
 the man was away everyday on a hunt for game.
And the man came home,
 his wife would that moment go for firewood,
  so that she might make ready to cook the
    meal.
The children were also very neglected.   15

And now presently they say the man was bothered,
 (and) thought,
  "I wonder what is going on!"
   he thought.
Then that was the way it always was,   20
 he would find his wife getting ready to cook the
    meal.
The man said nothing.

And then they say he thought,
 "Now I will ask my older son what is going on
   here at our home."
And then truly he asked his son in secret: 25
 "My son,"
  he said to him,

    "come and truly tell me,
        what is your mother doing?
  "Straightaway does she go to work as soon as I
        come home.   30
  "And both you and your little brother look as if
        you were weeping all the time."

And the little boy did not wish to say anything.
At last the man had spoken a lot to him,
He was told,
    "Well I really will tell you,   35
      but I am not anxious to tell you anything.
      "I will tell you,
        as I am very sad all the time,
        that my little brother cries every day,"
            he said to his
              father.   40
  "Then just as soon as you are gone in the morning,
      later our mother also dresses herself and
             carefully combs her hair.
    "And then she too goes away.
    "And then you almost precede her on the way
            home.
    She comes and takes off her clothes,   45
      and gives suck to my little
            brother,"
      he said to his father.
And the man said,
  "That is just what I wanted to know,"
        he said.   50

(man discovers wife is a manito)

And then they say the next morning the man lay in wait
           for his wife.
  Truly the next morning the man pretended that he
           was going away.
And near the place from where he could barely see the
           lodge,
  he remained in hiding.
He thought: 55
  "I will now see what she is going to do."

And then truly he was gone.
Now afterwards his wife truly came out of the lodge.
  My, but she was beautifully dressed.
  She was very beautiful.   60

Right over there by a straight course she went,
  by way of the path used in going after firewood.
And he did not exactly make out what his wife was up
       to.

And then again they say on the next day he did the same
       thing,
  he went over to the place where he barely lost
    sight of her on the day before.
And then he found a great tree standing alone,   65
  which was very red from the bark being peeled off
  on account of much travel upon it.

And then,
  "Then it is perhaps here that she goes,"
    he thought.
  And the beaten path (to the tree) was very plain.   70
And then he thought:
  "Then I will hide myself near by this place,"
    he thought.

And then again now truly his wife was coming into view.
Oh, and then she was truly clothed elegantly!   75
Now she came close by to where the tree was standing.
And then the woman pounded upon the tree,
  at the same time she said,
   "Oh my husbands!
    I am come once again,"   80
     she said.
Without ceasing they say out came crawling the snakes.
  In a little while she was crawled about by them,
   and made use of as a wife.

(man sends children away)

And then the man saw what his wife was doing.   85
  He went speedily away;
   around he turned,
    (and) went home.

And then he spoke to his children,
  he said to them: 90
   "I've seen what your mother is doing.
    "And then I've made up my mind to kill
      her.
  "And you my son,"
      he said to him,
  "you must take away your tiny little brother."   95
  "I want you to carry him on your back,"
      he said to him.

"And I will remain here until the arrival of
                  your mother,"
              he said to him.
"Do as well as you can my son,"   100
                  he said to him,
    "so that you may live,
          and also save the life of your tiny
                  little brother."

"Straight in yonder direction shall you go,"
                  he said to them,   105
      "straight toward the west,
            and then over that way will you go
              and see your grandmothers,"
              he said to his little
                      son.
"And then I say to you,
      she will pursue you.   110
          In spite of all will your mother
                  (follow you).
    And don't ever under any condition look
                  behind you!"
                  he said to him.   115
    "And also don't ever stop running!"
                  he said to him.
    "And by and by at that place will your
        grandmothers give you words of advice",
                  he said to him.

And then they say he took up the cradleboard on which   120
                  was tied his little son.
He lifted it upon the back of his son who was
                      older.
And with that cradleboard the boy almost touched the
                      ground.
And then as he started away,
    "Go fast,
        my son!
            You must go at full speed,"
                  said the man to him.   125
    "Then I will remain here."

(man burns woman)

And then truly the man remained.
    He put things in order,
          he gathered much firewood.
And then after he had finished work,   130
      he went inside.

He was prepared to kill his wife.
Now truly he suspected that she was coming.
And then he was ready with bow and arrow to shoot her
                  as she was coming in.
  As soon as she lifted the flap of the doorway,   135
      then he shot her,
          at the very center of her heart he shot
                  her.

And then he was asked by her,
  "Why do you do it?"
      But the man made no remark.   140
  And the woman came over there by the edge of the
                  fire and fell.

And then the man dragged her,
  and he placed her closer to the center of the
                  fire.
And then he built a great fire.
And then he burned her.   145
    And while she was burning up,
      he gazed upon his wife.
She said to him:
  "Now why do you treat me thus?
  "You have brought sadness upon our children by
           making orphans of them."   150
The man did not say anything;
  well he had seen what his wife had done;
  he was very angry with her.
And the woman said all sorts of things,
  that she might be pitied by her husband.   155
But the man had not a single word to say to her,
  then he simply worked with all his might to burn
                  her up.

Then the fire went down a little way,
    then again he was addressed by her,
      till finally the woman wept.   160
In vain she tried to appease the wrath of her husband,
  yet he gave her no pity.
And then they say the man became very tired with
          keeping up the fire all night long,
    (and) he wanted sleep.
Then all the time did his wife have the same power of
                  voice.   165
    Then again he built up a great fire.
It was morning they say when he burned her up,
  and he no longer heard her voice.

And then truly in good earnest he built up the fire.
And then they say by morning he had her all burned up.   170
And then he covered up his fire.
And then he too went away,
     but in another direction he went.

(boy receives awl and comb from his grandmother)

And then again the children are taken up in the story.
Now presently they say that one evening,   175
    while the boy was traveling along and carrying
          his little brother on his back,
   he became very weary.
He looked ahead,
   he saw that straight ahead was a little lodge
            standing.

And then he directed his way to it.   180
They say that as soon as he came near by,
   he heard somebody speak,
     saying:
      "Oh dear me!
        My grandchildren,   185
          both of you are to be pitied,"
            they were told.

Then they say that the boy wept bitterly,
   and also he that was carried in the cradleboard.
"Come in!"   190
   they were told by their grandmother.

And then truly they went in.
   They were fed by her,
     and they were put to bed by her.
And in the morning they say they were told by their   195
           grandmother:
  "Now then come and rise from your sleep.
    You need to be on your way again,"
         they were told.
And then they say that he was given an awl and a comb
         by his grandmother.
And then he was told: 200
  "Presently will you be pursued by your mother.
    Do as well as you can,
      my grandchild.
   Then the reason I have given you these things is
         that you may use them if,
    when she follows after you,   205

and you think her to be near by;
then you shall fling them behind
you.
"You shall throw the awl,"
he was told,
"and be sure not to look." 210

"Then again shall you do the same with the other one",
he was told.
and then you will be able to reach another
grandmother of yours."

And then his little brother was helped upon his back by
her.
And then they set out after they had been kissed by 215
their grandmother.
"And then go fast!"
they were told.

(boy throws awl, escapes mother)

And then truly away they went.
Now presently they say that he went running along,
now he heard the sound of somebody behind saying, 220
"Do stay there!
I want to suckle your little brother."
And then they say that the boy became mindful of what
he had been told by his father and grandmother.
And then he was very afraid.

And then he started to run; 225
he was not able to run very well,
then he would hit his heels with the
cradleboard.

And then again he heard his mother saying:
"Do stay there!
I want to suckle your little brother." 230
All the more did they weep when they heard their
mother,
and they did not want to listen to her.
And again the same thing as before were they told by
their mother:
"Do remain there I tell you!
"I really want to suckle your little brother I
tell you! 235
You are surely doing him injury,"
he was told.

And then truly he ran at full speed,
    nearer still could be heard the sound of her
                 voice.
And then he flung the awl.   240
And then a great mountain came to be;
    there were awls everywhere over it.
And then far away they heard the faint sound of their
                 mother.
And then a skeleton caught fast its bones in among the
                 awls.
And then they say it said to the awl: 245
    "Make way for me!
        I am following my children."
    But not in the least did (the awls) listen to her.
And then again she said to them:
    "Come on!"   250
        she said to them.
    "And as a reward I will be a wife to you all,"
        she said to them.
But not the least faith was placed in her word.
    And it was a long time before she was able to pass
            over the mountain of awls.   255

(boy throws comb, escapes mother again)

And again then she was in pursuit of her children.
And then again the children heard their mother,
    faintly they heard the sound of her voice coming
                 hither.
Again as before it came saying,
    "Bring him to me!   260
      "I want to suckle your little brother!"

And then again the boy wept aloud;
    all the harder did he begin to run;
And then again he bumped his heels.
Then again they heard their mother,   265
    ever nearer kept coming the sound of her voice.

And then again he began running.
Then again he heard his mother.
    Very close came the sound of her voice saying:
      "Bring me your little brother!   270
        I want to suckle him!"

And then all the harder did he start to run.
And then again he flung the comb behind.

And then a mountain range of combs strung out over the
country at the rear.
And then he began running at full speed;   275
again after a while they heard her,
feebly could she be heard.
The woman was unable to pass the place again for a long
time.

Then again the same thing as before she now said to the
mountain,
but no heed was given her;   280
and it was a long while before she was able
to pass.
And then again she called after them.
And then she said,
"Give me your little brother!
I want to suckle your little brother!"   285
And then only once they heard the sound of her voice.
And then the boy walked with a hurried step,
he was becoming very tired,
and it was now growing very dark.

(boy receives flint and punk from grandmother)

Now presently as he was walking along,   290
he looked and saw a little wigwam;
it was the home of another grandmother of
his.
He was pitied very much by her.
And then he was told:
"You are in distress,   295
my grandchild.
"Come in!"
he was told.
And then after they were fed,
she put them to bed.   300
In the morning they were again told by their
grandmother:
"Come,
my grandchild,
rise up!
Come!   305
now again you must be going."

And then again he was given by his grandmother,
as a means of protection,
a flint and some punk.
And then with her help his little brother was lifted
upon his back.   310

And then he was told,
  "You will still be followed by your mother.
  And now,
    my grandson,
      this punk which I am giving you is the
        last thing for you to throw.   315
  And then you will be able to come out upon a
          great river.
    Then there you will see a great Horned Grebe
      that will be moving about over the water
         in the river there.
  And then you will say to it:
    'My Grandfather!
      Please carry us across the water,   320
        for a manito is chasing us!' "
          he was told by his
            grandmother.
    "Then that is what you shall say to it,"
        she said to him.
"And after you have crossed the river,   325
  then again you will no longer be pursued.
  Carefully,
    my grandson,
      do you give heed to my
        instructions,"
        she said to him.   330

(boy throws flint, escapes mother)

And then the boy started off again.
Now presently again he went running along,
  now again he heard the sound of her coming behind
    with the clank of bones striking together.
At the same time she was calling after him
  and saying: 335
    "Stay there!
      I want to suckle your little brother!"

And then truly the boy started running with great
          speed;
  and he was crying loud,
    for he knew it was his mother who was
         pursuing him.   340
And he was mindful too that their mother had been
         killed,
  and they were afraid of her.
Again he heard her.
Still nearer came the sound of her voice,

saying to them, 345
    "Give me your little brother!
      I want to suckle your little
            brother,"
  they were told.

And then with speed he started running.
Again he heard her, 350
  very near came the sound of her voice.
The same thing as before she was saying:
  "Bring me your little brother!
    I want to suckle your little brother!"

Then truly the boy was greatly afraid. 355
    He almost forgot what had been told him by his
           grandmother,
    which (of the objects) he should first fling
           away.
It was a long while before he recalled (which) it
           (was).
    He suspected his mother to be very close behind.
And then he flung the flint, 360
And then suddenly there was a range of mountains—
        mountains of flint.
And then again some further distance on,
  he felt secure in having gotten so far away.
Then the woman slipped on the flint.
Then she reached the top,
    again she slipped back. 365
And then again she said to (the mountains)
  "Do please let me pass over you!
    In return I will be a wife to you,"
      she said to them.
And then it was a long time before she succeeded. 370
And then from the place up there she came sliding down.
And then again she went in pursuit of her children.

(boy throws punk, escapes mother again)

And then now presently again the boy went running along
        the way.
Now again somebody could be heard coming behind,
  saying to them the same thing they had heard
        before: 375
    "Give me your little brother!
      I want to suckle your little brother!"

And then the boy ran with even greater speed.

Again he heard her:
    "Give me your little brother!   380
        I want to suckle your little brother!"

Still nearer came the sound of her voice.
    And the little brother whom he bore on his back
                  had been crying,
      till now he could cry no more.
And then again he heard her,   385
    ever so close came the sound of her voice:
        "Give me your little brother!
          I want to suckle your little brother!"
And while he was hearing the sound of her voice,
    he hurled away the punk as the last thing,   390
        saying:
           "This is the last,
              my grandmother,
                  that you gave to me.
           Set it afire!"   395

And then truly there was a great mountain of fire
                      everywhere,
    stretching from one end of the world to the other.

And then they went on again.
And then the boy heard his mother wailing in a loud
                      voice.
    All the faster he went,   400
        and he too was weeping aloud.
Again he heard her,
    barely could the sound of her voice be heard as
               she wailed in great grief.
And then again they also wept in grief.
And then they say the woman passed round the boundaries
    of the fire till she came to the path of her
                    children.   405

(boy meets Horned Grebe, gets safely across river)

And now the children came out upon a river.
And then truly did they see what had been told them by
                  their grandmother.

And then truly the boy spoke to Horned Grebe:
    "Please,
        my grandfather,   410
          carry us over the water to the other
               side.

A manito is chasing us!"
            the boy said to him.
And then truly he was told what had been told him by
                        his grandmother:
        "If you will only do what I tell you,   415
            then will I carry you both across the water,"
                they were told.
        "We will,"
            the boy said to him.
        "You yourself only will I take across the water,   420
            but not your little brother,"
                he was told.
And then the boy said to him:
            "I will not listen to that sort of thing from you.
            I am very fond of my little brother,"   425
                the boy said to him.
"All right then,"
            the boy was told,
        "First I will carry you across the water."
And then the boy said to him: 430
        "How shall I be able to put my little brother upon
                    my back if I put him down?"
            the boy said to him.
"Oh, you will be able to do it,"
            he said to the boy,
        "Let him down!"   435
                he was told by his grandfather.

And then truly was he in the act of letting him down,
And then "Now he might fall,"
        he thought.
        Then again he hesitated.   440
"Let him down!"
        he was told by his grandfather.
            "He will not fall,"
                the boy was told.
And then truly at last he let him down carefully.   445
"First I will carry you across the water,"
                the boy was told.

And then the older boy gave a great sigh.
        At the same time he said to his grandfather:
            "My grandfather!   450
                Please carry my little brother to the
                            other side first,"
                the boy said to him.
And then truly his grandfather did what was asked of
                            him.

It was seen how very fond he was of his tiny little
                                    brother,
            and how careful he was not to lose him.   455

And then the boy was told:
    "All right!
        put him on,
            but don't touch me on the back!"
                he said to the boy.   460
And then he carried him over to the other side and put
                        him on the shore.

And then afterward the other was taken across.
And then both were on the other side.
And then he was told by his grandfather:
    "Put your little brother upon your back!"   465
        the boy was told.
And then he found it easier than before to lift his
                    little brother upon his back,
    as easy as it was when he first wanted to put him
                            down.

(woman meets Horned Grebe, falls into river)

And then again they continued on their way.   470
And now presently again the woman arrived at the river.
And then she too saw the Horned Grebe,
            and said to him:
    "Please,
        carry me over to the other side,
            my little brother!"   475
                she said.

"Oh, bother!"
"Come on!"
    she said to him.
        "I am anxious to pursue my children,"   480
                she said to him.
"Oh bother!
    No!"
                she was told.
"Come on!"   485
    she said to him,
        "and in return you can have your desires with
                        me,"
                she said to him.
"I don't want to,"
            he said to her.   490

"Come on!
    Hurry up!"
"Well all right,"
    he said to her.
        "But don't step over me,"   495
      he said to her.

And then truly was she being taken over to the other
        side.
And then as she was about to land the woman thought:
   "Then I will now be able to leap ashore,"
    she thought.   500
And then she stepped over Horned Grebe at the same time
       that she leapt.
And then down fell the woman into the middle of the
       sea.
And then this point ends the story of the woman.

Part II, Series I, No. 3, 45–63.

REFERENCES

Bahr, Donald. 1975. *Pima and Papago Ritual Oratory: A Study of Three Texts.* San Francisco: Indian Historian Press.

Banfield, Ann. 1973. "Narrative Style and the Grammar of Direct and Indirect Speech." *Foundations of Language* 10:1–39.

Bauman, Richard. 1983. "Reported Speech as Esthetic Focus in Narratives." Paper delivered at the University of Texas at Austin, March 1983.

Bierhorst, John. 1985. *The Mythology of North America.* New York: William Morrow.

Bright, William. 1979. "A Karok Myth in 'Measured Verse' ": The Translation of a Performance." *Journal of California and Great Basin Anthropology* 1:117–123.

———. 1980. "Poetic Structure in Oral Narrative." In *Spoken and Written Language,* edited by Deborah Tannen. Norwood, N.J.: Ablex.

Chatfield, William. 1979. Personal interviews, Minneapolis, Minnesota, with the author.

Ghezzi, Ridie Wilson. 1990. "Ways of Speaking: An Ethnopoetic Analysis of Ojibwe Narratives." Ph.D. dissertation, University of Pennsylvania.

Glassie, Henry. 1982. *Passing the Time in Ballymenone: Culture and History of an Ulster Community.* Philadelphia: University of Pennsylvania Press.

Hallowell, A. Irving. 1960. "Ojibwe Ontology, Behavior, and World View." In *Culture in History,* edited by Stanley Diamond. New York: Columbia University Press.

Hymes, Dell. 1976. "Louis Simpson's 'The Deserted Boy.'" *Poetics* 5:119–155.

———. 1980a. "Tonkawa Poetics: John Rush Buffalo's 'Coyote and Eagle's Daughter.'" In *On Linguistic Anthropology: Essays in Honor of Harry Hoijer,* edited by Jacques Maquet. (Reprinted in Sherzer and Woodbury, *Native American Discourse,* 1987.)

———. 1980b. "Verse Analysis of a Wasco Text: Hiram Smith's 'Al'Unaqa.'" *International Journal of American Linguistics* 46:2:65–77.

———. 1981. *"In Vain I Tried to Tell You": Essays in Native American Ethnopoetics.* Studies in Native American Literature I. Philadelphia: University of Pennsylvania Press.

———. 1983. "Agnes Edgar's 'Sun Child': Verse Analysis of a Bella Coola Text." In *Working Papers for the 18th International Conference on Salish and Neighboring Languages,* edited by William Seabing, 239–312. Seattle: Department of Anthropology, University of Washington.

———. 1984. "Language, Memory, and Selective Performance: Cultee's 'Salmon Myth' as Twice-told to Boas." In *Working Papers for the 19th ICSNL,* University of Victoria, B.C., August 1984, edited by Thomas Hukari. Distributed in a special issue of *Working Papers of the Linguistic Committee* 4:2:162–228. Reprinted 1985 in *Journal of American Folklore* 98:391–434.

———. 1987. "The Religious Aspect of Language in Native American Humanities." In *Essays in Humanistic Anthropology: A Festschrift in Honor of David Bidney,* edited by Bruce T. Grindal and Dennis M. Warren, 83–114. Washington, D.C.: University Press of America.

Jones, William. n.d. "Ethnographic and Linguistic Field Notes on the Ojibwa Indians." American Philosophical Society, Manuscripts Department.

———. 1916. "Ojibwa Tales from the North Shore of Lake Superior." With notes by Truman Michelson and Franz Boas. *Journal of American Folklore* 29:378–391.

———. 1917. *Ojibwa Texts.* Edited by Truman Michelson. Vol. 7, pts. 1 and 2. Publications of the American Ethnological Society. New York: G. E. Stechert.

McClendon, Sally. 1982. "Meaning, Rhetorical Structure, and Discourse Organization in Myth." In *Analyzing Discourse: Text and Talk,* edited by Deborah Tannen, 384–395. Washington, D.C.: Georgetown University Press.

Mishler, Craig. 1981. "He Said, 'They Say': The Use of Reporting Speech in Native American Folk Narrative." *Fabula* 22:239–249.

Overholt, Thomas W., and J. Baird Callicott. 1982. *Clothed-in-Fur and Other Tales: An Introduction to an Ojibwa World View.* Washington, D.C.: University Press of America.

Rhodes, Richard. 1979. "Some Aspects of Ojibwa Discourse." *Algonquian Conference Papers,* 10th (1978). Fredericton, New Brunswick, 102–117.

Sherzer, Joel, and Anthony C. Woodbury. 1987. *Native American Discourse: Poetics and Rhetoric.* New York: Cambridge University Press.

Silverstein, Michael. 1985. "The Culture of Language in Chinookan Narrative Texts: Or, On Saying That . . . in Chinook." In *Grammar Inside and Outside the Clause,* edited by Nichols and Woodbury, 132–175. Cambridge: Cambridge University Press.

Tedlock, Dennis. 1978. "Coyote and Junco." In *Coyote Stories,* edited by William Bright. *IJAL,* Native American Texts Series, Monograph 1. Chicago: University of Chicago Press.

———. 1983. *The Spoken Word and the Work of Interpretation.* Philadelphia: University of Pennsylvania Press.

Thompson, Stith. 1919. *European Tales among the North American Indians.* Colorado Springs: Colorado College (Colorado College Language Series, vol. 2, no. 34).

———. 1929. *Tales of the North American Indians.* Bloomington: Indiana University Press.

Toelken, Barre. 1969. "The 'Pretty Languages' of Yellowman: Genre, Mode, and Texture in Navajo Coyote Narratives." *Genre* 2:211–235.

―――. 1981. "Poetic Retranslation and the 'Pretty Languages' of Yellowman." In *Traditional American Indian Literatures,* edited by Karl Kroeber, 65–116.

Urban, Greg. 1984. "Speech About Speech in Speech About Action." *Journal of American Folklore* 97:310–328.

Vecsey, Christopher. 1983. *Traditional Ojibwa Religion and Its Historical Changes.* Philadelphia: American Philosophical Society.

Woodbury, Anthony C. 1985. "The Functions of Rhetorical Structure: A Study of Alaskan Yupik Eskimo Discourse." *Language in Society* 14:2:153–190.

CREATING MEANING AND EVOKING EMOTION THROUGH REPETITION

Shuar War Stories

Janet Wall Hendricks

In 1982 I was privileged to hear and record a life-history narrative of Tukup', one of the last surviving warriors among the Shuar of southeastern Ecuador.[1] The event took place in the home of Chumap', a man from the western, colonized region of the territory who was living in the *centro* Tukup' at that time.[2] The audience for Tukup's narrative included one of Tukup's wives; a son-in-law and his wife and children; two sons; Chumap', who served as the listener-responder,[3] and his wife; my family and I.

Tukup's narrative provides a first-hand account of intertribal and intratribal retribution for homicide. He tells his personal experiences in warfare: who he fought and why, where he fought, and how he fought. Each episode in the narrative is an account of a particular raid, the events necessarily in chronological order, as each raid was initiated as a result of a previous one.

As the events covered in the story comprise only short intervals in his life, Tukup's life history in no way "mirrors" his life in the manner expected of Western autobiography. Presumably much of his life was spent in hunting, fishing, cutting wood, training his sons, curing, and other endeavors. Tukup' did not necessarily see the narrated events as the whole of his life story, but rather they created an image of the person he wanted people to know.

Tukup's goals are achieved, in part, through his use of a variety of linguistic devices found in Shuar narrative style. One such device is repetition. This essay demonstrates the range of functions of repetition as employed in one episode of Tukup's life-history narrative. Like many Native American narratives, perhaps most, Tukup's narrative is poetically organized through semantic, lexical, grammatical, and intonational parallelisms that serve as cohesive devices at both the micro and macro levels of organization. However, these instances of repetition also further the narrator's intentions in a more direct way, by evoking emotions and creating specific meanings related to his rhetorical strategy. Such patterns of form-meaning covariation are central to an understanding of the text and the speaker's goals.

Life histories provide a method of discovering the individual in society, though one that has not been fully explored. The separation of life-history material collected during anthropological fieldwork from the linguistic analysis of narrative has limited our understanding of the social and cultural contexts in which an individual chooses to tell his story, and has isolated us from the artistry with which he tells it. Usually, readers are not given the words of native peoples, allowing them to speak for themselves, but rather a monologic translation that frequently ignores the presence of the ethnographer and others who may have attended or participated in the performance and that neglects the stylistic features of the life-history narration itself. A few recent life histories have sought to correct the first problem, that of addressing the role of the ethnographer, but have failed to include the native text (e.g., Shostak 1981, Crapanzano 1980). The problems of translating style and structure have been addressed with regard to formal speech styles such as myth narrations, poetry, song, and ritual speech (Tedlock 1972 and 1983, Hymes 1981, Sherzer 1983, Woodbury 1987, Sherzer and Urban 1986), but have not been applied to life histories.

Repetition is prominent in Native American narrative styles, though this feature is often lost in autobiographical texts.[4] Krupat (1985) points out that Native American autobiographies are the narratives of the ethnographers or other collaborators rather than the natives whose lives are presented. Typically, the collaborator is told the story by an interpreter who translates the Indian's words into English, later to be edited for print by the collaborator (e.g., Dyk 1938, Jackson 1955, Underhill 1979). In other cases, the narrative was recorded in the native language and then translated and extensively edited (e.g., Barrett 1906, Schultz 1962, Johnson 1977). When the interest was primarily linguistic, the native-language text was recorded, but usually published in a prose format with only a literal or a free translation and little attempt to analyze features of the text other than grammatical ones (e.g., Radin 1963, Bloomfield 1928).

In the English presentation of a life history, it was inevitable that the translator shaped the material, often deciding what was to be cut and what kept, and nearly always rearranging and editing the text, deleting repetitions and other stylistic devices. Typically, editors rewrote narratives to conform to the conventions of written standard English (Brumble 1981, 1988). Referring to Leo Simmons's editing of Don Talayesva's story in *Sun Chief* (1942), Clyde Kluckhohn said, "the serious student wants to know at first hand on what subjects the Hopi *did* tiresomely repeat himself. Every omission by the editor, every stylistic clarification takes us one more step away from what Don actually said" (1945:97). While the importance of repetition is noted in studies of myth narrations, the emphasis is usually placed on the esthetic functions of repetition and on its structural functions in creating the text's organization. Less attention is paid to the role of repetition in the expression of meaning and emotion, though these functions are often mentioned. Hymes notes that "the pointing up of significance by repetition" along with direct speech, are "vital features of American Indian narrative. To omit them suggests an insensitivity to the traditional style" (Hymes 1987:45). Hymes's interest in repetition, however, is primarily concerned with the ways repetition affects the structure of texts, as for example in the numerically constrained patterns in Chinookan myths (1981, 1987). He points out, for example, that repetitive initial particles such as "so," "then," and "now" are part of the poetic style, and cannot be omitted since they were "means of shaping the story, means of defining through repetition the structure the narrator intended the text to disclose" (1981:7). His insistence on accurate translation of texts is related to his view that American Indian narratives should be regarded as literature, and that when accurately translated their poetic features are apparent.

Tedlock (1983) argues that repetition creates intensity, and advises greater attention to pauses, loudness, and other features that may accompany repetitions. He also points out the structural uses of repetition in comparing repetition in Zuni oral narratives to that found in epic poetry (1983:52). Although he states that "poetic subtleties have a potential for radically altering surface meanings" (1983:54), he gives little attention to how the use of repetition does so. In lowland South American societies, parallelism is a dominant feature of ritual, ceremonial, and formal speech styles (Sherzer and Urban 1986:6), though the emphasis in most studies is on the semiotic and organizational functions of repetition rather than its contribution to narrative content or the communication of emotional content.

Tukup's narrative is unique in comparison to the life histories usually collected by anthropologists in that it is a single, uninterrupted narrative told in the native language without questions from the ethnographer. Also, as the narrative is relatively short, lasting an hour and fifteen minutes, it was possible to translate and analyze the entire text without extensive editing. Most life histories are based on a series of interviews with the informant, with the researcher adding direction to the content through his questions. The result is an interview situation in which the researcher controls narrative form as well as content rather than the native who is telling his story. Unencumbered by the disruptive influence of an on-site interpreter and undisturbed by the reflective options of series interviewing, Tukup' told his story to his family and to Chumap' in the discursive style of Shuar personal narratives. The only direct intrusion on my part was to ask him to stop once while I turned over the tape.[5]

In addition to its relevance to life-history studies, Tukup's narrative may have significant implications for the "discourse-centered" approach to the study of culture, society, and language, an approach that takes the view that "what is traditionally called 'culture' is constituted by means of discourse, just as it is transmitted by means of discourse" (Sherzer and Urban 1986:2). Focusing on the multitude of formal devices found in instances of speech, discourse-centered analysis asks how these devices communicate messages. The propositional function, which communicates information about the world, is only one among many functions of linguistic signs. Equally important are the pragmatic uses of language, which may be found at every level of discourse, from the choice of morphological or lexical items to the structure of the discourse itself.

With few exceptions, discourse-centered studies have looked to discourse to understand culture, rather than the individual. Graham (1986), for example, analyzes three forms of communication in Shavante in order to interpret notions of nature and culture in Shavante society. Keith Basso (1984) finds a portion of the Apache worldview in their use of placenames and narratives about the landscape. Such studies are less concerned with the speaker as an individual or with the pragmatic features of texts directly associated with the speaker's intentions than with discovering aspects of the language/culture relationship through close analysis of texts recorded in their natural settings. Although Tukup's narrative provides insights into Shuar warfare and culture, as a subjective document it also includes affective and pragmatic dimensions that may be discerned from an analysis of form-meaning covariation in the text. That is, analysis of Tukup's narrative demonstrates that the individual as well as culture is revealed through attention to discourse.

Speaking ability is highly respected among the Shuar, who believe that a man who speaks well has great power. Among the forms of speech which may contribute to a man's prestige and power are myth narrations, curing rituals, ceremonial dialogue, political oratory, and personal narratives. Shuar personal narratives are told not only in conversational contexts, but also as public performances, in settings where any number of persons constitute an audience for the performer, usually during formal visits. The content of the narrative may be a recitation of events that occurred during hunting or fishing trips, visits to distant neighbors, trading expeditions, or war raids. While Tukup's narrative covered many years instead of a single event, in many ways it corresponds to the personal narratives frequently heard in Shuar gatherings.

Personal narratives are an important part of the political process in Shuar society, and the manipulation of information is an essential skill of big men, who must control information to be politically effective. Exchange of information is especially important in feuds, when a man's very survival may depend on his ability to attract potential allies to provide support in raids, resources in case of flight, and information concerning enemy activities. A man is constantly required to give his point of view on the developments in a feud, his and others' participation in a particular raid, what his enemies are saying, and so on. This information has to be evaluated. Is the speaker lying or telling the truth? Does he know with any certainty what occurred?

As personal narratives are intended to persuade listeners to a particular point of view, the result is a narrative tradition in which stories are seldom told the same way more than once,[6] and in which the context of the story-telling event may be the single most important influence on its content. Although this performance may have been the first time Tukup' told his life story as such, each episode must have been repeated many times, both by Tukup' himself and by others, so that this particular performance was but one instance in a succession of performances, each one created specifically for the audience present.

This time Tukup' was not seeking allies for a retaliatory raid. However, he expects his performance to have political ramifications in terms of how others, especially the *murá shuar,* or hill people, perceive him.[7] My request provided Tukup' with an opportunity to tell his story to Chumap', a man of some consequence from Sucúa, where the headquarters of the Shuar Federation is located. Tukup' knew that Chumap' would repeat the story, as stories of important men are always repeated. Therefore, the image Tukup' projected to Chumap' would be the one repeated in other regions.

Throughout the narrative, Tukup's intent in addressing the story to Chumap' was to demonstrate his competence (and superiority) as a warrior and a leader, to justify his actions, and less explicitly to perpetuate the image others have of him, the "legend" of Tukup'. Self-glorification is typical of Shuar personal narratives and is related to the role such narratives play in attracting allies. However, it is more than that as well. Personal advancement depends largely on reputation, and Tukup' intended to use this opportunity to enhance his status. After hearing the tape, a Shuar elder commented, "he believes that he is a famous, noble man . . . and he has pride in this story, his words. . . . He speaks only for his own glory."

Tukup's narrative is also an act of public self-justification, though Shuar normative sanctions justify killing when motivated by revenge. Two reasons come to mind as to why Tukup' defended his actions. First, he wanted to set the record straight, at least for Chumap' and the people to whom he would repeat the story. Tukup' is known widely as a killer, and in some stories about him the killings are "for no reason." Of course, his enemies never believed that Tukup' had killed justly, just as Tukup' never believed his enemies had done so. This is the nature of feuds, that each side is convinced that its people have been wronged.

A second reason is that Tukup' was speaking to younger men with no experience in warfare, and especially to one man who was raised in a region that had given up warfare before he was born. Tukup' does not question his motivations and the narrative reveals no self-conflict concerning whether his actions were justified. His actions were well within the culturally accepted norms of his society. Thus, he is not justifying his actions to himself, but to an audience that had not lived through the constant feuding of an earlier period of Shuar history.

Another theme concerns the stories told about Tukup' and their political as well as personal implications. The ambiguities concerning his background, as well as the numerous stories of his power and courage, give Tukup' an aura of mystery and danger that he wanted to perpetuate. Many of the stories of Tukup' included claims that he was Achuar or half Achuar, and Chumap' had undoubtedly heard these stories.

The Achuar, traditional enemies of the Shuar, are culturally and linguistically very similar to the Shuar. One of the best-known distinctions between the two groups is also the least valid: the commonly held belief that the Achuar did not take heads and make *tsantsas*.[8] Tukup's narrative clearly demonstrates that the Achuar did indeed make *tsantsas,* at least in certain circumstances. However, the hostile attitudes expressed by the Shuar and Achuar toward each other run much deeper than minor cultural and linguistic differences. The Shuar frequently state that the Achuar are uncivilized savages, little better than animals. They insist that the Achuar are "of a different race," and that their language is not only unintelligible, but lacks the beauty and complexity of Shuar. As might be expected, the Achuar have similar things to say about the Shuar, adding that the Shuar have become like the white man, lying and cheating at every opportunity. Yet Tukup' seems to be neither Shuar nor Achuar, and he delights in leaving this component of his identity vague. The Achuar say that Tukup' is Shuar and have little to say about any connections he might have to the Achuar other than as an enemy. Although the Achuar have great respect for Tukup's power, few are willing to claim kinship with him. The Shuar in the Upano Valley, on the other hand, as well as the colonists who heard the stories from the Shuar, insist he is Achuar.

The confusion springs in part from stories about his exploits in war. The fact is that Tukup' fought on both sides at various times during his career, and each side is most familiar with the raids perpetrated against its own people. One Shuar informant told me that Tukup' is regarded as Achuar because he kills his own brothers, though the Shuar were also known for their internal feuds. The contradictory stories, as well as Tukup's reluctance to claim either the Achuar or the Shuar as his own people, reflect a reality in Tukup's life in that there is a sense in which he is both Shuar and Achuar. My research into Tukup's family history indicates that his parents were, in fact, Shuar from Chiwiasa, the "hill people" he so thoroughly criticizes in the episode presented here. Tukup's father, Kumpánam, left that region as a result of an internal feud and went to live near the Macuma River, an area inhabited by both Shuar and Achuar during Tukup's youth. His mother was also Shuar, though I could find no information concerning why she was living in the interior at the time of her marriage to Kumpánam. Eventually, Kumpánam became involved in local feuds and was killed by Achuar enemies. By that time he also had an

Achuar wife, and Tukup' was left to be raised by her brother, Pakunt, a well-known Achuar warrior.

Tukup's son Alberto gave a rather confusing explanation of Tukup's identity with respect to his tribal affiliation that reflects the complexity of his situation.[9] He said that Tukup' didn't really know the hill people, since his father had left Chiwiasa before he was born. He lived with the Achuar most of his life, making him "like a *mestizo*—half Shuar and half Achuar." Alberto added that "in his heart, Tukup' is Achuar." He thinks of himself as Achuar and he speaks Achuar. Then Alberto said that Tukup' claimed to be Achuar in the past, but now he says he is Shuar because now he speaks Shuar rather than Achuar. This explanation suggests that tribal affiliation is not determined by the parents' group alone. At least in regions where both Shuar and Achuar live, tribal self-designation seems to be related to socialization factors, the language one chooses to speak, and to a conscious choice as to which group one wishes to be affiliated with at any given time.

Although his son claims that Tukup' now says he is Shuar, the narrative is less explicit in confirming the claim. In fact, Tukup' does not specify the group to which he belongs in the narrative, and he is critical of both groups. That Tukup' was indeed concealing certain information regarding his identity was verified in a conversation between Tukup' and Chumap' immediately after Tukup' finished telling his story. Chumap' asks Tukup' if he is Achuar, obviously still confused about the matter.[10] Tukup's response was to laugh and ask, "Why do you want to know?"

Given the opportunity to straighten out misconceptions about himself, why would Tukup' want to perpetuate the myths? As the Shuar have become more acculturated, the Achuar have moved into the position of being the "savages," who possess greater traditional power, and who are now feared in the colonized areas more than the Shuar. As a powerful warrior and shaman, Tukup' may have wanted to reinforce the belief that he is Achuar, or at least has Achuar ancestors, though he regards himself as Shuar. However, in one part of the narrative he states that the Achuar were cowards, with the exception of the famous Achuar warrior Kashijint. And as the episode presented below demonstrates, he also wanted to distance himself from the Shuar of the western region, who no longer are perceived as men of power. Underlying the effort to reinforce the ambiguity surrounding his life may have been a belief that perpetuating the myths was essential to his survival and to the survival of his family. That is, he wanted to remain somewhat mysterious, and therefore dangerous, so that his enemies would be reluctant to attack.

In the episode that follows, two groups of people participated in the raid: Tukup', his brother, Piruchkun, and others directly under Tukup's leadership, and the hill people, a group of Shuar warriors led by Juank. Whereas in other episodes Tukup' emphasizes his distrust and dislike for the Achuar, here he distances himself from the hill people, the

Upano Valley Shuar who are his blood relatives. In this raid, Tukup' fails to carry out his obligation to avenge a relative's death. However, his manner of telling it suggests to the audience that Tukup' was not at fault for this failure, and that he acted at all times as a leader should. Rather, he lays blame on the hill people whom he invited to participate in the raid, emphasizing their cowardice and its tragic consequences. Here, as elsewhere, repetition is used to elaborate the message Tukup' wanted to convey by drawing the audience into an emotional frame of mind that generates sympathy for his point of view.

Nuna tura nuna iniáis	After doing that, leaving that
atak nuámtaik	later between them
ataksha	later
nusha Pitruk [jm]	that Pitiur
1115 nuka suntár Pitiur [jm]	and that soldier Pitiur
tura nankámnaiyamiayi.	then they began.
Nankámnaiyamiayi	They began
núwaitkiúsha áchiniáikiar nii yachijiaink. [jm]	catching each other like a woman, each with his own brother.

The opening stanza gives the background for the raid related in this episode. A man named Pitiur was involved in a feud with his brother, called "soldier Pitiur."[11] The phrase "catching each other like a woman" (1118) means that the brothers persisted in battle as a woman clings to a man, never letting him go.

Pénke nuínkia auka	Really then, those
1120 uunt tuíntsuk nújainkia	elders, wherever they were
máaniawármia [tsej]	they fought,
ti máaniawármiayi. [ja]	they fought a lot.
Naichapin máawarmíayi. [jm]	They killed Naichap'.
Wampiun máawarmíayi. [jm]	they killed Wampiu.
1125 Juwá máamiayi. [jm jm]	they killed Juwá.

Structural functions of repetition are often combined with rhetorical functions as in this instance of lexical parallelism in which Tukup' repeats a form of the verb *maatin* (to kill) in listing the people killed in a feud. The repetitions give a feeling for the interminable nature of Shuar feuding, and thereby support and justify Tukup's later retaliatory actions.

Tura naan Shikin máawarmiayi, [ja]	Then they killed Shiki,
Pitru uchirín. [jm]	Pitiur's son.
Natsa uuntan chinkín umpuntútsa wéan [ja-a]	When the older youth went to shoot birds
máwarmiayi. [tk]	they killed him.
1130 Túramatai	After doing that
ma tiítruki	indeed, having done so much

ma niíncha	indeed, for him also
sain Pakuntan	his brother-in-law Pakunt
máawarmíayi. [ja]	they killed.

1135 Ee Pakuntan máawarmíayi,	Yes, they killed Pakunt,
yatsúmir Pakúnmin. [ja]	my late brother Pakunt.
Uunta Kashijntiu uchirín sain [jm]	The elder Kashijint's son, the brother-in-law,
mantúawarmíayi. [ja]	they killed him for us.

Now, Tukup' comes to the point of this incident, that in this feud, Kashijint's son was killed. This death brings Tukup' and his brother Piruchkun into the feud, as Kashijint is Piruchkun's Achuar father-in-law. Repetition in lines 1135 and 1138 emphasizes the significance of this killing, saying first that they killed Pakunt, and then that "they killed him for us."

The verb *maatin* has been used ten times in the last five verses, so that the narration begins to sound like a litany of death and destruction. Throughout the narrative, Tukup' uses such repetitions to emphasize the persistence of feuds.

Túramátai ma mesét tiítrukim,	Having done that, indeed having made so much war,
1140 "Ame yatsuru	"You my brother,
au nekáprútsai."	test them for me."
"Amesh nuní ínkiuntrútkai," tákui	"And you find them for me over there," he said,
ma núnaka meséta mankárin umártatkui, [jm]	indeed, that was when I was to drink of death, of war,
"Ayu," tímiajai. [jm]	"Okay," I said.
1145 "Watsek,"	"Let's see,"
nekápnáiya winia yatsur Piruchkun	he who proved himself, my brother Piruchkun,
nu Kashinintiu nawántrin nuátka. [jm]	he was married to Kashijint's daughter.
ja	ja
Maj yatsuchiru,	*Maj* my little brother,
1150 "Ma iiksha nekápsátai," turútmíayi. [ja]	"Indeed, let's test ourselves," he told me.
ja	ja

In this stanza, Kashijint asks Tukup' and Piruchkun to help him, to find Pakunt's killer and retaliate. Piruchkun was Kashijint's son-in-law and therefore obligated to aid him, and as Piruchkun's brother, Tukup' also agreed to join. The first, third, and fourth verses of the series are linked by the verb *nekáprustin,* which means to test oneself against another, to prove oneself, or try out the enemy. Phrases such as "let's test ourselves" are a call to battle, in which warriors boast of their intentions to kill the enemy and call upon others to join them. Here, Kashijint uses the imperative form, saying "test (try) them for me" to encourage the young warriors to join in the raid.

	Túramtai werín	So being, when we went,
	aa puján	I was outside
	Kayápan [ja]	Kayáp's
1155	nekáska tej	which was well closed,
	enkékmíaji. [ja]	and we went in.
	Kayáp [jm]	Kayáp
	nuka nawén amák	following those tracks
	awáke	behind us,
1160	nusha awáke ma amák	and following the tracks from behind,
	winímiayi. [jm]	he was coming.

The opening verse of this stanza moves the warriors to the house of the enemy they intend to kill in retaliation for Kashijint's son. However, the enemy, Kayáp, was not in the house, but found their tracks and followed them. Here, repetition both indicates a continuous action and gives the audience a sense of suspense. That is, when Tukup' repeats that Kayáp was behind them, following their tracks, coming, the audience gets the feeling of a relentless pursuer, almost like a jaguar in his persistence. Tukup's party is not yet aware of the enemy behind them, but the audience is already anticipating the encounter with Kayáp.

	Túramu	So being,
	nuka	those
	muránia shuar [ja]	hill people
1165	ipiámiaji. [ja]	we had invited.
	Ea muránia shuaran wikia ipiámiajai. [jm]	Yes, I had invited the hill people.
	ja-a	ja-a
	Ma nuka	Indeed they
	ishámkarmiayi, amikru [jm]	were afraid, my friend,
1170	awáke wínian. [laughs]	of those who came from behind.

Tukup' now tells us that he had invited the hill people as allies on this raid. He repeats this in a two-line verse (1166–1167) for emphasis. The first indication of the importance of the hill people in this raid occurs in a comment addressed directly to Chumap' ("my friend") in which Tukup' says that the hill people were afraid "of those who came from behind." Also, the verse ties this stanza to the last by mentioning the enemies who were following them. Picking up one element from the previous stanza and repeating it is a common means of providing cohesion in the narrative. However, in this case, it also reminds the audience that Tukup' and his party were being followed and were therefore in danger.

	Iikia,	We,
	júni	over here

naan jáu ju ju ju ju yawá̱
jáu ju ju ju ju nuwa taa ajáiniákui,

that *jáu ju ju ju ju* of the dog,
jáu ju ju ju ju when the women said *taa,*

1175 "Pai áini entsáni yaja pujúrji," tusar'
juka awákeka akúpmamtíkrar' ikiúakur'
werímiaji. [ja]
jm [jm]

"Okay we are far away by the river," we said
sending some of us back, leaving them,
we went to see.
jm

"Entsá nijiá pujúreatsuash?" tusar' [jm jm]
1180 ma warí ajápen túrasha [ja]
nuka auka jaténkárin taa [jm]

"Perhaps he is washing the river?" we thought,
indeed because he was in the middle,
then, having arrived on his property,

entsán nijiá ikiuak
niinkia,
"Jintián iyútaj,"
1185 tusa áishmanka Kayápka
niínkia wé. [jm]

having quit washing the river,
he himself,
"I'm going to look in the path,"
said the man Kayáp
when he went.

Repeating the onomatopoeic sounds of the dogs howling adds drama to the narrative, helping the audience get a sense of what the raiding party was experiencing, as well as locating the participants. "We" were "over here," and Kayáp was coming in from a journey with his family. Tukup's party was listening as the dogs howled and the women called the dogs, and made plans accordingly. Still far away from the house, by the river, the raiding party is split into two groups. Tukup' went to the river, but sent some of the party back to see what was happening.

Tukup' thinks that Kayáp and his family had been fishing with barbasco poison (*entsá nijiá,* "washing the river"). Kayáp goes to look in the path, where he finds their tracks.

Tumáka ii kaúnkámun [jm]
nawén tsats^u
jukíyi. [jm]

Doing thus, of our arrival
the split tracks
he divided.

1190 Tuma tsekénki winiáj tukáma tsekénki winián

Then he came running, so doing, when he
came running

shaut wéakármiayi. [chuwa]
Muránia shuar pénke ashámkarmiayi.

quickly he approached.
The hill people were truly afraid of him.

Pénkesha ipiáticharmiayi.
ipiátutsuk uwémarmiayi.

And they didn't shoot him.
They let him go without firing.

Now the narrative returns to the scene mentioned earlier, that Kayáp was following Tukup's party, and to a pivotal theme, the hill people's fear. The second verse also illustrates an important form of repetition, the use of a repeated word to indicate a continuous action, what Grimes calls "iconic representation of extent" (1975:81). In line 1190, *tsekénki* (running) is said twice to suggest that Kayáp was "running and running," giving a sense of urgency in Tukup's situation by repeating the image of a relentless pursuer created earlier. In the next line, the onomatopoeic word *shaut* indicates the sound of rapid movement, such as the sound of hands slapping the water when someone is swimming, or as in this case, the sound of running footsteps. The combination of the repeated word *tsekénki* and the onomatopoeic *shaut* serve the function of expressing a continuous action.

The last line of this verse (1192) picks up the theme expressed earlier. Stating that the hill people were afraid (*ashámkarmiayi*) echoes the earlier statement in line 1169 (*ishámkarmiayi*). The repetition not only ties this verse to the earlier part of the episode, but emphasizes the theme concerning the hill people.

The next verse (1193–1194) gives the main point of this series, that the hill people let Kayáp go without shooting him. As in other peaks in the narrative, it is short and to the point, just two lines of two words each. In this case, both lines are complete sentences and further emphasize the significance of what happened by immediately repeating it in a slightly different way: "And they didn't shoot him. They let him go without firing."

An important detail in this verse is that Tukup' now says "they" instead of "we." This is in part because the group is split and he must indicate who carried out the action. However, earlier he said "we" referring to the same group (1178). There is a sense of separation here that is more than spatial; Tukup' is separating himself from the hill people in the sense of refusing to identify himself with them. They are his allies on this raid, but he is not one of them. The use of "we" is the appropriate form for talking about a raiding party, but when the hill people acted like cowards, they forfeited their right to be considered part of the group, resulting in Tukup's reference to them as "they" when he talked of their failure to shoot Kayáp and when he said they were afraid.[12]

1195 Túramtai [ja]	Having done thus,
ma	indeed
wakétki nush	and when he returned
pénker tátaka nusha amikru	he arrived well, and that, my friend,
kame	well
1200 ma ikiútakmiaji.	indeed, we left him.
Maj	*Maj*
urúku asartsuk ii nekármachiaj'. [jm jm]	we didn't know why we were doing this.
"Nákakar' máatai," timiaji. [je]	"Let's wait for him and kill him," we said.
"Yaunchu wakétracharish?" tusa	"Perhaps they've already returned?" he thought,
1205 "Winiá	"When he comes,
kashín winiá máatai," tíri,	when he comes tomorrow, we'll kill him," we said,
"Timiai ishínkiar'	"We'll go there
jíntia pak mátsamiaji." [jm]	to the path and attack quickly, *pak*."
Pénka pujúrmiaji.	We waited a long time,
1210 epetkar' pujúrmiaji.	leaving it, we waited.

Nántuka epetkar' tuke tuke ajapeantmiayi,   When we left it, the sun was in the middle,
tutúpin ajásai. [ja]   when it was midday.

In this stanza, all the participants are repositioned for the next incident. Kayáp returned to his house and Tukup's party left him there, reuniting to wait for another attack in the morning. Line 1204 quotes what Tukup' thinks or hopes Kayáp is thinking, that the raiding party has already left. Then, Tukup' and his party say they will wait until Kayáp comes out of the house the next morning, when they will go to the path and attack him at once.

In the following verse (1209–1212), Tukup' restates in narrative form what was quoted in the last verse, the fact that they waited, repeating it twice and adding that they left Kayáp at midday. Tukup' and his party probably arrived at Kayáp's house before dawn, since that is the usual time for a raid. All of the events so far narrated in this episode occurred from the time they arrived at dawn until noon when they left the path.

The repetitions in each of these verses give a sense of the duration of time of the events so far related, as well as providing cohesion in the stanza. In the first verse, Tukup' says "we left him"; then, "let's wait for him"; "tomorrow, we'll kill him"; and finally, in the last verse, he repeats that they left him and that they waited. A cohesive structure is produced by repeating elements in previous verses, but the rhetorical function is to create a sense of time passing and perhaps a sense of the tedium and tension associated with delays in executing a raid.

"Aukatma?"   "Perhaps it is he?"
Nu winia sair Juánk,   Then, my brother-in-law Juánk,
1215 "Aukatma auk náata?" tusa   "Perhaps it is he, is he so much?" he said,
"Tepérmáti ikiúktiai." [je]   "Let's quit laying here."

Nuka auka penké   But then, very
areantach winíniai winiá   close they came, coming
yaunchu apápénki winiá   they were already following us, coming,
1220 jintiák winiá [je]   coming by the same path.

Juank, one of the hill people, is now quoted, voicing his disagreement with Tukup's plan. The quoted rhetorical question in line 1213, "perhaps it is he?" is repeated in line 1215, adding "is he so much?" Juank is saying he doesn't think the enemy, Kayáp, is so important that they should wait all night. Juank wants to leave, rather than waiting to attack in the morning. This argument is another allusion to the cowardice of the hill people, a theme Tukup' clearly wants to keep alive.

The last few verses have suggested that Kayáp returned to his house. Tukup' stated earlier what he thought Kayáp would think and do, and what his party should do. However, in the next verse, we find that Kayáp was still after them, that he hadn't abandoned the chase after all. In lines 1217–1220, Tukup' says that the enemies were coming after them, following the same path Tukup' and his party were on earlier. Probably, Kayáp returned to his house to get other members of the household to help him go after Tukup'. The repetition of *winiá* (coming) in lines 1218–1220 suggests that the enemies were getting closer and closer. Of course, Tukup' and his party did not know they were being followed at this time, so telling the audience that Kayáp is right behind them increases the audience's sense of impending danger.

Ikiúrkir'	Leaving,
kanu aípkimiunam núchamtaik	at the same time, to where the canoe was
warúkar'	we climbed,
kanu achírar	getting the canoe,
1225 murá shuara au, "Wakétratji aí,	the hill people said, "We will return there,
Makuma nujíya aí.	up the Macuma.
Kanu iwiártuktárum nákak."	Take us straight up by canoe."
Tuiniákui,	When they said that,
"Iikia juke wéaji" tíri,	"We are going this way," we said.
1230 "Uchi	"Boys,
atum kanu iwiáktárum	you all go up by canoe,
aí íkiatíarar akúpkamjirum urum entsák	after we send you passed, then we'll return
wakétrami" tíri.	along the river," we said.

Tukup's party left their hiding place and went to where the canoes were hidden. In line 1222, "at the same time" refers to the previous verse, indicating that they went back to the canoe at the same time as Kayáp and his people were following them. The phrase links the two stanzas while giving a temporal reference for Tukup's action in this incident.

The hill people get the canoe and say they are going to return up the Macuma River. They tell Tukup' and his party to take them straight home, suggesting that the hill people had no further desire to participate in the raid, and that they wanted Tukup', as the leader of the raid, to take them home immediately.

Tukup's response is "we are going this way." He is not willing to take them home. Then, he tells the younger members of the party (*uchi*) to go upriver by canoe (1230–1232). Tukup' wanted to stay on the shore to see if he could find the enemy. Those in the canoe would go to Taisha, and later Tukup' would follow along the river. Juank had insisted on a retreat, but Tukup's only concession was to send the young boys home.

Wéarin ma ukúrin wéarin	When we went, indeed, when we went back
nush kukárak wéri	and that, we went on foot,
1235 nush wérumátaichu [jm]	and that, instead of going quickly,
"Imia mantámnatai" tsar',	"Let us kill many," we said,
"ii mantámnatnuik."	"for our own deaths."

Ataksha nu nákak jintia
ataksha ishíintiuka epétkaji. [jm]

1240 "Chíkich jíntia ínkiunka asamtai au winiátai"
tusar'. [jm]

Again that straight path
again we went over it.
"Where another path meets this one perhaps
he will come," we said.

Tukup's party is now separated from those who left by canoe. All of the last verse was a quote, but this one (1233–1235) is in narrative form and repeats part of what was said in the last quote to emphasize it and to link the stanzas. Tukup' says his party went slowly because they were on foot. Repetition of the verb *wetin* (to go) indicates both continuous movement and the slow pace of their trek. Again, participants are being moved in preparation for the next major incident.

Tukup' is still thinking of revenge, as is indicated in the reported speech of lines 1236–1237. They go back over the path, hoping to meet the enemy at a crosspath. Something of the tediousness of the hunt is suggested by the repeated word *ataksha* (again) and the addition of another word for "going" (*ishíintiuka*), the root of which includes the plural subject.

Tuma amáiniararin
penké
júnis atsúmiayi. [jm]

"Tarúmchayi" tíri
1245 ma nújainkia
chuntán achírar nuí amíkmir' Jempéktam [jm]

Jempékat
pujúyayi. [jm]

So doing, when we advanced,
nothing
there was nothing.

"He did not come," we said.
Then with that
they gathered chonta, where my late friend
    Jempékat,
where Jempékat
used to live.

The raiding party continued on the path, but Tukup' says they found nothing. Line 1244 repeats in quotation that they did not find the enemy. Having had little success, they go the house of Jempékat, Tukup's ally, to gather chonta fruit to eat.

Tuma asamtai
1250 nuna asákarin jeár'
ma nuínkia chuntán achírar

ma yuíniakᵘ ajáiniakui
murá shuar túmainiákui
páchichmiajai. [jm]

1255 "Tura warí
tsa tsa tsa tsa tsa
anentáimpratárum
wáinkiatá."

So being
when we arrived in his abandoned garden,
indeed, when they gathered chonta there,

indeed, when they ate,
the hill people, when they did this,
I didn't say anything.

"And why (are you doing this)?
no no no no no,
think well,
be careful."

Saimir Juánkim winia sair
1260 ma nusha wiki mámiajai auka [jm]
winia sair nasha [jm]
Juánkan [jm-m]
winian
winia sairnak. [ja]

My late brother-in-law Juánk, my brother-in-law
indeed, and I myself killed him later, that one
my brother-in-law, he also
Juánk
my own,
my own brother-in-law.

Tukup's repeats that they arrived at Jempékat's house, where the hill people gathered and ate chonta. Even though they took the fruit without asking, Tukup' didn't say anything at first because they were hungry. What the hill people were doing is repeated several times, emphasizing the point and also suggesting that they ate a lot, far more than would be expected without permission.[13] When they continue getting more chonta, Tukup' asks them why they are getting so much. He tells them to stop and to "be careful," that is, to be more thoughtful in their actions.

The next verse (1259–1264) is a curious addition to this section. Tukup' states that he later killed Juank, who was his brother-in-law. Alberto explained that Juank was involved in Piruchkun's murder. Achayát of Pumpuentsa killed Piruchkun, and Juank showed him where Piruchkun's house was. In revenge, Tukup' killed Juank. A question arising from this passage is whether Tukup's repeated criticism of Juank is entirely due to his actions in this raid or to his future role in Piruchkun's death. In either case, the following verses make it clear why Tukup' wanted to distance himself from Juank at this stage of the narrative, since Juank's actions ultimately lead to disaster (if, indeed, the disaster was Juank's fault).

1265 Túramu nusha
ma,
"Aaniuk" naatrumea?
Ju wéajai." [je]

"Ayu,
1270 watsek ámechuk táme
iistá,"
jee

nuyánka tsenkéakur'tiri.
Winia yatsurka
1275 Pirúchkunkia nii kanurín iwiák
niisha uúntrui Kashijntiui
uúntrin wéak"
wémiayi. [ja]

Then, he also
indeed,
"Evil one, perhaps you are a great man?
I am going this way."

"Good,
okay, as you say,
look,"
yes

then, when we separated, we said.
My brother
Pirúchkun, when he went up in his canoe
to where his elder Kashijint was,
going to his elder,
he went.

Returning to the narrated events, Juank is quoted as if he is speaking directly to the enemy. He repeats his earlier opinion that Kayáp is not so great as to be worth the wait, and adds that he intends to leave. Tukup' responds by telling Juank to do as he wishes.

These disagreements and changes of plans, here and elsewhere, suggest how little authority the leader of a raid has. Juank was only an invited participant, but he was not obligated to follow Tukup's leadership. Of course, another possibility is that Tukup' wants the audience to believe that he disagreed with Juank, considering that the consequences of the decision were disastrous.

Each group began to go its separate way: Juank and the hill people toward Taisha, Tukup' toward his home in Yaasnunka, and Piruchkun toward Kashijint's house. Repetition of verbs for "going" in the last lines of the verse emphasizes the sense of separation and movement: Piruchkun "went up (*iwiák*) in his canoe," "going (*wéakkᵘ*) to his elder," "he went (*wémiayi*)."

	Tumáarin	When we did thus,
1280	wisha yamá	and I, just then,
	júnisan jakéai	just when I started downriver,
	ju amikru yamá jéarua	this, my friend, from my new house,
	júni júni ikiátiaran ikiúakun	thus, when I left them, passing as far as
	au na	from there to
1285	Uktáyuru kanurí tepána [je]	where Otavio's canoe is,
	áiniai	when they began
	tk ipiátiarmiayi [chia]	tk they began shooting.
	Tikítcha,	And another,
	takea ipiátiarmiayi, [jm?]	*takea* they shot,
1290	jai murá shuaran. [je]	*jai*, at the hill people.
	tk shaaa . . .	*tk shaaa* . . .
	takéa tek aj aj, "Waríniak?" tárin	*takéa tek aj aj*, "What are they doing?" we thought,
	tak tak tak tak tak	again again again again again

Tukup' had separated from the others and had just started downriver by canoe, when he heard shooting. A precise measure is given of the distance traveled before the shooting began. Tukup' says that he had gone only the distance from his new house to where Otavio's (Tukup's son's) canoe is, near Otavio's house.

The next two verses use repetition and onomatopoeia to stress through sound symbolism what Tukup' has said in narrative form, that the enemy was shooting at Juank and the hill people. The repeated sound *tak* in line 1293 is an abbreviated form of *atak* (again), but its use here may also be regarded as onomatopoeic, as *tak* also expresses the sound of blows. These verses give the sense both of repeated action and the sounds of battle, dramatically drawing the audience into the scene. At the time of the performance, even though I did not understand Tukup's words, the meaning of these onomatopoeic passages was very clear to me. Like everyone else in the audience, I was transported to the scene of the battle by the rapid-fire sounds of shotguns expressed both in Tukup's words and his manner of delivery.

Jurétma au iistá utsutmam utsutmam ajáwa au
   amikrua

1295 jurétmachia au tákea tákea ajáwa au
   nekáprumniúkai?
[Niinkia pasur . . .]
tsentséret pe
tsentséret pe. Ausha
[niinkia pasurtum pasurtum . . .]

1300 auka
pt aujainkia yaunchuka auka amikru
auk auk áiniana, [jm]
jai
auk auk áiniana.

1305 Imiájni áents
tepérkaráinia. [ja]

That *jurétma,* see, it keeps pushing and
   pushing itself, my friend

That shotgun keeps going *tákea tákea,* perhaps
   it can feel it?
[They put . . .]
one right after the other,
one right after the other. And that
[putting them in . . .]

that one (shotgun)
pt, with those long ago, only those, my friend
there were only those, only those.
jai
there were only those, only those.

So many people
they attacked.

In an aside to Chumap', Tukup' explains why there was so much shooting. The shotguns being fired were of a type called *jurétam* by the Shuar.[14] Tukup' says the shotgun "keeps pushing and pushing" and he repeats that it keeps firing, *tákea tákea.* According to Alberto, the meaning of Tukup's statement is that the shotgun pushes like a woman against a man during intercourse. The word *jurétam* is derived from the verb meaning to give birth, but the question, "perhaps it can feel it?" and Chumap's response in line 1296 suggest that Alberto's interpretation is correct. Chumap's response is also a sexual metaphor, *pasurtin,* meaning to put leaves in a basket. The repeated *tsentséret* refers to a continuous sound, "one right after another." In line 1299, Chumap' adds a further response, "putting them in," again suggesting the sexual metaphor. Although Tukup' is no longer describing the battle, by repeating the sounds made by the shotgun in order to describe the shotgun itself, he has kept alive the sense of drama established in the previous verses.

The second verse in the aside (1300–1304) explains that long ago there was only this type of shotgun. The last three lines of this verse illustrate a pattern of repetition found throughout the narrative, usually marking the end of a section, in this case, the aside to Chumap'. The sentence-final verb phrase closing the verse ("there were only those, only those") is followed by Chumap's response (*jm*), after which Tukup' counter-responds with *jai* and a repetition of the sentence-final verb phrase. In the following two-line verse, Tukup' returns to the narrated events, quoting himself, saying that the enemy attacked many people.[15]

Tuma
Ankuashan [jm]
muráya shuaran [jm]

1310 auna Ankuashan nekás penkérin
   yapájkiarmiayi, [jm]

So doing,
Ankuash
of the hill people,
Ankuash, who was truly the best, they
   avenged themselves on him,

jai	*jai*
pákitkiusha. [jm jm]	like he was a wild pig.
jai [chuwa]	*jai*
Túramtai maj	So doing, *maj*
1315 suéya ímiajai jiiya tímiajai tuku	hitting him from the throat to the eye,
pee	passing through,
jankéya ímiajai ju míshaa ímiajai apújtuk	and from the jaw to the face, putting it
[chuwa]	through,
jankénka kushá kushát tk [nekasan]	leaving the jaw loose, just loose. tk [true]

This stanza describes in considerable detail the attack on the hill people. First, Tukup' tells us that Ankuash was killed (1307–1313). Though he was one of the hill people, Tukup' regards his loss as momentous. Ankuash was "the best of the hill people" in that he was the most courageous of them. The phrase "like he was a wild pig" has a double meaning, first that Ankuash was strong and healthy, "fat" like a pig, and second, that he was killed as if he were an animal.

The repetition of the interjection *jai* in lines 1311 and 1313, and elsewhere in passages describing raids, requires some explanation. *Jai* is an exclamation of strength, challenge, or defiance, regularly used in connection with warfare. Its use here seems to be to frame the phrase "like he was a wild pig," suggesting that Tukup's response to the incident is indignation. It also signifies his desire and promise to retaliate in kind. Typically, Tukup' does not describe his emotions directly, but evokes them through devices such as this repeated interjection.

Another interjection, *maj,* occurs in the following verse. Although Bolla translates *maj* as "an exclamation of wonder, of something strange, of something uncommon or rare" (1972:51), it seems to be used also as an exclamation of dismay or wonder in the sense of "how could this have happened?" Clicks, transcribed as *tk* or *pk*, are also common, and may indicate amazement or the kind of "clucking" heard in English over a sad or unfortunate event.

It is clear from this and other passages that Tukup' considers one of the most important details in warfare narratives to be the nature of the injuries received. They shot Ankuash in the throat and the ball came out in his face. Another ball hit him in the jaw, leaving the jaw loose.

Sairun Timiásrun	My brother-in-law Timiás
1320 tk nekás jankéchia tímiajai tukú	tk truly hitting him here in the jaw
pk titírinkia púj	pk his throat púj
nakárkarmiayi.	was split.
Pénke yajáuch' májkarmiayi.	Surely they treated him badly.

Next, Tukup' tells what happened to Timiás. He was hit in the jaw, splitting his throat. The repetition of clicks (*tk, pk*) throughout this stanza serves both to signify dismay as noted above and to punctuate the descriptions Tukup' is giving, adding a certain rhythm to them as well as emphasizing what is being said. Shuar men frequently use such clicks in their speech, especially when the story they are telling becomes particularly exciting or extraordinary. At the end of line 1321, *puj* is the onomatopoeic word for the sound of something breaking, such as an egg or a bowl. Line 1322 ends the principal sentence, but the verse includes an additional line, "Surely they treated him badly," in the form of a complete sentence for emphasis.

	Pitrun	Pitiur
1325	uuntan Kajékai uchirín	the elder Kajékai's son,
	nush múrayának	also from the hills,
	pk nekáska ju tuntúpech pikiásna tímiajai tukú	pk truly when they hit him here in the spine,
	pk nekás ju suntuch pujása ekétsa tímiajai	pk truly here where the joint in the back is,
	pee iniánkatsarmiayi	they made it pass through him rapidly
1330	kutírjai. [jai]	with the shotgun.
	Suwén tukúrchamiayi	But it didn't hit the jugular
	nusha chimírmiayi.	and he was cured.
	Timiásjai chimírmiayi [ja]	And Timiás was cured
	jankénka púj nakárkamaitiat. [laughs]	although it had split his jaw, púj.
1335	Tura	But
	nuka uuntka Ankuashka	that elder Ankuash
	jiniúm tukúmu asa	because he was hit in the eye
	ea jáka.	yes, he died.

Now, Pitiur's wounds are described. He was hit in the back and the ball passed through. Lines 1327 and 1328 are preceded by clicks (*pk*), and as in the previous verse, they occur before a statement about where an individual was hit.

The last two verses in the stanza state the consequences of the injuries. First, Tukup' says that Pitiur was not hit in the jugular, so he was cured. Then, Timiás was also cured, though his jaw was split. The onomatopoeic *púj* is repeated here (1334) which provokes a laugh from Chumap'. The amusement is perhaps at the image of Timiás being split open like an egg. Shuar humor is sometimes rather black.

The final verse of the stanza refers only to Ankuash. Tukup' says that because he was hit in the eye, he died. The verse consists of only one sentence, broken into four short lines, a pattern that is often used to emphasize an incident.

	"Chuwa," tímiajai, "watskea,"	"*Chuwa*" I said, "let's see,"
1340	nuí sairun Juánkan	then to my brother-in-law Juánk
	sairun Juánkminu	to my late brother-in-law Juánk,
	"Auka, áitkiataj," tusam,	"Then, "let's do this," you said,
	"Entsak jakértai" tamáitíatam	although I told you, "Let's go by river,"
	juní áitkia wekákam	doing thus you walked

1345 penker wakétrámnia.	when we could have returned easily.
Iik pújakúti mesérikia pénker."	If we had died there, it would have been better."
"Iiniak achírkutak itiármas	"When they came chasing us
jíntia íimiarin	meeting us on the path
mántamkúrkia pénker."	if they had killed us there, it would have been better."

This stanza begins with a reported speech series quoting Tukup'. The first line merely indicates that Tukup's will speak (*chuwa*,[16] *watskea*), and the next two lines indicate to whom he is speaking, Juank, the repetition conveying Tukup's anger at his brother-in-law.

Then, Tukup' reports part of a previous dialogue in which Juank and Tukup' disagreed about what they should do. Tukup' says that he told him they should all leave by canoe, but Juank wanted to take the hill people on foot. Tukup' is speaking of the recent exchange in lines 1267–1272 when the raiding party separated, in which Juank is reported in the narrative to say only that he is going another way and Tukup' tells him to go ahead.[17] Tukup' is placing the blame for their losses on Juank.

The semantic parallelism of lines 1346 and 1349 reiterates Tukup's condemnation of Juank, saying that it would have been better if they had died. His words also suggest an underlying reason for regretting the incident. If they had stayed together, fighting and dying together on the path, the fight would have been easier to explain to the hill people's families. Instead, only the hill people were attacked.

1350 Tura, "Aantar ju murá shuar nánkamin	Then, "In vain these hill people, in vain
jútikiájnia ju yawáitkiusha	that we did this as if they were dogs,
ii yawái jútikiajnia ju	like our dogs we did this,
sairu penkerkait."	my brother-in-law, is it good?"
"Iisíana watskea	"Look, let's see,
1355 urum enkérar[a] júkiarti	after we load them,
kanúnam enkérar yaruákarti	after we put them in the canoe and take them,
iik nekápsatai," tímiaji. [ja]	we'll try ourselves," we said.
"Jean nekapsatai."	"Let's try ourselves at the house."
Makuma nujín akára pámpatra asamtai wajáta	Crossing the Makuma upriver because the
katínki	current was low
1360 tímiai amáini wéarin	we went over to the other side,
murá shuar sapíjin,	the hill people, in fear (said),
"Itiúrak enkerárat?	"How will we get in?
Itiúrak jukíarat?"	How will we carry them?"

Still addressing Juank, Tukup' tells him that the hill people were killed for nothing (1350), and that they cannot be treated like dogs. Allies invited to war are called "my little dogs" because just as one carries dogs to the hunt, a warrior carries invited allies on a raid. However, on a hunt, if a dog is killed, the hunters leave it in the forest. Tukup' tells Juank that they can't just leave the wounded as if they were dogs. Because Juank doesn't respond, it isn't clear whether he wants to leave them or not, although the rhetorical question "is this good?" gives the impression that Juank was willing to leave the wounded.

Tukup' then tells the hill people what must be done, saying that they should take the wounded away in canoes, while he returns to fight. He says he and his group will try themselves, repeating the quote in the next line (1358), repetition providing cohesion between the verses and emphasizing Tukup's intention to fight. Having moved to the other side of the river, Tukup' is now on foot, walking along the shore of the Macuma.

Tukup' then quotes the hill people, who ask him how they will carry the wounded out. Again he notes their fear, this time of crossing to the other side of the river.

Túrayat, "Aták shuaraiti," tíar	Although doing thus, "It is the enemy again" they said,
1365 táker awájiarmiayi.	*táker* they fired.
"Tsaj? [chuwa]	"What happened?
Murá shuaran áinik amútrameaj. [laughs]	He is finishing the hill people for us.
Yaunchu amútrámkaji yamaikia." [tsa]	Soon he will have finished them for us." [no]
Mash ataksha, "Iistai," tiri ataksha wakétrar' katíarar'	Everyone again, "Let's go see," we said, returning across the river again,
1370 [Winia nui awajtumai'?]	[Did they do what I would have done?]
ataksha katíara kaúnkámiaji.	after crossing the river again, we arrived.

Tukup' continues to report the hill people's words. They hear firing (*taker*) and say, "it is the enemy again." Then, Tukup' reports his own thoughts upon hearing this second round of shooting. He asks, *tsaj?* ("what happened?"). The quote continues with Tukup' reporting what he thought, that they were going to "finish" the hill people. The relational suffix meaning "for us" in the verb "to finish" in the parallel lines ending the verse has a double meaning, suggested also by Chumap's laughter (1367). As the leader of the raid, the suffix is appropriate in that the hill people are part of Tukup's group, and when an enemy kills a member of one's party, he injures the whole group. However, Tukup' has made it clear that he has little respect for the hill people. Thus, the two lines could also mean that in finishing the hill people "for us" they've done Tukup's people a favor.

Everyone in Tukup's party crosses the river again to find out what happened. Chumap's rhetorical question (1370), asking if they did what he would have done, means that he wouldn't have been afraid to fight, but would have killed many people.

Ma kaúnkárin	Indeed, after we arrived
ma nújainkia	indeed with that
atáksha tk tk	again tk tk
1375 tarímiaji.	we arrived where they were.

Nuínk	There
aépas pujúriarmiayi,	they were lying
matsásar	crowded together
nújainkia.	with them

1380	[Uuntur yamárman sumák ántar emésar atús pujúrna aaniun takármaknaka wikia]	[My elder bought a new shotgun that doesn't work, if I had one like that . . .]
	Matsás pujúriarmiayi.	They were all together.
	[akákaitiainkish takákkunkau.]	[if I had it, I would cower too.]

The repetition of "arrived" in lines 1372 and 1375 refers to two separate instances of arriving. First, they arrived when they recrossed the river. In line 1373, *ma nújainkia* (indeed, with that) indicates an end to the action, and therefore, means that what follows is a new action, a new movement. The word *atáksha* (1374) can mean "again" or "later," and in this instance, means both. That is, "later" they arrived "again" where they had fought before. The two clicks (1374) are further indications of repetition, but also suggest anticipation of events to come. Tukup' seems upset by all the coming and going. His invited warriors are far more trouble than they are worth.

In line 1376, *nuínk* (there) links this verse to the last by reference to the place where they arrived. The wounded and those who were with them were gathered on the shore of the Macuma. From Tukup's statement that they were lying down, crowded together, one gets an image of a terrified group of people, huddled together, cringing at the possibility of another attack. At no time during this episode do the hill people fire at the enemy or behave as warriors in any fashion. Of course, Tukup' is presenting his version of the events, which may or may not be an accurate account, but his account does demonstrate clearly Tukup's opinion of the hill people, at least in their capacity as warriors.

In the final verse of this series (1380–1382), Tukup' repeats that the hill people were all together, again emphasizing the image of their cowardice. The rest of the verse consists of a comment made by Chumap'. He refers to a shotgun, owned by my husband, Chuck, which became a major source of amusement because it never worked. Chumap' says if he'd had a gun like his, he would have been afraid, too. The comment seems a bit out of place and Tukup' doesn't acknowledge it at all.

"Urúkarmea?" timiaji.	"What happened?" we said.
"Shuar jatítmakrin itiúrak jumákitiáj?"	"When the enemies come after us, how will we free ourselves?"

1385	Nuí iniumakar' tu matsáteaji.	Then, because we were afraid, we stayed together.
	"Tukúrmashtájiash," tiarmiayi. [ja]	"Perhaps they aren't going to shoot us?" they thought.
	"Chuwa yatsuchiru antsu	"*Chuwa*, my brothers, rather

jeá ejétai," timiaji. [jm]
1390 "Jeá ejétai
sapíjmiainiákᵘ ainiawai."

we'll go to the house," we said.
"We'll go to the house
because you all are afraid."

"Itiúrak enkérarat? Ti nekas

"How will they get in? Truly,

nunkánia timiai yaunchu yapájkiachjik?"

"did we not avenge ourselves downriver
before?' "

Addressing the hill people gathered on the shore, Tukup's party asks them what happened. The next three lines are their quoted response. They said that they were thinking about how they could defend themselves if the enemies come after them again. Then, because they were afraid, they stayed together. The hill people said nothing of the battle. Rather, they were explaining why they were hiding at the river. The rhetorical question (1386) indicates certainty; that is, they were sure the enemy was going to shoot them. The response suggests that Tukup's question had nothing to do with the attack. He wanted to know why they were behaving like cowards.

Tukup' continues the dialogue in line 1387, saying, "we'll go to the house . . . because you all are afraid." The hill people respond, asking how the wounded will be carried (1392). Line 1393 quotes what they expect the enemy to be thinking, that since they have killed three, why not go down river and finish the rest of them.

"Kunújai jakéa
1395 tusar epétak áinia
suntára amútramkaij'.
Nújainkia ti wishíkrampraij'."

"Let's go down with the canoe
and set traps
so that they won't finish our soldiers.
With that, so that they don't laugh at us."

"Watsek
ejé winia jearui ikiutai," timiajai. [ja]

"Look,
let's leave them at my house," I said.

Now Tukup' speaks again, suggesting that they take the canoe downriver and set traps so that the enemy can't kill all their "soldiers." If the enemies killed them all, they would laugh at them, saying Tukup's people didn't know how to fight. Tukup's party is indeed in danger of losing everyone, but his concern is that the Achuar don't laugh at them, laughter being the worst of insults. Then, Tukup' repeats the earlier quote saying that they should leave the wounded at his house (1398–1399).

1400 Turan
nújainkia
"Jukítiarum," timiajai.

So doing,
with that
"Carry them," I said.

"Entsáktarum páchitsuk entsákrum jukítiarum.
Tarách tampúmpruárum entsákrum jukítiárum

"Just load them, and loading them, take them.
Wrapping them in cloth and loading them,
take them,

1405 warí ímiajin
tukúrmasha."

because there are many
wounded."

Juka Timiásnaka entsáki júkiarmiayi,	Loading Timiás, they took him,
Timiásjai nájai Ankuashjai sumpitruawar.	and with Timiás also Ankuash, shortening the cloth.

Nuka naka	But that one,
1410 nuka yatsumir Pitrumkia nuka	that late brother of mine, Pitiur, he,
ímiajai tukúmaitíatank	although he was hit badly,
nii nawéjaink jéamiayi. [je]	he went on foot.
ja a	yes

Line 1400 begins a new stanza and a new series of actions in the episode. The repetitions so prominent in these verses indicate repeated actions. However, repeating the order to "carry them" and "load them" in the canoe also emphasizes the gravity of the situation. There were many wounded and they had to be carried to safety. That Tukup' had to repeat his orders to the hill people also stresses the incompetence and cowardice Tukup' attributes to his allies in this raid.

In the first two verses of the series, Tukup' orders his allies to carry the wounded and load them in the canoes, repeating the word *jukítiarum* three times. He explicitly states that there were many wounded. The word used here for "carry" is the same as that for "load," *jukítiatin*. The variations in the translation follow those given to me by both translators, the different interpretations of the word corresponding to whether the hill people were putting the wounded in the canoes or were transporting them. However, since the same word is used in Shuar, the repetitions and the implied sense of repeated action are even more insistent.

Next, Tukup' begins the narrative account of what was suggested in the previous quotations. They loaded Timiás and Ankuash, but Pitiur went on foot, though he too was wounded.

Túramatai	When they had done thus
1415 "Juka	"This one
juka	this one
entsáki éestarum," tiri.	go on loading them," we said.

"Ju"	This
ju atúmsha werítiárum	you all go this way
1420 juní werítiárum	go this way
isheamkairap ipiátakuisha."	and don't be afraid even if they shoot."

"Ishámkairap nákasrumek jukítiarum juka	"Don't be afraid, carry them slowly,
júnaka shuaran jukí wéan	go on carrying these people,
ipiátitiáji," tiri.	we will shoot," we said.

1425 "Juní tsekéaru asamtai	"Because they ran over here,
ii juínk tee ajasar' wajátsatai," tiri.	let's wait for them quietly over here," we said.

After Timiás and Ankuash are in the canoe, Tukup' told the hill people to load each wounded man until all were in the canoes. Repeated action is indicated by two lines, each with the single word *junka* (this one). The last line of the verse continues the command with "go on loading them."

Although the next verse (1418–1421) doesn't mention loading the wounded, it continues Tukup's admonitions to the hill people, telling them what direction to go and not to be afraid. This is followed by his advice to carry them slowly and to "go on carrying these people." Tukup' adds that he and his party will provide cover for those carrying the wounded. The final verse of the stanza is only two lines in which Tukup' states his plan of action: that they will wait, watching for the enemy, while the hill people finish loading the wounded in canoes.

Juka entsáki wénai	They went on loading them
auk auk auk auk	over there, there, there, there
ejéwar kanúnam ejéwar	taking them to the canoe, taking them,
1430 en̲kérármatai, "Pai."	when they got in, "Ready."

Again, Tukup' repeats the theme of loading and carrying the wounded, this time reporting the action taken (1427). That is, the hill people did as they were told and loaded the wounded. Here, "loading" is given as *entsáki* (putting in), and the action is emphasized by the repetition of *auk* (over there).

The repetitions throughout this series do more than indicate actions or words that are repeated. First, Tukup' uses these repetitions to indicate his distrust of and disrespect for his allies, the hill people. Second, he is stressing the magnitude of the tragedy that occurred in this failed attempt to retaliate against his enemies. By repeating over and over again the command to load the wounded in canoes he emphasizes the excessive number of wounded, a fact which he attributes to the incompetence of the hill people. Finally, the repetitions add an emotional quality to the passage. It is easy to envision a scene in which Tukup' and his people carefully place the wounded warriors in canoes, one after another, with a sense of failure and loss.

"Jakértarum tepésrum jakértarum,	"Go downriver, lying down, go down thus
shuar ipiáturmák^u tukúrmáirum	so that the enemy doesn't hit you when he
	shoots at you,
áya tepésrum."	only lying down."
"Naka wéarkrúmka	"If you go straight
1435 penké kajínmatsuk jakérum	going down without being careless,
nun̲káni akŕa timiai kanu anújkárum	when you pass the current and tie the canoe,
nákarsatárum." [jm]	wait for me."
"Atumin ipiáturárash, "Niiyap' en̲kémpraya,"	"Although they shoot at you, saying, "They
taun,	surely got in,"
atumin utsúpia ipiáturmakrumnish	although they shoot at you when they fire,
wi ánuk wéran	going along the shore
1440 niincha atak íiksanak entsánini kéas ajúntatjai	I will throw them back in the river again."
auka."	

"Antrarum ashámkairap," tiri itiúakur,

"Don't be afraid for nothing," we said as we left,

"Iikia juka éntsaka ánuar
wéa wéakuar'
jimiára akara nankáikirun nuí peémka
wajástárum," tímianum.

"Along the banks of this river
we'll keep going,
after passing two currents, stay and wait
there," we said.

Tukup' continues to give orders to the hill people, telling them to lay down in the canoe so they'll be safe (1431–1433). The enemies won't see them to shoot them. Tukup' then tells them to wait for him past the current, referring to a stretch of whitewater downriver.

Tukup's instructions extend into the next verse, emphasizing through repetition a theme mentioned earlier, that they should not be afraid because he will protect them. He repeats that the enemy may know they're in the canoe, but tells them not to worry. He will be on the shore and will "throw them in the river," meaning he will kill them. In the next verse (1441–1444), Tukup' tells them again not to be afraid, repeating that he would be on the shore to protect them and that they should wait for him after passing the two currents.

We cannot know, of course, how many times Tukup' actually told the hill people to stay down in the canoes or that he would protect them. However, the repetitions in the narrative clearly indicate Tukup's intent to influence the audience's perception of the roles played by the hill people and by Tukup'. The hill people are presented as cowardly, uncertain, and not very familiar with the strategies of warfare, while Tukup' is portrayed as calm and knowledgeable, as well as brave.

1445 Nuí jeármatai
suruká chumpímprar
juni ai, kaúntrámiaji winia jéarui. [jm]

When they arrived there,
everyone filling it,
it was like this, when we arrived at my house.

Ee tukúrma [je]
je

Yes, the wounded
yes.

1450 Nuí kanúnmanka númpaka méte piákai
aya nii numpénak shúpararara . . .
ajá ajáiniakua
anéantarmiayi. [chuwa]
jai [maj]

Although the canoe was filled with blood,
although only *shúpararara* . . . their blood
kept going.
they survived.
jai

1455 Ensta pajámuk urúka?
Imiainikmíayi,
ímiainikmíayi. [jm jm]

When water gets in, how is it?
It was as much as that,
It was as much as that.

They arrived at Tukup's house at night, and the canoes were filled with people. In this series of verses, Tukup' again uses repetition to emphasize the tragedy of the situation. First, he refers to the canoe being filled with people (*chumpímprar*). Then, after reiterating that it was the wounded in the canoes (1448–1449), he says that the canoe was filled with blood (*méte piákai*). The image evoked by the two instances of words meaning "filled" is powerful. Tukup' also dramatically describes the condition of the wounded by using the onomatopoeic *shúpararara,* the sound made when someone breathes blood. In spite of this, the wounded survived.

Then, Tukup' continues describing the scene, this time through a rhetorical question asking how water fills a canoe. There was as much blood as there would be water in a broken canoe. He repeats "it was as much as that" twice for further emphasis.

Tu túrunámtai	Thus, because it was so,
jéa kanára tsawárkur',	after sleeping at the house until dawn,
1460 "Urúkatárme? Watskea	"What will you all do? Look,
aépsárum pujúrú ajátárum	keep resting, do that,
wi iístájai," tímiajai. [ja]	I am going to see," I said.
je e	yes
"Murá shuartiram	"You hill people
1465 auketiatrumku tímiatniukarum	being such cowards, being so much,
iiru mátiárum watsek."	'look at me,' we'll see."

Tukup' stayed at the house one night, then said he was going to look for the enemies. He tells the hill people to rest while he is gone. Then, Tukup' tells the hill people that they are cowards and they should look at him.[18] That is, when they see him, they should see a warrior who wants to fight his enemies. Saying that he is truly a great man, a brave man, this is one of many passages in the narrative in which Tukup' glorifies himself, pointing out his aggressiveness as a warrior. Of course, the quote also makes an explicit comparison between Tukup' and the hill people, in which Tukup' must be seen as the better man. One has to wonder whether these are Tukup's acutal words or whether they are for the benefit of the audience. He would have to have been very confident of his position to call them cowards to their faces.

"Aepsárum	"While you lie here
jakakuish	if they die,
juínk ikiúrmastárum	bury them here,
1470 winia jeáruínink ikiúmastárum."	bury them in my house."
"Aantrarum	"You are wrong
yapájtiámpraj tirum	to want to avenge yourselves on us.
nuár yajauch majtúsairap.	Don't do anything bad to my wife.
Winia uchir yajauch mátrukáirap.	Don't do anything bad to my children.
1475 Iniámprúktatjarme."	I will defend you."
"Iniámprúktatjame	"I will defend you
auka améketkum	because if you were alone
iniámprumakcháinme.	you could not defend yourselves.
Pujúmata," tímiaji. [jm]	Goodbye," we said.

Tukup' tells the hill people that if the wounded die while they are there, they should bury the dead in his house. The verse reminds the audience that the hill people are going to wait, lying around comfortably, while Tukup' goes off to war again.

. The next verse indicates Tukup's apprehension that he will be blamed for what happened to the hill people. Tukup' invited the hill people, and now there are three wounded, and one dead. He tells them not to do anything to his family, not to avenge themselves on his family if some of the wounded die. This suggests that Tukup' may be held responsible for the deaths of people he invited on a raid. Also, if the hill people retaliated against Tukup's family in the event of another death, a new feud would have begun, this time between Tukup' and the hill people. Tukup' not only tells them not to do anything to his family, but also tells them he will defend them. In order to avoid another feud, Tukup' intends to avenge the injuries done to the hill people, his allies.

In the final verse of the episode, Tukup' repeats again that he will defend them. His explanation, that they cannot defend themselves, could have two interpretations. The hill people may be unable to avenge their own deaths because they are too few and too weak from injury to go on a raid, or the passage could also mean that they are cowards and are unable or unwilling to fight. I prefer the latter interpretation since it fits the image Tukup' has been creating for the hill people in this episode. In the last line, Tukup' says *pujúmata,* a salutation used in leave-taking. This leave-taking also ends the episode.

The structural devices employed in Tukup's narrative include such features as the use of particles to mark the beginning of verses and stanzas, response-counterresponse patterns of verses ending stanzas, converting the final element of one verse into the initial element of the next, and a variety of parallel structures at the lexical, semantic, and grammatical levels. The most obvious function of these devices is to provide cohesion between verses, stanzas, and even episodes. Tukup's narrative, however, demonstrates an instance of form-meaning covariation in which the structural uses of repetition become devices for creating meaning and evoking emotions that help realize Tukup's personal goals in telling the story. While repetition is used like a thread, tying parts of the story together poetically, it also serves to mark significance, create suspense and intensity, express and evoke emotion, and metaphorically represent extent (of time, motion, action).

The value of faithfully transcribing and translating oral texts in their entirety has been established many times in studies of narrative and ritual speech, stressing the importance of this method for the analysis of organizational structure and meaning. Tukup's narrative adds another dimension to this approach in that it demonstrates that understanding the speaker's intentions on a more personal level is also affected by the translator's fidelity to the original words of the speaker. Life histories have been described as the "retrospective re-creation of experience of a particular person for his own purposes at a definite point of his life" (Watson and Watson-Franke 1985:146). As collaborators in the interpretation of such documents, it seems especially important to adhere to the narrator's original words as closely as possible. Repetition, along with other features of narrative style, constitutes a part of the narrator's verbal strategy that cannot be discovered without close attention to the actual instance of narrative performance.

APPENDIX

Episode from Tukup's Narrative

Nuna tura nuna iniáis	After doing that, leaving that
atak nuámtaik	later between them
ataksha	later
nusha Pitruk [jm]	that Pitiur
1115 nuka suntár Pitiur [jm]	and that soldier Pitiur
tura nankámnaiyamiayi	then they began.
Nankámnaiyamiayi	They began
núwaitkiúsha áchiniáikiar nii yachijiaink. [jm]	catching each other like a woman, each with his own brother.
Pénke nuínkia auka	Really then, those
1120 uunt tuíntsuk nújainkia	elders, wherever they were
máaniawármia [tsej]	they fought,
ti máaniawármiayi. [ja]	they fought a lot.
Naichapin máawarmíayi. [jm]	They killed Naichap'.
Wampiun máawarmíayi. [jm]	they killed Wampiu.
1125 Juwá máamiayi. [jm jm]	they killed Juwá.
Tura naan Shikin máawarmiayi, [ja]	Then they killed Shiki,
Pitru uchirín. [jm]	Pitiur's son.
Natsa uuntan chinkín umpuntútsa wéan [ja-a]	When the older youth went to shoot birds
máwarmiayi. tk	they killed him. tk
1130 Túramatai	After doing that
ma tiítruki	indeed, having done so much
ma niíncha	indeed, for him also
sain Pakuntan	his brother-in-law Pakunt
máawarmíayi. [ja]	they killed.
1135 Ee Pakuntan máawarmíayi,	Yes, they killed Pakunt,
yatsúmir Pakúnmin. [ja]	my late brother Pakunt.
Uunta Kashijntiu uchirín sain [jm]	The elder Kashijint's son, the brother-in-law,
mantúawarmíayi. [ja]	they killed him for us.
Túramátai ma mesét tiítrukim,	Having done that, indeed having made so much war,
1140 "Ame yatsuru	"You my brother,
au nekáprútsai."	test them for me."

"Amesh nuní ínkiuntrútkai," tákui
ma núnaka meséta mankárin umártatkui, [jm]

"Ayu," tímiajai. [jm]

1145 "Watsek,"
nekápnáiya winia yatsur Piruchkun
nu Kashinintiu nawántrin nuátka. [jm]
ja

Maj yatsuchiru,
1150 "Ma iiksha nekápsátai," turútmíayi. [ja]
ja

Túramtai werín
aa puján
Kayápan [ja]
1155 nekáska tej
enkékmíaji. [ja]

Kayáp [jm]
nuka nawén amák
awáke
1160 nusha awáke ma amák
winímiayi. [jm]

Túramu
nuka
muránia shuar [ja]
1165 ipiámiaji. [ja]

Ea muránia shuaran wikia ipiámiajai. [jm]
ja-a

Ma nuka
ishámkarmiayi, amikru [jm]
1170 awáke wínian. [laughs]

Iikia,
júni
naan jáu ju ju ju ju yawá
jáu ju ju ju ju nuwa taa ajáiniákui,

1175 "Pai áini entsáni yaja pujúrji," tusar'
juka awákeka akúpmamtíkrar' ikiúakur'
werímiaji. [ja]
jm [jm]

"Entsá nijiá pujúreatsuash?" tusar' [jm jm]

1180 ma warí ajápen túrasha [ja]
nuka auka jaténkárin taa [jm]

"And you find them for me over there," he said,
indeed, that was when I was to drink of death,
of war,
"Okay," I said.

"Let's see,"
he who proved himself, my brother Piruchkun,
he was married to Kashijint's daughter.
ja

Maj my little brother,
"Indeed, let's test ourselves," he told me.
ja

So being, when we went,
I was outside
Kayáp's
which was well closed,
and we went in.

Kayáp
following those tracks
behind us,
and following the tracks from behind,
he was coming.

So being,
those
hill people
we had invited.

Yes, I had invited the hill people.
ja-a

Indeed they
were afraid, my friend,
of those who came from behind.

We,
over here
that *jáu ju ju ju ju* of the dog,
jáu ju ju ju ju when the women said *taa*,

"Okay we are far away by the river," we said
sending some of us back, leaving them,
we went to see.
jm

"Perhaps he is washing the river?" we
thought,
indeed because he was in the middle,
then, having arrived on his property,

entsán nijiá ikiuak
niinkia,
"Jintián iyútaj,"
1185 tusa áishmanka Kayápka
niínkia wé. [jm]

having quit washing the river,
he himself,
"I'm going to look in the path,"
said the man Kayáp
when he went.

Tumáka ii kaúnkámun [jm]
nawén tsats"
jukíyi. [jm]

Doing thus, of our arrival
the split tracks
he divided.

1190 Tuma tsekénki winiáj tukáma tsekénki winián

Then he came running, so doing, when he
    came running

shaut wéakármiayi. [chuwa]
Muránia shuar pénke ashámkarmiayi.

quickly he approached.
The hill people were truly afraid of him.

Pénkesha ipiáticharmiayi.
ipiátutsuk uwémarmiayi.

And they didn't shoot him.
They let him go without firing.

1195 Túramtai [ja]
ma
wakétki nush
pénker tátaka nusha amikru
kame
1200 ma ikiútakmiaji.

Having done thus,
indeed
and when he returned
he arrived well, and that, my friend,
well
indeed, we left him.

Maj
urúku asartsuk ii nekármachiaj'. [jm jm]
"Nákakar' máatai," timiaji. [je]

Maj
we didn't know why we were doing this.
"Let's wait for him and kill him," we said.

"Yaunchu wakétracharish?" tusa

"Perhaps they've already returned?" he
    thought,

1205 "Winiá
kashín winiá máatai," tíri,

"When he comes,
when he comes tomorrow, we'll kill him," we
    said,

"Timiai ishínkiar'
jíntia pak mátsamiaji." [jm]

"We'll go there
to the path and attack quickly, *pak*."

Pénka pujúrmiaji.
1210 epetkar' pujúrmiaji.
Nántuka epetkar' tuke tuke ajapeantmiayi,
tutúpin ajásai. [ja]

We waited a long time,
leaving it, we waited.
When we left it, the sun was in the middle,
when it was midday.

"Aukatma?"
Nu winia sair Juánk,
1215 "Aukatma auk náata?" tusa
"Tepérmáti ikiúktiai." [je]

"Perhaps it is he?"
Then, my brother-in-law Juánk,
"Perhaps it is he, is he so much?" he said,
"Let's quit laying here."

Nuka auka penké
areantach winíniai winiá
yaunchu apápénki winiá
1220 jintiák winiá [je]

But then, very
close they came, coming
they were already following us, coming,
coming by the same path.

Ikiúrkir'
kanu aípkimiunam núchamtaik
warúkar'

kanu achírar
1225 murá shuara au, "Wakétratji aí,
Makuma nujíya aí.
Kanu iwiártuktárum nákak."

Tuiniákui,
"Iikia juke wéaji" tíri,
1230 "Uchi
atum kanu iwiáktárum
aí íkiatíarar akúpkamjirum urum entsák
wakétrami" tíri.

Wéarin ma ukúrin wéarin
nush kukárak wéri
1235 nush wérumátaichu [jm]

"Imia mantámnatai" tsar',
"ii mantámnatnuik."

Ataksha nu nákak jintia
ataksha ishíintiuka epétkaji. [jm]
1240 "Chíkich jíntia ínkiunka asamtai au winiátai"
tusar'. [jm]

Tuma amáiniararin
penké
júnis atsúmiayi. [jm]

"Tarúmchayi" tíri
1245 ma nújainkia
chuntán achírar nuí amíkmir' Jempéktam [jm]

Jempékat
pujúyayi. [jm]

Tuma asamtai
1250 nuna asákarin jeár'
ma nuínkia chuntán achírar
ma yuíniakᵘ ajáiniakui
murá shuar túmainiákui
páchichmiajai. [jm]

1255 "Tura warí
tsa tsa tsa tsa tsa
anentáimpratárum
wáinkiatá."

Leaving,
at the same time, to where the canoe was
we climbed,

getting the canoe,
the hill people said, "We will return there,
up the Macuma.
Take us straight up by canoe."

When they said that,
"We are going this way," we said.
"Boys,
you all go up by canoe,
after we send you passed, then we'll return
along the river," we said.

When we went, indeed, when we went back
and that, we went on foot,
and that, instead of going quickly,

"Let us kill many," we said,
"for our own deaths."

Again that straight path
again we went over it.
"Where another path meets this one perhaps
he will come," we said.

So doing, when we advanced,
nothing
there was nothing.

"He did not come," we said.
Then with that
they gathered chonta, where my late friend
Jempékat,
where Jempékat
used to live.

So being
when we arrived in his abandoned garden,
indeed, when they gathered chonta there,
indeed, when they ate,
the hill people, when they did this,
I didn't say anything.

"And why (are you doing this)?
no no no no no,
think well,
be careful."

Saimir Juánkim winia sair

My late brother-in-law Juánk, my brother-in-law

1260 ma nusha wiki mámiajai auka [jm]
winia sair nasha [jm]
Juánkan [jm-m]
winian
winia sairnak. [ja]

indeed, and I myself killed him later, that one
my brother-in-law, he also
Juánk
my own,
my own brother-in-law.

1265 Túramu nusha
ma,
"Aaniuk" naatrumea?
Ju wéajai." [je]

Then, he also
indeed,
"Evil one, perhaps you are a great man?
I am going this way."

"Ayu,
1270 watsek ámechuk táme
iistá,"
jee

"Good,
okay, as you say,
look,"
yes

nuyánka tsenkéakur'tiri.
Winia yatsurka
1275 Pirúchkunkia nii kanurín iwiák
niisha uúntrui Kashijntiui
uúntrin wéak"
wémiayi. [ja]

then, when we separated, we said.
My brother
Pirúchkun, when he went up in his canoe
to where his elder Kashijint was,
going to his elder,
he went.

Tumáarin
1280 wisha yamá
júnisan jakéai

When we did thus,
and I, just then,
just when I started downriver,

ju amikru yamá jéarua
júni júni ikiátiaran ikiúakun
au na
1285 Uktáyuru kanurí tepána [je]
áiniai
tk ipiátiarmiayi [chia]

this, my friend, from my new house,
thus, when I left them, passing as far as
from there to
where Otavio's canoe is,
when they began
tk they began shooting.

Tikítcha,
takea ipiátiarmiayi, [jm?]
1290 jai murá shuaran. [je]

And another,
takea they shot,
jai, at the hill people.

tk shaaa . . .
takéa tek aj aj, "Waríniak?" tárin

tk shaaa . . .
takéa tek aj aj, "What are they doing?" we
thought,

tak tak tak tak tak

again again again again

Jurétma au iistá utsutmam utsutmam ajáwa au
amikrua
1295 jurétmachia au tákea tákea ajáwa au
nekáprumniúkai?
[Niinkia pasur . . .]

That *jurétma,* see, it keeps pushing and
pushing itself, my friend
That shotgun keeps going *tákea tákea,* perhaps
it can feel it?
[They put . . .]

tsentséret pe

tsentséret pe. Ausha

[niinkia pasurtum pasurtum . . .]

one right after the other,

one right after the other. And that

[putting them in . . .]

1300 auka

pt aujainkia yaunchuka auka amikru

auk auk áiniana, [jm]

jai

auk auk áiniana.

that one (shotgun)

pt, with those long ago, only those, my friend

there were only those, only those.

jai

there were only those, only those.

1305 Imiájni áents

tepérkaráinia. [ja]

So many people

they attacked.

Tuma

Ankuashan [jm]

muráya shuaran [jm]

1310 auna Ankuashan nekás penkérin

yapájkiarmiayi, [jm]

jai

pákitkiusha. [jm jm]

jai [chuwa]

So doing,

Ankuash

of the hill people,

Ankuash, who was truly the best, they

avenged themselves on him,

jai

like he was a wild pig.

jai

Túramtai maj

1315 suéya ímiajai jiiya tímiajai tuku

pee

jankéya ímiajai ju míshaa ímiajai apújtuk

[chuwa]

jankénka kushá kushát tk [nekasan]

So doing, *maj*

hitting him from the throat to the eye,

passing through,

and from the jaw to the face, putting it

through,

leaving the jaw loose, just loose. tk [true]

Sairun Timiásrun

1320 tk nekás jankéchia tímiajai tukú

pk titírinkia púj

nakárkarmiayi.

Pénke yajáuch' májkarmiayi.

My brother-in-law Timiás

tk truly hitting him here in the jaw

pk his throat púj

was split.

Surely they treated him badly.

Pitrun

1325 uuntan Kajékai uchirín

nush múrayának

pk nekáska ju tuntúpech pikiásna tímiajai tukú

pk nekás ju suntuch pujása ekétsa tímiajai

pee iniánkatsarmiayi

1330 kutírjai. [jai]

Pitiur

the elder Kajékai's son,

also from the hills,

pk truly when they hit him here in the spine,

pk truly here where the joint in the back is,

they made it pass through him rapidly

with the shotgun.

Suwén tukúrchamiayi

nusha chimírmiayi.

Timiásjai chimírmiayi [ja]

jankénka púj nakárkamaitiat. [laughs]

But it didn't hit the jugular

and he was cured.

And Timiás was cured

although it had split his jaw, púj.

1335 Tura

nuka uuntka Ankuashka

But

that elder Ankuash

jiniúm tukúmu asa
ea jáka.

because he was hit in the eye
yes, he died.

"Chuwa," tímiajai, "watskea,"
1340 nuí sairun Juánkan
sairun Juánkminu

"*Chuwa*" I said, "let's see,"
then to my brother-in-law Juánk
to my late brother-in-law Juánk,

"Auka, 'áitkiataj,' tusam,
'Ensak jakértai' tamáitíatam
juní áitkia wekákam
1345 penker wakétrámnia.
Iik pújakúti mesérikia pénker."

"Then, let's do this, you said,
although I told you, 'Let's go by river,'
doing thus you walked
when we could have returned easily.
If we had died there, it would have been
     better."

"Iiniak achírkutak itiármas
jíntia íimiarin
mántamkúrkia pénker."

"When they came chasing us
meeting us on the path
if they had killed us there, it would have been
     better."

1350 Tura, "Aantar ju murá shuar nánkamin
jútikiájnia ju yawáitkiusha
ii yawái jútikiajnia ju
sairu penkerkait."

Then, "In vain these hill people, in vain
that we did this as if they were dogs,
like our dogs we did this,
my brother-in-law, is it good?"

"Iisíana watskea
1355 urum enkérarᵃ júkiarti
kanúnam enkérar yaruákarti
iik nekápsatai," tímiaji. [ja]

"Look, let's see,
after we load them,
after we put them in the canoe and take them,
we'll try ourselves," we said.

"Jean nekapsatai."
Makuma nujín akára pámpatra asamtai wajáta
     katínki
1360 tímiai amáini wéarin

"Let's try ourselves at the house."
Crossing the Makuma upriver because the
     current was low
we went over to the other side,

murá shuar sapíjin,
"Itiúrak enkerárat?
Itiúrak jukíarat?"

the hill people, in fear (said),
"How will we get in?
How will we carry them?"

Túrayat, "Aták shuaraiti," tíar

Although doing thus, "It is the enemy again"
     they said,

1365 táker awájiarmiayi.
"Tsaj? [chuwa]
Murá shuaran áinik amútrameaj. [laughs]
Yaunchu amútrámkaji yamaikia." [tsa]

táker they fired.
"What happened?
He is finishing the hill people for us.
Soon he will have finished them for us." [no]

Mash ataksha, "Iistai," tiri ataksha wakétrar'
     katíarar'
1370 [Winia nui awajtumai'?]
ataksha katíara kaúnkámiaji.

Everyone again, "Let's go see," we said,
     returning across the river again,
[Did they do what I would have done?]
after crossing the river again, we arrived.

Ma kaúnkárin
ma nújainkia

Indeed, after we arrived
indeed with that

atáksha tk tk
1375 tarímiaji.

again tk tk
we arrived where they were.

Nuínk
aépas pujúriarmiayi,
matsásar
nújainkia.

There
they were lying
crowded together
with them

1380 [Uuntur yamárman sumák ántar emésar atús
    pujúrna aaniun takármaknaka wikia]
Matsás pujúriarmiayi.
[akákaitiainkish takákkunkau.]

[My elder bought a new shotgun that doesn't
    work, if I had one like that . . .]
They were all together.
[If I had it, I would cower too.]

"Urúkarmea?" timiaji.
"Shuar jatítmakrin itiúrak jumákitiáj?"

"What happened?" we said.
"When the enemies come after us, how will
    we free ourselves?"

1385 Nuí iniumakar' tu matsáteaji.

Then, because we were afraid, we stayed
    together.

"Tukúrmashtájiash," tiarmiayi. [ja]

"Perhaps they aren't going to shoot us?" they
    thought.

"Chuwa yatsuchiru
antsu
jeá ejétai," timiaji. [jm]
1390 "Jeá ejétai
sapíjmiainiákᵘ ainiawai."

"*Chuwa*, my brothers,
rather
we'll go to the house," we said.
"We'll go to the house
because you all are afraid."

"Itiúrak enkérarat? Ti nekas
nunkánia timiai yaunchu yapájkiachjik?"

"How will they get in? Truly,
did we not avenge ourselves downriver
    before?"

"Kunújai jakéa
1395 tusar epétak áinia
suntára amútramkaij'.
Nújainkia ti wishíkrampraij'."

"Let's go down with the canoe
and set traps
so that they won't finish our soldiers.
With that, so that they don't laugh at us."

"Watsek
ejé winia jearui ikiutai," timiajai. [ja]

"Look,
let's leave them at my house," I said.

1400 Turan
nújainkia
"Jukítiarum," timiajai.

So doing,
with that
"Carry them," I said.

"Entsáktarum páchitsuk entsákrum jukítiarum.
Tarách tampúmpruárum entsákrum jukítiárum

"Just load them, and loading them, take them.
Wrapping them in cloth and loading them,
    take them,

1405 warí ímiajin
tukúrmasha."

because there are many
wounded."

Juka Timiásnaka entsáki júkiarmiayi,
Timiásjai nájai Ankuashjai sumpitruawar.

Loading Timiás, they took him,
and with Timiás also Ankuash, shortening the
    cloth.

Nuka naka

1410 nuka yatsumir Pitrumkia nuka
ímiajai tukúmaitíatank
nii nawéjaink jéamiayi. [je]
ja a

Túramatai
1415 "Juka
juka
entsáki éestarum," tiri.

"Ju"
ju atúmsha werítiárum
1420 juní werítiárum
isheamkairap ipiátakuisha."

"Ishámkairap nákasrumek jukítiarum juka
júnaka shuaran jukí wéan
ipiátitiáji," tiri.

1425 "Juní tsekéaru asamtai
ii juínk tee ajasar' wajátsatai," tiri.

Juka entsáki wénai
auk auk auk auk
ejéwar kanúnam ejéwar
1430 enkérármatai, "Pai."

"Jakértarum tepésrum jakértarum,
shuar ipiáturmáku tukúrmáirum

áya tepésrum."

"Naka wéarkrúmka
1435 penké kajínmatsuk jakérum
nunkáni akára timiai kanu anújkárum
nákarsatárum." [jm]

"Atumin ipiáturárash, "Niiyap' enkémpraya,"
taun,
atumin utsúpia ipiáturmakrumnish
wi ánuk wéran
1440 niincha atak íiksanak entsánini kéas ajúntatjai
auka."

"Antrarum ashámkairap," tiri itiúakur,

"Iikia juka éntsaka ánuar
wéa wéakuar'
jimiára akara nankáikirun nuí peémka
wajástárum," tímianum.

But that one,
that late brother of mine, Pitiur, he,
although he was hit badly,
he went on foot.
yes

When they had done thus
"This one
this one
go on loading them," we said.

This
you all go this way
go this way
and don't be afraid even if they shoot."

"Don't be afraid, carry them slowly,
go on carrying these people,
we will shoot," we said.

"Because they ran over here,
let's wait for them quietly over here," we said.

They went on loading them
over there, there, there, there
taking them to the canoe, taking them,
when they got in, "Ready."

"Go downriver, lying down, go down thus
so that the enemy doesn't hit you when he
    shoots at you,
only lying down."

"If you go straight
going down without being careless,
when you pass the current and tie the canoe,
    wait for me."

"Although they shoot at you, saying, 'They
    surely got in,'
although they shoot at you when they fire,
going along the shore
I will throw them back in the river again."

"Don't be afraid for nothing," we said as we
    left,
"Along the banks of this river
we'll keep going,
after passing two currents, stay and wait
    there," we said.

1445 Nuí jeármatai	When they arrived there,
suruká chumpímprar	everyone filling it,
juni ai, kaúntrámiaji winia jéarui. [jm]	it was like this, when we arrived at my house.
Ee tukúrma [je]	Yes, the wounded
je	yes.
1450 Nuí kanúnmanka númpaka méte piákai	Although the canoe was filled with blood,
aya nii numpénak shúpararara . . .	although only *shúpararara* . . . their blood
ajá ajáiniakua	kept going.
anéantarmiayi. [chuwa]	they survived.
jai [maj]	*jai*
1455 Ensta pajámuk urúka?	When water gets in, how is it?
Imiainikmíayi,	It was as much as that,
ímiainikmíayi. [jm jm]	It was as much as that.
Tu túrunámtai	Thus, because it was so,
jéa kanára tsawárkur',	after sleeping at the house until dawn,
1460 "Urúkatárme? Watskea	"What will you all do? Look,
aépsárum pujúrú ajátárum	keep resting, do that,
wi iístájai," tímiajai. [ja]	I am going to see," I said.
je e	yes
"Murá shuartiram	"You hill people
1465 auketiatrumku tímiatniukarum	being such cowards, being so much,
iiru mátiárum watsek."	'look at me,' we'll see."
"Aepsárum	"While you lie here
jakakuish	if they die,
juínk ikiúrmastárum	bury them here,
1470 winia jeáruínink ikiúmastárum."	bury them in my house."
"Aantrarum	"You are wrong
yapájtiámpraj tirum	to want to avenge yourselves on us.
nuár yajauch majtúsairap.	Don't do anything bad to my wife.
Winia uchir yajauch mátrukáirap.	Don't do anything bad to my children.
1475 Iniámprúktatjarme."	I will defend you."
"Iniámprúktatjame	"I will defend you
auka améketkum	because if you were alone
iniámprumakcháinme.	you could not defend yourselves.
Pujúmata," tímiaji. [jm]	Goodbye," we said.

NOTES

1. Shuar orthography is based on Spanish and was developed by the Salesian missionaries for use in teaching religion and for use in the bilingual educational system. I have used this system because it has become accepted among the Shuar themselves and is used in the publications of the

Shuar Federation. However, there are some ways in which this orthography differs from standard notations that should be explained.

All Shuar vowels may occur as voiceless vowels at the end of a word. In Shuar orthography, voiceless vowels are usually represented by an apostrophe, though in some cases, particularly with the unvoiced /u/, a superscripted vowel is used, as in Chinkiasu. The apostrophe at the end of the names Tukup' and Chumap' represents an unvoiced /i/. In translating possessive forms, the single apostrophe serves as the possessive marker as well as the voiceless vowel, as in "Tukup's narrative."

Shuar vowels also occur as nasalized vowels and are represented by underlining the vowel, as in *ju*. The underlined /n/ is a velar phoneme, as in *pénker.*

2. A *centro* is the neighborhood or community level of organization within the *Federación de Centros Shuar,* an indigenous organization formed in 1964 to help the Shuar fight the onslaught of colonists from the highlands. In the late seventies, Tukup' settled in Ecuador, sent messages to his enemies that he no longer wanted to fight, built an airstrip, and petitioned the Federation for *centro* status.

3. Tukup's narrative is in the dialogic form typical of most Shuar discourse. When Tukup' began his narrative, Chumap' immediately fell into the role of listener-responder, punctuating the narrative with responses such as *ee* ("yes"), *pai* ("okay"), or simply *jm,* in much the same way as the Kalapalo "what-sayers" described by Ellen Basso (1985). These responses add to the rhythmic quality of the narrative and also help create the structure of the text by their presence at the end of lines and verses.

4. An abundant literature on life history and autobiography has emerged in recent years that addresses many questions of too broad a scope for the present essay. Issues such as autobiography and native genres of speech, the researcher as collaborator in native autobiographies, coherence among events in life histories, the discursive construction of events, and other relevant topics will be treated in a more comprehensive work on Tukup's narrative (Hendricks n.d.).

5. It is in the capacity as translator and interpreter that my role becomes significant in reproducing Tukup's narrative, and I do not minimize the importance of that role. However, I am convinced that my presence at the narrative event had little influence on how Tukup' told his story.

6. There seems to be no tradition of memorizing stories and repeating them verbatim. Siro Pellizzaro (personal communication) said that when he collected myths, he frequently asked a narrator to tell the same myth again as much as two years later. They never gave exactly the same version. Rituals and songs, however, are memorized.

7. The Shuar of the interior region and the Achuar frequently refer to the Shuar of the western region as *murá shuar* (hill people).

8. The Shuar are famous for taking the heads of their enemies, especially the Achuar, and making *tsantsas,* shrunken heads.

9. Alberto was one of the two translators I employed in transcribing and translating the narrative. As a member of Tukup's family, he also provided additional information concerning the family history.

10. Chumap's responses and comments are enclosed in brackets.

11. The name Pitiur is used here as a surname. In the last episode the two brothers are

distinguished by their nicknames, "Waking-in-the-vagina-Pitiur" and "Soldier Pitiur." The word *suntár* is derived from the Spanish *soldado*.

12. Being afraid, in itself, is not regarded by the Shuar as shameful or dishonorable in a warrior. Fear is commonly expressed in relation to warfare, and the dominant tactic of Shuar warfare, surprise attack, reinforces the implication that Shuar warriors are afraid. Such tactics hardly suggest the bravado so prominent in groups such as the Yanomamö (Chagnon 1968). However, what is reprehensible is the failure to kill an enemy who has exposed himself as Kayáp did. One gets the impression that the hill people were so afraid that they froze, unable to carry out the obvious duty to strike the enemy before he had time to get reinforcements.

13. That they did not have permission is indicated by the statement in line 1250 that the garden was abandoned. Fruit trees always belong to the owner whether he currently lives at that location or not.

14. I could find no more specific designation for this type of shotgun, only that it was a "repeater" and was commonly found among the Shuar during the time of the narrated events.

15. Both translators agreed with this translation, though I have found no other source that gives the verb *tepertin* a meaning of "attack." Usually the verb means "to lay down," so there is a possibility that a more exact translation would be something like "they put so many people down."

16. Shuar interjections such as *chuwa* are difficult to translate because they have no denotative meaning. Equating them with English expressions such as "Oh my!," "Gosh!," or "Gee whiz!" makes them too bland and somewhat frivolous. Stronger English expressions tend to have religious and/or sexual connotations that are equally inappropriate. In general, the context is sufficient to suggest the emotion attached to the interjection, and therefore, I leave them untranslated in most instances.

17. This is somewhat confusing since earlier in the episode, Juank wanted to go by river and Tukup' on foot (1224–1229). However, they did not separate at that time, but remained together until after the incident in Jempékat's garden.

18. Both translators gave the gloss, "being such cowards" to the word *áuketiátkurmeku* in line 1465, though the word is derived from a root with little semantic content. The root is *au* (that) followed by suffixes meaning "only," a verbalizer, and a second person plural suffix, resulting in something like "you all being only that." The meaning then, is that they are nothing, which is interpreted as being cowards. Similarly, *tínuítkiarum* is constructed from the adverb *ti* (much). Tukup' says "being so much" in the sarcastic sense of "you think you're so great."

REFERENCES

Barrett, S. M. 1906. *Geronimo's Story of His Life.* New York: Duffield.

Basso, Ellen. 1985. *A Musical View of the Universe: Kalapalo Myth and Ritual Performances.* Philadelphia: University of Pennsylvania Press.

Basso, Keith. 1984. "Stalking with Stories: Names, Places, and Moral Narratives among the Western Apache." In *Text, Play, and Story: The Construction and Reconstruction of Self and Society,* edited by E. M. Bruner. 1983 Proceedings of the American Ethnological Society.

Bloomfield, Leonard. 1928. *Menomini Texts.* Publications of the American Ethnological Society, vol. 12.

Bolla, Luis. 1972. *Diccionario práctico del idioma shuar.* Vicariato apostólico de Méndez y Federación Shuar. Quito.

Brumble, H. David, III. 1981. *An Annotated Bibliography of American Indian and Eskimo Autobiographies.* Lincoln: University of Nebraska Press.

———. 1988. *American Indian Autobiography.* Berkeley: University of California Press.

Chagnon, N. A. 1968. *Yanomamö: The Fierce People.* New York: Holt, Rinehart and Winston.

Crapanzano, Vincent. 1980. *Tuhami: Portrait of a Moroccan.* Chicago: University of Chicago Press.

Dyk, Walter. 1938. *Son of Old Man Hat: A Navaho Autobiography Recorded by Walter Dyk.* With introduction by Edward Sapir. New York: Harcourt.

Graham, Laura. 1986. "Three Modes of Shavante Vocal Expression: Wailing, Collective Singing, and Political Oratory." In *Native South American Discourse,* edited by J. Sherzer and G. Urban. Berlin: Mouton.

Grimes, Joseph E. 1975. *The Thread of Discourse.* Berlin: Mouton.

Hymes, Dell. 1981. *"In Vain I Tried to Tell You": Essays in Native American Ethnopoetics.* Philadelphia: University of Pennsylvania Press.

———. 1987. "Anthologies and Narrators." In *Recovering the Word: Essays on Native American Literature,* edited by Brian Swann and Arnold Krupat. Berkeley: University of California Press.

Jackson, Donald, ed. 1955. *Black Hawk: An Autobiography.* Urbana: University of Illinois Press.

Johnson, Broderick H. 1977. *Stories of Traditional Navajo Life and Culture, by Twenty-two Navajo Men and Women.* Tsaile, Ariz.: Navajo Community College Press.

Kluckhohn, Clyde. 1945. "The Personal Document in Anthropological Science." In *The Use of Personal Documents in History, Anthropology, and Sociology,* edited by Louis Gottschalk et al. New York: Social Science Research Council, Bulletin no. 53.

Krupat, Arnold. 1985. *For Those Who Come After: A Study of American Indian Autobiography.* Berkeley: University of California Press.

Radin, Paul. 1963. *The Autobiography of a Winnebago Indian.* New York: Dover Publications.

Schultz, James Willard. 1962. *Blackfeet and Buffalo: Memories of Life among the Indians.* Edited by Kieth C. Seele. Norman: University of Oklahoma Press.

Sherzer, Joel. 1983. *Kuna Ways of Speaking: An Ethnographic Perspective.* Austin: University of Texas Press.

Sherzer, Joel, and Greg Urban, eds. 1986. *Native South American Discourse.* Berlin: Mouton.

Shostak, Marjorie. 1981. *Nisa: The Life and Words of a !Kung Woman.* Cambridge, Mass.: Harvard University Press.

Simmons, Leo W. 1942. *Sun Chief: The Autobiography of a Hopi Indian.* New Haven: Yale University Press.

Tedlock, Dennis. 1972. *Finding the Center: Narrative Poetry of the Zuni Indians.* New York: Dial Press.

————. 1983. *The Spoken Word and the Work of Interpretation*. Philadelphia: University of Pennsylvania Press.

Underhill, Ruth. 1979. *Papago Woman*. New York: Holt, Rinehart and Winston.

Watson, L. C., and M. Watson-Franke. 1985. *Interpreting Life Histories: An Anthropological Inquiry*. New Brunswick, N.J.: Rutgers University Press.

Woodbury, Anthony C. 1987. "Rhetorical Structure in a Central Alaskan Yupik Eskimo Traditional Narrative." In *Native American Discourse,* edited by J. Shezer and A. C. Woodbury. Cambridge: Cambridge University Press.

TO BE OR NOT TO BE

Suicide and Sexuality in Huichol Indian Funeral-Ritual Oratory

Jay Courtney Fikes

T ranslating Huichol funeral-ritual oratory immediately confronts one with baffling concepts: physical transformations that presuppose the persistence of the
iyari (heart-soul) despite disintegration of the human body; an intensely emotional union Huichol singers achieve with Iromari/Caoyomari, their creator and
tutelary spirit. My enduring focus on understanding highly esteemed achievements such as
nahualism—becoming a wolf (Fikes 1985)—or achieving union with Caoyomari (deemed
vital for effective healing and singing), led me into a domain of analysis that transcends
the merely denotative. According to Rappaport,

> Highest-order meaning is grounded in identity or unity, the radical identification of self with other. It is
> not so much intellectual as experiential and is perhaps most often grasped in ritual and other religious
> devotions . . . In highest-order meaning . . . meaning becomes a state of being. (Rappaport 1979:
> 127–128)

To apprehend what Rappaport recognizes as higher- and highest-order meaning and
thereby elucidate the core of Huichol funeral-ritual oratory, rigorous semiotic analysis of
all texts in the relevant literary corpus is indispensable. In this case, to contextualize
correctly meaning inherent in Huichol funeral rituals required prior comprehension of
aboriginal temple rituals (Fikes 1985). Interpreting Bonales's funeral-ritual oratory was
also facilitated by my translations of funeral-ritual texts dictated by two other Huichol

singers, one of whom was a *cahuitero* acclaimed as the premier informant on ritual in Santa Catarina.

Jerónimo Bonales was one of four Huichol singers from the temple district of Santa Catarina whose songs I tape recorded (Fikes 1985:8–12). Nicknamed the "medicine" by his people, his skill as a healer was renowned even among Mexican peasants and Tepehuan Indians. He was the chief custodian of the Catholic church at Santa Catarina when we met in 1976. He gave me my Huichol name and allowed me to live with him and his family until his untimely death in 1981. Bonales died shortly after singing the funeral-ritual song translated here. This was his last ritual performance and the first time any Huichol funeral-ritual text recorded live has been published.

Bonales's funeral-ritual text was recorded live at a village located about four kilometers from the ceremonial center of Santa Catarina. Bonales's nephew, whom I'll call Pancho Torres, translated the song from Huichol to Spanish in May 1988. Pancho was born and raised in a Huichol village near Santa Catarina. His command of Spanish is excellent because he had lived in Mexico City for several years before returning to his village. I met Pancho on my first visit to Santa Catarina in 1976. I later became the godfather of one of Pancho's sons. In May 1988 we worked together for several days to complete the translation of his uncle's text. He dictated a free Spanish translation while I wrote it down. He answered my questions about the text and often discussed certain issues connected with it without any prompting. My relationship with Pancho and method of translating his uncle's text are essentially identical to that described for my work with Felipe Sánchez, my first interpreter and ritual kinsman or *compadre* (Fikes 1985:12–13).

CHAPALAGANA HUICHOL CULTURE AND HISTORY

More than eight thousand Huichol Indians inhabit the rugged Chapalagana river basin in northwestern Mexico. Chapalagana Huichol[1] have preserved a rudimentary form of slash-and-burn horticulture. Rains that fall between early June and October are indispensable for growth of corn, beans, and squash. Extended family compounds, villages called *ranchos* in Spanish, are concentrated in a habitation zone about fifteen hundred meters above sea level (Fikes 1985; Weigand 1972). Huichols have a system of bilateral kinship and inheritance but prefer to select first-born sons (of the first wife) as rancho leaders. Funeral rituals are performed under the direction of a Huichol singer. They occur in the village patio, in front of the family god-house or *xiriqui*.

Healer, singer, and cahuitero are distinct religious practitioners whose status depends primarily upon the extent of their community service as aboriginal temple officers.[2] Although their prestige may be considerable, Huichol healers and singers are merely part-time ritual practitioners. Carl Lumholtz, the first ethnographer to study the Huichol, discovered nineteen or twenty aboriginal temples, the chief component in ceremonial centers

(Lumholtz 1900:9–10; 1902:27). Huichol temple officers, recruited from various ranchos surrounding the closest ceremonial center, are expected to perform an annual ritual cycle for five consecutive years before selecting their replacements (Fikes 1985, 1992). All available evidence indicates that since A.D. 200 the aboriginal Huichol temple-ritual cycle has governed vital subsistence activities (i.e., deer and rabbit hunting, fishing, and maize horticulture) and regulated trade of sacred items (e.g., peyote, conch shells, and feathers) with members of neighboring cultures. The annual ritual cycle is performed to honor various ancestor-deities who personify natural phenomena. Rain-Mothers are particularly important. Temple rituals replicate the world-organizing precedents the ancestor-deities set and dispose them to protect human health and provide abundant subsistence.

The Huichol language most closely resembles that spoken by their western neighbors, the Cora Indians of Nayarit. Cora is the nearest living language to Nahuatl (Aztec). Similarities in social organization and religion between Huichol and Cora are profound and pervasive.

Despite Franciscan missionization, Huichols have preserved an aboriginal ritual cycle more elaborate than that of most other Indians of North and Middle America. Christian elements in aboriginal ritual are obvious, but syncretism has remained relatively insignificant, at least in Santa Catarina. It has been more than a hundred years since Franciscans resided in Santa Catarina. Since their departure Ash Wednesday ceremonies have disappeared, but Easter-week ceremonies led by cahuiteros remain important.

The 4,107-square-kilometer homeland reserved by Chapalagana Huichols is half the size it was before Spanish conquest. In 1722, after Spaniards conquered the Cora capital at the Mesa del Nayarit, the Spanish crown established three *comunidades indígenas* (indigenous Huichol communities): Santa Catarina Cuexcomatitlán, San Andrés Cohamiata, and San Sebastián Teponahuaxtlán. Only Santa Catarina, the Huichol comunidad indígena where my ethnographic research was conducted, has resisted subdivision.

WHEN AND WHY THE *HUTAIMARI* IS PERFORMED

Huichol burials occur shortly after death (Mata Torres 1974, Weigand and Weigand 1991). They are essentially self-contained rites that must be completed before conducting the more elaborate funeral ritual called *Hutaimari*. The orderly alternation of wet and dry seasons, which is so fundamental in Huichol horticulture and the aboriginal temple ritual cycle (Fikes 1985), is evident in the scheduling of the Hutaimari. This aboriginal Huichol funeral can be performed only during the dry season. Because darkness reaches its peak during the cloud-filled rainy season, Huichols feel it is hazardous for singers to attempt to locate the deceased. They fear that the darkness accompanying the rainy season might cause the Hutaimari singer to lose his way and become trapped in the underworld to the west.

The Hutaimari begins with the sacrifice of cattle (deer were surely hunted prior to Spanish contact) late in the afternoon on the eve of the ritual. After dark the singer and his two assistants are seated by a fire in the patio of the deceased's village, just west of the god-house. While facing east they sing until sunrise, and sometimes well into the next day. The climax of the ritual occurs when a blue fly, which represents the deceased, is summoned by the singer and given offerings by the relatives. Before sunrise certain plants are placed around the village to prevent the deceased from returning. Later the relatives and ritual attenders wash their hands and face with water to prepare for the ashes which are applied to four parts of their bodies. The Hutaimari ends with a feast, including soup from the sacrificed animal, and the distribution of the deceased's belongings (what we might define as the execution of the last will and testament).

Funeral ritual illustrates the fundamental Huichol concern: recreating and sustaining the world order originally established by their ancestor-deities (Fikes 1985). The prohibition against performing this ritual during the rainy season exemplifies their conviction that human health is dependent on ecological order. The transformation of the deceased's soul, a goal the singer advances by directing the deceased to a new plane of existence, is done not only for the benefit of the deceased, but to protect the health of surviving relatives. This ritual is also performed to enable singers to determine the cause of death, another issue important to survivors.

Elucidating the significance the *iyari* or heart-soul has for Huichols is indispensable fully to comprehend the Hutaimari ritual. A small, spineless cactus, peyote (*Lophophora williamsii*), is revered as the iyari (heart, mind, or memory) of their Creator, Caoyomari. Unlocking the wisdom of his heart-soul, which is incarnate in peyote, is what enables Huichols to heal and sing effectively (Fikes 1985:255). Merging their iyari with that of Iromari, Caoyomari's counterpart, permits Huichol singers to follow the deceased through the underworld. Their conviction that the iyari rather than the human body constitutes the essence of existence is epitomized by their fear that the singer can die if his iyari is trapped or lost somewhere in the underworld or Pacific Ocean due to insufficient light. As noted above, to protect singers Huichols perform funeral rituals only during the dry season, when the terrestrial world is full of light. Although the singer's body remains at the rancho where the Hutaimari is being performed, the journey he takes during this ritual is considered quite real. Similarly, during dreams one's iyari travels great distances outside the sleeping body (Fikes 1985:339; Negrín 1977:77).

Control of the iyari is essential for Huichols learning to take the physical form of the wolf, a teacher or "elder brother" whose prowess in rabbit, deer, and peyote hunting is revered. Their belief in wolf-nahualism presupposes that the iyari can exist independently of the human body (Fikes 1985). Accordingly, Huichols assume that when the *nahual*, animal form, is shot, the wound will appear at the corresponding location on the human body (Benítez 1968b:326–328). Transformation into rock crystal form, whether during life or after death of the physical body, also illustrates the Huichol faith that the iyari is the locus of intelligence, which exists independently of the particular body in which it may be present. While Bonales was still alive a Huichol man who knew him asserted that Bonales "is already a rock crystal." According to Lumholtz, "Both men and women may become *tevali'r* (crystals) while still alive, the condition being that they have been true husbands and wives" (Lumholtz 1900:64). To become a crystal requires sexual fidelity, abstaining from sexual involvement with anybody other than one's spouse. Sexual fidelity is also required to achieve wolf-nahualism (Fikes 1985). Becoming a wolf enhances one's skill in hunting, healing, and bringing rain, abilities of perennial value to the Huichol.

Huichol funeral-ritual texts invariably depict the deceased following a path toward the underworld in the west. The deceased's travels through and emergence from the underworld, equated with the Pacific Ocean, occur along a well known passageway filled with obstacles, trials, and traps. The character and destiny of the deceased are gradually disclosed as the singer reports on the individual's activities at various landmarks encountered along this afterlife route. The deceased's conduct in life determines whether the obstacles encountered on this journey will be surmounted and, therefore, what the fate of the iyari or heart-soul will be. Individuals known to have engaged in many misdeeds, typified by sexual promiscuity, are doomed to dwell in darkness in the primordial underworld. Righteous Huichols, those who fulfill ritual obligations and control their sexual passions, are entitled to enter the celestial realm ruled by the Sun-Father and Moon-Mother.

The cahuitero's text, which ends with the deceased acquiring a new name, confirms Zingg's insight (1938:153) that Huichol funeral rituals are a rite of passage, a transition from one social and physical status to another. In order to participate in the new mode of existence the deceased must be separated inexorably from human status. To accomplish this transformation the deceased must descend into the underworld, and return to the source of human life. Tatei Yocáhuima (Mother Black Dog), who lives at the bottom or middle of the ocean, must be visited before the deceased is allowed to ascend to heaven. In Bonales's text, the deceased ascends, with Mother Black Dog's aid, at *Haori tecua,* the peak of the ceremonial candle (see note 34).

The cahuitero's text suggests that the blood of bulls sacrificed on the eve of the Hutaimari is provided for ancestor-deities, on behalf of the deceased. Feeding ancestor-deities for the last time presumably completes one's earthly obligations and induces ancestors to allow one to enter the celestial or heavenly realm. In Bonales's Hutaimari text the deceased credits both male and female ancestor-deities with giving her offerings. Sharing their offerings with her (especially since it is her bull) demonstrates she has transcended human status. At the climax of the ritual Bonales performed the deceased appeared briefly (as a blue fly) to receive offerings from her relatives, including the blood or soul of her beloved bull. As she put it, "I already received the bull. Now there is nothing else left for me." Then she departed in the company of the male and female ancestor-deities. This is evidently the moment when her transition to the next world occurred (and is symbolized by the fly vanishing).

Both Zingg (1938:153) and I recognize preventing contact with the deceased as a funeral-ritual objective. It is accomplished by special use of sage and acacia plants (see note 16) and disguising one's self by hallowing the body with ashes at the conclusion of the ritual.

The crying evident in that phase of the ritual called *murucuitzica,* when family members are expected to confess their offenses against the deceased, surely provides catharsis. The deceased's explicit denunciation of their mistreatment of her may prompt further confession and catharsis. The relatives' repentance is followed by reconciliation. The deceased returns, is given offerings, and tearfully bid farewell. I suspect that devout Huichols are intent on liberating the deceased rather than improving their own mental health. They are told their confessions are required to induce the deceased to return in the form of the blue fly. Stopping in at the ritual to visit bereaved relatives and receive offerings must take place before the heart-soul can enter the celestial realm.

Huichol singers are responsible for determining and publicly proclaiming the reason the individual died. Singers apprehend the cause of death through union with Iromari. This ecstatic state of consciousness facilitates consultation with the deceased and is predicated upon visionary ability symbolized by the *nierica* or mirror (Fikes 1985:343).

According to Phil and Celia Weigand (1991), Chapalagana Huichols recognize at least four primary causes of death: old age, punishment for transgression of taboo, witchcraft, and suicide. Death of old age is desirable and results from a lifetime of righteous living. Reasons for premature demise—punishment for misdeed or neglect of ritual obligations, witchcraft or sorcery, and suicide—merit further discussion.

Some Huichols allegedly die prematurely because they violated rules of conduct or neglected their ritual responsibilities toward the ancestors. Huichol ancestors are thought to enforce the order they established by sending sickness or death as punishment for transgressing taboos. One of Klineberg's informants reported that "when children die it is because the father has committed adultery" (1934:452). One woman whose burial I witnessed in July 1981 was rumored to have died for failing to offer deer blood to the Rain-Mother known as Na'arihuame.

Witchcraft or sorcery is another cause of premature death. It may be suspected by the deceased and his/her relatives sometime before death. It can be proposed as the cause of illness. When Huichols are buried signs of witchcraft are often detected (Zingg 1938:160). Singers may discover while performing the Hutaimari that witchcraft caused the demise of the deceased. Those suspected of sorcery are in danger of being killed (Lumholtz 1902:238; Klineberg 1934:453). Zingg reported that one Huichol singer suspected of witchcraft established a new residence for fear he might be punished (Zingg n.d.:370; 1938:160). As Phil and Celia Weigand's research indicates, "acts of sorcery are dramatically punished," and accusations of sorcery are pursued with such vigor that feuds often result (Weigand and Weigand 1991:58–59). As we shall see, the wise and benevolent image associated with pious Huichol singers may be essential to maintain social order in such potentially volatile situations.

That the deceased committed suicide is insinuated in the opening words of Bonales's Hutaimari song. Acceptance of the singer's judgments as infallible is strengthened by the belief that he has attained the state of absolute objectivity resulting from identification with Iromari. As the deceased tells the singer, Iromari: "They (the ancestor-deities) have appointed you to be their investigator." In the very next sentence the deceased admits she "made the mistake of dying." Having the deceased diagnose the cause of her own demise may minimize potential social conflicts triggered by those whose opinions differ from the Hutaimari singer's diagnosis. Because her decision to commit suicide was partially motivated by the misbehavior of relatives, especially her husband, it must come as an unpleasant revelation. Acceptance of such a verdict is surely enhanced by attributing it to the deceased herself, who is prompted by inquiries of the ancestors (see note 40). Her remark, "You don't have my mouth covered to prevent me from speaking," can be viewed as another device to persuade her relatives to accept the singer's verdict. The conclusion that her suicide was chosen is indicated by having the deceased announce that her husband, whose infidelity caused the death of her children (see note 41), is not to be blamed for her death. She seems to bear full responsibility for her response to the anguish her husband's misconduct brought upon her.

Unlike sexual excess, which is clearly the cardinal sin among Chapalagana Huichols, suicide is tolerable if not honorable. I deduce this primarily because her suicide did not prevent her from entering the celestial realm. Mata Torres (1974) has summarized several cases of Huichol suicide, noting they are often accomplished by hanging with a noose, without coming to any definitive conclusions about its meaning. Mayan beliefs may provide leads useful for research required to reveal Huichol attitudes toward suicide. Mayans who committed suicide were admitted to paradise:

Many who were sick and weak shortened their lives in order to enjoy the privileged existence of suicides beyond the grave. There they were protected by Ixtab, goddess of all who had hanged themselves. She is represented with a noose around her neck. (Hultkrantz 1979:239)

SEXUALITY, SPIRITUAL PROWESS, AND SORCERY

The quintessential indicator of piety is sound sexual conduct. From birth to death Huichols are inundated by messages that cultivate the conviction that sexual purity certifies spiritual prowess. As noted, lifelong sexual fidelity is required for transformation into wolf or rock crystal form. Sexual fidelity is the leading indicator of singers' devotion to the dictates of the ancestor-deities. Serving the ancestors and concomitantly one's community is an ideal inculcated during the five-year term as an aboriginal Huichol temple officer. "A man who wants to become a shaman must be faithful to his wife for five years. If he violates this rule, he is sure to be taken ill, and will lose the power of curing" (Lumholtz 1902:236). Sexual fidelity for aspiring healers and singers is widely documented (Fikes 1985:54). Huichols who intend to become healers and singers are expected to be sexually faithful to their spouses because they are taking on the concerns of their ancestor-deities. They are learning to perpetuate the world established by their ancestors when they take responsibility for performing the annual cycle of rituals which sustain it. When Huichol temple officers take on the names of the ancestors they serve for five consecutive years they are expected to act as if they truly represent those ancestors. Huichol singers are empowered to perform rituals believed vital to insure abundant subsistence for all provided their conduct demonstrates propriety. Their intense identification with their creator and tutelary spirit, Caoyomari, exemplifies what Rappaport recognizes as a religious transformation wherein "ultimate sacred postulates" are validated by "numinous experiences."[3]

In funeral rituals Huichol singers unite with or incarnate *Iromari*. Singers merge with him because his visionary or detective ability was bestowed by the Sun-Father (Fikes 1985:133). Union with Iromari enables singers to report accurately what they observe while following the deceased's tracks or trail (*cacaiya*). Singers call themselves Iromari when performing the Hutaimari ritual because they experience a merging or oneness with him. When a singer's hands tremble while singing it signifies that union with Iromari or his counterpart Caoyomari has been achieved (Fikes 1985:99).

The singer who represents Iromari is cast in the role of impartial observer, reporter, and investigator. During the Hutaimari, singers frequently talk in the first person on behalf of the deceased. They are not possessed by the deceased. They faithfully report what the deceased wishes to communicate.

Believing that singers are in harmony with Iromari makes it easier to accept their diagnosis of the cause of death as accurate and impartial. Because accusations of witchcraft can provoke especially disruptive feuds (Weigand and Weigand 1991), the sanctity attached to the diagnosis reached by Iromari, whom pious singers incarnate, helps sustain a society unaccustomed to political institutions or power.

Unauthorized sex dissolves piety and imperils Huichol social order. Huichols immersed in selfish or personal affairs cannot be trusted as effective conduits for the creator or servants of society. Aspiring shamans who fail to abide by their vows of sexual fidelity "are in danger of becoming sorcerers" (Myerhoff 1968:98; 1974:100). Aspiring shamans whose sexual misconduct breaches their vow to the ancestor associated with the sacred plant known as *quieri* are presumed to be prime candidates for sorcery. "Soon they will cause so much harm that someone will eventually kill them for revenge" (Valadez 1986:38). Huichol aversion to sorcery is reinforced by their belief that illicit sex and aggression corrode commitment to the socially valued process of identifying with the Creator. Preoccupation with sex blocks the benevolence needed to perpetuate social and ecological harmony and achieve union with Iromari/Caoyomari. The horrors associated with sexual misconduct pervade Bonales's Hutaimari song. It jeopardizes subsistence (see note 21), human health (see notes 41, 46), spiritual achievement (mentioned above), and one's fate in the afterlife (see notes 21, 24, 29–32).

JERÓNIMO BONALES'S *HUTAIMARI* RITUAL SONG

(The deceased speaks as if she were alive) "I punished myself for the last time. Now I bid farewell to my family. I am leaving. At the same time I bid farewell to my Rain-Mothers and to *Tatei Nihuetzica*" (Our Mother Maize).

(Now the singer answers) "Being inside the xiriqui [god-house] that is how she bids farewell."

(Deceased) "The most painful part of it is that I have lost my relatives. If they hadn't died I would not have thought of dying. But as things turned out that is what happened. There is where I thought it better for me not to be around."

(Singer) "With this conversation she bid farewell from inside the xiriqui. She left there speaking like this."

(Deceased) "I am going to my Mother, to the place where I set out with my *cüpori*." [The deceased is returning to Tatei Matinyeri, which is her soul's birthplace.[4] The *cüpori* or "soul" is centered in the fontanelle or crown of the head (Grimes 1981:42; Negrín 1977:77).]

(Singer) "That is the way one encounters the speech given in front of Grand-father-Fire. After this discourse she followed the passageway saying," (Deceased) "Well I am leaving forever. I will never return here to be with all of you."

(Singer) "That is how she bid farewell. Then she disappeared. Nobody knew where she went. After being unable to detect the tracks, Caoyomari [the singer] is search-ing for the footprints of the deceased."[5]

(Deceased) "Yes, I thought of dying [killing myself]. Death has already touched me. Well, now I am leaving. I wonder where I'll end up."

(Singer) "The deceased has arrived at the aboriginal temple at Santa Cata-rina, where the gourd bowls with offerings are found. She arrived there bidding farewell in this way."

(Deceased) "I am making a journey. I came here to bid farewell for the last time because I will never again be present here. My own heart-soul made me end it. Now you understand my Rain-Mothers and my male relatives [*necaocaoma*]."[6]

(Singer) "I arrived asking at the aboriginal temple at Santa Catarina if they had seen her come by there. They said that they had only seen the shadow [or ghost] of the deceased. I assume that she arrived here. Here one sees the discussion she had when she was taking leave of my Sun-Father, my Rain-Mothers, and my male ancestor-deities."

(Deceased) "I take my leave because it is impossible for me to be with all of you again."

(Singer) "Upon saying that she arrived at Cürüxipa ["place of the cross", which in this context refers to the Catholic church at Santa Catarina], where the gourd bowls are placed. From the place where the children are assembled she took her leave. The last time she was present she gave this speech as she bid farewell." Iromari is trailing her, looking for her tracks. Iromari found the words of the deceased in her heart-soul [iyari].

(Deceased) "In my own heart-soul I declared that I should die. Well, absolve me then my Rain-Mothers and my male ancestor-deities. I regret very much having ended my life."

(Singer) "With that said she left. That is what my Rain-Mothers and male ancestor-deities told me. That is how my Rain-Mothers and male ancestor-deities understood it. After her speech they told her: "Look, we don't know where you will go and how you will go, or whether you will suffer or not because of what you did. Perhaps you did it because you wanted to suffer." Having said that they released her and let her leave. Then she arrived at Cürüxipa, the place of the cross. From there they did not permit her to ascend or even to speak. They quickly disapproved of her because she had taken her own life. They drove her away from Cürüxipa so that she could not ascend. "Because you wanted to take your own life we do not accept you. Even though you asked to die we knew all along that you still had more years to live. In this case, because you are the one who asked to die, we don't want to receive you." [They will not allow the deceased to stay in the celestial realm until she has discharged all her earthly obligations, including visiting her relatives.][7] That is what Tatei Nihuetócame, [the moon or celestial mother], the Rain-Mothers, and the place of the cross told her. Then the deceased began to ask where she would go. Here she is begging for a favor and crying. She says: "Where shall I go? If you all do not accept me where will I end up?" The Mother tells her, "Let us see if you really know our song. Go ahead, sing it if you really know it. Only under these conditions can we accept you." [Caring enough about ancestor-deities to learn the songs they dictate proves that the deceased would be righteous enough to merit their acceptance.][8]

(Iromari says) "I am seeing that the deceased is silent. She doesn't speak because she didn't ever learn what to say. The Mother notifies her: "You still haven't returned to the place from where your spirit [tocari] comes. [Her Mother tells her she must return to the underworld, which is regarded as the source of an individual's tocari, life energy.][9] And you must still go to the place where the guide of life is for us to determine what we will do with you, to decide if we will accept you or not." The deceased implored them, kneeling and crying. Several times she kneeled, insisting that they accept her. The Mother opposed her because she had thought of taking her own life. Because the Mother was unwilling to compromise, she hit the deceased with a *xruya* [a thorny acacia tree] branch.[10] "When you were alive you never paid attention to what I was telling you even though I am your Mother [Tatei Nihuetócame]. I don't know where you are going to go. Well then, if you are able, if you know the words of the ancestor-deities, go ahead and speak God's word. If you know it that is. "When the deceased tried to speak she sang like the *micüri,* burrowing owl. [The Huichol believe that singing/hooting like an owl indicates that the human aspect of the heart-soul is dissolving.][11] With this song [of the owl] we don't know where you will be going said the Mother. We won't say where you will go."

(Deceased) "So that is how it is. I don't know where to go. I can't ascertain where I will arrive. If that is the way you think, my Rain-Mothers and my male ancestor-deities, then I don't know what to do."

(Singer) Having said that, she disappeared. From that point on Iromari was following her. She left without knowing where to go, thinking in her heart-soul "I don't know where to go." She arrived at the place called "where the head stands." Arriving there she was told, "Pass by here below because you know that you have always esteemed me greatly." The deceased was feeling afraid to approach and look at her own head. The head was reminding her, "Well, remember that you were biting me when you were alive." The deceased was fearful and was saying "no, no, no." She became demoralized there. Iromari followed her tracks there. She had reached a certain place, but before arriving she didn't want to cross over where something had been put. That thing was proclaiming, "Come here and pass by." She was too discouraged to pass because she was seeing a ribcage. That is why she wasn't eager to continue. The ribcage told her, "Come here and lay down." The deceased was too frightened to lay down with the ribcage.[12]

(Singer) "I believe that these are the words of the ancestor-deities." Speaking that way Iromari [the singer] is walking behind her. The deceased went on following the path. The ribcage told her, "Follow your path, there goes the route of life. In addition, there go the tracks of the deceased ones." When she followed the path she came to a place where someone was waiting for her and suddenly she heard a whistle, as if someone was calling her. She continued, thinking "I know where I am going," and she went straight ahead.[13] As she proceeded she heard the whistle again because she was planning to go straight ahead. Where she arrived she suddenly heard a violin. They grabbed her and said "Now we are going to dance, that is if you were enjoying dancing while you were alive." She replied that she had never liked to dance to that music. The two who had grabbed her released her then. From there she continued, following the path until arriving at a place where the male ancestor-deities were assembled. Iromari went on speaking: "I believe that this is how our ancestor-deities are. I believe that this is how our human spirit [*tocari*] is." From there Iromari departed, following the tracks of the deceased. He came to a place where the blue fly [*haiyü yoahui*] is put.[14] There they wanted to delay the deceased but she replied, "I am on my way elsewhere, I can't stay here."

They released her and she continued straight ahead following the path. She arrived at a place where the Tatei Neixa [Dance of Our Mother or first fruits ritual] was being performed. They grabbed her and they made her dance around the fire, notifying her, "You will never again return to dance in this manner so you must take your leave." They released her and from there she came to a place where there was a Hicüri Neixa [the peyote dance performed at the end of the dry season]. There they asked her if she had enjoyed dancing it when she was alive. She said she had never danced this dance. Nevertheless, to make her bid it farewell, they made her dance a little. She told them "I can't continue dancing much longer because when I was living I was not dancing much because I didn't like it.[15] Anyway, I take my leave now that I shall never again see this dance." They released her from there and she continued until she arrived at the dance of Namahuita Neixa [a ritual performed early in the rainy season]. They quickly grabbed her and she replied: "I can't dance this dance because I never did it before. I believe one doesn't do what one doesn't want to do. There is no way I can do it." Then they released her. She kept on descending until arriving at a place where there was a dance of *xinari* [a sour cornmeal soup called "atole" in Spanish]. There she told them "I am not familiar with this dance." They let her go. She continued descending. She arrived at another dance called Tücühuaixi. They grabbed her to make her dance but she told them, "I have never danced this dance before." They released her and she continued descending. She came to a place where the deities called Tücühuaixi are assembled.[16] They wanted to delay her but they allowed her to pass. From there she departed, descending until reaching the place where the Cócoro Huimari [dove girl/maize goddess] is. When she arrived there the maize goddess asked her if she had ever eaten maize when the dove was living and she said no. Then the dove told her, "Well then, if you are going elsewhere I believe we are never going to understand each other. When you were alive, whenever you were inside the xiriqui you always requested that I answer your prayers."[17] That is what Mother Dove Girl was telling her. She also said, "Because you are going elsewhere, I don't know how your journey will go. I hope you arrive where Mother Blue Corn is found." She continued going down the path. She arrived at the place where one finds the crow perching. The crow asked the deceased, "Are you hungry? I am giving you a blue corn tortilla." Well, she [Yuama, the crow] wanted to give it to her but then she didn't. The crow said, "You didn't allow me to eat in the cornfield whenever I was hungry. That is why I didn't give it to you."[18] She continued traveling downward. She came to a place where the white water is. From there she continued descending. She arrived at the site where Tocácame [the enemy of humans and Lord of the Underworld] has the trap.[19] Nothing happened to her there. She continued traveling. She came to the spot where the possum has placed the trap. She passed by there without any problem.[20] She continued descending. She came to the place where the sharp stake stands. They were waiting for her and when she arrived they asked her, "Did you ever have any sexual relations [which are prohibited] with your brother-in-law? If you say you did I am going to impale you." She said she had nothing to confess. They permitted her to pass. She continued descending. She came to the spot where those who have committed sexual transgressions were impaled. She passed by easily. [This means she had not engaged in illicit sex. Those impaled here are being punished for breaking this taboo.][21] She arrived at the place where the female black dog is tied. She informed the dog[22] (who is Tatei Yocáhuima, Mother of the postdeluge Huichols), "I never made you suffer because I was always giving you tortillas." The dog answered, "That is true," and permitted her to pass. The dog-Mother said, "I don't know whether your journey is going well or badly. I hope you will arrive safely at your final destination." The deceased continued descending.

(*Iromari* says) "Her ghost or shadow [*a'etuli*] kept descending until it reached the site where the ram is tied. The ram was backing up in order to strike her. She went by quickly and when the ram came forward she had already passed. She arrived at a place where there is a drawing of flowers and they told her, "When you were living you enjoyed making designs of flowers. Let me see you do it right now." She was not able to do it the way she had before, when she was alive. "You never believed what we were telling you, that it was forbidden to copy the designs of flowers and draw them on the earth and on *tepetates* [an impermeable layer of volcanic tuff common in the Huichol region]." When she could no longer make the designs they freed her. She continued descending. She arrived at the site where the pine girl is. At that spot, according to information from others, she said, "Don't take offense, Huahuatzari and Ototahue. You are going to discover it. In agreement with this conversation, you Huahuatzari are interpreting with the antler from Grandfather-Fire.[23] From there she continued traveling. She arrived at the place where there is a broad-leafed oak tree. The tree asked her, "Were you in the habit of swinging from my branches? Come here and climb up." She begged his pardon. "Yes, I was swinging. I enjoyed playing. Forgive me. In my present condition I can't climb up." They released her from there and she continued descending. At the place called "where the broad-leafed oak tree is" the deceased said, "I am going to where my Mother and the relatives of my soul are."

(*Iromari* says) "What she declares is true. Proceeding down the path she says: "I am going to arrive where one finds those who live in the darkness of the underworld, the Yuhuitari."[24] The male ancestor-deities advised her, "If you are going there you will arrive at a place called the Lipicate [a place inhabited by the deities that set traps]. That is the site where there is a fig tree" [a tree in the genus *Ficus*, known in Spanish as *salate* or *amate*, a mispronunciation of the Aztec word "amatl"]. When she reached the fig tree the male relatives advised her: "Now you have arrived at the fig tree where you must confess all your sexual transgressions." She said, "Now I am going to the underworld, the place of darkness. Don't be upset with me my elder brother, and my honorable male ancestor-deities." She continued descending to a place called "violin peak." They seized her there. She said, "My Rain-Mothers, my male ancestor-deities, I am going to the place of darkness, the underworld." They released her at the peak of the ceremonial candle.

From there she continued until she arrived at a place where there is a *Aochue* tree with fragrant white flowers.[25] From there she continued until arriving at the place where the cross stands. Iromari was following behind her listening to her speeches. The deceased said, "My male ancestor-deities, I am leaving. Don't take offense. I will never return again with you." From there she continued until she arrived at a place called Tatzuraita, and to another place called Nupatzie.[26] There she started to become fearful. From there she arrived at a place where the male ancestor-deities are placed below, then at the place where the relatives [*noihuari*] are placed below, and at Yoz tecüa, the peak of God [a sacred mountaintop also known as Paritecüa].[27] There she told the male ancestor-deities: "If it is true that death has claimed me I must continue until I reach the underworld." She arrived at Tete yüa'cua [the round, or quaking, rock].[28] At that place she jumped on the rock and it made a sound. All of her ancestors in the underworld heard the noise. The noise was heard by all the Yuhuitari in the underworld and they said, "Our sister is coming now." They were content staring up above where she was. From there she went to the place of the fig tree. There the male ancestor-deities told her, "Now you must hit the fig tree." The deceased responded, "I don't have much wood" [which symbolizes sexual transgressions].[29] She only tossed two pieces of wood onto the fig tree. She said, "I have no more. When I was living they were telling me that I was committing many sexual misdeeds, but that is not true my male ancestor-deities. I bring no more."

(Iromari) "That is what the deceased told them." When she finished speaking she left. From there she came to a place where there was a kettle of boiling water. It was called where the Lipicate are stuck together.[30] There they told her, "Get into the water." She got in and got out of the first kettle. Then into and out of the second kettle. After that she said, "You all should remain here. I am continuing on my journey to reach my Mother." After leaving there she came to a place where the mules are confined.[31] Nothing happened to her there. She traveled until arriving at the place where she found *cuitemui* [an illicit lover in the form of a thick white worm].[32] Nothing happened to her there. From there she came to the shore of the ocean. They said to her, "How can you say that you are going to your Mother? Take a look at this ocean. Do you think you can cross it?" She pleaded with the Mothers to be granted permission to cross the ocean. Then Mother Black Dog emerged and told the deceased: "If you truly want to arrive with your Mother I will help you cross the water." The deceased replied: "Mother, please transport me to the other side because I am going to see my Mother."[33] From there they came to a place called where human life [*tocari*] is, and a place where the red sandal is, and then to Toránita. At Toránita she arrived with her Mother. Upon seeing her daughter the Mother said, "Yes, you are my consanguine. Now that we have seen each other you must return up above. It has to be that way. I am going to free you." The deceased asked the Mother, "Tell me Mother, where am I going to stay? Where are you going to send me?" The Mother released her from that place in order that she could return above [leave the underworld]. She came to a place called the shore of the ocean. They told her to cross over to the shore on the other side. She came to Haori tecüa,[34] the peak of the ceremonial candle. There the Mother told her, "You have to remain above here. Because you come to learn [about your destiny]. It must be that way." From there the Mother threw her all the way to Yoz tecüa [the place where the Sun-Father first emerged from the underworld]. The deceased, in the form of a ghost or shadow, was seeing the preceding discussion. Iromari has been following her, seeing clearly everything she was doing. From there they told her, "Ascend, up there you will remain."

(Iromari says) "We have already ascended to the great plains above. We are grateful for the favor you granted.[35] I asked to borrow your *nierica* in order to arrive with you Yuhuitari. Now that we have left you I bid you farewell my Yuhuitari. Remain just as you are. I can't ask you for anything else." From there they released the deceased because she had come back from visiting the inhabitants of the underworld, the Yuhuitari. There Iromari said, "Here I will follow the deceased, searching in the world of light [*Cueriyaoca*]. Because I don't know how to function without my nierica I asked you to lend it to me. It will remain here at the place called Taorunipa. [He returns the nierica to the Yuhuitari.] I must search for the deceased in the world of light, to find where she went." They told him, "She already ascended." The Yuhuitari had already discharged her. Iromari continued looking for her footprints, returning with the Yuhuitari. From there he continued looking for her. Iromari asked, "Where can I find her?" At the same time Iromari asked the Yuhuitari to prepare Huahuatzari and Ototahue to locate the deceased.[36]

"Be observant, Huahuatzari and Ototahue." Iromari said they freed her but he saw her footprints. Huahuatzari and Ototahue reported that the deceased had already gone back to the Yuhuitari. She remained there. [Iromari is now pleading for the Sun-Father to grant a favor.] "Examine her carefully because she has gone back to the Yuhuitari. When you consult your nierica my Sun-Father you will discover that she has gone back," Iromari said.[37] Iromari discovered her footprints near Huahuatzari and Ototahue. She was about to arrive at a very large place called Cueriyaoca. Once there, she made her way to the female ancestor-deities and inquired, "Where do I go? Where shall I stay?" The Yuhuitari told her, "Now that you have arrived with your Mother we release you but we don't know where you are going." They freed her at Cueriyaoca.[38]

(Iromari/singer says) "I believe that is the way it is." Iromari tried to continue trailing her. "I believe that is the way it is," said her consanguines and the Yuhuitari. The deceased was pleading to reside with her Mother but they didn't permit her to ascend to be with her Mother. Iromari continued following the footprints of the deceased. From there she was arriving in the south where one hears the song of the shaman. They asked her, "What are you doing walking around here with us? Why did you come here? You should be careful not to walk around here with us." That's what the male ancestor-deities and Rain-Mothers told her. She responded, "I didn't come here voluntarily. It was only because I died. Of course one can't come here for pleasure. Forgive me for what I did, because I decided to die. But that was only after my children had died. That was the event which caused my desire to die. It was to avoid the sadness. You are not to blame. Forgive me because I took my own life."

Her Rain-Mothers and male ancestor-deities asked her: "Why did your heart ache so much? You should not have tried to die. We knew you still had many more years left to live. It was you who decided to give up and die." That is what the Rain-Mothers and male ancestor-deities told her. They asked her: "What really happened? Was some sorcerer [*cuasuihuari*] involved?[39] Did you notice if anybody threatened you? Tell the truth." She did not know what to say. She talked about negative things without clarifying anything. Then she suddenly changed the topic of conversation.

(Iromari says) "I am now on the earth's surface. That is how they define it here at Yoz tecüa, at Paritecüa. I believe they speak the truth." There Iromari asked for his prayer-feather [*mohuieri*]. The Mother answered him, "Yes the deceased already went to visit the Yuhuitari. We know very well that she returned to Yoz tecüa and Paritecüa and Haoriyapa. We are listening and know that she has returned from her journey. The deceased asked to be forgiven, speaking like this, "I am to blame for my demise. I was thinking that nothing would happen, but death has already taken me. Forgive me."

Iromari found her there where her heart-soul was heard, where her *matzua* [pulse or wristguard] and her *mohuieri* [prayer feathers] were. Iromari saw the wind and listened to everything the deceased had said. I believe that is what they say where the ancestor-deities of the north are assembled. Iromari continued listening to her while she spoke with our elder brothers. They told her, "There is no remedy to restore you to life. You must remain in your present condition." She said, "Inasmuch as I am still manifested in the nierica I shall continue saying the same thing. [Pancho noted that she has arrived at a specific condition which one sees in the *nierica*.] In this way you are informed my family. All of you must remain here. That is how it must be." That is the way she addressed them. After that speech they were waiting for her at Yunoihuarie [the place where the consanguines or relatives are]. The deceased says, "Listen to it and remain the way you are my Rain-Mothers and male ancestor-deities. Stay here in the intersection." Having said that she made her way over to the Rain-Mothers and male ancestor-deities. She is passing by each one of the Rain-Mothers and male ancestor-deities, begging their pardon for all the mistakes she made. "My Rain-Mothers, here I am visiting with each of you even though I am not the equal of any of you. In my heart-soul I thought about ending my life. Forgive me." They replied, "Because your heart ached you thought of killing yourself. You should not have thought that way. Of course you said it in jest, but now death has taken you and you have come here. There is no remedy. You wanted to end your own life. We see that you ended your own life. You said in your heart that you were not willing to live, that you were not willing to exist where you were. You deserved your punishment. Now you are experiencing your punishment."[40]

(The deceased speaks) "They [her earthly relatives] say that many [sinful] things happened, but I am certain that it is not like that. That is why Iromari is investigating, looking at the birthplace of our souls. There one knows perfectly well that what I say is true. You, my male ancestor-deities and Rain-Mothers, know that I can't lie. This is all I have to say. This is the truth. One can do nothing more. You already know this Huahu-atzari and Ototahue. Don't think badly of me any more. Don't examine me any more because I am no longer alive. I am bidding all of you farewell so that you don't examine me again after this. I can't implore you for anything more. This is the last time I will bid you all farewell. Don't think badly of me my Rain-Mothers and male ancestor-deities. Remain in your residence, my ancestor-deities. Because none of you have to die like I do you shall remain there forever. I abandoned myself to death." The deceased said the same thing again while sobbing. "While my life still existed, without knowing it I abandoned myself to death. I will not be present in the same way I was when I was living and walking inside the xiriqui (god-house) with the women, and when I was walking there with the singers. At this moment I can't be present at the xiriqui. Because I can't do anything more I can't return there. Because it grieved me to be at the temple in Santa Catarina, because of the rumors which were heard while I was committed to a sacred obligation [she was the wife of a singer]. Because this obligation was violated my children died.[41] After they died I thought that I should abandon myself to death. It is too late. Now I have done it. Don't give it another thought my male ancestor-deities. Forgive me. At that moment, on seeing that my children were gone, I decided to disappear too. I declared that I wouldn't live here. Besides, the father who raised me had died too. So I decided to die too. Pardon me if you listened to what I thought, my Sun-Father. Pardon me if you listened to what I thought, my Sun-Father. I definitely thought to live in darkness. Because I thought only about the fact that my father was deceased I decided to die. Focusing on all these events I thought that I should no longer live. That is how I thought, focusing on these events. You heard me my Sun-Father. I alone plunged myself into the darkness. Even though my children were talking to me, trying to convince me not to dwell on death, I still decided to dwell in the darkness. I paid no attention to those who advised me to avoid thinking about dying. I wasn't in agreement with them and so I decided to die. Now that Iromari is looking for me I can be found right here with my Mother. I couldn't ascend to be seated at my Mother's side. I am standing here below my Mother. Why didn't they allow me to ascend to her side? I am enduring being here. I am not doing anything bad. Being present here with my Mother I am discovering everything. During my lifetime I did not tarnish myself much with mistakes committed while I was the singer's wife. I was married to Iromari at the same time. I remained sexually faithful, intent on complying with whatever my husband told me. We went together to visit various ancestor-deities. You, the singer, are the one who knows about our obligation. You know well what was said at Cueriyaoca [where one finds the deer]. You went to Paritecüa. You remember everywhere you passed along the way. You know well that a little deer was standing at Cueriyaoca. I am hearing [remembering] your voice clearly. It is you. We grasped the sacred arrow [needed to hunt the deer properly] and held it in our hands. I was hoping to learn more, but now I can't because I am gone. I regret being dead but now I can't do anything about it. I am to blame for my death. There is nothing to do about it. My husband is not to blame for my death. Keep that in mind my Rain-Mothers and my male ancestor-deities. That is why I am clarifying the cause of my death. I am uncovering all the events in my life. Now Iromari is searching for me. Well, here he can find me, here he can locate me."

(Iromari tells her) "Now that I have found you your relatives have told me to tell you that I have to deliver you. You must go to them."

(The deceased answers) "I am not going to go because my relatives didn't pay attention to me. When they did, they didn't accept my advice. That is why I don't want to go to them. When I was living they didn't respect me and now that I am not alive they will respect me even less. That is why I don't want to visit with them. At this very moment I am below my Mother and I can't go to my relatives. I prefer to ascend to my Mother." Having said that she tried to ascend but they didn't permit her to do so. [According to Pancho she knew why she had died all along but did not confess the reason until she was standing below her Mother, Tatei Nihuetócame.][42] They put her on a cross and she remained there. She couldn't ascend. The deceased said, "I did not contradict my Mother and I was not accustomed to insulting her. But my relatives weren't respecting me the way I respected my Mother. That is why I don't want to visit them. Considering everything they were saying to me, I decided to die. When my husband was drunk he was in the habit of saying mean things to me, but he said them while drunk, so I can excuse him. But because I can't arrive there alive I won't go.[43] Yes, until right now you were searching for me and you were thinking you would see me. But I will not arrive alive and I don't want to go. I will not arrive alive and I don't want to go. You don't have my mouth covered to prevent me from speaking. So I am speaking plainly about the reasons for the events already mentioned. Iromari was looking for me by means of his nierica and he found me here. He was even searching for me in the underworld. Now he has me here. I can't ascend with my Mother. Even though I tried they wouldn't allow me to ascend. Anyway, I find myself here below, hoping for the answer from my Mother, to learn where she is going to send me and where I shall stay. At the same time, Iromari, concentrate on hearing the words of my Mother, to learn where she is going to send me. You, Iromari, understand the words of the wind, and you know the Rain-Mothers and the male ancestor-deities. They have appointed you to be their investigator. Well, yes, I made the mistake of dying. I believe it was I who surrendered. In order to prevent me from dying, you Iromari, were trying to convince me to acknowledge the error that made me ill. But I tried to deny it. It was as if I had given myself life. Thus my only opportunity to get well eluded me. At that time I thought only about disappearing forever. I couldn't imagine that my Rain-Mothers and my male ancestor-deities were listening to me. Only now do I realize, now that I find myself outside my home, and now I am unable to return. Yes, I was responsible for allowing myself to die. I did it. Nothing can be done now. I didn't consider the relatives who survived me. I intended to kill myself. I can't ever return. My relatives remain there.

I will never visit them alive. You are still there too my husband. When you were able to look at me you often hit me. I meant nothing to you. I was your companion, being the singer's wife. I punished myself. Nothing can be done now. [She appeals to *Iromari* for permission.] Free me from my sacred obligation [of collaborating with her singer/ husband]. You must free me from my obligation and not punish me. I don't know where my husband found the nierica. It was he who installed me behind his *maxa ohueni* [literally, deer chair, commonly known as the Huichol singer's or shaman's chair]. It was he who obligated me to be present at the singer's seat. I accepted as if it were my own thought. I conducted myself with great respect for you my male ancestor-deities and Rain-Mothers. Because I am no longer living excuse me for what I was asking you to do. I will never do it again. But it wasn't for no reason. It was because my children had died. That is why I decided not to live. Now that you have found me, Iromari, I am clarifying the motive for my death. During my lifetime I knew perfectly well that when my husband went to hunt deer my prayers were accepted there at Cueriyaoca. My husband quickly found the deer [which in this context Bonales called his *mohuieri*, prayer-feather, to focus on the deer being the offering for the ancestors]. I didn't look for the deer, Iromari did. I never touched one mohuieri [in this context prayer-feathers are handled only by deer hunters]. You know this is true my Sun-Father. I did not request this responsibility that I had. Rather it was my Sun-Father who permitted me to have it. Now that I am gone I will not exercise this responsibility. I don't know how the person destined to be in my place will discharge this obligation. I arrived this far. Don't examine me, my Sun-Father. Now you are listening to me up above, at the peak of the ceremonial candle."

(Iromari says) "The Sun-Father is judging her."

(The deceased says) "Yes I said this. Now one hears the words Crüxtecüa [peak of the cross], Paritecüa, Yoz tecüa [peak of God]." Having spoken these words she passes before each of the male and female ancestor-deities. In conjunction with her speech Iromari appointed Huahuatzari and Ototahue to go seize the deceased in order to deliver her to her family. Even though she does not want to go, they begin to insist, telling her: "Your relatives say that we must take you to them."

(Iromari says) "She seems confused. Above all else, she says she is too discouraged to come back to her relatives. I believe she must pass by this place called "the hill with pine trees," Hüriyapa.

(To the deceased *Iromari* says) "From this spot one must look at all the plains and the hills which one passed during one's life. I understand that this is the way it must be." Standing beneath the cross Iromari spoke these words and continued searching for her. Huahuatzari, Ototahue, and Iromari seized her where she was standing below her Mother. She tried to ascend, but they didn't permit her to ascend to reach her Mother. At that moment they seized her. Huahuatzari, Ototahue, and Iromari detained her. Iromari says, "Now we have caught you so that Grandfather-Fire can judge you.[44] *Huahuatzari* and *Ototahue* have caught you. They will release you straightaway so you can go bid farewell to your relatives, to your male ancestor-deities and Rain-Mothers. All the ancestor-deities grant you permission to reveal yourself and bid farewell to your family for the last time. That is what the Yuhuitari say."

(The deceased says) "Yes, that is how my family wants it to be. However, I see that not all of my relatives are present. Although I won't arrive alive I would still like to encounter all of them. I don't want to arrive with them because they are not all present. Yes, I am going because I have to pay my last respects to your nierica, my husband, in order to prevent being punished for failing to be at your side. I never tarnished your nierica. I always saved myself, never provoking any sexual transgressions. Whenever you brought me to the temple at Santa Catarina I was present with you, whenever they engaged you as the singer there. I always accompanied you carefully. Yes, it was my fault that I am not present now. At this moment I find myself deceased. I deeply regret having thought about taking my own life. At any rate, I will be present so that Iromari can erase me from the place where I was seated at your side.[45] I believe it is wrong for my soul to remain at your side forever [the deceased must take leave of her husband, the singer]. I accomplished everything you ever told me to do. Now I recognize that death is my loss. That is why I appeal to Iromari to free me from my obligation. That is why I am showing myself [to my relatives]. If it weren't for that I wouldn't be present."

(Iromari says) "Our Sun-Father says that she must arrive with her relatives in order to obliterate the trace of where she was living, where she was enjoying life."

(The deceased says) "You all chastised us, we who were attempting to obtain nierica [the visionary ability required by Huichol healers and singers]. But you were the ones who failed to live up to your sacred vows. Due to your mistake over there we paid the penalty. I, being your wife, received the punishment.[46] Even though I am not familiar with our traditions, I did my best to conduct myself properly in the presence of the ancestor-deities as long as they granted me life. However, I assume that when one dies the soul [iyari] is penalized until Iromari liberates it [releases it from where it walks on the earth]. I also occupied the woman's chair behind my husband, the singer. I was also huimarita [a collaborator with her singer/husband]. I believe I was included among the tzaorixi [the wisest of the singers], among the male ancestor-deities, and among the women who collaborate with their singer/husbands. Only a few women attain this honor. Not all women are entitled to belong to this elite group. All women are eligible to attend the dance at the place of the cedar. Not everyone is qualified to guard the nierica. We are all permitted only at the dance at the place of cedar used to make the violin [anybody in this proletarian group may have sex without obligation, unlike the healers and singers for whom sex is especially restricted].[47] We are all acceptable only at Iromarita [in the dark underworld where unrestricted sex exists]. We thought that what we were doing [having illicit sex] was concealed. But we are living on a planet where there is light, and our ancestor-deities are observing, watching over us and what we do. You singers surely realize you are within sight of the ancestor-deities. Yes, I made a mistake by ending my life, despite knowing that I was still healthy. At this time I consent to come back to you my relatives, even though I am not alive. If it is really true that you are waiting for me, I will arrive with you my relatives. But I will not arrive as a person. I will arrive solely as a blue fly [*xraipü yoahui*]. I will be hovering above. My Rain-Mothers and male ancestor-deities I already received all that you offered me, including my bull, the being I most loved while I was alive [she refers to the bull which was sacrificed the previous after-noon]. I believe you killed the animal my father had given me as part of my inheritance. I heard that bull breathing as its life expired. I already received the bull. Now there is nothing else left for me. I agree to return even though I will not arrive alive."

(Iromari says) "I am seeing her. The bull will remain inside her mouth as a blood [soul] offering. I believe our Rain-Mothers and male ancestor-deities are accompanying her. [Pancho explains that at this moment the singer, Iromari, offers her all the edible offerings which have been placed on top of the altar, the wooden platform on the north side of the xiriqui.] Keep all the food and the bull inside your mouth. In spite of the fact there is little food accept it. Your relatives are offering you this meal."

(The deceased says) "If this is how it is, my beloved relatives, I agree to receive what you are all offering me. Iromari, you will never die like I did. While I was living whenever we met each other we were obliged to each other by covenant. Now that I am gone the covenant is canceled. I expect that the visionary skill will be taught forever because you don't die the way we must. I believe that in this manner the *niericate* are assigned. I made myself perish. This was because my father and my children had died. Because of them my heart ached. I suppose my thoughts were heard by the male and female ancestor-deities. I must have directed many negative thoughts [words] to them be-cause I died soon thereafter. Don't give it much deliberation, Iromari. I finished myself."

(Iromari asks her) "Tell the truth. Has anyone bewitched you to terminate your life? If that is what happened tell the truth; after all, we are gathered at an arena within sight of our ancestor-deities."

(Ototahue says) "Some persons have visionary ability and prayer-feathers that are used exclusively for doing witchcraft. That is why we are questioning you, to deter-mine if that is what happened."

(The deceased answers) "I suppose that is correct. But I didn't detect anything. I myself committed the error of concluding my life."[48]

At this point Bonales interrupted his singing and according to Pancho ordered the relatives "to light the candles and prepare the foods so that when the *xraipü* [blue fly] arrives they will be attentive." I stopped taping to go see the fly.

NOTES

1. Chapalagana Huichol inhabit the aboriginal Huichol homeland, in the Chapalagana River region, and must be distinguished from refugee Huichol residing south of it (Fikes 1992). My

use of the word Huichol should not lead readers to conclude that regional variation in language and culture is unimportant. The linguist, Grimes (1964:13), has distinguished three major dialect divisions which correspond to natural barriers in the Chapalagana River region. Weigand (1981) and Negrín (1985:13) have independently identified four major aboriginal zones.

2. The Huichol word *mara'acame* designates an animal, plant, or person credited with having "supernatural" power. It is a generic term which does not distinguish between healers, singers, and *cahuiteros*. In the Huichol hierarchy of religious practitioners healers are accorded less prestige than singers, who are, in turn, less influential than *cahuiteros*. The authority of the *cahuitero* plays a crucial role in selecting candidates to unpaid political offices imposed by the Spaniards (Fikes 1985:75).

3. Emotionally charged numinous experiences, such as merging with Iromari in ritual, convey a degree of certainty which surpasses the intellect. Such experiences facilitate faith in sacred propositions, e.g., that Iromari and Caoyomari exist.

> Sacred propositions and numinous experiences are the inverse of each other. Ultimate sacred postulates are discursive but their significata are not material. Numinous experiences are immediately material (they are actual physical and psychic states) but they are not discursive. Ultimate sacred postulates are unfalsifiable; numinous experiences are undeniable. In ritual's union ultimate sacred propositions thus seem to partake of the immediately known and undeniable quality of the numinous (Rappaport 1979:217).

4. *Tatei Matinyeri*, the Mother of all Huichols, resides at sacred springs in the desert where peyote grows. *Tatei Matinyeri* is the Huichol Mother's womb, the opening through which souls descend from heaven to earth. Huichol peyote pilgrims use water from this Mother in the peyote dance ritual (Fikes 1985:196–197, 350).

5. My translator said Caoyomari here, but Iromari is mentioned everywhere else in this text. Iromari is only active at night, and must depart at sunrise (Fikes 1985:338). He is represented by singers performing fishing rituals, possibly because fishing, like the *Hutaimari* ritual, involves actions with occur beneath the earth's surface, in the primordial underworld.

6. In all my funeral-ritual texts, male and female ancestor-deities are mentioned together, one after the other, as components of a single unit. The "they" that often appears in this text refers to these ancestor-deities, unless otherwise noted. Necaocaoma, translated as "my male ancestor-deities," could more literally mean my fathers, or perhaps my fathers' fathers. I translate *Neteiteima* as "my Rain-Mothers," although for some informants it may mean my mothers' mothers, or perhaps female ancestor-deities in a generic sense. Grimes (1981:99) reports that Huichols inhabiting the western part of the territory (nearer the Cora) have preserved more archaic words, and notes that *tei*, the word my eastern Chapalagana Huichol informants use for "mother," means "aunt" among the western Huichol.

7. Although Bonales's understanding of Christianity may have led him to insinuate that suicide is sinful, it is the supreme Huichol deity, the Sun-Father, whose birth provides the paradigm for human ascension to heaven. The Sun-Father first emerged from the underworld at Pariteqúa. A text dictated by the *cahuitero* indicates that the Sun followed the same path taken by the moon. The

trail blazed through the underworld by these celestial parents established the path Huichols must follow. In ascending to heaven, righteous Huichols follow their precedents in a manner Eliade would define as an "imitatio deo" (Fikes 1985:122–123).

8. Sacred songs, those appropriate for healing and performing rituals, are allegedly dictated by ancestor-deities such as Deer-Person, Grandfather-Fire, and the Sun-Father (Fikes 1985:132). To learn songs Huichols must demonstrate devotion to the ancestors who teach them. This is done by fasting, being sexually faithful to one's spouse, doing without sleep, and making all relevant offerings to ancestor-deities.

9. The underworld is the source of the rainy season, which facilitates terrestrial life (see note 24). My Huichol informants regard life, night, and rainy season as synonyms, using the word *tocari* to refer to them (Fikes 1985:125, 353). Negrín (1977:77) translates *tocari* as the energy or force humans need to live.

10. Jim Bauml (letter of May 24, 1991) identified the *xruya* plant (called *huisache* in Spanish) used in this ritual as *Acacia pennatula*. The divine Mother's punitive behavior suggests that the deceased must undergo the full cycle of trials and tribulations before acceptance of the ancestor-deities is earned and passage to the next phase in life's cycle can occur. The Black-Dog Mother, Tatei Yocáhuima, dwelling in the underworld and the Celestial Mother, Tatei Nihuetócame (see note 35), are both authorized to judge the deceased. Their judicial power over the deceased resembles the control Huichol mothers are expected to exercise over their children.

11. The burrowing owl, *micŭri*, is presumed to be an ally of *Tocácame* (see note 19), and a thief, or perhaps hijacker, of a person's *iyari*, heart-soul. The voice and even the body of the deceased may become an owl. Felipe Sánchez calls these owls, and certain other creatures which manifest the deceased in animal form, *itaicari*. Data from the *cahuitero,* and from Negrín (1977:130), inform my translation of *itaicari* as spook.

12. The deceased's horror at contemplating her own head shows that her *iyari* remains alive and well outside her decomposing body. If her *iyari* hadn't survived the death of her body she would be unable to contemplate her head and ribcage.

13. Blowing the whistle announces the start of the standard cycle of obstacles, distractions, and tests through which the deceased must pass. Hultkrantz's generalization about North American Indians seems appropriate to this Huichol situation.

> Spooks and apparitions appearing as rattling skeletons or ethereal translucent spirits frightening the wits out of people with their shrill whistling are recruited partly from the unburied bodies, partly from the putrefying corpses in the burial grounds (Hultkrantz 1979:137).

14. Her release shows she passed some kind of trial imposed by the deceased and the blue-green fly, *haiyŭ yoahui*. This flying insect may belong to the genus *Phaenicia* (Grimes 1981:119).

15. That she hardly ever danced the peyote dance is practically impossible. Her answer evidently indicates that she wants to avoid communication with those deceased Huichols dwelling in the underworld who are forcing her to dance.

16. Tŭcŭhuaixi is best translated as "corpse carriers." According to Grimes (1981:109),

"tŭcŭ" means to carry, "huai" is corpse, and "xi" is a plural morpheme. In the *cahuitero's* funeral-ritual text the *ŭruhuaixi* or *hŭhŭhuaixi* are people whom Iromari summons to bury the deceased.

17. Answering the prayers of the deceased refers to the growth of maize associated with this Maize Mother (whose *nahual* or messenger is the dove). According to Preuss (1907:190) the white-winged dove, *Zenaida asiatica,* is a manifestation of the "earth and corn goddess" called *Tatei Cócoro Huimari.*

18. This crow, perched near a ladder at the entrance to the Pacific Ocean (underworld), refused to give the deceased a tortilla because she (like all Huichols) had treated crows as pests or competitors when she lived on the earth's surface.

19. Tocácame, the owner of the primordial underworld, is a nefarious being who sets traps to rob humans of their heart-souls. According to Lumholtz (1900:61), *Tocácame* is nocturnal and eats only humans. His body is smeared with blood, and the large arm and leg bones hanging all around him make a rattling noise as he walks. "Even the most powerful shamans fear him."

20. The possum's trap snares only the souls of people who have eaten his sacred meat. Because the deceased passed possum's trap without incident we know Bonales considered her devout. Reverence for possums is evident in ritual (Lumholtz 1902:264–266) and justified by the belief that possum stole fire for the Huichol.

21. Being impaled here is the punishment reserved for all Huichols who have sex with any Huichol except their spouse. The premium Huichols place on sexual purity is undeniably pre-Christian, being connected with hunting and fishing ritual (Fikes 1985:225–226; McCarty and Matson 1975:216; Ortega 1754:26).

22. Totziama or Yocáhuima is the Mother of post-deluge Huichols, rabbits, and deer. Dwelling in the middle of the Pacific Ocean, she receives dead deer and their antlers, presumably to reincarnate them. She is represented by the Huichol women who are responsible for soliciting deer and rabbits and identified with the dogs which help Huichol deer hunters (Fikes 1985:217–220, 354, 358). In Fernando Serratos's funeral-ritual text the deceased carries five tiny tortillas, which are actually included in burials, to feed dogs found in the underworld. This enables the deceased to walk past the dogs who are busy eating tortillas.

23. The *cahuitero's* deer-hunting ritual song credits the Yocáhuima (see note 22) with granting Huahuatzari the favor of killing deer (Fikes 1985:217). Huahuatzari, a master of deer associated with the south, and *Ototahue,* a master of deer associated with the north, are summoned in rabbit and deer-hunting rituals to aid hunters (Fikes 1985:335). Both these envoys or investigators belong to a select group of tutelaries known as *ahuatámete,* "those who obtain antlers" (Fikes 1985:328). They are able to sing with antlers (Fikes 1985:344) and to locate the quarry sought by the Huichol singer. Their antlers are a guide or antennae for Iromari, for whom they work to locate the deceased.

24. *Yuhuitari* means rainmakers or "those inside the rain," a category that evidently includes deceased persons whose sexual promiscuity prevented them from entering the celestial realm. The rainmaking ability associated with these underworld inhabitants may explain why they are invited to attend the peyote dance ritual, Hicüri Neixa, which marks the transition from the dry to the wet season. Similarly, as Hultkrantz recognized (1979:139), Pueblo Indians equate rain spirits with deceased ancestors.

25. According to James A. Bauml (letter of May 24, 1991), the scientific name of

Aochue is *Magnolia schiedeana.* In the *cahuitero's* Good Friday speech, the Virgin Mary, called Tanana, is equated with the Virgin of Guadalupe, and acknowledged as having sent an Aochue flower to the bishop to announce that she wished to have a temple built in her honor. This connection between the Virgin, the Aochue, and the Christian church (mentioned on Good Friday morning in the church), is subtly evoked by Bonales at this point in his Hutaimari as a metonym for Christ. The next stop for the deceased is the place of the cross.

26. Tatzuraita means the place of the *tatzurai,* a bird called *Xenops minutus,* the Plain Little Xenops. This bird, mentioned in Serratos's funeral-ritual text, is said to insult and tease the deceased at a particular place on the Pacific Coast.

27. Huichols have no concept of a "transcendent deity" (Bateson 1972; Fikes and Nix 1989). They equate the God brought by Franciscans with their own Sun-Father, referring to the sacred mountaintop where the Sun-Father first ascended to heaven, *Paritecŭa,* as God's peak, *Yoz tecŭa.* Yoz is heard because the "d" sound in Dios (God in Spanish) does not exist in Huichol phonetics.

28. My translator remarked without prompting that this round rock makes a sound like a drum. In Serratos's funeral-ritual text the whole coast shook the moment the deceased stepped on it. Grimes (1981:134) defined *yŭaca* as to quake or tremble.

29. My translator explained that each piece of wood represents a penis, or sexual transgression connected with the deceased. By throwing the wood into the fig tree, the deceased disposes of her sins. The sexual transgressions discarded here are all sexual acts involving Huichol men other than her spouse.

30. The "they" the deceased obeys by immersing herself in boiling water must be the *Lipicate.* When the deceased departs and tells them, "You all should remain here," it suggests she passed their test, thereby avoiding their trap. They intended to dissolve her heart-soul by transforming her into a spook animal or *itaicari* (see note 11).

31. My translator freely revealed that any Huichol who engages in sexual intercourse with a Mexican is obliged to enter this corral and have intercourse with a mule. The fact that nothing happened here to the deceased indicates that she had abstained from sexual involvement with Mexicans.

32. The fact that the deceased is not detained here indicates she had refrained from illicit sex.

33. The Black Dog-Mother dwelling in the Pacific Ocean is Tatei Yocáhuima (see note 22), the twin or counterpart of Tatei Huerica Huimari, the celestial Mother. Here Black Dog-Mother is credited with transporting the deceased across the ocean. Later Black Dog-Mother must decide whether or not to help the deceased ascend to heaven (see notes 34–35). All available evidence suggests that the underworld Mother and the heavenly Mother are complementary. As Hultkrantz noted, complementarity or dualism between the celestial eagle and an underworld counterpart is fundamental and pervasive among North American Indians (1979:24, 50–51).

34. The Mother at Toránita is Totziama or Yocáhuima (Fikes 1985:354, 358). The deceased emerges from the underworld only after having returned to the source of human life, known as Tocari Mehuatemani, and then to Toránita. With her help the deceased is able to ascend after reaching the shore on the other side of the ocean. Haori tecüa, the peak of the ceremonial candle or

antler, is a launching pad, or place where distinct planes of existence intersect. It seems to be the bottom end of the "axis mundi" (Eliade 1964) or "world navel" (Ortiz 1969) whose exit or top is Paritecúa, the birthplace of the Sun-Father. Later Bonales uses Haoriyapa (place of the antler or ceremonial candle) as a synonym for Paritecúa. Still later in this text Bonales refers to this sacred mountaintop as Crúxtecúa, the "peak of the cross," to reconcile Christ's ascension with the Sun-Father's emergence.

35. Iromari, the singer, thanks Black Dog-Mother for helping the deceased leave the underworld. If her transgressions had been excessive, the deceased would have been obliged to remain in the underworld. Now that her trek through the underworld is complete the deceased may, after visiting her relatives at the ritual, dwell in the celestial world with her Mother, Tatei Nihuetócame.

36. The Yuhuitari, who are demigods, will locate Huahuatzari and Ototahue, who in turn will find the deceased for Iromari. These two ahuatámete are envoys indispensable to Huichol singers performing hunting and funeral rituals (see note 23).

37. Returning to the Yuhuitari implies she doesn't want to visit her relatives, whose transgressions against her contributed to her suicide (see note 46). Asserting that she went back to the Yuhuitari may induce her relatives to confess their offenses.

38. Cueriyaoca, the place where rabbits and deer are killed (Fikes 1985), is identified here as the place where the deceased is released by the Yuhuitari. Later the deceased reminds Bonales that a little deer was waiting at Cueriyaoca, indicating it symbolizes anyplace where "souls" being pursued materialize.

39. Funeral-ritual texts dictated by Serratos and the *cahuitero* emphasize place names and events associated with the afterlife journey of all Huichols instead of examining the biographical details of a particular person. Because their texts were not recorded during actual funeral rituals they were not obliged to consider sorcery as a cause of death. Bonales's text mentions sorcery but rules it out as the cause of death by having the deceased admit she took her own life (see note 48).

40. The cause of her death has been ascertained beyond a reasonable doubt because the ancestor-deities are presumed to be hyper-intelligent, capable of reading one's thoughts, even if they are never voiced. "You said in your heart . . ." means the ancestors discerned her unspoken death wish.

41. "When children die it is because the father has committed adultery" (Klineberg 1934:452). Huichol singers who commit adultery are expected to be punished by the ancestor-deities. The rumors about her husband's sexual infidelity, plus the grief she felt after her children died, account for most of the reason she "thought that I should abandon myself to death."

42. My translator stated that she should not confess in front of the *Yuhuitari* because they are sinners, "slaves of *Tocácame* . . . trapped in eternal darkness." Her assertion, that because her relatives didn't respect her she wanted to ascend to her Mother, may prompt them to confess their transgressions against her.

43. The crying I heard during this phase of the ritual, called *murucuitzica,* occurs as adults ask to be forgiven for their offenses. Their confessions are surely triggered by the deceased repeating her complaint, that her relatives were disrespectful, and then accusing her husband of abusive behavior.

> While the singer is explaining the thoughts of the deceased . . . her relatives must confess all their offenses and ask her to pardon them in order to induce her to come back and bid them farewell for the last time. (Pancho Torres)

Her relatives surely feel better after they confess. They do so believing the deceased may not ascend to heaven without first bidding them farewell and receiving their offerings.

44. Declaring that Iromari and his two envoys (see notes 23 and 36) must force the deceased to bid farewell to her relatives probably promotes further confession and catharsis. Grandfather-Fire's role as judge of the deceased was anticipated near the beginning of the Hutaimari, when Bonales referred to "the speech given in front of Grandfather-Fire."

45. In order for Iromari to "erase her" from the position she occupied as her husband's partner (and thereby nullify her pact with Iromari) she must return to her relatives. Appealing to Iromari to free her from her obligation to her husband assumes that both spouses made a pact with Iromari, and that the abilities needed for effective hunting, healing, and performance of ritual are partially shared between husband and wife.

46. Orthodox Huichols would interpret her children's death as the ancestors' punishment for her husband's illicit sexual affair, euphemised as "your mistake over there." Asserting that she was punished for his infidelity means she feels her children's death made her lose heart and eventually die.

47. Huichols regard dancing to violin music, a diversion taught by Mexicans, as tantamount to having illicit sex. According to Pancho Torres, Huichol violins are made of cedar and dancing to violin music provides Huichols with an opportunity to have sex in the darkness. By postulating an opposition between dancing and guarding the *nierica* the deceased proclaims the Huichol conviction that spiritual achievement and sexual promiscuity are incompatible. Unlike plebian Huichols, healers and singers are entrusted with preserving social (and ecological) order. They are required to put spiritual achievement above sexual adventure.

48. Bonales died within days of performing this funeral ritual. I had no opportunity to ask him if the deceased was killed by witchcraft. I presume the deceased's answer, "that is correct," refers to Bonales's general proposition (which was expressed by *Ototahue*), that persons skilled in witchcraft exist. This is consistent with her admission that she "committed the error of concluding my life."

I remain deeply indebted to Bonales, Pancho Torres, and my other Huichol friends for their devotion to educating me about their customs. I appreciate the encouragement and constructive criticism offered by Phil C. Weigand, the guidance provided by Arnold Krupat, and ethnobotanical data supplied by James Bauml.

REFERENCES

Bateson, Gregory. 1972. *Steps to an Ecology of Mind*. New York: Ballantine Books.

Bauml, James. Letter dated 24 May 1991.

Benítez, Fernando. 1968a. *En la Tierra Mágica de Peyote*. México: Biblioteca Era.

———. 1968b. *Los Indios de México*. Vol. 2. México: Biblioteca Era.

Eliade, Mircea. 1964. *Shamanism: Archaic Techniques of Ecstasy.* Translated by Willard Trask. Bollingen Series no. 76. New York: Pantheon Books.

Fikes, J. C. 1985. *Huichol Indian Identity and Adaptation.* Ph.D. dissertation, Ann Arbor: University of Michigan.

———. 1992. *Carlos Castaneda, Academic Opportunism, and the Psychedelic Sixties.* Lanham, Md.: Madison Books.

Fikes, J. C., and Nelleke Nix. 1989. *Step Inside the Sacred Circle.* Bristol, Ind.: Wyndham Hall Press.

Grimes, Joseph E. 1964. *Huichol Syntax.* The Hague: Mouton.

Grimes, Joseph E. et al. 1981. *El Huichol: Apuntes Sobre el Lexico.* Technical Report to NSF distributed by the Department of Modern Languages and Linguistics, Cornell University.

Hultkrantz, Ake. 1979. *The Religions of the American Indians.* Translated by Monica Setterwall. Berkeley: University of California Press.

Klineberg, Otto. 1934. "Notes on the Huichol." *American Anthropologist* 36:446–460.

Lumholtz, Carl. 1900. *Symbolism of the Huichol Indians.* American Museum of Natural History, Memoirs 1 (2). New York.

———. 1973 [1902]. *Unknown Mexico.* Vol. 2. Glorieta, New Mexico: Rio Grande Press.

Mata Torres, Ramón. 1974. *Vida y Arte de los Huicholes.* Primera Parte (La Vida). No. 160. México: Artes de México.

McCarty, Kieran, and Daniel S. Matson. 1975. "Franciscan Report on the Indians of Nayarit, 1673." *Ethnohistory* 22 (3):193–222.

Myerhoff, Barbara G. 1968. *The Deer-Maize-Peyote Complex among the Huichol Indians of Mexico.* Ph.D. dissertation, University of California at Los Angeles.

———. 1974. *Peyote Hunt: The Sacred Journey of the Huichol Indians.* Ithaca: Cornell University Press.

Negrín, Juan. 1977. *El Arte Contemporáneo de los Huicholes.* Guadalajara: Universidad de Guadalajara.

———. 1985. *Acercamiento histórico y subjetivo al Huichol.* Guadalajara: Universidad de Guadalajara.

Ortega, José. 1944 [1754]. *Conquista del Nayarit.* México, D.F.: Editorial Layac.

Ortiz, Alfonso. 1969. *The Tewa World.* Chicago: University of Chicago Press.

Preuss, Konrad T. 1907. "Die Hochzeit des Maises und andere Geschichten der Huichol-Indianer." *Globus* 91:185–192.

Rappaport, Roy A. 1979. *Ecology, Meaning, and Religion.* Richmond, Calif.: North Atlantic Books.

Valadez, Susan. 1986. "Mirrors of the Gods: The Huichol Shaman's Path of Completion." *Shaman's Drum.* Fall 6:28–40.

Weigand, Phil C. 1972. *Cooperative Labor Groups in Subsistence Activities among the Huichol Indians.* Mesoamerican Studies no. 7. Carbondale: Southern Illinois University Museum.

———. 1981. "Differential Acculturation among the Huichol Indians." In *Themes of Indigenous Acculturation in Northwest Mexico,* edited by P. C. Weigand and Thomas B. Hinton, 9–21. Tucson: University of Arizona Press.

Weigand, Phil C., and Celia Garcia Weigand. 1991. "Death and Mourning among the Huicholes of Western Mexico." In *Coping with the Final Tragedy: Cultural Variation in Dying and Grieving,* edited by David Counts and Dorothy Counts, 53–69. Amityville, N.Y.: Baywood.

Zingg, Robert M. 1938. *The Huichols: Primitive Artists.* New York: G. E. Stechert.

———. n.d. *Huichol Mythology.* Unpublished manuscript on file at the Laboratory of Anthropology, Santa Fe, New Mexico.

"ANOTHER HOME RUN FOR THE BLACK SOX"
Humor and Creativity in Hopi Ritual Clown Songs

Hans-Ulrich Sanner

Anyone who has spent enough time among the Hopi[1] to establish relationships of friendship and mutual trust will probably agree that humor and joking play a tremendous role in their society.[2] Authors like Brinton (1975:219ff) and Deloria (1969:148ff) have shown that this is generally true of many Native American peoples. Consequently, a good sense of humor is perhaps more "typically Indian" than, say, safeguarding Mother Earth or having an inclination to wear feathers. However, among white people the old stereotype of the "stolid Indian" has been persistent up until now. The "granite-faced grunting redskin," as Deloria calls this image, well known from older Hollywood westerns, may have gone out of fashion. And yet, the wise old Indian shaman or prophet to whom we now listen as he tells us cosmic truths about how to save the world from ecological disaster wears a granite-face, too. The Hopi Indians of Arizona in particular have been highly popularized because of such "cosmic truths."[3] This essay deals with their (unfortunately) much less known "comic truth," or at least one fascinating aspect of it.

I had my first personal encounter with the Hopi fondness for humorous wordplay in the summer of 1988 when I was spending some time on the reservation in order to check on the possibilities for a fieldwork project about Hopi ritual clowns. In the course of my endeavor to make initial contact with possible informants I was sent to the house of a man whom I was told might be willing to help me out. When I arrived at the house I noticed a trailer parked in front of it. Three Hopi men were busy moving furniture from the trailer into the house. Being an anthropologist in the field, I felt awkward and superfluous in the presence of men doing "real work." I kept what I considered a polite distance, watching them moving chairs and planks and waiting for a chance to confess the purpose of my visit. Finally one of them, an elderly man with glasses and a baseball cap, came over to me, pointed toward the scene and explained with a grin what was going on: "We are INDIAN MOVEMENT!" We started to laugh, and I relaxed. So that was the true meaning of "Indian Movement"!

Puns and wordplay, either spontaneous or as preconstructed jokes, are frequent elements of Hopi everyday conversation, in both Hopi and English. Of course, some Hopi are more talented in that regard than others, and a good punster is likely to be held in high esteem because of his ability to make people laugh and thereby provide happiness—a central value in the Hopi worldview.[4] Humorous wordplay also has its role in religious ceremony, especially in connection with ritual clowning. The clown songs (*tsukutawi*, pl. *tsukutatawi*) that shall be presented as a genre of literature in this essay are based on humor that runs much in the same vein as the quip about "Indian Movement." They differ from other instances of both everyday and ceremonial humorous wordplay in that they present humor in a set literary mode and structure and constitute a religious ritual with definite meaning and purpose.

THE CONTEXT OF CLOWN SONGS

Kachina Dance and Clown Ceremony

Several layers of context have to be considered here, at least briefly. The clown songs are in essence a ritual of confession. This ritual is an important element, in fact it is the conclusion, of an elaborate ceremony called *tsukulalwa* (clowning). The clown ceremony in turn is an integral part of many outdoor Kachina dances in early summer.

Much has been written about the role of Kachinas in Hopi life.[5] Kachinas are the spirits of the ancestors, but also the spirits of many kinds of plants, animals, and phenomena of the natural world. Their home is in the other world, but they visit the Hopi villages in the period roughly between the winter and summer solstices. During this "Kachina season" a sequence of ceremonies celebrates and highlights their presence. Impersonated by masked and costumed male dancers, the Kachinas entertain and delight the Hopis with their colorful appearance and their beautiful songs and dances. They also bring various kinds of gifts and food, especially for the children. Kachinas are messengers of the gods. They carry the people's prayers to the spirit world and return as rain for the corn plants that sustain the Hopi life.

Between April and late June two-day Kachina dances are performed on week-ends in the plazas of the Hopi villages. Each village usually stages one or two of these "ordinary" Kachina dances in one season. Frequently, a group of sacred clowns (*tsutskut*) appears in the plaza after noon on the first day. The men who impersonate the clowns are not, as in former times, initiated members of a special clown society; they have been chosen a few days previously by the sponsor of the dance or by the Kachina group. It is an honor for a man to be appointed, because clowning is a religious duty involving responsibility and hard work for the benefit of all.[6]

While the dancing Kachinas may be said to represent nature and the harmony and beauty of the spirit world, the clowns—boisterous, loud, and presumptuous—depict mortal humankind with all its shortcomings and failures, but also its hopes and struggles for a good life. In the words of one Hopi, "*Pam yaw tsuku pay yep hin qatsiniqw put yaw pam tu'awi'ytangwu*": "The clown depicts how life is here." "*Tsutskut qatsit pas tuwi'yyungngwu*": "The clowns really know about life," and therefore they are predestined to hold a mirror up to the people so that they can take a look at themselves, laugh, and, with luck, learn. During the one and a half days of their performance, the clowns enact various funny skits and satires that comment on current problems and concerns of Hopi society. However, these skits are only up-to-date illustrations of a deeper truth. The overall clown ceremony follows a traditional pattern of dramatic ritual development that reflects and enacts a central conception of Hopi philosophy: the life cycle of the people from a paradise-like beginning to a stage of utmost corruption and decadence that will inevitably lead to supernatural punishment and a renewal of life. According to Hopi eschatology, this has happened several times before, and it will happen again, perhaps soon.[7]

As the dance proceeds and the sun crosses the sky toward his house in the west, the clowns become more outrageous and disrespectful. Several kinds of fear-inspiring Warrior Kachinas (*kipokkatsinam*) start appearing, warning the clowns that something terrible will happen if they don't change their ways. All this time the other Kachinas keep dancing and singing, undisturbed. As the clowns pay no heed to the warnings, punishment finally becomes inevitable. Toward the end of the day, the Warrior Kachinas join forces for a raid (*kiipo*). They rush into the plaza, throw the clowns to the ground, tie them together, strip them, drench them with buckets full of water, and whip them with branches of certain plants. Then they withdraw, leaving the tortured clowns to recover. They have been purified, but in a deeper sense the drenching and whipping has been an invocation of rain. The water has also washed away the paint from their bodies and faces, revealing their individuality.

After a little while the Warrior Kachinas return to the plaza with gifts of food. Upon noticing their former tormentors, the clowns start to run and hide, much to the amusement of the audience. Sometimes they find clever ways of hiding, but eventually the Warriors detect them all and lead them to one end of the plaza, where they carefully line them up. Then the Warrior Kachinas and clowns make friends with each other (*naa-kwatslalwangwu*). Each Warrior shakes hands with each clown and gives him something as a gift: some roasted corn, *piiki* bread, an orange, an apple. The surplus is distributed among the audience.

Making a Confession

The ritual of confession that follows will be introduced here in the words of a Hopi onlooker. As with all Hopi interlocutors whom I shall quote in this essay, I choose to refer to him by use of initials in order to provide a general anonymity. The following text was extracted from a long general account given by NI in Hopi, based on his observation of countless clown ceremonies in the village of Hotevilla on Third Mesa:[8]

After they have carefully distributed [these things] among the clowns and given [the rest] to the people, they make the clowns sing [*tawtoynayangwu*]. [First] they pull out the Clown Chief [*tsukumongwi*] and . . . here in Hotevilla they pull him over to the west side [of the plaza]. When they have managed to bring him there, then there always has to be one [Warrior Kachina] that can talk; a Warrior Kooyemsi [for example] can talk. Then the clown says: "All right. What shall I do?" And that Warrior Kachina tells him: "You shall sing!" So that's what the clown does. He does it like this: "*Aa' ii'. Aa' ii'.*" That's how he always starts off, and then he sings a satirical song about anybody [*pam naap hakiy tawsomi'ytangwu*]. It could be about his mother, his father, his grandmother, his younger brother, his older sister, or his female clan-relatives. He sings about those who are related to him [*put aw hakim hin yanyungqam*]. One by one, they bring the clowns over there. When one has finished, the next one has his turn. When all of them are through singing, they say: "All right, may it be so!"

The gifts that the Warrior Kachinas have brought for the clowns are considered blessings. But in order to earn and truly deserve them, each clown must first make a confession (Lomatewama 1988:11). So they tell him: "*Um tawmaniy!*" "You shall sing!" They take him over to the opposite end of the plaza, away from his fellow clowns, who are waiting side by side. Then the Warriors—sometimes twenty, thirty, or even more Kachinas—gather in a U-shape around him, with the opening toward the other end of the plaza where his gifts are waiting for him. Surrounded on three sides by those fierce-looking beings uttering muffled calls, the clown has no choice but to sing and dance his way out of there, across the plaza.

Many clown performers emphasize that this ritual of confession (*nahoslawu*) is the hardest part of clowning, and there are several reasons for that. First of all, it is not so much the presence of the Warriors that may be frightening, but the fact that the attention of the audience is focused on him at that moment. At that point, the plaza and the surrounding housetops are still occupied by sometimes two or three hundred people, and many of them are eager to hear the clown tell his stories. As a result, he may get scared and even forget the lines of one of his songs. In this case, his fellow clowns usually help him along. NI explains:

It happens that they actually get scared, and the word just leaves them. That's what WA [a clown performer] was talking about. You really have to memorize it as best as you can, so when you get scared, when you look around and see all those people eyeing you. . . . That probably scares you! Scares the daylight out of you.

Of course, there are expectations from the side of the audience. Who will he sing about? Will he succeed in being funny? Members of the Eagle Clan, which owns and hands down the clown tradition at Third Mesa, told me that of the two or three songs a clown usually sings, one should always be about himself. Only then will it be a true confession. However, the clown also has to confess in behalf of "those who are related to him" by blood, clan, or marriage. In the tradition of the Eagle Clan, the clowns represent *tsukutiyo* ("clown youth") and *tsukumana* ("clown maiden"), the ancestral brother and younger sister (*naasiwam*) of the clan. In the ceremony, the *tsukumana* is impersonated only by a doll, but in the end the male clowns confess in her behalf as well.[9] In my record of clown songs, the persons who figured most frequently were the clown himself and a (younger or older) sister. Other relatives addressed were the clown's wife, an uncle (mother's brother), mother or father, a (younger or older) brother, the clown's children, and a grandmother or grandfather. NI and other interlocutors made a point that two kinds of kin can never be sung about: the paternal aunts and the sons-in-law. It has been well documented that "auntie" (*ikya*) and nephew (*imööyi*) share a joking relationship that emphasizes (sexual) fondness of each other (cf. Hieb 1972:234–248); they "never put each other down." I noticed many times and was told that a son-in-law is praised in an exaggerated manner and jokingly referred to as a "superman" (*hongvitaqa,* "strong man"), even if he is anything but that. It may thus tentatively be concluded that when certain kin cannot be criticized (jokingly) in everyday social life, it cannot be done in a ritual clown song either.

The clown has "to point at" someone of his own kin, exposing his/her imaginary or real weakness. Often, there is some truth behind the story, and some songs imply serious criticism. In any case, humor is the key to the success of a song. The following statement by AT of the Eagle Clan, referring to clowning in a more general sense, reveals the important socio-psychological dimension of Hopi humor:

This may be just one man's opinion, but if it was done just merely to discipline someone morally and to remind him of the teachings, and there was no laughter or anything like that involved, it would be very DULL. They would just sit there and look. You know, it would be uncomfortable for a lot of people; certainly would be unpleasant for the people who are the objects of it. So what they then DO is, they introduce things into it that are amusing, that are FUNNY. That way they make it entertaining as well as a form of discipline to the people who are being exposed.

I have heard that some people get mad when a clown sings about them, although there is nothing they can do about it. On the other hand, there are people who do not mind composing songs about themselves for a relative who will perform as a clown. Consider the following remark by NI that also shows how the idea for a song was born:

See, I'm often thinking about songs like that for TY [NI's grandson]. And the other day, out of the blue, he mentioned something about rubbing alcohol, and I meant to do something about that, including MYSELF, even though I'm making it for TY. So TY can sing and include me in there.

      I don't know exactly how to put it, I haven't worked on it. But it seems to be a good thing, on rubbing alcohol.[10]

Although the clown is immune in his sacred role, and although it is actually a blessing to be named in a song, it is obviously embarrassing for some of the performers to sing about their relatives. Several younger men have told me that this is the main reason why they would not want to clown. Could it be that embarrassment grows—both on the side of performers and those who are being sung about—when the belief in the sacredness and immunity of the clown wanes?

      Besides the stage fright and the psychological stress that a clown has to cope with, there are physical strains involved. I can only describe here what some men have told me and what I have seen, but of course one must have been out there in the plaza as a clown to know what it really feels like. The confessions stand at the end of a long and strenuous performance. The clowns are worn out. After staying up all night in their kiva they have spent almost two days in a dusty plaza, very often in scorching weather. Now they start feeling their sunburns and the wounds and scratches that they have received during the punishment. They may still be soaking wet, with mud and sand in their pants and shoes, itching on their skin. I have seen clowns shivering from a cool evening breeze or after a most welcome rainstorm. Some clowns are hoarse from yelling in the plaza all day long. Still, they all have to sing their songs and confess.

CLOWN SONGS IN ETHNOGRAPHY

Before presenting and discussing my own field data, let me first consider what has previously been written about clown songs. An examination of the ethnographic record indicates a long-standing tradition of these songs and also sheds some light on the history of research.

      The earliest mention dates back to the 1890s and is found in the work of two pioneers of Hopi ethnography, Alexander M. Stephen and J. Walter Fewkes. Their descriptions of the ritual, down to the typical movements and gestures of the clown, show the striking correspondence with today's procedure, one hundred years later:

the other [Warrior Kachina] then leads the clowns, one at a time, to the north end of this double line [of Kachinas]. He must then tell a droll story in ransom for the pile of food assigned him by the [Warriors] and this he proceeds to do, holding his hands up to his breast and making some sidelong hops with feet close together, toward the food piles. As he hops thus, he shouts out: "*Ahai'! Ahai'! Pasha'nihinta!* Attend to this true story!" And then he tells it, and it is usually very gross. (Parsons 1936:404ff)

Fewkes (1892:48) provides a similar description, and concludes: "The meaning of this I cannot interpret, but it afforded great amusement to the spectators." He probably would not have told us anyway. Why? Stephen, who understood some Hopi, calls these stories "smutty" (Parsons 1936:480). This is, of course, an ethnocentrism; however, Stephen was an accurate ethnographer who—unlike some of his contemporaries, including Fewkes—did not refrain from describing things considered "vulgar and obscene" by Victorian standards (cf. Titiev 1944:41):

The first clown advised the band to go to Oraibi and steal horses and ravish the women. The second told his father's amorous adventures with a Pah Ute woman at Moenkopi. The third told of an Oraibi who copulated with his wife with a big cannon, the wife giving birth to young firearms. The fourth told of his father's amorous adventure when a youth. He and a young girl were storing corn in an unoccupied room. He tried to copulate with the girl but she was a virgin and he could not make entrance. He tried all day and just about dark was making another effort and was lying in a position above the girl when his father came in and, seeing the boy's posture, gave him a kick in the buttocks which resulted in a successful defloration. The fifth one, however, took up a distinctly moral discourse. (Parsons 1936:480ff)

It cannot be inferred if any of the stories involved humorous wordplay. Stephen's more detailed rendering of the fourth story indicates that the humor—at least in this example—had a different source (The father's attempt to punish the boy leads to the opposite). Except for the fifth song that was deliberately serious and may be interpreted as serving ritual "reconciliation" (Handelman 1981:350ff), all the songs were about sexuality, and at least some of them involved a relative of the clown. In his autobiography, Don Talayesva, a Hopi from Orayvi, Third Mesa, mentions a song that he had performed during a clown ceremony around 1920. Clearly, this one is based on wordplay and contains the basic features of today's clown songs:

Then we sang funny songs with double meanings. The theme of my song was: "My mare is very mean, she bucks and kicks. I have turned her loose dragging a rope. Whoever catches her may ride her." I explained that the song meant I had a cross, hot-tempered wife who was difficult to manage; that she had thrown and kicked me; and whoever caught her might ride. The people laughed. (Simmons 1942:278ff)

Louis Hieb (1972:221–223) and Emory Sekaquaptewa (1980:16ff) have pointed out the nature of clown songs as both humorous entertainment and religious confession, providing three examples in English. Their insights have stimulated my own research into the matter.[11]

     Basic methods and problems in ethnographic fieldwork on humor have been discussed by Apte (1983:195–201). At least a few words must be said here concerning the nature and scope of my field data. I estimate that every year more than one hundred new clown songs are performed at Hopi. Only a Hopi who is fluent in his language and who has been watching dances from year to year can estimate and appreciate the full range of *tsukutatawi*. Between 1988 and 1990 I "collected" roughly thirty examples, most of which had been originally performed in recent years. As non-Hopi are strictly forbidden to make recordings of any kind during public ceremonies (a fact that I do not regret), and as I am not fluent in Hopi (a fact that I do regret), my collection consists mainly of retold versions of clown songs. Furthermore, the collection is heterogeneous in quality. A few of the songs are recorded incomplete as notebook entries, providing merely the keyword and punch line. More than half of the songs were told on tape—some in Hopi, some in English—by either onlookers or clown performers. I witnessed many more confessions "live" in the plaza, but due to my insufficient fluency in Hopi I failed to get the joke in most cases. Some of them were kindly explained to me by Hopi friends after the dance. As for data on humor, the dependency on native informants may have disadvantages with the participant observation (and immediate "understanding") of humorous events (Apte 1983:197). Hieb (1972:222) writes that "Hopis consider these stories to be 'pretty raw stuff' and are reluctant to relate them." From my own experience, I cannot confirm the latter part of his statement (as for the "raw stuff," see below). I made no systematic attempt at collecting as many songs as possible. In many cases it was a Hopi interlocutor who, at some point during a conversation or interview, started to tell "a good song" he had heard or performed himself. Naturally, a person is inclined to tell a "good" joke rather than a "poor" one. The ethnographer makes a further subjective selection when it comes to presenting the data. Examples of both "good" and "bad" humor—however defined, and by whomever defined—can be useful for the understanding of cultural systems (Apte 1985:24). For the purpose of this essay, however, I choose to present primarily such clown songs that I myself found funny and witty and that were also funny and witty to those Hopis who related them or with whom I discussed them. I hope readers will enjoy them as well. Humor, of course, is a relative thing, and its appreciation depends on many factors, both within a culture and between cultures. Equally, some clown songs bring down the house, while others hardly get any laughs. When NI first told me the "Mississippi" confession presented below, I had a good laugh about it. I told him that I liked this one, and he replied:

THINGS like that, they vary. You know, it stands out, it's pretty hard to forget. And sometimes some other songs, aaw! they're not that good, so you don't pay that much attention to it. . . . Some are real good, it stays in your head, it's pretty hard to forget.

THE ART OF CLOWN SONGS

Following Hockett's definition of jokes (1972:154), Hopi clown songs constitute an art form, specifically a genre of literature. Clown songs are performed regularly in a specific setting or context (see above) and they create humor within the bounds of a set literary mode and structure. The art of how these songs are created and performed, how their humor "works" and relates to a cultural background, and how they are evaluated by an audience can best be explained with a number of examples. It must be kept in mind that the following narratives, as given by several Hopis, are retold versions of clown songs. They are field data "constructed from talk and action" (Van Maanen 1988:95). There is no room here for a thorough "specification of discourses" (Clifford and Marcus 1986:13); however, a short introductory account of "who said what and when" will at least be provided for each of the following detailed examples.

Example I: "Outstanding"

The following clown song was narrated by AT during a long conversation about several aspects of clowning. He had heard and seen it performed a while ago, and it was clearly one of his favorites at that time. The text is not an exact repetition of the actual clown song, but a free rendering of its content in English. After addressing the ethnographer in the first sentence, the narrator subsequently switches to the first person singular, in imitation of the clown telling his story.

This clown during his confessional was talking about people being OUTSTANDING, you know, very outstanding people. When somebody accomplishes something or does a good deed or becomes very prominent for an achievement of some kind, he's an outstanding citizen. That's what the word means.

BUT, that's not what I am talking about, that's not what I mean. See, I got these uncles, they are always drinking. Everytime they get a little money they buy booze and they drink, and they get drunk in the end and do all kinds of things, and then eventually their wives throw them out.

And my uncle so-and-so, last weekend he got hold of some booze somewhere and he did the same thing again. He got drunk and got so obnoxious in the house that his wife threw him out and wouldn't let him back in. So now he is OUTSTANDING [laughs aloud].

Clown songs are always performed in Hopi, but the keyword or key phrase is frequently English nowadays. In the above case, the humor results from discovering an ambiguity in the English word "outstanding." As is customary, the clown first describes what the word really means. Then he leads his audience to discover a hidden meaning in the word. While talking about the deed and mishap of his uncle, the clown manipulates the word "outstanding" and its correct use in such a way that it turns out to be a fitting description of his uncle's mishap. The result is laughter. This example may be termed an imperfect pun (cf. Hockett 1972:157ff) because "standing out" must be extended to "standing outside." The resulting humor is perhaps enhanced by perceiving a further incongruity, namely that the poor guy who has been kicked out is actually far from being outstanding. The two types of humor involved—linguistic manipulation and incongruity—are readily accessible to both Hopis and non-Hopis. However, the song also pertains to specific Hopi cultural knowledge. The next example, while having a similar topic and technique as the one above, puts more emphasis on this cultural aspect.

Example II: "Home Run for the Black Sox"

The following text has been extracted from a long narration in which an elderly man from Hotvela tells in Hopi about his clowning (*tsukulawu*) in the early 1960s.[12] The clown song appears in natural temporal sequence toward the end of his narration. Again, at the beginning (and also at the end) of the text he is addressing the ethnographer, while the central portion reproduces the mode of the original performance. The italics mark the English words used in the song.

At that time, as I recall, I had a song about *baseball*. Remember, *baseball teams* are named in various ways: As you will recall, some are called *Red Sox,* and some others also *White Sox.* But me, I am playing for the *Black Sox,* I said.

But it's not really that! Look, I have a wife here on the southwest side [of the village]. And when I get drunk she sends me away, she throws me out of the house. And then I always go home to my mother's house on the northeast side. She lives there. That's where I go to, and after I have gotten there people always find out about it, and then they laugh about me. They laugh about me. "I heard that WA has made a *home run* again," they say and laugh about me. And then, my mother who lives there; she is an old woman. And therefore, she doesn't *wash* my *socks* for me, and so after a while—too bad— they turn black.

And that's the reason why I play for the *Black Sox team,* and also why I make a *home run.* They throw me out, and so I run [home] to my [mother's] house.

That's what I was singing about, as I recall, and the people really enjoyed it.

Other than in the example above, the clown confesses his *own* bad habit of getting drunk and consequently getting kicked out. Instead of being "outstanding," he finds another way of making creative and humorous use of the case: he makes a "home run for the Black Sox"—that is, he runs home for the black socks. Clearly, there are two punchlines here that can be enjoyed independently, but taken together they make the story more effective.

Furthermore, the song wittily links a cultural theme of Anglo society (baseball) with a cultural theme of Hopi society. Hopi is a matrilineal and matrilocal society. Traditionally, women own the houses, and upon marriage a man moves into his wife's household where he—structurally—remains an outsider (Titiev 1944:15ff; Schlegel 1977). Upon temporal separation or divorce, a man has to leave the house of his wife. Most likely he will go back to the house of his mother (or sisters), which he considers as his *home* throughout his life. In that connection, the baseball term "home run" can be easily perceived as ambiguous by Hopis, and therefore lends itself well for use in a clown song. (In fact, I have heard about another song where "home run" was used in a similar way.) In a discussion about the truth behind the "Black Sox" confession, NI explained:

It could be all true, and it could be all made up. But to us listening to him, whoever knows him that much, and it actually happens, so it could be true, or just made up.

And I know HIM. He's like me, he drinks, and . . . You know, our wives, they just don't like us drinking like that, so they . . . it actually happens that way. They really get after us. And sometimes even get us out of the house and tell us to go home: "Go to your mother, go to your mother's house!"

You can't do anything about it but do what you are told. Go to your mother, and you have to stay with your mother for a length of time until such time they decide to take you back, so . . . so that's what it is. So it could be true.

Readers will note that most of the examples deal with alcohol abuse. Of the thirty-one songs I collected, thirteen were about alcohol. This is another cultural theme to be considered. Alcohol consumption is generally regarded as unethical (*qahopi*) by Hopis. Nonetheless, and despite general prohibition, drinking is a widespread phenomenon on the reservation today. Alcoholism is a major disruptive force and the primary mental health problem of modern Hopi society (cf. Hopi Health Department 1981–85). It has to be remembered that a clown song is indeed a confession. Because many Hopis have an alcohol problem themselves or among their relatives, and because this goes directly against the ethical *ideal,* it is no wonder that the topic figures prominently in clown songs. Acting out the problem and the gossip about it in a funny way may be a genuine relief to both clown and community. Most likely, humor will not solve the problem, but perhaps it helps to cope with it.

The two examples discussed so far show another trait of many current clown songs: they play on a word or phrase of the English language ("statistics" again: twenty-one out of thirty-one songs had an English keyword). This clearly reflects linguistic acculturation and Hopi bilingualism. Leap (1973:292) defines bilingualism as "one means through which a speaker is able to exploit new language environments." He argues that "bilingualism is a process, not a state" (ibid.). Indeed, Hopi bilingualism has been in a constant state of flux for decades. About thirty years ago, Kennard (1963:36) stated (referring to Second Mesa Hopi) that in the 1930s "everyone above the age of 40 was monolingual, and those below that age had varying degrees of control of English. Today, the only monolingual Hopi are over 70 years of age." During the last thirty years there has been a dramatic development, with bilingualism expanding and now gradually giving way to English monolingualism among the younger generation. NI described the current situation with a sarcastic remark: "What is 'good Hopi' now is a combination of English and Hopi." The issue cannot be discussed here in detail, but it must be emphasized that the ongoing rapid loss of the Hopi language is a serious threat to Hopi culture; the consequences are already painfully being felt, especially in ceremonialism and the teaching of Hopi traditions.[13]

My point here is that the art of clown songs reflects the changing language situation and exploits the opportunities of bilingualism in a creative and humorous way. In this respect, the high frequency of clown songs with an English keyword is perhaps typical for those generations of Hopis who learned Hopi as a first language but are also fairly articulate in English. Redfern (1984:164) points out that punning appeals particularly to writers in exile. The same can be said about bilingual Hopis: "You see the second language from the outside, and its mechanisms, its automatisms, are that much more apparent to you" (ibid.). The following clown song is a fine example of bilingual humor, in that it splits a non-Hopi keyword into a meaningful combination of Hopi and English words.

Example III: "Mississippi"

NI first told me about this clown song in English during an interview in 1989. The song had been originally performed by a clown in Hotvela, probably some years earlier. In 1990, I asked NI to narrate it in Hopi. Upon my request, he told it in the same mode as the clown had done (he didn't jump along to it, though). This text may serve to exemplify the typical outward form of a clown's *taawi* in both English translation and Hopi original.

Aa' ii', aa' ii'. MISSISSIPPI. MISSISSIPPI. Aa' ii', MISSISSIPPI, MISSISSIPPI. Aa' ii'.
  I guess you think of it in a certain way: look, you will recall that somewhere here, somewhere in the east flows the Mississippi. That's how it is called, Mississippi River. Remember, that is a big river over there.
  But it is not THAT! I have a mother out here, in [village] X. I have a mother, and she is old now. And because she has gotten old she keeps a chamber pot [*sisipi*] in the house. Now, when she feels an urge to piss she goes there, to the chamber pot. And sometimes when it is real urgent she won't hit it. First it goes to the side of it, and then she hits it right. And then it starts running down along her legs and along the ground.
  THAT is the reason why she is miss-*sisipi* [Mississippi]. Because she misses the chamber pot, and because it starts running down her legs and also along the ground. That's why she is miss-*sisipi*. That's what it is talking about.

Aa' ii', aa' ii'. MISSISSIPPI. MISSISSIPPI. Aa' ii', MISSISSIPPI, MISSISSIPPI. Aa' ii'.
  Suupan kya umuy wuuwayaqw meh ura yangqe haqe', hopkyaqe haqe' i' *Mississippi* muuna. Pan maatsiwa, *Mississippi River*. Wukomuna ura pam pangqe'e.
  Noq pay qa PAM i'i. Pay nu' yepeq X yu'yta. Nu' yu'ytaqw pay pam pi pu' wuyooti. Pam wuyootiqe pay pam aapave sisipi tavi'ytangwu. Pu' hisatniqw sisiwkukmoke' pu' put awningwu, sisipi aw'i. Pu' ephaqam pas payninik pay qa su'aqwningwu. Pay aqlavo mootiniqw pu' paasat su'aqwningwu. Noq pu' pay hokyayat ang munvangwu pu' tutskwava.
  Paniqw oovi pam *miss*-sisipi [Mississippi]. Pam sisipi *miss*tangwuniqw oovi pu' hokyayat ang munvangwuniqw oovi pu' tutskwava piw munvangwuniqw oovi'o. Paniqw pam *miss*-sisipi. Pay it lalvaya.

I had no opportunity to discuss this clown song with its author; yet I have an idea as to how the song may have come into being. First, it was noticed that a part of the word Mississippi is homophonous with the Hopi word for chamber pot, *sisipi*. The remaining part (mis-) still made sense, identified as an English morpheme (miss). The challenge to the artist, then, was to exploit the discovered bilingual ambiguity in "Mississippi" and make a good story out of it. This would fit the assumption of humor theorists that "the creator of a joke first notices an ambiguity (either linguistic or conceptual) and then creates an incongruity by responding to the hidden rather than the intended meaning of the ambiguity" (Shultz 1976:15). On the other hand, the idea may as well have originated from an actual observation, namely that somebody "missed the *sisipi.*"

In any case, the result is convincing in more than one way. An old person may indeed sometimes "miss the sisipi." It is certainly funny to perceive and resolve the incongruity of a big river with a little old Hopi woman. However, incongruity does not account for all the humor here, because the author additionally applies a humor technique that leads to "heightened congruity" (cf. Eichinger Ferro-Luzzi 1990): he likens his mother to the actual river flowing (*muuna*) because, as he explains, her water (urine) starts flowing (*munva*), first down her legs and then along the ground (*tutskwava*).[14] As a result, she is "miss-*sisipi*" and "Mississippi" at the same time.

A further possible source of humor in this clown song may tentatively be considered here: making fun of the aged. I know of four other clown songs that center on the frailty or limited capability of an old person (e.g., a grandmother), poking mild fun at a peculiar habit (this is an aspect, although not the central one, in the "Black Sox" confession discussed above). Lorenz and Vecsey (1986:215ff) hold that "the old person who is crippled or useless demonstrates to Hopi neighbors a form of antisocial behavior" and is consequently considered *qahopi* (see also Brandt 1954:373). This point needs careful examination through fieldwork. However, clown songs are confessions of "wrongdoings," that is, they are basically dealing with unethical (*qahopi*) behavior. Given that songs about old relatives frequently aim at their condition of being old and feeble, this might indicate that such condition is being perceived of as *qahopi*.

Example IV: "*Wupnaya*"

At least one clown song that has a Hopi keyword will be presented here because the monolingualism of this type frequently demands and allows humor strategies that play on ambiguities or subtleties within the Hopi language.[15] A few songs still operate exclusively on levels of traditional Hopi culture: they make no reference to any aspect of Anglo culture and its inroads into Hopi culture. The topics, then, may be marital trouble, sex habits, or *qahopi* behavior like laziness or gluttony. However, I choose to present an example here that plays on both Hopi tradition and culture change. The aspect of change, again, is alcoholism. This song was told to me, along with others, in 1988 by a man in his forties who lives in one of the most conservative Hopi villages. Being an initiated member of a high-order priesthood society and an active participant in Hopi religion on the one hand, and a Vietnam veteran on the other hand, he is clearly torn between two worlds, like many of his generation. Alcoholism easily results. I emphasize this point because to me the ability of Hopi society and Hopi individuals to deal with the dark sides of life in a humorous way denotes vigor.

To make the humor of this *tsukutawi* intelligible to non-Hopis, a few things have to be explained first. The background of the song is Hopi naming practices. Throughout life, a Hopi individual is ritually bestowed a new name upon acquiring a new social or ceremonial status. On the twentieth day after birth, a baby is named by its paternal clans-women. The names, one of which will finally "stick," refer to a typical trait or activity of the clan's totem—the animal, plant, object, or being that the clan is named after.[16] In our case, the clown performer had been named *wupnaya* by a woman of his father's Eagle Clan. This name needs to be explained as well. In early summer, Hopis go out to gather ritually young eagles that will play an important role in one of the major ceremonies. Held by a rope, a young Hopi male makes a risky climb down a steep mesa wall to an active nest. From there, the eaglet is hauled up to the mesa top.[17] The Eagle Clan name *wupnaya*—"they brought it up"—refers to that action.

It should be noted that there is no way to translate the following clown song adequately because part of the humor is rooted in the "textual features" of the Hopi original and is therefore lost in translation (cf. Kroeber 1981:3). Only Hopi listeners can perceive of *wupnaya* in various ways simultaneously: as a name and as an action. The lacking pronouns can also be read into it in several ways: "they brought it/him up"; "we brought it/him up"; "we brought you up."

Aa' ii', aa' ii'. WUPNAYA, WUPNAYA. Aa' ii', aa' ii', WUPNAYA, WUPNAYA. Aa' ii'.

   See, you think that this is the name of someone here in [the village] Y, right? Wupnaya.

   Well, that is ME! I am named like that! Remember, the Eagle Clan named me thus, Wupnaya ["brought it/him up"]. Now, it happens that I get drunk. And everytime that I get drunk I fall down somewhere. Out there on the west side [of the mesa] I fall down. And afterwards, they always bring me up from there. And then they always say to me: "Well, we brought you up!"

   That is the reason why my name is Wupnaya ["Brought him up"].

Aa' ii', aa' ii'. WUPNAYA, WUPNAYA. Aa' ii', aa' ii', WUPNAYA, WUPNAYA. Aa' ii'.

   Meh, umuy wuuwayaqw ura hak pan maatsiwa yep Y, nooqa'? Wupnaya.

   Pay NU'U, nu' pan maatsiwa. Ura pan ima kwaangyam nuy tungwaya: wupnaya. Pu' nu' yantingwu, nu' hoonaqtingwu. Hoonaqte' pu' nu' haqami posngwu. Iikye' taavangqöyva nu' posngwu. Pu' pangqw nuy wupnayangwu. Pu' pangqaqwangwu: "Pay itam wupnaya!", kitotangwu, hakiy aw'i.

   Paniqw oovi nu' wupnaya pan maatsiwa.

The clan name that was given to him when he was a baby turns out to be a description of his *qahopi* behavior as an adult. Hopis consider young eagles to be innocent and spiritu-ally pure. In the song this purity is contrasted with the profane impurity of the drunk man. There is clearly an incongruity involved that allows an ethical comment, but I doubt that this is the source of the humor. Rather, it is the construction of heightened congruity that makes the song funny: the clown explains that he usually falls down on the westside of the mesa, probably a little way down (this is of course an exaggeration, but in a way it may also be convincing because the villagers know that he really lives close to the mesa edge). And then they always bring him up (*wupnayangwu*) from there to the mesa top. What happens to him is exactly what happens to the eaglet he was named after. *Wupnaya*, indeed!

FORM AND PERFORMANCE: SOME STRUCTURAL ASPECTS OF CLOWN SONGS

The discussion of the four examples above has focused on the content and context of clown songs, trying to examine their humor and how it relates to the social and cultural background. Not much has been said so far as to matters of form, style, and performance. As I am neither an ethnolinguist nor a literary critic, I will make no attempt at an in-depth analysis of these aspects.[18] However, I will try to point out some basic structural features of this genre of literature, as well as some aspects of its verbal performance and audience response.

The text of a clown song (cf. examples 3 and 4) is the core of the performance. A skillful clown may increase the humor and success of a song considerably through a variety of performance techniques, while on the other hand an uninspired performance may waste even a good song (we all know this from joketelling). A self-confident performer may try to produce an air of expectation and excitement among the audience first. One time at Hotvela, I watched an older clown who made a big fuss when his turn came to make a confession. He went into a funny argument with the Warrior Kachinas, hopped up and down in feigned nervousness, and pretended that he had not prepared any songs. Sure enough, all the attention of the onlookers turned on him, and then he started singing his songs, and they turned out to be the funniest ones of all.

Each clown song is set off from the overall ritual performance by framing devices that clearly mark its beginning and its end. The text structure of the most common type of clown song shall be defined and presented here as a coherent sequence of four segments. Important aspects of performance will be treated in combination with the text. For an illustration of each segment, I will use the corresponding lines of example III, "Mississippi."

1. *"Aa' ii', aa' ii'*. MISSISSIPPI. MISSISSIPPI. *Aa' ii'."*

The first segment marks the beginning of the song and gives the keyword or key phrase. The framing device employed here is a chant: *Aa' ii', aa' ii'*. With this the clown informs his audience that the story will begin now, similar to a traditional storyteller who always starts off with the word *aliksa'i*.[19] In rhythm to this call, the clown jumps sideways and moves his arms up and down in front of his breast, as if he was shaking water off his hands. Then he halts and exclaims the keyword, usually twice. Then he jumps and shouts some more. On hearing the keyword, expectations will arise among the audience as to what the clown will make out of it and who it will refer to. A relative of the clown may anticipate (or even know) that he or she will be the target. An attractive keyword brings smiles and eager anticipation onto many faces; an air of amusement and curiosity—always crucial for the success of humor—is being set already.

Note that performing a clown song is called *tawma,* literally "singing while in a linear motion" (cf. Malotki 1979:346ff). Some clowns will make people laugh by making giant jumps in order to cross the plaza really fast without singing much. However, they never get away with this because the Warriors will immediately protest and pull the clown back. It is only the first segment of a clown song that is actually sung. The rest of it rather resembles an oration. At the end of a phrase the clown will frequently raise the pitch of his voice and stress the endings, for example, *lalva*YAY instead of *lalvaya.* This use of the exclamatory suffix *-y* is typical of prayers spoken in public ceremonies (Malotki 1979:379).

2. "*Suupan kya umuy wuuwayaqw.*" "I guess you think of it in a certain way." "*Meh, uma wuuwayaqw.*" "See, you think, that . . ."

MISSISSIPPI, WOODEN INDIAN, HUMPTY DUMPTY, HIGHWAY DINER, PETER MACDONALD, GOLFBALLS, KOOTSURU, AASOSI: no matter what the keyword is, most listeners will recognize it and have an immediate association as to its meaning. Of course, Hopis who do not understand much of their language might not know what *kootsuru* means, and some old Hopis may have never heard about Humpty Dumpty. In any case, the second part of the song serves to confirm the common association by explaining what the word really means (someone who didn't know before gets a chance to learn). The phrases above are two variations of how the clown addresses the expectation of his audience. To my knowledge, a form of the verb *wuuwa* (think) is always employed in this type of song. Next, the clown gives a short and serious outline of what the word means; for example, he identifies "Mississippi" as the well-known big river in the east. These factual statements typically contain the particle *ura* that has an evocative function (Malotki 1979:323), and that I choose to translate either with "remember!" or "as you will recall." All in all, the clown defines the serious meaning of the keyword that the hidden meaning will play upon.

3. "*Noq pay qa* PAM *i'i. Pay nu' yepeq X yu'yta.*" "But it is not THAT! I have a mother out here in (village) X."

Having evoked the actual meaning of the keyword, the clown immediately announces that this is *not* what he is referring to. He prepares the audience for a hidden meaning in the word. There are other ways of announcing the shift in meaning: "*Noq pay qa pas antsa,*" "But it is not really that," or, "*Noq pay qa put lalvaya,*" "But it doesn't talk about that." Next, the clown names the relative he refers to in the song (except when he sings about himself); "Well, I have a . . . (older or younger sister or brother, wife, mother, father, uncle, etc.). It is important to note here that the clown addresses two audiences at the same time that surround him in a narrow and wide circle: the Warrior Kachinas and the Hopi onlookers. On naming the person that he sings about, the clown usually locates that person in the audience and points in her or his direction. For example, when singing about his wife he might say: "*Pay nu' nööma'yta. Pam ayangqw tayta!*" "Well, I have a wife. She is watching from over there!" Right then, all the Warriors and the people in the audience will turn their heads in her direction. She may try to hide from the looks, covering her face with a shawl. In order to tease his wife and create laughter, a good clown will turn to the Warriors and tell them: "*Meh, pu'sa hamanti. Pu' hin unangwa'yta. Aqw huvam yorikya.*" "Look, only now she is getting bashful. She is excited now! Look at her!" In communicating with the Warrior Kachinas, a clown can make fun of them, too: "*Qa pas inumisatayta'a. Nu' pay qa uukwatsi.*" "Don't you stare at me! I am not your friend!" Talk like this adds to the excitement of a good performance.

Now that everybody has been informed about the keyword and the person it refers to, the task for the clown is to link the two in a humorous way. There is no limit to the humor techniques that can be applied in doing so; a small number of them have been illustrated by the above examples. Note that the song always exposes behavior or a trait that is (supposedly) typical of the person addressed. This is shown by the use of the habitual suffix -*ngwu* (cf. Malotki 1979:351).

The third segment of a clown song may be called the "build-up" of the joke, but frequently there is no clear distinction between build-up and punch line. Accordingly, the reaction to many songs is not one outburst of laughter, but rather laughter and mirth in various degrees at different parts of the song. For example, we have seen that "Home Run for the Black Sox" contains two independent punch lines. Or, consider the "Mississippi" confession: as soon as the clown mentions the *sisipi,* some people may realize what the story will be driving at, and start smiling or laughing right away.

4. "PANIQW *oovi pam* MISSISSIPPI. *Pam sisipi* miss*tangwuniqw oovi pu'.*" "THAT is the reason why she is MISSISSIPPI! She misses the chamberpot and . . ."

Although usually the hidden meaning of the keyword can be gradually detected while the clown is still "building up," the fourth part of the song may nevertheless be called the actual punch line or climax. It brings out the point, summing up the story and its humor in a nutshell. The pieces are being put together now, and the people can enjoy the humor to its fullest. The mirth created by a good song is more than just a response to a humorous stimulus (as some humor theorists would have it); it is also a sign of appreciation and admiration for the artist's cleverness and skill. "*Pay* IT *lalvayay.*" "Now, THAT's what it is talking about," the happy clown may say at the end. The joyous laughter blends with the noise made by the Warrior Kachinas, who hoot and ring their cowbells in approval.

A DIFFERENT TYPE OF CLOWN SONG

While most clown songs roughly follow the pattern described above, there is a slightly different type of song that needs to be mentioned briefly: instead of announcing a key-word, the performer starts with a question. In an abbreviated form, I shall provide one example here that was told to me by SA, a young clown performer from Kiqötsmovi, Third Mesa. This one also serves to finally illustrate the "raw stuff" mentioned above, those clown songs that center on sexuality and lovemaking and that are being enjoyed by Hopi listeners of all age groups.

Aa' ii', aa' ii'. How come when you get to a *burger stand* they always ask you: "*You want everything on it?*" That way it is very DELICIOUS! Aa' ii', aa' ii'. How come when you get to a *burger stand* they always ask you: "*You want everything in it?*" That way it is REAL GOOD!
　　　But it doesn't talk about that.

Aa' ii', aa' ii'. Ya sen hintiqw hak ura *burger stand* aw pituqw hakiy tuuvingtotangwu: "*You want everything on it?*" Yaw pante' pas is ALIningwu. Aa' ii', aa' ii'. Ya sen hintiqw hak ura *burger stand* aw pituqw hakiy tuuvingtotangwu: "*You want everything in it?*" Yaw pante' pas KWANGngwu.
　　　Pay qa put lalvaya.

The central part of the song follows the same structure as the type discussed above. In this case, the clown named his wife and explained that he unfortunately has a small penis. So, every time they start making love he puts one finger in there additionally, and his wife gets aroused. Finally, he puts two fingers in, and that's when she gets *all* aroused. The song concludes:

And that is the reason why it is so DELICIOUS when you "put everything in it"!

Noq paniqw oovi yaw hak *put everything in it*niqw yaw pas is ALIningwu.

It makes sense, doesn't it? Some Hopis may enjoy this story also because it ridicules a typical facility of white man's culture. Furthermore, it contains an interlingual pun, and "such puns are especially noted when one of the meanings is obscene" (Apte 1985:181): SA explained to me that he pronounced the word burger (in burger stand) in such a way that it sounded like *puuku*, a Hopi word for sexual intercourse (namely, "to deflower").

　　　Again, it shows that there is no limit to the topics and kinds of humor employed in Hopi clown songs, as long as they serve the purpose of making a confession, making sense, and making people laugh.

CONTINUITY AND CHANGE

I have presented Hopi ritual clown songs as a genre of literature embedded in an important religious ceremony. Along with their religious meaning as a form of confession, these songs provide humorous entertainment, cultural information, and ethical commentaries for bilingual Hopi audiences. While the creation of clown songs by Hopi individuals follows a conventional structural form, there is much room for the creative application of a great number of topics and humor techniques. A few of them have been discussed here in detail. The common denominator of the humor may be labeled "meaningful word-play": each song is based on an ambiguous keyword or key phrase, the hidden meaning of which serves to expose a (supposed or real) bad habit, moral weakness, or peculiarity of the clown performer himself or of one of his relatives. The analysis of several clown songs has shown that while incongruity is a frequent element, it cannot be said to be the essence of the humor; in some cases, humor is the result of heightened congruity (Eichinger Ferro-Luzzi 1990).

More than one man has told me that he has a good song made up already in case he is chosen as a clown someday. Until then, the song will be his secret. The art of clown songs, the ability to create laughter and provide meaning, comprises a number of skills: the clever and unexpected organization of the humor material and its link to some deeper truth (Leventhal and Safer 1977:341), but also a variety of performance techniques. The quality of clown songs is immediately evaluated by Hopi audiences through laughter and mirth; it is furthermore evaluated and discussed by Hopis after the dance. The best songs are remembered for a long time and may be told over again informally.

Clown songs both comment on and reflect changes in Hopi culture and language. Certain aspects of culture change can undoubtedly become integrated well into Hopi traditions. Bilingualism has opened a whole new field for creativity in clown songs. However, the question remains what will happen if the Hopis find no way to stop the current rapid loss of their language. Although it is possible to create clown songs in English, it must be doubted whether they could still be meaningful in terms of Hopi religion, ethics, and identity. The clown ceremony is an impressing symbol of what is happening in Hopi society today. On one symbolic level, the confessions depict what will happen on the Last Day (*nuutungk talöngvaqa*) when this present world will come to an end. There are varying clan traditions as to who will judge the people as well as on which criteria when it comes to that day. According to one tradition, it is the Aa'alt Priesthood Society that will judge:

Our old people talk about the day we will all be judged by the Ah-alt (Two horns). We will all be lined up in a single file.

Then we will be pulled one by one to be judged. The head priest will grab a hold of our hair and pull us toward him.

Then he will ask us: 'Are you a Hopi?'

We will nod our heads indicating that we are.

Then he will say to us: "If you are a Hopi, then speak to me in Hopi!"

If we know how, we will speak to the priest in Hopi. He will lead those who can speak Hopi to one side. Those who cannot speak Hopi he will put on the other side of him. This is how he will judge and divide us.

Now those people who can speak Hopi will earn a right to stay here on our land for awhile longer.

Those who cannot will be told to seek places to live elsewhere. (Hopi Mental Health Department 1983:48)

In a way, this separation occurs already, every time the clowns make their confession and sing their songs. Those who know the Hopi language and understand the songs are united in laughter and perhaps a feeling "of belonging," while the others remain outside: white visitors who may wonder what this is all about, but also a growing number of young Hopi who don't speak the language and know little about the clan system and the backgrounds of their culture.

Getting hooked on American television and video is certainly one of the major threats to Hopi language. However, as my last example will demonstrate, it can also be a source of inspiration for Hopi clowns who are keen observers of the world around them. The idea for this clown song told by SA had originated in a beer commercial on TV. The advertising jingle went: "Budweiser—You said it all!" In the song, SA transformed the jingle—a symbol of Anglo-American culture and its materialistic temptations—into a comment on unethical behavior (aggressiveness, bragging) that results from giving in to these temptations.

Aa' ii', aa' ii'. [sings] BUD—WEISER. YOU SAID IT ALL! Aa' ii'. [again] BUD—WEISER. YOU SAID IT ALL!

Well, you think that there is this white man's liquor, the one called BUDWEISER. Remember, they always sing that on TV: "BUDWEISER. YOU SAID IT ALL!"

But I am not talking about THAT! See, I have an uncle, he is called Bud. And he is NO GOOD, he is always drinking. And when he gets drunk he becomes real WISE, and then he wants to argue with you. So when he argues with you, you cannot say ANYTHING to him, so you just tell him: "Hey BUD, YOU SAID IT ALL!"

NOTES

1. This essay contains material from my forthcoming doctoral dissertation entitled "Changing Hopi Society in the Mirror of the Clown Ceremony." Fieldwork was made possible through funds of the "Deutscher Akademischer Austauschdienst" (DAAD). A sincere word of thanks is due to a number of people: Herschel Talashoma Sr. of Paaqavi, without whose knowledge and skill as an interpreter of Hopi language and culture this work would not have been possible. For the same reason, I extend my gratitude to Abbott Sekaquaptewa of Kiqötsmovi. Furthermore I wish to thank Sonny from Kiqötsmovi and all the other Hopi clowns who made me laugh (and sometimes shiver), and who shared some of their knowledge with me. I am also indebted to a number of scholars for valuable assistance, criticism, and a delightful conversation: Professor Armin W. Geertz, Dr. Louis A. Hieb, Dr. Emory Sekaquaptewa, Professor Alice Schlegel, Dr. Bernd Peyer, and Professor Peter M. Whiteley.

2. The Hopi today number approximately 10,000 people, the majority of whom live in eleven villages at the southern end of the Black Mesa massif in northeastern Arizona. The villages are situated on and below three mesa extensions that have been termed—from east to west—First, Second, and Third Mesa. The data presented in this essay have been collected predominantly in the Third Mesa villages of Hotvela (Hotevilla), Kiqötsmovi (Kykotsmovi), and Paaqavi (Bacobi), and in the Second Mesa village of Musangnuvi (Mishongnovi).

3. My native Germany is one of the centers of romantic Hopi worship, hence unqualified "pop literature" and pseudo-ethnography abounds. For an example, see Kaiser (1990), and the subsequent critique in Geertz (1991); see also Geertz (1987a). During a long interview session a young clown performer gave me an interesting Hopi perspective on Germans in Hopiland: "That's what sort of freaks me out. Everybody that comes out here, it's always a German! They always gotta . . . dig further. 'How come this happens? How come that happens?' (. . .) Germans are a dime a dozen out here. They come out here and they try to learn. LEARN, you know! Ain't nobody gonna tell them the truth." Fortunately he added, "I'm telling you some truth." (Either way, thanks for being honest with me, Sonny!)

4. According to Geertz and Lomatuway'ma (1987:47 n. 19), someone who is known to amuse others and make them laugh is referred to as "a person who prolongs his own life" (*pam qatsiwuphoya*) in that manner. Malotki (1991:66f.) provides a Hopi exegesis of the term.

5. Some major sources on Hopi Kachinas are: Earle and Kennard (1938); Titiev (1944: 109–129); Wright (1973); Hartmann (1978). For a Hopi perspective, see Sekaquaptewa (1976).

6. The clown ceremony has been described and analyzed by Hieb (1972). Sekaquaptewa (1980) and Lomatewama (1988) provide short accounts from a Hopi perspective. See also my forthcoming dissertation.

7. The topic of Hopi eschatology resp. prophecy is being treated in extenso in a forth-coming book by Armin W. Geertz. See also Geertz (1987b, 1989), and Hopi Health Department (1981–1985).

8. All the Hopi texts presented in this essay in translation and original were first recorded on tape and subsequently translated in the field by Herschel Talashoma Sr. The transcriptions and final translations are my own, based on the existing grammatical and lexicographic material of the Hopi language. A few of them have been checked and corrected by Dr. Emory Sekaquaptewa and by Abbott Sekaquaptewa. The responsibility for any errors, misspellings, or incorrect translation in the final product are my own.

The ortography used in the text is the one developed by Ekkehart Malotki on the basis of Third Mesa dialects (cf. Malotki and Lomatuway'ma 1984:340–343). Second Mesa Hopis may forgive me that the phonological properties of their dialects have been adjusted according to Dr. Malotki's orthography.

The English words in parentheses either replace pronouns in the Hopi text or have been added to clarify certain actions. Hopi key terms are given in italics in parentheses. Those words that were emphasized by the speaker are written in capital letters.

9. The art of song-satire is not an exclusively male occupation at Hopi, however. NI characterizes the confession as *tawsoma,* which literally means "song-tied." This term is usually applied to a type of satirical song that occurs in a different ceremonial context: The women of the important Maraw Sisterhood compose and perform songs that criticize in a joking way the *qahopi*

behavior of individual members of the corresponding Wuwtsim Brotherhood (Geertz 1990:327f.). Geertz presents a bilingual example of such a song. According to Voth (1912:56f.), "song–tie" (*tawsoma*) implies that the man who is mentioned in the song is bound to give a present (of food) to the women who taunted him. I have no information if such an obligation exists in connection with clown songs.

10. NI went on to explain the ambiguity that he had discovered in the word and how he might exploit it for a humorous description of his own *qahopi* behavior.

11. After I had finished this manuscript, Armin Geertz sent me a copy of a freshly published article by Ekkehart Malotki (1991). It contains an interesting brief section on Hopi humor, including three texts of *tsukutatawi* in original and English translation. They are fine examples of linguistic humor, exploiting the sound similarity of certain Hopi words.

12. The narration was recorded in 1979 by Armin Geertz. I wish to thank him for kindly letting me have the tape that contains the text and the field translation by Herschel Talashoma for my own use. The transcription and final translation are my own.

13. The causes and consequences of language loss, as well as how they may be counteracted from within Hopi society, are discussed in the four *Reports of the Annual Hopi Mental Health Conferences* (Hopi Health Department 1981–1985). See also Whiteley (1988:196). Malotki (1983:616–622) discusses phases and mechanisms of Hopi linguistic acculturation and provides examples.

14. *Tutskwa* means "ground, earth, land." Upon my question, Herschel Talashoma confirmed that the form *tutskwava* applies also to a river flowing "through the land." Consequently, *tutskwava* may be perceived as a pun in this case, meaning both "along the floor" and "through the land."

15. For further examples of monolingual clown songs see Malotki (1991). (Cf. note 11 above.)

16. Bradfield (1973, 2:26–35) provides a good summary and discussion of Hopi naming practices.

17. A marvellous photo showing that procedure is found in Page and Page (1982:199), along with a detailed description of eagle gathering rituals.

18. Kroeber (1981) provides an excellent overview of recent approaches to the textual presentation and interpretation of Native American literatures.

19. Compare the analysis of framing devices in one type of Zuni storytelling by Tedlock (1983:160ff.).

REFERENCES

Apte, Mahadev L. 1983. "Humor Research, Methodology, and Theory in Anthropology." In *Handbook of Humor Research,* edited by P. E. McGhee and J. H. Goldstein. Vol. 1: Basic Issues: 183–212. New York: Springer-Verlag.

———. 1985. *Humor and Laughter: An Anthropological Approach.* Ithaca and London: Cornell University Press.

Bradfield, Richard M. 1973. *A Natural History of Associations: A Study in the Meaning of Community.* 2 volumes. London: Gerald Duckworth.

Brandt, Richard B. 1954. *Hopi Ethics: A Theoretical Analysis.* Chicago: University of Chicago Press.

Brinton, Daniel G. 1975. "Aboriginal American Authors and Their Productions." In *Literature of the American Indians: Views and Interpretations,* edited by A. Chapman, 185–223. New York: Meridian Books.

Clifford, James, and George E. Marcus, eds. 1986. *Writing Culture: The Poetics of Ethnography.* Berkeley: University of California Press.

Deloria, Vine, Jr. 1969. *Custer Died For Your Sins: An Indian Manifesto.* New York: Avon Books.

Earle, Edwin, and Edward A. Kennard. 1971 [1938]. *Hopi Kachinas.* New York: J. J. Augustin. New York: Museum of the American Indian, Heye Foundation, 2d rev. ed.

Eichinger Ferro-Luzzi, Gabriella. 1990. "Tamil Jokes and the Polythetic-Prototype Approach to Humor." *Humor* 3:2:147–158.

Fewkes, J. Walter. 1977 [1892]. "A Few Summer Ceremonials at the Tusayan Pueblos." In *A Journal of American Ethnology and Archaeology,* edited by J. W. Fewkes, 2:1–159. New York: AMS Press.

Geertz, Armin W. 1987a. Hopi-Forschung, literarische Gattungen und Frank Waters' *Das Buch der Hopi.* In *Authentizität und Betrug in der Ethnologie,* edited by H. P. Duerr, 111–136. Frankfurt am Main: Suhrkamp Verlag.

———. 1987b. "Prophets and Fools: The Rhetoric of Hopi Indian Eschatology." *European Review of Native American Studies* 1:1:33–45.

———. 1989. "A Container of Ashes: Hopi Prophecy in History." *European Review of Native American Studies* 3:1:1–6.

———. 1990. "Hopi Hermeneutics: Ritual Person among the Hopi Indians of Arizona." In *Concepts of Person in Religion and Thought,* edited by H. G. Kippenberg et al., 309–336. Berlin and New York: Mouton.

———. 1991. "Hopi Prophecies Revisited: A Critique of Rudolf Kaiser." *Anthropos* 86:199–204.

Geertz, Armin W., and Michael Lomatuway'ma. 1987. *Children of Cottonwood: Piety and Ceremonialism in Hopi Indian Puppetry.* American Tribal Religions Volume 12. Lincoln and London: University of Nebraska Press.

Handelman, Don. 1981. "The Ritual Clown: Attributes and Affinities." *Anthropos* 76:321–370.

Hartmann, Horst. 1978. *Kachina-Figuren der Hopi-Indianer.* Berlin: Museum für Völkerkunde.

Hieb, Louis A. 1972. "The Hopi Ritual Clown: Life as It Should Not Be." Ph.D. dissertation, Princeton University. Ann Arbor: University Microfilms, 1986.

Hockett, Charles F. 1972. "Jokes." In *Studies in Linguistics, in Honor of George L. Trager,* edited by M. E. Smith, 153–178. The Hague and Paris: Mouton.

Hopi Health Department, eds. 1981–1985. *Reports of the (Annual) Hopi Mental Health Conferences 1–4, 1981–1984.* Edited by the Hopi Health Department, The Hopi Tribe. Kykotsmovi.

Kaiser, Rudolf. 1990. "Prophecies and Eschatological (Millennial) Traditions of the Hopi-Indians in Arizona." *Anthropos* 85:65–71.

Kennard, Edward A. 1963. "Linguistic Acculturation in Hopi." *International Journal of American Linguistics* 29:36–41.

Kroeber, Karl, ed. and comp. 1981. *Traditional Literatures of the American Indian: Texts and Interpretations*. Lincoln and London: University of Nebraska Press.

Leap, William L. 1973. "Language Pluralism in a Southwestern Pueblo: Some Comments on Isletan English." In *Bilingualism in the Southwest*, edited by P. R. Turner, 275–293. Tucson: University of Arizona Press.

Leventhal, Howard, and Martin A. Safer. 1977. "Individual Differences, Personality, and Humour Appreciation: Introduction to Symposium." In *It's a Funny Thing, Humour*, edited by A. J. Chapman and H. C. Foot, 335–349. Oxford and New York: Pergamon Press.

Lomatewama, Ramson. 1988. "A Hopi Mirror." *Native Peoples. The Journal of the Heard Museum*, 8–13.

Lorenz, Carol Ann, and Christopher Vecsey. 1986. "Hopi Ritual Clowns and Values in the Hopi Life Span." In *Humor and Aging*, edited by L. Mahemow et al., 199–220. New York: Academic Press.

Malotki, Ekkehart. 1979. Hopi-Raum. Eine sprachwissenschaftliche Analyse der Raumvorstellungen in der Hopi-Sprache. Tübingen: Gunter Narr Verlag.

———. 1983. *Hopi Time: A Linguistic Analysis of the Temporal Concepts in the Hopi Language*. Berlin and New York: Mouton.

———. 1991. "Language as a Key to Cultural Understanding: New Interpretations of Central Hopi Concepts." *Baessler-Archiv, Neue Folge* 39:43–75.

Malotki, Ekkehart, and Michael Lomatuway'ma. 1984. *Hopi Coyote Tales: Istutuwutsi*. American Tribal Religions, vol. 9. Lincoln and London: University of Nebraska Press.

Page, Susanne, and Jake Page. 1982. *Hopi*. New York: Harry Abrams.

Parsons, Elsie Clews, ed. 1936. *Hopi Journal of Alexander M. Stephen*. Columbia University Contributions to Anthropology 23, in 2 parts. New York: Columbia University Press.

Redfern, Walter. 1984. *Puns*. Oxford and New York: Basil Blackwell.

Schlegel, Alice. 1977. "Male and Female in Hopi Thought and Action." In *Sexual Stratification. A Cross-Cultural View*, edited by A. Schlegel, 245–269. New York: Columbia University Press.

Sekaquaptewa, Emory. 1976. "Hopi Indian Ceremonies." In *Seeing With a Native Eye: Essays on Native American Religion*, edited by W. H. Capps and E. F. Tonsing, 35–43. New York: Harper and Row.

———. 1980. "One More Smile for a Hopi Clown." In *The South Corner of Time: Hopi Navajo Papago Yaqui Tribal Literature*, edited by L. Evers, 14–17. Tucson: University of Arizona Press.

Shultz, Thomas R. 1976. "A Cognitive-Developmental Analysis of Humour." In *Humour and Laughter: Theory, Research, and Applications*, edited by A. J. Chapman and H. C. Foot, 11–36. London and New York: John Wiley.

Simmons, Leo W., ed. 1942. *Sun Chief: The Autobiography of a Hopi Indian*. New Haven and London: Yale University Press.

Tedlock, Dennis. 1983. *The Spoken Word and the Work of Interpretation*. Philadelphia: University of Pennsylvania Press.

Titiev, Mischa. 1944. *Old Oraibi: A Study of the Hopi Indians of Third Mesa.* Papers of the Peabody Museum of American Archaeology and Ethnology vol. 22, no. 1. Cambridge: Harvard University.

Van Maanen, John. 1988. *Tales of the Field: On Writing Ethnography.* Chicago: University of Chicago Press.

Voth, Henry R. 1912. *The Oraibi Marau Ceremony.* Field Museum of Natural History Publication no. 156, Anthropological Series 11(1). Chicago.

Whiteley, Peter. 1988. *Deliberate Acts: Changing Hopi Culture through the Oraibi Split.* Tucson: University of Arizona Press.

Wright, Barton. 1973. *Kachinas: A Hopi Artist's Documentary.* Original paintings by Cliff Bahn-imptewa. Flagstaff, Ariz.: Northland Press.

THE WRITING OF THE INUIT OF CANADA'S EASTERN ARCTIC

Perry Shearwood

he Inuit of Canada's Eastern Arctic use syllabics to write in their language, Inuktitut, unlike Inuit in other areas who use the Roman alphabet or, in the case of Siberia, the Cyrillic alphabet. The use of the syllabic writing system postdates contact with Europeans. In addition, many Inuit are literate in English and, in the case of Arctic Quebec, in French. The use of writing has made possible an emergent literature, important as both an expression of Inuit identity and a source of universal interest.

RELIGIOUS LITERACY

The first use of syllabics was for religious literacy. Missionaries developed the system to Christianize the Inuit so that they could express their belief by reading the Bible, the prayer book, and the hymnal. Syllabics originated far to the south of the land of the Inuit. In 1840 the Reverend James Evans, a Wesleyan missionary, began work at Norway House in what is now Manitoba (Harper, "Writing," 8; Murdoch). Based on his knowledge of Pitman's shorthand and his previous efforts to create a script for the Ojibway in Southern Ontario, he devised a method of writing down the Cree language. Evans translated religious material into Cree and built a printing press.

The use of the system proved popular and spread quickly. It was adapted to

Inuktitut by John Horden and E. A. Watkins, Church of England missionaries in the James Bay and Hudson Bay areas (Harper, "Early Development"). Horden was based in Moose Factory and used syllabics in his work with the Cree there. Watkins, after arriving at Moose Factory in 1852, then took up his post at Fort George (now Chisasibi in Arctic Quebec). He also traveled to Little Whale River and Great Whale River (Kuujjuaraapik) to bring Christianity to the Inuit there. He was at first reluctant to use syllabics but by 1856 introduced the Inuit to the system, using for that purpose a selection of the Gospels printed for him by Horden. This book is the first known to have used Inuktitut syllabics.

The syllabary was based on the concept that each character represented a consonant sound; the vowel sound was revealed by the orientation of the character. The four possible orientations in the early versions corresponded to what the missionaries perceived as the four phonemically distinct vowels of Inuktitut. A modification to the syllabary suggested by Horden was the use of a dot over the character to indicate a long vowel. In 1865, Horden and Watkins suggested the use of superscript characters to indicate syllable-final consonants, a solution similar to that proposed by Robert Hunt in his work with Cree.

In 1876 Reverend Edmund James Peck arrived at Little Whale River and, assisted by local Inuit like John Melucto and Adam Lucy, took up the work of translating religious material into Inuktitut syllabics and teaching the local people to read (Harper, "Writing," 14). In 1894 he continued his work far to the north when he established a mission at Blacklead Island in Cumberland Sound, near the present-day community of Pangnirtung on Baffin Island in the Northwest Territories. Peck devoted his life to translating the Gospels into Inuktitut and spreading the word about Christianity in his travels. In this he was assisted by local catechists like Luke Kidlapik and Joseph Pudloo.

In the vast reaches of the Eastern Arctic, proselytizing required extended travel, by dog sled in the winter and by boat in the summer. The spread of literacy preceded the arrival of the missionaries, for syllabics was imparted informally by traveling Inuit. In Maurice Flint's account of the missionary career of Canon John Turner, he describes a sled journey in the Igloolik area (43). In dire straits because of lack of dog food, Turner and his companion are fortunate to encounter the hunter Piugattuk. They camp together, and in the morning Piugattuk brings out his New Testament and asks to have various passages explained. Shortly afterward, he is baptized into the Anglican church.

The Roman Catholic church established a mission at Chesterfield Inlet, N.W.T., in 1912, and by 1931 a mission was built near Igloolik on Baffin Island. The Catholic priests also adopted the use of syllabics for the publication of religious material, but with some modifications of the Anglican system. There was competition and even hostility between the two religious factions. Previously existing family and hunting-territory relations were replicated and solidified in adherence to one religion or another.

Throughout the history of syllabics, a certain tension has existed between the view of this writing system as a necessary expedient in promoting the quick conversion of the Inuit to Christianity and the view of it as authentically Inuktitut and enduring. This ambivalence is more manifest in the Roman Catholic perspective. Charles Choque, an Oblate missionary of long experience in the North, commented at the time of the introduction of the new Standard Orthography for syllabics in the seventies:

The more we insist on using syllabics, the more we will lead the Inuk to believe that this system is linked to his culture, when it is only an outside contribution which is archaic and outmoded. The more we insist on using syllabics, the more we keep the Eskimo in a closed area, writing with symbols that set them apart from other Eskimos, in the East as in the West, the more access to literature, news, magazines, reports will be limited. (21)

Despite this viewpoint, all Inuktitut-language religious material in the Eastern Arctic is in syllabics, and no serious effort has been made to introduce Inuktitut material using the alphabet. Inuit identify themselves simultaneously as Christian and distinctively Inuit by reading religious material in their own language and in their own script. The relationship of this Biblical literacy to contemporary literature in Inuktitut has a parallel in North American and European literacy. Lockridge, in a comparison of literacy in colonial New England with that in the rest of the Atlantic world, identifies a widespread Biblical literacy in Sweden, Scotland, and New England that preceded formal public schooling: "In America as in Europe, in so far as literacy moved rapidly toward universality, the prime motive force was the conservation of piety (101)."

While the missionaries intended that the Inuit use syllabics for religious purposes, the Inuit soon began to use writing for interpersonal communication and archival purposes. For example, Therkel Mathiassen of the Rasmussen expedition, which visited the Igloolik area in the early 1920s before the establishment of a mission there, noted that most Inuit were using syllabics and often wrote letters to each other (233). Letters were entrusted to family members for delivery during their travels. The ease with which syllabics was learned and the frequent difficulty of face-to-face communication, given a nomadic existence in search of game over vast areas, combined to make writing a popular technology. This appropriation of syllabics for the Inuit's own needs presages the dynamic tension between a literature serving an Inuit audience and one for a larger audience whose concerns are the universally aesthetic or the anthropological.

THE ORAL TRADITION

Inuit culture has a rich tradition of tales and sung poems, and examples of these were transcribed and even scored by Europeans at the time of initial contact with the Inuit. Franz Boas, in his classic work *The Central Eskimo,* includes material he collected himself in his travels on Baffin Island, as well as songs collected by Parry and Lyon at the time of the first contact in 1822–23 between Europeans and the Inuit of the Igloolik area.

Boas compares these works musically to Indian and Chinese structures and Gregorian chant:

As to the contents of the songs, they treat of almost everything imaginable: of the beauty of summer; of thoughts and feelings of the composer on any occasion, for instance, when watching a seal, when angry with somebody, &c.; or they tell of an important event, as of a long journey. Satiric songs are a great favourite. (241)

On his epic journey across Arctic America, Knud Rasmussen also collected the poetry of the Inuit. The child of a Greenlandic mother and a Danish missionary father, Rasmussen was able to communicate with the Inuit of the Eastern Arctic in their own language. He had been trained in ethnography in Copenhagen, and his work and that of his colleagues is a monumental contribution to Northern studies. A work by Ivaluartjuk from the Igloolik area exemplifies the genre:

> Cold and mosquitoes,
> These two pests
> Come never together.
> I lay me down on the ice,
> Lay me down on the snow and ice,
> Till my teeth fall chattering.
> It is I,
> Aja-aja-ja.
>
> Memories are they,
> From those days,
> From those days,
> Mosquitoes swarming
> From those days,
> The cold is bitter,
> The mind grows dizzy
> As I stretch my limbs
> Out on the ice.
> It is I,
> Aja-aja-ja.
>
> Ai! but songs
> Call for strength,
> And I seek after words,
> I, aja-aja-ja.
>
> Ai! I seek and spy
> Something to sing of,
> The caribou with the spreading antlers!
>
> And strongly I threw
> The spear with my throwing stick.

And my weapon fixed the bull
In the hollow of the groin
And it quivered with the wound
Till it dropped
And was still.

Ai! but songs
Call for strength
And I seek after words,
It is I.
Aja, aja-haja-haja.
(Rasmussen 18–19)

Translated into English and detached from its oral performance, this rendering can only allow us to imagine the power of the original. For me, this poem evokes intimacy with the land in its harshness and abundance and the primacy of the hunt for the Inuit.

Work of this nature survives, particularly together with the drum dance. A contemporary example is "Song Composed for the Visit of Their Excellencies Governor General and Mrs. Michener to Igloolik, Mayday 1969" by Tamnaruluk (François Quassa), which is part of the collection *Paper Stays Put,* edited by Robin McGrath.

McGrath, in a recent critical essay, traces the publication of the oral literature collected by Boas, Rasmussen, and others and presents some of the poems in such a way that they are accessible to the general English-speaking reader, comparing them to poetry in English. At the same time, she puts forward an important caveat differentiating the contemporary Canadian poetic tradition and that of the composers of these poems (27). Traditional Inuit believed in the practical application of poetry in a manner analogous to the efficacy of prayer. To extend McGrath's point, language in this context had power that is of a different magnitude than that of the poems neatly ranged in an anthology. If we wish to call this literature, let us do so with a recognition that this is our category and not that of the maker.

THE MOVEMENT INTO THE SETTLEMENT

In the late fifties the Canadian federal government began implementing a policy of moving the Inuit off the land and into the settlement. The general policy was in response to factors enumerated by Chartrand: "first, the collapse of the fur trade . . . second, widespread famines and severe health problems; third, the knowledge of the existence of valuable resources in the north; and fourth, international geopolitical interest in the face of the Cold War" (241). Permanent residential housing, schools, and nursing stations were built. This enforced modernization was preceded by little or no consultation with the Inuit. In the Eastern Arctic, minimal preparation had come in the form of contact with traders, missionaries, and government agents, attendance at residential schools, and the publication of two volumes by the Canadian government. The federal Department of Mines and Resources published *The Book of Wisdom for Eskimo* in 1947 in syllabics and English with a revised version following two years later (Harper, "Writing," 31). In 1964 the Department of Northern Affairs published *Qaujivaallirutissat* or the *Q-Book* in syllabics, English, and Inuktitut Roman orthography (Harper, "Writing Systems," 44). These works fulfilled the didactic function on a secular basis that Inuktitut-language Bibles and prayer books had done on a religious one. While paying respect to the Inuktitut language and traditional ways, their main thrust was to reassure the Inuit that any change was for the best and should be accepted unquestioningly: "Some Eskimos say that the old ways were the best, but the life of a hunter is a hard life and there are not enough animals left to give the Eskimo all the food, clothing and shelter he needs" (Canada, Northern Administration Branch, 62).

TOWARD A PUBLISHED VOICE

Contemporary with the change in Inuit life in the Eastern Arctic was the appearance in publications like *Eskimo* (from 1946 on), *Inuktitut* (from 1959 on), and *Inuit Today* (between 1971 and 1983), among others, of writing by Inuit. The personal diaries kept as records of important events by Inuit and the transcriptions of oral narrative by visitors were the twin forerunners of these published accounts. Petrone, as part of her thorough compilation of Inuit writing in English, has described the underlying themes of these autobiographical narratives:

the importance of the family and the establishment of kin relationships; preoccupation with the seasons and the weather; the complex, rich, and sometimes terrifying spiritual dimensions of this life; the significance of psychic travel and dream visions; the love of story, dance, and song; and a sound respect for the practical and pragmatic. The theme most noteworthy, however, is the Inuit's unique sense of the land. (104)

In addition, people used their ability to write to respond to the experience of contact. Letters to the editor expressed opinions and suggestions about recent developments. The traditions, stories, and techniques, all at a greater or lesser risk of falling into disuse, could be preserved in writing.

Following publication in serial format was the appearance of books of Inuit writing. Initially these were often the results of collaboration between Inuit and Qallunaat, such as that between Peter Pitseolak and Dorothy Eber, which resulted in *People from Our Side* and *Peter Pitseolak's Escape from Death;* between Father Maurice Metayer and Nuligak, which led to the publication in English of *I, Nuligak;* and between Davidialuk Alasuaq Amittu and Bernard Saladin d'Anglure in producing the French-language

La Parole changée en pierre. Minnie Aodla Freeman recounted her experiences in southern Canada in *Life Among the Qallunaat.* The first novel in Inuktitut, *Harpoon of the Hunter* by Markoosie, appeared in successive issues of *Inuktitut* magazine in the late 1960s and was later translated into English and published as a book. As recently as 1983, the only book in syllabics to be written by a Canadian Inuk was *The Autobiography of John Ayaruaq,* published by the federal government in 1968 (Harper, "Writing," 31). *Sanaaq* by Salome Mitiarjuk Nappaluk was published in syllabics in 1984.

A common theme running through these works is survival or death in the face of an unforgiving environment. The terrifying descriptions of drowning due to treacherous conditions on the sea ice in *Harpoon of the Hunter* are typical. To survive in a harsh world was difficult, and thus the elders were accorded respect for their wisdom. A birth was to be celebrated, as in *La Parole changée en pierre,* because it meant the group would one day have another hunter:

Upon entering the igloo, the happy father had difficulty in hiding his joy for finally having a son. A future hunter could assist him one day, then replace him as the provider of game, who could also through the lives of children that he will procreate in his turn, perpetuate that of his ascendants. (Quoted in Petrone 219)

STANDARDIZATION

One question that must be addressed in considering an emerging literature as exemplified by the works mentioned above is whether a standard writing system is a necessary precondition to the establishment of that literature. Inuktitut syllabics was originally devised by those who did not speak it as a first language, and therefore certain infelicities were present. In addition, there were variations in orthography according to region and religion. Together with this was an attitude by those in positions of authority that the use of syllabics was a stopgap measure and the use of the Roman alphabet would be more economical in terms of typesetting and also permit wider communication, in that Inuit in Canada's Western Arctic, Labrador, Alaska, and Greenland already use the Roman alphabet to write their language. Tentative initiatives toward standardization by the federal government associated with the linguists Gagné and Lefebvre were received without enthusiasm by the Inuit, who saw them as attempts to replace syllabics, which had come to be regarded as authentically Inuit, with use of the Roman orthography.

Then, in the early 1970s, the Inuit Tapirisat of Canada, the political organization that represents the Inuit, approached the federal government for funding the study of the question of standardization. The Inuit Language Commission was created under the auspices of the Inuit Cultural Institute of Eskimo Point (now Arviat) in the Keewatin region of the Northwest Territories. Its mandate was to study the possibility of developing a writing system that would accurately reflect each dialect and yet be standardized enough to permit communication across dialect areas. Representatives of each region where Canadian Inuit live sat on the commission, and hearings were conducted across the North.

The standard orthography proposed by the commission was ratified in 1976. It is sometimes known as the I.C.I. orthography. It was now possible to transliterate on a standard basis between syllabic and Roman orthographies. (Eventually this could be done by computer.) For this reason the new standard has also been called the dual orthography. Vowel quality is indicated in syllabics by the orientation of the characters; while Inuktitut has only three vowels, previously there had been four possible orientations, one representing a diphthong. This column of the syllabary was now eliminated and the diphthong represented by two characters. Further, the use of finals was made standard. Syllable-final consonants in Inuktitut are lightly sounded. Given sufficient context, it is not essential for comprehension that they be written, and many older Inuit do not use them when writing. As well, a character was created to represent the voiceless lateral fricative in addition to the modification of other characters. The standard orthography was accepted with enthusiasm by government agencies, more reluctantly by the churches, and hardly at all by most older Inuit. The most salient characteristic of the standard orthography is seen as the compulsory use of finals.

Some older Inuit in the Baffin region (those born before 1950) wondered why the system had not been left as before and saw it as imposed from outside, that is, from the Keewatin. Others saw not using the proper finals as a limitation on their ability to write syllabics. People in this position have no difficulty in reading material written in the standard orthography. Younger people, however, reported finding it hard to understand writing by older people written without finals. I would suggest that writing without finals is appropriate to the most usual productive use of literacy by older Inuit, letters or notes to people they know, while the demands now being placed on syllabics as a language of publication and education make the use of the standard orthography almost a necessity. Collaboration between younger and older Inuit in the production of texts could bridge this gap.

INUKTITUT AS A LANGUAGE OF LITERATURE

Today, most Inuit in the Eastern Arctic have the choice of reading and writing in English or Inuktitut. The implications of this choice are considerable, and the matter reminds me of the controversy among African writers about whether to use African languages, as proposed by Ngugi wa Thiong'o, or languages of wider communication, as advocated by Chinua Achebe. Published material by Inuit has often appeared in both English and Inuktitut, with a potential audience of readers of both languages. For example, *Inuktitut* magazine [sponsored previously by the federal government and now by the Inuit Tapirisat of Canada) has in recent years been published in two editions: one in English, Inuktitut syllabics, and Inuktitut Roman orthography, and the other in English, French, and Inuktitut syllabics. The former edition is distributed free to households in the North, and a survey of Northern households revealed that 63.3 percent of individuals surveyed had received a copy as of 1983.

The magazine is read primarily in the North in Inuktitut (59.7%) and then English (40.3%). Of those who read in Inuktitut, 73.2% read exclusively in Inuktitut. Of those who read in English, approximately half also read in Inuktitut. . . .

     As could be expected, exclusive Inuktitut readers tend to be older Inuit of both sexes. Bilingual readers are mostly below 35 and read in English because it is preferred or faster than Inuktitut. Interestingly enough, only 16.2% are unable to read Inuktitut.

     A vast majority of respondents (95%) claimed it is important to publish materials in Inuktitut.

(Nortext Information Design 101)

My own recent research in an Eastern Arctic community corroborates these findings. Those surveyed who were born after 1945 will prefer to read bilingual material in English rather than Inuktitut, citing dialectal differences or greater experience with reading English. They tend to read more frequently in English than Inuktitut, although they do read in both. They are proficient readers in both languages, but reading material in Inuktitut has in the past been limited in quantity and variety. Chartrand has drawn attention to the key role played by language in the maintenance of a distinct Inuit identity (242). The role of literature in the maintenance of this identity is being addressed by recent action in the Baffin region.

RECENT INITIATIVES

In 1985 the Baffin Divisional Board of Education became the first Native-controlled board of education in the Northwest Territories. Building on previous initiatives in bilingual education in the region beginning in the 1970s, the board has developed an integrated Inuktitut program of studies for Kindergarten through Grade 9 called Piniaqtuvut. In addition, the board has published 130 children's books in Inuktitut syllabics by Inuit authors since 1987. About half of the books are being reprinted in the dialects of the surrounding regions for other school boards in both the Northwest Territories and Northern Quebec. More than 175,000 copies of the books are in the school systems or in production in the Baffin, Keewatin, Kitikmeot, and Northern Quebec dialects of Inuktitut and in James Bay Cree ("Baffin School Books").

     A related initiative is the Baffin Writers' Project. This locally controlled project, documented in two recent articles by, respectively, Sandy McAuley and Victoria Freeman, is using the technology of desktop publishing, strong community involvement, and visits by professionals, particularly Inuit and other Aboriginal writers, to jumpstart a literary renaissance. The project is publishing the journals *Kivioq* and *Titirausivut,* the second for student writers. An important element of the philosophy of the project is expressed as follows:

High-quality reading materials in Inuktitut carry two messages beyond their literal text. First, they imply that Inuktitut is as worthy a language to learn as any other that appears in attractive interesting-to-read books. Second, because those who write in Inuktitut are Inuit, sufficient attractive Inuktitut books in print suggest that being a writer is something to which a young Inuk can reasonably aspire. (McAuley 48)

An example of the work published by the Baffin Divisional Board of Education is *Akumalik* by Monica Ittuksardjuat. This beautifully illustrated and produced book, written in Inuktitut syllabics, tells the story of a young girl writing to her cousin and of her disappointment when the letter goes astray. Although *Akumalik* evokes themes of the importance of family relationships, the intimacy of camp life, and travel across the land, it is not situated in a timeless, traditional present. Instead, it is located at a particular point in the child's development and the history of the culture at which literacy facilitates interpersonal communication at a distance. Writing can be the means to constitute a subject both Inuk and modern.

The Inuit of Canada's Eastern Arctic have already made significant contributions to Canadian and world literature. As they look forward to greater autonomy with the formation of Nunavut in the near future, the importance of writing in articulating their destiny cannot help but grow.

ACKNOWLEDGMENTS

I would like to acknowledge the financial support of the Government of Ontario, the Northern Scientific Training Programme, and the Social Science and Humanities Research Council. I would like to thank the people of Igloolik, N.W.T., the staff of the Igloolik Research Centre, and my colleagues at Ontario Institute for Studies in Education. All errors and omissions are my own.

REFERENCES

Achebe, Chinua. 1966. "The African Writer and the English Language." *Insight* October–December 19–20.

Ayaruaq, John. 1968. *The Autobiography of John Ayaruaq.* [Inuktitut Syllabics Version]. Ottawa: Queen's Printer.

———. 1969. "The Story of John Ayaruaq." [English Version]. *North* 16:2:1–5.

1990. "Baffin School Books Marketed Across Canada." *Nortex News,* Spring 4.

Boas, Franz. 1969 [1888]. *The Central Eskimo.* Lincoln: University of Nebraska Press.

Canada. 1947. Bureau of Northwest Territories and Yukon Affairs. *The Book of Wisdom for Eskimo.* Ottawa: Bureau of Northwest Territories and Yukon Affairs, Lands, Parks and Forests Branch, Department of Mines and Resources.

———. 1964. Northern Administration Branch. *Qaujivaallirutissat/Q-Book.* Ottawa: Department of Northern Affairs and National Resources.

Chartrand, Jean-Philippe. 1987. "Survival and Adaptation of the Inuit Ethnic Identity: The Importance of Inuktitut." In *Native People, Native Lands: Canadian Indians, Inuit and Metis,* edited by Bruce Alden Cox, 241–255. Ottawa: Carleton University Press.

Choque, Charles. 1975. "Has the Eskimo Language a Chance of Survival?" *Eskimo* 32:20–21.

Flint, Reverend Maurice. 1949. *Operation Canon: The Reverend John Hudspith Turner.* London: Bible Churchmen's Society.

Freeman, Minnie Aodla. 1978. *Life among the Qallunaat.* Edmonton: Hurtig.

Freeman, Victoria. 1990. "The Baffin Writers' Project." *Native Writers and Canadian Writing,* edited by W. H. New, 266–271. Vancouver: University of British Columbia.

Gedalof, Robin, ed. 1980. *Paper Stays Put: A Collection of Inuit Writing.* Edmonton: Hurtig.

Harper, Kenn. 1983a. "Inuktitut Writing Systems: The Current Situation." *Inuktitut* 53:36–86.

———. 1983b. "Writing in Inuktitut: An Historical Perspective." *Inuktitut* 53:3–35.

———. 1985. "The Early Development of Inuktitut Syllabic Orthography." *Inuit Studies* 9.1:141–162.

Ittuksardjuat, Monica. 1988. *Akumalik.* Iqaluit: Baffin Divisional Board of Education.

Lockridge, Kenneth A. 1975. *Literacy in Colonial New England.* New York: Norton.

Markoosie. 1970. *Harpoon of the Hunter.* Montreal: McGill-Queen's University Press.

Mathiassen, Therkel. 1928. *Material Culture of the Iglulik Eskimos: Report of the Fifth Thule Expedition 1921–1924 Vol. 4 No. 1.* Copenhagen: Gyldendalske Boghandel, Nordisk Forlag.

McAuley, Sandy. 1991. "By Our Kamik Strings—The Baffin Writers' Project and the Process of Empowering Literacy." *Our Schools/Our Selves* 3.1:17:45–57.

McGrath, Robin. 1990. "Reassessing Traditional Inuit Poetry." *Native Writers and Canadian Writing,* edited by W. H. New, 19–28. Vancouver: University of British Columbia.

Murdoch, John. 1981. "Syllabics: A Successful Educational Innovation." Ph.D. dissertation, University of Manitoba.

Nappaluk, Salome Mitiarjuk. 1984. *Sanaaq.* Québec: Association Inuksiutiit Katimajiit Inc., Department of Anthropology, Laval University.

Ngugi wa Thiong'o. 1986. *Decolonizing the Mind.* Portsmouth, N.H.: Heinemann.

Nortext Information Design. 1983. *Inuit Culture and Linguistics Evaluation Study Report.* Prepared for Evaluation Branch, Corporate Policy, Department of Indian and Northern Affairs.

Nuligak. 1966. *I, Nuligak.* Translated and edited by Maurice Metayer. Markham, Ont.: Peter Martin.

Petrone, Penny, ed. 1988. *Northern Voices: Inuit Writing in English.* Toronto: University of Toronto Press.

Pitseolak, Peter. 1975. *People from Our Side: A Life Story with Photographs by Peter Pitseolak and Oral Biography by Dorothy Eber.* Edmonton: Hurtig.

———. 1977. *Peter Pitseolak's Escape from Death.* Edited by Dorothy Eber. Toronto: McClelland and Stewart.

Rasmussen, Knud. 1929. *Intellectual Culture of the Iglulik Eskimos: Report of the Fifth Thule Expedition 1921–1924, Vol. 4, No. 1.* Copenhagen: Gyldendalske Boghandel, Nordisk Forlag.

Saladin d'Anglure, Bernard. 1978. *La Parole changée en pierre: Vie et oeuvre de Davidialuk Alasuaq, artiste Inuit du Québec arctique.* Québec: Gouvernement du Québec.

Shearwood, Perry. 1987. "Literacy among the Aboriginal Peoples of the Northwest Territories." *Canadian Modern Language Review* 43:4:630–642.

POEMS AND SONGS OF THE CUICAPICQUE, CONTEMPORARY NAHUATL POETS

Miguel León-Portilla

Translated, with notes, by Willard Gingerich

Nothing could better serve as introduction to an initial group of modern poets in the Nahuatl language, ancient but still-living tongue of the Aztecs, than the words Miguel Espinosa Barrios, native teacher of Hueyapan, Morelos, affixed by way of introduction to the first issue of a newspaper which, with Robert Barlow, he began publishing on May 12, 1950. Introducing the distribution of *Mexihcatl Itonalama*, "The Mexican's Newspaper," he announced with obvious pride and a touch of exaggeration that the paper was directed to the "two million indigenous Mexicans who speak this language." We know now that the number of persons who kept this language alive in 1950 was slightly less than a million, while at present (1990) they approach one and a half million.

The significance of the words of Miguel Barrios is the manner in which they anticipate the contemporary renaissance among those who, having Nahuatl as their mother tongue, are now studying its grammar and creating its new literature:

Mexihkatl Itonalama has as its purpose the stimulation of reading and writing in Mexicano [Nahuatl] among the two million Mexican persons who speak Mexicano. To this end it will make use of descriptions of their customs, their traditional fiestas, dances, songs, dramas, and contemporary events—climatological and social. It will also publicize pre-Cortesian customs with the intent of showing that, in spite of the Spanish conquest, there remains an intimate line of relation from the past to the present. It will show that Mexico ought to be Mexico through the Mexicans themselves, since our ancestors gave the name "Mexico" to our country and a coat of arms to the flag that sustains us.

INITIATION OF THE NEW PERSONAL CREATIONS IN NAHUATL

From among all the songs and poems that began to be composed a little before Miguel Barrios would write the paragraph quoted above, and from other more recent productions, a selection is gathered here. Beginning with the identified creators of songs who wrote prior to 1950, I will adduce several poems from the work of the following.

Enrique Villamil (c. 1890–c. 1960) was also a native of Tepoztlán Morelos. He was a jealous guardian of the traditions of his homeland, among them those of the pueblos of Tepoztécatl. He wrote and published various works, some of great lyrical strength. Reproduced below is *Quenin ca in yolli,* "What is Life," and *Caxtilteca in Tenochtitlan huan tlacoltica yohualli,* "The Spaniards in Tenochtitlan and the 'Night of Sadness'."

Pedro Barra y Valenzuela (1894–1978), a native of Chicontepec, Veracruz, cultivated historical investigation and the study of the language as well as literature in Nahuatl. The scarcity of the facts concerning Barra y Valenzuela that have come down to us testify to the low esteem which until recently has been accorded anything relative to the language that was once the *lingua franca* of Anahuac, "the Land by the Seas." He published a book of poems in Nahuatl with Spanish translation, *Nahuaxochmilli,* "Nahua Garden" (México: Editorial Polis, 1939), as well as *The Nahuas, History, Life and Language* (ed. Bartolomé Brucco, México, 1953). From among his poetic productions I have chosen several of great sensibility which sing the marvels of the native fauna and flora.

Santos Acevedo López y de la Cruz (1903–   ), a native of Xochimilco, fought in the Mexican revolution and achieved the rank of lieutenant colonel. A descendent of Martin de la Cruz, the Nahua doctor who wrote on prehispanic medicine, he has been the chronicler of Xochimilco and author of a sizeable number of works about the city. He has published a volume of poems entitled *Macehualcuicatl,* "Songs of Common Man" (México: Vargas Rea, 1957). Several of his compositions have also been circulated through *Estudios de Cultura Náhuatl,* v. 15, pp. 237–244.

It bears mentioning that other songs and poems were also circulated by the newspaper, fruit of the creativity of the above-mentioned Miguel Espinosa Barrios, who sometimes used the pseudonym of Miguel Xochipapalotl Atezcatl. Also included in the paper were compositions of Macedonia Mendoza, of Xochimilco, author of brief poems characterized by their subtle irony and occasional veiled erotic overtones; María de Jesus Villanueva, of Tuxpan, Jalisco, who must be considered one of the last literary practitioners in the dialect of that region; Zacarías Sánchez, Leandro García, and other *cuicapicqui* of that fertile town of Tepoztlan; Eloy Alvarez of Cuauhchinanco, Puebla; Eduardo Rosas, of Acalpixca, D.F.; Victoriano Velasco, of Xochimilco; Marciano González, of San Pedro Actopan, D.F.; and Tomás González of Atlahpolco, D.F. As we can see, the number of those who continue cultivating the art of the *cuicatl* in Nahuatl is not as diminished as we might suppose.

A YOUNGER GROUP OF NAHUATL POETS

In more recent times a new flourishing of poetry in Nahuatl has occurred, owing to individuals in different regions of Mexico who, with dialect variations, maintain the life of this language. Among the motivations that impel the authors of this poetic activity to seek self-expression, two in particular stand out. One is to reaffirm the cultural identity itself; the other, to make it possible that living speakers of the language have access to a new literature, one near their own sentiments, concerns, and aspirations as felt by others within that same culture. Another characteristic that these modern forgers of song share is having had some form of academic preparation. Just as some have earned the title of Normal Teacher, others have studied at the National School of Anthropology and History or in the School of Philosophy and Letters of the National Autonomous University, Seminar on Nahuatl Culture, or in one of the provincial universities. It is important to note, however, that in every case we are speaking of individuals whose maternal language is Nahuatl and whose profound concern is to strengthen and extend it.

One such author of an already ample and widely recognized poetic corpus is Natalio Hernández Hernández, born in Ixhuatlan de Madero in the state of Veracruz. Since obtaining his title as normal teacher he has dedicated himself completely to the tasks of education as well as to the cultivation of his native tongue, which is Nahuatl in one of its Veracruz Huastec variants. Gifted with exceptional qualities of leadership, he has been one of the promoters and president of the Organization of Nahua Professionals, *Nechicolistli tlen Nahuallajtonaj Masehuallamachtianij.* Employed in the field of bilingual education under the Secretary of Public Education, he has sponsored the publication of Nahuatl grammars designed specifically for native speakers in a variety of dialects. To teacher Natalio Hernández we owe the following books, among others, in which his poetry is collected: *Xochicoscatl* "Flower Necklace" (Editorial Capulli, 1985) and *Sempoalxochitl* "Twenty Flower" (Universidad Nacional Autónoma de México, 1988). His creations have circulated also in newspapers and journals, including *Estudios de Cultura Náhuatl* from the National Autonomous University, and *Caravelle,* University of Toulouse. The acute sensibility to which his poems give testimony, as well as the intensity with which he often affirms the affection and pride he feels for his culture, have awakened á vital interest and appreciation in his ever-expanding circle of readers. We should add that Natalio Hernández has performed readings of his work in indigenous communities as well as in cultural salons, among them the National Museum of Anthropology.

Delfino Hernández Hernández, brother of Natalio, was also born in Ixhuatlan de Madero, Veracruz. He also earned the title of Normal Teacher and has followed a career parallel to that of Natalio. In addition to having worked for the Secretary of Public Education, teacher Delfino Hernández gives classes in Nahuatl at cultural centers sponsored by the Instituto Nacional de Bellas Artes throughout Mexico. (As a student in the Seminar of Nahuatl Culture of the National Autonomous University, he has approached the understanding of Nahuatl literature, in its classical form, with attention and zeal.) In his poetry and narratives, both exhibiting deep sentiment and a magisterial style, he stands out as one of the most distinguished creators of contemporary Nahuatl literature. His work has won him honors in a variety of literary competitions. Through the circulation of this work in newspapers and journals, including *Estudios de Cultural Náhuatl,* as well as through readings he has given in various places, he has become one of the most widely recognized of all authors who write in Nahuatl. We also owe to him several grammatical works, some for use in primary schools and others for advanced students of the language.

A native of Xalitla, in the state of Guerrero, Alfredo Ramírez, who holds a master's in ethnology from the National School of Anthropology and History, dedicates a part of his time to poetry. In his productions, where one feels the beat of inspiration from the ancient songmakers, the *cuicapicqueh,* feelings, images, and ideas flourish, reflections of his own ambiance and way of life. In comparison to other contemporary poets for whom Nahuatl is the maternal tongue, the poetry of Alfredo Ramírez conveys what one might call a more personal tone. No small number of his compositions are songs of sadness, modern *icnocuicatl,* "orphan songs," new jades that prove that the capacity for original literature endures even today in the cultural world of the Nahuas. Alfredo Ramírez, a former member of the Seminar of Nahuatl Culture, has published various of his works in *Estudios de Cultura Náhuatl* and in other journals and papers.

Many will be surprised to learn that, in addition to these three conspicuous contemporary Nahuatl poets, there are others—not a few—who are beginning to be recognized. I refer not to the well-known and already recognized masters of Nahuatl writing such as Librado Silva Galeana and Carlos López Avila, natives of Santa Ana Tlacotenco in the Federal District and known especially for their narratives, but to various others also from the Huastec region of Veracruz. I will limit my mention here to a small anthology titled *Xochitlajlolkoskatl: Poesía Náhuatl Contemporánea,* compiled by Joel Martínez Hernández, a teacher, and published by the Autonomous University of Tlaxcala in 1987. From its riches of nearly one hundred poems, I offer below a small sample. Looking upon such a rich stream, which grows by the day, one can only think of the prophetic words of that prehispanic songmaker who said, "My songs shall not cease, nor my flowers die; singer, I raise them up."

Of the new treasure of "flowers and songs" in Nahuatl those presented here in the original language and translation are only a sample. The history of modern Nahuatl literature and its rich universe of poetic expression awaits further study.

Enrique Villamil

Caxtilteca in Tenochtitlán Ihuan Tlacoltica Yohualli

Cuauhtemoc in aztecatl,
Telpochtli yolchicactic,

Tlatelolco Tlacatecatl,
Ca itlaquen pehpetlactic.

Ihcuac Cortes oacico,
Altepepa Tenochtitla,
Mexihca oquinchanhuice,
Moctezuma tzacualtitla.

Huan ocachtin tlacateca,
Teilpiloyan oquintlali,
Cuauhtemoc ihuan azteca,
Iciuhqui oquincentlali.

Man Cortes otlamihmicti,
In teopa Huitzilopochtli,
Cenca oquitlahuelmichti,
In yochicahuac telpochtli.

Oyec ompa in choquiztli,
Huei in yeztli ototocac,
Pampa open yaohuiliztli,
Huan yehua omocenmacac.

Man Cortes ocholohuaya,
Ca Popotla nahualtica,
Huan tlaxcalteca oyaya,
Oquinchiato nahualtica.

Ompa miac oquinmihmictihque,
Caxtilteca huan tlaxcalteca,
Cortes oquimohcamictihque,
Huan ocachtin itlacateca.

Ahuehuetontli itzintla,
Campa Cortes in chocac,
Huan mimique tlatzintla,
Tlapal yeztli ototocac.

Nochi tlen oquihuicaya,
In chalchihuitl in Mexihco,
Iman in oquintocaya,
Oquicatehque Mexihco.

Ica iyolo in cocoltic,
Cuauhtemoc in yaohtic,
Iyezmihmil oquipalehui,
Huan ihquion omoyolcehui.

The Spaniards in Tenochtitlan and the Night of Sadness[1]

Cuauhtemoc[2] the grand Aztec,
young man of warrior spirit,
Lord of Tlatelolco[3]
splendidly arrayed.

When Cortés arrived here
at the city of Tenochtitlan,
he seized the Mexica homes
and imprisoned Moteuczoma.

And other warriors also
he imprisoned as well;
Cuauhtemoc and the Aztecs
quickly assembled.

When Cortes led a slaughter
on the temple of Huitzilopochtli,
great anger rose up
in the valiant young man.

On the battleground
blood was scattered and sown;
commotion sounds
and they surrendered themselves.

When Cortés escaped
with all his Tlaxcalans
to Popotla by night,
they fell on him furiously.

Spaniards, Tlaxcalans
there they killed many,
terrified Cortés
and all the Spanish lords.

Under the ahuehuete tree
there Cortés wept,
seeing the dead laid out
and so much blood running.

So much fine Mexican
jade they carried,
but pursuing them without quarter
the Mexica recovered it all.

For strong was his heart
Cuauhtemoc, the warrior;
his race he sustained
and his people he pacified.

Pedro Barra y Valenzuela

In Huitzitzillin

Xochitic molinia ce chalchiujyojyoli:
quilcajtoc huitzitzili ihuehue tapazoli.

The Hummingbird

In and out of the flower flits
    a living emerald;
the hummingbird forgets its old nest.[4]

In Ocotl

Ixtlahuatl quipotonia,
tlapechtzotzoltic techmaca
tla itzoncal mocelia.

Cente cihuatl tlapapaca
ocotla itzintla, [Zen cualli]
Itonalcuica temaca
ipan iteno ameyalli.

The Pine

The fields fill with fragrance,
it gives us soft beds
when its hair renews.

A woman washing, washing
under the pines—so good;
she gives away her day-song
on the bank of the spring.

In Cacalotl

Ehecaticpac tzahtzi ica cualantli,
quipolotoc iozto
ipan yayactic tepetl ixilantli

The Crow

On the wind he squawks with irritation;
can't find his cave
in the mountain's grey belly.

In Zolli

Zacaitic nehnemi, nel mahmahui,
xinachtli tlapepena pan tlazolli
Huihhuitoni, tlehco, quen tlahuitolli,
huan ichoquiliz, pan ehecatl quiahui

The Quail

Through grass it goes, full of fright,
picking out seeds among the garbage.
It starts, it rises arrow-like
and its chirring on the wind rains.

Santos Acevedo López

Ixtelolotli Capollin

No nic itoa quenin mo ixtelolotli
Huelittiliz ome capolme,
qui no huelittaliz amaxocotl,
yohualli ihuan huel cemixquic tlampil huiloni,
¡Amo mo no nitla xoloxoatzintl,
mo nitla tlapochiuia, tetech acyohuac!

¡Ihuan quenin notiahui qui nitla chihua,
ihuan quenin tiahui nitla neltoca:
nelnozo manel ce nitla cuepa,
no nitenamiqui ocequi cihuatl! . . .

Moztla yquac tlahuizcalehua
mo nite chia tetzalan nopalin
ihuan nepa mo nicte ma no quiteotl
quenin no tiahui inic Nogales
zanye oncan nitla nitla tehuatza caztila hemilli
qui nahui yeica macuilli tomin.

Eyes of Cherry

They tell me your eyes
are like two cherries,
or like blackberries
in the night and any other hour;
Don't you scowl, little thing,
I'll carry you off in the morning!

And what do you know, what do you do,
and what do you think—

just as I turn and spin around
here's another lady before me!

Tomorrow at dawn
I'll wait for you in the nopales
and give you my farewell;
I'm off to Nogales, where
the toasted beans go
at four for five reales.[5]

Natalio Hernández Hernández

Nomaseualchinanko

Axkemaj nimistsilkauas nomaseualchinanko
nochipa nimitsijlamikis ika noyolo
nimits tokajtis ika nomaseualtlajtol
"Tlaltolontipaj" ljkinoj momaseualtokaj.

Noyolo mokuesoua kemaj nitlaijlamiki
kemaj nikijlamiki kalpolmej tlen onkayaya:
Tsapoyoj, Reyistlaj, Tlapani uan Mankojyoj
tlen totatauaj ijkinoj tlatokajtlalijtejkej.

Axkemaj nikilkauas kampa san noikxipaj ninemiaya
kuaojmej kampa nionkuajkuauiyaya,
ojmej kampa niouiyaya mila,
ueyojmej Kampa niouiyaya niontiankisoua.

Kuali nikijlamiki kenijki nimopapaleuiaya
Iniuaya sekinok telpokatlakamej,
ipan se tonatlj se ueyi mili tijmeuayayaj
ika miak pakililistli titokayayaj,
ika miak pakililistli tokistlakuali tijmaseuiyayaj.

Melauak yejyektsij kenijki nimoskaltijtiakl
papamej ika kualkaj nex ixitikoj,
akuajtajmej ika tiotlak nechkuikatikoj,
kayochi ika tiotlak nech majmatiko,
sakamistli nojkia ika tiotlak piomajmatiko
uan kemaya pioichtekiko.

Ika miak pakilistli nikintlachiliaya
xochimej tlen mojmostla ual kueponiaya
chimalxochitl tlen iuaya tonatij ual kauaniaya;
tlatokxochitl, kuetlaxxochitl, xiloxochitl,
teokuitlaxochitl, oloxochitl, sempoalxochitl
uan miak sekinok xochimej nikinjlamiki,
tlen onkaj hasta kenamaj ipan nomaseualchinako.

My Native Town

I'll never forget you, my native pueblo,
always my heart will remember you.
I will liberate you in my Indian voice,
"*Tlaltolontipa*"[6] I will call you.

My heart saddens with the memories
when I imagine again the barrios that were:
Tsapoyo, Reyistla, Tlapani, el Mangal—
calpullis[7] founded by our grandfathers.[8]

I will never forget walking barefoot
two miles to bring firewood,
two to go to the fields,
long miles to the market.

Remembering well how I assisted in the labor brigades
together with other young men;
In one day we could clear a large field,
and with great delight we planted,
with the same delight we shared the crops.

The truth is I grew in rectitude and grace.
Toucans woke me early,
the *akuajtajmej* sang to me in the afternoon;
the *kayochi* came in the afternoon to scare me,
the *sakamistli* also came in the afternoon
to frighten the hens
and sometimes stole them away.

With great contentment I observed
the flowers that bloomed day by day;
the *chimalxochitl*[9] that turned with the sun,
tlatocxochitl, cuetlaxxochitl, xiloxochitl,
teocuitlaxochitl, oloxochitl, cempoalxochitl
and many other flowers I remember now,
which even today still adorn my native town.

Delfino Hernández Hernández

Kauitl Ixayak

Yaluaya nimoitak ipan teskatl
kauitl kiijtlakojtok,
uajka mokajki telpokayotl.
Yolik ixmiktiajkej se uan se
nochi xochitl tlen ipan noyolo kueponiyayaj.
¿Nelia ueuekisa ni kauitl?

Amo, amo neli. Kauitl amo pano.
Tojuantij kena ax ouij tipanoj.
Tlaj tijneki tikitas ken tipanoj ipan kauitl,
xijpoua kexpa tepejtok xiuitl,
xijpoua kexpa monextijtok sitlalkueyitl eluikak,
kexpa istak astamej panotokej eluikak,
kitemouaj kanij momanauisej ipan sekuistlaj,
ouamili san kej ipa yaluaya uan namaj,
onkaj tlapatskilistli.
Yese ayok tlen tlamantli mokaua kej ipa.
Ichpokamej ueuiyak intsonkal tlen nechnauajkej
kemaj nipili nieliyaya, namaj nojkia tlaiskaltijkejya.
Ontlanesi, ontlanesi, sekinok tlakamej ualouij totepotsko,
nochi moyaualoua uan teipaj nochi moixpatla.

Time's Face [10]

Yesterday I looked in the mirror,
time has destroyed it,
my youth lies far off.
Slowly they lost their faces,
the flowers that bloomed from my heart.
Is it true that time grows old?
No, no, not true. Time doesn't pass;
We are the ones who pass through time.
If you wish to observe our passing
count the falls of leaves
count the appearances of *Sitlalkueyitl,* the star
count the passages of white cranes searching
across the winter sky for shelter.
The canebreaks look the same, but
nothing is the same.
The girls in heavy braids who once carried me
as a child already have their own fresh plants.
The sun rises and rises again; other beings
appear walking behind us.
Everything turns, and turning, all faces change.

Alfredo Ramirez

Zan Ce' Otli'

Nocniuhtzin,
¿tlin topan nochiua?
xniau, nanunca
uan xniaznequi',

quemantica'
caznonyatiaz.
¿Quemanon?
xnicmati'.
Amantzin
niau, ninenemi' uan ninenemi'
ipan ce' otli' ueyac uan patlauac,
¿uan tla quemantica' nipoliui' quen teua'
ipan un otli' ueyac uan patlauac?,
iuan tlaquemantica' tinechelnamiqui'
xnechtetemo' umpa niez.
Umpa nimitzchixtoz
xniaz umpa ninemiz.
Cuac teua' taziz campa ninemiz,
umpa timoyecnotzazque
campa neua' nitlayocoxtinemiz.

Only One Road

Friend,
What happens with us?
I'm not moving, I'm here
and don't desire to move.
But one day
perhaps I'll be going somewhere.
When?
I don't know.
Right now.
I go, walking and walking along
on a broad and long road.
And suppose one day I get lost
like you, on this broad, long road—
and if one day you think of me,
look for me, I'll be there.
I'll be there waiting for you;[11]
I won't leave, I'll be walking around.
When you arrive where I'll be walking,
there will be clean conversation between us,
there, where I'll be waiting in imagination.

Joel Martínez Hernández

¿Keski Nauamaseualme Tiitstoke?

Seki koyomej kiijtoua
timaseualmej tipoliuisej

timaseualmej titlamisej
totlajtol ayokkana mokakis
totlajtol ayokkana motekiuis
koyomej ika yolpakij
koyome ni tlamantli kitemojtokej.
¿Kenke, tle ipampa,
kitemojtokej matipoliuikan?
Ax moneki miak tiknemilisej
se tsontli xiuitl techmachte
tlen kineki koyotl.
Koyotl kieleuia totlal
kieleuia tokuatitla
kieleuia toateno
kieleuia tosiouilis
kieleuia toitonalis.
Koyotl kineki matinemikan
uejueyi altepetl itempan
nupeka matixijxipetsnemikan
nupeka matiapismikikan
nupeka matokamokajkayauakan
nupeka matokamauiltikan.
Koyotl kineki matimochiuakan tiitlakeualuan.
Yeka kineki matikauakan
tokomontlal
tokomonteki
tomaseualteki
tomaseualtlajtol
yeka kineki matikilkauakan
tomaseualtlaken
tomaseualnemilis
tomaseuallalnamikilis.
Koyotl achto techkoyokuepa
uan teipa techtlachtekilia
nochi tlen touaxka
nochi tlen titlaeliltia
nochi tlen mila tlaelli
kichteki tosiouilis
kichteki totekipanolis.
¿Tlen kichiuas maseualli?
¿Monenkauasej?
Moneki se ome tlajtolli
tiktlalisej pan toyolo
timoyoliluisej
tiixpitlanisej
tonejmachpan tinemise.
Miak pamitl tekitl tikixnamikisej

aman axkan san se pillajtolli tikijtosej
sen kamatl inmonakastitlan tikaxiltisej.
¿Kanke uan keski timaseualmej
tiitstokej pan ni Mexko tlalli?
Tojuanti tinauamaseualmej
axkana san sejko, amo san sikan, tiitstokej
tixitintokej, titepejtokej
pan kaxtolli uan se Estados
tiitstokej pan ontsontli uan chikueye altepeme
Yeka moneki tikkuamachilisej
axkana san tochinanko
axkana san toaltepeko tiitstokej
tojuanti tinauamaseualmej
nouiyan Mexko tlalli tiitstokej.
Kemantika tikitaj tikakij
timaseualmej titlamijtokej
tla tikitaj tlakapoualis ni tikitasej:
pan 1895 xiuitl tiitstoyaj 659,650
pan 1910 xiuitl tiitstoyaj 516,410
pan 1930 xiuitl tiitstoyaj 664,293
pan 1960 xiuitl tiitstoyaj 842,239
pan 1970 xiuitl tiitstoyaj 935,290
ok tikitasej keski tiitstokej pan 1980 xiuitl.
Yeka kuali tikijtosej
mejkatsa kinekiskia matipoliuikan
nauamaseualmej axkana tipoliuij
nauamaseualmej timomiakilijtokej.

How Many Native Nahuas Are We?

Various "coyotes" [12] (not native) have said
that we native people will disappear,
we native people will be extinguished,
that our words will no longer be heard,
our words will no longer be in use.
The heart of a coyote delights in this,
the coyotes pursue this goal.
Why, and for what cause
should they desire our disappearance?
It doesn't require much pondering;
Four hundred years have taught us
what the coyote wants:
Coyote covets our land,
covets our forests,
covets our rivers,
wants our exhaustion,

wants our life-sweat.
Coyote wants us to live
in the margins of great cities
and to live there naked,
to die there of hunger,
to be made the token of his manipulations,
and to be made the butt of his jokes.
Coyote wants to make us over into his wage laborers.
For this he wants us to abandon
our common lands,
our common labors,
our native labor,
our native language.
For this he wants us to forget
our native dress
our native mode of life
our native mode of thought.
First Coyote transforms us to coyotes
and then robs us
of everything that is ours:
of everything we produce,
of everything the fields produce;
he steals our weariness,
he steals our work.
What is a native man to do?
surrender himself without a fight?
It requires that we place
a few words in our hearts,
that we speak to ourselves,
that we let the light fill our faces,
that we live in consciousness.
We must confront many tasks;
for now we say only one noble word,
we fit a phrase for your ears.
Where, how many native people are we
living here in the lands of Mexico?
We Nahua people are not found
in one place, we are dispersed,
we are scattered in sixteen states
in eight-hundred-and-eight towns.
And so we must recognize
that we exist not only in our hamlet,
not only in our own town;
we Nahua people live throughout all
the lands of Mexico.
Sometimes we hear or we see

that we native people are diminishing;
but if we observe the census we see:
In the year 1895 we were 659,650
in the year 1910 we were 516,410
in the year 1930 we were 664,293
in the year 1960 we were 842,239
in the year 1970 we were 935,290
and we shall see how many we are in 1980.
So we can say confidently,
even though they wanted us to disappear
we Nahua people are not disappearing,
we Nahua people are flourishing.

NOTES

1. This song is written in the traditional ballad meter of the *corrido*.

2. The last native ruler of Tenochtitlan, who at age eighteen inherited the last desperate defense of the city against Cortés when his uncle, Cuitlahuac, died of smallpox. He would not surrender or even meet with Cortés and was captured on the lake attempting to flee when the entire city had been flattened around the last defenders. Coming before Cortés, he handed him his dagger and said, "Here, now kill me."

3. Site of the final defense of the city.

4. This haiku-like piece is reminiscent of Emily Dickinson's description of the hummingbird in #1463: "A Route of Evanescence / With a revolving wheel— / A Resonance of Emerald— / A Rush of Cochineal . . ."

5. One-eighth of a peso.

6. "Round-swelling Land," which carries implications of fertility and beauty.

7. Ancient Nahuatl name for the ethnic/religious/clan neighborhoods of which the Nahua cities were composed in pre-Columbian times.

8. Perhaps truer than even the poet knows; modern names of barrio neighborhoods in several villages in the state of Puebla have been identified in early sixteenth-century native land record codexes for those villages—records far more precise and carefully measured, by the way, than anything created by contemporary Spanish surveyors.

9. Sunflower; lit. "shield flower"

10. Reminiscent of Yeats's "Wild Swans at Coole."

11. Whitman, "Song of Myself," section 52: "I stop somewhere, waiting for you."

12. This Mexican "coyote" is quite different from the trickster of western U.S. stories and has his own tradition.

PART 2

Authors and Issues

MYSTERY NOVELS TO CHOCTAW PAGEANT

Todd Downing and Native American Literature(s)

Wolfgang Hochbruck

A s the importance of ethnic minority texts gradually increases in American literature, the question of which texts should be considered part of an ethnic literary tradition becomes unavoidable. Knowing that no single definition will account for all possibilities and satisfy everybody, this essay will still try to provide a working platform from which to evaluate the relatedness of texts to that body of texts for which the term Native American literature is currently the most frequently used. It will therefore outline some of the problems connected with an attempt to define Native American literature and then proceed to suggest a solution.

THE (RE-)SEARCH FOR NATIVE AMERICAN LITERATURE

Point One: Native American literature did not exist before Scott Momaday's *House Made of Dawn*. This may sound odd since authors of American Indian descent like John Rollin Ridge, Mourning Dove, and D'Arcy McNickle had published novels and short fiction before Momaday was even born. However, they hardly received a substantial critical response to their works. "Native American literature" was not perceived as an interrelated corpus of texts. Therefore, when *House Made of Dawn* won the Pulitzer Prize for fiction, it was ubiquitously hailed as the first novel by a Native American. The book triggered off a host of publications by Native American authors, so the tag is still fitting in that it preceded a new subcategory of ethnic writing. In terms of literary history, the tag of "first Native American novel" has since been tugged upstream and is now docked at John Rollin Ridge's *Life of Joaquin Murieta* (1857); the earliest literary texts written by Native Americans that we know of today date back to the 1600s. What this means is that the corpus of texts subsumed under Native American literature is expanding in two directions. Not only are authors constantly adding new texts, but other, earlier texts are also being republished and made available, some of them, like Ella Deloria's novel *Waterlily,* for the first time. For Native American literature, therefore, literary history proceeds both ways from *House Made of Dawn.* Any attempt to discuss contemporary and particularly older Native American texts in the context of their literary history must necessarily also take into account their (post-)colonial context.

Point Two: When in the 1970s scholars started looking for pre-Momaday specimens of "Native American literature," they usually followed the "paramount storyline" (Clifton 1989:31)[1] adopted by many anthropologists and other scholars, which lamented the inevitable destruction of Native American communities. Unwillingly continuing the stereotype which saw Native Americans in the arts as limited to "Indian" material culture, folklore, and the oral tradition, they usually combined a biographical approach with a search for "Indian" topics. The results were predictable. In the first major study on Native American fiction, Charles Larson (1978) unearthed several novels of doubtful authorship while overlooking a number of other books like John Rollin Ridge's *The Life of Joaquin Murieta* (1857), a populistic piece of cloak-and-dagger fiction with hardly any "Indian" content. There are—horribile dictu—some rather condescending passages about the comically uncivilized "Digger" Indians. According to the rules set by the post-1960 paramount storyline, *Murieta* hardly qualifies as Native American literature at all. The question of "Indian" vs. non-"Indian" material, setting, and plot constitutes yet another problem in identifying the corpus of literary texts called Native American literature. In the second wave of research for Native American texts, the usual approach taken was biographical. If authors claimed or were found to be of Native heredity, their products were considered to be Native American literature.

Point Three: The biographical approach brought up the question of who is an "Indian" author, a question that by its own phrasing fails to pay proper attention to the fact that many Native Americans identify themselves as members of their own nation, but not as "Indians" nor as Americans or Canadians (Feest 1983:93ff). The term "Indian" authorship presupposes a pan-Indian body of literary texts as well as a concept of intertribal or metatribal sense of identity with the open space between the tribes being inhabited by individuals who live a pan-Indian identity with no particular tribal affiliation. Scott Momaday's belief that "an Indian is an idea which a given man has of himself" (1975:79) involuntarily left additional space for "Indian" authors like Jamake Highwater, who certainly was a result of his own idea of himself.[2]

The problem, it seems, is not easy to solve. In another attempt to come to terms with "Native American (respectively Canadian) literature," Thomas King, in his introduction to the first anthology of Canadian Native fiction, cautiously suggested: "Perhaps our simple definition that Native literature is literature produced by Natives will suffice for the while providing we resist the temptation of trying to define a Native" (1986:5). This fairly broad definition, however, leads to the classification of Canadian Métis authors with Native Indians regardless of their different ethnic self-image. Arnold Krupat's approach is certainly more pertinent. Krupat suggests that "Indians must be culturally Indian, with such cultural 'identity' not wholly a random or arbitrary choice (e.g., the Indian person having some actual heredity link to persons native to America)" (1990:207). Pointing in the same direction is a definition formulated by Brian Swann, stating, "Native Americans are Native Americans if they say they are, and"—and this appears to be the crucial point in a societal form that still relies more on the community than on the individual—"if other Native Americans say they are and accept them" (1988:xx).

Attempting to eliminate an author's Native heredity as one of the constituting factors of North American Native literature does not seem to make much sense (even though some of the biographical studies in James Clifton's *Being and Becoming Indian* [1989] seem to point in this direction). There is, however, ample reason to relativize the importance of "blood" as a literary kinship marker. The idea that a certain "blood" percentage (however inadequately measured) or blood relationship alone shape an author's perception of the world bears (at least to a German critic like myself) unpleasantly racist implications. To add to the confusion, some authors like Frank Waters, who has been said to be "part Indian" (Adams 1987:935) or to have "a small part Cheyenne blood" (Davis 1976/77:62) or not to be of Indian ancestry at all (Cook 1977:4) have never expounded on their Indian bloodline, while authors of black and Indian mixed descent like Alice Walker are usually categorized as "black." Certainly in most of her works Alice Walker's commitment is unilaterally with black Americans, leaving no doubt but that she rightfully should be placed with the Afroamerican literature section. But Melba Boyd's essay on Walker's novel *Meridian* (Boyd 1990) casts some doubt on this sort of categorization, at least as far as *Meridian* is concerned. Boyd uses the term "mestizo" for persons of mixed ethnic origin like Walker and herself who are "living on the edge of American ambiguity" (115). Rather than introduce new interethnic terminology, Fredrik Barth in his study *Ethnic Groups and Boundaries* observed that given certain conditions a person may change his or her ethnic affiliation (1969:21ff). More conceiveably in the context of literature, a person of mixed origin may choose to write one text from the perspective of one group of his/her origin, and another text from a second or even third. With reference to the definition of Native American literature, this would suggest a focus on individual books.

But even with useful definitions (like the ones by Krupat and Swann) to identify

Native American authors, the question of Native American texts remains rather open. As far as contemporary literary efforts are concerned, Arnold Krupat again offers a definition that appears useful, but focuses primarily on the conditions of literary production:

> *Indigenous literature* I propose as the term for that form of literature which results from the *interaction* of local, internal, traditional, tribal, or "Indian" literary modes with the dominant literary mode of the various nation-states in which it may appear. Indigenous literature is that type of writing produced when an author of subaltern cultural identification manages successfully to merge forms internal to his cultural formation with forms external to it, but pressing upon, even seeking to delegitimate it. (Krupat 1989:214)

While the above definition would also rule out many early texts written by Native missionaries and students, it would still include works like Momaday's dissertation on the American poet Frederick Goddard Tuckerman, who influenced Momaday's poetry. One result of the interaction between dominant culture and indigenous person not covered by Krupat's definition is also scholarly books or articles written by authors with Indian forebears. In contrast, Jack Forbes's attempt to see as contemporary Indian literature mainly "the discourse appearing in 'Indian published periodicals'—poetry and fiction, some of the time, to be sure, but most often nonfictional, topical writing" (in Krupat 1990:206)[3] would exclude most of the novels, poetry, and short fiction commonly being read (and taught in classes) as "Native American literature."

Furthermore, one of the basic principles of Native American societies has always been to place community before the individual. So what if a piece of literature is specifically aimed at a readership that does not perceive of the author as homeless, be it transcendentally or not? If Native American Indian social life is more community-oriented than Euroamerican social life, should not, then, the question of what is and what is not Native American literature be approached from the same angle? By analogy to Swann's definition of "Indian," a piece of Native American literature would have to proclaim itself to belong with this group of texts, and it would have to be accepted as such by Native Americans or even Native American communities. Perhaps looking at the whole problem from the perspective of the individual piece of literature and its intended interpretive community or communities (Schöler 1987:27; Fish 1980:331) might provide a workable solution. At the same time it should of course be kept in mind that the response by the respective interpretive communities also plays a role in the creation not only of narrative meaning, but also in the grouping of a text within a class or section of literature or outside it. Lastly, conventions of genre (which in turn depend on the expectations of the intended audience) shape a text. Together, the criteria of intention, genre, and response should provide a workable basis from which to evaluate texts.

This (to some extent provisional) essay will therefore attempt to approach the problem of defining Native American Literature on the basis of the individual text. In doing so, it will (re-)introduce Todd Downing (1902–74), who was a remarkable man of letters, scholar, and teacher of Choctaw descent and whose career in writing spans not only fifty years but also a variety of genres.[4]

THE WRITING CAREER OF TODD DOWNING

Todd Downing, born in 1902 to a well-to-do family in Atoka, Oklahoma (in 1902 still in the Choctaw Nation), was an enrolled member of the Choctaw Nation and spoke Choctaw fluently (Smith 1983:247ff). With nine mystery novels published between 1933 and 1941 (Hagen 1969:123) and numerous other publications Todd Downing remains one of the most prolific Native authors to the present day.

Downing's career as an author included many different kinds of writing for a variety of audiences or interpretive communities. As a student at the University of Oklahoma, he wrote a gossip column for the Oklahoma Daily under the pen-name "Professor Hoople." His M.A. thesis won a national prize and the annual award of the Institute de las Españas for excellence in Spanish studies. From 1927 to 1934, Downing worked as business manager and review author for *Books Abroad*. The first review he wrote touched on a Native American subject, but this may well have been coincidence (Downing 1927:26). Not until the later years of Downing's employment with *Books Abroad* do his articles show a focus of interest on two particular fields, one of them being the mystery novel, the other being Mexico, with special attention to Indian cultures. In his crime novels, Downing combined the two; all except *Death Under the Moonflower* use Mexico for at least part of their setting (Hubin 1984:122). The Indian content of his first novel, *Murder on Tour* (Downing 1933), however, is limited to Aztec waitresses, the ruins of Toltec and other Mexican cultures, and the fact that the murderers have also been stripping ancient gravesites. Their robbery not only means the loss of archaeological material, but also enhances the danger of an Indian uprising:

Among the ignorant ones, the country people, there are strange rumors. In Oaxaca the story goes about that the old kings are returning after their sleep of centuries—to sit upon their thrones. It is said that in Tzintzuntzan the Tarascans wait for their ancient capital to be established again. You understand . . . the danger—to us. (Downing 1933:73)

The case is solved in time to prevent a possible uprising of Indians and other "ignorant ones," an attitude that reminds one of John Rollin Ridge's "Digger" (Miwok) Indians in *Murieta*. As it is, nothing in *Murder on Tour* would indicate or make the reader guess that the author himself could be of Indian descent.

The Cat Screams (Downing 1934) is different. Downing achieves density of structure by limiting the story's space and the number of characters, and he creates atmosphere largely through the use of Mexican Indian folklore, including allusions to a possibly supernatural background to the several ghastly murder cases. The witchcraft-world of Indian *brujos* and *curanderas* is present throughout. A small clay figure of the Mexican god Xipe plays a significant role in the solution of the case, and Indian myths and cultures are treated with reverence, even though the servant boy whose illness confines the characters of the novel to their quarantined hotel dies not of a curse but acute appendicitis. With the density of its form, its respectful treatment of indigenous material and its rather hideous drug-related killings, *The Cat Screams* reads like a predecessor of Tony Hillerman's novels in topic and form if not in style and tone. The main difference from Hillerman's novels is that the main protagonist is white: "A man with a white skin, he [the detective Hugh Rennert] told himself, had no business thinking in this country" (1933:121). The difference is one of genre convention and audience expectations. Hillerman (non-Native) is able to use characters like Joe Leaphorn and Jim Chee because under 1970s and '80s conditions his national and international audience will accept them as amiable and believable. Downing (Native) depicted Hugh Rennert (who appears in *Murder on Tour* as well) as interested in Mexican cultures and able to speak "the soft Mexican tongue" (1933:64) but apparently guessed that his audience would accept a police officer of Indian origin only in the form of a slightly comical Mexican: "Backed against the wall of the washroom was the Aldamas police officer who looked like a pureblood Indian, acted like an Andalusian and was named Miguel O'Donojú which is Spanish for Michael O'Donohue" (Downing 1941:221ff).

   The Cat Screams was Downing's most successful book; it was not only chosen as a selection for The Crime Club but also republished in Great Britain, Sweden, and Germany. Unfortunately, Downing did not continue in the vein of *The Cat Screams* but reverted to mysteries more like *Murder on Tour,* the last of which was *The Lazy Lawrence Murders,* published in 1941. After his contract with Doubleday had expired, Downing worked as an advertising copywriter and edited *Pan Americanismo,* the monthly magazine of the Pan-American Association of Philadelphia (Smith 1983:247).

   For the purposes of this essay it is important to notice that so far all of Downing's writings had been aimed either at specialized groups (students, readers of foreign books) or at a national and international audience. None of the published works discussed bears any marks by which the reader could have identified Downing as Native American. Epistemological or discourse structures denoting Downing's Choctaw experience are simply absent. This does not mean to imply that Downing ever tried to deny the Choctaw part of his heritage; he was, for example, a member of Okla-she-da-ta-ga, the Indian club of the University of Oklahoma. This Choctaw side is just never mentioned on the book covers or in the texts. *The Cat Screams* does suggest an intimate knowledge of Indian material but contains no direct or indirect indication of its author's ethnic background. Writing for different audiences as he did, Downing was held by the expectations of these audiences and the genre conventions of his time.

   In 1940 Doubleday published Downing's first volume-length piece of nonfiction. *The Mexican Earth* (1940) is not so much a travel account as an Indian history of Mexico.

What is new in terms of the relationship between reader, author, and text is that in *The Mexican Earth* Downing identifies himself as a Native person. The particular sequence relates his encounter with an American student of the Aztec language and indigenous art in the summer school of the National University of Mexico:

> The high light of her day seemed to be the time she had joined ("horned in on" I would have said) a family of Indians at their midday meal. . . . "I hate to think of going back home," she told me over her filet mignon. "I'd like to live down here, where I could be with Indians all the time. I think it's wonderful—the way they're coming into their own." And on and on. . . . I said: "You have Indians out in California, don't you?" She frowned. "Oh, that's different. They're not—well, yes, I guess they are the same race. But—" The young man who was my host rattled silverware and introduced a new topic of conversation. . . . Later, in his room, he laughed and said to me: "Miss Blank is quite a card, isn't she? Uh—you understood she was just kidding you, of course. She knew all the time that you're Indian yourself." (Downing 1940:9ff)

In this passage Downing takes sides, and he chooses the side of the indigenous Mexicans. The problem he addresses, however, is not so much one of personal identity but of that peculiar position the "Indian" holds in society.

> Indian. *Mestizo*. White. In these days of so much chest thumping and shouting in parade-ground voices about race, it seems futile to try to get in a sane word on the subject, even if that word be confined to the problems of Mexico. Paradoxically, consideration of the question there is made more difficult by the fact that, so far as the American tourist is concerned, surface appearances show the question to be settled fair and square and to the greater glory of the Indian. He has been "taken up" enthusiastically, his virtues worried out of him and extolled. The Americans who were so articulate during the Díaz dictatorship thirty years ago still stay with the beer and skittles of the changeless American colony but are seldom heard from now. Yet I find an individual of this passé type only a little more irksome than the one who puts too much effort into letting the world know that he is free of prejudice. At home he exclaims loudly: "Why, some of my best friends are Jews!" In Mexico he waxes sentimental over every pot in a market place, defective or not, simply because it is Indian. His words do not ring true to an Indian of Oklahoma. I doubt that they do to an Indian of Mexico. (8–9)

Downing sums up his contemplations: "The person likely to be most free of prejudice is the one who is unconcernedly silent about race and nationality and creed" (9). This, apparently, was his ideal.

Downing considered *The Mexican Earth* to be his most important book, and the National Library of Mexico called it "one of the best books published in English about Mexico" (Bolen 1973). *The Mexican Earth* was aimed at a national audience (as were Downing's crime novels), but in terms of genre conventions its form was more open to personal statements. Calling attention to the fact that the author himself is an Oklahoma Indian, Downing pointedly draws a line of difference between himself and his audience. Read as a book by an American Indian author, *The Mexican Earth* belongs to a different field of literary experience than the crime novels by the same author, whose Indian identity is not mentioned. With *The Mexican Earth* Downing joined those Native American authors that like him and before him had tried to educate a generally non-Native readership about Indian problems and issues.

According to one source (Gridley 1947:33) Downing was writing a non-mystery novel in the early 1940s. The manuscript appears to have been lost after Downing's death in 1974, so there is no way to tell whether it touched on Native issues and used Indian characters or not. Either he did not complete it or it suffered the same fate as Ella Deloria's *Waterlily* and was rejected by the publishers. The 1940s and '50s apparently were not particularly suited for the publication of novels by Native American authors, let alone the establishment of the Native American novel as a distinct ethnic genre. Even though the first decades of the century had seen an upsurge in Native American literary activity, "creative writing played only a small role in Indian literature until the later 1960s" (Peyer 1990:vii). Authors like John Milton Oskison, John Joseph Mathews, and D'Arcy McNickle had published during the 1920s and '30s, and then they were not identified as Native American authors on the dust jackets of their books (Larson 1978:3). On a national scale, a pan-Indian readership hardly existed, and the very sort of romantic racism Downing criticized in *The Mexican Earth* prevented the recognition of the increasing number of texts by authors of Indian descent. Publishers and general audience likewise could or would not conceive of American Indians as authors of novels.

In Oklahoma, things were somewhat different. A large percentage of the population was either Native Indian or of tribal descent, and after more than a hundred years of tribal written culture, Native American literary production was apparently taken for granted. Considerable numbers of Indian readers also meant that Oklahomans took notice of the efforts of Native authors. In 1936, an article in the *Chronicles of Oklahoma* by Muriel Hazel Wright, herself a noted Choctaw historian, had mentioned Todd Downing alongside Will Rogers, Lynn Riggs, John Joseph Mathews, and John Oskison (Wright 1936:161). In 1939, a brief sketch of Downing's life and writing career before the war appeared in the *Handbook of Oklahoma Writers* (Marable/Boylen 1939:9ff). In 1951, Wright again mentioned him in her *Guide to the Indian Tribes of Oklahoma:* "Choctaw prominent in the history of the Indian Territory and Oklahoma since 1898 include . . . Todd Downing, novelist" (1951:114). On this regional scale, the novels by Oskison and Mathews as well as the newspaper columns by Rogers, Posey, and others were read by Natives and non-Natives alike, and generally the authors were approved of by their respective communities. From the variety and number of publications one may even conclude that on a regional Oklahoma level Native American literature existed (and had established itself firmly) in the 1800s. Since Downing wrote mostly on Mexico and used Mexican settings he would not seem to fall in this category, but, as the above quotations prove, he was known and considered important as an Oklahoma Indian who had become a celebrity as an author.

After his return to Atoka to care for his parents, Downing worked as a high school teacher. One more mystery story appeared in 1945 (Downing 1945). Since there were no reprints of his earlier works knowledge about them gradually declined.

A regional result of the upsurge in the political awareness and self-confidence of American Indians during the 1960s was the establishment of the Choctaw Bilingual Education Program which hired Downing. Downing, by now almost seventy years old, had always expressed the opinion that "belonging to two or more cultures doubles your enjoyment of life" (Morrison 1975:416). He was obviously the right man in the right place. His sister Ruth remembers that "He was happiest when teaching in this program" (personal communication).

Concentrating his efforts on the region and on the Choctaw Nation meant that Downing started writing for yet another audience in his career as an author. His Choctaw-language course *Chahta Anumpa* (Downing 1971) was first published as a serial in the Atoka *Indian Citizen*. Nobody seems to have been more surprised by the immediate success of this series than the author himself. In the foreword to the third edition, he wrote,

Many moons ago (as Choctaws do not say) Mr. B. R. Cook . . . suggested that I write a series of Choctaw lessons for his newspaper. I hesitated. "Do you think many people would be interested?" I asked, having had experience in turning out manuscripts in which few people *were* interested. . . . To my surprise, Mr. Cook decided to run the entire series three times, to meet the demands of readers who wanted a complete file of the lessons. These developed into the present *Chahta Anompa*—and now it is going into a third edition. (1971:4)

Downing designed *Chahta Anompa* to serve as a combined introduction to language and culture alike. It included stories about the great nineteenth-century leader Pushmataha as well as the Choctaw creation myth and the Lord's Prayer in the Choctaw language. Written for publication in a newspaper read by Natives and non-Natives, it reached a wider audience than language courses created specifically for use in the classrooms. However, *Chahta Anumpa* was adopted for language teaching courses not only at Southeastern State College (now University), but also for Choctaw language courses at Vanderbilt University (Bolen 1973). Likewise, the pageant *Journey's End*[5] was written for Downing's home community—in other words, for an intended audience that was regionally specific but not limited in terms of linguistic or ethnic group:

We reenact some of the great scenes from Choctaw history: the confrontation of Pushmataha and Tecumseh in 1811; the signing of the treaty of Dancing Rabbit Creek in 1831; the wintertime removal of our people to new homes across the Mississippi River; the signing of the Atoka Agreement in 1897; and the final merging of Indian Territory and Oklahoma Territory into the State of Oklahoma in 1907. (Downing 1971:15)

The performances of *Journey's End* needed and found the cooperation of both Choctaws and non-Indians, even though the text is not without bitterness. For example, the Choctaws are shown to have been forced into signing away their lands in the treaty of Dancing

Rabbit Creek, while greedy whites are already waiting on their doorsteps. Not only that; history seems to repeat itself when the same wording is used before the Atoka Agreement is signed:

Hardwick: Well, some of them are bellyachin'—sayin' this is their land and they've got treaties with the Federal Government guaranteein' their right to it. But old Andy [President Andrew Jackson] has put it to 'em straight from the shoulder. . . . So it's in [their] best interest to go peaceable. . . . I've got my eye on old Noxabee's place. Rich bottom land with a good house and the best live stock in these parts. (Act I, Scene 1)

Harding: Well, some of them are bellyachin'—sayin' this is their land and they've got the Treaty of Dancing Rabbit Creek guaranteein' their right to it. But their Governor, Green McCurtain, has put it to 'em straight from the shoulder. . . . So it's in their best interest to go peaceable. . . . I've got my eye on a good Boggy Bottom farm. The owner's a sick old woman and I can bamboozle her easy. (Act II, Scene 6)

These accusing scenes stand in somewhat awkward contrast to the pageant's finale where the entire cast (and, probably, the audience) sings "Oklahoma." Considerations concerning the prospective audiences and sponsors of the performances probably helped shape the text to a certain degree. The pageant was, after all, presented and perhaps sponsored by the Atoka County Historical Society and the Atoka County Chamber of Commerce and attended not only by Choctaws but also by the non-Indian inhabitants of the Atoka region. A more radical version of the text is easily imaginable, considering not so much the history of Choctaw-white relations but the radical rhetoric of the day as used by the spokespeople of militant Native groups like AIM. This rhetoric of conflict, however, can be used only where antagonisms are either already at hand or intended. Downing even refrained from making dramatic use of the Battle of Boggy Depot near Atoka, where on February 13, 1864, Union soldiers had massacred wounded Confederate Indians. On the other hand, he also declined to enliven the scenery with Choctaw dances or anything of the kind.

 Journey's End is not a particularly well-integrated piece of literature. In fact, it seems to have been written rather hastily, so that the predicaments of working for a multiple audience remain visible in their effect on the text. Choctaw grievances over white men's greed on the one hand and "Oklahoma" on the other stand in curious contrast.

 The problem of a multiple audience with differing demands that Downing was facing on a regional scale when he wrote *Journey's End* is by and large the same all contemporary Native American authors face. If they want to be accepted not only by their own communities but by an intertribal and pan-Indian audience and by a mixed audience on a national or even international scale, they have to shape their texts carefully according to the demands of their audience(s). Homogeneous audiences like the ones Downing had written for during his early career in the 1930s do not pose such problems. To his home audience, Downing was not only a distant "Indian" author but a well-known member of the community. The influence of such an audience of course by far exceeded that of a general national audience like the one that read *The Mexican Earth*.

DIFFERENT AUDIENCES AND "NATIVE AMERICAN LITERATURE"

The problem of a double or multiple audience and of presenting literary pieces that are read, understood, and accepted by all parts of their audience(s) leads back to the contemplation of the range and types of Native American literature this essay started with. As has been pointed out, Downing's various works—ranging from a master's thesis and scholarly book reviews to advertising copy, from mystery novels and an Indian history of Mexico to a pageant and a language course—were written for a number of different audiences. These audiences were all addressed in different ways, and their demands as well as certain genre conventions were instrumental in shaping the texts. The pageant *Journey's End* was seen and performed by both Native and non-Native inhabitants of the Atoka region; the language course was primarily of importance to Choctaws. The crime novels and stories of his early career were meant for a general audience on a national level, as was *The Mexican Earth*. In his youth, when working with *Books Abroad*, Downing wrote book reviews for an intellectual audience; the same holds true for his work with *Pan Americanismo* and for the "Professor Hoople" columns. All of these works were written by the same person to whom the definition of "Native American author"—given the definition of American Indian heredity and, of course, his own statement in *The Mexican Earth*—obviously applies. On the other hand, none of Downing's texts would readily fit the commonly accepted image of Native American literature as determined by the successful works of Momaday, Silko, Erdrich, and Welch, which were written for an audience of mixed racial descent and ethnic identity.

The individual case of Todd Downing and the various relationships between him as author and the varying interpretive communities for his works suggests a model for a definition of Native American literature using a variable scale. At this point, seven types of texts that outline specific intended audiences and their responses are distinguishable.

1. Texts intended for a limited local or regional audience which is either (predominantly) Native or consists of different ethnic groups living in the same area, usually the writer's own people; these texts may be about Native or non-Native issues.

2. Texts intended for an extended (predominantly) Native audience, written on behalf of the writer's own people, about Native issues in general or about non-Native issues.

3. Texts intended for a larger non-Native audience, written on behalf of the writer's own people or about Native issues in general;

4. Texts intended for a general readership of mixed ethnic identity about Native issues, using Native characters, motives, material, etc.;

5. Texts intended for a specialized audience about non-Native issues;

6. Texts intended for a local, regional, or general audience without particular reference to Native issues.

7. Texts originally from a tribal, communal, or personal oral tradition, transcribed and edited.

The first group of works includes all Native regional newspapers, leaflets, and magazines, some of which are also read by non-Native audiences. This field is the closest to contemporary Native American everyday life; the authors usually reside in the community. Bilingual or monolingual Indian-language texts are most likely found here. This group of texts is the one that historically came first; also, the relationship between author and audience is closest in this group. One can agree with Jack Forbes (see above) that it forms the nucleus of Native American literature. *Chahta Anumpa* and most of Downing's articles for local newspapers come under this heading as well as, considering the special conditions in Oklahoma, *Journey's End*. In terms of genre, apart from journalistic texts and speeches, short forms (poetry, tales, sketches, short stories) dominate. A modern novel of predominantly regional importance to the Choctaws and their neighbors is John T. Webb's *Never On My Knees* (1988).

The second category includes most of what Jack Forbes (1987:3ff) wanted to see as the core of Native American literature: the magazines, newspapers, and booklets printed for a largely Native American audience by Native American pubishers. Scholarly magazines like the *Wicazo Sa Review* that also reach a non-Native readership come also under this heading, as well as the few cases in which an author explicitly addresses only fellow Native Indians like Lee Maracle's *I Am Woman* (1988:11). Historically, this group is basically an extension of the first under the conditions of a postcolonial mass-media society.

Although they deal with Native American subjects and issues, works in the third group were—like Downing's *The Mexican Earth*—originally written for a generally non-Native audience but by authors who consciously and for a purpose identified themselves to their audience as being American Indians. It includes the works of most Native American authors, who, like Samson Occom, George Copway, and Charles Eastman were read by a general audience prior to 1960. One of the reasons for this of course is that Native American authors of this period could not count on a larger Native audience to be literate, let alone able to buy expensive books. Only those of their books that conformed to the audience's expectations were a success on the market. Because writing in this group does not necessarily require direct contact between the writer and his or her own community, authors posing as representatives of their nations like Copway (Smith 1988) or imposters of Native persons like Highwater/Markopoulos are most likely to be found in this group, too. One has to keep in mind, though, that already an eighteenth-century author like Occom wrote for different audiences (see Peyer 1982:12, 193). Historically, the third group did not exist as "Native American literature" before the formation of a tentative canon of works in the 1970s and '80s. Only then did these works gain additional importance as ancestral voices to works that largely belong with the fourth group according to the above system of classification. This literary heritage, however, does not conform to the definition of *tradition*. It is neither traditional in the sense of the old oral tradition nor really a literary tradition, since only a few authors were aware of their literary predecessors before their works were republished.

Works that are consciously written about or use Native issues and materials and that are intended for both Native and non-Native audiences on a larger scale compose the fourth category of texts. This is where the majority of contemporary authors would be listed, and this is the core of what Krupat calls "indigenous literature," which in similar form exists under similar conditions also in countries like Canada, Australia, and New Zealand. Usually these works are read by a white audience (which is necessary for a success in the book market) as well as by members of the minority cultures—though the response may be different, as in the case of Charles Storm/Hyemeyohsts, whose *Seven Arrows* met with praise from the reviewers but was rejected by many Cheyenne (Costo 1972). Slowly, the formation of a tentative canon can be observed (Ruppert 1981:87) as authors like Momaday, Ortiz, Silko, Vizenor, and Welch are read, reread, taught, and to an extent also copied by younger writers who in turn enter the market with new publications (this process is visible for example in the collection *Touchwood*, edited by Gerald Vizenor).

The fifth group includes works like Downing's M.A. thesis and Momaday's dissertation or, more generally, all works by authors of Native descent in the natural sciences, business, law, and so on (except, of course, those which deal with specifically Indian-related themes and topics).

The sixth group consists of all those works by Native literary men and women who do not deal with Native issues or present their material from an expressedly Native Indian point of view. For example, a lot of Will Roger's political satires and other journalists' writings belong in this category as well as works of book length like Martin Cruz Smith's (Seneca-Yaqui) *Gorky Park* (1981) or, for that matter, all of Todd Downing's crime novels.

The seventh group, finally, is made up of texts that were originally part of an oral tradition, be it tribal, communal, or personal. It covers biographies and autobiographies (Krupat 1985:32) as well as ethnographic collections. Obviously, this inclusion leads into a grey zone: most of the collaborators on Native autobiographies were non-Natives; likewise, only few ethnographic collectors could claim a tribal heritage like Ella Deloria or William Jones.[6] Many texts in this group bear only a doubtful semblance to the oral originals they profess to represent.

All of these groups coexist, although the third is historically almost closed since there is no need any longer for tribal writers to write for audiences that do not include fellow Native Americans. Exploitive tracts that profess to teach American Indian religious secrets have fortunately been losing importance over the past years. Furthermore, imposters are more easily discovered today than even a few decades ago.

Together, the groups form a continuum rather than clearly defined sectors. As in the case of Todd Downing, one piece by an author may belong to the first group, another one to the fourth, still another to the fifth. In fact one and the same author may during his writing career cover all. One and the same piece may also belong to more than one category at the same time: as a text, the Nanabush-legends printed in the Anishinabe *The Progress* belong with group seven; since they appeared in an early tribal newspaper, they also belong with group one (Hochbruck 1991:168). Leslie Silko's *Storyteller* (1981), obviously a fourth-group collection, is also of regional importance to the Lagunas. Finally, individual pieces may change groups: should, for example, Todd Downing's *The Cat Screams* be reedited with an introduction pointing out the author's Choctaw heredity, this would affect the readers' perception of the text. The change of context and the presentation of the text to a new interpretive community would produce a substantial alteration in the reading of the text. Instead of a simple crime novel they would now read a crime novel by an Indian author, a reading which probably would give additional weight to the Indian material Downing incorporated into the text. *The Cat Screams* would shift from group six to four.

Looking at the present condition of Native American and Canadian Indian writing and publishing, the interaction between groups one, two, and four is apparent. An author may start writing for local newspapers and then get a chance to publish on a national level, or else an author of national renown may publish essays in American Indian publications of group two.

Groups five and six are usually not directed at a Native audience, nor do they touch Native issues or topics. Their relation to the focal term Native American literature is therefore based exclusively on the fact that they were written by authors of Native ancestry. According to the system suggested above, they are not evicted from the ranks of Native American literature, but neither are they given the same status as texts from the historical, sociocultural, and literary core of this indigenous literature.

To define "Native American literature" neither by topic alone nor by the quantity of Indian blood in a certain author alone, but along the criteria outlined above—that is by range, topic, intention, and intended audience—provides a base to evaluate any given text within the system and to arrive at conclusions as to its importance for the whole body of Native American literature. Silko's *Storyteller,* belonging to two groups, is apparently of more importance than Storm's *Seven Arrows* within this system, even though sales figures would suggest the opposite. To draw an analogy to Brian Swann's definition of "Indian": if a book by a Native American author is obviously intended as Native American literature, and if its audience (both Native and non-Native) reads and accepts this book as Native American literature and its author as Native American, then it should be accepted as such.

NOTES

1. I am grateful to Arnold Krupat for pointing out this important essay to me as well as for his helpful comments on an earlier version of this essay. Thanks also to Beth Satre for revising the manuscript. The author takes responsibility for any remaining mistakes or inconsistencies.

2. Jamake Highwater, a.k.a. Gregory Markopoulos, a person of Greek origin who used the fact that a Blood elder adopted him into his family to pose as a Native American author for several years.

3. Krupat discusses an article by Jack Forbes, "Colonialism and Native American Literature: Analysis," which initially appeared in the *Wicazo Sa Review* (1987) 3:17–23.

4. A more extensive introduction to the life and works of Todd Downing will be included in a volume on Downing currently prepared for publication by this author. I am thankful to Ruth S. Downing and Nenad Downing, Chattanooga, and to Margaret Hames and Homer Blaker of Atoka, Oklahoma, for sharing their time, memories, and other information about Todd Downing with me.

5. The program leaflet of the 1971 performance identified Gladys Wilson and Cassie Williams as authors of Act II, Scene 1: 'Geary Station on the Butterfield Trail, September 1858'; and Scene 2: 'A Choctaw School 1860' respectively. A copy of the typescript was made available to the author by Margaret Hames.

6. The seventh group was left out in the original draft of this paper; however, I decided to include it after a discussion with Bernd Peyer.

REFERENCES

Adams, C. L. 1987. "Frank Waters." In *A Literary History of the American West,* edited by J. G. Taylor, 935–957. Fort Worth: Texas Christian University Press.

Barth, Fredrik. 1969. "Introduction." In *Ethnic Groups and Boundaries: The Social Organization of Culture Difference,* edited by Fredrik Barth, 9–38. Bergen and Oslo: Universitets Forlaget.

Bolen, Robert. 1973. "Choctaw Teacher Doubles As Author." *The Southeastern,* December, n.p.

Boyd, Melba Joyce. 1990. "The Politics of Cherokee Spirituality in Alice Walker's *Meridian.*" In *Minority Literatures in North America,* edited by Wolfgang Karrer and Hartmut Lutz, 115–127. Frankfurt and Bern: Lang.

Clifton, James A. 1989. "Alternate Identities and Cultural Frontiers." In *Being and Becoming Indian,* edited by J. A. Clifton. Chicago: Dorsey.

Cook, Liz. 1977. "American Indian Literatures in Servitude." *Indian Historian* 10:3–5.

Costo, Rupert. 1972. "Seven Arrows Desecrates Cheyenne." *Indian Historian* 5:2:441–442.

Davis, J. L. 1976/77. "The Whorf Hypothesis and Native American Literature." *South Dakota Review* 14:59–72.

Downing, Todd. 1927. "Jean Feron: La Métisse. Montreal. Edouard Garant. 1926." *Books Abroad* 1:1:26.

———. 1933. *Murder on Tour.* New York: Putnam.

———. 1934. *The Cat Screams.* New York: Doubleday.

———. 1940. *The Mexican Earth.* New York: Doubleday.

———. 1941. *The Lazy Lawrence Murders.* New York: Doubleday.

———. 1945. "The Shadowless Hour." *Mystery Book Magazine* 2:1.

———. 1970. *Journey's End.* Typescript.

———. 1971. *Chahta Anompa: An Introduction to the Choctaw Language.* Durant, Okla.: Choctaw Bilingual Education Program.

Feest, Christian F. 1983. " 'Indianness' and Ethnicity." In *Le facteur ethnique aux Etats-Unis et au Canada,* edited by Monique Lecomte and Claudine Thomas, 89–97. Lille: Université de Lille.

Fish, Stanley. 1980. *Is There a Text in This Class?* Cambridge, Mass.: Harvard University Press.

Forbes, Jack. 1987. "Colonialism and Native American Literature: Analysis." *Wicazo Sa Review* 3:17–23.

Gridley, Marion E., ed. 1947. "Todd Downing." In *Indians of Today.* Chicago: Indian Council Fire.

Hagen, Ordean A. 1969. *Who Done It? A Guide to Detective, Mystery, and Suspense Fiction.* New York and Los Angeles: Bowker.

Hochbruck, Wolfgang. 1991. *'I Have Spoken'. Die Darstellung und ideologische Funktion indianischer Mündlichkeit in der nordamerikanischen Literatur.* Tübingen: Narr.

Hubin, Allen. 1984. *Crime Fiction 1749–1980: A Comprehensive Bibliography.* New York: Garland.

King, Thomas. 1986. "Introduction: An Anthology of Canadian Native Fiction." *Canadian Fiction Magazine* 60:4–10.

Krupat, Arnold. 1985. *For Those Who Come After.* Berkeley and Los Angeles and London: University of California Press.

———. 1989. *The Voice in the Margin: Native American Literature and the Canon.* Berkeley and Los Angeles and Oxford: University of California Press.

Larson, Charles. 1978. *American Indian Fiction.* Albuquerque: University of New Mexico Press.

Marable, Mary, and Elaine Boylen, eds. 1939. "Todd Downing." In *A Handbook of Oklahoma Writers,* 9–10. Norman: University of Oklahoma Press.

Maracle, Lee. 1988. *I Am Woman.* North Vancouver: Write On Press.

Momaday, N. Scott. 1975. "The Man Made of Words." In *Literature of the American Indian,* edited by A. Chapman, 96–110. New York: Meridian Books.

Morrison, James D. 1975. *"Chahta Anumpa:* An Introduction to the Choctaw Language." *Chronicles of Oklahoma* 53:415–416.

Peyer, Bernd, ed. 1982. *The Elders Wrote: An Anthology of Early Prose by North American Indians 1768–1931.* Berlin: Reimer.

———. 1990. *The Singing Spirit: Early Short Stories by North American Indians.* Tucson: University of Arizona Press.

Ruppert, Jim. 1981. "Literature on the Reservation—Source for the Future of American Indian Literature." *MELUS* 8:2:86–88.

Schöler, Bo. 1987. "Interpretive Communities and the Representation of Contemporary Native American Life in Literature." *European Review of Native American Studies* 1:2:27–30.

Silko, Leslie. 1981. *Storyteller.* New York: Seaver Books.

Smith, Charlene Wilson. 1983. "Todd Downing." In *Tales of Atoka County Heritage,* edited by Atoka County Historical Society, 247–248. Atoka, Oklahoma.

Smith, Donald B. 1988. "The Life of George Copway or Kah-ge-ga-ga-bowh (1818–1869)—and a Review of His Writings." *Journal of Canadian Studies* 23:3:5–38.

Smith, Martin Cruz. 1981. *Gorky Park.* New York: Ballantine Books.

Storm, Hyemeyohsts. 1972. *Seven Arrows.* New York: Harper and Row.

Swann, Brian. 1988. "Introduction." In *Harper's Anthology of 20th Century Native American Poetry,* edited by Duane Niatum, xiii–xxxii. New York: Harper and Row.

Vizenor, Gerald, ed. 1987. *Touchwood: A Collection of Ojibway Prose.* St. Paul: New Rivers Press.

Webb, John T. 1988. *Never On My Knees.* Durant: Choctaw Nation of Oklahoma.

Wright, Muriel H. 1936. "Contributions of the Indian People to Oklahoma." *Chronicles of Oklahoma* 14:156–161.

———. 1951. *A Guide to the Indian Tribes of Oklahoma.* Norman: University of Oklahoma Press.

THE FRONTIERS OF NATIVE AMERICAN WOMEN'S WRITING

Sarah Winnemucca's *Life among the Piutes*

Brigitte Georgi-Findlay

The study of the history, literature, and popular mythology of American westward expansion and the frontier West has, during the past decades, undergone some crucial reconsideration, if not revision, through the inclusion of two new angles of vision: the focus on the tribal people dispossessed by the westward movement and, more recently, on the largely ignored and for a long time invisible participation of women in this move west. These two relatively new fields of study, it would appear, do not have much in common with each other—except, of course, for their combined efforts to rewrite previously excluded groups of people as presences and agents into American history and literature. Thus it should not come as a surprise that both areas have kept rather aloof from each other and have only recently approached each other in studies focusing on Native American women. Both areas of study, however, may be made profitable for each other also in the reconsideration of the frontier experience in American literature and culture, from which both Native American and female voices have long been absent. Focusing on one of the first autobiographical narratives written by a Native American woman, Sarah Winnemucca Hopkins's *Life among the Piutes: Their wrongs and claims* (1883),[1] I aim at such a reconsideration of the frontier experience from the female and the Native American point of view, by drawing on some of the critical questions raised by both fields of study.

Historical research on the American frontier has tended to view westward expansion as a predominantly male activity, and studies dealing with the "popular mythology of the frontier"[2] have defined it as a cultural idea almost exclusively linked to and shaped by male concerns, although admittedly assigning women an important symbolic presence.[3] Both have for a long time based their evidence on texts written by white men. However, recent historical research, mostly undertaken by women, has established women's presence on the various western frontiers on the basis of their published and private writings in the form of travel narratives, memoirs, diaries, and letters.[4] In their writings, these westering women have recorded their encounters with native women—sometimes expressing unconcealed racism and ethnocentrism, sometimes full of fear and distrust, and sometimes with a refreshing openness and willingness to understand the "other," as represented by tribal cultures and people, in a way that leaves us wondering about the impact of these encounters on tribal women, both on a cultural as well as an interpersonal level. One of the main problems in the study of the female experience of the frontier is, of course, the problem of written evidence. Researchers have so far mostly focused on the experience of Euroamerican middle-class women for the obvious reason that these more or less educated women furnished the largest part of the written material on the female frontier. During the 1980s, however, large retrieval efforts have resulted in the recovery and establishment of an ever increasing store of women's texts on the frontiers, which has also multiplied the complexity of perspectives.[5] Aware of the immense variety of women's experience, researchers increasingly emphasize the need to consider the impact of many cultures when studying women and call for a "new multicultural framework."[6] Of course, the admittedly problematic text status and limited amount of the material which is available to study the experiences especially of Native American women, consisting to a large degree of originally oral narratives and raising serious questions of authorship, have prevented researchers so far from taking a closer look at native women's texts. However, studies on Native American autobiographies on the one hand, and of women's autobiographies on the other hand, have already developed methodological approaches to the interpretation of these difficult texts.[7] As a matter of fact, it is remarkable that the studies of both Native American and women's autobiographies deal with similar difficulties and often come up with similar conclusions. Here I only want to point to the questions of authorship and voice, the role of the "framing" of texts through prefaces, appendixes, and generic conventions, to the special circumstances of text production, distribution, and reception, as well as to the issues of power and authority surrounding editor-narrator relations. Both areas of study often come to the conclusion that the characteristics identified as generic to the American autobiography are largely based on the study of texts by male white Americans; both often contend that the concept of self-projected in the "master texts" of the American autobiography informs neither—or only marginally—the autobiographical narratives of tribal people nor those of women.[8]

While researchers on the female frontier have recently called for a multicultural framework in the study of women's experiences of the western frontiers, Native American studies, both anthropological and literary, have begun to focus on Native American women and to put emphasis on the construction and role of gender in North American tribal cultures.[9] Although the studies of Native American literature have come to acknowledge the prominence of contemporary native women writers and the important thematic and formal role of gender in contemporary Native American literary works,[10] they have not considered well enough the role of gender in earlier Native American literature. These literary expressions of Native Americans in the eighteenth and nineteenth centuries have been interpreted mainly in the context of political Indian-white relations, of acculturation and assimilation, an approach which is of course fully legitimized by the circumstances surrounding and motivating the production of these early texts.[11] I would argue, however, that we have not considered well enough the role of gender in the history of Indian-white relations, of cultural contact, colonization, and assimilation—especially in the interpretation of the texts written, authored or coauthored, or narrated by Native American women. Shouldn't we wonder whether the experience and process of assimilation is different for native women than for native men?[12] How did cultural contact, colonization, and change affect tribal women? How did it affect their views of themselves as tribal persons and as women, and how did they express these views in their autobiographical narratives?[13] And how did these women place themselves within the changing world of the western frontiers? These, I would suggest, are the questions that may add new angles of vision to the study of early native women's texts.

One of the first autobiographical texts written by a Native American woman, Sarah Winnemucca Hopkins's *Life among the Piutes,* seems to me to be a case in point, since it demonstrates the need for an interpretation that is sensitive to the complex role of gender and gender relations in the narrator's appeal for the vindication of her people's rights. In the following I want to suggest that this text may be read in more than one context. It may be read, of course, as a Native American autobiographical narrative that incorporates a political message. Yet, I would argue, it is not only a political statement on Indian-white power relations toward the end of the nineteenth century, but is itself shaped by the realities of sexual politics in Indian-white relations. At the same time, it may be read as an example of women's writing on the western frontier, a reading which is suggested by the fact that the text is anthologized in collections of western women's writing.[14] Sarah Winnemucca was born, as she states in her autobiographical narrative, "somewhere near 1844" near the sink of the Humboldt River in what is now western Nevada. She came from a Northern Paiute[15] family that from the time of first contact with whites had advocated peaceful coexistence. Her maternal grandfather Truckee, who she claimed was the chief of all the Paiutes, welcomed early explorers and settlers and served as a guide to various emigrant parties traveling to California. He had fought in California with John C.

Frémont in his Mexican campaigns and befriended white families and individuals throughout northern Nevada and California. Sarah's father, Old Winnemucca, succeeded Truckee as chief.[16]

By the time she reached adulthood, Sarah Winnemucca was in the public eye as an "Indian Princess"[17] and a spokeswoman of the Paiute tribe. At the age of twenty, she appeared on stage with her family, acting in Indian *tableaux vivants* and interpreting for her father in his attempts to mediate between the Paiutes and the citizens of Virginia City. At twenty-four she was a figure of some prominence and influence, serving as a liaison between the Paiutes and the whites in her people's native Nevada and in Oregon, where they were assigned to the Malheur Reservation, soon living lives of poverty dependent on the whims of an Indian agent. During the Bannock War of 1878 she acted in the controversial role of the army's emissary to recalcitrant bands of Paiutes and Bannocks, bringing them onto the reservations. Already in 1870, a letter she had written on the plight of the Paiutes was published by *Harper's Weekly,* attracting the attention of eastern Indian reformers particularly after its republication in the appendix of Helen Hunt Jackson's *A Century of Dishonor* (1881). After the Bannock War, Sarah accompanied her father and her brother Natchez to Washington to talk to President Hayes and to obtain from secretary of the interior Carl Schurz permission for the Paiutes to return to the Malheur Reservation in Oregon, after they had been crowded onto the Yakima Reservation in Washington. The government, however, provided neither supplies nor transportation for the tribe's return. Disillusioned with federal Indian policy and its agents, Sarah started taking the Paiute cause to the public. Encouraged by the success of her first lecture in San Francisco in 1879, she went east on a lecture tour. Giving nearly three hundred talks between April 1883 and August 1884, from Boston and New York to Baltimore and Washington, she exposed inequities in federal Indian policy and the corruption of federal Indian agents and called for the restoration of lands in severalty to the Paiutes. In Boston she met Elizabeth Palmer Peabody, the promoter of kindergarten education and publisher of the works of the transcendentalists, and her sister Mary Mann, who took up the Paiutes' cause.[18] Under their direction, she also spoke in the homes of Ralph Waldo Emerson, John Greenleaf Whittier, and those of congressmen, among them Senator Henry Dawes.[19] Evidently encouraged by the two women, Sarah Winnemucca, now Mrs. Hopkins, wrote her autobiographical book *Life among the Piutes,* which was edited by Mary Mann and published in 1883 by Elizabeth Palmer Peabody. This book, which contains the text of a petition requesting the grant of lands in severalty to the Paiutes at Malheur Reservation, is together with her lectures generally claimed to have lent support to the passage of the General Allotment Act, also known as the Dawes Act, in 1887.[20]

Consequently, Bernd C. Peyer has read Sarah Winnemucca's autobiography, together with other autobiographical texts of the period, as a political text in the context of Indian-white political relations in the last quarter of the nineteenth century. In his reading, these texts reflect changes of the time both in federal Indian policy and in the public interest in Indian affairs. Thus the lessened focus on the religious conversion experience, which had been so prominent in earlier autobiographical works, is explained by the secularization of Indian education, which no longer aims predominantly at the education and training of preachers. At the same time, the end of any major Native American military resistance by 1890 at the latest and the confinement of tribes on reservations gave rise to a scholarly and humanist interest in the history and fate of Native Americans, which, together with the founding of numerous organizations of "friends," created a greater market for Native American literature with an emphasis on traditional life. Thus, Peyer argues, the works written by Native Americans during this period, among them that of Sarah Winnemucca, include much more ethnohistorical detail and, as the situation on the reservations quickly became unbearable, turn more and more critical of the conquering society.[21]

In a similar fashion, A. LaVonne Brown Ruoff notes that Winnemucca's text, unlike the earlier autobiographies of William Apes and George Copway, is not influenced by religious autobiographies, and that its central theme is not the conversion experience, but Indian-white relations.[22] Contradicting Bernd Peyer, however, she contends that hostile government policies and public attitudes created a climate generally unfavorable to the development of Native American literature during this period. White audiences, she argues, were far more interested in reading the accounts of the explorers, settlers, and gold miners who conquered the West than they were in reading of Native American suffering brought about by this conquest.[23] This would suggest that Native American literature of the time had, so to speak, to compete with western literature. Yet, although Ruoff discovers allusions to dime-novel westerns in Winnemucca's text, she does not elaborate further on this interesting intertextual aspect and on the whole seems to privilege a reading of the autobiography as a political statement supporting the General Allotment Act. In another publication Ruoff argues that *Life among the Piutes* should be understood in the light of contemporary literary trends and types, such as the captivity narratives and the slave narratives. She points to a number of features that the text has in common with such narratives, such as some sexual violence and lots of daring adventures.[24] In reaction to this argument, H. David Brumble regards it as unlikely that Winnemucca herself was familiar with such literature. He asks that we "not simply *assume* the degree of literacy and the breadth of reading which Ruoff's argument would require of Winnemucca"[25] and argues that Winnemucca's autobiography was not influenced by written captivity or slave narratives, but seems instead to owe a good deal to preliterate autobiographical traditions. He proposes to look at Winnemucca instead as a well-experienced *speaker* who adapted Paiute oral conventions to the uses of the pen and to the entertainment and persuasion of white audiences. By the time she came to write her narrative down, he argues, Winnemucca would have delivered it, in parts, on many occasions, and she would have had a lively sense of how white audiences had responded to the various versions of particular episodes. Thus we need not assume that Winnemucca was at all aware of literary models, but we have to take into account that she had learned a great deal about her white audience.[26]

My reading of *Life among the Piutes* sustains Peyer's and Ruoff's interpretations of the autobiography as a text of some political impact in the area of Indian policy, although I cannot fully follow the connections Peyer draws between changes in federal Indian policy and the impact of these changes on the content and style of Native American literature in the last quarter of the nineteenth century. As the title suggests, the work may be identified as both autobiographical and ethnographic. In it Winnemucca tells the story of Indian dispossession and legal incapacitation, exemplified in the case of her tribe, the Northern Paiutes. Its publication may be seen as a sign of increasing humanitarian concern among eastern reformers for the plight of Native Americans, and also of changes in the federal Indian policy leading to the Dawes Act of 1887. Moreover, H. David Brumble's reading of the text as following a preliterate autobiographical tradition seems to be a convincing explanation for the striking differences distinguishing it from both the earlier and later Native American autobiographies of William Apes (1829), George Copway (1847), Charles Eastman (1902, 1916), and Joseph Griffis (1915). These differences consist, for instance, in the absence of turning points or conversion experiences as well as in Winnemucca's reference to her actions as solely motivated by the service to her people. As Brumble suggests, she seems mainly concerned with setting down her deeds, assuming, with other male Native autobiographers, that she may rise in the regard of her tribe by the telling of these deeds, thus implicitly assuming an audience with Paiute habits of mind, not Christian.[27] From this vantage point, he comes to the conclusion that "for all her acquaintance with the Transcendentalists, for all her Indian activism, Winnemucca retained an essentially tribal sense of self,"[28] an interpretation that justly contradicts Bataille's and Sands's claim that Winnemucca's autobiography is "heavily biased by her acculturated and Christianized point of view."[29] Although it supports his interpretation in many of its main arguments, my reading of the text will try to expand its focus by pointing to another one of its dimensions which has so far not been considered. Concurring with Brumble's thesis that Winnemucca was less aware of literary models than of the potential response of her white—and potentially tribal—audience to her speeches, I want to suggest that Winnemucca's identity as a woman and the way her womanhood is, so to speak, "incorporated" into her text, form an important part of Winnemucca's dialogue with her public that should not be underestimated. I would even go so far as to suggest that the very fact that Winnemucca was a woman was crucial in the public reception of her person, her lectures, and her book by a contemporary audience.[30] A reading of the text from this perspective, however, will necessarily lead to a modification of Brumble's suggestion that Sarah Winnemucca retained an essentially tribal self throughout her autobiographical narrative.

When I reread Winnemucca's *Life among the Piutes* in terms of what it might reveal about being a Native American woman in the transitional culture of the frontier

West, I was appalled at the sense of personal pain, yet also of personal pride, pervading the text; but I was also surprised at the way this woman had written herself, or possibly, had been written into the text. What difference did it make, I wondered, that the author of this bitter attack on the reservation system was a woman, and a Native American woman at that? Hers is a distressing story that aims at her audience's emotional commitment and concern. That the author is a woman seems to be part of this effect; that the editor is a woman is evidence of the fact, of which a contemporary public doubtless had been aware, that toward the end of the nineteenth century women played an important part in the reform movements of the time, and particularly in the Indian reform movement, where women's organizations in fact had initially formulated policies that were later endorsed by other groups and adopted by the government.[31]

Although most critics note Sarah Winnemucca's exceptional position as the female public voice of her tribe, none of them has considered the implications of this exceptionalism in the text itself. In his preface to the 1969 reprint of the text, M. R. Harrington remarks that "not often has an Indian woman been allowed to become so vocal and to bring the history of her people before the public." Ruoff as well notes this exceptionalism and points to Winnemucca's emphasis on the roles played by women in achieving peace for her people, yet does not go beyond relating the narrative of Winnemucca's daring exploits to the western dime novels featuring adventurous heroines.[32] Peyer points to Winnemucca's position as the first major female Native American writer, and Fowler argues that the events of Winnemucca's life suggest clearly some of the motives that led her to speak for Indian rights at a time when a Native American *woman* would hardly be respected for doing so.[33] Only Brumble registers Winnemucca's own explanation of the position of women in the tribe and draws the conclusion that "Winnemucca wants to be remembered in this way, as a woman who was brave as any man, as a woman who did great things."[34] I would go even farther and argue that the female presence of Sarah Winnemucca in her text extends this traditional tribal role by incorporating references to concepts of Victorian womanhood, and is thus in fact much more ambiguous than Brumble suggests.[35]

The reports on Sarah Winnemucca's public appearances support the idea that she was aware of the effect she had on her public in the romantic role of the "Indian Princess," a role certainly not entirely of her own making.[36] In a similar fashion, she seems to capitalize on this romantic public image in her lectures and her autobiographical narrative for the purpose of winning her audience's sympathy for her tribe. However, in *Life among the Piutes* this self-stylization as an Indian princess takes on exactly the paradoxical quality of the image of the Indian woman in American culture, which Rayna Green had stressed: Sarah faces what Green describes as the basic crux of the Native American woman, the impossibility "to be seen as real . . . As some abstract, noble Princess tied to 'America' and to sacrificial zeal, she has power as a symbol. As the Squaw, a depersonalized object of scornful convenience, she is powerless."[37] Linked to the main narrative dealing with the story of her tribe, we discover a subtext of personal defense, which has led Brumble to read the text as "an extended self-vindication, as an attempt to defend her own reputation and that of her family and her tribe," relating it to a preliterate, tribal conception of autobiography "as a way to answer slander," and arguing that "Indians of many tribes were answering their accusers with autobiographical narratives long before the Paiutes came into contact with the white man."[38] As a matter of fact, Winnemucca's own person is at times so overwhelmingly present in the narrative of her tribe's plight that we might be tempted to read the text as an enterprise of self-aggrandizement in the tradition of the male American autobiography—an enterprise that, to my knowledge, no American woman had undertaken so far. It also seems to be no coincidence that, as Catherine S. Fowler has pointed out, Winnemucca emerges in the works of cultural anthropologists as a controversial figure, a woman with two faces.[39] Considering the fact that she is writing against the silencing of Native American tribal voices in the context of a paternalistic federal Indian policy, her focus on her own person may of course be seen as a strategy of authentication, of claiming authority and representativity as a spokeswoman of her tribe. And yet what distinguishes Sarah's strategy of claiming authority from other native authors' strategies, say, for instance, from that of Charles Eastman, is not only the absence of the discourse of conversion, but also the awareness, ever present in her text, that this claim of authority is in a problematic way tied to issues of gender. I would argue therefore that the subtext of personal defense implies that Winnemucca had to defend herself against attacks particularly aimed at her as a woman. This becomes especially clear when we consider the framework of the book, which is provided not only by a foreword of the editor, but also by an appendix—a well-known and important textual device in the publication of Native American autobiographies as well as of slave narratives—that includes affidavits testifying to the respectable and reliable character of Sarah Winnemucca Hopkins, and thus implying, although rather subtly and unobtrusively, that her respectability must somehow have been questioned. Read against this framework, the issues of sexuality and morality written into the text take on a new meaning: what is negotiated in her presentation of Indian-white relations is not only the issue of the dispossession of tribal land, an issue a white audience dedicated to the rhetoric of national westward expansion would not have espoused without restrictions, but also the outrageous issues of sexual violence and miscegenation revealed in the violation of native women's bodies by white men.

The personal attacks against Sarah Winnemucca, as they are indirectly referred to in the affidavits in the book's appendix, seem even tame compared to the press reports and letters written about Sarah and sent to officials in Washington: Sarah is described as nothing less than a prostitute, an easy woman, a common camp follower.[40] Now we begin to identify the voices Sarah must implicitly have been writing against: those who disclaim her authority as a political spokeswoman by disclaiming her respectability as a woman, by exposing the woman who speaks and acts in public as a "public woman,"[41] by putting the Native American "princess" in her negative stereotypical place as savage woman, as "squaw," a promiscuous consort lacking "civilized" womanly virtue and restraint. As a matter of fact, even today's critics feel compelled to apologize for Sarah Winnemucca's supposedly unwomanly habits.[42] If we take further into consideration that Sarah reportedly had to defend herself against other Native women's insults as well as that her book was written during a lecture tour in the East, encouraged by, edited, and promoted by women active in or affiliated with various reform movements known for their concern for morality, domesticity, and the integrity of the family, we may assume the high importance this issue of respectability—and, implicitly, of sexuality, seduction, and slandered virtue—must have had in the production, promotion, and reception of the text.[43]

Life among the Piutes is apparently the result of a collaboration, or rather, of a dialogue of voices, female and male, eastern and western, Indian and white. Yet it is not the collaboration of a tribal person with one of the increasing numbers of anthropologists, as will be the case with many of the Native American autobiographies produced in the first decades of the twentieth century, which were informed by the scientific concerns of the young discipline of cultural anthropology.[44] It is a collaboration between women of two cultures. Arnold Krupat has suggested that "to see the Indian autobiography as a ground on which two cultures meet is to see it as the textual equivalent of the frontier."[45] In this sense, Winnemucca's *Life* could be read as a textual equivalent of a woman's frontier which is defined by the boundaries and reciprocal relationships between her native culture on the one hand and both eastern and western cultures on the other hand.

In her preface, Mary Mann describes the book as "an heroic act on the part of the writer," and as "the first outbreak of the American Indian in human literature, [which] has a single aim—to *tell the truth* as it lies in the heart and mind of a true patriot, and one whose knowledge of the two races gives her an opportunity of comparing them justly." She describes the motivation of Sarah Winnemucca, who is, in view of the attacks upon her respectability, significantly referred to as Mrs. Hopkins, to write the book: "Finding that in extemporaneous speech she could only speak at one time of a few points, she determined to write out the most important part of what she wished to say." She draws attention to the importance of the book at a particular historical instance: "At this moment, when the United States seems waking up to their duty to the original possessors of our immense territory, it is of the first importance to hear what only an Indian *and an Indian woman* [my emphasis] can tell." Why should it be of the first importance, at that particular historical moment, to hear what only an Indian woman can tell? Because, I would suggest, Indian reform is regarded, at this historical moment, as a domain which is of particular concern to women. The book is thus placed in a feminine discourse which assumes moral responsibility in the realm of political reform.

Mary Mann further informs her readers that the writing of the book was Sarah's "own deep impulse, and the dying charge given her by her father, the truly parental chief of his beloved tribe." Sarah Winnemucca herself will, in her narrative, legitimize her own role as spokeswoman with her family position as granddaughter of Truckee, whom she introduces as chief of the entire Paiute nation[46] and as daughter of Winnemucca, whom she describes as the legitimate successor of Truckee. Thus she suggests that her authority is based on kinship and relation: she is spokeswoman first by way of relation, and only secondarily by way of education. The idea is also underlined by her devaluation of her educational training. In this she distinguishes herself from other authors of Native American autobiographies who present themselves as educated Christians.

Mary Mann describes her own editing as "copying the original manuscript in correct orthography and punctuation, with occasional emendation by the author." The final version of the text is credited as Sarah's own: "In fighting with her literary deficiencies she loses some of the fervid eloquence which her extraordinary command of the English language enables her to utter, but I am confident that no one would desire that her own original words should be altered." To a friend, however, Mary Mann had confided that she had found the work of editing the manuscript rather difficult, which suggests not only that she may have interfered in the original text more than she cared to admit in her preface, but also that she may have realized the oral dimension of Sarah's written text:

I wish you could see her manuscript as a matter of curiosity. I don't think the English language ever got such a treatment before. I have to recur to her sometimes to know what a word is, as spelling is an unknown quantity to her, as you mathematicians would express it. She often takes syllables off of words & adds them or rather prefixes them to other words, but the story is heart-breaking, and told with a simplicity & eloquence that cannot be described, for it is not high-faluting eloquence, tho' sometimes it lapses into verse (and quite poetical verse too). I was always considered fanatical about Indians, but I have a wholly new conception of them now, and we civilized people may well stand abashed before their purity of life & their truthfulness.[47]

Sarah Winnemucca's *Life among the Piutes* is arranged in eight chapters, following in general a linear chronology of events from her childhood to the present in 1882-83. As a child she witnesses the first encounters between Paiutes and white people in the 1840s and 1850s and the impact of the westward movement on the overland trails on tribal life. Retrospectively, she describes the first coming of white people as the central event of her childhood, the event that marks the beginning of the story of her life, and that— as in many other Native autobiographical narratives—is seen prophesied in visions and dreams.[48] Thus she puts herself in the position of both tribal historian and autobiographical narrator. From the beginning of her text, she uses direct speech and dialogue as narrative devices, which give the text an extraordinary vividness and preserve a sense of the oral quality of her narration; at the same time they add a dramatic element to her story, especially in the rendering of speeches. The purpose of this first chapter is clearly to establish the peaceful intent of the Paiutes in their relations with whites, revising the idea of hostile savages promoted by bloodcurdling tales of emigrant trains attacked by Paiute bands in the years of increasing emigration to California. As a matter of fact, the coming of the emigrant trains every summer lends a structure and repetitive rhythmic pattern to the narrative, which reproduces the movement of white people closing in upon the migratory Paiutes from all sides. The Paiutes' frontier, the encounter with a foreign people on the territory they call their homeland, of course does not resemble the Turnerian concept of *the* American frontier. Although the Paiutes are reaching out to welcome the strangers, they are encircled and finally expelled from their homeland.

When she was a very small child, Sarah tells her readers, a party of white people was seen traveling eastward from California. They were people who kept at a distance (5). During the following years these emigrants came closer with every annual emigration. More emigrants came, and one summer—which must have been 1846, two years after Sarah's birth—her grandfather goes to California with a party of Paiutes to help Frémont against the Mexicans. Very late that same fall, Sarah reports, the emigrants kept coming and were forced to live among the Paiutes during the winter. The following spring, there were "fearful news coming from different tribes, that the people whom they called their white brothers were killing everybody that came their way, and all the Indian tribes had gone into the mountains to save their lives" (11). Then Winnemucca describes the psychological effect of these news on her tribe by dwelling on the special sense of fear and horror this brought to the lives of women and children. Women covered long distances when gathering food, and the dramatic episode Sarah tells of her mother burying her in order to hide her from white people serves to demonstrate this sense of fear and horror shared by women and children. In an inversion of the pattern of the Indian captivity narrative, she casts white people in the role of savages and cannibals, and dwells on the emotional effect of this incident on herself:

Oh, can any one imagine my feelings *buried alive*, thinking every minute that I was to be unburied and eaten up by the people that my grandfather loved so much? . . . Oh, can any one in this world ever imagine what were my feelings when I was dug up by my poor mother and father? (12)

The idea that white people were cannibals, that "we shall all be killed and eaten up" (11) seems to have haunted especially the women after talk had come up that a party of emigrants "ate each other up in the mountains last winter"—a possible reference to the Donner party, thus locating the incidents in the year 1846.

Drawing a connection between past and present, Winnemucca now uses sentimental language to narrate the story of her life in terms of a tragic plot:

I was once buried alive; but my second burial shall be for ever, where no father or mother will come and dig me up. It shall not be with throbbing heart that I shall listen for coming footsteps. I shall be in the sweet rest of peace—I, the chieftain's weary daughter. (12)

This use of the stylized phrase of the "chieftain's weary daughter" is the only instance in which Sarah Winnemucca draws openly on the romantic figure of the Indian princess. It has to be noted that in other instances she uses her claim of being the chief's daughter not in order to possibly attain an exotic effect, but in order to establish her authority to speak up and act for her people.

When Sarah was about ten years old, her grandfather "prevailed with his people to go with him to California" (21). As his daughter, Sarah's mother accompanies him with her children, and they spend part of a year near San Jose. The trip to California marks Sarah's first direct contact with white emigrants and their way of life; at the same time her own presence in the narrative becomes stronger. Increasingly interlaced in the story of Indian-white relations, dominated by her grandfather's policy of peaceful coexistence, is the story of Sarah's own extreme reaction to his efforts: she pictures herself as a unique child who was crying more, was afraid more than any of the other children (28), a child who kept her distance from her grandfather, whom she held responsible for having exposed the family to the white "owls," and thus acts badly and rebellious. She pictures herself frantic with fear whenever confronted with white people, dancing round "like the wild one, which I was" (25).

Thus we see Sarah first as a child who is extremely violent in her instinctual resistance to contact with white people, and it is significant that this resistance, which she obviously shares with her mother, is only slowly overcome by white women's acts of kindness in order to be reinstated by acts of violence committed by white men. The first white person Sarah encounters is indeed a woman who gives the children sugar (23). And when little Sarah lies sick with the unforeseen effects of having eaten too much cake, she remembers, "some one came that had a voice like an angel." This was "the good white woman" who had come every day to see her, had made her well, and had given her her own dead child's clothes (31–33). Soon, however, the theme of sexual violence is introduced. The band leaves Stockton for the San Joaquin River, where the Paiute men work as vaqueros for a rancher. Here she reports, still from the perspective of the child, of the first incident of sexual violence by hinting that white men had attempted to rape her sister (37). This first part of the narrative establishes her as a child who feels instinctively threatened by white men taking the role of "hostiles" or savages uprooting Paiute family life. It establishes her as a special child, the daughter and granddaughter of chiefs, who perceives herself first in relation to her family, then in relation to her tribe, which is the subject of her second chapter. That this second chapter is titled "Domestic and Social Moralities" and not, as might have been expected, "Domestic . . . Manners," seems to underline the general intent of demonstrating the moral integrity of traditional Paiute upbringing and training: "Our children are very carefully taught to be good" (45). It is a chapter in which Sarah assumes the position of tribal ethnographer, at the same time inscribing herself, as female member of the community, into the description of the Paiute Flower Festival, a female puberty ceremony. It is also a chapter that discusses the issue of gender relations before and after white contact. Here it is significant that Sarah Winnemucca repeatedly emphasizes the controlled and morally pure quality of gender relations in a tribal context: "Our young women are not allowed to talk to any young man that is not their cousin, except at the festive dances" (45). Her description of the Flower Festival gives a sense of the possibilities for self-admiration and self-esteem available to Paiute girls, imagining, dancing, and singing themselves as flowers in bloom, admired by the young men who sing and dance with them. This moral integrity of gender relations and of women's self-esteem, Sarah argues, suffered a deterioration after Indian-white contact: "My people have been so unhappy . . . The mothers are afraid to have more children, for fear they shall have daughters, who are not safe even in their mother's presence" (48). Indian-white relations, she suggests, had a different dimension for native women than for native men. Her description of traditional marriage customs then emphasizes the women's freedom in choosing a husband, the husband's duty to assume all his wife's household work during a certain period before the birth of the first child, and the extent of power wives have over their husbands. When Sarah Winnemucca points to the possible superiority of Indian education over white child training, this is supported by the editor who in a footnote recommends the principles of Indian training as being "worthy the imitation of the whites" (51).[49] Sarah Winnemucca's account of the principles of Indian training leads her to emphasize the role of women in tribal politics, stating that "if the women are interested they can share in the talks" of the tribal council:

The women know as much as the men do, and their advice is often asked. We have a republic as well as you. The council-tent is our Congress, and anybody can speak who has anything to say, women and all. They are always interested in what their husbands are doing and thinking about. And they take some part even in the wars. (53)

At the same time she comments on the gendered power relations in white America: "If women could go into your Congress I think justice would soon be done to the Indians" (53). If we read this text in the context of white women's demands for political participation and the growing presence of women in public affairs, a context possibly mediated by Sarah's interaction with her editor as well as with other white women, this chapter may be seen to serve as another legitimation of Sarah's own role as public woman and tribal spokeswoman, and of the roles of woman scout and woman warrior she will subsequently assume further in her account. Thus, in the second chapter, she establishes her role as tribal spokeswoman by pointing to the role of women in the political affairs of the tribe and, in contrast to white "domestic feminism," emphasizing the absence of a separation of female and male spheres in tribal culture. At the beginning of the third chapter, she announces: "I will now stop writing about myself and family and tribe customs, and tell about the wars, and the causes of the wars. I will jump over six years" (58). She locates the events within her own history, remembering that she and her sister "were living at this time in Genoa with Major Ormsbey's family, who took us as playmates for their little girl. While with them we learned the English language very fast, for they were very kind to us. This was in the year 1858, I think" (58). When, in 1873, Sarah Winnemucca was interviewed by a reporter of the *Nevada State Journal,* she revealed that she was adopted by a Mrs. Roach, worked for several white families, and that she and her sister, while they lived in Major Ormsby's household, worked at household chores and helped serve passengers.[50] In her autobiography, however, she leaves out this part of her circumstances which reveals the common practice of frontier families to adopt Paiute children, who were expected to earn their keep, and mentions the educational effect of this practice. Yet this first experience in education is not centered on by Sarah Winnemucca as a crucial formative event. As a matter of fact, her allusions to her education are always cursory, never at the narrative center. Her emphasis is on the repetitive acts of violence marking the beginning of strained Indian-white relations in Nevada. Even the racist attitudes that terminated her attendance of a San Jose convent school remain uncommented. She simply states that they "were only there a little while, say three weeks, when complaints were made to the sisters by wealthy parents about Indians being in school with their children" (70).

Shortly after the children had to leave school, the "war of 1860" broke out, as she reports, with the kidnapping and rape of two twelve-year-old Paiute girls by white men (70–71). After a war of three months, a treaty was made, giving the Pyramid Lake Reservation to the Paiutes (73). Reservation life begins, which for the people will mean dispossession, increasing encroachment upon their land by cattle ranchers, dependence on Indian agents, hunger, starvation, and powerlessness. The description of this process of dispossession will now be at the center of Sarah's narrative, which exposes the lawless practices of Indian agents, criticizes the reservation system sharply, and argues that Indian affairs should be assigned to the military.

Again the facts of her personal life are only cursorily mentioned. The following passage is typical of the way in which Sarah Winnemucca writes her own story, as a secondary but striking presence into her narrative:

I will tell you the doings of the agents in that agency. The first six who came I did not know. In 1866, after my poor mother and sister Mary died, I came down from Virginia City to live with my brother Natchez, while there were some white men living on the agency. (79)

Telling the story of her people's plight, she only hints at the personal tragedies in her life, leaving the reader wondering about the causes of her separations from her people, about her work and her life. Canfield reveals in her biography that Sarah Winnemucca must have come into the public eye as an "Indian princess" at about that time.[51] Yet Sarah does not tell of this; neither does she tell of her father's loss of authority and trust with the white settlers at about 1866. Is her move to live with her brother, one wonders, a forced or voluntary removal from the white society of Virginia City?[52]

As soon as Sarah is on the reservation, she seems to be in a prominent position as interpreter and peacemaker, serving as go-between in the dealings of the Paiutes with their Indian agents. We see her as the one who, with her brother, warns the agent of plans to kill him (79–80), we see her jumping "on a horse, bareback" (80) to go and meet her brother at a time of danger, and we see her receiving a letter by an officer, addressed to her, and asking her and her brother for a meeting with the soldiers (82). It becomes clear that this prominent position is not only related to her family's position in the tribe, but also to her ability to speak English, to read and write, although she discounts the latter abilities (82–83). She begins to talk for her people with the soldiers. Yet it is significant that in this role she pictures herself as reluctant and needy of protection, "because I was afraid of the soldiers" (84). We see Sarah crying all the while when she is asked by the soldiers to help them bring her father's band onto the army post (85). Her brother, upon leaving his sister to the care of the Colonel, asks "that no soldiers talk to her" (100). When talking to some other Indians, he expresses his fears that the soldiers "might abuse her" (101–102). When her brother is gone, she goes to the commanding officer and tells him: "Colonel, I am here all alone with so many men, I am afraid. I want your protection. I want you to protect me against your soldiers, and I want you to protect my people also" (103). That she deemed it necessary to stress her respectable womanhood repeatedly in these allusions to her endangered virtue demonstrates the force of the voices she is speaking up against. It also demonstrates that her narrative is located, either by herself or by her editor, within a feminine discourse of respectable womanhood, with a stress on morality as a key term. This is further underlined by the fact that the book was published under Winnemucca's married name. This denial of erotic relations between the "Indian Princess" and the soldiers, and the attempt to de-eroticize her own presence as an Indian woman among white men form important strategies of the book; these go, however, curiously unnoticed in some of today's historical literature, which seems to thrive on this eroticism.[53] Of course, Sarah Winnemucca's favorable view of the army is shaped by practical, although controversial, considerations based on the Paiutes' experience:

Can you wonder, dear readers, that I like to have my people taken care of by the army? It is said that I am working in the interest of the army, and as if they wanted all this care. It is not so; but they know more about the Indians than any citizens do, and are always friendly. (93)

Yet these considerations are everywhere linked to the theme of sexual violence. Apparently in order to demonstrate the need for the army's protection against white settlers, she adds an episode that emphasizes the unprotected situation of native women in the area. Sarah Winnemucca may be influential as a political spokeswoman, yet she is constantly molested as a woman—except when she is among the soldiers:

The last time sister and I were on a visit to our people at our old home, just before I was married, we stopped with a white lady named Nichols, at Wadsworth, Nevada. . . . Some one tried to break through our bedroom door. . . . This is the kind of people, dear reader, that the government sends to teach us at Pyramid Lake Reservation. (94)

After we have seen her as peacemaker and interpreter trying to dissuade her people from going to war, there is a break of about six years in her narrative again. Chapter VI begins with a reference to the year 1875: "In 1875 I was in Camp Harney, Oregon, to see my father. It was in May" (105). Invited to act as interpreter for her people at the Malheur Reservation in Oregon, she accepts the offer, "for I had no other way of making a living for myself" (105). She pictures the people as living happily and prospering under agent Parrish, with his brother's wife, the "white lily," as a kind school teacher, loved by everyone, and assisted by Sarah. Yet again a time full of hope for a better and possibly self-determined future comes to an end when the civilian agent, in the course of the implementation of Grant's Indian policy, is supplanted by a religious man. Under the new agent Rinehart[54] the Paiutes are again dependent and starving. As the voice of her people, Sarah becomes the target of the agent's anger. Caught up in the conflict between the Department of the Interior and the War Department for control of Indian affairs, she is inevitably discharged from her position and expelled from the reservation. Moreover, agent Rinehart will try to destroy her credibility by denouncing her as a harlot and camp follower, when she reports him to Washington.

Of course, Sarah Winnemucca's main purpose is to tell about her people and not about herself. Yet at chronological breaks like these, one becomes aware of the sometimes dangerously voyeuristic nature of the interpretation of any life story—with the lure of exoticism added in the case of a Native American woman's life story. Why else should we be so curious about these years missing in her story? Canfield reveals what seems to be left out here, and what a contemporary audience potentially was, at least in part, aware of: a letter by Sarah Winnemucca criticizing the reservation system, passed on to the Indian Commissioner Parker; an article on her in the May 7, 1870, issue of *Harper's Weekly;* a Boise, Idaho, editor's unfavorable reaction to Sarah's publicity, picturing her as an unwashed, unattractive savage; an August 1870 interview in the San Francisco *Alta California;* an 1871 elopement with and marriage to a Lieutenant Bartlett, a marriage that was unacceptable to her father and brother, who did not want to see her any more; a letter to General Ord, again critical of the reservation system, with repercussions both in Nevada and Washington; after the breakup of her marriage, work as a hospital matron at Camp McDermitt; after an argument with the commanding officer a move to Winnemucca and work as a glovemaker, milliner, and interpreter. During that time she repeatedly makes the local news: she is reported to have fought with another Paiute woman who slandered her virtue and she is said to be living with an Indian named Jones.[55] Subsequently she is reported to live in Winnemucca, where within a few weeks the *Winnemucca Silver State* commented on her activities. She had gotten into another fight with another Indian woman, and was soon thereafter accused of cutting a man with a knife. Sarah had felt that her dignity was threatened because a man had touched her without permission. The "Piute Princess," as the newspapers called her, was put in the county jail overnight. In November 1876 Sarah got married, apparently for the third time. Her husband was Joseph Satwaller.[56]

What personal tragedies are hidden behind the lines of her autobiographical narrative? As a woman of two worlds, Sarah Winnemucca must have provoked criticism from both sides, walking a tightrope between two cultures. She must have found herself in the position of an outsider, not living on the reservation, but in various frontier towns, trying to make a living, and at the same time trying to speak up for her starving people in interviews, and to get her family's love back. Yet it is significant that she chooses not to talk about her life in Virginia City and the other frontier towns, and instead talks about her deeds in the service of her people. While her life as a woman in frontier towns is the focus of press reports, and may well have contributed to her popularity built on the image of the Indian princess, she herself is concerned with placing her life both within the context of the story of her tribe, and, possibly with a view to a female audience, within the context of feminine respectability.

When she takes up the narration again, after her dismissal from her interpreter's position, it is three years later. In the winter of 1878, we find her "living at the head of John Day's river with a lady by the name of Courley" (137). Having apparently had no news from Malheur for quite some time, she is asked for her help by her people: new trouble is ahead on the Bannock reservation after two white men were killed and a Bannock girl was raped; Bannocks keep trying to get the Paiutes to go to war with them against the whites. Yet Sarah repeatedly declines, since she feels powerless on account of "being a woman" (139). At last she agrees to go to Washington for them, an enterprise that will have to be postponed after the outbreak of the Bannock war. She asks to be of service to the army and acts as scout in the military campaign against the Bannocks, a service that will provoke criticism from her own people. The account of her participation in this campaign, however, is one of the most vivid parts of her book, where she now pictures herself as a female daredevil, courageous and unafraid, undertaking what neither Paiute nor white men would undertake "for love or money," leading scouting parties of fearful men (151, 155) and rescuing her people held prisoners at the camp of the "hostile" Bannocks. At the same time she takes care to emphasize that despite all this she has not lost her genteel standards of womanhood. We see her riding in the sidesaddle, wearing a riding dress (152). On the way to the camp of the "hostiles," as she terms the Bannocks, she is in the position of leader, giving orders, encouraging fearful men, guiding them over difficult terrain only she is familiar with. The only impression of the country we get is that it is rocky, full of steep mountains, and without water (155, 158).[57] Even during her daring exploits, she remains a lady; her brother tells her to "take off your hat and your dress and unbraid your hair" (158), thus again revealing her genteel appearance to her readers. Yet the heroic nature of her action is immediately revised as the act of a daughter, when she quotes her father welcoming her with the words: "Oh, my dear little girl, and what is it? Have you come to save me yet? My little child is in great danger" (159). After the rescue of her father's band from captivity, Sarah and her sister-in-law Mattie undertake the dangerous enterprise of bringing a message back to the troops: "Away we started over the hills and valleys. We had to go about seventy-five miles through the country. No water" (164). Thereafter, the two women start for Camp Lyon, and Sarah declares that she "was as mad as could be because I wanted to go right after the hostile Bannocks" (165).

It is clear that the role in which she casts herself here is the role of a warrior. When she is asked by General Howard to go with a dispatch to Camp Harney, she refuses an escort: "No, Mattie and I will go alone, for no white man can keep up with us. We can go alone quicker than with soldiers" (167). Yet one of the soldiers insists, "as there were bad white men who might harm us" (167). When a battle ensues between soldiers and "hostiles," she "did not feel any fear. I asked the general to let me go to the front line where the soldiers were fighting" (176). She draws attention to the heroism of this army, applying a cultural key term usually including Native Americans: "Dear reader, if you could only know the difficulties of this wilderness you could then appreciate their loyal service" (176). Subsequently, she casts herself in the role of the Indian fighter: "we struck the Indian rear guard. . . . We went in hot pursuit of the Indians" (178–80).

When she returns to her band's camp, she is welcomed by her family as a woman warrior, putting the Paiute men to shame. It is important how she relates this story of her elevation to the status of a warrior: it is contained in the speeches of her father and brother. Her brother scolds his young men: "I am afraid, my young men, you are not doing your duty; for I have here in my camp a warrior who has just arrived" (189). Old Winnemucca speaks in the same way to his people:

Oh! for shame! for shame to you, young men, who ought to have come with this news to me! I am much pained because my dear daughter has come with the fearful things which have happened in the war. Oh, yes! my child's name is so far beyond yours; none of you can ever come up to hers. Her name is everywhere and every one praises her. Oh! how thankful I felt that it is my own child who has saved so many lives, not only mine, but a great many, both whites and her own, people. Now hereafter we will look on her as our chieftain, for none of us are worthy of being chief but her, and all I can say to you is to send her to the wars and you stay and do women's work, and talk as women do. (193)

Thus Sarah Winnemucca has legitimized her role and established her authority as spokeswoman on multiple levels: by way of family and kinship, by pointing to the role of women in the political affairs of the tribe, and by becoming a tribal warrior hero, elevated by her chieftain father to the status of female chieftain. I agree with H. David Brumble that it sounds rather like the assertion of her deeds in the traditional manner of a coup tale[58] than like an apology when Sarah sums up her work for the army:

This was the hardest work I ever did for the government in all my life. . . . Yes, I went for the government when the officers could not get an Indian man or a white man to go for love or money. I, only an Indian woman, went and saved my father and his people. (164)

Yet while Sarah Winnemucca may present her acts in terms of a Paiute role model, her voice still remains that of an individual woman under attack from two sides. Moreover, as she now reveals, the fact that she had never spoken with her own voice, but always in the words of others, becomes the more problematic with the breakdown of tribal authority structures. Probably Sarah would not have helped gathering together the Paiutes if she had known what was ahead of them. Soon she receives order that they were to be taken to the Yakima Reservation in the middle of winter, and it becomes increasingly difficult for Sarah to act as the voice of the people and of the soldiers at the same time: she is held responsible for the army's and government's promises conveyed by her to her people. The increasing difficulty of speaking in the words of others is revealed in a dialogue between her and Mattie. Mattie replies to Sarah's fear that her people will think her to have worked against them: "Well, sister, we cannot help it if the white people won't keep their word. We can't help it. We have to work for them and if they get our people not to love us, by telling what is not true to them, what can we do? It is they, not us" (204). It is the beginning of a tragedy, of the Paiute trail of tears to the Yakima reservation in the winter of 1878–79 where they will go hungry again as they had done before. It is also the beginning of a personal tragedy: her people do not believe her any more and refuse to speak to her (208). The public lecture platform becomes her new domain of activity. She reports that she went away in November 1879 to Vancouver, Washington Territory, to see General Howard, going on to San Francisco to lecture: "Well, while I was lecturing in San Francisco, a great deal was said about it through the Western country. The papers said I was coming East to lecture" (207). When she was getting ready, a telegram arrived from Washington, asking her, her father and brother, and another chief to see the president (207). Her editor notes,

Mrs. Hopkins has not told in the text of the very great impression made by her lectures in San Francisco, showing up the iniquity of the agent Reinhard. It was, doubtless, the rumor of the excitement she caused which led to her being sent for to Washington. Reinhard could not contradict her there, where he and she were so well known, and therefore he probably wrote to Washington and told some story for himself. (217)

Thus, although Sarah herself understates the political effect of her lectures, her editor elevates her to a central position as political spokeswoman of the tribe in Washington. And in fact, Canfield's research suggests that Sarah's popularity may well have had a political impact. Yet it also suggests that any public comment on Sarah, whether positive or negative, was tied to conceptions of her womanhood, either as the good, motherly "Indian Princess" or the bad, lewd "Indian Squaw." On her arrival in San Francisco, Sarah Winnemucca found herself something of a celebrity, who had been in the public eye during the Bannock War. The newspapers headlined her as "The Princess Sarah," or wrote of her as "Nature's child." [59] The *San Francisco Chronicle* reported:

Sarah has undergone hardships and dared dangers that few men would be willing to face, but she has not lost her womanly qualities, and succeeded during her visit in coaxing into her lap two little timid "palefaced" children usually shy of strangers, who soon lost their fear of her dark skin, won by her warm and genial ways.

In the same paper, however, she was also described as having had "an extensive and diversified matrimonial experience, the number of her white husbands being variously estimated at from three to seven." Sarah subsequently gave an interview in which she refuted that report, mentioning her marriage to Bartlett and subsequent divorce and a second marriage to an Indian, who grossly mistreated her.[60] That her popularity had political repercussions is demonstrated in the letters agent Rinehart sent to the Indian Department, in which he called Sarah a "low, unprincipled Indian woman of questionable virtue and veracity as well, who was formerly Interpreter at the Agency and who was discharged for untruthfulness, gambling and other bad conduct."[61] That her lectures did have a political effect is also suggested in her description of the Paiutes' visit to Washington in January 1880. There she is asked by Secretary Schurz not to lecture (221) and the whole group is kept from reporters and other interested parties (219). At the White House, however, "[a] great many ladies were there to see us" (222), among them apparently Elizabeth Palmer Peabody,[62] while President Hayes only grants them a handshake.

The group's mission is met with only a limited success. Although Secretary Schurz has granted the Paiutes to live on the Malheur Reservation, the government provides neither supplies nor transportation for the tribe's return. Before she knows this, however, Sarah goes on another mission with another Paiute woman, trying to get her people to go to the agency. Again she emphasizes the boldness of the undertaking for two unaccompanied women, when she quotes her cousin Joe Winnemucca welcoming her with the words: "That can't be, you two women, all alone" (227). He accompanies the women to the next place, warning them:

He said there were very bad men there. Sometimes they would throw a rope over our women, and do fearful things to them. "Oh, my poor cousins," he said, "my heart aches for you, for I am afraid they will do something fearful to you. They do not care for anything. They do most terrible outrageous things to our women." (228)

Sarah herself is rather explicit about the subject of rape here, yet she speaks not as a helpless, fearful frontier woman but as a Native American woman who can defend herself to a certain extent: "If such an outrageous thing is to happen to me, it will not be done by one man or two, while there are two women with knives, for I know what an Indian woman can do. She can never be outraged by one man: but she may by two" (228). And, she adds:

It is something an Indian woman dare not say till she has been overcome by one man, for there is no man living that can do anything to a woman if she does not wish him to. My dear reader, I have not lived in this world for over thirty or forty years for nothing, and I know what I am talking about. (228)

When they leave the house the next morning, their host's Spanish boarders are after them "like wild men" (229). However, they manage to reach the next house safely. In a breathless manner she dwells on the dangers the road poses to Native American women, dangers which are linked to the absence of white women: "No white women on all the places where we stopped,—all men,—yet we were treated kindly by all of them, so far"

(230–231). When they spend the night at a place where cowboys stay over night, she is molested, yet manages to give the man "a blow right in the face" (231). When they arrive at Camp Harney, there "were only three ladies at the post. The captain's wife and the other officers' wives were kind to me while I stayed there" (232). In this context it should be noted that her remarks on and descriptions of white women always serve rather strategic functions in her narrative. There are good women like the emigrant woman who nursed her back to health when she was a child, or like the "white lily," whom she assisted as teacher of the Paiute children. There are also army officers' wives who represent genteel womanhood and protection against potential molestations, and who supply Sarah with dresses (169). Yet she also presents another kind of womanhood, such as the woman who wants to see Sarah hang, for reasons we are not informed about: "Dear reader, this is the kind of white women that are in the West. They are always ready to condemn me" (168). In another passage, she describes an Indian agent's wife: "She had a Bible with her. Ah! ah! What do you think the Bible was? Why it was a pack of cards. She would sit every day and play cards with men, and every evening, too. She was an Indian agent's wife" (223). On the whole, she seems to present western women with an eye to an eastern female audience and their assumed standards of morality.

The last part of the book is dominated by a note of personal defense against attacks from two sides. Back at the Yakima reservation, some of her people accuse her of having sold them to the soldiers, yet she is defended by the women: "We knew she would not do such a thing" (235). She herself tells her people:

You can say what you like about me. You have a right to say I have sold you. It looks so. I have told you many things which are not my own words, but the words of the agents and the soldiers. I know I have told you more lies than I have hair on my head. I tell you, my dear children, I have never told you my own words; they were the words of the white people, not mine. (236)

At the end of her narrative, Sarah Winnemucca is a woman in between, attacked from all sides—a woman desperately alone, yet trying to assume a collective voice. As if she had given up her own voice as speaker, and deferred the talking to her readers, she now appeals to them in the name of all tribes:

Hear our pitiful cry to you, sweep away the agency system; give us homes to live in, for God's sake and for humanity's sake. I left my poor people in despair, I knew I had so many against me . . . I see that all who say they are working for Indians are against me. (243)

And she goes on to appeal not only to her readers' national values, but also to their sense of morality. Again she speaks as part of a group, of Indians confronting whites:

For shame! for shame! You dare to cry out Liberty, when you hold us in places against our will, driving us from place to place as if we were beasts. Ah, there is one thing you cannot say of the Indian. You call him savage, and everything that is bad but one; but, thanks be to God, I am so proud to say that my people have never outraged your women, or have even insulted them by looks or words. Can you say the same of the negroes or the whites? They do commit some most horrible outrages on your women, but you do not drive them round like dogs. Oh, my dear readers, talk for us, and if the white people will treat us like human beings, we will behave like a people; but if we are treated by white savages as if we are savages, we are relentless and desperate; yet not more so than any other badly treated people. Oh, dear friends, I am pleading for God and for humanity. (244)

And thus ends her autobiographical narrative: "Finding it impossible to do any thing for my people I did not return to Yakima, but after I left Vancouver Barracks I went to my sister in Montana. After my marriage to Mr. Hopkins I visited my people once more at Pyramid Lake Reservation, and they urged me again to come to the East and talk for them, and so I have come" (246).

Appended to the main text is a note by the editor asking readers to sign the petition made by Sarah Winnemucca to the next Congress, asking to restore Malheur Reservation in severalty to the Paiutes, and to let the portion of Paiutes removed to Yakima return to Malheur. The language of the petition reveals its link to a female rhetoric of domesticity:

And especially do we petition for the return of that portion of the tribe arbitrarily removed from the Malheur Reservation . . . in which removal families were ruthlessly separated, and have never ceased to pine for husbands, wives, and children, which restoration was pledged to them by the Secretary of the Interior in 1880, but has not been fulfilled. (247)

Mary Mann finally draws attention to the last three pages of the appendix, which

will show that the friends of the agents she criticizes are active to discredit her; but it has been ascertained that every definite charge made to the Indian office has no better endorsement than the name of Reinhard, who is characterized, to my personal knowledge, by some of the army officers who have known of his proceedings, as "a thoroughly wicked and unscrupulous man." (248)[63]

The appendix is not only commented on by the editor, but also held together by Sarah's voice who finally places her text within the context of a campaign aimed at discrediting her as a spokes*woman:*

I know now, from the highest authority, that the government was deceived by the agent, Renehart, who said the Indians would not stay at the Malheur Reservation. After being driven away by starvation, after having had every promise broken, falsehoods were told about them and *there was no one to take their part but a woman. Every one knows what a woman must suffer who undertakes to act against bad men. My reputation has been assailed, and it is done so cunningly that I cannot prove it to be unjust. I can only protest that it is unjust, and say that wherever I have been known, I have been believed and trusted.* . . . Those who have maligned me have not known me. It is true that my people sometimes distrust me, but that is because words have been put into my mouth which have turned out to be nothing but idle wind. Promises have been made to me in high places that have not been kept, and I have had to suffer for this in the loss of my people's confidence. (258)

Sarah Winnemucca Hopkins's *Life among the Piutes* has answered many of my initial questions about the role of gender in Indian-white relations and about the way cultural contact affected Native American women's lives. Indian-white relations, as they emerge in Sarah's narrative, are highly charged with the issues of sexual violence and sexual stereotyping. Sarah herself uses her text to fight against stereotypical images of Native American women, and although she draws on the image of the Indian princess, it mainly serves as a legitimizing strategy to underline her authority as spokeswoman. Her narrative represents the attempt of a Native American woman to become real as a woman beyond stereotypes. It also counters the image of Sarah as the "fallen woman" by depicting her relationship with her sister-in-law and other women, and by presenting her, also through the voice of her editor, as part of a female community. Acculturation, however, is a double-edged sword in Sarah's narrative, as ambiguous as the image of Sarah's personality which emerges in this text. As the product of an encounter between female voices, East and West, white and Indian, the narrative presents a rather complex concept of the woman and tribal person. By referring to the role of women in the political affairs of the Paiute band, and by emphasizing the absence of the separation of female and male spheres in the tribe, Sarah Winnemucca draws authority for her public role as spokeswoman from both this position of women within the tribe and from her kinship position as daughter and granddaughter of chiefs. Placing her life story within the context of the story of her tribe, she takes on the various roles of peacemaker, interpreter, helper of both whites and Paiutes, as scout, chieftain, and woman warrior, thus legitimizing her public role with role models which are apparently in accord with Paiute concepts of womanhood. Her acts of heroism and self-reliance thus have their roots in her conception of her Native American womanhood.

On the other hand, Sarah Winnemucca draws upon images of genteel Victorian womanhood by presenting herself, within the context of feminine respectability, as a lady in appearance and manners, distancing herself from the image of the erotic or even lewd Native American "squaw." Yet whenever she emphasizes her own morality and modesty, she explains their rationale by pointing to her Paiute upbringing, and it is the voice of the editor that relates principles of Paiute womanhood to those of white respectable womanhood. When Sarah Winnemucca is seen crying, she cries over the plight of her people, which of course may have a special effect on her audience since it shows her as a sensitive woman. However, references to other aspects of "true womanhood," such as piety, submissiveness, and domesticity, are significantly lacking. Sarah Winnemucca does not present herself as a religious woman. Neither does she claim for herself a "civilizing" influence on her people. References to these aspects of ideal white womanhood are, however, contained in her remarks on white women which underline her own arguments by valuing genteel army wives and kind pioneer women over rough frontier women and immoral Indian agents' wives. Although Sarah hints at her domestic work for white women in Nevada and Oregon, there are no references to herself as a domestic woman. The idea, or rather the ideology, of "domestic feminism" so often elaborated on in the literature on white nineteenth-century women is only appealed to in references to her people's search for a permanent home where families can be reunited. She herself presents herself rather as a working woman who, although proud of her achievements, describes them as acts of necessity and duty.

Sarah Winnemucca's narrative exemplifies the necessity for a multicultural framework in the study of women's experience, which so far has focused predominantly on white middle-class women—a framework that should also allow for an analysis that takes class into account. What is presented in Sarah Winnemucca's *Life among the Piutes,* is the image of a complex personality who draws her strength from a cultural encounter whose negative impact, in the form of the white control of Native American lives, is at the center of her story. How far Sarah had control over her own narrative in the encounter with her editor and publisher, still remains to be debated. Nevertheless, although the nature of these women's collaboration still needs to be investigated more thoroughly, I would venture the thesis that this text is very much Sarah's own in the sense that she can present the complexity of her situation, both as a mouthpiece of many voices, and as a woman who is forced to find her own voice in order to defend her personal dignity. Sarah Winnemucca emerges, on the one hand, as an individual who has to defend her reputation as a modest and respectable Native American woman against both white and Indian voices, a woman who stands alone under attacks from various sides. On the other hand, she transgresses the boundaries imposed on white respectable womanhood. We see her as a tribal person committed to her people through bonds of love and kinship, drawing strength for her heroic deeds from an allegedly tribal, or rather Indian, role model of the woman warrior. It is her gender which, in the eyes of both her supporters and her attackers, singles her out. She has spoken out both as a daughter and a Paiute spokesperson, never claiming a voice of her own. But she was most vulnerable and alone when she had to find her own voice as a woman between two worlds.

NOTES

I would like to thank Eve Keitel for her thoughtful reading of this article's various drafts.

    1. Hopkins (1969).

    2. The term has been used by Slotkin (1973).

    3. Slotkin (1973) shows how women have been used as the motive behind male manipulation and destruction of both the natural world and the indigenous inhabitants of the frontier. Women are symbolically present in the popular mythology of the frontier as civilizing maternal forces from whom men flee into the wilderness or as legitimation for the conquest of Indian land.

    4. See Jeffrey (1979); Faragher (1979); Schlissel (1982); Myres (1982); Riley (1988). The only major work dealing with the imaginative constructs women have projected onto the west-

ern frontiers in their literary writings is Kolodny (1984). A textual study of women's private writings has been undertaken by Hampsten (1982). Articles of an interdisciplinary sort on western women have been collected in Armitage and Jameson (1987) and Norwood and Monk (1987).

5. See Riley (1985:83–84).

6. See Jensen and Miller (1980:185). See also DuBois and Ruiz (1990). Riley (1984:xvi) has examined the relationship between white women and Native Americans, taking as her basis the diaries and letters of westering women. Yet she puts no special focus on the relations between white and Native American women. The perspective of her study is "that of white history rather than white-Indian or Indian history." Myres (1982) has included Native American women's perspectives, based on a reading of oral and written sources. The articles included in Myres (1982) and Norwood and Monk (1987) demonstrate this growing concern for a multicultural framework in the study of western women.

7. On Native American autobiography see Krupat (1985); Brumble (1988); Sands (1982:55–65); Theisz (1981:65–80). On women's autobiography and personal narratives, see Personal Narratives Group (1989); Hoffmann and Culley (1985); Brodzki and Schenck (1988); Buss (1989:1–17).

8. Krupat (1985:31) has argued that the principle constituting the Native American autobiography as a genre is the principle of "original bicultural composite composition." Krupat (1989:133–134, 141, 149) refines this definition by describing the model of the Native American autobiography as a dialogic model of the self. In their introduction, Brodzki and Schenck (1988:2) state that "the implicit attitude toward the masculine representative self . . . is reflective . . . of a generic exclusivity in the critical treatment of autobiography, rendering this model inadequate for a theory of women's autobiography." They regard "self-definition in relation to significant others" (Brodzki and Schenck 1988:8) as the most pervasive characteristic of the female autobiography.

9. See Albers and Medicine (1983); Green (1983); Powers (1986); Liberty (1982:10–19); Mathes (1980:20–25). See also Williams (1986).

10. See the literary criticism on Silko's novel *Ceremony,* for example, Herzog (1985:25–36); Rubenstein (1987); Allen (1986:118–126).

11. See Peyer (1981:1–12; 386–402).

12. This issue is discussed in Armitage and Jameson (1987:51ff). Various papers in this collection, particularly those by Kirk and Smith, explore whether gender has an impact on intercultural relationships, and whether women and men view people of different cultures differently.

13. The value of an interpretation of Native American women's life stories for an understanding of the complexities of cultural contact and change is increasingly acknowledged. One of the first works analyzing these life stories was Bataille and Sands (1984). Carr's (1988:131–153) excellent essay on native women's life stories of the twentieth century, which has profited from recent research in both feminist and poststructuralist theory, demonstrates the fruitfulness of an approach that is sensitive to the textuality and the special "framing" of these texts.

14. See Fischer (1977); Luchetti (1982); Moynihan, Armitage, and Dichamp (1990).

15. In the historical and anthropological literature, there are many variations for the spelling of *Paiute*. I have used the popular blanket term *Paiute* throughout the text, except in direct quotations.

16. See Hopkins (1969:5), chaps. 1–4; Fowler (1978:33–42); Ruoff (1982:151–152).

17. The term *Indian Princess* occurs very often in the literature on Sarah Winnemucca. Gehm (1975) uses the term rather uncritically, without being aware of the ideological implications of this stereotype. Green (1975:698–714) has explored how the paradoxical but positive image of the Indian Princess, "exotic and sexual, yet maternal and contradictorily virginal" (Green 1975:709–710), is paired with the negative image of the Indian Squaw in the national imagination. Both the native woman's "nobility as a Princess and her savagery as a Squaw are defined in terms of her relationships with male figures" (Green 1975:703), either as exotic helper and guide, whose "sexuality can be hinted at but never realized" (Green 1975:711) or as real woman and sexual partner, in which case the positive image is converted into a negative one.

18. Peabody's letters of the years 1883–1887 show how Sarah and the Paiute case figure prominently in the old lady's correspondence before her death in 1894. See Ronda (1984:esp. 397–398, 414–415, 439–440, 442–443).

19. For these biographical details, see Canfield (1983).

20. See Fowler (1978:38); Brumble (1988:61); Ruoff (1982:151).

21. See Peyer (1981:6, 392).

22. See Ruoff (1987:1041).

23. See Ruoff (1987:1040).

24. See Ruoff (1990). I am relying here on Brumble's interpretation of Ruoff's article, since I have not yet been able to locate the publication.

25. See Brumble (1988:63).

26. See Brumble (1988:69–71).

27. See Brumble (1988:65–66).

28. See Brumble (1988:71).

29. See Bataille and Sands (1984:21).

30. This argument is partially supported by Canfield's biography of Sarah Winnemucca, which is an invaluable source on the reception of her lectures, since it collects evidence from both the eastern and the western contemporary press. Although she is concerned mainly with the accurate historical compilation of the "facts" of a life gathered from various sources, and does not consider the textual implications of her sources, Canfield (1983) provides a fascinating reconstruction of the life of Sarah Winnemucca.

31. See Mathes (1990:15–16, esp. 14).

32. See Ruoff (1987:1041).

33. See Peyer (1981:392); Fowler (1978:33).

34. See Brumble (1988:65).

35. Much of the scholarship on nineteenth-century women's history is based on the assumption that women's lives, particularly among the emerging bourgeoisie in the first half of the nineteenth century, were lived in a separate domestic "sphere," on which basis they were able to claim a kind of social power distinct from that of men. Reified in prescriptive literature, realized in daily life, and ritualized in female collectivities, this "woman's sphere" came to be seen as the foundation of women's culture and community within the Victorian middle class. See Hewitt (1990:1–14). Welter (1966:151–174) has first identified the construction of a new ideology of gender that defined the "true woman" as pious, pure, domestic, and submissive. Other formative works on Victorian womanhood are Cott (1977); Smith-Rosenberg (1975:1–29).

36. Note the way Sarah appears as the "Indian Princess" in De Quille (1947:11–12, 201–202).

37. See Green (1975:713).

38. See Brumble (1988:68, 69).

39. See Fowler (1978:33): "Robert Heizer (1960:3) suggests that her 'selfless motives and tremendous energies and high purpose make her a person to admire in the history of our far West.' Omer Stewart (1939:129) on the other hand, described her as 'ambitious, educated, . . . trying to attain self-aggrandizement by exalting her father.'"

40. See Canfield (1983:172ff) where she quotes affidavits to Washington, signed by nine gentlemen of Canyon City: "That this woman has been several times married, but that by reason of her adulterous and drunken habits, neither squawmen nor Indians would long live with her, that in addition to her character of Harlot and drunkard, she merits and possesses that of a notorious liar and malicious schemer [*sic*]."

41. Ryan (1990:48–94) discusses this double bind of women who began to claim the public, political arena for themselves in Victorian America.

42. See Fowler (1978:37): "In all fairness to her detractors, Sarah was short tempered, particularly in the context of offenses to her people, and she was known to take a drink and to scream and swear on occasion. She also had three husbands, two of them White men."

43. Note especially the titles of Peabody's and Mann's publications that emphasize the "moral" as a key term, although it might have had a different significance for nineteenth-century readers than for a twentieth-century audience. See Peabody and Mann (1870); Peabody (1874).

44. See Krupat (1985:33).

45. See Krupat (1985:33).

46. See Hopkins (1969:5); further references to the autobiography will appear in the text.

47. Quoted in Canfield (1983:203).

48. See the autobiography of Black Hawk (1964); see also *Co-ge-we-a, the Half-Blood* (Mourning Dove 1927).

49. Here Mann admires the Native American emphasis on teaching "a great deal about nature; how to observe the habits of plants and animals," criticizes Indian-white relations, and charges her own country, by quoting from Helen Hunt Jackson's *A Century of Dishonor,* with Christian bigotry: "Thus Christendom missed the moral reformation it might have had, if they had become acquainted with the noble Five Nations, and others whom they have exterminated" (Mann 1870:52).

50. See Canfield (1983:11).

51. See Canfield (1983:36–42).

52. Brimlow (1952:118), attempts to fill this gap: "Intermittently, Sarah had been doing housework for white families in Virginia City. She observed the frothy night life and participated in sociable dances, but she spent some of the hard-earned money on books to piece out her education." In a footnote he adds, with an obvious allusion to De Quille's romanticization of Sarah Winnemucca: "Written and oral evidence, for the most part, refutes stress misplaced on Sarah's frailty of character in this period. Obviously miscalculated is making Sarah a Gold Canyon frontier dance-hall girl in the early 1850s, as related in print from time to time. She had not attained teen age until about 1857."

53. See Brimlow (1952:121), who describes events later in Sarah's life:

Coincidentally with the winding up of Crook's campaign, Sarah and Natchez accompanied Company M, First United States Calvalry, from western Nevada to Fort McDermitt. On the slow journey by horseback, she warded off flirtations by emboldened troopers. She was not unattractive. A tri-cornered scarlet shawl kept alkali dust out of her glossy black hair. Her well-spaced black eyes often blinked mirthfully and her deep-red lips puckered teasingly. At the left side of a two-inch beaded belt, cleating a ruffled pink waist and a dark green overskirt, swung a sheathed knife. High-laced shoes peeked from underneath fringes of petticoats.

54. Both Canfield (1983) and Gehm (1975), in their biographies of Sarah Winnemucca, spell the agent's name as Rinehart, while in *Life among the Piutes* it appears as Reinhard or even Renehart.

55. See Canfield (1983:60–82).

56. See Canfield (1983:92).

57. This absence of explicit landscape description in Native American women's (and men's) texts is emphasized by Brumble (1988:198). He argues against Bataille's and Sands's (1984:3) assertion that one of the "basic characteristics" oral Indian literature "shares" with American Indian women's autobiography is the "concern with landscape." In an interesting article on Hispanic women artists of the Southwest, Stoller (1987:125–145) argues that Hispanic women artists, like Indian artists, have felt little need to represent their physical environment in other than abstract forms.

58. See Brumble (1988:66).

59. See Canfield (1983:164).

60. See Canfield (1983:163).

61. Quoted by Canfield (1983:163).

62. That Peabody was present at this occasion is suggested by Gehm (1975:20–21).

63. Peabody (1874:415) emphasized the same in a letter she wrote to the editor of the *Boston Daily Advertiser* in 1883: "Now I want to tell you how she has been misrepresented in some quarters—& how every thing has been thoroughly investigated & every thing is perfectly right about her. She has shared our bed & board for months this last summer and fall. I want the Daily Advertiser to recognize her & her cause—& think you will agree." One can imagine how important the support of this woman must have been for Sarah Winnemucca Hopkins at this difficult time in her life.

REFERENCES

Albers, Patricia, and Beatrice Medicine. 1983. *The Hidden Half: Studies of Plains Indian Women.* Washington, D.C.: University Press of America.

Allen, Paula Gunn, ed. 1982. *Studies in American Indian Literature.* New York: Modern Language Association.

————. 1986. *The Sacred Hoop: Recovering the Feminine in American Indian Traditions*. Boston: Beacon Press.

Armitage, Susan, and Elizabeth Jameson, eds. 1989. *The Women's West*. Norman and London: University of Oklahoma Press.

Bataille, Gretchen, and Kathleen Sands. 1984. *American Indian Women: Telling Their Lives*. Lincoln and London: University of Nebraska Press.

Black Hawk. 1964. *Black Hawk: An Autobiography*. Edited by Donald Jackson. Urbana: University of Illinois Press.

Brimlow, George F. 1952. "The Life of Sarah Winnemucca: The Formative Years." *Oregon Historical Quarterly*, June 2:103–134.

Brodzki, Bella, and Celeste Schenck, eds. 1988. *Life/Lines: Theorizing Women's Autobiography*. Ithaca and London: Cornell University Press.

Brumble, H. David. 1988. *American Indian Autobiography*. Berkeley: University of California Press.

Buss, Helen M. 1989. " 'The Dear Domestic Circle': Frameworks of the Literary Study of Women's Personal Narratives in Archival Collections." *Studies in Canadian Fiction* 1–17.

Canfield, Gae Whitney. 1983. *Sarah Winnemucca of the Northern Paiutes*. Norman: University of Oklahoma Press.

Carr, Helen. 1988. "In Other Words: Native American Women's Autobiography." In *Life/Lines*, edited by Bella Brodzki and Celeste Schenck, 131–153. Ithaca and London: Cornell University Press.

Cott, Nancy. *The Bonds of Womanhood: 'Women's Sphere' in New England, 1780–1835*. New Haven: Yale University Press.

De Quille, Dan (William Wright). 1947 [1876]. *The Big Bonanza*. New York: Knopf.

DuBois, Carol, and Vicki L. Ruiz, eds. 1990. *Unequal Sisters: A Multicultural Reader in U.S. Women's History*. New York and London: Routledge.

Faragher, John Mack. 1979. *Women and Men on the Overland Trail*. New Haven and London: Yale University Press.

Fischer, Christiane, ed. 1977. *Let Them Speak for Themselves: Women in the American West*. Hamden, Conn.: Shoestring Press.

Fowler, Catherine S. 1978. "Sarah Winnemucca, Northern Paiute, 1844–1891." In *American Indian Intellectuals*, edited by Margot Liberty, 33–42. St. Paul: West Publishing.

Gehm, Katherine. 1975. *Sarah Winnemucca: Most Extraordinary Woman of the Paiute Nation*. Phoenix: O'Sullivan.

Green, Rayna. 1975. "The Pocahontas Perplex: The Image of Indian Women in American Culture." *The Massachusetts Review*, Autumn 16:698–714.

————. 1980. "Native American Women." *Signs*, Winter 6:248–267.

————. 1983. *Native American Women: A Contextual Bibliography*. Bloomington: Indiana University Press.

Hampsten, Elizabeth. 1982. *Read This Only to Yourself: The Private Writings of Midwestern Women, 1880–1910*. Bloomington: Indiana University Press.

Herzog, Kristin. 1985. "Feeling Man and Thinking Woman: Gender in Silko's *Ceremony*." *MELUS*, Spring 12:1:25–36.

Hewitt, Nancy A. 1990. "Beyond the Search for Sisterhood: American Women's History in the 1980s." In *Unequal Sisters,* edited by Carol DuBois and Vicki L. Ruiz, 1–14. New York and London: Routledge.

Hoffmann, Leonore, and Margo Culley, eds. 1985. *Women's Personal Narratives: Essays in Criticism and Pedagogy.* New York: Modern Language Association.

Hopkins, Sarah Winnemucca. 1969 [1883]. *Life among the Piutes: Their Wrongs and Claims.* Edited by Mrs. Horace Mann. Bishop, Calif.: Sierra Media.

Jeffrey, Julie Roy. 1979. *Frontier Women: The Trans-Mississippi West 1840–1880.* New York: Hill and Wang.

Jensen, Joan, and Darlis A. Miller. 1980. "The Gentle Tamers Revisited: New Approaches to the History of Women in the American West." *Pacific Historical Review* 49:2:173–212.

Kolodny, Annette. 1984. *The Land Before Her: Fantasy and Experience of the American Frontiers, 1630–1860.* Chapel Hill and London: University of North Carolina Press.

Krupat, Arnold. 1985. *For Those Who Come After: A Study of Native American Autobiography.* Berkeley: University of California Press.

———. 1989. *The Voice in the Margin: Native American Literature and the Canon.* Berkeley: University of California Press.

Liberty, Margot. 1982. "Hell Came with Horses: Plains Indian Women in the Equestrian Era." *Montana, The Magazine of Western History,* Summer 32:10–19.

Luchetti, Cathy, in collaboration with Carol Olwell. 1982. *Women of the West.* St. George, Ut.: Antelope Island Press.

Mann, Mary Tyler, and Elizabeth Palmer Peabody. 1870. *Moral Culture of Infancy and Kindergarten Guide.* New York: Schenterhorn.

Mathes, Valerie Sherer. 1980. "American Indian Women and the Catholic Church." *North Dakota History,* Fall 20–25.

———. 1990. *Helen Hunt Jackson and Her Indian Reform Legacy.* Austin: University of Texas Press.

Mourning Dove (Hum-ishu-ma). 1929. *Co-ge-we-a, The Half-Blood: A Depiction of the Great Montana Cattle Range,* as told to Sho-pow-tan. Boston: Four Seas.

Moynihan, Ruth B., Susan Armitage, and Christiane Fischer Dichamp, eds. 1990. *So Much to Be Done: Women Settlers on the Mining and Ranching Frontier.* Lincoln and London: University of Nebraska Press.

Myres, Sandra L. 1982. *Westering Women and the Frontier Experience, 1800–1915.* Albuquerque: University of New Mexico Press.

Norwood, Vera, and Janice Monk, eds. 1987. *The Desert Is No Lady: Southwestern Landscapes in Women's Writing and Art.* New Haven and London: Yale University Press.

Peabody, Elizabeth Palmer. 1874. *Record of Mr. Alcott's School, Exemplifying the Principles and Methods of Moral Culture.* 3d ed. Boston: Roberts Brothers.

Personal Narratives Group, ed. 1989. *Interpreting Women's Lives: Feminist Theory and Personal Narratives.* Bloomington: Indiana University Press.

Peyer, Bernd C. 1981. "Autobiographical Works Written by Native Americans." *Amerikastudien/American Studies* 26:3/4:386–402.

————. 1981. "The Importance of Native American Authors." *American Indian Culture and Research Journal* 5:3:1–12.

Powers, Marla. 1986. *Oglala Women: Myth, Ritual, and Reality.* Chicago: University of Chicago Press.

Riley, Glenda. 1984. *Women and Indians on the Frontier, 1825–1915.* Albuquerque: University of New Mexico Press.

————. 1985. "Women on the Great Plains: Recent Developments in Research." *Great Plains Quarterly* 5:2:81–92.

————. 1988. *The Female Frontier: A Comparative View of Women on the Prairie and Plains.* Lawrence: University Press of Kansas.

Ronda, Bruce A., ed. 1984. *Letters of Elizabeth Palmer Peabody: American Renaissance Woman.* Middletown, Conn.: Wesleyan University Press.

Rubenstein, Roberta. 1987. *Boundaries of the Self: Gender, Culture, Fiction.* Urbana and Chicago: University of Illinois Press.

Ruoff, A. LaVonne Brown. 1982. "Old Traditions and New Forms." In *Studies in American Indian Literature,* edited by Paula Gunn Allen, 147–168. New York: Modern Language Association.

————. 1987. "Western American Indian Writers, 1854–1960." In *A Literary History of the American West,* edited by The Western Literature Association, 1038–1057. Fort Worth: Texas Christian University Press.

————. 1990. "Nineteenth-Century American Indian Autobiographers: William Apes, George Copway, and Sarah Winnemucca." In *Redefining American Literary History,* edited by A. LaVonne Ruoff and Jerry Ward. New York: Modern Language Association.

Ryan, Mary. 1990. *Women in Public: Between Banners and Ballots, 1825–1880.* Baltimore: Johns Hopkins Press.

Sands, Kathleen Mullen. 1982. "American Indian Autobiography," in *Studies in American Indian Literature,* edited by Paula Gunn Allen, 55–65. New York: Modern Language Association.

Schlissel, Lillian. 1982. *Women's Diaries of the Westward Journey.* New York: Schocken Books.

Schlissel, Lillian, Vicki L. Ruiz, and Janice Monk, eds. 1988. *Western Women: Their Land, Their Lives.* Albuquerque: University of New Mexico Press.

Slotkin, Richard. 1973. *Regeneration through Violence: The Mythology of the American Frontier, 1600–1860.* Middletown, Conn.: Wesleyan University Press.

Smith-Rosenberg, Carroll. 1975. "The Female World of Love and Ritual: Relations between Women in Nineteenth-Century America." *Signs,* Autumn 1:1–29.

Stoller, Marianne L. 1987. "Peregrinas with Many Visions: Hispanic Women Artists of New Mexico, Southern Colorado, and Texas." In *The Desert Is No Lady,* edited by Vera Norwood and Janice Monk, 125–145. New Haven and London: Yale University Press.

Theisz, R. D. 1981. "The Critical Collaboration: Introductions as a Gateway to the Study of Native American Bi-Autobiography." *American Culture and Research Journal* 5:1:65–80.

Williams, Walter L. 1986. *The Spirit and the Flesh: Sexual Diversity in American Indian Culture.* Boston: Beacon Press.

TOWARD AN ANTHROPOLOGY OF ANTHROPOLOGY
Culture Heroes, Origin Myths, and Mythological Places of Southwestern Anthropology

William Willard

I t may be that nineteenth-century anthropology in general was "imbued with a pervasive ideology of social progress" and "dominated by hopes for a general science of Man, for discovering social laws in the long evolution of humans toward ever higher standards of rationality" (Marcus and Fischer 1986:17). In the American Southwest, however, the ethnological tone was imbued with romanticism, and archaeology was dominated by the search for exotic objects for museum collections. The individuals who contributed to the development of the tone of Southwestern ethnology must realistically be considered in terms of their personal agendas. These agendas cannot be discounted in considering how and why a professional culture developed in the ways that it did and still does. For some, even most, early Southwest anthropologists it wasn't contributing to theory and subscription to an ideology that brought them to the subject, it was simply that they liked the adventure of being among Other people (in Todorov's sense) and the uncommitted nomadic quality of camp life. Oliver La Farge caught this sentiment in a short story:

I figured that I'd do another week's work on it before moving on, and that next year when the University gave me a regular expedition again—the funds were promised—I'd excavate this place thoroughly. This year I was simply scouting, enjoying the frequent changes of camp, and finding it a relief not to have any students to take care of. (La Farge 1935:90)

The professional anthropological literature about the indigenous cultures of the American Southwest probably surpasses that of all other ethnographic regions in the Americas for its magnitude and richness of detail (Basso 1979:14). That great literature tells very little about the people who wrote that literature. But there is another source of information for an anthropological study in the smaller body of oral and written texts about the people who produced the great wealth of the professional literature. James Watson's *Double Helix,* for an example from another discipline, is the kind of writing that tells how a profession really functions with professional rivalry and personality conflicts, individual likes and dislikes. Here we factor into our awareness the kind of information that Paul Rabinow called corridor talk, in the domain of gossip networks.

Rabinow advocates moving corridor talk into discourse to develop an anthropology of anthropology. Corridor talk is, in Geertzian phraseology, the stories "they" tell themselves about themselves. The importance of the stories they tell themselves about themselves is that there is "a body of tales, some verging on or already passed into myth. Such may serve as one of many mechanisms which give group members a sense of oneness and uniqueness" (Woodbury 1986). This body of tales tells who and how the culture of anthropology has been shaped. It is, again in Geertzian terms, an ensemble of texts that can be read to examine the culture of the group to which it pertains. An anthropology of Southwestern anthropology derived from reading the non-academic and fictional literature is an application of the notion that "one can start anywhere in a culture's repertoire of forms and end up anywhere else. One only has to learn how to gain access to them" (Geertz 1973:453).

Access to the culture of anthropology through certain works of fiction is access to a medium where the corridor talk, what is not said in the academic literature, can be acquired. Writing that is clearly labeled fiction provides a way to publish academic corridor talk. The authors have deniability; those who know "the truth" read to see how much was left out, and those who do not know are only reading fiction.

ORIGIN MYTHS

In a broad but real sense that does not take into account the intellectual beginnings of American anthropology, the origins of Southwestern anthropology are rooted in a political event, the Treaty of Guadalupe Hidalgo of 1848. This treaty marked the end of the U.S.-Mexican War of 1845 and the cession of the northern quarter of Mexico to the United States. The Bureau of American Ethnology from its founding on March 3, 1879, took as part of its mission dispatching expeditions to the new American Southwest to collect information about the alien Other people of the indigenous communities of the region.

The Bureau of American Ethnology expeditions into the unknown new territories of the Southwest were interested in everything. Material culture, architecture, language, folklore, archeology, anything, was collected because it was all new information.

Cushing

Frank Hamilton Cushing at Zuni is the culture hero who established the accepted rites of passage for cultural anthropology for the next century. He came to the Southwest in August 1879 as an employee of the Smithsonian Institution assigned to a Bureau of American Ethnology expedition headed by James and Matilda Cox Stevenson. His assignment is prologue in every sense of the word for his activities at Zuni. As Basso writes,

the newly founded Bureau of American Ethnology arranged for one of its employees, Frank Hamilton Cushing, to travel to the Territory of New Mexico to inquire firsthand into the customs and beliefs of the People of Zuni Pueblo. (1979:14)

Cushing lived at Zuni for four and a half years in the native governor's house.

His life in the governor's house (actually the governor's wife's house in matrilineal Zuni) has the aura of myth. When he first came to Zuni, he lived in the style of the local people (see *Zuni: Selected Writings of Frank Hamilton Cushing*). He slept on sheepskins on the floor, wore the clothing of the men of the pueblo, and ate the village food of mutton stew, tamales, paper bread, and *tortillas de maiz*. He took a break from his fieldwork in 1882 to take four Zunis and one Hopi to tour the eastern cities, particularly Boston and Washington. Cushing may have attracted as much attention as the Zuni and Hopi travelers, in his silver-ornamented buckskin clothing, turquoise necklaces, long hair, head wrap, and eagle feather. (See Hinsley's "Zunis and Brahmins" for a fuller description of that trip.)

His second stay was different. He came back with his new wife Emily, his sister Margaret, and an anonymous "negro cook brought from Washington, and trained in an old Virginia family, [who] presided at the fireplace" (Baxter, cited in Green 1979:249). The Cushing entourage took the governor's first floor, while the governor lived with his wife's household on the second floor. On the first floor austerity was replaced by a hybrid sort of "divan Japonais en Zuni" (Hinsley 1983:59) with sofas, Japanese fans, Navajo rugs, mirrors, and assorted wall hangings. The Cushings and their visitors were served from a well-supplied larder of food and bottled beverages. Adolph Bandelier, who was surveying ruins near Zuni, wrote of the arrival of a messenger from Cushing with a four-mule train of provisions, including thoughtful gifts of cigars, beer, and a bottle of whiskey. Cushing had dispatched the provisions after hearing that Bandelier had fallen from a wagon and had been run over by it. Bandelier was resting from the incident at the small farm village of Nutria, twenty-five miles from Zuni. The whiskey, Bandelier wrote, was of much comfort.

Cushing's departure from Zuni was dramatic. Some land pirates had tried to grab part of the pueblo's land through legal chicanery. Cushing countered with a successful campaign that included reportage in northeastern newspapers. U.S. Senator John A. Logan of Illinois, involved in both this and another Zuni land grab, the father-in-law of one of the other land thieves—Major William F. Tucker, stationed at Fort Wingate, New Mexico Territory—threatened to use his senatorial privileges to cancel funding for the Bureau of American Ethnology, Cushing's employer, unless he was removed from Zuni. The heroic defender and champion of the pueblo thereupon left, defeated by corrupt and vindictive senatorial privilege (see Wilson 1956).

The Frank Cushing origin myth, viewed from the perspective of the American Indian Coyote myths, presents a very Coyotelike culture hero with both positive and negative sides. Like Coyote he frequently took an assertive approach in his gathering of information. He did not allow any resistance to his appearance in any setting at the pueblo, whether it was a secret religious society meeting or moving into a household. He was not unopposed in his aggressions. Adolph F. Bandelier, an 1883 visitor to Zuni, recorded his impressions:

Mr. Cushing has trouble in the pueblo. There is a man here called Roman Luna, half-Navajo, who is his bitter enemy. He tried to take his [Cushing's] life and has stirred up an insurrection against him and the chiefs. The latter are on his [Cushing's] side. As war chief of the tribe, Cushing is accused of not having done his duty. He offers to resign.

Bandelier's romantic image of the intrepid ethnologist facing down Roman Luna in front of an ellipse of the men of good standing in the big plaza at Zuni is only one example of the literary wealth in the journals:

Behind the principals the rest of the men, including many Navajo men, stood or squatted, because it was a general meeting of the pueblo and as such all the men "in good standing" with the pueblo had access to it. In the great debate before the council, Roman Luna spoke long and loud. Frank Cushing spoke very calmly and persuasively. The two spoke in the big plaza, encircled by the high walls of the houses, crowded with men smoking corn husk cigarettes, a pungent haze of smoke from burning pinyon pine-wood and tobacco hanging over their heads. The adversaries presented their arguments to the half circle of principals and the packed crowd of Zuni and Navajo men behind them.

Later after nightfall when the voting had been completed, the head-chiefs all came to the governor's house, smiling and glad. They brought news from the council. Cushing had previously re-signed, and they now came to beg of him to withdraw his resignation and accept his position as war chief again. (Bandelier, *Southwestern Journals*, February 1883, 38–39)

Cushing's stay at Zuni, when the Stevenson expedition moved on, established the model for the participant-observer role for the fieldwork, which is the hallmark of American anthropology. He lived as the Zuni people did, ate Zuni food, wore Zuni clothes, and learned to speak the Zuni language. He became a participant in the things that Zuni people did. These remain the components of the accepted observer-participant fieldwork method of American anthropology. Many others came to Zuni to have something magic rub off onto their own lives from the Zuni people and the Cushing legend, as Terry Boren saw it happening in a Navajo context (Boren 1987).

Archaeology

In the origin myth of archaeology, Cushing and Bandelier share the position of culture heroes and mythmakers. They were associated with both the great eastern archaeological expeditions into the Southwest and the founding of the great regional archaeological institutions.

In the beginning, when Bandelier visited Cushing in Zuni Pueblo in 1883, he came there as a part of his survey of archaeological sites in New Mexico, Arizona, Sonora, and Chihuahua. The survey and its funding source presaged the next chapter in the Frank Cushing mythology and Adolph Bandelier's own next enterprise. The survey was funded by the Archaeological Institute of America of Boston, a private organization of New Englanders interested in Southwestern antiquities.

Six years later, Bandelier and Cushing were employed by the Boston-based Hemenway Southwestern Archaeological Expedition. This time the money came from one person, Mary Hemenway of Boston, who gave twenty-five thousand dollars a year to keep the expedition in the field. The expedition camped in the middle Gila River valley of Arizona from 1886 to 1889. Cushing was the expedition leader. Various expedition members carried out large scale excavations, collected skeletal material for physical anthropological studies, did documentary research, made observations among the Pima villages, and studied pre-Columbian irrigation. Bandelier was employed as the expedition's historiographer to do documentary research in Spanish colonial and church archives in Santa Fe and Mexico City. The Hemenway Expedition carried out the first archaeological excavation that could be called scientific in the Southwest (Haury 1945:vii, 3–4).

Frank Cushing did not write any final reports (Schroeder 1979:6). The only scientific report of the archaeological work carried out was compiled years later in Emil Haury's *The Excavation of Los Muertos and Neighboring Ruins in the Salt River Valley of Southern Arizona.* Emil Haury put the volume together from published works of participants, incomplete manuscripts, notes, maps, and the recollections of F. W. Hodge, secretary of the expedition and the last surviving member. Hodge failed to recollect for Haury that he still had the records of the expedition in his possession (after Hodge's death, Bernard L. Fontana found the records while preparing an inventory of his papers).

Hodge did remember Frank Cushing's omission of a final report;

If a paucity of material was left by the director of the expedition, it was due also in part (Cushing was in poor health much of the time) to an overwrought imagination and a species of egotism that brooked no opinion adverse to his own and accepted no suggestion of scientific help on the part of others. (Haury 1945:viii–ix)

THIEVES OF TIME

The American settlers who came to the new territories after the Treaty of Guadalupe Hidalgo turned to anything that would bring in money: construction work, driving freight wagons, mining, cowboying, anything. Then a new source of cash income turned up. Willa Cather wrote about how it happened in "Tom Outland's Story," a story within the story *The Professor's House:* "This German, Fechtig, come along; he'd been buying up a lot of Indian things out here, and he bought your whole outfit and paid four thousand dollars for it" (Cather 1925:238). The whole outfit was the loot from a find two cowboys had made in an Anasazi Pueblo.

The story is based on the real cowboys, Richard Wetherill and Charlie Mason, who in 1888 discovered the Mesa Verde ruins:

I wish I could tell you what I saw there: just as I saw it, on that first morning, through a veil of lightly falling snow, far above me, a thousand feet or so, set in a great cavern in the face of the cliff, I saw a little city of stone, asleep. I knew at once that I had come upon the city of some extinct civilization, hidden away in this inaccessible mesa for centuries, preserved in the dry air and almost perpetual sunlight like a fly in amber, guarded by the cliffs and the river and the desert. (Cather 1925:202)

Willa Cather wrote about both the appropriation of one local culture's artifacts for another's national cultural symbols and the cash-market profit motive for pothunting for those same artifacts;

There's only one man in thousands that wants to buy relics and pay real money for them. Who else would have bought it, I want to know? We'd have had to pack it around at Harvey Houses, selling it at a dollar a bowl, like the poor Indians do. (Cather 1925:241)

Willa Cather thought of the Anasazi ceramics as national treasures to be preserved for all Americans:

I never thought of selling them, because they weren't mine to sell—nor yours! They belonged to this country, to the State, and to all the people. They belonged to boys like you and me, that have no other ancestors to inherit from. You've gone and sold them to a country that's got plenty of relics of its own. You've gone and sold your country's secrets, like Dreyfus. (Cather 1925:243)

Willa Cather had arrived in the Southwest at the invitation of Mabel Dodge Luhan who asked her to stay at Mabel's Great House in Taos, New Mexico. Mabel Dodge Luhan turns up in nearly any narrative about the Southwest after 1920. She was a great patron of the many American and European artists and writers who were invited to stay at her house in Taos. An important feature of stays at the Great House was touring the region under the guidance of Mabel's husband and sometime Taos Pueblo official, Antonio Luhan. Willa Cather's access through Mabel and Tony to the Southwestern tales provided her the inspiration to write Tom Outland's story. The story is an earnest statement on the justification for one culture's appropriation of another culture's archaeological history.

Cather wrote a word portrait of the level of federal interest in Southwestern antiquities of the time as contrasted to simple earnest Tom Outland. Tom came to Washington to find some federal agency or institution to receive the objects he and another cowboy had found;

> At last the Commissioner returned, but he had pressing engagements and I hung around for several days more before he could see me. After questioning me for about a half an hour, he told me that his business was with living Indians, not dead ones, and that his office should have advised me of that in the beginning. He advised me to go back to our Congressman and get a letter to the Smithsonian Institution. The head clerk followed me down the corridor and asked me what I would take for that little bowl he had taken a fancy to. He said it had no market value, I'd find Washington full of such things, there were cases of them in the cellar at the Smithsonian that they'd never taken the trouble to unpack, hadn't any place to put them. (Cather 1925:226–227)

The Smithsonian's Secretary was interested in Tom's story and set up a meeting with Dr. Ripley, who was the authority on prehistoric Indian remains (Cather 1925:234).

Ripley asked the right questions and seemed to be interested. The problem was there was no money to excavate, but there was a bill in Congress to appropriate money to the Smithsonian. If the bill was passed, there might be money to send an expedition to the Southwest. Ripley took Tom's pottery to study and never returned it. Two months later, Congress had appropriated money to the Smithsonian, but not enough to fund a Southwestern expedition. Tom had to send a telegram to Roddy Blake, the other cowboy, for money to come back to Colorado.

The real Richard Wetherill and his brothers went on to become the best-known nineteenth- and early twentieth-century Southwestern commercial pothunters. They were the first Americans to see many Anasazi ruins, and were the guides for late nineteenth- and early twentieth-century archaeological expeditions to the Southwest. The archaeologists whom the Wetherills guided came in expeditions to collect spectacular artifacts for Northeastern museums and collections. In the transfer process, the readiness of wealthy collectors to pay cash for Southwestern antiquities stimulated the development of a commodity market for artifacts. Settlers who could not make a living on hardscrabble farms were inspired to become pothunters by the market.

In Frank Cushing's time, Eastern museums began to send their own expeditions to do purposeful archaeology in the Southwest. At first, there was little difference between commercial pothunting and official archaeological expeditions. Both the expeditions and the pothunters were representative of the antiquarian attitudes of the nineteenth century, when museums increased their prestige and reputation by collecting large numbers of artifacts (Chase, Chase, and Topsey 1988:58).

The next phase was the appearance of privately funded archaeological institutes located in the Southwest, administered by either very wealthy individuals or by men with access to wealthy patrons. The first of these was the School of American Archaeology, established in 1909 in Santa Fe, New Mexico, as an offshoot of the Archaeological Institute of America. The school's director, Edgar L. Hewett, changed its name in 1916 to the School of American Research, so as to include the painters who were moving to Santa Fe. With the passage of time, the institutes and the archaeologists associated with them became mythological presences of Southwestern archaeology. They began the professionalization of the field, which has evolved "from curio-collecting to radio-carbon-dating and pollen analysis" (Judd 1968) and has developed even more sophisticated methods since Judd wrote those words.

The privately funded archaeological institutions included the Gila Pueblo Archaeological Foundation in Globe, Arizona, founded in 1928 by Harold S. Gladwin and Mrs. Winifred Jones MacCurdy; the Museum of Northern Arizona in Flagstaff, Arizona, founded by Dr. Harold S. Colton and his wife, Mary-Russell Ferrell Colton, in 1928; the Laboratory of Anthropology, Incorporated, in 1930 by John D. Rockefeller, Jr.; the Museum of International Folk Art, founded by Elizabeth Bibell Heard in Santa Fe; and the Amerind Foundation, Incorporated, founded in 1937 in Dragoon, Arizona, by William Shirley Fulton and his wife Rose. The directors of these institutions are ancestors of Southwestern archaeological culture, who in effect divided the Southwest among themselves, so that any one wishing to do archaeological work in the region needed the positive sanction of the powerful directors. These powerful directors also began to find negative sanctions to apply against the pothunters.

These legendary persons met with other archaeological figures to establish an annual cultural ritual of professional recognition. Forty-one ancestral figures (a "Past Is Present" column says there were perhaps more than fifty; *Anthropology Newsletter,* September 1991), met by invitation at the first Pecos Conference on August 29–31, 1927, at what is now a mythological place, "the excavation camp of Phillips Academy, Andover, at Pecos, New Mexico." Alfred V. Kidder, director of the Phillips Academy project was the host and inviter. He maintained his field camp at Pecos for fifteen years, excavating the ruins of Pecos Pueblo. The event became the traditional annual gathering which brought together "the cream of Southwestern practising archaeologists, to spend time arguing on such questions as 'when is a kiva not a kiva?'" (Morris 1978:39).

ETHNOLOGY

Southwestern ethnology began with Cushing as a salvaging of indigenous cultural diversity. The diversity was seen as destined to disappear through the overpowering assimilative force of American culture. Ethnologists were to capture the authenticity of the changing native cultures for the ethnological record.

In the twentieth century there was an intensification of the salvage effort in tandem with the sink-or-swim Cushing style applied to university students training in the observer-participant role. The first source of the university students was Columbia University, where Franz Boas defined anthropology and how it should be done. Fieldwork training was sanctioned by Boas's own experience in the Arctic and on the Northwest Coast. There was a difference in this new phase. Now it wasn't just a lone observer-participant. Dennis Tedlock described it thus: "Beginning in the second decade of the present century, a veritable army of Boasian fieldworkers descended upon Zuni" (Tedlock 1983:37).

Two of the Boasians, Ruth Benedict and Ruth Bunzel, came in the summer of 1924. Their style of living was neither as Spartan as Cushing's first stay nor as well supplied as his second. They lived in a rented house with a bed and table at the edge of Zuni village. Ruth Benedict spent long hours writing down the folktales and myths people told her, while Ruth Bunzel studied potterymaking. They did not collect in the high-handed Cushing style. Instead, they paid people to talk to them. Both were successful in publishing from their fieldwork notes. Dennis and Barbara Tedlock have memorialized Ruth Benedict's long-term success, noting that "the most widely read piece on Zuni is Chapter 4 in Benedict's *Patterns of Culture*" (1979:473).

Benedict and Bunzel went on to stay in other pueblos. Ruth Benedict's letters from Cochiti Pueblo speak of the joys of finding four boxes of Aunt Jemima pancake flour for sale at a Pueblo store, and of the entertainment of meeting

One amorous male I think I have got rid of, dear soul! He's stunning, with melting eyes and the perfect confidence which I can't help believing has come from a successful amour with a white woman. He hopes I'll be another Mabel Dodge; he's all ready to take Tony's part and I will say he's a better catch than Tony. (Benedict 1925)

After Ruth Benedict's achievement at Zuni, she became the supervisor who field-marshaled the Boasian troops' summer fieldwork rituals in the 1920s and 1930s.

The body of tales is an important part of the anthropology of Southwestern anthropology. The tales tell about the practice of fieldwork from the mythological times of the culture hero, Frank Cushing, in the place of origin at Zuni Pueblo, where the concept of fieldwork and the way it was to be done began. The tales carry the history from legendary times through the changes in the practice of the profession and the styles of the practitioners. Once upon a time anthropologists were ethnologists and archaeologists from Northeastern universities and federal agencies, intent on academic prestige to advance their careers. A recent "Past Is Present" column in the *Anthropology Newsletter* speaks of anthropologists in the 1930s who went out to the Southwest to do "fieldwork summers with the Navajo," and "with the Walapai," mass nouns that imply that they were interviewing all of the Navajo and Walapai on the planet. Actually of course, an individual anthropologist talked with some small number of Navajo and Walapai individuals who, because they were paid and had nothing pressing to do that summer, answered questions and told stories (*Anthropology Newsletter,* September 1991).

The intended audience for ethnologic information shifted in the 1930s from an academic focus to include government agency administrators. The shift marked a federal-Indian policy change as a result of the national elections of 1933. John Collier was appointed as chief administrator of the Bureau of Indian Affairs. Collier was convinced that anthropological fieldwork could provide information for the improvement of the BIA. During his eleven years as commissioner he hired anthropologists for positions at all levels throughout the agency. In addition he contracted with the Society for Applied Anthropology, university anthropology departments, and individual anthropologists for fieldwork projects to provide specific kinds of data, an applied anthropology.

Oliver La Farge was one of Collier's applied anthropologists and also a prolific writer of fiction about characters and situations in the Southwest. Because of his access, he is a prime source for corridor stories and the "political correctness" of the time. One of his short stories, "The Little Stone Man," is something of both in that at least some of the characters are identifiable as anthropologists of the time and as a statement of political correctness for the time. The story is about naive Charlie Bond, who had grown up in close association with people of the pseudonymous pueblo of San Leandro. The pueblo religious leadership asks him to locate a stolen stone figure, the stone man of the title. Charlie recovers the figure and in the process of returning it to the Pueblo religious officials learns something about the stone figure. Charlie goes away to the fictitious Talvert University to become an anthropology major. Because he is from the Southwest he is invited to a social meeting of eminent anthropologists, where he meets a visiting Dr. Sorenson of Northern California University. Dr. Sorenson uses his eminence and detailed knowledge of San Leandro to manipulate naive Charlie into revealing just enough new information about the stone figure for Sorenson to add to what he already knew and what he had guessed to write an article about "Anthropomorphic Fetishes at Modern Pueblos" and get it published in the pseudonymous *Southwestern Anthropologist,* with a footnote crediting Charlie for his assistance. There were, of course, San Leandro pueblo members at the University of New Mexico who read the *Southwestern Anthropologist.* The War Captains and their assistants meet Charlie when he tries to return to San Leandro. They tell him: "You get out Bond, or we put you out. We beat the hell out of you" (La Farge 1988).

There is a second story, "The Ancient Strength," which has portents for the ways pueblos will seek the return of lost land in the future. The place of the story is San Leandro again. The pueblo has a claim to the El Cajón grant of some twenty thousand acres of land and the water rights of the permanent stream of water on the land. If the pueblo government can show legal evidence that the land and water rights belong to them by aboriginal use and occupancy, then there could be compensation for their loss of the same.

The role of the archaeologist, a man named Hendricks, is to provide archaeological evidence that would date the use of the El Cajón land by the San Leandro people through matching potsherds uncovered at a settlement of Civil War time on the lost land with pottery of the same kind from the communal trash heap of San Leandro. La Farge explains the importance of pueblo trash heaps. There are some religious associations about a supernatural presence called Ash Boy, involving the ashes of kiva fireplaces and other less identified materials and places in the midden, as well as the use of rubbish for dating occupation of a particular place. For two thousand years, Basketmakers, Anasazi, and Pueblos have had the institution of an annual village cleaning with a dumping of the collected refuse in a fresh layer on top of last year's trash for the entire time that a village is occupied. Therefore, a pueblo trash heap is a layered historical record of the Pueblos' past and, if excavated by a professional archaeologist in a professional way, is acceptable as scientific evidence to validate a historical claim in court.

The archaeologist Hendricks is approached by the law firm representing the pueblo to come to excavate the trash heap with the approval of the pueblo council. Men from San Leandro know Hendricks from working as shovel bums on digs for him. Hendricks is an assistant professor in the anthropology department of Northern California University. He is a specialist in Pueblo-Anasazi archaeology and has "worked in Pueblo country for more than a dozen seasons" (La Farge 1988:194). The law firm has offered forty dollars a day to Hendricks to do the work and appear as an expert witness. An older anthropologist, Sorenson, advises Hendricks, "Anyone in the academic line who doesn't pick up a little extra money when he can do so properly and legitimately should have his head examined" (La Farge 1988:197).

The council decides not to approve the dig in the trash heap because the digging would disturb the spiritual solidarity of the pueblo. Hendricks tells the council, "I think you are exactly right. I think the important thing is for you to keep everything whole" (La Farge 1988:212). The story marks the beginnings of the practical use of archaeological authority and the authenticity of professional standards for field methods by pueblo governments to make legal claims for lost land and water rights.

Clyde Kluckhohn was one of the most influential individuals among the applied anthropologists during and after the Collier years (1933–44). He came to the Southwest in 1922 for health reasons, to spend time with near-relatives, the Vogt family. The Vogt ranch was near Ramah, New Mexico, not far from Zuni. He learned the Navajo language and became familiar with the Navajo culture of the people who lived around Ramah. Kluckhohn moved to Harvard from the University of New Mexico and took his interest in fieldwork with him. He brought Harvard students to the Southwest for the transforming experience of fieldwork, just as the Boasians had, except Kluckhohn preferred placing his students in Navajo communities.

David Aberle said that Kluckhohn was a magnificent interpreter of Navajo culture to various American publics in the sense of showing members of one culture how the world looks to another culture (Aberle 1973:88). And John Adair wrote a chapter entitled "Clyde Kluckhohn and Indian Administration" in *Culture and Life,* a collection of essays about him. The judicious academic prose here shows the importance of Kluckhohn as an influential academic anthropologist with a nearly lifelong political involvement in Navajo affairs. Aberle believed that Kluckhohn and other applied anthropologists of the Collier years were under the "happy assumption that if they [the federal administrators] were enlightened by the anthropologists, the powerful would act to help the powerless" (Aberle 1973:88).

In a historical sense Frank Cushing could be viewed as having pioneered the role of an applied anthropologist in the Southwest long before John Collier employed any anthropologists to enlighten federal administrators. The perils of being or of being perceived as an applied anthropologist remained for all who came after Cushing. During Collier's tenure he ingeniously found ways to protect the anthropologists who worked for the BIA. But anthropologists who were not in protected positions could find themselves in very uncomfortable circumstances caught between the powerful and the powerless.

There is a novella, *Chapayeca,* by G. C. Edmondson, a veteran science-fiction writer and a man with access to the store of anthropological tales about Yaqui ethnological fieldwork. The novella draws from the store of tales about American anthropologists doing fieldwork in Yaqui communities in the American state of Arizona and in the Mexican state of Sonora. The central character is Nash Taber, a pseudonymous anthropologist who has specialized in ethnographic studies of the Yaqui culture of Sonora. The novella goes beyond fieldwork to the professional perils of a faculty person in the academic milieu of an anthropology department. The chairman of the anthropology department with which Nash Taber is affiliated at a nameless Southwestern university threatens him with an ultimatum to publish something new, or else. Taber reflects on his personal situation:

As a young man he'd gotten by on brilliance, never learning the outs of infighting. But he was no longer young. At thirty-nine he should have been easing into administration but here he was on another goddamn field trip. And he'd better turn up something earth shaking or there wouldn't be any next time. (Edmondson 1971:12)

Nash Taber travels across the border to one of the Yaqui River towns in Sonora to find an ethnological problem to work into a new publication. When he is questioned by a Mexican army officer, the presence of Mexican troops occupying the Yaqui country is introduced. The officer is interested in Taber's possible association with intransigent Yaquis who may be planning another uprising against the Mexican occupation.

The reality behind the fiction is that Edmondson has access to the fieldwork stories of Ralph Beals and Edward Spicer for Yaqui/anthropologist/Mexican military relationships. Ralph Beals's encounters with Yaqui intransigents began on a blazing summer day in southern Sonora in 1918 when I crouched under a stunted mesquite bush while a mounted Yaqui war party crossed the trail ahead in skirmish formation the drummers at each end of the line tapping their drums to keep the formation. (Beals 1978:355)

In the 1930s he had an encounter with the Mexican military command in Sonora:

The General improved my opinion of Mexican army intelligence considerably. He knew about my visit in Pascua village near Tucson, including the names of all the people I had talked with, and requested that I tell him about our discussions. I was able to satisfy him with some rather general and nonincriminating statements and he issued me a permit to enter and reside in the villages under martial law, subject to conditions established by the officers on the spot. I was required to live in the only inn within Yaqui territory. For the first month or so of my stay I was also forbidden to leave the inn unless accompanied by a lieutenant of the Army, a young man who spoke fluent Cahita. I was also secretly visited by a representative of the rebels who wanted me to visit them in the Sierra Bacatete, an invitation I declined not from fear of the Yaqui but of the certainty that I would land in a Mexican jail on my return. (Beals 1987:2)

In 1942 Edward Spicer, his wife, and their year-old son went to live in the Yaqui River town of Potam. They were already familiar with Yaqui ways from living in the Arizona Yaqui community of Pascua. Spicer writes,

When we took a trip one Sunday with Angwamea and some others, making a tour of the western pueblos from Rahum to Pitahaya, we went, as is usual for any Yaqui to do, immediately to the soldier's guardia on arrival in Rahum. There we found about a dozen men, young and old but mainly old, sitting on benches talking. One was the aged pascola dancer I had seen at the Rahum fiestas in Potam; he was gay and bantering in mood and spoke only Yaqui to us. Another was a tall, slender old man in the usual blue jeans. He spoke in Spanish later on, but at first tried my mettle by using only Yaqui. (Spicer 1954:6)

The Spicers remained there only so long as the Mexican military command permitted. In April 1942 they were evacuated from the Yaqui Military Zone on order of the commanding general (Spicer 1954:3). Later when the Spicers were permitted to return for a visit they found that Yaquis regarded them as having been there to promote Yaqui independence.

Chapayeca interweaves history and fantasy into a fictional piece, with a depiction of involvement of anthropologists in Yaqui activities and the very real non-fictional way Mexican military authorities have viewed those involvements.

In 1966 Neil Judd listed the tasks of anthropology:

There is still work to do—the River Valley salvage program, researches in Canada and Mesoamerica, reinterpretation of archaeological data by means of radiation, soil, and pollen analyses, culturization in the several tribes and guiding more isolated peoples to a better way of life. Both the army and navy now rely upon anthropology to pave the way with stranger groups in distant countries. (Judd 1967:35)

A novel published in the same year puts Judd's thinking into Southwestern context. *The Burning Sky* by "Robert Duncan Hall," is on the surface a fantasy about a lost outpost of the Hohokam culture discovered in a remote corner of the Arizona desert. It is also a collection of corridor talk from a gossip network about private archaeological institutions, Southwestern archaeologists, and the role of applied anthropologists working for federal agencies. One of the characters in the novel spells out what will happen when the news of the lost Hohokam becomes public. The federal government will send a team of applied anthropologists to find out how to deal with these people. Once that is known then arrangements will be made to place them on a federal Indian reservation, to be administered by the Bureau of Indian Affairs. Then missionaries will be sent to convert them to Christianity. These lost Hohokam formerly lived in a multistoried Great Pueblo building. Contract archaeologists will come in to sift through the building, remove all the remains of the dead ancestors and all the artifacts left behind when the pueblo was abandoned. The situation presented is probably accurate for the time of the novel and of earlier years. After the 1960s there was a federal policy shift away from the heavy authoritarian methods of dealing with indigenous people of the past, which would not allow for the forced missionization, excavation, and matter-of-fact assumption of total authority. Federal agencies wanted reports authenticated with the authority of academic degrees to validate bureaucratic actions taken under federal policy rules.

OTHER AUDIENCES, OTHER AGENDAS

The literature of the 1970s shows that another shift had taken place, away from academic audiences and agendas. The non-academic audiences and agendas were not interested in the collection of either ethnological data or archaeological artifacts to contribute to the state of knowledge. David Seal's novel *Powwow Highway* has a bit from a non-academic gossip network which places some Southwestern anthropologists in a reverse of the kind of role the Mexican army officer placed Nash Taber in, regarding Yaqui independence. One of the *Powwow Highway* characters, Buddy Red Bird, says that the anthropologists on the faculty of one of the large Southwestern universities are all FBI provocateurs. They are just pretending to be American Indian Movement sympathizers (Seals 1990:266).

Dean Ing wrote about an American Indian archaeologist, Dr. Koshare, who was a native of a pueblo, working in what he originally thought was an atypical Anasazi site (1987). Koshare is an archaeologist with a Ph.D. from Arizona State University. It is equally important to note that the governor of the pueblo where the story action takes place has an investment broker with whom he is in close communication. Pueblo governers can refer to our anthropologists and tell visitors they should read a particular ethnography because that is the best one on us. They may mean that the anthropologists they refer to are also Pueblo members. Now that there are American Indians who have graduate degrees in anthropology, the roles of anthropologists have shifted to the natives.

Tony Hillerman introduced his Navajo policemen in 1970 and has gradually, through a series of novels, introduced fictionalized corridor stories about the practitioners of Southwestern anthropology. The Navajo tribal policemen, Joe Leaphorn and Jim Chee, are former anthropology graduate students, with master's degrees from Arizona State University for Leaphorn; Jim Chee studied at the University of New Mexico. There is an incorporation from another source, the Navajo origin myth. The origin myth focuses on the hero twins, Child of or Born from Water and the Monster Slayer. The twins are the children of the sun; their mission was to destroy dangerous monsters and to make the world safe for the Navajo people.

The Hillerman novel *The Talking God* (1990) moved the formal legal and political debate that surrounds the commerce in antiquities, grave goods, and human remains to the pages of popular fiction. Until the 1980s the graves, shrines, and former habitation sites of indigenous people in the Southwest were regarded as productive of materials for study by archaeologists and for museum collections, or of objects for the commercial trade from pothunters to dealers to museums and private collectors.

When the physical anthropologist Loren Eiseley wrote a reflective essay on finding a dead child bundled in a Southwestern mountain cave, he saw the child protectively accompanied by objects it could not have used in its life, all that its culture could provide where human affection could not follow (Eiseley 1969:29). Eiseley reflected that the child and its grave goods should have been left where its people had placed it.

A "thief of time" 1988 Arizona court case involved a similar find. Someone like Kunetka's dealer and Hillerman's collector was involved on one side of the case. Several archaeologists assisted as expert witnesses against a dealer-pothunter charged with the unlawful removal, possession, and sale of a naturally mummified infant girl with extensive grave goods from a cave site in the Tonto National Forest of central Arizona. The mummy and its Hohokam culture grave goods were dated at A.D. 600, plus or minus twenty-five years. The dealer was found guilty of the charges.

Vine Deloria, Jr., once posed a series of questions that Hillerman essentially addresses in his fiction:

1. Are American Indians human beings?
2. How valuable are Indian human remains for science?
3. How long should human remains be available to science?
4. Is there a freedom of religion issue here?
5. Should burial offerings be included within the religious freedom protections?

(Deloria 1989)

Hillerman's *The Talking God* and its 1989 predecessor *The Thief of Time* deal with these questions in simplified and personalized human terms. The Navajo Hero

Twins, Leaphorn and Chee, through their patient investigations of reservation crimes take the readers through the federal laws and regulations. They find out about poverty-driven local Indian and non-Indian diggers in the Anasazi ruins, and they have revealed to them the humanity and the professional careerist ambitions of archaeologists.

Leaphorn and Chee bring their remembrances of anthropology courses about the Anasazi and their knowledge of contemporary Navajo culture into play to solve a series of killings of pothunters and the disappearance of an archaeologist who is a specialist on Anasazi ceramics. Readers learn about Chaco Canyon, Navajo religion, Anasazi petroglyphs, Anasazi settlement patterns, the contemporary problems of Navajo society, and Anasazi burial practices. Pothunters, Hillerman suggests, may be driven to loot in the ruins by poverty as the Wetherills were and by Christian conversion in the case of some Navajos. The readership will not learn about the Wetherill's presence at Chaco as commercial pothunters for the Hyde expedition here, but they may develop the idea that if there is anything worse than a pothunter, it must be the wealthy degenerates who are ready to pay for stolen artifacts of authenticated quality and sufficient rarity for their collections. For these people the Other exists only to supply products to the market of rare and exotic commodities. There is a portrait of just such a collector whose only interest in the fate of the missing archaeologist, Dr. Eleanor Friedman-Bernal, is revealed when he asks Leaphorn to "Call me back with all the details. When you find her body." Then he will have a story to tell his social equals about his Anasazi ceramic.

There has been a change in American sentiment about the looting of the graves and burial goods of indigenous people. Duncan, in writing about a private archaeological institute in the mid-sixties, could say that a notorious pothunter could come to the institute to sell his looted artifacts. He could write that "Leeper was a pot hunter, one of a breed of spoilers who had contaminated a good many sites in their search for artifacts to sell" (Duncan Hall 1966:24). But he could also write that the people of the institute did not let their scorn for Leeper prevent them from buying his artifacts.

A tribal policeman novel by James Kunetka, *Shadow Man*, features Tomas Reyes of San Ildefonso pueblo. The story focuses on Los Alamos, New Mexico, mixing an archaeologist, the theft of Star Wars data out of Los Alamos National Laboratory, collectors of antiquities, and a dealer in stolen antiquities who may have a university background in anthropology. Angela, the dealer, is an amoral director of a network of contract thieves and killers who loot Anasazi sites, rob special objects from kivas, museums, and private collections on assignment. The real-life original of Kunetka's fictional Angela and her network may well have been responsible for a 1989 report about the seizure of a stolen kachina mask at the October New York Fall Antiques show at the Pier. The chief priest of the First Mesa Kachina Society of the Hopi Tribe of Arizona, an FBI agent, and the Hopi tribal director of cultural preservation seized the mask at the antique show. The mask had been stolen sometime during March 1989 (*Indian Affairs* Fall 1989:4).

Federal recognition of the shift in national sentiment came in the form of legislation, Public Law 101–601, the Native American Graves Protection and Repatriation Act. The Act (Section 12) defines a burial site, cultural affiliation, cultural items—which means human remains—and associated funerary objects, unassociated funerary objects, sacred objects, and cultural patrimony. There are several more definitions in this section on federal agencies and land, Native Hawaiian and Native American, tribes and organizations of both identities, museums, and right of possession, all necessary for future legal actions. Section 4 deals with the "Thief of Time" problem, illegal trafficking. Fines and imprisonment penalties are listed. The Treaty of Guadalupe Hidalgo inaugurated the processes that led to this political document.

In the American Southwest of the nineteenth century Frank Cushing, the culture hero of the origin myth, began much that became traditional for anthropologists: observer-participation, collecting ethnological information and archaeological artifacts, advocacy for "their people" against would-be alien exploiters. After him many others came, each with their own agendas. Some sought the limited fame of academic recognition through careers that gave them professional reasons to spend time in hard-to-get-to archaeological camps, or among indigenous people in equally distant places. The place to learn about the individual agendas that shaped Southwestern anthropology is in the store of tales, the corridor talk, the stories they tell themselves about themselves, the stories passed or passing into myth which serve as an important mechanism to give group members a oneness or uniqueness. If we look only in the professional literature we will usually find the lives of the academic disciplinary saints. The corridor talk transmuted into fiction may give a different perspective, and possibly one that is less hagiolatric.

Frank Cushing and the other nineteenth-century ethnologists and archaeologists have passed into myth. Those who followed them in the first fifty years of this century either are or are becoming mythological figures. Political events shaped the ways in which the mythological figures followed their individual agendas, in the spirit, if not the manner of Edmondson's Nash Taber, who "as a young man had gotten by on brilliance."

In the second fifty years of the twentieth century political events required adaptations to changing realities in which the audiences for anthropology were shifting to federal agencies, tribal governments, and state agencies. Along with the change of audiences, the anthropological culture incorporated individuals from a new population, the indigenous people. The native people of the Southwest became more than a useful research population providing living laboratories for alien researchers and shovel bums for archaeological digs. In 1970 Tony Hillerman could plausibly create a series of popular novels about two tribal policemen who are Navajo tribal members and are university graduates with degrees in anthropology, whose roles are modeled on the hero twins of mythology.

There is professional academic recognition of the change in the Southwest volume of the *Handbook of North American Indians*. The editor of the volume is Alfonso

Ortiz from San Juan Pueblo. The author of the Zuni section is Edmund Ladd, from Zuni Pueblo. Velma Garcia Mason, from Acoma Pueblo, writes about Acoma.

In 1991 the September *Anthropology Newsletter* has an advertisement for an assistant director for the Pueblo of Zuni's Archaeological Program. On page 46 of the *Newsletter*, there is a news item headed "Anthropologist Helps Zuni Tribe Win Multi-million Dollar Land Settlement."

Things have changed since Frank Cushing first came to Zuni.

REFERENCES

Aberle, David F. 1973. "Clyde Kluckhohn's Contributions to Navaho Studies." In *Culture and History,* edited by Walter W. Taylor, John L. Fischer, and Evon Z. Vogt. Carbondale: Southern Illinois University Press.

Adair, John. 1973. "Clyde Kluckhohn and Indian Administration." In *Culture and Life: Essays in Memory of Clyde Kluckhohn,* edited by Walter W. Taylor, John L. Fischer, and Evon Z. Vogt. Carbondale: Southern Illinois University Press.

Association on American Indian Affairs, Inc. 1989. *Indian Affairs,* Fall 120:4.

Basso, Keith H. 1979. "History of Ethnological Research." *Handbook of North American Indians, Southwest,* vol. 9, edited by Alfonso Ortiz, 14–21. Washington, D.C.: Smithsonian Institution.

Beals, Ralph L. 1978. "Sonoran Fantasy or Coming of Age?" *American Anthropologist,* June 80:355–362.

Beals, Ralph L., and N. Ross Crumrine. 1987. "Reflections, Contrasts, and Directions." In *Ejidos and Regions of Refuge in Northwestern Mexico,* edited by N. Ross Crumrine and Phil C. Weigand. Anthropological Papers of the University of Arizona No. 46. Tuscon: University of Arizona Press.

Benedict, R. F. 1925. Letter to Margaret Mead, 8 September 1925.

Boren, Terry. 1987. "Sliding Rock." In *A Very Large Array: New Mexico Science Fiction and Fantasy,* edited by Melinda M. Snodgrass. Albuquerque: University of New Mexico Press.

Brunhouse, Robert L. 1976. *Frans Blom, Maya Explorer.* Albuquerque: University of New Mexico Press.

Caffrey, Margaret M. 1989. *Ruth Benedict: Stranger in This Land.* Austin: University of Texas Press.

Cather, Willa. 1925. *The Professor's House.* New York: Knopf.

Chase, Arlen F., Diane Z. Chase, and Harriet W. Topsey. 1988. "Archaeology and the Ethic of Collecting." *Archaeology,* (January/February), 56–87.

Deloria, Vine, Jr. 1989. "A Simple Question of Humanity: The Moral Dimensions of the Reburial Issue." *Native American Rights Fund Legal Review,* Fall, vol. 14, no. 4.

Dennis, Phillip A. 1989. "Oliver La Farge, Writer and Anthropologist." *Literature and Anthropology,* edited by Phillip A. Dennis and Wendell Aycock, 209–219. Lubbock: Texas Tech University Press.

Duncan, Robert Lipscomb (Robert Duncan Hall). 1966. *The Burning Sky.* New York: Morrow.

———. 1988. Letter.

Eastlake, William. 1975. *Dancers in the Scalp House.* A Richard Seaver Book. New York: Viking Press.

Edmondson, Gary C. 1971. *Chapayeca,* reprinted as *Blue Face.* New York: Daw Books.

Eiseley, Loren C. 1969. *The Unexpected Universe.* New York: Harcourt, Brace and World.

Geertz, Clifford. 1973. "Deep Play: Notes on the Balinese Cockfight." In *The Interpretation of Cultures: Selected Essays by Clifford Geertz.* New York: Basic Books.

Gibson, Arrell Morgan. 1983. *The Santa Fe and Taos Colonies: Age of the Muses, 1900–1942.* Norman: University of Oklahoma Press.

Gish, Robert F. 1989. "A review of 'Yellow Sun, Bright Sky: The Indian Country Stories of Oliver La Farge'." *Journal of the Southwest,* Autumn 31:3:435–437.

Green, Jesse, ed. 1979. *Zuni: Selected Writings of Frank Hamilton Cushing.* Lincoln: University of Nebraska Press.

———, ed. 1990. *Cushing at Zuni: The Correspondence and Journals of Frank Hamilton Cushing, 1879–1884.* Albuquerque: University of New Mexico Press.

Haury, Emil W. 1945. "The Excavation of Los Muertos and Neighboring Ruins in the Salt River Valley, Southern Arizona. Based on the Work of the Hemenway Southwestern Archaeological Expedition of 1887–1888." *Papers of the Peabody Museum of American Archaeology and Ethnology,* vol. 24, no. 1. Cambridge, Mass.: Harvard University.

———. 1988. "Gila Pueblo Archaeological Foundation: A History and Some Personal Notes." *Kiva.* Quarterly Journal of the Arizona Archaeological and Historical Society, vol. 54, no. 1.

Hillerman, Tony. 1988. *Thief of Time.* New York: Harper and Row.

———. 1989. "Making Mysteries with Navajo Materials." *Literature And Anthropology,* edited by Phillip A. Dennis and Wendell Aycock, 5–13. Lubbock: Texas Tech University Press.

———. 1989. *Talking God.* New York: Harper and Row.

———. 1990. *Coyote Waits.* New York: Harper and Row.

Hinsley, Curtis M., Jr. 1981. *Savages and Scientists: The Smithsonian Institution and the Development of American Anthropology 1846–1910.* Washington, D.C.: Smithsonian Institution Press.

———. 1983. "Ethnographic Charisma and Scientific Routine: Cushing and Fewkes in the American Southwest, 1879–1893." In *Observers Observed: Essays on Ethnographic Fieldwork,* edited by George W. Stocking, Jr. Madison: University of Wisconsin Press.

———. 1984. "Zunis and Brahmins: Cultural Ambivalence in the Gilded Age." In *Romantic Motives and the History of Anthropology,* edited by George W. Stocking, Jr., 169–207. Madison: University of Wisconsin Press.

Ing, Dean. 1987. *Anasazi.* New York: Baen.

Judd, Neil M. 1967. *The Bureau of American Ethnology: A Partial History.* Norman: University of Oklahoma Press.

———. 1968. *Men Met along the Trail: Adventures in Archaeology.* Norman: University of Oklahoma Press.

Kluckhohn, Clyde. 1944. *Navaho Witchcraft. Papers of the Peabody Museum of American Archaeology and Ethnology,* vol. 22, no. 2. Cambridge, Mass.: Harvard University.

Kunetka, James W. 1988. *Shadow Man.* New York: Warner Books.

La Farge, Oliver. 1935. "Higher Education." In *All the Young Men.* Boston: Houghton, Mifflin.

———. 1965. *The Door in the Wall: Stories by Oliver La Farge.* Boston: Houghton, Mifflin.

———. 1988. *Yellow Sun, Bright Sky: The Indian Country Stories of Oliver La Farge.* Edited with an introduction by David L. Caffrey. Albuquerque: University of New Mexico Press.

———. 1988. "The Ancient Strength." In *Yellow Sky, Bright Sun.*

———. 1988. "The Little Stone Man." In *Yellow Sun, Bright Sun.*

Lister, Florence C., and Robert H. Lister. 1968. *Earl Morris and Southwestern Archaeology.* Albuquerque: University of New Mexico Press.

Malinowski, Bronislaw. 1954 [1926]. "Myth in Primitive Psychology." In *Magic, Science and Religion,* 72–119. Garden City, N.J.: Doubleday.

Marcus, George E. 1991. "A Broad(er)side to the Canon Being a Partial Account of a Year of Travel among Textual Communities in the Realm of Humanities Centers and Including a Collection of Artificial Curiosities." *Cultural Anthropology,* August 6:3:385–405.

Marcus, George E., and Michael M. J. Fischer. 1986. *Anthropology as Cultural Critique: An Experimental Moment in the Human Sciences.* Chicago: University of Chicago Press.

McNickle, D'Arcy. 1971. *Indian Man: A Life of Oliver La Farge.* Bloomington: Indiana University Press.

Mead, Margaret. 1959. "Apprenticeship under Boas." In *The Anthropology of Franz Boas: Essays on the Centennial of His Birth,* edited by Walter Goldschmidt. The American Anthropological Association, vol. 61, no. 5, Pt. 22. Memoir no. 89.

Modell, Judith Schachter. 1983. *Ruth Benedict: Patterns of a Life.* Philadelphia: University of Pennsylvania Press.

Morris, Anne Axtell. 1978 [1933]. *Digging in the Southwest.* Santa Barbara and Salt Lake City: Peregrine Smith.

Public Law 101-601-Nov. 16, 1990. 101st Congress. Native American Graves Protection and Repatriation Act, Hawaiian Natives Historic Preservation. 25 USC 3001.

Rabinow, Paul. 1986. "Representations Are Social Facts: Modernity and Post-Modernity in Anthropology." In *Writing Culture: The Poetics and Politics of Ethnography,* edited by James Clifford and George Marcus. Berkeley: University of California Press.

Reed, Erik K. 1954. "Transition to History in the Pueblo Southwest." *American Anthropologist,* Southwest Issue 56:561.

Schroeder, Albert H. 1979. "History of Archaeological Research." *Handbook of North American Indians, Southwest,* vol. 9. Washington, D.C.: Smithsonian Institution.

Seals, David. 1990. *The Powwow Highway.* Plume Contemporary Fiction. New York: Penguin.

Spicer, Edward H. 1954. *Potam: A Yaqui Village in Sonora.* American Anthropology Association, vol. 56, no. 4, Pt. 2. Memoir no. 77.

Taylor, Walter W. 1954. "Southwestern Archaeology, Its History and Theory." *American Anthropologist* 56:561.

Taylor, Walter W., John L. Fischer, and Evon Z. Vogt, eds. 1973. *Culture and Life: Essays in Memory of Clyde Kluckhohn.* Carbondale: Southern Illinois University Press.

Tedlock, Dennis. 1983. *The Spoken Word and the Work of Interpretation.* Philadelphia: University of Pennsylvania Press.

Tedlock, Dennis, and Barbara Tedlock. 1979. "Sources" in "Zuni Prehistory and History to 1850" by Richard B. Woodbury in *Handbook of North American Indians, Southwest,* vol. 9. Washington, D.C.: Smithsonian Institution.

Todorov, Tzvetan. 1987. *The Conquest of America: The Question of the Other.* New York: Harper and Row.

Vogt, Evon Z., and Ethel M. Albert, eds. 1966. *People of Rimrock.* Cambridge: Harvard University Press.

Watson, James. 1980. *The Double Helix.* Norton Critical Edition, edited by Gunther S. Stent. New York: Norton.

Wilson, Edmund. 1956. *Red, Black, Blond, and Olive: Zuni, Haiti, Soviet Russia, Israel.* New York: Oxford University Press.

Woodbury, Nathalie F. S. 1991. "Past Is Present." *Anthropology Newsletter,* September.

———. 1986. "Past Is Present." *Anthropology Newsletter,* September.

LOOKING THROUGH THE GLASS DARKLY
The Editorialized Mourning Dove

Alanna Kathleen Brown

ourning Dove's life coincides with a very harsh period in Indian-Euro-american relations. She was born in April between 1882 and 1888,[1] during the final decade of the Indian wars. Before Mourning Dove's birth, Custer and his cavalry had met their deaths at the Battle of the Little Big Horn (June 25, 1876), and Chief Joseph had fought his way toward Canada in protest to the opening of Nez Percé lands to settlement (May–September 1877). The massacre at Wounded Knee, South Dakota (December 29, 1890), which ended open military hostilities between the U.S. government and indigenous peoples, occurred after her birth.

Mourning Dove was to live almost all of her adult years in the period of extreme assimilation pressures which followed, pressures intended to wipe out Indian cultures in the twentieth century. Even before the Wounded Knee massacre, the federal government had established a Court of Indian Offenses (1883), which made it a crime for Native Americans to speak their own languages, to practice traditional religious rituals, or to wear traditional dress or their hair at male-warrior length. By 1887 the General Allotment, or Dawes, Act had already begun to force Indians into a cash nexus while systematically opening up reservation lands for white settlement. Indian tribes lost two-thirds of their original treaty lands between 1887 and 1934. During what is now called the assimilation period (1880s–1934), Bureau of Indian Affairs schools and mission schools also were intensively used to eradicate Native tribal identities. Children were removed from their homes, punished for speaking indigenous languages, and drilled on English as well as white behavioral norms and Christianity, while Indian customs and religious beliefs were ridiculed. Mourning Dove died August 8, 1936, just two years after John Collier was appointed to direct the Bureau of Indian Affairs and more humane federal Indian policies were put into effect. Hers is one of the very few Indian voices that directly reflects on that assimilation period from an Indian perspective.

It is important to recognize that Mourning Dove was of the first generation of inland Salish-speaking peoples to grow up on a reservation. She was sent to the Goodwin Mission School near Kettle Falls, Washington, in 1895 and 1898–99 at the urging of Catholic priests. When the government balked at funding Catholic education for Indians, and established government schools, Mourning Dove was transferred to the newly created Fort Spokane School for Indians, which she attended from 1899 to 1902. Of her own volition, she continued a white education when she chose to become a matron of the Fort Shaw Indian School in Montana in exchange for classes (1904–08). Moreover, to pursue a writing career she attended a secretarial school in Calgary, Alberta, to master typing skills in 1913. Yet Mourning Dove ultimately rejected absorption into the dominant culture, and chose to use that education to preserve the oral traditions of her people and to record the events of her times.

Mourning Dove's final manuscripts, now published as *Mourning Dove: A Salishan Autobiography* (1990),[2] include recollections of her early childhood, when the family followed traditional migration routes, to her experiences of being sent off to mission and then BIA schools, to the settlement of Indians onto farm plots, to a mineral-rights and then a homesteaders run on the Colville Reservation. Her novel *Cogewea, the Half-Blood* (1927),[3] explores the difficult situation of a young mixed-blood woman on the Montana frontier at the turn of the last century; and her collection of tribal legends, *Coyote Stories* (1933),[4] is an important act by a Native American storyteller to preserve some of her cultural heritage in the face of what then appeared to be inevitable cultural genocide. But as with many non-white women writers of the nineteenth and early-twentieth centuries, Mourning Dove initially came into print through the aid of white male collaborators. Their assumptions as well as their editorial work deeply colored, even altered, the tone and substance of Mourning Dove's original manuscripts.

Her first editor, mentor, and ultimately, friend, was Lucullus Virgil McWhorter,[5] a man of enormous energy with an intense passion for justice. They met in 1914 when Mourning Dove was in her late twenties or early thirties, and McWhorter was fifty-four. McWhorter was already a published author and an activist on behalf of Indian rights. He immediately saw the literary promise in Mourning Dove's novel manuscript and her collection of twenty-two legends. He offered to edit and help publish her work. However, as a settler in the Yakima Valley of Washington, he was horrified by the greed and Christian hypocrisy of those surrounding him. He suffered at the thought of the passing away of peoples and cultures while settlers like himself chose to be obtuse and racially arrogant. In his need to educate and awaken the consciences of white readers, McWhorter not only edited Mourning Dove's novel, but he also added numerous passages of ethnographic commentary and attacks on religious and government corruption. The result is that *Cogewea* is rent by two voices and two purposes.

Dean Guie,[6] a young man in his twenties, became the second editorial force in Mourning Dove's life when McWhorter gave up hope of publishing *Okanogan Sweat House,* a collection of thirty-eight Salish tales transcribed by Mourning Dove. McWhorter had been working to publish the legends for fourteen years. His editorial changes had been modest, for McWhorter understood the importance of keeping the stories as close to oral presentation as possible, and he admired Mourning Dove's storytelling skills. Dean Guie, on the other hand, was not an advocate of Indian cultures. He had been born into a Northwest that was now settled, and the Indians represented vestiges of the past. He viewed them with curiosity and believed Indians to be immature culturally. Thus Guie thought that Native legends were best suited for juvenile audiences. He selected just over twenty-seven of Mourning Dove's original tales, changed the title of the collection to appeal more to children (*Coyote Stories*), added animal illustrations, and edited Mourning Dove's transcriptions to suit the 1930s literary standards for young adults.

Cogewea, the Half-Blood was printed in 1927 and had very weak sales.[7] *Coyote Stories,* published in 1933, was surprisingly successful, and in a second printing by 1934. But decades passed, and Mourning Dove's works were virtually forgotten until the impetus of the civil-rights movement of the 1960s and the women's movement of the 1970s led scholars to recover works that would expand American literature to include non-white and women writers. Donald Hines retrieved the original manuscript chapters for *Okanogan Sweat House,* which Mourning Dove had typed and McWhorter had edited by hand, and published *Tales of the Okanogans* in 1976.[8] Alice Poindexter Fisher (Dexter Fisher) completed a dissertation on Zitkala-Sa and Mourning Dove in 1979,[9] and two years later she edited a reprint of *Cogewea* for the University of Nebraska Press. The publication of *Tales of the Okanogans* was important because it included all thirty-eight of Mourning Dove's original stories, and, even given a different arrangement of the tales, Hines stayed much closer to Mourning Dove's original transcriptions than did Dean Guie. The republication of *Cogewea* was important in two ways. Fisher accomplished her goal of bringing a grandmother of the Native American literary renaissance to the fore, and, indirectly, she also helped bring the issue of collaboration into focus.

With regard to the latter, several works of major significance, including Kate Chopin's *The Awakening* and Zora Neale Hurston's *Their Eyes Were Watching God,* had affirmed the importance of recovering a literary past for those excluded from the traditional canon. But a number of nineteenth- and early twentieth-century American works were dominated by strong collaborative voices, *Cogewea* among them. Such collaborations presented new critical problems for scholars. Dexter Fisher chose to go to the correspondence between Mourning Dove and McWhorter housed in the archives of the Holland Library, Washington State University, Pullman, and to create sympathetic portraits of their lives drawn from their letters. Unfortunately, she did not examine the text to illustrate how Mourning Dove's and McWhorter's collaboration actually worked, nor did she include some major insights about the transition from an oral to a written tradition which she had explored in her dissertation.

Since the republication of *Cogewea, the Half-Blood* in 1981, *Coyote Stories* has been reissued (1990), and Mourning Dove's incomplete final manuscripts have come into print (*Mourning Dove: A Salishan Autobiography*, 1990), the latter two edited by Jay Miller. One would expect that critics would explicate issues of collaboration more fully by 1990, and that greater care would be taken to present Mourning Dove's voice accurately, but not so. Miller has chosen to "correct" Mourning Dove's Indian English and to arrange her final manuscripts to fit ethnographic categories of description. Moreover, he consistently challenges Mourning Dove's understanding of her own experiences and culture through the corrective lenses of the accepted ethnohistorical data of the dominant culture, and through the recollections of a brother born in 1910, a generation after her. Such editorial choices obscure the subtlety and humor of Mourning Dove's own use of language and subvert her authority about her own life. Those editorial choices also block the possibility of expanding ethnohistorical data to include a more comprehensive grasp of Native American lives, both female and male. But in the reactionary 1980s, cooptation has been an effective tool in thwarting the transforming social challenges of the previous two decades.

As this synopsis suggests, through Mourning Dove's work we have an unusual opportunity to examine the changing currents of twentieth-century American thought and the effects on the editing of an Indian woman's materials. Each of the editors has believed himself or herself to be bringing Mourning Dove's writing to the fore, and each to some extent has achieved that goal. But each editor also has undercut his and her objective. As we approach the five hundredth anniversary of Columbus's voyage, it is critical for us to understand how little we yet know about Native peoples, how effectively we continue to obscure their voices.

Let us take a closer look at the work of each of these editors.

L. V. McWhorter's enthusiasm about Mourning Dove's novel[10] can best be illustrated by a letter he sent his dear friend, J. P. MacLean, on January 3, 1916. He notes that the story is set on the Flathead Indian Reservation in Montana around 1900, and continues:

The story is a true depiction of events there at that time. It graphically portrays the social status of the Indian, especially the half-bloods; or "breeds." It is given from the Indian standpoint and by one well qualified to write on the subject. Mourning Dove rode in the great roundup of the buffaloes sold to the Canadian Government; and is well versed in the ways of the range.

After summarizing the plot and acknowledging that the last three chapters are "still in the crude," McWhorter states his dilemma:

I am now asking your opinion as to annoting this work. This can be done, I believe, to advantage; but I am not well enough versed in romance writing to speak on the subject. I could give several incidents which have come under my personal observation, which would strengthen the statements of the writer. Also, notes could be given explaining that certain narrations are true and as gathered from the old Indians.

> Then again, Mourning Dove is averse to having her picture and a sketch of her life go in the book. She says that this would be alright for an historical work, but for fiction, she thinks it out of place. I have explained to her, that hers is NOT fiction in the full sense of the word; and that we can overcome the seemingly "ego"; in the copyright and publication of the volume. I do not want to do any thing which might detract from the beauty and worth of the book; but I am anxious that this feature go in. (35–36; 392)[11]

This letter summarizes Mourning Dove's original plot, highlights what McWhorter found to be valuable about the text,[12] and acknowledges his inexperience about taking on the role of editor for such a work.

By August 25, 1924, however, in a letter to the Honorable Joseph W. Latimer, McWhorter describes the value of the novel in a distinctly different light:

Mourning Dove, a woman of the Okanogan tribe, has written a story depicting the status of the Indian, including the half-bloods, in contrast to the social and political standards of the land. It is correct in its essence, and is historically and ethnologically annotated. The manuscript deals with the blight of the Bureau system, and is outspoken in denunceation of the Government's policy towards its "wards." . . . At this time when the public's attention is being drawn to the curse of the Indian Bureau, I feel that the publication of this work, coming as it does from the pen of an Indian, would be a potent factor in bringing about a reformation and cleaning up of the Indian Department. (10–11; 294)

The shift in purpose and content reflects McWhorter's move from editor to co-writer of Mourning Dove's text.

A number of personal frustrations led McWhorter to overstep appropriate editorial bounds. The rising cost for paper during World War One as well as changing readership tastes caused two publishers to withdraw their offers to print *Cogewea* between 1917 and 1919. Both McWhorter and Mourning Dove were deeply disappointed by these setbacks. Meanwhile McWhorter continued to be embroiled in a defense of Yakima treaty rights, and that devotion cost him dearly when community leaders thwarted McWhorter's bid to be appointed the government agent for the Yakima tribe.[13] He also took it upon himself to act on behalf of those with personal complaints of injustice. An appeal from Mourning Dove's best friend, Jenny Lewis, about the damage to her daughter's allotment on the Flathead Reservation, is a case in point:

one thing I dont like about Toots land   the Reclamation put a ditch or a drainage deitch and covered it up and sure has left it in an awfull condition   they were to send some men and consider the damages and come to some settlement but havent heard a word   also at one end of her place they put a dranage ditch and it caved in along the river bank and will ruin that fraction if it keeps up   when I try to find out who did it the city says its the county   and when I go to the county commissioners they say they have nothing to do with it   so I seen an attorney about it and he wanted 700 dollars to take up the case   it is the Indian agents place to see to this (February 16, 1917 [6–8;345*B*(1)])

Such appeals reveal both how poorly the Indians had been educated to address the issues they faced, and how conscious government ineptness worked to benefit white settlement. The corruption of the lawyer also is self-evident. $700 was an outrageous price to charge. As McWhorter dealt with case after case like Jenny's and the Yakima tribes' situations, his rage grew. So did his isolation within the white community. He was not forgiven for being an "Indian lover" by those who wanted to profit from the opening up of reservation lands.

McWhorter's intrusion into Mourning Dove's novel, *Cogewea,* was a direct result of his compelling desire to redress the wrongs of a blatantly exploitative environment. Chapters XV and XVI of the novel best illustrate McWhorter's voice and themes. As he wrote to Mourning Dove on November 7, 1922: "Am rewriting a few pages, and dividing one chapter (XV), where I am now working. It is where Densmore and Cogewea left the grandmother's tepee. It is a natural division, and as I am adding to the chapter created by the division, both chapters will be [of] goodly length" (2;1635*D*).

When Mourning Dove's episodes were particularly moving and effective, McWhorter often felt compelled to expand on those story units to drive home particular points. In Chapter XIV, Stemteema has just recounted "The Dead Man's Vision" about the advent of European migration and the devastating effect that that migration would have on Native cultures. The narrative is a powerful and disturbing one for white readers. Following this narrative, McWhorter intervened by creating a dialogue between the heroine and villain that questions the religious superiority of the dominant culture and the duplicity of government agents. This intrusion severely disrupts the narrative, but McWhorter was blind to that disruption in his need to expose the villainy around him. Consider the following passage:

Skilled in the art of white washing, brooded the girl, the Indian Bureau was an octupus [*sic*], with life extracting tentacles reaching into every Indian reservation of the Union. A vampire! whose wing cools with the breeze of never-to-be-filled promises, the wound of its deadly beak, while it drains the heart's blood of its hapless "ward." Where rested the wrong? The Bureau! a branch of the Government. The Government? the dollar-marked will of the politician. The politician? the *priest,* and the *Levite,* who "pass on the other side" from the bruised, and robbed victim of systematized plunder-lust, lying naked by the trail. Should an occasional *Samaritan* stoop to minister to the sufferer's wants, he is rebuked by the Bureaucrats, and warned that such charity is ill advised; wasted where not an exigency. (Chapter XVI, 140–141)

Emphatic to the point of being comical for contemporary readers, the passage condemns the Indian Bureau for betraying its moral obligations to its wards, assaults the moral weaknesses of politicians who betray democratic values for the dollar, and refers to the

"Good Samaritan" parable to expose the religious hypocrisy McWhorter believed people used to hide their selfish actions from themselves. It is also a passage of self-defense. McWhorter saw himself as the despised Samaritan, one living a truly moral and compassionate life.

Of course, there were many times when McWhorter's insertions reflected the ethnohistorian rather than the pedagogue, and then his tone was neither frantic nor severe. The explanations about Indian music (73–74), pipe smoking (120–121), and the sweat-lodge (238–240) are good examples. He also took on the role of commentator, particularly with regard to the dilution of Indian rituals such as the warrior dance (75), or intervened as an interpreter, such as explaining the belief around good fortune/bad fortune and the rocks used to create a sweatlodge (241). It must be remembered that so little was known about Indians in McWhorter's time that McWhorter felt compelled to explain and reinforce Mourning Dove's representation of Indian life.[14]

Two other beliefs impacted McWhorter's editing. He believed, as did his contemporaries, that Indian cultures were so rapidly disintegrating that they would disappear in the twentieth century. He selected the introductory chapter quotations from the writers Henry Wadsworth Longfellow, Lord Byron, Sir Walter Scott, and even Badger Clark and Herbert E. Palmer, to evoke a sense of pathos about that passing. He also decided to "elevate" Cogewea's language by constantly adding Latinate phrases in order to convey the intelligence of Native peoples. While Indian cultures might be dying out, it was as if McWhorter wanted to refute the Social Darwinism that assumed that the passing away of inferior peoples was inevitable, an unfortunate but necessary sign of cultural evolution.

While one can admire McWhorter's courage and personal convictions, it still is profoundly unfortunate that he could not draw the line between his own beliefs and needs, and honor the voice and content of Mourning Dove's novel by being a circumspect editor. His writeovers and additions to Mourning Dove's original manuscript were so extensive that some people questioned Mourning Dove's authorship upon the publication of *Cogewea,* and even as recent a critic as Charles Larson in *American Indian Fiction* (1978),[15] asserted that it is impossible to separate the voices in the novel.

Dean Guie presents us with different problems. The adult world he entered was far different from the settlement experiences of McWhorter and Mourning Dove. McWhorter was sixty-nine when he invited Guie to work on *Okanogan Sweat House* in February of 1929. Mourning Dove was in her forties, and Guie was a newly married man at the beginning of his work career. It appears that Guie was initially asked only to proofread the text (February 18, 1929 [67–68;526]). But by June 1929 it was clear that Guie had offered to illustrate the book, had suggested that the title of the work be changed (63;526), and had urged McWhorter to redirect the legends toward a juvenile market (June 26, 1929 [90–91;386]). By July 19, 1930, he asked to be acknowledged as the editor of the text (8;322) in spite of Mourning Dove's known aversion to such a situation since the confusion surrounding the authorship of *Cogewea.* Guie did work diligently to edit the tales for a young adult white audience, but his first commitment was to his evolving career, and secondarily to preservation of the Native American oral tradition.

Guie's attitude at that time toward Indian culture is revealed in his responses to a July 1930 letter Mourning Dove mailed to McWhorter. The letter describes the Blue Jay Medicine Dance:

The Blue Jay dance is practiced by the Lake and Chewelah Indians, which was as one tribe in former periods before the Indians land was taken away from them and were divided. They were originally as the Lakes, and formly lived near the Arrow Lakes in B.C. Canada.

This dance starts about midwinter. The medcine men gather in the big typee, and the greatest medcine man is choosen to take the stand in the middle where the "medcine pole" is set decorated with feathers, strips of skins, and bits of bones collected by all of them from different animals that represents their "medcine powers"[.]

As the man in the center rocks the pole in rythm of their weird song one by one the men began to dance in a hopping and skipping form till they gradually dance higher and higher into the air, as they shed their clothing peice by peice till they acted with fear to the other Indians who join them in dancing and soon fly out the typee only to come back before morning with their feet blackened from the calfs down to the tips of their toes with charcoal, and their arms painted the same in black from elbows to the finger tips. To keep them themselves warm they say. Because outside of a breech-cloth on these insaned dancers nothing is on them in the freezing weather, and for the rest of ten days dancing they roam the hills like animals afraid to get near the people without food nor clothing. The only time they come among the people is at night while dancing, and they dance only on one foot at a time skipping and hopping about, always watching. Their ears are filled with pine gum as food. They spoke backwards, and could find anything, and could cure all kinds of sickness without even touching the patients, by paying them small toys, or bright articles.

On the last night these Blue Jays are gathered in, by getting the strongest men of the tribe to dance and mingle with them, and catching them which seems to sap their strength which seems very strong as the human hands takes them, and they fall in a faint. The old women bring their scented mountain herbs and make smoke for inhaleing the Blue Jay back to sanity again. These are very strong medcine men. Very rare now. They never freeze their feet nor body. (34;269)

McWhorter chose to share the letter with Guie, and on July 13, 1930, Guie responded:

Getting back to the Blue-Jay dance, I wonder if those dancers roam around naked all the time, as they apparently do, or whether they have a rendevous in some hidden place where they keep warm and "hide out" until time for them to reappear? Might be possible as M. Dove says they only show up after dark to dance. I imagine that last part, where they are seized by the strong men of the camp is a bit of sham, like so much primitive ceremonial stuff. It surely is interesting to know about it. (9;322)

Nine days later, Guie was still thinking about the description of the Blue Jay Medicine Dance, and he added the following postscript:

P.S. Don't tell M. Dove that I questioned the "honesty" of those Blue-Jay dancers. That would be good stuff, if she can tell you more about it. If you could get a lot of "dope" on dances of that kind, would be good for an article, I believe. (July 22, 1930 [5;322])

These responses communicate Guie's ethnocentricity. He objectifies, even ridicules, an Indian ritual to deny its ceremonial power, and then on reflection, he considers the market for such Indian material. That ethnocentricity also blinded Guie to a central aspect of the stories he had been editing for over a year. On May 3, 1930, McWhorter wrote to Mourning Dove, telling her not to worry about explaining the dual animal/human nature of the characters in the legends to Guie:

Guie is puzzled about the "Animal People" and where it appears as the hero is really a human being, as in the case of Cold Wind legend, where the hero is a boy. I can understand all this, and I can explain it to him when he comes home. I will speak to him on this item, which puzzles him, and tell him I will explain fully when he returns here. (41;269)

It is easy to understand how one with Guie's perspective would adapt the literature of a "primitive" people for a juvenile market. What is unexpected is that Guie wanted his editorial work to have ethnographic authority. To this end he badgered McWhorter and Mourning Dove on numerous questions of translation. Guie trusted white male authority. When Judge William C. Brown of Okanogan, Washington, wrote McWhorter one meaning for the word "Okanogan" and Mourning Dove told McWhorter another, it was Mourning Dove who was pressed by Guie on the accuracy of her explanations:

Need some more help from Mourning Dove for that introduction. I want to make that as air tight as possible in regard to the religious beliefs of the Okanogans and also in regard to the translation of the name. In this last I think she should be more definite than in her letters on the meaning of Okanogan. She said it was a corruption of the original word, "Okan-nock-kin" or "Ok na-kan"—that the last sylable [*sic*] "kin" or "kan" means "head of" or "top of" or "tip." Also that the first syllable has a sound like the word meaning "seeing."
    Now, ask her what she means by the first syllable, whether it is "Okan" or just plain "Ok," and to give the words for "see" "to see" and "seeing."
    Ask her, too, if they have any word corresponding to "nock" or "na."
    In that letter from Judge Brown he says that some of the more intelligent Indians think it means "Shining Heads" or "Shining Tips" referring to mountains between Okanogan and the Methow valley. Ask her if there is any part of the word that is like the word for "shining." (April 21, 1930 [76;269])

Having already responded to previous queries along the same vein, Mourning Dove finally asserted:

There is no word "shining" in the word Okanogan, but the word could be derived from Wick-na-kan. It is in reason that Indians coming a long ways would be attracted by the glaicer shining top of Mt Chopka situated in the heart of the Okanogan tribe of Indians, and so everything in connection with this tribe has been called Okanogans. River, lake, valley, and Indians. In speaking of Indians for explination no doubt the Indians explained to Judge Brown why the word was derived from the effects of seeing the shining tips of the mountains as they came in view for many miles away before reaching the Okanogan valley. This is all in reason, but Judge cannot talk Indian and he comes to conclusions too quick. (May 19, 1930 [38–40;269])

Nonetheless, Guie did not cease challenging her on this point, or on others that attracted his attention.

If the Bureau of Ethnography or another "reputable" source provided information pertinent to the tales, Guie would push Mourning Dove to bring her stories into sync with his ethnohistorical sources (i.e., the mystic power number of the Salish-speaking peoples). He also drew on scientific and geographic sources to make the tales "more accurate." Such editorial work reveals a very problematic issue for Native American studies. How often did and do translators, collaborators, or editors adapt Native American accounts to fit preconceived notions of authoritative text? Over time, to what extent do such exchanges, as well as language acquisition, alter the nature of the known and the traditional?

It must be said that Guie knew his American audience. *Coyote Stories* was a stunning publishing success, particularly given that the book came out at the heart of the Great Depression. It was in its second edition by 1934, and it has been reissued by the University of Nebraska Press (1990).

However, in 1976, another version of *Okanogan Sweat House* was published, *Tales of the Okanogans,* and Donald Hines specifically distanced himself from Guie's work: "Important, this edition does not bear the handiwork of Dean Guie, for the original edition was extensively rewritten and made 'proper.'"[16] A comparison of the ending of "Owlwoman and Coyote" from Mourning Dove's 1921 manuscript, with "Chipmunk and Owl-Woman" from *Coyote Stories,* and "Coyote Kills Owl-Woman" from *Tales of the Okanogans,* will make the editorial choices Guie and Hines made quite clear.

Mourning Dove's original manuscript reads as follows:

Coyote told the children to help him with all their forked sticks to keep her in the fire, at which they gladly did, at last she was burnt to death. Roasted like the many children that she ate.

Coyote then sent all the children back home, after Owlwoman's eyes bursted and from there flew a small little owl to light the tree where it hooted its night call. Coyote then told the bird that in the future, the owlwoman's remains will be only a thing to scare a bad child into sleep, because it will only travel by night, because it is blind in daylight, and only can see in darkness. Because its eyes are burnt out with the pitch. So it is to this day, Indian children are still afraid of the Owlwoman. (143–147; 346)

Guie rewrote that passage to read:

He called to the children, and they brought the forked sticks which they and Coyote used to hold Owl-woman in the fire. Covered as she was with pitch, Owl-woman burned like pitchwood.

In that way perished the wicked Owl-woman. Bad persons always must pay for the evil workings of their mind.[17]

Hines edited the passage into:

Coyote told the children to help him with all their forked sticks to keep Owl-woman in the fire. They did so, and at last she was burned to death. She was roasted instead of the children.

Coyote then sent all the children back home. After Owl-woman's eyes burst, from them flew a small owl, alighting on a tree where it hooted its night call. Coyote told the bird, "In the future, Owl-woman's remains will only be a thing to scare a bad child into sleep. You will only travel by night because you will be blind in the daylight, only able to see in darkness, because your eyes were burnt out with the pitch." So it is to this day. Indian children are still afraid of Owl-woman.[18]

Obviously, Hines followed the manuscript the most closely, while Guie chose to write a new ending.

Hines also chose to recount all thirty-eight of Mourning Dove's original legends, stories that Mourning Dove had asked McWhorter to be sure Guie included in *Coyote Stories:*

To me it would be correct to put in all the legends whether interesting or not, for the sake of my people the Indians of this location where I worked for years to collect for publication, which the "poor dears" did not know I was going to write stories for printing purposes while they told me in every day "talk."

Of course it looks sneaky, but it was the only means that I could be able to collect datas, otherwise it would have been hard for me to get the material which should be preserved for the coming generation of Indians.

You will see that in my recasting I have purposely omitted a lot of things, that is an objection to printing and reading, but an Indian that knows the story can read between the lines just the same. So it is best that we save it all. (February 12, 1930 [69;526])

She would be pleased that the stories are preserved in Hines's edition. Unfortunately, *Tales of the Okanogans* is out of print.

Yet given much that is good about Hines's work, there are still issues that must be addressed. It might have been publishing pressures, or Hines's own belief that he should correct Mourning Dove's grammar and make the sentences flow more smoothly, but Hines's editing does dilute the oral force and accuracy of Mourning Dove's translations because he corrected so extensively. He even went so far as to rephrase some sentences and to substitute other words for Mourning Dove's, and such choices also have slightly altered the tone of the tales.

Mourning Dove was a gifted storyteller. The legends she transcribed are highly readable in their Indian English, and the stories invite dramatic oral interpretive gestures and vocal emphasis. Even the rhythmic variations of Mourning Dove's sentences suggest the flow of dialogue as it might move in Salish. Moreover, who but Mourning Dove is qualified to determine what English word best translates the Okanogan meaning that she heard? Hines is a far better editor than Guie, but he did slip into errors of judgment we still see today. Even in the 1990s, the editing of oral material can follow literary requirements that eliminate the appeal to the ear and an imagined live audience.

Dexter Fisher's editorial work on Mourning Dove encompasses a larger frame of reference than Hines's goal of recovering Mourning Dove's original Okanogan narratives. Her introduction to the 1981 reprint of *Cogewea, the Half-Blood* is a synthesis of approximately two-fifths of her dissertation, *The Transformation of Tradition: A Study of Zitkala Sa and Mourning Dove, Two Transitional American Indian Writers* (1979). In that dissertation, Fisher introduces her readers to an overview of Indian history, which is rarely incorporated into American studies. She also takes great care to raise questions about the difficulty of shifting from an oral to a written tradition, and examines the situation of those caught between two cultures. The dissertation is a compassionate and intelligent examination of the pressures that led Zitkala Sa and Mourning Dove to produce some of the earliest autobiographical accounts, fiction, and transcriptions of tribal legends that we have in English by Indian women writers. It was a groundbreaking work for 1979, and is still of significant interest, although some of her points about Mourning Dove's collaborators, L. V. McWhorter and Dean Guie, as well as the timing of certain events, are inaccurate.

Unfortunately, Fisher's introduction to *Cogewea* is such a tight summary that the exploratory energy of the dissertation is lost. In twenty-four pages Fisher does include an overview of Okanogan history and pertinent rituals, and backgrounds on McWhorter and Mourning Dove. She also discusses issues around the publication of the novel, the themes that distinguish the co-writers of *Cogewea,* references to the assimilation pressures of the time, and the importance of the character Stemteema as an oral historian and spiritual teacher. It is a very informative introduction. Nonetheless, two things are missing: a delineation of McWhorter's inserts from Mourning Dove's text, and the inclusion of Fisher's most subtle and significant dissertation points.

On page v of her dissertation abstract, Fisher writes: "For those early Indian writers, the movement from an oral mode of cultural expression to a written form was difficult and challenging." On page vi, she recognizes the difficult mediation role those early writers took on:

As the observer and preserver of culture and tradition, the Indian writer stands outside the tribal circle, while the oral storyteller is the center of the circle, and that may point to the single greatest difference between oral and written forms. The one is the expression of the community, the other of the individual.

Fisher's exploration of these issues is important, yet that discussion is barely referred to in the republication of *Cogewea*. Without access to correspondence, it is impossible to know why such an editorial choice was made, but a consideration of the scholarly climate surrounding Fisher may shed some light.

In the early 1970s feminist scholars were committed to rediscovering texts by women that could survive the rigors of scholarly criticism. It was believed that such works could effectively expose the sexism and racism of the traditional canon while recovering women's voices in the process of creation. In this context, *Cogewea* would have been a problematic text. It could not stand on its own merits. A sociohistorical analysis was essential for placing the novel, and even then, the problem of collaboration loomed large. Fisher may have chosen a conservative approach for her introduction just to get *Cogewea* published and into discussion. Perhaps she felt unsure about exploring the more theoretical aspects of her dissertation in such a scholarly climate.

The other problem with Fisher's introduction, the failure to discuss the aspects of the collaboration that could enable a reader to distinguish Mourning Dove's and McWhorter's voices, may only be a flaw in retrospect. The republication of *Cogewea* (1981), following Charles Larson's critique of the novel in the appendix of *American Indian Fiction* (1978), actually brought issues of collaboration to the fore. It would be only five years (1986) before Mary Dearborn would focus an entire book on this subject, *Gender and Ethnicity in American Culture,* with a good part of Chapter One focused on *Cogewea.* The recovery of multiethnic texts in the 1970s and early 1980s has opened up whole new areas of critical inquiry for American scholarship.

In the same year that *Cogewea* was republished (1981), Jay Miller was introduced to Mourning Dove's work. He was asked to review her unpublished manuscripts by the University of Washington Press. As Miller comments:

I was both impressed and vexed by the submission. It was the most sustained discussion of Interior Salish life by an insider that I had ever seen, full of historical and ethnographic gems, but badly disjointed and ungrammatical.[19]

For the next nine years, Miller went about correcting her Indian English, organizing her material ethnographically, and annotating Mourning Dove's memories of Salish life either by challenging or supporting their "historical" accuracy. It was amazing good fortune suddenly to have the opportunity to edit such texts. However, it was not fortunate for Mourning Dove.

As already noted, Miller chose to "correct" extensively Mourning Dove's Indian English and organized her materials to fit within the parameters of an ethnographic study. Such choices obscure a writer's tone, emphasis, and purpose. Done extensively, the author's voice can be subsumed into that of the editor's. Second, Miller was careless about details, large and small. McWhorter and Mourning Dove met in 1914, not 1915. Mourning Dove's original gravestone said Mrs. F. Galler, not Mrs. Fred Galler. Such examples of minor errors pepper his work. More importantly, Miller is not knowledgeable about the Mourning Dove/McWhorter collaboration and the Mourning Dove/McWhorter and Guie collaboration. That leads to a number of misleading statements and assertions. For example, in *Coyote Stories,* Miller blames Mourning Dove, not Guie, for severely modifying the tales to meet the standards for juvenile literature.

Third, as can be seen in a major essay, "Mourning Dove: The Author as Cultural Mediator,"[20] Miller creates a frenetic, imbalanced persona for Mourning Dove, one whose writing and political ambitions ultimately undermined her marriage (176–177). What Miller fails to mention is Fred Galler's severe alcoholism and the outbreaks of violence that marred the marriage in its later years. Galler may well have harbored, or shared with others, a deep-seated jealousy and resentment of Mourning Dove's growing stature as an author as well as her election to the Colville Tribal Council (1935). The records from Medical Lake, Washington, the place where Mourning Dove died on August 8, 1936, record that there were old and new contusions all over Mourning Dove's chest and legs when she arrived at the hospital on July 30, 1936. Ten days later, the family was told that she died of a brain hemorrhage. Miller refers only to the death certificate, which gives the cause as "exhaustion from manic depressive psychosis," a commonly used diagnosis for patients who died at Medical Lake during the 1930s.

Fourth, Miller is prone to using ethnographic and male authority to comment constantly on Mourning Dove's texts. His notes appended to *Coyote Stories* and *Mourning Dove: A Salishan Autobiography* correct, add, and now and then compliment Mourning Dove on her accuracy. Authority resides in other male speakers' or writers' recollections of the events, historical and contemporary. A glaring example comes in the *Autobiography* when Mourning Dove has just described the severe hardships on her people after farming is implemented, migration routes are disrupted, and then a severe winter occurs. Mourning Dove describes the near starvation of her family and the loss of livestock and horses. Miller's note begins as follows: "Although this chapter is full of high drama, Charles Quintasket described it as 'the Hollywood version.'" Then Miller projects onto Mourning Dove rationales for her choices: "Mourning Dove probably chose a tragic version because it was more dramatic, made a better story, and saved her father from possible envy by neighbors who were not as wise or lucky."[21] Jay Miller, through his own editing or through the voices of others, does not permit Mourning Dove to tell her own story.

Miller's fifth and most subtle distortion of Mourning Dove's final unpublished manuscripts, "Tipi Life" and "Educating the Indian," was to forge them into an "autobiography" as Euroamericans understand that term, and not to let Mourning Dove's accounts grow out of the Native American oral tradition. Mourning Dove, above all, even through years of interaction with white collaborators, drew on the storytelling foundation of her people. That is why *Cogewea* and her final manuscripts are filled with anecdotes. The meaning emerges through the story. Personal identity is secondary to the issues that address the survival of the tribe.

As the overview of Mourning Dove's five editors indicates, even in the twentieth century we still hobble our way toward letting a Native storyteller speak out her own truth in her own way. The passions, the needs, even the personal prejudices of her editors obscure her voice. So do their expectations around format and grammatical correctness. In light of this review, it is helpful and disturbing to reflect on a letter Columbus sent to Ferdinand and Isabella of Spain, nearly five hundred years ago to the day (April 29, 1493):

As soon as I reached that sea, I seized by force several Indians on the first island, in order that they might learn from us, and in like manner tell us about those things in these lands of which they themselves had knowledge; and the plan succeeded, for in a short time we understood them and they us, sometimes by gestures and signs, sometimes by words; and it was a great advantage to us.[22]

From the very start of European exploration, through the long period of settlement and creation of nationhood, the seizing of lands and of indigenous peoples has been a proclaimed right. But in our need to appear humane in the process, at least to ourselves, we have created situations of enforced conversation, and we have insisted that the monologue was, instead, a dialogue. It is profoundly difficult to break through the structures and ego expectations of dominant power. Until we do, we not only look "through the glass darkly," we help to obscure the image and to erode the cultures we believe we convey.

NOTES

1. Mourning Dove always refers to 1888, the Tribal Enrollment Services records indicate 1887, and the Allotment records indicate 1882, 1886, and 1887, for her birth year. This information was gleaned from Mourning Dove's probate records, which the family has generously shared with me.

2. Mourning Dove, *Mourning Dove: A Salishan Autobiography,* edited by Jay Miller (Lincoln: University of Nebraska Press, 1990).

3. Mourning Dove, *Cogewea, the Half-Blood* (Lincoln: University of Nebraska Press, 1981).

4. Mourning Dove, *Coyote Stories,* edited by Heister Dean Guie (Lincoln: University of Nebraska Press, 1990). Mourning Dove's original title for this collection of Salish tales was *Okanogan Sweat House.* The thirty-eight stories included in that manuscript were reprinted as *Tales of the Okanogans,* edited by Donald Hines (Fairfax, Wash.: Ye Galleon Press, 1976). *Coyote Stories* includes just over twenty-seven of the original tales. For further discussion, see Alanna Brown, "The Evolution of Mourning Dove's *Coyote Stories,*" *SAIL* 4.2 & 3 (Summer/Fall 1992).

5. L. V. McWhorter was born in what became the state of West Virginia, 29 January 1860. In 1903 he moved to the Yakima Valley in Washington and lived there until his death on 10 October 1944. Nelson A. Ault's "Introduction" to *The Papers of Lucullus Virgil McWhorter,* reprinted by the Friends of the Library, State College of Washington, Pullman (1959), from Research Studies of the State College of Washington 26.2–4 and 27.1–2, gives a good overview of McWhorter's life and a listing of his extensive correspondence now housed at the Holland Library, Washington State University, Pullman, Washington.

McWhorter also was known by two other names. "Big Foot" was a term of endearment. "Shopowtan" (Old Wolf) was the official Indian name given to him when he was adopted into the Yakima Tribe for all his efforts on their behalf. He was largely responsible for preventing the Yakimas from being dispossessed of millions of dollars worth of land and water rights. McWhorter is also known for his pamphlet, *The Crime Against the Yakimas* (n.p.: Republic Print, 1913); and for his book, *Border Settlers of Northwestern Virginia* (n.p.: Republican Publishing, 1915); for editing a reprint of *The Wonders of Geyser Land* by Frank D. Carpenter (1878), retitled *Adventures in Geyser Land* (Caldwell, Id.: Caxton Printers, 1935); and for privately publishing a pamphlet on the *Tragedy of the Wahk-Shum* (1937); followed by two books, *Yellow Wolf: His Own Story* (Caldwell, Id.: Caxton Printers, 1940), and posthumously, *Hear Me, My Chiefs! Nez Perce History and Legend* (Caldwell, Id.: Caxton Printers, 1952).

6. When Heister Dean Guie began to work on *Okanogan Sweat House*, the manuscript that ultimately became *Coyote Stories*, his primary credentials were that he had written for his hometown newspaper, the *Yakima Herald*.

Social connections in Yakima undoubtedly brought McWhorter and Guie together. During their collaboration on the legends, Guie lived with his wife in Seattle, Washington. Guie corresponded with McWhorter. McWhorter corresponded with Mourning Dove and Guie.

7. In a letter to Mr. Harl J. Cook, dated 16 November 1928 McWhorter comments on the costs to Mourning Dove and McWhorter of the tardy publication of *Cogewea*: "We lost heavily in advanced sales, many subscribers demanding refund of their money and never renewing. Instead of the 1,250 copies expected to be sold when the book would be ready the actual sales were less than a quarter thousand" (McWhorter Collection, Holland Library, Washngton State University, 9–10, 401). *Cogewea* was contracted for publication in early 1925 and was finally published in late 1927 after McWhorter threatened to sue for mail fraud.

8. Mourning Dove, *Tales of the Okanogans* (Fairfax, Wash.: Ye Galleon Press, 1976). The original story manuscripts are at Holland Library, Washington State University, Pullman, Washington.

9. Alice Poindexter Fisher, "The Transformation of Tradition: A Study of Zitkala-Sa (Bonnin) and Mourning Dove, Two Traditional Indian Writers." Ph.D. dissertation, City University of New York, 1979. A summary of that dissertation by the same title is published in *Critical Essays on Native American Literature*, edited by Andrew Wiget. (Boston: G. K. Hall, 1985), 202–211.

10. Through 1921 Mourning Dove signed her name Morning Dove. Then on 27 December 1921 she visited a museum and discovered that she had been misspelling her name. The Okanogan word for the bird, Mourning Dove, is Humishuma. She published *Cogewea, the Half-Blood* and *Coyote Stories* using both the Indian name and its English translation. Her Christian name was Christine Quintasket. She was married twice, first to Hector McLeod (1908) and then to Fred Galler (1919).

11. This letter is in the extensive twenty-year correspondence between Lucullus Virgil McWhorter and Mourning Dove, which is housed at the Manuscripts, Archives and Special Collections Division of the Washington State Universities Libraries, Pullman, Washington 99164. The correspondence is kept in individual folders and each sheet of paper within a folder is numbered. Some folders have several files, and if so, further letters indicate the file within a given folder. Some sheets have the same number with additional letters to indicate their order in a file. This 3 January 1916 letter is sheets 35-36 of folder 392. All further correspondence from the L. V. McWhorter collection will be indicated by date, page numbers; folder number. The quoted material will maintain the writer's original spelling and grammar with the exception that a period or comma in brackets is my insertion in order to help reader clarity. Such additions have been kept to a minimum. There also may be explanatory notes about dates. Such dates reflect my best judgment on the placement of letters based on their content and other technical assessments. Approximately 15 percent of the Mourning Dove/McWhorter correspondence is partially dated or has no date at all. A few letters are dated incorrectly.

The letters are published with the knowledge and permission of the family elders, Mary Lemery and Charles Quintasket.

12. For a discussion of the autobiographical content and inclusion of oral traditions in *Cogewea,* see Alanna Brown, "Mourning Dove's Voice in Cogewea," *The Wicazo Sa Review* 4.2 (Fall 1988): 2–15.

13. In a 29 July 1921 letter to McWhorter, J. P. MacLean writes:

> I am not surprised that the Indian looters will oppose your appointment as Indian agent. These robbers do not want friends of the Indians as agent. The appointment of the Secretary of the Interior must be taken for granted that the president will show no favor to these persecuted people. If the Indian was a voter it would be different. He may fight the battles of his country, he may be taxed, robbed and kicked about, but he shall not vote or accorded justice. You are perfectly free to use the above in any way you may see fit. (14;1635A)

14. Mary Dearborn's introductory chapter for *Pocahontas's Daughters: Gender and Ethnicity in American Culture* (New York: Oxford University Press, 1986), is an insightful look into collaboration for earlier multi-ethnic American women writers. Unfortunately, the discussion of *Cogewea* in Chapter 1 is based on inaccurate information and assumptions about Mourning Dove's and L. V. McWhorter's working relationship. Thus Dearborn reads into the text more convoluted purposes than are actually there. But in spite of her misreading of *Cogewea,* she makes some valid and interesting points about the pressures on collaborators to interpret, even neutralize, the fiction of non-white writers for the dominant culture. McWhorter, however, sometimes chose to challenge, even antagonize, the dominant readership.

15. Charles Larson, *American Indian Fiction* (Albuquerque: University of New Mexico Press, 1978), 173–180.

16. Donald Hines, "Foreword," *Tales of the Okanogans,* 10.

17. Mourning Dove, *Coyote Stories,* 58–59.

18. Mourning Dove, *Tales of the Okanogans,* 102–103.

19. Mourning Dove, *Mourning Dove: A Salishan Autobiography,* xxxii.

20. Jay Miller, "Mourning Dove: The Author as Cultural Mediator," in *Being and Becoming Indian: Biographical Studies of North American Frontiers,* edited by James A. Clifton (Chicago: Dorsey, 1989), 160–182.

21. Note 7 for Chapter 14: "The Big Snow and Flood Rampage," *Mourning Dove: A Salishan Autobiography,* 229–230.

22. A copy of this Columbus letter was passed out at a conference session. Unfortunately I do not know the translator or the publication source. It is drawn from Leander de Cosco's translation from Spanish into Latin done for the court records of Ferdinand and Isabella of Spain.

THE GREAT STILLNESS
Visions and Native Wisdom in the Writings of Frank Bird Linderman

Celeste River

. . . they were firm believers in luck, and in the *medicine* conferred in dreams. Men often starved, and even tortured themselves, in preparation for desired *medicine-dreams*. Then, weakened both physically and mentally by enervating sweat-baths and fatigue, they slipped away alone to some dangerous spot, usually a high mountain-peak, a sheer cliff, or a well-worn buffalo-trail that might be traveled at any hour by a vast herd of buffalo; and here, without food, or water, they spent four days and nights (if necessary) trying to dream, appealing to invisible "helpers," crying aloud to the winds until utter exhaustion brought them sleep, or unconsciousness—and perhaps a *medicine-dream*. If lucky, some animal or bird appeared to the dreamer, offering counsel and help. . . . Thereafter the bird or animal appearing in the *medicine-dream* was the dreamer's *medicine*.—Frank Bird Linderman, "Out of the North"

Recently a family member sent me an old, tattered manila envelope, covered with red geometric designs and figures and the words "Blackfeet Indians of Glacier National Park" written across the faded blue border. In pencil on the front of the envelope are the identifying words I wrote long ago for grade school show-and-tell: "Celeste R. Grade 3. Age 8. October 22, 1954."

This packet of drawings first came into my life when I was seven, while on a camping trip through the West. For many years after, while growing up near Chicago, I often sat for hours looking at the twenty-four prints by German artist Weinold

Reiss—famous for the colorful designs and clothing, the exotic hairstyles, the strong but saddened faces he depicted of the Blackfeet—wizened elders, men and women in their prime, innocent children.

Frank Bird Linderman's name is on that envelope. In 1935 he was commissioned by the Great Northern Railway to write an "authoritative article" about the Blackfeet to accompany Reiss's drawings in a publication called *Blackfeet Indians*.[1] The booklet containing his story, "Out of the North," is missing from the old manila packet, but the pictures of the people have come back into my life as familiar friends.

When I was fourteen I spent two weeks in Montana on a fire lookout, on the east side of the Mission Mountains, overlooking the Swan Valley. While there I was enthralled by the grandeur and ineffable silence of the surrounding mountain peaks, the valley far below us, the expansive sky above. Never before had I experienced such power in nature as when, on stormy nights, lightning bolts flashed and cracked around us, and rolling thunders rumbled and shook the mountains. At dawn I was amazed to find the valley below had filled with a white sea of mist that slowly lifted to reveal faraway trees, rivers, waterfalls, and lakes, in delicate detail. Most brilliant was Swan Lake, at the north end of the valley—a deep, shimmering reflection of the play of light across the sky.

A child lives in mystical time. During my childhood visits to Montana I did not perceive where I was—that the places were near each other, that a man named Linderman had been there before me. Years later, after moving to Missoula and becoming involved in research on Linderman's life and writings, it dawned on me that he had loved the same natural place, the same natural people—the same heart of the Rocky Mountains that inspired my youthful imagination. In the late 1880s he had often camped at the foot of Swan Lake, and was the first white man to trap in that area.

Most of Linderman's literary works have been out of print for years, lost in the penumbra of eclipse. As I gradually located and read his books and collections of his correspondence I was touched by the history of the man and the content of his writings—especially the direct integrity of his character, and the honest relationships he had with Montana's old full-blood tribal leaders.

Linderman was an early advocate of religious freedom for the American Indian. He respected the dignity of the people, their spiritual beliefs, the wisdom of their relationships with nature. His writings honor their worth. With his literary skills he drew word-pictures that bring us into the mind and experience of tribal historians, the storytellers, who communicated openly with him.

Linderman's published works included four books of Indian legends, from Chippewa, Cree, Blackfeet, Kootenai, Crow, and Gros Ventre oral traditions; two novels about a free-trapper on the Missouri River, which Linderman used to transmit knowledge of the Plains Indians' way of life and spiritual beliefs; and two classic Native American autobiographies about the lives of a Crow chief and a Crow medicine woman. Of these, the last two are still in print. Four other previously unpublished manuscripts have been published since the 1960s, including Linderman's personal memoirs, his recollections of his friendship with Charley Russell, and a biographical novel about a prairie Gros Ventre named Frozen Water, whom he called "Wolf."

STONE ARROW POINTS

Linderman wrote about the Indians of the plains and forests of Montana with a sensitivity that derived from his knowledge of their spiritual and ceremonial life, and their life in the world of nature. He was not a man who would brag about the high level of brotherhood he knew with the Indians, a trust that allowed him into their personal and ceremonial lives. Instead, he wove allusions to his privileged knowledge into stories that are found within the fabric of his literary works.

An elegant example of Linderman's insight is found in the introduction to *Kootenai Why Stories* (1926) when Walks-in-the-water invites him to enter the Great Stillness—the profound silence that dwells in the voice of nature:

> *"Su-ap'-pe,* Whiteman, if you would listen to Kootenai tales of *Old*-man, come with me. I will take you to the lodge of Two-comes-over-the-hill. His lodge is tall and white with a smoky top, and it stands to-night alone under the moon by the lapping waters of Flathead Lake.
>
> "The Great Stillness is there, *Su-ap'-pe.* And yet there are noises. But these only make the Stillness deeper. When the noises come you will listen until they come again. It is while one waits for the noises that the Stillness is deepest. Then it is like a soft robe about him, and his heart sings. At first there will be only the lapping of the waters—lapping, lapping, as though little children were playing. Then far out on the dark lake, where the waves reach far but touch nothing, the Spotted Loon will laugh, and the Gray Goose will gonk at the light in the white lodge of Two-comes-over-the-hill.
>
> "These are the noises that are in the Great Stillness, *Su-ap'-pe.* Will you come?" (xvii–xviii)

The Indians recognized Linderman's sensibility, his willingness to apprehend the no-thing, the stillness—that place "far out on the dark lake, where the waves reach far but touch nothing."

Born in Ohio on September 25, 1869, and raised in the Midwest, Linderman fulfilled his boyhood dream and became a hunter and trapper in the remote Flathead and Swan valleys of northwestern Montana Territory, from 1885 to 1892. Few whites had settled in the area, since the country was too heavily timbered for large cattle ranges and gold had not been found there. When he arrived in the Flathead Valley on March 20, 1885, the sixteen-year-old pioneer did not know if the Indians he would encounter were friendly or hostile.

In his memoirs, *Montana Adventure* (1968), written in the early 1930s, he described the first leaky cabin he built, near the present site of Bigfork, Montana, and his tenderfoot experience the first time he met an Indian. As it turned out, he and Red-horn became lifelong friends:

My Indian visitor instinctively knew that I was a rank pilgrim. His smile said as plainly as words that he thought me a babe in the woods. However, he was exceedingly polite, and tried to treat me as he would a grown man. This made a deep impression on me. . . . For many years after our meeting I knew my first Indian intimately. His name was Red-horn, a renowned Flathead warrior who had counted several "coups" and had taken more scalps than any other living member of his tribe. It was Red-horn who gave me my first glimpse of what men in the old Northwest called the "moccasin telegraph." (8)

The following winter (1885–86) thirty lodges of refugee Chippewa (Ojibwa) and Cree Indians camped near Linderman. A news story written in the 1930s recounts what happened when, after taking part in the Riel Rebellion in Saskatchewan, Canada, they followed the son of their leader Big Bear to the Flathead valley:

Little Bear [Imasees], who was a fierce and resourceful warrior, fled to Montana, crossing the line in the main range of the Rocky Mountains in bitter winter weather.

Nearly dead from starvation they reached the Flathead valley. Frank Linderman, now a resident on the shores of Flathead lake, was then a hunter and trapper in the Flathead country, and it was he who saved the starving Crees and Chippewas from perishing, by furnishing them with elk and deer meat. They have never forgotten this kindness, and to this day consider Linderman the greatest of white men.[2]

When he met them "they were pictures in the extreme and full of fight," Linderman said, in a letter written in 1918. Because he had had trouble with the Kootenais, who at that time were hostile to the few whites living in the area, he "sought to strengthen the friendship between the new arrivals" and himself.

He soon learned that the Chippewa and Cree "were wholly unspoiled by contact with the whiteman." In trying to retain the freedom of their ancestral way of life, their chief, Big Bear, who was a strong spiritual leader, had kept them from the influence of missionaries. They had never accepted the religion of the white man and were devout in the observance of their own ceremonies and ritual. Not much was known about them, because they did not mix with the white man and had not adopted his customs.

Wishing to communicate with the Indians, Linderman learned their sign language and began to absorb the knowledge of the tribal historians, the storytellers. As a boy he had collected the stone arrow points he found while trekking through the countryside in Ohio. Curious about the origin of these mysterious pieces of stone, he questioned the old ones he now sat among, and in the process found himself learning about the origins and wisdom of the people:

I soon satisfied myself that the stone arrow-point belonged to some other race than the Indian but in arriving at this decision I ran across many stories which I thought worth saving.

I was careful in securing these stories and tried many individuals among the older Indians I knew but found them to be as careful as myself in handling them. They differed somewhat at times but in the main were alike. In the work of gathering the legends I became interested in the Indian's religion and found much worth knowing.[3]

Linderman was fascinated by the wisdom and humor of his Indian friends. During his years in the barely settled wilderness of northwestern Montana Territory he learned the Indian's ways and lived as they did. This fact established his lifelong friendships with the native people. In a letter to his family, written in 1914, he reminisced about his early days in the Flathead Valley and Swan Lake area:

I know every inch of that whole country on both sides of the ranges like a book. I have camped in every place along the shore of the lake when whitemen were not wanted there . . . and Manitou was king. Both that country and I were young.[4]

By the time he left the wilderness in 1892 to marry Minnie Jane Johns (they had met in Demersville, a now-extinct settlement on the Flathead River) he had collected many stories, especially from his friends Full-of-Dew, a Chippewa medicine man, and Muskegon, a Cree.

When he left the wilderness Linderman became a self-taught assayer, a prospector, and eventually, in 1899, the owner of the *Sheridan Chinook* newspaper in Madison County, Montana. In 1903 and 1905 he represented Madison County in the eighth and ninth legislative assemblies. When he was appointed assistant secretary of state in 1905, the Lindermans, who by then had three young daughters, moved to Helena, the state capital.

While serving as assistant secretary of state Linderman, and consequently his family, became deeply involved in the fate of the wandering bands of Montana Chippewa and Cree Indians, who were increasingly destitute and starving. With no treaty rights, no reservation lands, and no rations, they wandered the state; most were unable to attain permanent jobs and they were not allowed to hunt on public lands. They lived in camps on the outskirts of white communities, where they survived by hunting through garbage in back alleys for food and clothing, and collecting offal from the slaughterhouses.

In their dire need the Chippewa and Cree turned to Linderman for help. He was a man they knew they could trust to represent their interests in the white world. They lined up daily at his office in Helena, coming to him for advice and help, and for many years he organized campaigns to collect money, food, and clothing for them. In 1908 a group of influential Montanans including William Bole, editor of the *Great Falls Tribune,* Paris Gibson, the founder of Great Falls, and artist Charles M. Russell, joined him to help the homeless Indians.

Finally, in 1916, the Rocky Boy Indian Reservation was established—by law, not by treaty—for the Montana Chippewa and Cree, at the abandoned Fort Assiniboine Military Reservation in the Bear Paw Mountains. This was an amazing feat because it occurred during the height of the homestead rush in Montana, at a time when many Indians were losing their treaty lands to land grabbers and the allotment process.[5]

During this time Linderman's first book was published by Charles Scribner's Sons. *Indian Why Stories, Sparks from War Eagle's Lodge-fire* (1915), illustrated by

Russell, is a collection of Chippewa, Cree, and Blackfeet legends as told by a tribal grandfather named War Eagle in the book, whose prototype was in fact Linderman's Chippewa friend, Full-of-Dew (also known as Paneto).

In 1917 Linderman moved from Helena to a secluded log home he built at Goose Bay, on Flathead Lake, to pursue his dedication to preserve what he knew of the old West in "printer's ink." His second book of Chippewa and Cree legends, *Indian Old-Man Stories, More Sparks from War Eagle's Lodge-fire,* illustrated by Russell, was published by Scribner's in 1920.[6]

Several other books were published by Scribner's during the next few years, including his first novel, a book of stories about the traits of animals, and a book of Kootenai legends, but in 1930 Linderman changed publishers. The John Day Company reprinted his first novel and published a book of Crow legends, his second novel, and his two best-known books, the stories of Plenty-coups and Pretty-shield. Linderman continued to write and lecture, advocating justice and respect for Indian people, until his death on May 12, 1938.

In his lifetime Linderman was given several Indian names. In the early days, because of his ability to make the calls of all the birds of the region, the Chippewa and Cree called him Sings-like-a-bird, and old Kootenais named him Bird-singer. In later years, the Chippewa and Cree called him Co-skee-see-co-cot, Man-who-looks-through-glass, and his Blackfeet name was Iron-tooth. Because of the adeptness with which he was able to communicate in sign language, the Crow chief, Plenty-coups, gave him the name Mah-paht-sa-mot-tsasa, Man-who-knows-sign-talk, or, Sign-talker.[7]

SIGN-TALKER

In his collaborations with Indian storytellers Linderman's main function was that of an informed journalist and editor. He was a creative listener, a poet, an adept sign-talker, and a raconteur. These skills and his experience as a newspaperman served to develop the techniques he used when collaborating with the great Crow chief Plenty-coups in 1927–29, and the Crow medicinewoman Pretty-shield in 1931, to record their autobiographies, published in 1930 and 1932 respectively.

Linderman wrote to his family in November 1928, about his interviews with Plenty-coups, "I learn that I'm a wise interlocutor in drawing these vigorous memoirs from the Chief, and that there is no doubt of their historical value."[8] In great part his success was due to his understanding of the Plains Indians' universal sign language. At the beginning of his work with Pretty-shield he asked her to use signs:

"Talk signs to me, and Crow to Goes-together [the interpreter]," I said in the sign-language.

. . . "Yes," she signed, her eyes telling me that she perfectly understood the reason for this request. She never forgot it. Her sign-language told her story as well as her spoken words. (*Pretty-shield*, 16)

Linderman understood the shaped imagery that sign language gives to thought. Many of his sentences and phrases reflect the whole-thoughts and worldview of the Indians, transmitted through their pictorial language. For example, he used the phrase "on this world," in reference to this earthly life. When Pretty-shield told him about the quality of her peoples' way of life at the time when she was born, he wrote that she said, "We were a happy people when I came onto this world, Sign-talker" (*Pretty-shield*, 20). When Plenty-coups said he was looking forward to life after death, Linderman transcribed:

"I am old and am living an unnatural life. I know that I am standing on the brink of the life that nobody knows all about, and I am anxious to go to my Father, Ah-badt-daht-deah, to live again as men were intended to live, even on this world." (*Plenty-coups*, 78)

Linderman explained, "Ah-badt-dadt-deah literally translated means The-one-who-made-all-things" (*Plenty-coups*, 79). In his Crow and Gros Ventres stories, when referring to Animal-persons, ancestral Spirits, or the Supernatural Ones, the aboriginal people used variations of a phrase, "The-ones-who-live-without-fire."[9] The complete imagery of these hyphenated phrases, and others such as "The-seven-stars" [Big Dipper], "The-beyond-country," or "the-grass-that-the-buffalo-do-not-eat" (*Pretty-shield*, 221, 42, 146), show how native people communicated whole thoughts through gesture language, and consequently, with linguistic sound.

Sign language—which evolved out of pictography long before the written word—is a three-dimensional, visual language. It is ideographic writing in the air. With sign language, meaning is not separated into individual words; rather, complete ideas are transmitted as information flows from image to image.

When interviewing Indian storytellers Linderman was using two different sensory pathways, receiving both the verbal/auditory information coming through an interpreter and the gestural/visual dialogue passing directly between himself and the storyteller. This gave him a deeper understanding of the Indian mind and spirit because, using languages of both sound and sight, and through his experiential knowledge of their way of life, he was able to realize a greater degree of similarity between his and their thoughts.[10]

Because he was a poet himself, Linderman appreciated the poetics of the Indian storytellers. For instance, when talking about something as mundane as "early morning" he wrote that Plenty-coups said "the night was westward," and elsewhere, "just when the night was leaving to let the morning come" (*Plenty-coups*, 36, 59).

About his style of translation of the Indian legends Linderman wrote, "I propose to tell what I know of these legends, keeping as near as possible to the Indian's style of storytelling" (*Indian Why Stories,* x). While working on illustrations for *Indian Old-man Stories* Russell, who was a master storyteller, commented on Linderman's representation of the aboriginal legends:

> I think you have written those last Ingun storys better than the Why yarns [*Indian Why Stories*] youv made them more flowery and you know that the red man was a fancy talker.[11]

When writing the Indians' stories Linderman chose his words with meticulous care, not only for factual accuracy, but to record the color and ambiance of the storytelling. In the introduction to *Recollections of Charley Russell* (1963) editor H. G. Merriam (a Rhodes scholar in 1907, founder of the creative writing program at the University of Montana, and publisher of *Frontier and Midland,* the premier literary magazine of the Pacific Northwest during the 1920s and 1930s) said, of Linderman's literary worth and authenticity. "Frank Bird Linderman was one of Montana's most accomplished writers. He possessed a fine conscience in his effort to interpret the red man, an almost fanatically painstaking regard for accuracy, a sense of form, and an ear for language" (xxi).

In the foreword to his first novel, *Lige Mounts: Free Trapper* (1920, reprinted as *Morning Light,* 1930), Linderman stated his intention to portray the Indians' dialogue honestly:

> In order to give the reader an idea of the dignity with which the old-time Indian conversed, I have assumed that in speaking the Cree language, which he had learned perfectly, or in translating conversations from the Cree, Lige Mounts used nearly perfect English. (*Morning Light,* viii)

Linderman was aware of the problems involved in the translation of bicultural, composite works, but his knowledge of sign language helped him. In the foreword to Pretty-shield's story he addressed these problems and his method of dealing them:

> Such a story as this, coming through an interpreter laboring to translate Crow thoughts into English words, must suffer some mutation, no matter how conscientious the interpreter may be. . . . However, in this, as in all my work with Indians, my knowledge of the sign-language made it always possible for me to know *about* what Pretty-shield said, so that, even though she wished to do so, the interpreter could never get very far afield without my knowing of the divergence. (*Pretty-shield,* 11)

Also, the Indian storyteller could know the gist of what Linderman was asking or saying, even before the interpreter had translated his words. Through the voice of Lige Mounts, Linderman explained this process in his second novel, *Beyond Law* (1933):

> I spoke in English, so that Mr. Cameron could know I wa'n't saying anything I ought not to, and so our interpreter could repeat my words in the Crow tongue. But I used the sign talk, too, so that the Injins knowed what I said long before our man repeated my speech in the Crow language. (178)

Linderman's method of transmitting to us the distinctive and changing mood around the Indians' storytelling was unusual in his day, because he transcribed related dialogues that took place with others during the sessions, and he described the "performed quality" of the oral narrations. Again, he attempted to employ careful, descriptive writing in all dimensions—observing nonverbal information coming from the surrounding atmosphere and environment, and noting other nonverbal messages such as facial expressions, body language, pauses, interruptions, and changes in rhythm, tone, and volume of voice— more accurately to translate the oral traditions of the native people.

Linderman was ahead of his time in his use of these notations, and in his comprehension of the knowledge of an Indian woman, in Pretty-shield's story. Most of our early records of Native American oral tradition are literal transcriptions that do not include the performed quality of the narrations, nor the balance of a woman's story and perspective. The lasting value of Linderman's literary work is found in the fact that through his words we experience the humanness of the Indian storytellers, and gain a better understanding of their awareness in the world.[12]

In 1927 the University of Montana awarded Linderman, who often lectured at the university, an honorary doctorate for his literary work and his research in the field of Indian customs, beliefs, and traditions. Merriam, who knew Linderman personally for twenty years during the 1920s and 1930s, explained Linderman's understanding of the Indian people:

Linderman knew Plains Indians as friends whom he admired. He also, being curious about their inner life as well as the outer, before white contamination, treasured their legends and beliefs and their relationship to all that is in heaven and earth. (*Recollections of Charley Russell,* xx)

Others recognized Linderman's sensitivity to the Indian psyche as well. In May 1930, soon after the publication of Plenty-coups's story, Rev. John Frost, a Crow from Plenty-coups's home at Pryor, Montana, wrote Linderman that the book "brings out the Indian as near as can be in writing or words." Frost closed his letter with a prayer for Linderman:

May the Great spiret give you maney snows so you can give your race the insides of the Indian's heart[.] that they may know we Indian as we are, not what others think. I am your frind.[13]

In a 1930 review of Plenty-coups's story, New York literary critic Frederic F. Van de Water commented on Linderman's ability to give the reader, in writing, reflections of the Indian mind:

Here, for the first time to our knowledge, an Indian speaks directly to you of the old free life of a half century gone. . . . Through the endearing simplicity of Mr. Linderman's prose comes a comprehension of the Indian mind, its mysticism and arrow straight directness of purpose; of the Indian ethics which held war the raw essence of sport and esteemed bravery and truth above all other virtues.[14]

However, despite Linderman's many years of friendship with Indians, he felt no white man could ever completely understand them. In 1920 he wrote, "After so many years of acquaintance the Indian remains to me still a man of mystery" (*Morning Light,* vii).

NATIVE WISDOM

Besides his mastery of sign language Linderman understood other languages hidden to most, but familiar to the native people. He knew the songs of the birds and heard the voice of nature in the big trees, the winds, and the waters. He was a student of nature, of the secret habits of wild animals, and of the people he met throughout his life. In a letter to his daughters written in 1917, he related the silent reserve of the owl to other profound beings:

The owl is silent—the most silent of all the birds when silence pleases him but when he desires sound, he can make the Timberlands ring with his voice. The owl is weather-wise, too, but stingy with his knowledge, as are all other profound beings.[15]

Linderman, who considered Montana "the real Indian home," knew many of the old full-blood tribal leaders and medicine men in Montana and found them to be careful with their knowledge, like the owl. In his memoirs he described his Chippewa friend, Full-of-Dew, as "a silent man, always anxious to learn, a profound mystic":

"Who *is* Manitou?," I asked, as always when opportunity offered.

He looked about, his eyes settling for a moment on the far mountains white with snow. "The mountains, the lowlands, the rivers, the birds, my fire, the people, the big trees," he said slowly. Then he added, "I believe that the big trees speak to you, Co-skee-see-co-cot, but not to many other white men." (*Montana Adventure,* 160–161)

After Linderman visited the Crow Reservation, in 1926, to meet with old warriors who told him stories for his fourth book of Indian legends, *Old Man Coyote* (1931), John Frost wrote to him about the songs of the talking waters:

I do hope that we will meet againe some time at the Water of manney Toungs[.] What I mean by that is what you heard in the Creek while lying awake awaiting the returne of your unwelcome visoters the Skunks.

I thought we Indians were the onely one that understod the Language of the waters and the swis[h] of the pines. When I am sad I go into the Mountans and listen to the manney songs of the Creeks and the sootheing words of the Pines.

you could of not suprised [me] aney moor by saying what you heard in that Creek than if you had taken a gun shot at me[.] I would not open up my heart to anone else but you for they would say I was crasey but you understand.[16]

Ten years earlier, in 1916, Linderman had met for four days of "medicine talk" with Chief Big Rock, a Chippewa medicine man he had known for thirty years, to record information and prepare for his writing of *Indian Old-Man Stories*. A news story about the event, which took place in Great Falls in a tipi owned and furnished by Charley Russell, emphasized the solemnity of the occasion:

The origin and the ancient customs, superstitions, traditions and religion of the Chippewas were discussed and explained by Big Rock in great detail, and all was set down. During the four days no one [else] was admitted into the lodge until sunset.[17]

During the four days in the medicine lodge of Big Rock Linderman took part in a "medicine-smoke," which he described in the foreword to *Indian Old-Man Stories*. He said all essential points of the Chippewas' religion are found in the sacred pipe ceremony, and he described the setting within the lodge and details of the ritual:

Even though surrounded by mists of superstition there is yet beauty in the rites and ceremonies of the Indian. Dignity is always present. . . .

      An imaginary trail led straight across the lodge from west to east. It was not occupied nor littered. It was the way for the spirits of all departed beings, and was spoken of as the "Buffalo's trail." A painted lodge is a constantly offered prayer, and as it must face the East, the imaginary trail is also the way of the sun. . . . The first fire in the imaginary trail was the Sacred fire—the Holy fire, and was but four glowing coals that had been taken from the regular lodge-fire and deposited in a square within a square of the perfectly cleaned earth. Each spear of grass and foreign thing was carefully removed before the coals were deposited, and only sweet-grass or sweet-sage was burned upon the coals. In the smoke of the incense given off by the fuel, the pipe-bowls, stems, and even the hands of the company were cleansed at the beginning of the ceremony. (xiii–xvi)

The news story quoted above, about the "medicine talk" in Great Falls, opened with a visualization of the voice of Manitou that reflects Linderman's style of writing and his eloquent love of nature:

Manitou, the God of the red man, and protector of his children on earth, speaks in the sighing of the summer wind across the prairie, as well as in the thunder that rolls across the mountain tops, and his voice is the voice of the giver of all good.

In a short story, "The Indian's God," found in *On a Passing Frontier* (1920), Linderman spoke through a character named Uncle Billy, who told a story about the Indians' reverence for nature:

First of all I noticed that every beauty spot in nature was a shrine to him. He didn't tell me so, but I saw it and felt it. Before a brilliant sunset or a noisy waterfall he'd stand in silent admiration; an' I learned, after a while, that in each case he offered up his prayer to The Greaty Mystery. He had but one prayer, an' he told me that one: Let my children all grow old. That was all, an' it was never varied. It made me ashamed of myself an' my race. Once he told me that the birds were little people, an' after I'd learned to look an' listen, myself, I noticed that they had each just one sure-enough song, an' some of 'em only a single note. Then I thought of his only prayer.

Again, this time through the voice of Uncle Billy, Linderman asked "Who is God?":

I could talk to you for an hour about things I learned from that Injin. But he was an unwilling teacher, because he seemed to think that all live things believe an' think just as he did. Once I asked him: "Who is God?" an' he replied: "The sun, the earth, the flowers, the birds, the big trees, the people, the fire, an' the water is God. Sometimes they speak to me, an' I'm glad in my heart. Big trees speak the loudest to me. Others hear other things best."

He seemed surprised at my question—seemed to think I must be jokin' him. But I'm mightly glad he answered as he did, for it blazed a new trail for me. I feel better toward my fellows an' I only pray for peace. It took a long, long time, but now I know

> "The redman dares an only prayer;
>   One perfume has the rose;
> When mornin' dawns, the robin sings
>   The only song he knows.
> The silent are the giant things
>   That make the temple grand
> Amid a peace that nature meant
>   All men should understand."
>   (124–126)

Uncle Billy said his Indian friend had only one prayer, which he offered to The Great Mystery without variation: "Let my children all grow old." Knowing the beauty of that simple prayer, Uncle Billy felt ashamed of his race—the white man.

Years later Chief Plenty-coups told Linderman something his people had noticed about the foolish ways of the white man:

We saw that the white man did not take his religion any more seriously than he did his laws. . . . We kept the laws we made and lived our religion. We have never been able to understand the white man, who fools nobody but himself. (*Plenty-coups*, 228)

Plenty-coups had lived by the wisdom he learned from the elders of his tribe. For example, as a young warrior, while on a raid against an enemy band of Sioux, he reminded his friend Big-shoulder that the old men of the tribe said change is inevitable:

The old men have told us that nothing here can last forever. They say that when men grow old and can no longer eat hard food, life is worth little. They tell us that everything we can see, except the earth and sky, changes a little even during a man's natural lifetime, and that when change comes to any created thing it must accept it, that it cannot fight, but must change. We do not know what may happen today, but let us act as though we were the Seven-Stars [Big Dipper] in the sky that live forever. Go with me as far as you can, and I will go with you while there is breath in my body. (144)

Plenty-coups recalled another time when a chief named Long-horse, preparing to die in battle, told the men who were with him: "Remember that nothing is everlasting except the Above and the Below" (282). Such cultural insights helped the Crows adapt, and survive the changes forced upon their world in the late 1800s.

RELIGIOUS FREEDOM

Uncle Billy Hammerhill was an alter ego Linderman created when he owned the *Sheridan Chinook,* at the turn of the century. The sage old prospector, whose character was based on "old-timers" who lived in the hills around Sheridan, often expressed his wisdom in aphorisms. One of Linderman's favorite Uncle Billy sayings was, "A heathen is a party who don't believe in your God."

In his files Linderman kept a story from the *Demersville* (Montana) *Interlake* of December 21, 1890, which he said "gives in a nutshell much of the Indian point of view" and hints at "the struggle of the red man to forsake the religion of his forefathers for that of the 'blackrobes'." The story contained an epitaph from the headboard of an Indian grave found at a place called Half Moon:

Borned in Winnipeg, 1780, one Chippeway woman by the name of Wolf Woman. Have request she would not be baptze fore her children was not baptze and they was in hell she would go and be with them, age 110.[18]

This poignant epitaph shows the underlying reason for Linderman's keen dislike of the missionaries' religious dogma, a belief system that insisted on stamping out the indigenous peoples' wisdom.

Linderman recognized the purity of his Chippewa and Cree friends' beliefs and traditions, and he used his literary works to educate readers about the spirituality of the Indian as he knew it. In his first novel his protagonist, Lige Mounts, asked Bluebird, a young Cree woman, to tell him about Manitou:

"We do not speak His name often," she began softly. "The sun, the earth, and everything that lives is Manitou, even the ants and the tiny things that live under the leaves that lie on the ground beneath the forest trees. . . . Greater and more wonderful than the moon and stars is the sun, but *All* is Manitou. The Sun, the father, makes the grass and the flowers to grow upon Earth, the mother, of all things. And through the great Sun we thank Manitou with the Sun-dance each year." (*Morning Light,* 270)

During Linderman's lifetime the U.S. government forbade the practice of the Sun Dance and other essential spiritual traditions of the indigenous people. In 1916 Linderman wrote to Cato Sells, the commissioner of Indian affairs, that in his opinion it was "wicked, and not in keeping with good judgement to prohibit the sun-dance." He said the Sun Dance was "a very serious effort on the part of the Indian to serve his God" and that, by allowing its practice, Sells would "find the Indian far more satisfied in mind." On the same day he wrote to the Cree leader, Little Bear (Big Bear's son, Imasees), at Box Elder, Montana, "I told you not to tell the white man about [giving] the sun-dance, but I think you have told it. If you give the sun-dance be quiet about it." [19]

In the foreword to *Indian Old-Man Stories,* a book of Chippewa and Cree legends and knowledge, Linderman said white men trying to learn about the religion and customs of the Indian "sometimes jumped at conclusions" and "recorded untruths," this often occurring because of the Indians' practice of giving "direct answers to single direct questions" (x). Linderman explained what it was about the Indian that made him an unwilling teacher:

> The novice, writing of Indian beliefs and customs, is a dangerous man if his findings are to be recorded as historical fact. For after all my study, the Indian is still much of a mystery to me. He has trusted me and has always been willing to tell me of himself, but he is fair and attributes to *you* a mind as great or greater than his *own.* There is the trouble. Ask him: "Is the sun God?" and he may reply "yes"— simply "yes," for he believes that you know that ALL is God. He reasons if you desired further information you would ask for it in a direct question. Therefore, out of respect for you, he volunteers no information—no extra measure. You must know much of the Indian or you will learn nothing directly from him. He is a poor teacher, and your beliefs or findings concerning him are your own, and of no importance to him. He insists that this should be so, for, above all, the Indian is an individualist in all things. (viii–ix)

When, in 1924, the editor of *The Forum* magazine asked Linderman to express his thoughts on "our national duty toward the Indians" for a symposium about "the Indian problem," the Montana author outlined his front-line ideas for "bettering the Indian's condition." He made a brief but strong statement on the Indians' right to religious freedom:

> Leave the Indian his God. Let him practice his own religious rites. Whatever else the Indian may be he is not a bigot. Let us be as broad as is our helpless ward. (Here I would write pages.) [20]

He did write pages about the Indians' spiritual beliefs, and their tolerance of others' religions. He said Indians had great respect for the individualism of the other, and would never presume to try to change someone's beliefs or give them a "better God."

In *Morning Light* the story's protagonist, Lige Mounts, said the Indian "never scorns another's creed":

> Whatever an Injin believes in he never insists on you accepting it as your own belief, and he thinks no less of you if you *don't* believe like he does. He holds that you have a right to your opinion and claims that same right for himse'f. He never scorns another's creed, no matter how much it may differ from his own. (220)

In *Beyond Law* (published eleven years later), Lige talked about civilization and religion, and said an Indian would never quarrel with another man "about his religion":

Young Mr. McLeod talked a heap about what he called civilization. We argued some, he holding that it, and Christianity, was the world's best lights, and I agreeing that they *could* be, if they was rightly understood and practiced. I reckon he got a little r'iled when I pointed out to him that mighty nigh the first thing that what he called civilization did, was to mess up its neighbor's drinking water—and quarrel with him about his religion, a thing an Injin never does. (72)

Further on, Lige had more to say about the different ways of the white man and the Indian. Linderman thought this information was important enough to be repeated in different contexts:

That is our way, the white man's way. Whatever we can't understand is plumb outside of reason. A white man thinks nobody is right that ain't white, an Injin, that right ain't partial to color, and will bed down with anybody that'll give it room. As soon as a white man steps in he is hell-bent to teach, and too bullheaded to learn. Injins never teach, nor preach, without being asked. Even then they are mighty sparing. . . . And religion! That, to an Injin, is a man's own business.

Continuing, we recognize Uncle Billy's voice in Lige Mounts's words:

With us a heathen is mighty nigh anybody that don't believe in *our* God. I've lived with Injins a heap. With all their shortcomings, and they've got as many as most folks, I know these things are true. They didn't tell me they was true themse'fs. They just let me see them one by one and day by day till I learned them as well as a white man can. We can't ever sure-enough know Injins. No white man ever has or ever will. . . . Once an old Crow chief told me the white man was mighty smart but not very wise. It took me quite a spell to figure out what the old fellow was shooting at. (175–176)

The "old Crow chief" was Plenty-coups, who told Linderman, when they were collaborating on Plenty-coups's autobiography:

Our Wise Ones learned much from the animals and birds who heal themselves from wounds. But our faith in them perished soon after the white man came, and now, too late, we know that with all his wonderful powers, the white man is not wise. He is smart, but not wise, and fools only himself. (*Plenty-coups,* 265)

When Linderman wrote the narrated autobiography of Plenty-coups, he purposely chose to title the book *American: The Life Story of a Great Indian, Plenty-coups, Chief of the Crows,* to focus attention on the original status of the American Indian. But he went beyond this. In his unusual work of recording the stories of a Crow medicine woman—a wise-one—he stood in defense of the *whole family* of Indian people. He emphasized the family by naming Pretty-shield's narrated autobiography *Red Mother,* despite fellow author and historian Hermann Hagedorn's warning: "It suggests Russia and nothing else, and I think will be thoroughly misleading." [21] The titles Linderman chose for his books about Plenty-coups and Pretty-shield, *American* and *Red Mother,* were direct, bold statements about the value and humanity of the original, native, American.

When author and literary critic Frederic F. Van de Water eulogized Linderman's literary skills and the value of his writings, in a 1939 tribute titled "The Work of Frank B. Linderman," he said Linderman's books speak with "absolute authority, for their author had been a Doer before he became a Teller"—a man who knew well the "free Plains Indian, the red horse-people of the old West." Van de Water continued:

His collections of Indian folk stories have high ethnological value and something rarer and more precious than any scientific worth. In these, one can see the foreshadow of the impulse that eventually came to fruition in *American* and *Red Mother.* Here are sympathy and affection and a desire to comprehend a strange people. Indians to Frank Linderman were not specimens or spectacles. They were his teachers, as well as his pupils. He had none of the racial arrogance that scoffs at what it cannot understand. He wanted to know the ways and laws of a vanished culture and because of his approach, which was simple and earnest and abidingly friendly, like all his approaches in life, he understood them all—Crees, Ojibways, Piegans, Bloods, Blackfeet, Gros Ventres, and Crows—better than any man on this continent who ever has put pen to paper, and a suspicious people completely trusted him.

That mutual comprehension created *American,* the life story of the old chief of the Crows, taken down from his own lips, and its companion volume, *Red Mother,* the narrative of a medicine woman of the same tribe. (*Frontier and Midland* Spring 1939:151)

Linderman had rapport with Plenty-coups and the other old Indians who told him their stories. To them he was a confidant, a man who would write the truth of their experience. Pretty-shield told him, when talking about her father, "I am hiding nothing from you, Sign-talker" (*Pretty-shield,* 43). And, at the end of their collaboration, Plenty-coups told Linderman:

I am glad I have told you these things, Sign-talker. You have felt my heart, and I have felt yours. I know you will tell only what I have said, that your writing will be straight like your tongue, and I will sign your paper with my thumb, so that your people and mine will know I told you the things you have written down. (*Plenty-coups,* 308–309)

VISIONS, DREAMS, AND MEDICINE POWERS

Linderman and Plenty-coups sat under the rustling leaves in the shady grove of tall cottonwood trees beside the old chief's home near Pryor, Montana, for their storytelling sessions during the hot summer days of 1927 and 1928. Coyote-runs, Plain-bull, and other old men who had known the chief since boyhood were always present. As Plenty-coups told Linderman, "I am an old man, and they will help me to remember," to which Coyote-runs added:

If you do not tell all—if you forget—I will touch your moccasin with mine. . . . Your medicine-dream pointed the way of your life, and you have followed it. Begin at the beginning. (*Plenty-coups*, 4, 5)

As a boy Plenty-coups's future was given direction by his grandfather, who named him Aleek-chea-ahoosh, Many Achievements. In a dream the elder man had seen that his grandson would count many coups, he would be a chief, and would live to be old. Plenty-coups said as a young boy he had felt obliged to live up to his name, to excel and become a leader among those his own age. "And now," he said, "I was beginning to think of dreaming" (27–38).

When he was nine Plenty-coups went into the mountains to fast and dream. A Person, who appeared to him as a "queer light," took him into a sacred lodge:

I looked to see what Persons sat on the south side, and my eyes made me afraid. They were the Winds, the Bad Storms, the Thunders, the Moon, and many Stars, all powerful, and each of them braver and much stronger than men. (38–39)

Here, in the text, Linderman said he believed the old Crow chief "wished to convey" to him that he "recognized" the Persons on the south side of the lodge as "the great forces of nature." Plenty-coups went on with his story. A kind voice coming from the north side of the lodge urged him to sit among the Persons there. When he did so, understanding came to him in this way:

On neither side were the Persons the same as I. All were different, but I knew now that they had rights in the world, as I had, that Ah-badt-dadt-deah had created them, as He had me and other men. Nobody there told me this, but I felt it in the lodge as I felt the presence of the Persons. I knew that to live on the world I must concede that those persons across the lodge who had not wished me to sit with them had work to do, and that I could not prevent them from doing it. I felt a little afraid but was glad I was there. (39)

Young Plenty-coups was learning to live in harmony with the forces of nature.

The Persons on the north side of the lodge were the Little-people, or Dwarves, who the Crows believed made the ancient stone arrow points. All the Persons in the lodge were old warriors, and had been counting coups. In front of each was either "a white coup-stick bearing the breath-feathers of a war-eagle" or the "heavy first-feathers whose quills were strong enough to stick in the ground." Several times the chief of the Little-people told Plenty-coups to stick a feather in the ground, then recited some brave deed as though he were Plenty-coups. These coups stories were prophetic, and reaffirmed the dream of Plenty-coups's grandfather.

The Persons on the south were impressed by Plenty-coups's achievements and the Bad Storms told the Dwarf-chief, "You should give him something to take back with him, some strong medicine that will help him." The Dwarf-chief responded:

He will be a Chief . . . I can give him nothing. He already possesses the power to become great if he will use it. Let him cultivate his senses, let him use the powers which Ah-badt-dadt-deah has given him, and he will go far. The difference between men grows out of the use, or non-use, of what was given them by Ah-badt-dadt-deah in the first place.

Then the Dwarf-chief spoke directly to Plenty-coups:

Plenty-coups, we, the Dwarfs, the Little-people, have adopted you and will be your Helpers throughout your life on this world. We have no medicine-bundle to give you. They are cumbersome things at best and are often in a warrior's way. Instead, we will offer you advice. Listen!
    In you, as in all men, are natural powers. You have a will. Learn to use it. Make it work for you. Sharpen your senses as you sharpen your knife. Remember the wolf smells better than you do because he has learned to depend on his nose. It tells him every secret the winds carry because he uses it all the time, makes it work for him. We can give you nothing. You already possess everything necessary to become great. Use your powers. Make them work for you, and you will become a Chief. (42–43)

When Plenty-coups awoke in the early morning light he "went over it all" in his mind. He considered the advice of his Helpers and made up his mind that his own powers, and his will, would work for him. He told Linderman about his boyhood resolve:

I saw and understood that whatever I accomplished must be by my own efforts, that I must myself do the things I wished to do. And I knew I could accomplish them if I used the powers that Ah-badt-dadt-deah had given me. I *had* a will and I would use it, make it work for me, as the Dwarf-chief had advised. I became very happy, lying there looking up into the sky. My heart began to sing like a bird, and I went back to the village, needing no man to tell me the meaning of my dream. I took a sweat-bath and rested in my father's lodge. I *knew* myself now. (44)

Linderman had been looking into the nature of visions, dreams, and medicine powers for many years when he wrote, in 1931, about the elusive impressions of medicine dreams:

Nothing is more bewildering to me than recording the dreams of old Indians. Trying to determine exactly where the dream begins and ends is precisely like looking into a case in a museum of natural history where a group of beautiful birds are mounted against a painted background blended so cunningly into reality that one cannot tell where the natural melts to meet the artificial. (*Pretty-shield,* 10–11)

In *Plenty-coups,* before relating the chief's two medicine dreams, Linderman described the context of the vision quest. This passage is similar to the one he wrote in his article "Out of the North," about the Blackfeet, but it is an earlier version, written before 1930:

The Indians of the Northwest are great believers in dreams. They starve and torture themselves in preparation for "medicine-dreams" and then repair alone to some difficult spot, generally a high mountain peak. There, without food or water, they spend four days and nights—if necessary, appealing to "helpers." Their condition, both physical and mental, is unbalanced by weakness brought on by abstaining from food, taking enervating sweat-baths, and continually courting fatigue. Their resulting dreams are weird and often terrifying, though sometimes wonderfully prophetic of the future. In a medicine-dream some animal, or bird, or "person" appears and offers "help." Sometimes these apparitions only give advice or teach the dreamer by parables which are later interpreted by the "wise ones" (medicine-men) of the tribe. Thereafter, or until he has had a greater dream (which seldom happens), the creature that offered help in his dream is the dreamer's medicine.

But "medicine" is a confusing term. It is not especially a curative. It is more nearly a protective property. It is a talisman or charm, a lucky piece that no old Indian will forego. It is always kept near him. Often, in formal camps, it is hung on a tripod back of his lodge if the lodge faces east. (*Plenty-coups*, 28–29)

Linderman tried to further his readers' understanding of the term *medicine* as he concluded the passage about medicine dreams in "Out of the North," written for *Blackfeet Indians* in 1935 (see epigraph):

Thereafter the bird or animal appearing in the *medicine-dream* was the dreamer's *medicine*.

He believed that all the power, the cunning, and the instinctive wisdom, possessed by the appearing bird or animal would forever afterward be his own in time of need. And always thereafter the dreamer carried with him some part of such bird or animal. It was his lucky-piece, a talisman, and he would undertake nothing without it upon his person. (14)

Linderman's respect for the indigenous peoples' spiritual beliefs, traditions, and worldview, and his continuing efforts to help them politically and economically, earned him the trust of the old Indians. In the foreword to *Indian Old-Man Stories* he talked about his understanding of the Indians' reverence for all created things, and their recognition of the medicine powers of the animals and birds:

I believe that his [the Indian's] silence in the great out-of-doors is because of his reverence for other created things which can neither speak nor move. Created by the same power, he shrinks from flaunting his special favors before them, and so is silent, lest his power to move and speak make them jealous before his god. He believes that to all of His creations the All-wise gave some peculiar power, and instead of being jealous of these gifts, which he often recognizes as greater than his own, he respects them as special marks of respect from the hand of his own Maker. Strength, bravery, endurance, speed, and cunning—everything that contributed to make his own wild life a success, or marked him with distinction as an individual among his kind, is reverenced when possessed in an equal or greater degree among the lower animals and birds. (x–xi)

Plenty-coups told Sign-talker about the great medicine dream he had when he was ten, from which he gained the wisdom and protective power—the "medicine"—of the tiny chickadee:

"Listen, Plenty-coups," said a voice. "In that tree is the lodge of the Chickadee. He is least in strength but strongest of mind among his kind. He is willing to work for wisdom. The Chickadee-person is a good listener. Nothing escapes his ears, which he has sharpened by constant use. Whenever others are talking together of their successes or failures, there you will find the Chickadee-person listening to their words. But in all his listening he tends to his own business. He never intrudes, never speaks in strange company, and yet never misses a chance to learn from others. He gains success and avoids failure by learning how others succeeded or failed, and without great trouble to himself. There is scarcely a lodge he does not visit, hardly a Person he does not know, and yet everybody likes him, because he minds his own business, or pretends to.

    "The lodges of countless Bird-people were in that forest when the Four Winds charged it. Only one is left unharmed, the lodge of the Chickadee-person. Develop your body, but do not neglect your mind, Plenty-coups. It is the mind that leads a man to power, not strength of body." (*Plenty-coups,* 66–67)

The old chief recalled the first time when, as a young warrior on a raid against the enemy, he invoked the power of his medicine—"the stuffed skin of a chickadee, which I held in my hand." Linderman breathed life into the great warrior's telling of the story:

Plenty-coups showed intense feeling. He stood up, his moccasined feet spread wide to support his aged body, and addressed his open empty hand as though he were once more alone on that wind-swept hill. He was living his youth again. The chickadee was in his hand. He could see it there, and spoke to it as he had spoken that day so long ago when his medicine was his very life. . . .

    "O Chickadee!" he said, "I saw the Four Winds strike down the forest. I saw only one tree, your tree, when they had finished. The Four Winds did not harm you, Chickadee. You told me to use the powers that Ah-badt-dadt-deah had given me, to listen as you did, and I should succeed. I have tried to follow your advice, shall always follow it. Help me now! . . .

    "I tied the stuffed Chickadee beneath the left braid of my hair, just back of my ear," he went on. (142–143)

Like Plenty-coups, Pretty-shield also talked about the powerful little Chickadee, and one day told Linderman the story of her grandmother's vision and medicine power:

At first grandmother did not see the chickadee. She could hear the bird talking and laughing to itself, but could not see it until it came to sit on a willow right above her head. "Look," it said, going up into the air, flying higher and higher. Straight up it went, growing larger and larger and larger, until it was as large as a war-eagle [mountain, or golden eagle]. "See," it called down to my grandmother, "there is great power in little things. . . . I am a woman, as you are. Like you I have to work, and make the best of this life," said the bird. "I am your friend. . . . Have you listened?" asked the bird, settling down again, and growing small. (*Pretty-shield,* 159–160)

Pretty-shield's own medicine-power, her wisdom, was given to her by the ant people. One day, after she had been fasting and mourning the death of a baby daughter for two moons, a female Person standing beside an ant hill beckoned to her:

"Rake up the edges of this ant hill and ask for the things that you wish, daughter," the Person said; and then she was gone. Only the ant hill was there; and a wind was blowing. I saw the grass tremble, as I was trembling, when I raked up the edges of the ant hill, as the Person had told me. Then I made my wish, "Give me good luck, and a good life," I said aloud, looking at the hills. (166)

Plenty-coups and Pretty-shield both told Linderman many stories about healings and medicine powers demonstrated among their people in the old days before the buffalo disappeared. During one afternoon storytelling session Plenty-coups was recounting well-known prophetic dreams of his tribesmen. Linderman wrote, "Some of them are remarkable and leave one wondering." Most amazing was the story of Medicine-raven (also known as Medicine Crow):

Medicine-raven, a close friend of Plenty-coups, had such a dream in the Crazy Mountains, and it was so baffling in its mistiness that even the Wise Ones could not interpret its meaning. Many years passed before the Crows understood the great dream of Medicine-raven, who lived to see some of his dream's prophecies come true, but died before "wagons traveled in the air," as they did when he dreamed in the Crazy Mountains, at the age of nineteen. (*Plenty-coups*, 241)

CONCLUDING THOUGHTS

Plenty-coups and Pretty-shield trusted Linderman enough to tell him about their visions, dreams, and medicine powers, but, despite his highly developed interviewing techniques, he could not coax them to talk about their lives after the buffalo were gone. In the fore-word to Pretty-shield's story he wrote:

Like the old men Pretty-shield would not talk at any length of the days when her people were readjusting themselves to the changed conditions brought on by the disappearance of the buffalo, so that her story is largely of her youth and early maturity. "There is nothing to tell, because we did nothing," she insisted when pressed for stories of her middle life. "There were no buffalo. We stayed in one place, and grew lazy." (*Pretty-shield*, 10)

Although Linderman said it was hard to get the old Indians to talk about the desolation they experienced in the late 1800s, he thought it was an important historical period that people in the future should understand more honestly. In his last major work, *Wolf and the Winds* (1986), written in 1935–36, he described the isolation, confusion, and despair suffered by the indigenous people of Montana after the great herds of bison were destroyed.

Wolf and the Winds is a biographical novel about a Gros Ventre of the Prairie (the White-Clay-Men) whose medicine power was The Winds. When he was fifteen Wolf went into the Bear Paw Mountains to dream. His supplication to The-ones-who-live-without-fire was for knowledge from "a Helper," so he could be of service to his people. Many outward aspects of Wolf's vision quest were similar to those of Plenty-coups's journey into self-knowledge. But, while Plenty-coups's vision guided him to adapt to the changes that were coming, Wolf's vision caused him to reject the ways of the white man.

Linderman wrote to an editor in 1937, about *Wolf and the Winds*, "It is, I believe, my best work; and I can promise you that nothing like it has ever been done." Yet the manuscript was not published until fifty years later, in 1986. Like the other old Indians he wrote about, Linderman knew the man he called Wolf. In handwritten notes he said:

His name was Frozen Water and he was a big man among the Gros Ventres once. . . .
　　　The cowmen who knew him called him "Bill Jones" and one day Chas. Russell, then a cowboy, painted a small portrait of Frozen Water and presented it to him. It was then that I became convinced that the old fellow appreciated his situation—his acts—for he would pull the picture from the case in which he carried his telescope and gazing at it would repeat the only English words he knew, "Bill Jones, son of a bitch." [22]

In *Wolf and the Winds* Linderman wrote beautifully crafted descriptions of certain ritual enactments such as the sweat lodge, Wolf's medicine dream, his courage when going on horse raids, and his perceptions of the world. In this fictionalized version of Frozen Water's life story, as in his other works about Indians, Linderman chose to portray the "finer qualities" of the Indian because he believed "it is only the discovered good in man that builds humanity" (*Montana Adventure*, 163).

　　　A master storyteller himself, known for his ability to hold audiences spellbound for hours, Linderman's style of retelling the old Indians' stories reveals his clear-headed respect for their beliefs. He preserved in writing the insights and wisdom of the elders, for both Indian and non-Indian generations to come. In *Montana Adventure* he expressed his regret at the passing of the old warriors, and his gratitude for having known them:

Old Indians have always impressed me. In their presence, especially when they are telling me of old customs, or speaking solemnly of their religious beliefs, I feel nearly as they do, I am quite certain. I have tried to break down that something which separates me from them by thinking as old Indians think, perhaps with only imagined success. And yet I believe that I understand many points of their philosophy of life that I cannot yet express in words. Perhaps I never shall learn; certainly not from the offspring of these warriors, who know next to nothing about their people's ancient ways. Now is too late to learn. The real Indians are gone. I am grateful for the privilege of having intimately known many of the old warriors themselves; may they find peace and plenty in the Shadow-hills. (183)

Linderman persevered in his literary work for the sake of his old Indian friends whose elders had taught them that "nothing here can last forever," that human beings have to learn to accept change. Like them, he experienced a sense of loss that is common to the continuing human experience—change brings a sense of loss.

　　　I believe Linderman chose to emphasize the sense of loss—not in a maudlin way, but with exquisite veracity—in order to establish the value of that which could, truly, be gone forever. He was an assayer, trained to prove the worth of earthly treasure. In his writing he chose to weigh and record not only the earthly, but also the spiritual value of the Indians' way of life.

　　　When an official for the Great Northern Railway asked Linderman in 1935 to write the essay for *Blackfeet Indians,* he wrote back that he would "undertake the writing of the story at once," and closed with a statement about his experiential knowledge:

I'm sorry that so many of the real old Piegans have gone to the Shadow-hills. Nevertheless I know several who are yet living, men who knew me when I was a wild-man myself. Besides this I already know considerable about the Blackfoot Nation through early association.[23]

Linderman was a rare combination in the West—literate, well-read, yet he had been "a wild-man" himself. He had lived in the wild, had learned to adapt and co-operate with nature, and he wrote about "the free life" with recognized authority and literary skill.

Many Americans think the Indian days are dead and gone, but today in Montana, with a sizeable number of Indians from eleven tribal groups and seven reservations, we know that descendants of the "old warriors" are very much involved in their history and culture. We also know, from the quality of his relationships with Indians, and from the insights contained in his writings, that Linderman remains one of the trusted messengers between the old-time Indian and the rest of the world.

ABBREVIATIONS

FBL   Frank Bird Linderman Estate Files

MHS   Montana Historical Society

ML.UM   Frank Bird Linderman Papers, Collection 7, K. Ross Toole Archives, Maureen and Mike Mansfield Library, University of Montana, Missoula, Montana [ML.UM Box #:File #]

MPI   Frank Bird Linderman Papers, Museum of the Plains Indian, Browning, Montana [MPI Box #:File #]

NOTES

1. Linderman was asked to write "an authoritative article" about the Blackfeet because he had "an established reputation as an Indian writer" and "a deep sympathy for and a human understanding of these people." (O. J. McGillis for the Great Northern Railway Company to Frank Bird Linderman, 10 December 1934, ML.UM 2:9.) After the publication of *Blackfeet Indians* (1935) McGillis wrote, "I know from my contacts with eastern book sellers that they recognize you as *THE* authority on the plains Indians." (McGillis to Linderman, 22 November 1935, ML.UM 2:9.)

2. News story about Little Bear's people and young Linderman: "Giving the Red Man a Chance," n.p., n.a., n.d. (between 1932 and 1937), MPI 2:3; letter about the Cree's and Chippewa's condition when he met them and had a reason to befriend them. (Linderman to Mrs. Albert J.

Roberts, 12 March 1918, FBL.) They were "unspoiled by contact" and had not accepted the white man's religion or adopted his customs. ("Manitou, God of the Red Man," *Great Falls Leader* (Montana), n.a., n.d. (1916), FBL.)

3. Linderman learned to treasure the Indians' stories, as he had the stone arrow points. (Linderman to Roberts, 12 March 1918, FBL.)

4. Linderman to Norma Linderman (Waller), 24 June 1914, FBL.

5. Facts about Linderman's life, and background on the Chippewa's and Cree's deplorable condition can be found in Linderman, *Montana Adventure* (1968); for details on Linderman's role in acquiring the Rocky Boy Indian Reservation see Celeste River, 1990, "A Mountain In His Memory," thesis, University of Montana.

6. Reference to War Eagle's prototype found in foreword to *Indian Old-Man Stories* (1920:viii), "Many years ago I was in the lodge of Full-of-dew, who is War Eagle in this book and in 'Indian Why Stories'"; comment about preserving the old West in "printer's ink" found in Linderman to Harry Cunningham, 28 June 1922, ML.UM 3:42.

7. Linderman's Indian names found in MPI 2:29, and in biographical sketch on Linderman in *Blackfeet Indians* (1935:67).

8. Linderman to Wilda Johns Linderman, 25 November 1928, FBL.

9. For more from Linderman on "The-ones-who-live-without-fire" see *Wolf and the Winds* (1986:12), *Old-Man Coyote* (1932:11), and handwritten research notes in MPI 2:17.

10. Information on sign language from "The Stories of Plenty-coups and Pretty-shield Transmitted by Frank Bird Linderman" written by Celeste River (unpublished 1988) for a linguistics seminar on the translation of Native American oral texts, taught by Tony Mattina at the University of Montana.

11. Charles M. Russell to Linderman, 19 May 1919, ML.UM 4:6.

12. Information on Linderman's method and style of translation from River, "The Stories of Plenty-coups and Pretty-shield Transmitted by Frank Bird Linderman."

13. Reverend John Frost to Linderman, 16 May 1930, MPI 2:14.

14. Frederic F. Van de Water, *New York Post* book review quoted in *Cutbank Pioneer Press* (Montana), 9 May 1930, MHS news file. (Van de Water wrote *The Glory Hunter*, a biography of Gen. George A. Custer, in 1934.)

15. About the owl and other profound beings see Linderman to daughters, 29 April 1917, ML.UM 3:18; about Montana "the real Indian home" see Linderman to Wilda Johns Linderman, n.d., FBL.

16. Frost to Linderman, 24 July 1926, MPI 2:14.

17. News article about the meeting with Big Rock in Great Falls, and the voice of Manitou: "Manitou, God of the Red Man," *Great Falls Leader,* n.a., n.d. (1916), FBL. (If Linderman didn't write this article, he certainly had a hand in it.)

18. News story about the *Demersville Interlake* (Montana) article, in which the epitaph had been quoted in 1890: n.p., n.a., n.d., ML.UM Folio 4; Linderman file notes about the epitaph, MPI 2:8.

19. Linderman to Commissioner of Indian Affairs Cato Sells, 10 June 1916, MPI 1:28; Linderman to Little Bear, 10 June 1916, MPI 1:18.

20. "Leave the Indian his God" in Linderman to Henry Goddard Leach, 14 February

1924, MPI 2:27; for reference to a "better God" see Linderman's discussion in *Montana Adventure* (1968:181–182).

21. Hermann Hagedorn to Linderman, 23 May 1931, ML.UM 2:18.

22. Linderman to John T. Winterich, ed. *The American Legion Monthly,* 20 January 1937, ML. UM 1:3; notes from "Frozen Water (Bill Jones)," FBL.

23. Linderman to McGillis, 11 February 1935, ML.UM 2:9.

REFERENCES

Linderman, Frank Bird. 1915. *Indian Why Stories: Sparks from War Eagle's Lodge-Fire.* Illustrated by Charles M. Russell. New York: Charles Scribner. Reprint; 1926; New York: Charles Scribner. Cadmus Books; 1945; New York: E. M. Hale.

———. 1918. *Indian Lodge-Fire Stories.* Illustrated by Charles M. Russell. Scribner series of school reading version of *Indian Why Stories.* New York: Charles Scribner.

———. 1920. *On a Passing Frontier: Sketches from the Northwest.* New York: Charles Scribner.

———. 1920. *Indian Old-Man Stories: More Sparks from War Eagle's Lodge-Fire.* Illustrated by Charles M. Russell. New York: Charles Scribner. Reprint; 1926; New York: Charles Scribner. Reprint; 1937; New York: Blue Ribbon Books.

———. 1921. *How It Came About Stories.* Illustrated by Carle M. Boog. New York: Charles Scribner. Reprint; 1926; New York: Charles Scribner. Reprint; 1937; New York: Blue Ribbon Books.

———. 1921. *Bunch-Grass and Blue-Joint.* New York: Charles Scribner. Verse.

———. 1922. *Lige Mounts, Free Trapper.* Illustrated by Joe de Yong. New York: Charles Scribner. Novel. Reprint; 1930, under the title *Morning Light;* New York: John Day. Reprint; 1931 and 1933, under the title *Free Trapper;* London: Faber and Faber.

———. 1926. *Kootenai Why Stories.* Illustrated by C. L. Bull. New York: Charles Scribner. Reprint; 1937; New York: Blue Ribbon Books.

———. 1930. *American: The Life Story of a Great Indian, Plenty-coups, Chief of the Crows.* Illustrated by H. M. Stoops. New York: John Day. Reprint; 1930; Yonkers, N.Y.: World Book. Reprint; 1930, under the title *Plenty-coups, Chief of the Crows;* Bison Book; Lincoln: University of Nebraska Press. Reprint; 1963, under the title *Plenty-coups, Chief of the Crows;* Magnolia, Mass.: Peter Smith. Reprint; 1972, under the title *Plenty-coups, Chief of the Crows;* New York: John Day.

———. 1932. *Old-Man Coyote.* Illustrated by H. M. Stoops. New York: John Day. Junior Guild selection.

———. 1932. *Red Mother.* Illustrated by H. M. Stoops. New York: John Day. Reprint; 1972, under the title *Pretty-shield, Medicine Woman of the Crows;* Bison Book; Lincoln: University of Nebraska Press.

———. 1933. *Beyond Law.* New York: John Day. Novel. Reprint; 1957. Corgi Books; London: Transworld.

———. 1933. *Stumpy.* Illustrated by H. M. Stoops. Animal story. New York: John Day. Junior Guild selection. Reprint; 1933; Cadmus Books; New York: E. M. Hale.

————. 1935. "Out of the North." *Blackfeet Indians.* Illustrated by Winold Reiss. St. Paul: Brown and Bigelow for the Great Northern Railroad.

————. 1962. *Recollections of Charley Russell.* Edited by H. G. Merriam. Norman: University of Oklahoma Press. Reprint; 1984 and 1988.

————. 1968. *Montana Adventure.* Edited by H. G. Merriam. Lincoln: University of Nebraska Press. Reprint; 1985; Bison Book; Lincoln: University of Nebraska Press.

————. 1985. *Quartzville.* Edited by Larry Barsness. Illustrated by Newman Myrah. Missoula, Mont.: Mountain Press.

————. 1986. *Wolf and the Winds.* Introduction by Hugh A. Dempsey. Norman: University of Oklahoma Press. Novel.

VIZENOR'S *GRIEVER*

A Post-Maodernist Little Red Book of
Cocks, Tricksters, and Colonists

Bernadette Rigal-Cellard

T he hero of Gerald Vizenor's *Griever: An American Monkey King in China*[1] is a professor participating in the post-Cultural Revolution Sino-American exchanges at Zhou Enlai University in Tianjin. The novel opens with his letter to an addressee named China. One can't tell at this point whether it is the country or a woman, and it is the first of a long series of conundrums. His adventures are later related in the third person. He soon appears as an avatar of Naanabozho, the trickster and culture hero of Vizenor's people, the Anashinaabeg (named the Chippewa). A spectator as well as an actor, Griever, half human, half simian, draws upon Native American and Chinese traditions to subvert the socialist system. This hilarious and apparently rambling novel is in fact highly structured thanks to the hero's search for ancient manuscripts, found and lost in the very beginning. Such a quest will allow Griever to locate the deviationists of the so-called Maoist "liberation," all the survivors from the tribal past and living, like Griever, at the margins of the human and the animal, of the real and the legendary.

For the purpose of this essay I will limit myself to the analysis of four points. I will study, first, "cocks and tricksters," or Griever as the hero of the "in-between," to see how Vizenor has intertwined modern realities with the mythic characteristics of the trickster; second, "colonists," or the project Vizenor posited when he located *Griever* in China, that is how he uses contemporary China as the signifier for all colonizing regimes; third, the intertextuality which, by privileging the strategy of the pilgrimage, places the novel within the dialectics of a displacement between two poles, less spatial or temporal

317

than spiritual; and fourth, I will try to define the originality of *Griever* as a text—a "post-maodernist" one—belonging to various traditions and to the highly personal imagination of Vizenor.

GRIEVER, THE TRICKSTER OF THE IN-BETWEEN

The trickster in North American culture has been studied at length, and in order to see more clearly to what extent Griever resembles his tribal brother Naanabozho I will draw from Vizenor's other works and Franchot Ballinger's and Barbara Babcock's essays,[2] which, elaborating on major previous studies and completing them with recent perceptions, seem the most exact and exhaustive to date. To begin with a simple description, one can say that the Chippewa trickster is in many ways similar to the clowns of other North American tribes, and to the European fools, who all have the function of reversing the social and ceremonial order, within well delimited lines, so as to expose conventions for what they are. Vizenor himself constantly assumes the role of the trickster as he attacks not only the institutions that have "invented" the "Indians," but also those Indians who have adhered to the stereotype and molded themselves into it. In China, Griever's pleasure will consist in scandalizing those citizens who have accepted the new model forced upon them by the Communist regime.

According to Jung and Radin the trickster is a creative but also destructive and primitive force, and would correspond to the first period of a man's life, the one dominated by instinct and cruelty. He would possess no value, whether moral or social, would not distinguish between good and evil but would be responsible for both.[3] Though some of Radin's insights are appreciated, his work is now criticized because, as Babcock puts it, his book "has produced a plethora of psychologically reductive interpretations" (165). Vizenor, for one, refutes the psychoanalytical "word constructions" of Radin, Jung, and Freud (he counts the latter as a member of the Gang of Four in *Griever* [118]), and always puts on stage not asocial or amoral but compassionate tricksters whose mission is "to balance the world between terminal creeds and humor with unusual manners and ecstatic strategies" (*Earthdivers* xii). As for Griever, whose name reveals his propensity for empathy, Vizenor makes a point, at the very beginning of the novel, of having the wise warrior clown Wu Chou assure China Browne that he was "never evil, never, never" (24). Everytime someone is hurt or defeated, Griever buries his rage in "panic holes," shouting into the earth his affliction, or trying "to protect the people he loves," "to balance the world," (70–71) and he is the only professor outraged by the shooting down of the Air Korea airline (68).

Babcock uses Victor Turner's terms "Betwixt and Between" to attempt to situate the trickster, whose main characteristic is precisely his refusal to be pinned down. Vizenor sends his hero to the "middle land" (28) and creates him in his own image, that of the mixed-blood, living "in between" two races, two worlds, belonging to neither and yet to both, which endows him with a superior power of judgment. "Even at home on the reservation he was a foreigner" (42), and in China "the new sounds of [the] place hold [him] for ransom at some alien border" (13). The narrator quotes ironically Hannah who hates miscegenation because "no one knows who [mixed-bloods] are. [They] are neither here nor there, not like real bloods" (78). That lady obviously misses the point.

Babcock notes that the trickster blurs temporal and spatial distinctions: "there is a violation of the diurnal pattern of expectation in that the individual conducts his activities at night" (159). Now, though we suppose that Griever teaches according to expectation, he is often on the move in the dark hours, as when he escapes "at the crack of dawn" (27) or when he goes up the radio tower (133). Further, the trickster shows his preoccupation with the "between categories" through his power "to live interstitially" (Babcock 154), and *Griever* abounds in interstices. The floor, the walls, people are described with cracks, scars (Hester, China), gaps (Hua Lian's eye sockets). Page 27 reads like an exercise in synonyms for "interstices": "narrow seams," "crack of dawn," "scars" (twice), "the cleaves and rutted pattern," "gashed," "faults on faces and the earth." In relation to this, Babcock states that the trickster tends to inhabit crossroads, marketplaces, and doorways, for "they are usually situated between the social cosmos and the other world or chaos" (162). Griever lives at the crossroads that the International Center represents; skims marketplaces, parks, and country roads in search of the characters he dreams of; and is often poised on the windowsill, ready to jump out since the doors are locked at night (his "living sideways," to use Ballinger's title phrase, is nevertheless a free choice and not just the consequence of Egas Zhan's locking doors at night).

With respect to appearance, Vizenor loves indulging in the description of original attire in the Chinese opera tradition, with colorful masks and motley clothes, again a typical trait of tricksters, fools, and clowns the world over. Wu Chou gives Griever a gorgeous costume: "a beret, fashioned like a biretta with two blue tassels attached, and a lemon-colored raglan coat with blue piping on the collar and lapels" (140), and he appears with a sporran (a sort of Scottish loincloth!) on the picture Wu Chou gives China (25). When he attends the opening of Maxim's de Beijing, Griever wears his costume and the other patrons, whether jetsetters or uppity Chinese, wear "class neckties, cashmere blazers, narrow shoes" (202). Amusingly, as if Vizenor wanted to parody anthropological definitions of tricksters by making sure Griever displays as many of them as possible, the costume episode is linked to the mirror motif, which Babcock (163) classifies as number 8 before number 9, "motley dress." Griever asks for a mirror to see his mask; Wu Chou answers, "monkeys are immortal and immortals never appear in mirrors" because "The Monkey King is . . . not a photograph" (140).

Such a line recalls the love-hate relationship with photos that Vizenor's work betrays. For example, he publishes pictures of himself and of friends in *Interior Landscapes* and historical ones in *The People Named the Chippewa*, while decrying, in the text, their reductive role which colonizes people, as in the case of John Ka Ka Geesick whose "feathered visage encouraged the romantic expectations of tourists. . . . The eldest of the tribe was possessed in photographs."[4] Elsewhere Vizenor dissects the beautiful and beautified picture of Edward Curtis: "his pictorial tubes are secular reversals of a ritual striptease, frozen faces on a calendar of arrogant discoveries."[5] The fact that the Monkey cannot be in a photograph proves his resistance to colonization. Griever himself has to be photographed in a make-believe desert setting to comply with the identification mania of the bureaucracy; the identity picture becomes thus a pass and a trap.

Another episode with mirrors points to a different meaning. In a Disneyland-effect scene, Griever rides a train that lurches through a mountain tunnel with soldiers who turn into monkeys. When Griever looks out of the window "his face was captured in a simian reflection. . . . He frowned, smiled, winked, and the animal cast back the same expression in reverse order" (117). Griever is both monkey and human. The tiny mirrors that Shitou wears on his arms and waist testify to his own trickster nature as well. Both characters possess the "two-fold physical nature and/or a 'double'" of traditional tricksters who also tend "to be of uncertain sexual status" (Babcock 163). Griever becomes a female in the final scene of "Free the garlic" to suck Sugar Dee's nipples (55). Other personages change their outlooks, either through wigs, as Li Wen (83), or painted masks: Hua Lian, Wu Chou, and again Griever. In *Bearheart*[6] Parasimo wears meta-masks; Proude Cedar Fair regularly turns into a bear, as well as Saint Louis Bearheart, and we will discuss later these bear and monkey transformations. Erdupps McChurbbs, one of Vizenor's favorite tricksters, also possesses "the imaginative power to change his shape in visions and memories. . . . From time to time his hands and feet and ears and other parts are different sizes" (*Earthdivers* 81).

The simian nature of Griever helps him "efface spatial boundaries" (Babcock 159): Griever mounts things (134, 138, 145, 152, etc.), bounds (68, 135, etc.), and leaps (138), and his speed protects him from retribution. Nevertheless, he is not half as talented as the original Mind Monkey who could leap 108,000 *li* in one bound (1 *li* = 600 meters); he needs a plane to land in China and an ultralight to leave it. All these migrations confer to *Griever* the peripatetic structure (though not one as consistent and linear as in *Bearheart*) typical of the picaresque and pilgrimage stories that have influenced Vizenor.

Sex and lust, other features of the trickster, play an important role in *Griever*. All commentators explain that extravagant libido allows for social transgression. Here, Griever, as "the ritual violator of interdiction" (Babcock 166), breaks the tacit endogamous socialist law by sleeping with Hester Hua Dan, the daughter of the watchdog Egas Zhan. Griever departs from the trickster model who is supposed to "have an enormous libido without procreative outcome" (Babcock 162), since Hester will bear their child. However the law (that of the state and that of the anthropological categories) will prevail, for, after finding the note "I am pregnant" that Hester scribbled to Griever during the new-law-and-order speech of the Mayor of Tianjin, Egas drowns his own daughter in the pond among the blue bones of the babies, victims of the antinatalist policy of China (57, 132–133, ff.).

This occurrence, which intertwines life with death, fits again in the pattern: the trickster is both creative and destructive. Though he should not care about the end results of his acts (or precisely because of this), Griever screams his pain and horror in one of his panic holes, thus shedding his jester mask to reveal his compassionate humanity. Whereas in the traditional situation of a Native community the trickster's act would have allowed his audience to perceive all the complexity of reality (Babcock 182), in this particular example the deaths we witness are not meant to make us realize the complexity of life and death, but the actual nature of totalitarian societies. Death in *Griever* loses its inescapable yet natural and cyclical value to become exclusively an instrument of coercion, first from the part of the regime, then from the part of Vizenor/Griever to force our understanding of the essence of those constraining political systems.

The other sex episodes of the book provoke laughter, and one can see in the Octavio Paz quotation in the epigraph "The word is . . . a return to the body" an amused allusion to all the scenes that do end up on "a return to the bawdy/body." For example, at the end of "Obo Island," Griever's "penis leaped from his underwear and bounced" on Kangmei's buttocks, making her fall on the toilet papier-mâché monster representing Egas Zhan so that "the trickster bruised his penis on the broken cast" (177). The description Wu Chou gives to China, "Griever was the cock of the town" (21) (a dirty variation on, I guess, "the talk of the town"), summons up the strange couple formed by Griever and his "cock," always perched on his master's shoulder. At a second level, I see it in an allusion to those tricksters who carried their outsized sex organ on their backs in a box, and at a third level, the satire of Vizenor, certainly amused and irritated by the interpretations, which he must know, that never see in such a detail the humorous fantasy of the Natives, forever framed in an imperturbable pose *à la* Curtis. Instead, they explain this "boxed-in sex" as the proof that sex is "under control, a control which is essential to good social order but which is undoubtedly beyond Trickster's ability."[7] Griever's cock is not "boxed-in," not "caged-in," but definitely liberated.

The saucy and sacrilegious episode in King's College in Cambridge also allows for several readings. Griever dreams that he is in the chapel with China Browne (134–135) who shows him the statue of an androgyne. He touches a thigh, that of the statue or that of China one can't tell, since the statue blends with China. One can note that the young woman herself, though a Native American, blends with Chinese women since she is a bandaged-feet fetishist, and with Hester in particular, Griever's exotic lover, for both girls are portrayed as having a scar on their faces (20, 26, 88). The statue, being "a dark wooden androgyne," evokes the "dark wooden Indian," the mute hieratic redskin that signaled tobacconists' shops or adorned bourgeois mansions. Further, because of its union of the male and female polarities, its union of natural oppositions, the androgyne can be read as another figuration of the trickster who, able to transmute himself into his opposite, reconciles what Manichaeism would separate, for, as Susan Stewart wrote, "As the embodiment of disparate domains, trickster is analogous to the process of metaphor, the incorporation of opposites into a new configuration" (in *Earthdivers* 105). Such a notion was already contained in the title of the second chapter "Holosexual Clown." A "word game" on the model of "holotrope" that Vizenor explains as meaning whole, signifier and signified and communal,[8] "holosexual" implies "sexual in his totality," and also calls for the inevitable comic misunderstanding:

> "Holosexual."
> "No, not gay." (And one wishes the next line did not spoil the pun by explicating it:)
> "Holosexual, not homosexual."
>
> (21)

Postmodernist critics cherish "androgynous," along with "polymorphous," because they feel these terms translate accurately the plurality of expressions and meanings of the postmodernist texts. Ihab Hassan, in his list of differences between modernism and post-modernism, opposes these two terms to the modernist category "genital/phallic."[9] Though Vizenor considers himself and his tricksters as resolutely postmodernist, I would rather perceive Griever as embodying, once more, all these antithetical elements, thus being at the same time a postmodernist *and* a modernist. (And I wonder how Vizenor fares with feminist and postfeminist critics at home!) Monkey Griever reminds me of the famous wisdom "brass monkeys" so dear to the British who brought them back from their Asian tribulations. One shuts his eyes with his hands, the second his ears, the third his mouth ("see no evil," "hear no evil" . . .), and there is sometimes a fourth one who hides his genitals. Griever would be a fifth one who would not shut or hide anything at all.

The last role of the trickster that I will present here is that of the liberator, linked to what precedes for, says Vizenor: "the trickster is androgynous, a comic healer and liberator in literature; *the whole figuration* that ties the unconscious to social experiences" (*Narrative Chance* 188). Liberation, Griever's rallying cry, is all the more subversive in a country that has enslaved its citizens precisely in this very name. His liberating acts turn out to be farcical since what he truly liberates is not so much human beings as chickens. We know that he also set free experimental frogs (51) and a pretty nightingale (33), and that in a holistic conception of nature one values animals as much as people, but Vizenor deliberately imagined the chicken liberation sequence as a "comic opera" (40) that paro-dies war epics. Plump in the market place, Trickster, the Foreign Devil, fights against Cutthroat who butchers up chickens before selling them. In true grand-guignolesque fash-ion, blood spills everywhere, feathers fly about, Cutthroat drinks warm blood, chickens are carried away on bicycles or naked on nooses, and the crowd cheers on the valorous knights, who, of course, cannot understand what the other is saying. At the end, Griever pays for a rooster which he baptizes Matteo Ricci and opens the cages of the hens under the cries of the delighted peasants:

> "Free the pears."
> "Free the garlic, make me rich."
>
> (53)

This act somehow functions as a sequel to "Paraday Chicken Pluck," in *Earthdivers*, during which Erdupps McChurbbs observes plucking operations performed in booths named for varieties of domestic chickens—"Cornish Plucking Booth," "Plymouth Rock Plucking Booth." Why such crazy performances? Probably because chickens, a bit like monkeys, epitomize the "colonialized" animal and get plucked as Native American "inner chickens" are by teachers, salespeople, psychiatrists, social workers. In the words of Libertina to Erdupps: "We are all related to the wild red jungle fowl inside; how else could we have survived all the pecking and the plucking throughout our lives" (*Earthdivers* 104).

One expects more seriousness when the Mind Monkey encounters the Execution Caravan. Nevertheless here again parody reigns supreme. The caravan includes the traditional bandit types: the murderer, the prostitute, the thief, the rapist, plus the new ones: the heroin dealer and the art historian. Griever, on one of his "power trips," orders their liberation by the soldiers, to no avail of course. Suspense mounts when, after shouting a new aphorism, "Confucius and Mao Zedong were liars" (152–153), Griever hijacks the truck. The liberation of the prisoners will not last long since the soldiers catch up with them and, at least for the rapists, carry out the "sentence at the site" (155). Griever himself can only escape thanks to his friend Hua Lian. She hides him under her skirt, where the stench of her crotch almost asphyxiates him. The episode dissolves in an obscene and misogynous Tex Avery cartoon scene with Griever dusting "her feet with Double Happiness Pearl Foot Powder and her crotch with Springtime Thunder" (156).

The trickster denounces Mao and Zhou Enlai but his book does not dig at China so much as it digs at those who look for logical sequences in a novel. The outcome of the useless chase points to Vizenor's philosophy. He does not pretend to give a solution to China's problems, nor miraculously to save the prisoners (most of whom are guilty, anyway). Yet we should not call him frivolous, for he truly succeeds in deconstructing systems through an apparently insane chain of events. The end of the book testifies further to this. Once Griever beholds the body of his lover he decides to escape, and not to risk his life helping the Chinese. His flight in an ultralight looks like a parodic airlift, American way, recalling one farther south, since he only saves himself and an American Chinese, plus his cock and silkworm seeds.

Interestingly, this ultralight was made and sent by China's brother, a mixed-blood from the reservation. This flying machine signifies various things: the reification of the trickster's capacity for flying; the modern version of the traditional Chinese kite; and Native American technology, which attacks the stereotype. All these senses may account for such an exit, since as Mind Monkey Griever could have leapt out of China (leaving in an ultralight is hardly more plausible, but Vizenor never attempts at verisimilitude [10]). We are then to understand that the great brotherhood of traditions not only survives, but thrives, not static but mobile, if mechanical.

Thus, it would seem that Griever exhibits quite a lot of the trickster's idiosyncrasies. Yet, he is more than a case study for itemized anthropological requirements. He is a being of the mind, of fiction, the figment of Vizenor's imagination. In his creative act this author draws upon traditional stories, the present world scene and his own personality, itself the invented sum of past and present, so much so that Griever can be perceived as Vizenor's persona, or vice versa as shown in this passage that, significantly, contains the title of Vizenor's autobiography:

Griever is a mixedblood tribal trickster, a close relative to the old mind monkeys; he holds cold reason on a lunge line while he imagines the world. With colored pens he thinks backward, stops time like a shaman, and reverses intersections, interior landscapes. . . . Griever discovers events, an active opera and an audience all at once on rough paper. (34)

SOCIALIST CHINA AS THE SIGNIFIER OF MIND COLONIZATION

Aside from the personal experience (recorded in the epilogue), the choice of China betrays Vizenor's attraction to a brotherly Orient, the cosmogony and the philosophy which are close to his people's, to an Orient that would have known better than the West how to maintain a privileged rapport with its mythical past, as China has with, among other stories, the thousand operas derived from *The Journey to the West*. Then, before this empire cracked and drago(o)ned into materialism (the seeds of which were brought from Europe, from where else ?), one feels his frustration, leading to derision, a tactic Vizenor masters beautifully.

As an American in China, Griever is endowed with the exotopy essential, in the eyes of Bakhtin,[11] if one is to understand truly the object of one's study. Yet, his observations on China do not really matter as such, they matter in so far that they also speak obliquely about other countries. We are then confronted with a strategy similar to Montesquieu's in *Les Lettres Persanes,* even if the means are slightly different, Montesquieu having invented two Persians, Usbeck and Rica, who visit his country and write home critically about his society. Here, through China and the minute evocation of its idiosyncrasies, Vizenor levels the causticity not only at its regime, but at all mind-colonizing societies, including his own.

To begin with, Griever distinguishes between the ruling hierarchy and the tribal deviationists. Then he assimilates those marginalized individuals into the Native Americans. In the third line of the novel, Griever describes China (to China) as an "enormous reservation" (13). Further, "the sweet taste of lard reminded him of winter on the reservation" (29). An old woman looks like his grandmother (41). The running motif of the trees and the "save the park" battle cry of Hua Lian transpose in China Proude Cedar Fair's agony about the loss of his ancestral cedars (but when in *Bearheart* trees constituted the prime mover of the pilgrimage, here the theme is treated in lighter tones as shown in Griever's flat comment on Hua Lian's impassioned declaration about trees: "Rather abstract conservation" [121]). Various characters springing from Vizenor's other works contribute as well to the familiar "reservation air" of *Griever:* Mouse Proof Martin (124), Sister Eternal Flame (212).

Egas Zhan, the cadre of the "Foreign Bureau Affairs," functions as the Chinese counterpart of the federal officers and the Bureau of Indian Affairs officials ever present in Vizenor's narratives. Fittingly, his "colonial name" derives from that of Egas Monitz, "the father of the lobotomy who won the Nobel Prize" (15). The lobotomy emblematizes brain-destroying systems, while the Nobel Prize consecrates its universality. However, perhaps because lobotomy plays already such a role in Ken Kesey's *One Flew Over the Cuckoo's Nest,*[12] with the archetypal wise and mute Indian who kills his friend, the good white, rather than have him vegetate after his lobotomy, this reference to Egas Monitz sounds to me a bit like a facile ploy. The metaphor is spun out again at the end when Egas kills his granddaughter (the baby Hester bears) named Kuan Yin after the "bodhisattva who captured the mind monkey" in *The Journey to the West* (233), performing thus the ultimate lobotomy.

Obviously, then, China, as a signifier, points to the American, or generally Western, rupture between the survivors of the past on the one side and "terminal creeds" and "time measured ideologies"[13] on the other, from which the trickster will try to liberate the frogs, the chickens, the prisoners, and so on. To illustrate this cultural dichotomy, Vizenor weaves non-fiction into fiction when he exploits the old map of the colonial concessions, which, as he explains in the epilogue, he found in a drawer at the university. The map perpetuates the past, for "Dreams retreat to the corners like insects, and there we remember our past in lost letters and colonial maps, the remains of foreign concessions" (22). Griever's peregrinations are always rigorously localized on this map, and the toponyms in the novel seldom belong to contemporary reality: Maréchal Foch, Saint Louis, Astor House on London Meadows, Victoria Road (105), and the like. Victoria Park, one of the privileged spaces of the novel, "is the atrium in colonial concessions, carved from class reveries" (111). Nevertheless, one should not detect some form of nostalgia for a positivized antebellum grandeur in those elegiac reminiscences; one should decode them rather as mock elegiac since the map perpetuates not the ancient past of China but the recent past of European colonization. The equation of foreign and Maoist "colonizations" clearly transpires in the false coincidence that has Griever encounter the grim parade of the prisoners on their way to their execution (in the United Kingdom cemetery) just when he is meandering in the French and English concessions, precisely at "the intersection of Oxford and Cambridge" (148–149). Space contains past and present fused together in a meaningful sequence that can be held as emblematic of the novel's chronotope, to use Bakhtin's term.

One remembers then that Griever baptized his noble cock Matteo Ricci, an "invention" bordering on anathema. Vizenor briefly explains his choice: "Ricci was a missionary, an Italian Jesuit. . . . He was taken prisoner right here on the trail of the hare and hounds. . . . Three hundred eighty-four years and seven days ago, to be specific" (52). Though at first one might think he honors the memory of Ricci (the prisoner), he rails in fact at the Western obsession with precise historical duration, and at the patron of missionaries, for Ricci was not simply a missionary, but the *first* evangelist of Cathay, this European version of China. He organized there four Jesuit missions from 1582 to 1610 (to be specific). "His work," reads the *Encyclopedia Britannica,* "was the foundation of the subsequent success attained by the Roman Catholic Church in China." He and his missionaries adopted the costumes and manners of Chinese literates; he was given a Chinese name, Li Madou, and is there the best-known European of past centuries, better than Marco Polo, also present from the first paragraph in *Griever.*

In this name Griever deconstructs the term "christening" itself. First, baptizing a rooster is inconceivable from a strict religious point of view. Second, the cock automatically refers to the penis. Third, in the Buddhist context to which *Griever* somewhat "belongs" thanks to *Journey,* rooster Matteo can be seen as the reincarnation in a much lower form of the original one punished through the law of karma for his actions. Fourth, the couple Griever/Matteo recalls the couple Tripitaka/the Monkey, but since Griever is already the Monkey, who does Matteo represent? The Monk? Thus, the act of nomination, simultaneous with and an essential component of conquest and the planting of the flag or of the cross, is burlesquely subverted here.

Again, what Vizenor attacks is not so much the Maoist revolution as the colonization that prepared it, the one begun by the missionaries, followed by the military and the merchants, of the same nature as the colonization of America. Yet, Vizenor forgets to mention that if those Europeans could succeed it was because the emperors appreciated them and hired them, using them for their own purposes. Marco Polo worked some twenty years at the service of Kublai Khan, and Matteo Ricci evangelized the Chinese with the blessing of Emperor Wan Li. Of course, Vizenor will retort, this proves, if need be, the collusion between rulers and missionaries, then as now. One could also argue that Chinese people have always been "colonized" by their own rulers, the mandarins or the communist cadres, and that the Westerners' "sin" was to understand how they could benefit from such class rivalries and later inner decadence. Japan tortured and executed the Jesuits and the Christianized Japanese once they became too popular, and sealed the country off.[14] Later, the Japanese were particularly apt at exploiting to their advantage the second wave of exploration, led by Commodore Perry, and today who colonizes whom?

Before *Griever,* Vizenor's narratives were already obsessed with the colonization of America by priests and fur traders, an act destructive but also creative of another race, his own, that of the Métis. Vizenor does not reject his European (French) ascendency, and he makes his these words by Louis Riel, a leader of the Métis who declared a new mixed-blood nation in the nineteenth century and was executed for high treason: "If we have ever so little of either gratitude or filial love, should we not be proud to say, *We are Métis.*" [15] A bit as if he regretted not bearing also his paternal grandmother's birthname, Vizenor gives it to another of his avatars, Clement Beaulieu, the author who appears notably in *Wordarrows.* [16]

In *Griever* Vizenor has his hero quote at length an article on the orphanage of the Lazarist Sisters of Saint Vincent de Paul. In 1870 rumors circulated according to which, in order to practice satanic rituals, the nuns extracted the babies' eyes and hearts: the mob attacked the Sisters, "ripped their bodies open . . . impaled them . . . and burnt them." In typically Vizenorian style, Griever laconically reacts thus: "Griever was astonished that the other missionaries survived that night; but he was even more surprised to find apple pie on the menu in the old colonial hotel restaurant" (109–110). The matter-of-fact surrealism of Griever's reaction matches the surrealism of this Catholic orphanage in Chinese land. Two pages further, Vizenor still sees behind the surface purge the indelible marks left in stones and parks by foreign colonization:

nine nations succeeded in their vaults and domes, spires, groins, cusps and lobes on arches, and in their moats and stunted trees, sculpturesque gardens, monolithic markets, the same old pillars hauled back from the shadows. (111) [17]

With his ever keen eye for imported artifacts, Vizenor denounces the ideology that operates first through the trading of objects, then through architecture and nominalization to consecrate the conquest of land, peoples, and minds. It is significant that *Griever* is informed by the vision in the beginning and the recurrent motif of the explorers on the silk roads: some traded silk and spices, some (or the same) "looted the temples and ruins in the ancient cities on the rim of Taklamakan" (14), paving the way for the later conquerors of Asia. The fact that the manuscripts Griever searches for were originally stolen from one of those temples to reappear later in the British Museum, the shrine of British imperialistic acquisitions, points to the same vision of history. [18]

The surrealism of missions is perpetuated by the new hypocritical cultural and touristic colonization of the American professors, "the decadent missionaries of this generation" (13). One of them, yet different from them, Vizenor/Griever ridicules his colleagues through the transcription of their Ubu-like dialogues. Never bothering to mix in, they always repeat the same words with their fake sophistication. They grow animated only to rehash their monomanias and laugh at the backward Chinese who pretend to buy computers when they can't even use an electric can opener (184). This object is so emblematic of American civilization that Vizenor has his trickster read a letter informing him that the only factory on the reservation, the electric can-opener plant, closed down "to keep the bingo going" (125).[19] These Americans were perceived, with the typical view of colonized people, as huge and had to use sinks built too high by the Chinese. It is amusing to note that while some Indian tribes held the conquistadores to be gods, the Chinese held them to be "barbarians" (16).

Vizenor's genius for nominalization operates humorously through the professors' names. Though fairly evocative, those of Colin Marplot Gloome, Gingerie Anderson-Paterson, or Carnegie Morgan, do not connote as much as those of Luther Holes and Hannah Dustan. Luther Holes, "the valetudinarian and guest house sycophant" (66), derives his name from one of Vizenor's mock heroes, the father of Protestantism and in the coprophilia register the brother and antithesis of Naanabozho: when the trickster could float in his own excrements, so voluminous were they, Luther, constipated, could only soliloquize on his hard toilet seat. As in the "cock case," Vizenor derides psychoanalysis, which interprets Naanabozho's cloacal emergence myth along with Luther's quixotic "theological combat, daily and strenuous" in terms of anality and regression. No doubt Vizenor, like us, enjoys this vision of Luther repulsing the devil "with a fart, a turd, or the sight of his naked behind," and he lambasts through Professor Luther and his Holes the "theorists burdened with coprophilia [who] would have done much better to construe shit as universal comic sign than to bind the literal malodor in social science monologues" (*Narrative Chance* 203).

Hannah Dustan represents the modern Hannah Duston, the muscular white female who, taken as a captive with her maid and child, never let herself be lured into Indianness as so many others did, but stole her captors' tomahawk and killed them in their sleep. Leslie Fiedler identifies her story as one of the four founding myths, that of the castrating white woman wielding her tomahawk against her white males, husband or son, as well as against the Indians; the reversed mother myth of Pocahontas; and also the reverse of the friendship myth between Indian and white males in which the tomahawk reverts to the sacred pipe.[20] In *Griever* Vizenor takes his revenge by turning Hannah into a heavy framed mottled red skin: "her face, arms, and shoulders were blotched with dark pigmentation from sunburns," and perhaps by dint of wielding the tomahawk, she always conducts "each spoken word with a shoulder, arm and mad hand gesture" (75). She resembles the social workers on the reservation, always the butt of jokes in Native American stories. Worse still, Vizenor gives her nightmares about her mixed-blood children whereas, like the model she is a vowel away from, "she is a hereditist, withstands miscegenation, and neither speaks nor listens to people that she determines are mixedbloods" (77). In such a caricatural character Vizenor elaborates on the central concern of his work: relationships between the sexes, the races, the classes, around which the whole question of colonization and alterity revolves.

His narrative histories as well as his novels, precisely built on a peripatetic structure inviting encounters, always stage the various modes of confrontations between people: aggressivity, contempt, sarcasm, humor, compassion, never neutrality. Here Griever's exotopy allows him to observe intra-Chinese relationships, but, adversely, it prevents him from understanding the utterances of the Chinese. Many voices are heard in the novel, but translation poorly approximates their meaning, so that the "polyphony" leads to the burlesque rather than to universal comprehension.[21] As Anthony C. Yu perceived in his review of *Griever:* "cultural distance is indeed a prominent theme of the book."[22]

Tzvetan Todorov analyzes the conquest of America and its relation to China from precisely the perspective of cultural distance, as shown in his subtitle, *La question de l'autre*[23] (the question of the other). The book deciphers the radically different perceptions of signs (signs of the culture, the gods, the future) the Mexicans and the conquistadores had and how the Spaniards quickly grasped how to interpret the others' languages and mores in order to replace them gradually by their own. Todorov goes beyond the usual hagiography—Columbus sailing for China and bumping into America—to stress his often overlooked finality and mentality. His intention was to meet the Great Khan, who, according to Marco Polo, had asked "for scholars to instruct him in the faith in Christ,"[24] and behind this motivation lurked his grand design. Columbus expected the Great Khan to reward him in gold (supposed to "grow" in China[25]) that he would use to finance a new crusade to reconquer Jerusalem.

Todorov points out that Colon obeyed a "finalist strategy": he "knew," thanks to biblical prophecies and various relations, what he was going to find, and what he found was what he expected: gold, Chinese/Indians, strange creatures, paradise on earth. He never attempted to question his presuppositions. Alterity as a problem or as a concept no more existed for Columbus, "the psychopath" who invented the Indians,[26] than later for the American professors in *Griever* who see China through a finalist, reductive viewpoint, or even for the Chinese whose xenophobia transpires in their aversion to miscegenation and their seclusion of the Algerian clockmakers and African students (185–186). Alterity began in 1492, the year the Spaniards finally succeeded in driving the Moors out: "In that very year [Spain] repudiates its inner Other [*son Autre intérieur*] . . . discovers the exterior Other [*l'Autre extérieur*]."[27]

In *Griever,* Vizenor certainly endows his stranger with a sense for alterity, which he precisely trains on "others" to try to reverse their value systems, not as Columbus did to force them to adopt his own, but to understand how systems operate. In her conclusion Babcock summarizes the various explanations of the function of trickster narratives. The fourth interpretation sees them as "contributing to a reexamination of existing conditions and possibly leading to change," for "any form of symbolic inversion has an implicit radical dimension." And she quotes Harvey Cox: "From the oppressor's point of view satire can always get out of hand or give people ideas, so it is better not to have it at all," to which she adds, "as is indeed the case in modern totalitarian states" (Babcock 180).

All this is illustrated by the obligation Griever's friends have to hide away so that ordinary citizens will not get corrupted by their contact (85), or in *Bearheart* by the federal dictatorship hunting down tricksters.

Yet, as Native Americans in modern America, Vizenor's tricksters operate from a standpoint more complicated than that of the traditional trickster. They have more to achieve than he who "epitomizes the paradox of the human condition . . . [and who] embodies the fundamental contradiction of our existence: the contradiction between the individual and society, between freedom and constraint" (Babcock 163). The society Vizenor's trickster lives on the margin of is not the one he has left or one for which he would simply perform the salutary "margin of mess." He lives on the margin of a society itself relegated, as a whole, to the margin of another society, and in this he is a degree beyond the fool, the rogue, the picaro, the hippie. His function, as apparent in all of Vizenor's narratives, consists first in reassuring the marginalized group that it need not fear the marginalizing one. Second, since the trickster's idiom—English—is that of the dominators, he is also warning *them* to watch out. His game of satire, of reversing the order of things, aims at pointing out to the minority culture how colonized it has been, and at proving to the majority culture that he is not "fooled" by it. More than "of two worlds," he is "of three worlds."

Griever himself advances a step further. First, he subverts modern China by using his American stance (as is implied in the title of the book): he replaces the Chinese hymn "The East Is Red" by the "Stars and Stripes Forever," (135) which he also sang when he subverted the market system (24–37); he recommends the positive values of a bourgeois culture against socialism (150), and, as in Montesquieu, his caricature of the Chinese definitely operates by juxtaposing two "incompatible frames of reference" (Babcock 181). Second, he subverts the Chinese system from the inside by holding the Mind Monkey stance: traditional China railing at materialistic China. Third, by using his stance as a Native American, he subverts Americanness itself by parodying it, with his ironical allusions to typical American traits (as embodied in the professors). The "Stars and Stripes" episode is then best qualified as double subversion through derision: how could a genuine Native American willingly play an American military anthem?[28] Thus, even if China is itself the butt of satire, in depth it is a foil, an isolated topos on which universal antagonisms are acted out, and an exotic locale to enliven the lesson the trickster is performing for us readers.

Finally, *Griever* blends fiction with nonfiction, myth with history, the fabulous with the real, to point to a certain meaning of history and to re-create a form of mythic thought. Vizenor uses the colonial past of China to show the rupture brought about by the intrusion of history along with colonization, not so much in China (the Chinese "knew" history before the Europeans arrived) as in America. In the Chinese space, mythic cultures clash or fuse with recent or present history, and its scars (a word often repeated) are those of all victimized societies. Vizenor's characters try to mend this rupture by belonging at the same time to myth and to history: Wu Chou, a mythic man, went to school with Zhou Enlai; Sandie, another mythic man, studied at Berkeley; Griever is historically an American professor and mythically a Mind Monkey. In "Execution Caravan" he demands the release of the prisoners in the names of two mythical personages—the Jade Emperor and Su Wukong—and of Wei Jinsheng, a contemporary editor still in jail "for his outspoken advocacy of freedom and human rights." [29] Vizenor's legacy might well be the same appeal to myth, history, and present to liberate all of us on our way to the execution site.

INTERTEXTUALITY AND THE PILGRIMAGE STRATEGY

My concern here will be with the two references explicitly acknowledged in *Griever: The Monkey Grammarian*, quoted in epigraph, and *The Journey to the West*. I do not think the finality of *Griever* duplicates that of Paz's book. Rather, the kinship between the two works springs from the project of *The Monkey Grammarian*, an essay that relates Paz's pilgrimage "on the paths of creation" (specifically written for the series "Les sentiers de la création" of Editions Skira) to the source of language, at the temple of Monkey Hanumān in the *Ramāyāna*. Now, not only was this Monkey the ninth author of grammar, but he could fly, jump in one bound from India to Ceylon, move the Himalayas, take hold of the clouds, and so on. He is Griever's brother. Paz goes back and forth from his writing table in Cambridge to India along with Beauty. The writer identifies himself with Monkey, who smiles at the analogies that are offered to his mind between calligraphy and vegetation, woods and writing, reading and paths.[30] Paz's pilgrimage in an India both archaic and ever-present ends on a self-centered return to the act of writing as the negation of writing taken as a path. Even if Vizenor greatly mistrusts writing, the similarity between the two men would rather be in their common preoccupation with, on the one hand, their cultural past and its creative and destructive myths, and on the other hand, with the primeval spiritual past of India and China, in order to try to reconcile their personal experiences of cultural dualism with the source of universal wisdom.

The text that really inspired Griever, *The Journey to the West*,[31] never boringly narcissistic, harbors thousands of profound and entertaining treasures which underlie an authentic metaphysics of existence. Probably written in the sixteenth century by Wu Ch'êng-ên after a seventh-century event to which various versions, incorporating many influences, notably that of the *Ramāyāna*, were added, *The Journey* has inspired Chinese operas and many books to this day. In the United States, Maxine Hong Kingston refers to it in her first two novels, and uses it as the informing structure of *Tripmaster Monkey*.[32]

Griever departs from *The Journey* in many respects. The Chinese tale, with its scenic description of fabulous adventures on the way west from the Emperor's palace to the region of Buddha, describes in fact an internal journey, in purely allegorical fashion. Vizenor's alchemy also operates through words, but his concern is not with a psychological and philosophical internalization. He is not instructing us in the arcanes of Buddha-hood, of Confucianist self-cultivation, of Taoist physiological alchemy preparing the soul and body for immortality, as *The Journey* does, becoming "the larger and universal pilgrimage of life wherein all mortals must journey toward death," since "ascending the Western Heaven means in colloquial Chinese to die."[33] *Bearheart,* better than *Griever,* reproduces this pattern in that, as they advance, its pilgrims must get rid of their misconception of Indianness or die before the enlightened few reach the sacred place that takes them into the Fourth World of immortality. *Griever* is far more lighthearted. Another major difference lies in the mover of the Chinese pilgrimage. The four Disciples of the Monk must search for the Buddhist scriptures because they must atone for their original transgression of divine law. In *Griever* the positive characters suffer because they undergo the effect of the transgression *by the others* of cosmic law. And if *Griever* can be termed an "antipilgrimage" (to use the term Yu applies to *The Journey* [1983:226]), it is insofar as the hero and his wise friends do not learn anything on the way for, as tricksters and shamans, they already possess eternal knowledge.

Nonetheless, *The Journey* has lent more to our book than the few pages quoted in "Opera Comique" (127–131), and I will stop at "the monkey business" and the quest for manuscripts, the main two components derived from the Chinese pilgrimage. The success of Vizenor lies in his smart intertwining of these traditional Chinese motifs with Chippewa lore, so that one of my "pleasures of the text" lies in trying to sort out what belongs to *The Journey* and what does not. Griever's transformation into a monkey denotes his trickster capacity for metamorphosis. Being human and simian, he can be considered as both the Monk Tripitaka and his Monkey Sun Wu-k'ung, who underwent seventy-four transformations. Still, these two pilgrims are not libidinous: the Monkey is pure mind activity and the Monk has spent ten lives in abstinence. Griever's libido clearly springs from "reservations." One must note, however, that for a Vizenorian hero, his lust is rather subdued, mainly compared with that of some of the pilgrims in *Bearheart.* Griever, grant it, displays a breast fixation, but it is precisely to mock "this land of bare bulbs and no cleavage" (13), and of puritan public sexuality, as well as to mock this fairly general American fixation.

In *The Journey* the lustful one is appropriately Pigsy, the Pig with Intelligent Power who was banished for having tried to seduce the Moon Goddess. In *Griever,* Pigsie, "the lascivious peasant," coaches a burlesque basketball team of barrows, a great Orwellian vision. His companion, Sandie, has also flown in from *The Journey.* The Sand Bonze, he was banished for having broken a bowl at the Festival of Immortal Peaches (referred to on page 168), and is here "the most earnest and courteous of the wanderers," who has studied political science and economics at Berkeley, has helped muster the swines, and now makes a living as a government rat hunter (163–165).[34]

Griever's transformation into a monkey has several layers of meaning. Usually, Vizenor's tricksters turn into bears, the sacred animals of his people, to which *Bearheart* pays homage. Bears are not a Chinese motif; in *The Journey*, for example, they only appear as humanized monsters, never endowed with the value they hold in North America.[35] In *Griever* bears guide the trickster's visions. Vizenor astutely links these bears with the monkey by having Griever/the Monkey reach out to the bear on his balcony in order "to be the bear" (16), and by decreeing that Shitou, also a Mind Monkey, lived with a bear woman and begot thus healers in the tribal cultures of the world (17). Further, Griever "is related to the stone in his own tribal origin stories," hence to Shitou who "is a stone" and breaks stones (72), and to *The Journey*'s Mind Monkey, who was born of the immortal stone: "Griever dreamed he was born from a stone on Flower Fruit Mountain. He became a mind monkey" (128). Finally, Griever and the Mind Monkey share the same ticks (31–129). Perhaps as a warning to himself, to his own wild imagination, Vizenor quotes the passage of *The Journey* in which Bodhisattva Kuan Yin tames the Monkey's restless mind by constraining his head in a gold inlaid band that will fall off once he himself attains buddhahood. Constantly alert mental activity must be constructively harnessed, according to Buddhist wisdom. The pain Griever feels on his forehead (130) should be taken as a sign that he now knows how to focus his thoughts in the right direction.

Finally, the choice of a monkey can be construed as the reversal of the popular conception of this animal. It stands as the paradigmatic zoo tenant (bears also for that matter, but to a somewhat lesser degree). Hence, irony works through the reversal of situation: the free and powerful monkey playing tricks to caged-in human beings. This device of having an animal comment on society has often been used in oral stories and written ones, as in Apuleius's *Golden Ass* or Soseki's *I Am a Cat*.[36]

Griever's quest for manuscripts similarly intertwines Chippewa and Chinese details. On the plane, the Native American character receives the informing vision that will guide him, if not along his life, at least along his Chinese trip. The plane cabin is not exactly what one has in mind when one thinks of the vision rite, but it shows that our hero adapts very well to modern life, which is one of the points of the novel. He dreams of the silk roads, then of a fire bear on his balcony. Later the bear will guide him to the Kingdom of Khotan and show him "a bear with a black opal ring surrounded with azure blue stones" and "a small blue rabbit around her neck," also a motif from *The Journey*. The vision fades to continue with murals of bears, monkeys, and shamans. Griever is told to choose some birchbark manuscript. As he is returning to his apartment he loses it on a cart (16–18). The visions contain all the recurrent mythic elements that give its coherence to the novel: the black opal ring that Griever will see on an old Chinese woman in the crowd; the blue stones, lapis lazuli, always associated with good people and children; the bones, which will turn out to be those of babies; the shaman whom Griever will search and find along with the opal and the manuscript.

Griever then has, like *The Journey*'s pilgrims, traveled west (supposing he has flown over the Pacific) to find the original manuscripts of his tradition, for, though they came from a silk-road temple, their being in birchbark identifies them with the Chippewa scrolls bearing pictograms.[37] Griever concludes his pilgrimage when he discovers Shitou and Obo Island. "Obo" is a tribal Chinese term meaning "cairn" (164), and considering the looks and activities of its islanders one could risk calling it "Hobo Island." Obo, significantly one of the few noncolonial placenames of the novel, comes forth as *the* sacred topos of *Griever*'s China. A burlesque Noah's Ark on which barrows dribble basketballs (166), the island harbors all the shamans and tribal survivors Griever dreamed of or met in the streets, in particular Kangmei, in whom we earlier recognized the shrouded woman on whose cart Griever had lost his manuscript (18, 141). Before settling on the island she had circled it with her prairie schooner and fly seeds under her armpits (!). She happens to be the daughter of an American from Oklahoma, Battle Wilson, who entrusted her with the mission to give back to their tribal owners the scrolls that he had retrieved from the British Museum.

To celebrate his success in recovering the precious scrolls, Griever will, on the pattern of *The Journey,* be offered a gorgeous meal. The pattern of Vizenor's parody is equally followed: the author "apes" once more the Chinese tale. The magnificent banquet happens to be the one for the opening of Maxim's de Beijing. Griever goes to "mock a precious moment in the wild histories of capitalism" (201), and he invents a menu for Pierre Cardin. His fun will be "interruptus" by the doorman who expels him, not because he perturbs the celebration with paper planes, nor because Matteo Ricci "craps on a starched napkin," but because he wears no necktie (206), which actually happened to Vizenor and is far more absurd in what it reveals about social mores, transplanted or not.

As to the recipe for immortality, it turns out to be a cooking recipe, that of "blue chicken, made with mountain blue corn and pressed blue berries" (230). Subversion of the quest, negation of the very idea of pilgrimage, desacralization through the burlesque anticlimax of a "cooking recipe." Still, the recipe proves polysemous. After all, the scriptures Tripitaka and his disciples were given at Buddha's monastery were blank volumes. Thinking they have been deceived, the pilgrims go back to ask for written ones. Their wish is granted. They take these volumes to the emperor. They themselves understand that truth cannot be contained in words, and having reached enlightenment they are brought back to the seat of everlasting life, well beyond the written stage. The banquet partakes of buddhahood: "Long life's attained through strange food and fragrant tea," reads *The Journey* (vol. 4:389). Vizenor introduces with Griever's recipe some form, if less arcane, of culinary symbolism. The derisory revelation the scrolls contain might signify, on the one hand, that it is illusory to look for texts that would grant immortality; illusory to seek to return to a mythified past, because one must adapt to survive and to perpetuate ancestral wisdom, without refusing the present, and in so doing live on the hinge between two worlds, within and without, "to create a new consciousness of existence" (*Earthdivers* ix).

And yet, because this Oklahoma blue-chicken recipe (a Native American version of Kentucky fried chicken) includes the blue corn consumed by bear shamans, and because the book closes on the uncooked cock crowing over this final revelation, we may conclude that there was, indeed, in *Griever* as well, a pilgrimage to the source of Native American tribal wisdom. Consequently, Obo Island, hovering over the cesspool of contemporary China, appears as Naanabozho's Island, the land of emergence that allowed him to escape his own excrement floating around his nose.[38] How then, with such an inspiring model, could Vizenor not be a fantastic trickster himself?

THE ORIGINALITY OF *GRIEVER:* LANGUAGE AND TEXT

As in all his essays, Vizenor is so preoccupied with the act of writing that each of his fiction pieces must be considered as an actualization of his theoretical ideas. I will discuss only two characteristics of *Griever* in this respect: first, how Vizenor strives via the text to perpetuate the oral tradition; second, how *Griever* displays many postmodern features.

Rather than sink into silence, Vizenor has sublimated his mistrust of the written word by opting for a language that, thanks to the visual metaphor would break loose from the page to transmute itself into a voice. The act of writing, perceived as the echo of the oral tradition now on the decline, comes forth as the lesser of two evils, and it partakes of the ambiguity inherent in all the literatures that are the direct heirs of oral storytelling (and all literatures have had to solve it at some point). How does Vizenor cope with it in *Griever*? After the epigraph and chapter title, the reader is faced with the handwritten-like "Dear China," and the last line, excepting the epilogue, is the signature "Griever de Hocus" in a similar hand. The book is consequently a long story embedded within two letters. Moreover, because the title of the novel refers to China the country, one legitimately thinks he is writing figuratively to the country. When one finally guesses who the addressee is, one can feel "voyeurized" by the epistolary genre, or excluded from this "intra-Native American" exchange. The latter point might also imply that after so many decades of misunderstanding between the races, the book is destined to be read by someone who will understand from the inside. Over the necessary blending of the Native Americans into the Chinese, thanks to the girl who is both, one can pinpoint here another of Vizenor's word plays, a hermeneutic code that teases the reader.

The first word of the letter itself, "listen," posits a semi-oral dialogic strategy. We are going not so much to "read" a story as "hear" it. "Listen" oralizes the text. *Bearheart* started similarly with a "Letter to the Reader" (but the reader was not given a name) that embedded the pilgrimage narrative. *Griever*'s second chapter, by having the addressee China come on stage in China and Wu Chou sing the praise of the teacher, functions as the chorus in classic drama or as the intrusion of the storyteller commenting on the valor of the hero. Furthermore, it builds suspense: its use of the preterite when referring to Griever, the picture scene and the young investigating woman, sound like the postmortem recollection of the departed loved one: "Listen, he was unbelievable, but he freed birds. . . . The world gave him so much trouble for his time" (21). *Bearheart's* "heirships documents" turn here into the scrolls that recount the past from the silk culture to the tribulations of the teacher, and with Wu Chou opening them for China, the magic unfolds also for us. Yet, such a typical suspense story opening must be seen as parodic: Mind Monkeys don't die. The scrolls that once bore the chicken recipe cleverly fuse words with visual and oral operas.

A similar transmutation occurred in the first chapter. On the plane, Griever was reading a book and "the words became a real desert scene . . . but when I tried to hold the words down, a voice echoed from the page. The plane was transformed into a mansion" (14). The written word has here as much power as an oral one in creating an informing vision. One can see that even though Vizenor constantly nags at the printed word, he himself not only publishes a lot of printed texts, but also manages to transcend their neutralizing effect on the imagination. The following passage demonstrates this very poetically:

Griever listened to the rapid beat of his heart. . . . He was transformed from a flower to a bird, from a primrose to water ouzel in a warm rain. Plump children, wheeled over mountain meadows from the tribal past, were plucked from cosmetic chains, freed like small bears from a cold circus. (54)

Like Aesop's tongue, however, words can be the best and the worst thing: Griever is hauled back from his vision by the oral word of the archetypal moron in the next seat: "She held me down to the words, a good tourist" (15). The small talk they exchange is representative of many dialogues in *Griever.*

Short, poorly structured, unfinished bits of sentences are heard everywhere. People talk a lot, but most of the time their conversations do not amount to much. At first, one could construe them as obeying the postmodernist credo in nonmimetic, nonrepresentational fiction. Yet, far from being just absurd and burlesque, these reported dialogues ring authentic, "representational," of verbal exchanges between foreigners. I already pointed out that cultural distance was responsible for the strange conversations between Griever and the Chinese. In the middle of the book, when Griever searches for his bicycle, he also searches for words. The woman shaman Ha Lian relates that Confucius said that "words are rituals, catechisms a slow dance" (115), but then she refuses to answer him: "The words bounced back from an invisible cultural seal" (116). The impossibility of understanding the Chinese illustrates the impossibility of communicating with all the others, whether they speak a foreign language or not.

The teacher's dialogues sound hardly more elaborate and prove true the assertion according to which once writing appeared speech gradually stopped being concerned with important matters, since these were to be recorded in books.[39] The trivialization of orality is clearly displayed in *Griever*. Oral stories implied that each reproduction of the previously heard speech automatically became a re-creation, each speaker adding to the passed-on story. In his narratives, Vizenor achieves a somewhat similar effect by using certain episodes ad infinitum over the years and expanding their meaning by changing their textual environment. Further, aware as he is that translated myths lose their meaning, he constantly endeavors to translate them as accurately as possible. *Griever* belongs to the tradition, for it is an exercise in translation: of the tricksters tales, of *The Journey* operas, of Sino-American small talk that allows for such hilarious scenes:

> "When did he live there?" . . .
> "Gold mountain, but he's not that old."
> "Yes, cold."
>
> (170)

> "You eat pie."
> "What kind of apples are these?"
> "We eat pie."
> "Not with chopsticks."
> "You eat spoon."
> "Confucius was a dream buried in wild histories. . . ."
> "You like pie."
> "Ceramic spears burst overhead."
> "We like pie."
>
> (110)

Translation sometimes fails entirely, as is exemplified by the tribal woman who "did not understand what she heard in translation" (92), that is, what Griever is trying to pass on to her. Dialogue is then impossible, and significantly his lover is the "interpreter," words and bodies thus united, but destroyed or expelled finally by the political system.

All the laconic and absurd dialogues evoke those of other contemporary American authors—Barthelme for example, for whom the reproduced disintegration of language serves as the metaphor of the loss of valid communal relations. The trickster's role consists in preventing further disintegration, and Vizenor's work definitely invites a dialogistic rapport within traditions and literary works and with his readers, the basis for a transfrontier *communitas*.

Vizenor derides another type of language in *Griever:* official jargon and "cultural catch phrases" (132). When Wu Chou was at school with Zhou Enlai, they played with "new words on the run" (23), and once in power Zhou Enlai imprisoned creative language and banished Wu Chou to a farm: "we now speak a rather formal and footsore language" (23). The communists purged tribal languages as the American government did for the Native tongues in the federal schools. Typically, the reported speeches of officials will be utterly different from the others, with stilted, well-structured sentences, as seen in the Mayor of Tianjin's speech, or, in *Bearheart* (189–204), in the Mother Earth discourse of Belladona.

Before concluding I wish to sum up the characteristics of *Griever* as a text. Along with most of Vizenor's works, it has been labeled postmodernist. The term itself seems to me rather awkward since it suggests that literary periods succeed one another in a linear manner, progressing from the dark ages to a sort of perfected form, to which "postmodernism" would be as close as possible. They would thus resemble the Hegelian view of the vector of history, so often attacked by Vizenor himself—whereas he tells us that the postmodern has been in native cultures all along (*Narrative Chance* x). *Griever* itself stands in fact as the latest production in a literary cycle of metamorphoses: the *Rāmāyāna, Golden Ass, The Journey,* Chippewa trickster tales, and so on.

In any case, *Griever* does correspond to definitions of postmodern literature[40] in that it freely mixes genres, time sequences, styles, myths, and facts. Its "postmaodernist" characteristics essentially are the borrowings from:

1. The picaresque novel (itself derived from *The Golden Ass*), and its chain of events: *Griever* is triggered by "a stupid thing" (18), and the archetypal cart that carries the hero into fabulous adventures; the characters as type: the professors, the prisoners . . .

2. Rabelais's erotic and culinary grotesque, as seen in the bawdy episodes and the mock pantagruelian meal at Maxim's (204–205).

3. Gothic tales: the shrouded woman, blind people, the jailer Egas . . .

4. Detective stories: the search for the manuscript, the ring, and the stone shaman.

5. Western movies, with the cowboy walking out of a saloon (parodic, for the holster is empty and is to store scrolls anyway):

> He dressed and hurried down the carpeted stairs to the entrance hall. There, he fastened the polished leather holster to his waist and wheeled through the double doors into the middle land. (28)

6. Road stories and mad car or truck chases: when he hijacks the prisoners' truck (153).

7. Cartoon scenes: when he dusts Hua Lian's crotch with perfumed powders ready at hand in the park toilets; or the train-in-the tunnel scene with the special-effects mirrors (117).

8. The use of burlesque, idiosyncratic verbal inventions, not just in the metaphors but in the vocabulary itself, as in the four modernizations: "transportation was limousinized, food was banquetized, clothes were westernized, and the nation was pavilionized" (175).

9. Collages: extracts from *The Journey,* from an article on the Lazarist Sisters (109), from the mayor's speech, and so on. This particular point entails the next two.

10. The precision of the references of these quotes, either in the text or the epilogue. Vizenor does not use *The Journey,* either, in an arcane way. Some would (and have) duplicated the pattern without giving clues to its origin. *Griever* departs from most postmodern fictions which "serve as 'esoteric writing' waiting to be deciphered, as if in terms of an initiatory rite."[41]

11. Vizenor's quasi-parody of contemporary Native American texts, which often quote

extensively traditional myths, stories, or chants (by Momaday, Silko, Allen, and also by himself in his own earlier works). *Griever* is anchored in tradition but it is universal, not limited to one culture.

Griever is all this, and much more than just the sum of the various ingredients, thanks to Vizenor's imagination. As Maeterlinck wrote: "Imagination is the memory of the future." [42]

CONCLUSION

Griever demonstrates how Vizenor uses creative parody, but not just for the pleasure of it. All his writings are in fact didactic, for they subvert racism, social mores, institutions, the establishment in a burlesque manner, to make us aware of their surreptitious corrosive power. *Griever* acts out the forceful revenge of the Damned of the Earth ("Monkey Kings are myths for the poor and oppressed" [154]), not in Fanon style, politics, fire, and violence, but in trickster fashion with communicative wit. Not mind over matter, but flesh and spirit all together to provoke the reader into laughter and active participation. We readers constitute the society for which trickster Vizenor/Griever the deconstructionist, "the negation offering possibility" (Babcock 182), runs and bounds upon the stage, but who, unlike Shakespeare's poor player, is to be heard again: Vizenor has announced that once he lands in Macao, Griever will get embroiled in more adventures.

Furthermore, though Vizenor's work is marvelously original, his deepest preoccupation links him to many so-called "ethnic" American authors, whether Native or hyphenated. [43] They always distinguish between the inescapable reality of a cold, sterile, and frigid materialistic American society and the transcendent reality of memory, of belonging, of meaningful traditions. For most of them, salvation can come only from a fantasy over the past, personal or collective, from writing, from the verb as carrier of memory, from an imaginary and perpetual displacement signaling the refusal to be trapped in imposed stereotypes and territories. *Griever* goes further in this direction than most Native American novels, which are attached to a certain territory, the space within the reservation or without, just before retreating back in. *Griever* explodes the limits of the reservation and, as a prelude to *The Heirs of Columbus*, [44] dares to reverse Columbus's journey. Griever the "Indian" in turn goes to the land of the Great Khan to see for himself the people for whom his ancestors were mistaken. Though he comes from a reservation and says he goes back to it, we actually never see him back there, and China Browne testifies that he has not come back (the mention of his pseudo-return could be one more piece of parody in a Native-literature context). This book goes even further than *Bearheart* which was still a mere displacement between two Native reservations. Neither does Griever exhibit the divided self of most Native American heroes. As a Métis, Vizenor believes in living on the margins, those of an ever expanding free territory. Writing becomes this open, imaginary "in-between" space, perpetually recreated, and writing acts as one therapy (along with teaching and lecturing) for survival because the textual space can embody and resolve at the same time all irreducible antagonisms.

NOTES

1. Gerald Vizenor, *Griever: An American Monkey King in China* (Minneapolis: University of Minnesota Press, 1990). Subsequent references will be identified by page number in the text.

2. Franchot Ballinger, "Living Sideways: Social Themes and Social Relationships in Native American Trickster Tales," *American Indian Quarterly* 13:1 (Winter 1989):15–30. Ballinger studied Vizenor's tricksters in "Sacred Reversals: Trickster in Gerald Vizenor's *Earthdivers: Tribal Narratives on Mixed Descent*," *American Indian Quarterly* 9:1 (Winter 1985):56–59. Barbara Babcock, "'A Tolerated Margin of Mess': The Trickster and His Tales Reconsidered," Andrew Wiget, ed., *Critical Essays on Native American Literature* (Boston: G. K. Hall, 1985), 153–185.

3. Paul Radin, *The Trickster: A Study in American Indian Mythology* (New York: Schocken Books, 1956), quoted in Vizenor, *Earthdivers: Tribal Narratives on Mixed Descent* (Minneapolis: University of Minnesota Press, 1981), xii.

4. Vizenor, *The People Named the Chippewa* (Minneapolis: University of Minnesota Press, 1984), 143. Vizenor, *Interior Landscapes: Autobiographical Myths and Metaphors* (Minneapolis: University of Minnesota Press, 1990).

5. Vizenor, "Socioacupuncture: Mythic Reversals and the Striptease in Four Scenes," in Calvin Martin, ed., *The American Indian and the Problem of History* (New York: Oxford University Press, 1987), 181.

6. Vizenor, *Bearheart: The Heirship Chronicles* (Minneapolis: University of Minnesota Press, 1990).

7. Ballinger ("Living Sideways," 26) uses Wiget's interpretation. Emmanuel Désveaux, in his *Sous le signe de l'ours* (Paris: Editions de la Maison des Sciences de l'Homme, 1988), gives, among many legends of the Northern Ojibwa, the story of a "sleighed-in" penis (129–130).

8. Vizenor, "Trickster Discourse: Comic Holotropes and Language Games" in the book of critical essays he edited: *Narrative Chance: Postmodern Discourse on Native American Indian Literatures* (Albuquerque: University of New Mexico Press, 1989), 187–211.

9. Ihab Hassan, *The Postmodern Turn* (Columbus: Ohio State University Press, 1987), 91.

10. Vizenor, *Narrative Chance*, 190, explains the difference between verisimilitude as "appearance of realities" and "mythic verism," a "discourse, a critical concordance of narrative voices, and a narrative realism that is more than mimesis."

11. He explains this principle in two articles translated into French by Tzvetan Todorov in his *Mikhaïl Bakhtine: le principe dialogique* suivi *de Ecrits du Cercle de Bakhtine* (Paris: Le Seuil, 1981), 154–169. Exotopy is clearly linked to alterity to which we will return later.

12. Ken Kesey, *One Flew Over the Cuckoo's Nest* (New York: Vintage Press, 1962).

13. Vizenor often uses these words and in particular in *Earthdivers*, 81.

14. For a radically counter-vizenorian perception of the evangelization of Asia, see Shusaku Endo, *Silence* (London and New York: Quartet Books, 1978).

15. Vizenor quotes Joseph Kinsey Howard's *The Strange Empire of Louis Riel* in *Earthdivers*, x.

16. Vizenor explains this naming choice in the preface of *Wordarrows: Indians and Whites in the New Fur Trade* (St. Paul: University of Minnesota Press, 1978), x.

17. One could argue once more that the rational perversions of nature (moats, sculpturesque gardens, stunted trees, . . .) are by no means a Western specialty but also are typical of the Far Eastern custom of trimming nature to the metaphysical concept of what it should be like.

18. Because Vizenor's fiction is grounded in history I cannot help adding that his vision here only takes into account one side of history for the purpose of the narrative and overlooks internecine Asian wars and colonizations as if the continent had been a haven of peace before the Europeans arrived.

19. Because of the role it now plays on the reservation, bingo is another favorite topic of Vizenor. See his article, "Minnesota Chippewa: Woodland Treaties to Tribal Bingo," *American Indian Quarterly* 13:1 (Winter 1989):31–57, and also his subsequent books, *Crossbloods: Bone Courts, Bingo, and Other Reports* (Minneapolis: University of Minnesota Press, 1990), and *The Heirs of Columbus* (Middletown, Conn.: Wesleyan University Press, 1991).

20. Leslie Fiedler, *The Return of the Vanishing American* (Paris: Le Seuil, 1971), 84–99. Making Hannah Duston the paragon of White American Femininity, domineering and castrating, is, of course, a reductive male approach and it is a good thing that women like Annette Kolodny are also addressing this mythical domain to allow us a different perspective.

21. Vizenor is definitely illustrating here the point he often makes about the loss of meaning once oral stories become written and printed stories, or when they get translated into another language. In particular see his own texts in *Narrative Chance*.

22. Anthony C. Yu, "Fulbright Monkey in China," *Los Angeles Times* (11 October 1987): n.p.

23. Tzvetan Todorov, *La conquête de l'Amerique: La question de l'autre* (Paris: Le Seuil, 1989), in which he analyses alterity in French philosophical thinking over the centuries. Todorov chose the spelling "Colon" over the traditional ones because it was the one Christobal ("carrier of Christ") himself favored as, one could say, a "holotrope," both signifier and signified, "colon" being French for "colonist."

24. Colon, *Lettre rarissime* (7:7:1503) in Todorov, *La conquête de l'Amerique*, 18.

25. The Chinese will, in their turn, dream about American gold and invent their own "Gold Mountain," a myth Maxine Hong Kingston uses in her novels and that Vizenor uses in *Griever* (170) for a play on words.

26. Vizenor, in *The People Named the Chippewa* (107), quoted his friend Harold Goodsky who was trying to understand the meaning of the word "Indian": "Who am I? . . . I was chained in a dream and thought about us all being named by a psychopath like Columbus."

27. Todorov, *La conquête de l'Amerique*, 54–55, my emphasis.

28. There are of course many American patriots among Native Americans, but that too is ridiculed here.

29. Anthony C. Yu, "Fulbright Monkey in China."

30. Octavio Paz, *Le singe grammairien* (Genève: Skira, les Sentiers de la Création, 1972), 46.

31. Yu, trans. and ed., *The Journey to the West*, 4 vols. (Chicago: University of Chicago Press, 1977–1983). I wish to thank Anthony Yu for sending me his review of *Griever* and André Lévy, the French translator and editor of the Chinese masterwork, who happens to teach at my own university, for his kind help in clarifying some of its arcane passages.

32. Maxine Hong Kingston, *Tripmaster Monkey: His Fake Book* (New York: Knopf, 1989). Salman Rushdie's *Satanic Verses* (London: Penguin Books, 1988) also derives part of its peripatetic and impressive imagination from *The Journey*. This Indian trickster is the (still) living proof that humorless totalitarian regimes will not tolerate "a margin of mess."

33. Yu, "Two Literary Examples of Religious Pilgrimage: The *Commedia* and *The Journey to the West*," *History of Religions* 22:3 (February 1983):227.

34. This particular detail and many others call to mind the BBC productions of Monty Python in the early 1970s. Watching their reruns while working on Vizenor demonstrates the similarity of invention. No. 20 has a government rat catcher slip through wainscotting in a council house and finds sheep in the mouse hole, plus one of Her Majesty's ministers chants his program while stripteasing on stage. These burlesque parodies, interspersed with montages of animated cartoons with grotesque people and animals, "deconstruct" British society and TV programs in a perfectly English satirical and surrealistic vein.

35. See in particular A. Hallowell, "Bear Ceremonialism in the Northern Hemisphere," *American Anthropologist* 28:1 (1926):1–175, and E. Désveaux's *Sous le signe de l'ours*.

36. Lucius Apuleius, *Golden Ass: The Metamorphosis*, William Aldington, trans. (London: Norwood, 1986). Natsume Soseki, *I Am a Cat* (Rutland, Vt.: Tuttle, 1986).

37. Selwyn Dewdney, *The Sacred Scrolls of the Southern Ojibway* (Toronto: University of Toronto Press, 1975). These Chippewa scrolls, which bore signs or pictograms (or in *Griever* a written recipe), testify to an ancient graphic system, a form of writing, even if pre-alphabetic. As such they influenced the social organization and the knowledge system of the group. See Jack Goody, *The Domestication of the Savage Mind*, French translation: *La raison graphique* (Paris: Editions de Minuit, 1979), 142–143. Vizenor, who lists Dewdney in the bibliography of *The People Named the Chippewa*, knows that his own tradition practised a form of writing, drawn or incised into a flat medium and that would have certainly evolved into something more elaborate even without the Conquest. His condemnation of the whites, who by introducing history killed myth and by imposing writing killed the oral tradition, seems not to take into account those tangible proofs of early Chippewa forms of writing. What is more, writing, the great culprit, is an Asian, not a European invention. Having his trickster search for "manuscripts" may seem strange for an author riled by the written word, unless we are to see in it another form of parody that would take us back to Paz's words about how writing expels the meaning writing is searching for.

38. This primeval coprophilia is the one that has sent many analysts on the repressed anality track. For a presentation of Naanabozho, see John A. Grim, *The Shaman: Patterns of*

Healing among the Ojibway Indians (Norman: University of Oklahoma Press, 1983), 85–92; and Vizenor, *The People Named the Chippewa*, as well as *Summer in Spring: Ojibwe Lyric Poems and Tribal Stories* (Minneapolis: Nodin Press, 1981).

39. Raphaël Pividal, *La maison de l'écriture* (Paris: Le Seuil, 1976), 25.

40. See in particular Ihab Hassan's works, most of them are reedited in *The Postmodern Turn* and Vizenor, *Narrative Chance*.

41. Campbell Tatham quoted in Ihab Hassan, *The Postmodern Turn*, 79.

42. Maurice Maeterlinck, *L'Autre Monde ou le Cadran Stellaire* (Paris: Fasquelle editeur, 1942), 75. "L'imagination est la mémoire de l'avenir."

43. I draw these conclusions from six years of collective work within the Centre D'Etudes de l'Amérique anglophone, at Bordeaux University, on multiculturalism and literatures in the United States and Canada.

44. Vizenor, *The Heirs of Columbus*.

THE MULTIPLE TRADITIONS OF GERALD VIZENOR'S HAIKU POETRY

Kimberly M. Blaeser

Native American poets attempt in their insistent utterances to lessen the distance created by print, to transform the "passive word of the written page" into an "active immediacy." . . . The poems do not withdraw into style, but project into life.—Brian Swann

By understanding more about our immediate locale, the native soil we stand on and the other living things that share our world, we expand our imaginations and expand our culture.—Rick Simonson and Scott Walker

A mixed-blood of Ojibway and French ancestry, Gerald Vizenor has enriched his writing throughout his career with the interweaving of multiple traditions. His writing has worked to establish links, combine forms, play one idea or genre off of another. His novel *Griever: An American Monkey King in China,* for example, played upon the likeness of the Native American trickster figure and the Chinese Monkey King. His recent theoretical work has repeatedly drawn parallels between the Native American and the postmodern literary traditions. His historical accounts and journalistic writing have been fleshed out with the imaginative, the creative, the fictional. This cross-cultural, mixed-genre tendency of Vizenor's is clearly manifested as well in his haiku poetry, which seeks to combine the traditions of the Ojibway dream song and the Japanese haiku.

The Native American imprint on Vizenor's haiku, however, involves more than the narrowly defined dream-song tradition and expands beyond the bounds of Ojibway culture. Many of Vizenor's haiku, for example, readily exhibit a connection to the trickster tradition in Native American literature and to pan-Indian concepts of spirituality. In addition, by its minimalistic nature, haiku tends to lend itself to reading in a third tradition, that of reader-response aesthetics—for which Vizenor and other contemporary scholars find precedent in the oral tradition of many tribal cultures (Kroeber 1979; Krupat 1987; Jahner n.d.). An understanding of haiku in Vizenor's style, then, has clear links to multiple literary and theoretical traditions.

HAIKU FORM, OJIBWAY DREAM SONGS, AND WHETHER THE TWAIN MEET

Having served in Japan in the military in 1954 and 1955, Vizenor developed an interest in Japanese culture and especially in haiku thought. Later in both his undergraduate and graduate work at the University of Minnesota he was involved with the Asian studies program. His publications from the 1960s include collections of haiku and reexpressions of traditional Ojibway songs, two kinds of expression he saw as similar in form and intention. About the haiku form he said, "There is a visual dreamscape in haiku which is similar to the sense of natural human connections to the earth found in tribal music, dream songs" (1984a: 3). And about Ojibway dream songs he said, "They are sort of the Ojibway haiku—in song" (Blaeser 1987).

Reviewer Robert Glauber, writing in 1966 after the release of Vizenor's collection of Ojibway songs *Summer in the Spring,* was one of the earliest commentators to make a connection between the two forms in Vizenor's work. In *The Beloit Poetry Journal,* he noted:

Here is a fascinating collection of Ojibway pieces that strongly remind one of haiku. All are brief and extremely evocative. One cannot say, however, if the Japanese quality is actually in the original or has only crept into Vizenor's "interpretations." (39)

The line of inquiry suggested in Glauber's brief comments might be satisfied by the knowledge that Vizenor's "interpretations" were really "reexpressions" of Frances Densmore's translations of Ojibway song poems and that a haiku-quality was earlier noted in these original translations. However, that information leads to a more central question about whether the Japanese quality was inherent in the original Ojibway dream songs or merely "crept into" Densmore's translations. Lively scholarly debate continues on this issue.

Although scholars date the origin of the Japanese haiku differently, all agree it has a long literary and cultural history, and many fine studies analyze this history as well as the form, philosophy, and function of haiku (Chamberlain 1910; Keene 1955; Suzuki

1959; Yasuda 1957). Briefly, the haiku is a short poem (generally classified as a lyric) usually made up of seventeen syllables in three lines which follow a 5–7–5 syllable pattern. Although English and Japanese haiku may differ in regard to the use of poetic techniques like rhyme and alliteration, both rely mainly on cadence, not meter, for their rhythm. The poem most frequently has as its subject some aspect or observation of nature and usually includes a seasonal element. Tightly constructed, it offers vivid images with little or no commentary or interpretation. The Japanese haiku form has frequently been associated with the Zen philosophy and, like Zen, celebrates the "suchness" of things themselves and frequently has its origin in an experience of personal enlightenment. Vizenor published six collections of haiku between 1962 and 1984, and many of his poems have been anthologized.

Like haiku, the Ojibway dream songs also stem from a moment of intense personal awareness which, as the name indicates, may have come during a dream or visionary experience. The subjects of the songs might be an image in nature, an action, the experience of a moment, a state of mind, or an emotional response. Frances Densmore transcribed close to four hundred Ojibway songs of various types in the early years of the twentieth century (1910, 1913). Her original transcriptions of the dream songs included descriptions of their musical or oral performance or enactment as well as explanatory notes that attempted to provide details regarding social or cultural background particularly pertinent to the songs and to provide some understanding of the songs' allusions. However, the literal translations of the songs themselves given by Densmore and later "interpreted and reexpressed" by Vizenor in *anishinabe nagoman* and *Summer in the Spring: Ojibwe Lyric Poems and Tribal Stories* (1970, 1965) tend in form to be very brief, averaging about four lines in length.[1] The lines themselves consist of one to generally no more than six words or vocables and are presented with little or no punctuation or capitalization and usually without obvious grammatical connections to the other lines of the song.

Similarities in the forms and subjects of haiku and dream songs have been recognized and commented on since shortly after the original publication of Densmore's two-volume *Chippewa Music* in 1910 and 1913. The comparisons were frequently made with reference to a third (and at that time both new and radical) poetic movement, imagism. The imagists, who were fascinated with the haiku as well as with other "primitive" forms like the Chinese written character and Native American song poems, championed a new form of poetry: compact in form, based not on meter but on natural rhythm, using common speech, presenting precise images and refraining from comment. A review of Densmore's *Chippewa Music* published by Carl Sandburg in 1917 playfully noted the similarities between the Ojibway songs and the imagist movement: "Suspicion arises that the red man and his children committed direct plagiarism on our modern imagists and vorticists" (255). Later observations continued to point to similarities between haiku, imagism, Chinese poetry, and Native American song poems. In 1918 Mary Austin wrote about the "extraordinary likeness between much of this native product [translations of Native

American songs and chants in *Path on the Rainbow*] and the recent work of the Imagists, *vers librists,* and other literary fashionables" (267). Margot Astrov, writing in 1946, was more specific about what constituted the similarities between haiku and Native American songs. The tribal songs, she says, are "remindful of the best of Japanese Haiku that turn the listener into a poet himself, for it is his part to fill the sketch into completeness" (16). In his 1951 study *The Sky Clears: Poetry of the American Indian,* A. Grove Day analyzes the attraction Native American poetry held for the proponents of Imagism saying they:

found in the short verses like the Chippewa songs collected by Miss Densmore the sort of compressed word-pictures they also sought in other foreign forms like the Chinese poems collected by Ernest Fenellosa [*sic*] and the rigid seventeen-syllable Japanese form called the haiku. (32)

Many contemporary scholars, including James Ruppert, Michael Castro, Kenneth Rexroth, Larry Evers, Felipe Molina, Karl Kroeber, and Lester Standiford, have discussed this historical apprehension of similarity between these three forms and have debated the accurateness of such a claim. In addition, some scholars have questioned the accuracy of the work of Densmore and other early collectors. Although it is not within the scope of this essay to take up each of these debates and all associated issues, I raise these topics in order to give some indication of the place of Vizenor's work in this larger scheme.[2]

Vizenor has himself commented on the twentieth-century poets' exploration of the trend of relationships between haiku, tribal songs, and the imagist movement, and claims:

The first American imagist poets were the American Indians. . . . Many modern imagist poets have sought models of concise poetic expressions in Oriental literature. They may have found these qualities in the lyrical poetry and songs of the American Indians. (1966a)

Castro, however, believes, "These similarities are, in fact, superficial at best and more apparent than real" (1983:22). He claims that "when the translators used imagist concepts and techniques to produce their English translations, the results were bound to bear a striking resemblance to imagist forms" (22). However, this objection of Castro's can be answered at least in part by Rexroth's observation about the differences in poetic type that result from Densmore's translations of songs from various tribes:

The resemblance to Japanese poetry is indeed startling, particularly in the Chippewa songs. This is not due to the influence of Amy Lowell and other free-verse translators on Miss Densmore. On the contrary, she worked with the Chippewa many years before such Japanese translations and their imitations in modern American verse came into existence. As the years have gone by she has moved on to tribes which do not show the same kind of resemblance either in music or in lyric. (283)

Yet, even if we accept that Densmore's poetic style may have arisen organically from the various tribal songs themselves, Castro, Kroeber, Molina, and Evers raise other important points about the methods and problems of translation that cannot be ignored. For example, Castro notes:

The originals on which these poems are based are not written. They are sounded, not silent. Their dimensions of music, movement, and relation are more complex, more physical, for they are literally embodied in their singers. The translation, because it shifts the ground of the poem from the media of the singer's body and voice to the medium of the page, can only provide, at best, the roughest equivalent of the original. (23)

Here and elsewhere he challenges the very application of the term "poetry" to oral tradition, and, noting the diminished dimensions of the translations and the changed contexts of the finished products, he seems to question the wisdom of attempting to make of vital activities mere written words.

Castro's uneasiness with the attempts of translation and his keen awareness of the transmutations (or mutations) that result parallel the concerns of Vizenor himself. Vizenor has spoken of his original wariness of the written word and has bemoaned the inadequacies of translation; however, his response is not to forgo the attempt: "I don't think the oral tradition can be translated well, but I think it can be reimagined and reexpressed and that's my interest" (Bowers and Silet 1981:49).

One exploration of the translation dilemma particularly pertinent to a discussion of Vizenor's work is Arnold Krupat's, "Post-Structuralism and Oral Literature" (1987). Krupat discusses the opposing tendencies of translators who seek *either* "unmistakable" *or* "undecidable" meanings (118) and suggests not only that both methods are lacking, but that

what each method in itself is and can offer is always a function of what it is not and what it can never produce. What the very best mythographers make present to us can only fully be understood in relation to what they have left out, to the absences whose traces we must somehow take into account if we are to understand anything at all. (122–123)

While translators will continue to "fix" tests after whatever fashion they deem most worthy, readers, Krupat holds, must read the texts "as in need of unfixing" in order to gain understanding of the works as part of the oral as well as the written tradition (124–125).

Vizenor's style seems to encourage a similar method of viewing and of reading literature. To meet the challenge not only of translation or reexpression of oral tradition, but to meet the broader challenge of all writing—the translation or reexpression of life deeply experienced into static words—Vizenor frequently creates an "open" text, a text that advertises its absences and requires the response of the reader to bring it to fruition, a text that works to activate the reader's imagination and thus to engage the reader in the process of "unfixing" the text. By making what is present attempt to include what is absent by allusion, Vizenor attempts to break through the boundaries of print. Among his earliest experiments in this vein are his haiku collections.

Vizenor, unlike Castro, finds the similarities between tribal song poems and haiku to be more than superficial. One important similarity between the two that Vizenor identifies involves their ultimate purpose, their supraliterary (perhaps even antiliterary) intentions. Both, Vizenor feels, intend to surpass or forgo the goals of any philosophy of literary esthetics for the sake of actual experience, for a moment of enlightenment.

It is exactly this supraliterary quality which many, including Castro, have pointed to as distinguishing tribal song poems from the mainstream literary movements, including imagism. For example, Rexroth writes that American Indian "poetry or song does not only play a vatic role in society, but is itself a numinous thing" (282); A. La-Vonne Ruoff writes of the Native American's "attempt to order its spiritual and physical world through the power of the word, whether chanted, spoken, or sung" (1990:19); and Kroeber speaks specifically of the Ojibway dream song as "a transactional event, a process by which dream power is realized as cultural potency" (1978:272). Castro, too, points out that, in their origin most tribal songs were not "aesthetic objects," but sources or channels of power: "Indian poetry seeks to be effective, not merely affective" (24). The following statement from Densmore illustrates this effective intention of the Ojibway dream songs specifically:

The songs in this group are not composed in the usual sense of the term, but are songs which are said to have come to the mind of the Indian when he was in a dream or trance. Many Indian songs are intended to exert a strong mental influence, and dream songs are supposed to have this power in greater degree than any others. The supernatural is very real to the Indian. He puts himself in communication with it by fasting or by physical suffering. While his body is thus subordinated to the mind a song occurs to him. In after years he believes that by singing this song he can recall the condition under which it came to him—a condition of direct communication with the supernatural. (1910:118)

Although Vizenor does see a distinction in purpose between much mainstream poetry and the tribal songs, he sees the haiku poetry as like the tribal songs in this respect, as likewise pursuing (although admittedly perhaps not to the same degree) an experiential not merely a literary reality. This supraliterary quality of haiku was likewise identified by imagist poet John Gould Fletcher: "The merit of these haiku poems is not only that they suggest much by saying little; they also, if understood in connection with the Zen doctrine they illuminate, make of poetry an act of life" (1947:ix–x).

Vizenor, then, sees in the haiku method a way of writing that most nearly approximates the essence of an oral tradition and, therefore, as a form which can most nearly embody a tribal worldview. In his own characterizations of the haiku form—as he identifies what kind of experience gives origin to haiku, how the haiku engages the reader, what demands it makes on the reader, what powers it awakens, and what quality of experience it leads to—he weaves the Japanese tradition of Zen and haiku with Native American spirituality and oral tradition (or perhaps he merely expresses the similar vision held by the two traditions).

HAIKU POETS AND TRIBAL DREAMERS:
SINGING NATURE'S SONGS

One striking similarity between the two literary expressions is the quality of the experience that gives rise to the creation of the poetry. The "haiku moment," the kind of encounter from which haiku issues, has been described by haiku poet and theorist Otsuji (pen name for Seki Osuga) as

the instant when our mental activity almost merges into an unconscious state—i.e., when the relationship between the subject and object is forgotten . . . when it is said that one goes into the heart of created things and becomes one with nature. (Yasuda 1957:10)

Note the obvious similarity between the state described here and that described in Densmore's comments on dream songs. Dream songs, she writes, are "songs said to have come to the mind of the Indian when he was in a dream or trance" (1910:118) when "the dreamer contemplates nature in a certain aspect so long and so steadily that he gradually loses his own personality and identifies himself with it" (1910:126). Frequently the dreamer claims to have learned the song from some other being or spirit (deer, thunderbird, trees, and the like) (1913:37). This state Densmore describes as "a condition of direct communication with the supernatural" (1910:118) wherein the dreamer often "learns from manido?" (1913:37).

In their study of Yaqui deer songs (the Yaqui near-equivalent of Ojibway dream songs), Evers and Molina describe a similar state that gives rise to the deer songs: "The hunters learned the secrets of the deer and their language and that deer language came to be translated into the deer songs of the hunter." When the songs are performed, they explain, "the deer dancer takes on the spirit of the deer, giving him physical form even as the deer singers . . . bring his voice" (1987:47). Yaqui poet Refugio Savala has also explained that deer songs "come from the wild—just like when you dream, you go to a place in nature" (Evers and Molina 1990:40).

When Vizenor himself enumerates the similarities between haiku and dream songs, he, too, identifies this common state of mind or spirit. Both haiku and dream songs he sees as reflecting "the kind of touch with nature, the twist on natural experience that's almost a transformation, human consciousness derived from other living things" (Blaeser 1987). Ideally, then, both forms of poetry emanate from a moment of vision, what Zen calls enlightenment or "satori," what Rexroth has called "transfiguration and transcendence," and what Vizenor calls "dreamscape."

Both haiku and dream songs also seek not merely to give voice to this visionary experience, but also, acting as stimuli, to assist the reader or listener in the attainment of a similar moment of spiritual awareness or illumination. For example, Mary Austin, an early student of Native American poetry, emphasized the "state of mind evoked by tribal song" and writes of the "inherent power of [tribal] poetry to raise the psychic plane above the accidents of being" (1918:270). Evers and Molina describe the deer songs as "speaking the sacred" and comment on "the inspiration manifested in the deer song," and Savala compares singing the deer songs to praying: "It is like a prayer because the songs are inspired" (40). Similarly when Suzuki talks of the purpose of haiku and Japanese art, he notes both their spiritual quality and their transcendent effect:

The mysteries of life enter deeply into the composition of art. When an art, therefore, presents those mysteries in a most profound and creative manner, it moves us to the depths of our being; art then becomes a divine work. . . .

Great works of art embody in them *yugen* [also called *myo*, meaning mystery and spiritual rhythm] whereby we attain a glimpse of things eternal in a world of constant changes: that is, we look into the secrets of Reality. (219–220)

So it is in Vizenor's haiku theory and practice. The power of his haiku lies in its engagement of the reader's imagination and its ability to move the reader beyond the words to an individual moment of illumination, its ability to incite the reader to find what he calls "a dreamscape in natural harmonies beneath the words" (1984a:[11]). He writes:

The reader creates a dreamscape from haiku; nothing remains in print, words become dream voices, traces on the wind, twists in the snow, a perch high in the bare poplar. (1984a:[1])

THE NOTHINGNESS THAT IS NOT ABSENCE: READER RESPONSE AND HAIKU DREAMSCAPE

Note that Vizenor credits the reader not the poem with the creation or attainment of dreamscape. The haiku poem serves only to spark the reader's own powers. The dreamscape of haiku lies not in words, but in experience. Similarly in the Native American tradition, both the role of the singer and the role of the community is to hear more than is sounded or spoken. Molina and Evers make use of a Yaqui story of a talking stick to make this point, explaining, "The focus of the story is not so much on what the talking stick sounded like as it is on what the young woman is able to hear" (37).

Scholars of haiku like Dorothy Britton, Kenneth Yasuda, and Donald Keene (all of whom are familiar to Vizenor and mentioned or quoted in his own discussions of the art of haiku) frequently emphasize the reader's role in haiku. For example, Britton says:

These short verses are thought-provokers. The haiku poet rarely describes his own feelings, but lets the juxtaposition of his images make us feel his emotions instead. Seemingly objective, a good haiku should rouse in the reader's mind a deeply subjective response and set in motion a world of thoughts. A haiku makes demands. So much is left unsaid that its three brief lines need more than a casual reading. One should try to immerse oneself in the poem and let the images propel one's thoughts to deeper meanings. (1980:17)

In his introduction to *Matsushima* (1984a:[1–11]), when Vizenor discusses the participation of the reader, he quotes both Donald Keene—"a really good poem, and this is
especially true of haiku, must be completed by the reader"—and Daisetz Suzuki—"the
meaning of such objects . . . is left to the reader to construct and interpret it according to
his poetic experience or his spiritual intuitions" ([3]).

This participation of the reader is not only a recognized result of haiku, but an
important goal of the form, one clearly linked to the philosophy, method, and purpose of
the poetic process. Haiku's conscious attempt to engage the reader has its source in what
I have called the form's supraliterary intentions. The goal of haiku is its own annihilation.
Haiku exists solely to be obliterated and replaced by experience. Kenneth Yasuda makes
the distinction between poetry which is *about* experience and poetry which *becomes*
experience itself (44). The best of haiku, becomes experience. "The visual description
[of haiku]," claims Vizenor, "is enough to enter a visual experience. You don't need the
poem anymore" (Blaeser 1987). Therefore, as literature, haiku must work for its own
effacement. In Vizenor's discussion in *Matsushima* of these supraliterary aspirations of
haiku he quotes from R. H. Blyth:

A haiku is not a poem, it is not literature; it is a hand beckoning, a door half-opened, a mirror wiped
clean. It is a way of returning to nature. . . . (Vizenor 1984a:[2])

He also makes use of Roland Barthes's assertion that haiku is the "literary branch" of
Zen and that it is "destined to halt language" (1984a:[9]).

Both of these statements, which speak of the haiku desire to escape the capture
of language and literature, become more understandable when we consider the attitude of
Zen toward conceptualization. Daisetz Suzuki explains:

Zen is not necessarily against words, but it is well aware of the fact that they are always liable to de-
tach themselves from realities and turn into conceptions. And this conceptualization is what Zen is
against. . . . Zen insists on handling the thing itself and not an empty abstraction. (5)

Suzuki says Zen distinguishes between "living words" and "dead words," the dead ones
being "those that no longer pass directly and concretely and intimately on to the experience. They are conceptualized, they are cut off from the living roots" (7). The haiku
master then aspires not to create a work of art, but a work of life. Japanese art, including
haiku, avoids merely "copying or imitating nature" says Suzuki (36), and instead attempts to "give the [artistic] object something living in its own right" (36) to "go beyond
logic" (360) and point to "the presence in us of a mystery that is beyond intellectual
analysis" (220). A haiku that fulfills these intentions is the enlightenment or satori of Zen
artistically expressed.

In these referential artistic aspirations of haiku, although there is not a direct
correspondence, we can see some similarity to the goals and artistry of dream songs and

a connection to the broader practices of tribal oral tradition. Traditional tribal songs, like haiku, resist conceptualization; language remains connected to being. The songs did not so much report as participate in or embody life. "The words and rhythms themselves," Vizenor claims, "had intuitive power" (1966a:19). In tribal cultures, coup stories were the medium by which one told *of* one's deeds; dream songs were the means to renew a visionary connection or to access or share a power channel. H. David Brumble comments on a scene from *Two Leggings: The Making of a Crow Warrior* that illustrates this re-access of power through a dream or vision song:

The people assumed that the vision had a store of power, and that this power could be shared by the people if the vision could be enacted. . . . Two Leggings, for example, after building the miniature sweat lodges, sang for his raiding part the song he had heard in his vision. (45)

Molina and Evers, in describing the role and power of deer songs, also explain how the songs do not merely report but foster continuing communication with "the wilderness world" of the Sonoran Desert: "Deer songs continue in Yaqui communities as a very real vehicle for communication with the larger natural community in which the Yaquis live" (18). This communication with "plants, animals, birds, fishes, even rocks and springs" (18) certainly stands outside intellectual and logical realms and participates in the realm of experience and of mystery that Suzuki speaks of. Having their source in a visionary experience of a natural dimension outside the limits of time and space, these songs embody that mystery and invite its rediscovery.

How are the lofty goals of these two poetic forms achieved in practice? Both haiku and dream songs proceed by means of an "open text," a text that works by suggestion, implication, absence, allusion, juxtaposition, one that works through intentional gaps, indeterminancy in various forms, and the practice of many kinds of restraint in language.[3] For example, Yasuda describes the haiku method as "the representation of the object alone, without comment, never presented to be other than what it is, but not represented completely as it is" (7). Similarly, in describing Native American song poems, Margot Astrov claims "few of these short songs are complete in themselves" (15). She explains:

The singer sketches only a thought or an impression and it is left to the poetical imagination of the listener and his resources of mythic knowledge to supply the gradations of color and mythical context. (15–16)

The restraint on the part of the author or singer allows for and encourages the participation of the reader or community. In Native American song poems, the associations may not be "poetic" as much as cultural and mythical, but the implications of absence still hold sway. One of the better known illustrations of the allusive quality of tribal oral literature is that given in Ruth Underhill's *Papago Woman* when Maria Chona, Underhill's Papago informant, offers the following explanation before supplying Underhill with a rendition of a certain tribal song: "The song is very short because we understand so much" (1979:51).

Suzuki identifies part of what this common guardedness in language preserves when he talks about the appropriateness and purpose of restraint in haiku:

When a feeling reaches its highest pitch, we remain silent, because no words are adequate. . . . When feelings are too fully expressed, no room is left for the unknown, and from this unknown start the Japanese arts. (257)

Activated by the suggestion of the haiku are the reader's imagination, intuition, and primal memory, all of which work to fill in the essence that language cannot capture, to discover things that have not been written. The goal according to Suzuki is "to grasp life from within and not from without" (24). What Vizenor calls the "internal transformation" comes about when "the listener-participant makes that [the haiku] a personal experience-event from his or her own experience" (Blaeser 1987).

With the actualization of haiku, the words of the poem in essence dissolve or deconstruct, having been transformed or rendered into experience. The deconstruction of the words or the "art" thus accomplish the ultimate unveiling. According to Vizenor:

The images in haiku remain connected to our bodies; the words are rendered visual, transformed in primal memories, simple experiences, natural harmonies, and a dreamscape on the earth. Deconstruct the printed words in a haiku and there is nothing; nothing is a haiku, not even a poem. The *nothing* in a haiku is not an aesthetic void; rather, it is a moment of enlightenment, a dreamscape where words dissolve; no critical marks, no grammatical stains remain. (1984a:[5])

For Vizenor, then, haiku-like dream songs succeed to the degree that they deconstruct as literature and undergo a transformation into experience and enlightenment—into dreamscape.

VIZENOR'S HAIKU METHOD EMPLOYED

The open text of Vizenor's haiku generally works through images of the natural world, through unusual juxtapositions and through unfulfilled expectations. In his poetry, he employs natural images but refrains from dictating connections or meaning. Instead, he holds faith with the visual imagination of the reader. He describes his haiku method:

There is tension in haiku thought; little in human experience is without tension, but the tension in haiku is subtle, unresolved in narrative schemes. Tension is suggested, the reader touches the places in his memories. (1984a:[4])

The tension in Vizenor's haiku often stems from the juxtaposition of the sentimental with the mundane or of two apparently incongruous images. In this way, Vizenor's haiku seem to meet the qualifications set out by Donald Keene for effective haiku: "The nature of the elements varies, but there should be . . . two electric poles between which the spark will leap" (40). In Vizenor's poetry, the first line (or two lines) in his haiku frequently sets up edenic expectations and the final line (or lines) deflates these romantic notions of reality, thus propelling his reader beyond the conventional, fictionalized, or romanticized images of life toward an experience of authentic underlying harmony. This subtle undercutting of expectations or, in other poems, the unusual depictions of the ordinary or the revelation of surprising connections, has the effect of eliciting an internal gasp of recognition or producing an inadvertent glottal stop, either of which then provides the momentum for bridging the gap between mere words and experiential reality.

Although not all the haiku engage the reader in exactly the same way, a look at several from Vizenor's various collections illustrates his common methods and intentions and the probable effects on the reader. In the following poem from *Seventeen Chirps,* for example, Vizenor depicts a scene of natural, almost reverent, solitude with its first two lines:

> Morning mist
> Rowing over the leaf pond
> (1964a:[11])

The lines invite the reader to enter the scene through imagination: Damp morning mist seeming to hover or float silently over a pond, the invigorating moist chill of dawn still in the air, the slight musty smell of dampened leaves, and a hushed atmosphere that engenders stillness in any watcher. And then, the last line cuts across the scene with the shrill call: "Chick a dee dee dee!" Just as one standing at the scene might start at the tranquility so suddenly broken, so does the engaged reader seem to react. The ignited spark of excitement awakens a memory or a knowledge that, for an instant, transports the reader to the reality of just such an adrenergic experience, to an experience more alive than words on a page.

However, what the reader ultimately experiences is not so much a physical moment as it is an unbidden perception of an intersection with the eternal, with the unbounded oneness. On one level the poem is the depiction of physical tranquility followed by the momentary disruption of that tranquility, which only serves to awaken an awareness of the underlying all-consuming tranquility. The sound of the bird startles the reader over the hurdle of time and place into the realm of what Zen calls Emptiness. Thus he or she discovers the point of intersection of the momentary and the eternal, and thereby is enlightened regarding the intersection of all dualities.[4] Vizenor attempts to describe this kind of primal transcendence, the "moment of enlightenment" in haiku, when he writes,

"Words are turned back to nature, set free in the mythic dreamscapes of a haiku" (1984a:[5]). He continues the explanation by quoting from Susan Griffin's *Woman and Nature: The Roaring Inside Her:*

Behind naming, beneath words, is something else. An existence named unnamed and unnameable. . . . But in a moment that which is behind naming makes itself known. . . . This knowledge is in the souls of everything, behind naming, before speaking, beneath words. (1978:190–191)

Evers and Molina report the Yaqui understanding of a similar realm and refer to this "source of all things" (44) in various ways in their study. For example, they describe one of the supernatural worlds, the *sea ania* or flower world, as "located in the east, in a place 'beneath the dawn'" and as being "a perfected mirror image of all the beauty of the natural world of the Sonoran desert" (47).

Suzuki, like Vizenor and Griffin, also speaks of the buried knowledge that can be uncovered within each person, and he delineates the several layers of consciousness he believes make up the human mind. These include: "dualistic consciousness," the limited level at which we generally move; a "semi-conscious" plane consisting of our ordinary memory; the "Unconscious" made up of buried memories; the "collective unconscious" credited with being the "basis of our mental life"; and finally, the "Cosmic Unconscious" which is "the storehouse of all possibility," "the principle of creativity . . . where is deposited the moving forces of the universe" (242–243). Although successful haiku should reflect and have the inherent capability to propel us to the level of the Cosmic Unconscious, the reader in activating a haiku may or may not tap all these levels of understanding.

Indeed, not all readers' experiences will necessarily be uniform or even similar, nor is this the author's intent. The goal is not to understand the author, to "get" the author's meaning, but to move beyond the words on the page and experience natural, underlying harmonies that are part of our primal memory—to create life from static words.

In a haiku like the following from *Matsushima,* for example, the awareness it recalls, the certain perspective on natural experience, stimulates in the reader endless connective memories of other instances of similar awareness:

<blockquote align="center">

cedar cones
tumble in a mountain stream
letters from home
([23])

</blockquote>

In the first two lines, Vizenor simply visually describes a natural scene allowing us to imagine it photographically. In the final line of the haiku, however, Vizenor suggests a perspective that nudges the reader out of his or her observer status and gives him the role of discoverer. With the phrase "letters from home," Vizenor offers an image of the chain of natural relationships observable in nature and the potential for discovery; he offers a cultural interpretation of a natural phenomenon. The cedar cones may have tumbled into the mountain stream from one natural setting (perhaps even from a cedar grove familiar to the writer) and arrived by water at another place only to be discovered by him there. Thus, they become "letters from home," remindful as they are of another place or environment, a different order. The responses of the reader might then entail memories of the multiple other instances when scents, sounds, or sights have in the past caused that same thrill of recognition.

A second kind of recognition awakened by the closing line in the haiku is that of the movement or life in nature. Although we may see something in nature hundreds of times, if we view it only in tableau our view is limited. In the poem, the last line recounts that moment when something startles us into an awareness of the interconnections within the moving cycle of nature. The discovery about the cedar cones might be not only where they come from but the realization of how they travel from place to place or how the trees might spread to new locales. With the final line, the haiku incites us to recall the moments when the surprise of such discoveries in nature have caused us to look around inadvertently for a presence or have accelerated the beating of our heart. The heightened intensity of the moments these haiku create or recall comes from awareness of life unseen, which always affects us more readily than the seen because it involves greater potential for discovery and ultimately leaves our expectations aroused. Vizenor depicts another such moment in *Raising the Moon Vines* with the following haiku:

> Under the crossing log
> Fresh openings in the ice
> Haloed with footprints.
> (89)

The poem obviously describes markings left by an animal that had come to the water to drink. But by describing the markings as "under the crossing log" (therefore not as readily observable) and the openings as "fresh," Vizenor heightens the sense of discovery and the awareness of vital processes occurring literally under our noses. By employing the connotations of "halo" and using the word as verb, not noun, he implies a sacred quality or aura and links that with the activities not the tableau of natural life.

The invitation inherent in Vizenor's haiku is to be a participant in such sacred activities. The distinction between observing and being engaged in is key in Zen and in a Native American perspective of life and literature for the idea of beholding nature automatically creates a division and sets up a subject/object relationship, making of nature a thing, not a being. We understand our true position in nature when the separation brought about by ego vanishes to the degree that we not only experience the "merging of the self with the other," but remain unaware of that oneness. When we become conscious of our altered state, we have already reverted to the isolation of self-absorption. Vizenor's po-etry, then, clearly reflects and requires not mere observation of but participation in nature. Recognizing the cycles that the fresh tracks or the tumbling cedar cones represent is not like passively observing physical creatures or elements in nature as abstracted "scenery" or conceptualized objects. We experience the reality of the cones, the tracks—a reality more spiritual than physical, more internal than external—because through what Suzuki called our Cosmic Unconscious we see in them the ultimate movement of all nature.

Although the sight of natural creatures—the flash of white tail as a doe leaps out of our sight, the porcupine that waddles off the path—inevitably excites the observer, the pleasure depicted in Vizenor's lines is more intense because it involves a moment of new awareness. Vizenor's haiku moment more clearly parallels our experience when we dis-cover not the creatures themselves, but the traces of them—the still-steaming scat in the snow, the trampled impression where deer had lain among the pines or the fresh animal tracks of the *Moon Vines* haiku. His is a moment of intuiting the hidden life beyond the evidence or the unraveling of one of the mysteries of nature. The verbalization of such an experience is not the "aahh" of delivered pleasure but the "ahah!" of active discovery. The moment is not closed out as it is when the physical animal leaps out of sight, but continues to haunt our every step because its connective possibilities are endless. Any discovery tends to increase our attentiveness to our surroundings and our susceptibility to additional discoveries. In various ways, then, the perspective on nature depicted in the foregoing haiku causes the realm of the poems to expand with the responses of the reader.

Indeed, haiku experiences are always subjective; readers will respond to the sug-gestiveness of haiku in their own way, to the degree that they are able. As Vizenor notes, "There isn't any predestination [in haiku]" (Blaeser 1987). For example, in the following haiku from *Matsushima* the three images allow for multiple levels of interpretation:

> sunday morning
> children waddle in the park
> geese to water
> ([70])

A reader might envision a scenario involving an after-church outing, with little girls in frilly dresses and their first shiny patent-leather shoes buckled across white, lacy anklets, and little boys in navy and white sailor suits. The baby plumpness of the children and their still-uneasy balance cause them to waddle like the geese they've come to feed. When the children run, inquisitive little hands outstretched to touch feathers and beaks, the geese retreat to the safety of their pond. Such an imaginative fleshing out of the poem's images, replete with squeals of delight and squawks of displeasure, would certainly create a vi-brant reader experience and fulfill the intentions of the form. However, the open text implies and allows for a bolder reading from a tribal worldview. The last two lines, "children waddle in the park / geese to water" seem to advertise an omission and compel the reader to make a connection: children waddle in the park / like geese to water; or to complete the symmetry: children waddle in the park / geese waddle to the water. This participation in the creation of the meaning results not in closure, but in the further opening of the text. By supplying the link or the echo in the lines, we are drawn to acknowledge the implied correspondences between the children and the geese. The children may be "playing" geese or "becoming geese" by imitating the motion of the gaggle. The lines might also imply similarities other than movement between the geese and the children: the ecstatic feeling of play, the lack of schooled restraint, and an intangible natural bond or earth connection. If we take these ideas further, through the tribal idea of the shared reality of different elements of creation, we can arrive at the idea of transformation or the possibility of a dream experience of being another creature. As these hypothetical readings illustrate, the possibilities of the interpretation or co-creation vary depending on the participation and identity of the reader.

Vizenor talks about these variations and acknowledges that while any person of any experience can find an entrance point in his haiku that can lead the reader to illumination, the implications for tribal readers may be more expansive. Vizenor employs the term "primal memory" (as opposed to the "racial memory" N. Scott Momaday has spoken of), but he does feel that, because of embedded cultural tradition and beliefs, most Native Americans have more ease of access to the realm of dreamscape via haiku.[5] The issue for Vizenor is not race but established patterns of thinking, what John Dewey call "funded experience": "those memories, not necessarily conscious, but retentions that have been organically incorporated in the very structure of the self" (1934:89). For tribal people, Vizenor explains:

What makes it unique . . . is it is only a few generations to our experiences of the past. And it's an immediate recognition of the kind of climate, topography, vegetation and climate. I mean it's in the genes if it can be. And it's in the language and the vocabulary. It [primal memory] is a little more focused and direct. That's awfully mystical, but there is . . . a source of energy there. (Blaeser 1987)

Thus, in many cases a person's earth connections and intuitions may have been further honed by the location, activities, and belief systems of tribal cultures, while they may have been dulled by disuse or weakened by the skepticism of science in mainstream cultures. And because haiku thought is frequently grounded in seasonal associations, the more familiar the associations to the reader, the more readily he or she can create with them.[6]

VIZENOR'S "STREET DANCER": THE TRICKSTER VOICE IN HAIKU

Although sensuous nature imagery characterizes much of Vizenor's haiku, his poems do not deal exclusively with humankind's experience of or interaction with the natural world.

Vizenor talks about the range and voices of his poetry in his introduction to *Matsushima,* and he identifies what he calls "the soul dancer in me" who, in his haiku, "celebrates transformations and intuitive connections between our bodies and the earth, animals, birds, ocean, creation" ([6]); he also identifies other "interior dancers" involved in his haiku. Among these other voices, the one most prominent in his work is the "street dancer" who, he says, "is the trickster, the picaresque survivor in the wordwars, at common human intersections, in a classroom, at a supermarket, on a bus" ([6–7]). However, because both Zen and a tribal worldview see humankind not only as involved with but also as a part of nature, as Otsuji notes, "Human affairs as they appear in haiku are not presented as human affairs alone" (Yasuda, 44). We find this "street dancer," for example, in poems that have as their subject the human relationship to the larger world, unusual intersections between human nature and the natural world, and unusual intersections between civilization or technology and nature. This "trickster" frequently appears in the haiku, which offer illuminating twists on the way we perceive ourselves or in those which challenge our overserious or isolationist view of our actions.

Take, for example, this poem from *Empty Swings:*

> Newspapers are piled
> Day by day under the window
> Raising the cat.
> (1967:[50])

Vizenor takes a mundane, seemingly inconsequential, daily action and suddenly shows it to have impact on another living creature. I doubt that the poem intends to provoke any sustained thought about the cat whose perch is inadvertently raised day by day by the action of his or her human companion. Instead, I imagine its value to lie in the wry comment it makes on our failure to concern ourselves with the larger relationships and the larger consequences of our actions. I see no note of indictment in the haiku; rather, I see a playful and harmless little jab at our self-centeredness meant to jar us, if only momentarily, from our habitual monocular viewpoint. Vizenor's haiku in the voice of the trickster or the "picaresque survivor" definitely calls us to reconsider our narrow views. Consider this poem that gives title to the *Seventeen Chirps* collection:

> It took seventeen chirps
> For a sparrow to hop across
> My city garden
> ([47])

This haiku seems intended to nudge us toward a new perspective on how we evaluate by enumerating—even when the event ill suits enumeration. Of course, the larger implication probably involves how much we miss by insisting on applying our standards of judgment to all we encounter. Or consider how the following haiku challenges our feeling of superiority over other creatures by grouping the egotistical human, as represented by the poet, with the lowly beast, as represented by the cow. It shows both creatures as equally subject to the rough track of the pasture and the pestilence of the flies. Operating as "a great equalizer," this haiku depicts both human and beast at the same action:

> Through knobby pasture
> Both the poet and the cow
> Swishing flies away.
> (1964b:52)

In his haiku Vizenor employs many of the same methods to shake up the self-satisfied reader that the traditional tribal trickster tales used to reproach wayward tribal members. For example, the tribal tales frequently worked to enlighten the audience to their own flaws by exposing the ludicrousness of the trickster's actions; so, too, does the trickster voice of Vizenor's haiku employ this same tactic. Note that the following haiku from *Empty Swings* has as its nominal subject the imagined complaints of mice:

> Sliding in the loft
> The mice complained all Winter
> About the coarse hay
> ([26])

However, by projecting a typical (and unflattering) human reaction onto the mice, Vizenor really highlights the silliness of our own petty complaints and dissatisfactions. In another haiku from the same collection, Vizenor offers a similar perspective of mundane human complaints and a comment not only on humanities' pettiness, but perhaps on the practice of making petty complaints pass as poetry:

> Poet at the fence
> Would horses write about their burden
> Apple cores and blinders.
> ([63])

But in each haiku, Vizenor administers his mild reprimand with humor, much as a favorite uncle might tease or tickle a pouting child into better spirits.

But whether achieved through humorous or solemn means, the instant of revelation remains key in Vizenor's poems. Barbara Babcock has characterized trickster literature as having an "evaluative" function, "contributing to a reexamination of existing conditions and possibly leading to change" (180). Note how each of the following Vizenor haiku reveals something startling about the society humankind has created and, by so doing, questions the justice or wisdom of such a social arrangement:

> The old man
> Admired the scarecrow's clothes
> Autumn morning.
> (1964a:[4])

> Against the zoo fence
> Zebras and Sunday school children
> Hearing about Africa.
> (1967:36)

The first, of course, depicts both the tragic social and economic imbalance of society and indicts a throwaway culture that shows so little compassions for the poor in our midst. The second registers the irony of a zoo system devised by our consumer culture that results in creatures unfamiliar with their own "natural habitats," and it depicts both human and animal as equal exiles.

Both haiku work to actualize the experience of the poem through the creation of a moment of unbalance. Their unusual perspectives startle the words into life and thus lead the reader to contemplate more than the scene depicts and to invite a reevaluation of conditions. The moments of illumination in Vizenor's haiku may vary in type and intensity from the new twist offered by a trickster perspective to the spiritual reverberations activated by a natural encounter, but they all stem from the open quality of the text, involve the engagement of the reader, and inevitably outstrip the written words.

"OJIBWAY HAIKU—IN SONG"

The same method surfaces in Vizenor's transcription and reexpressions of Ojibway dream songs. Both in the rhetoric he uses to explain the working of the song poems and in the form of their actual translation, many similarities to his views and techniques of haiku surface.

In his introduction to his translations or reexpressions of the poems, Vizenor describes "the song poems of the *anishinaabeg*" as "imaginative events, magical and spiritual flights, and intuitive lyrical images of woodland life" (1981:11). Note that he sees dream songs, like haiku, as relying on imagination and intuition and involving images of woodland life. His reference to them as "events" and "magical and spiritual flights" is similar to his descriptions of haiku as "word cinemas" and "traces on the wind" (1984a:[7 and 1]). Vizenor also says the Anishinaabeg song poetry is

a sympathy of cosmic rhythms and tribal instincts, memories and dream songs, expressing the contrasts of life and death, day and night, man and woman, courage and fear. (1981:13)

Again the descriptive phrases here bear a striking resemblance to those Vizenor uses in discussing haiku. He speaks of "cosmic rhythms," "tribal instincts," and "memory" in this introduction to the dream songs; he speaks of "natural harmonies" and "primal memories" in his introduction to haiku (1984a:[5]). In describing dream songs, he speaks of "contrasts"; in describing haiku, he speaks of "tension" (1984a:[4]). Finally, in his introduction to the lyric poems, Vizenor credits dreams with achieving a connection "between the conscious and unconscious worlds of the people" (1981:11) just as he credits haiku with bringing about "transformation" and "a moment of enlightenment." The correlation between Vizenor's descriptions of each only confirms his evaluation of their similar forms, philosophies, and intentions.

His methods of expressing them in words is likewise similar as illustrated by the following pair of dream songs:

> with a large bird
> above me
> i am walking
> in the sky
>
> i entrust
> myself
> to one wind.
> (1981:35)

Note how each employs the same economy of words and makes the same kind of demands on the reader's imaginative powers as do Vizenor's haiku. Note, also, how our expectations are undercut in the same manner as in the haiku. For example, in the first song, the opening three lines might cause us to envision a man walking and looking up to watch a bird as it flies. But the last line surprises us by locating the man "in the sky." We are thus called to displace our conventional thinking, just as we were in Vizenor's haiku. The possibilities for interpretation are left open, much as they were in the haiku about the children and the geese. We may understand the dream song in terms of imaginative experience, dream experience, or transformation. In any case, our engagement in the song has undoubtedly transported us beyond the simple phrases of the text to the "visual dreamscape" experience likewise achieved by the haiku. The correlation is complete.

Another example from among Vizenor's reexpressions of tribal dream songs serves to emphasize the "funded experience" or the knowledge presupposed on the part of the hearer or reader and the imaginative demands made by the song:

> two foxes
> facing each other
> sitting
> between them
> (1981:34)

The breathtaking quality of this song poem only becomes apparent if the reader/listener has some experience or understanding of foxes on which to draw. Visually, the image multiplies in intensity with knowledge of the penetrating quality of a fox's gaze. Add to this visualization a familiarity with the fleet movement the creatures are capable of, familiarity with the sometimes playful wrestling the young especially engage in with one another, and knowledge of the animals' instinctive avoidance of human contact, and the first two lines—"two foxes / facing each other"—set up an expectation of impending motion. Taken in this context, the last lines—"sitting / between them"—implies an unlikely and therefore extraordinary experience on the part of the singer. Whether we take that experience to be physical, spiritual, imaginative, or some combination of these, an appreciation of its uniqueness can come about only as the reader imaginatively fleshes out the words of the song poem with the help of an understanding both of foxes and of the realm of magical possibilities available to a tribal person who is in the appropriate state of mind. Like the haiku, the song poem only suggests; the reader creates: she or he first imagines and then experiences.

HAIKU IN PROSE: BASHO'S *HAIBUN*

Just as Vizenor's early involvement with the haiku form, philosophy and methods undoubtedly affected his reexpressions of tribal dream songs, it has left its mark on most of his subsequent writing as well. Vivid nature imagery, building by suggestion, tension created by unusual juxtapositions, trickster consciousness, reader engagement—all of these traits surface again and again in Vizenor's work as methods to move beyond the written text itself.

Certain prose passages in Vizenor's writing greatly resemble his haiku and function in much the same way. The following prose statement is from Vizenor's first novel *Darkness in St. Louis Bearheart:* "The ritual of a spider building his web on the wind. . . . That is survival!" (1978:187). The following haiku is from his *Seventeen Chirps* collection:

> Patient spider
> Day after day in the wind bottle
> Building his web.
> ([30])

The extremely similar images used in each of the passages set up reverberations that extend well beyond an understanding of the spider's life: although the haiku does not name but instead embodies the quality of continuance, the revelation of each is about the spirit and deepest meanings of survival.

Here and elsewhere we can see in certain lines of Vizenor's prose what Makoto Ueda, in talking about the prose of haiku master Basho, called *haibun:* a kind of prose "written in the spirit of haiku" (Vizenor 1984a: [10]). For example, also from Vizenor's *Darkness in Saint Louis Bearheart*, come these passages:

We speak the secret language of bears in the darkness here, stumbling downhill into the fourth world on twos and fours, turning underwords ha ha ha haaaa in visions. *The bear is in our hearts. Shoulders tingle downhill on dreams.* The darkness moves through us in ursine shivers. (vii, italics mine)

Cedarfair circus in the morning. Clown crows. Incense from moist cedar. Time turns under the warm figures of breathing. Moths and the sound of dew coming down the fern and pale waxen faces on popular [*sic*] leaves near the river. (1, italics mine)

Both italicized sections report images in the same succinct fashion as Vizenor's haiku; both suggest, by juxtaposition, connections between the phrases; and both rely for their meaning on the engagement and participation of the reader. As they imply a connection with certain tribal ideas or experiences in nature, the reader's own knowledge of these things must be plumbed in order to arrive at the full significance of the passages. The first italicized passage involves the tribal ideas of dream vision, guardian spirit, and transformation. The second assumes an understanding of the position and role of animals in tribal culture and also contains references to the role of the clown, to the cleansing power of cedar smoke, and to the ceremony of sunrise prayer.

Let me comment more fully on the second passage as the better example of the haiku since it has the standard seventeen-syllable, three-line form (although Vizenor does not confine himself to this form even in his haiku poetry) and analyze it more completely. I see the movement in this passage working in a fashion similar to that of many of Vizenor's haiku, with the first two lines setting a scene and the last changing the quality of that scene. Here in the prose, the line "Cedarfair circus in the morning" evokes a sense of time and place: morning at Cedarfair circus (which, in the larger context of the book, we know to be a large circle of cedar trees near a river). The second line, "Clown crows," adds the presence of animal life with the word "crows" and implies a tribal consciousness by imparting to the birds a significant role with the epithet "clown." Many ideas are taken for granted in the application of such a title—the possibility of human-animal transformation, the illusory nature of physical forms, the possibility of reciprocal human-animal relationships, and the importance of the role of clown or trickster—all of which establish a tribal milieu. The last line, "Incense from moist cedar," could conceivably be taken merely as sensory description, adding the smell of cedar to the scene. But, considering the previous implications of tribal significance, I think the line turns on the universal connotations of the word "incense" combined with the tribal connotations of the word "cedar." Incense carries with it the suggestion of religious ceremony, and cedar smoke or incense is used for purification in tribal rites. Thus, taken together, the lines conjure something more than just an experience of early morning in a cedar grove. When the smell of damp cedar in the morning awakens in the writer/reader the memory of incense or becomes incense, the significance of the experience intensifies to take on religious dimensions. The passage may work to expose an innate connection between the natural and the religious. Or perhaps the last line may intend to transform the scene and recall the solemn morning rite of sunrise prayer.

In any case, the similarities between prose of this sort, Vizenor's reexpressions of dream songs, and his haiku are apparent. All work to invite the reader to break through the boundaries of print and find the essential experience beyond the words. As Suzuki has noted: "With all the apparatus of science we have not yet fathomed the mysteries of life. But, once in its current, we seem to be able to understand it" (24). The task of haiku in Vizenor's style is to thrust us into "the current of life" where we can find for ourselves a moment of understanding—of enlightenment.

Vizenor has bound in the form and philosophy of the "open text" of his haiku multiple traditions: traditions of both writing and speaking, of postmodern and tribal aesthetics, and of Native American and Japanese cultures. Such a linkage seems a fit illustration of the ultimate "nexus of infinite interrelationships" (Suzuki 1959:349) haiku profess to uncover.

NOTES

1. Vizenor does, however, offer explanatory notes for many of the songs, some of which include quotations and pieces of information offered in Densmore's original.

2. Vizenor accepts and bases his own reexpressions on the work of Densmore. Note, for example, how close is the language of the following version of one dream song the second version of which is Vizenor's: "as my eyes search / the prairie / I feel the summer in the spring" and "as my eyes / look across the prairie / I feel the summer in the spring." In one of his dream song collections Vizenor describes Densmore as "one of the most sensitive musicologists and ethnologists working with the anishinaabeg" (1981:19). He has spoken "in praise of Densmore" calling her work "brilliant and honest" and describing her efforts to somehow record not only the songs themselves, but the musical notations and the song pictures as well: "No one," he says, "has done a work as honest with such dedication as hers. She recorded, transcribed, transliterated and translated" (Blaeser 1987).

If the accuracy of Densmore's work is challenged (as it is in Evers and Molina's *Yaqui Deer Songs*), then Vizenor's "reexpressions," of course, become suspect as well. However, even if the translations are not sound word for word, certain key characteristics do surface and the intentions and practice of creating dream songs can themselves be compared to the intentions and practices of haiku art.

3. In Vizenor's haiku method, as well as in his broader literary theory and practices, many connections can be made to the reader-response aesthetics of the postmodernist school of criticism. I explore these interrelationships in *Gerald Vizenor: Writing—in the Oral Tradition*.

4. The movement in this haiku can be compared to that of a poem by seventeenth-century haiku master Basho, a haiku that is recognized by many as the one which gave birth to the present school of haiku poetry. One translation of Basho's poem reads: The old pond, ah! / A frog jumps in: / The water's sound. The dynamics of this poem as analyzed by both Daisetz Suzuki (1959:227–229, 238–240) and Donald Keene (1955:38–39) include a collision between the tranquility of the ancient pond (standing for the "eternal and the constant") and the disruptive sound of

the loud splash of water (standing for "the momentary"). The imaginative experience of the collision then results in an awareness of the point of intersection (of the eternal and the momentary) "on the other side of eternity, where timeless time is"; and thus leads to an understanding of the unity of the two worlds—the "sensual" and the "supersensual."

5. Matthias Schubnell (1985:54) talks about Momaday's idea of racial memory and the various terms he employs to describe it: "Momaday uses several terms to describe the extension of individual memory into anteriority: 'blood memory' or 'blood recollection,' 'whole memory,' 'memory of the blood,' and 'racial memory.' They all describe a verbal dimension of reality which perpetuates cultural identity."

Vizenor, however, says, "I think there is something going on there, too, but I would rather go for a larger collective unconscious. . . . I had a time with that—[the] racial unconscious. I think we can draw more immediate, closer environmental experience which is racial, but I'm less about it [race] than I am about an intersection in the world" (Blaeser 1987).

6. Suzuki, for example, comments: "The images thus held up and arranged in a haiku may not be at all intelligible to those whose minds have not been fully trained to read the meanings conveyed therein" (243).

Vizenor notes how important a sense of place can be in the rendering of haiku and notes how the natural and seasonal qualities vary with location (Blaeser 1987). The haiku images, he says, "set up possibility," and he compares them to the "naming of a town." The images reveal "the place, the time, the relationship so we can understand." He says, for example, "If I say winter in Minnesota, you know there's a connection visually and by experience."

Many others have taken up this idea of the place specific quality of primal knowledge. For example, in *The American Rhythm*, Mary Austin advances the idea of the "landscape line" which acknowledges a concrete connection between environment and literary rhythm and form (1923), and James Ruppert uses the term "geographical determinism" to describe a similar relationship in "Discovering America: Mary Austin and Imagism" (1983). In his essay "Landscape and Narrative," Barry Lopez claims, "the shape of the individual mind is affected by land as it is by genes" (1989).

REFERENCES

Astrov, Margot, ed. 1946. "Introduction" to *American Indian Prose and Poetry: An Anthology*, 3–72. New York: Capricorn Books.

Austin, Mary. 1924. "Review of *Dawn Boy* by Edna Lou Walton." *Saturday Review of Literature* 10 April.

———. 1970 [1923]. *The American Rhythm: Studies and Reexpressions of Amerindian Songs*. New York: Cooper Square Publishers.

———. 1972 [1918]. *American Indian Poetry: An Anthology of Songs and Chants*. In *Literature of the American Indians: Views and Interpretations. A Gathering of Memories, Symbolic Contexts, and Literary Criticism*, edited by Abraham Chapman 266–275. New York: New American Library.

Babcock, Barbara. 1985. "'A Tolerated Margin of Mess': The Trickster and His Tales Reconsidered." In *Critical Essays on Native American Literature,* edited by Andrew Wiget, 153–185. Boston: G. K. Hall.

Blaeser, Kimberly. 1987. Personal interview with Gerald Vizenor, 27–29 May. This series of interviews was conducted at the University of California–Berkeley. All of the formal sessions were tape recorded and later transcribed. Funding was provided by the University of Notre Dame Graduate School through a Zahm Research Travel Grant.

Bowers, Neal, and Charles L. P. Silet. 1981. "An Interview with Gerald Vizenor." *Melus,* Spring 8.1:41–49.

Britton, Dorothy. 1980. "Introduction" to *A Haiku Journey: Basho's "Narrow Road to a Far Province."* Tokyo and New York: Kodansha International.

Bruchac, Joseph. 1987. "Follow the Trickroutes: An Interview with Gerald Vizenor." *Survival This Way: Interview with American Indian Poets,* 287–310. Tucson: University of Arizona Press.

Brumble, H. David, III. 1988. *American Indian Autobiography.* Berkeley: University of California Press.

Castro, Michael. 1983. *Interpreting the Indian: Twentieth-Century Poets and the Native American.* Albuquerque: University of New Mexico Press.

Chamberlain, B. H. 1910. *Japanese Poetry.* London: John Murray.

Day, A. Grove. 1964 [1951]. *The Sky Clears: Poetry of the American Indians.* Lincoln: University of Nebraska Press.

Densmore, Frances. 1972 [1910]. *Chippewa Music, Vol. I.* Bureau of American Ethnology Bulletin no. 45. New York: Da Capo Press.

———. 1972 [1913]. *Chippewa Music, Vol. II.* Bureau of American Ethnology Bulletin no. 53. New York: Da Capo Press.

Dewey, John. 1934. *Art as Experience.* New York: Mentor, Balch.

Evers, Larry, and Felipe S. Molina. 1990. *Yaqui Deer Songs/Maso Bwikam: A Native American Poetry.* Tucson: Sun Tracks—University of Arizona Press.

Fletcher, John Gould. 1947. "Introduction" to *A Pepper Pod.* New York: Knopf.

Glauber, Robert. 1965–1966. "Review of *Summer in the Spring* by Gerald Vizenor." *The Beloit Poetry Journal,* Winter 16.2:39.

Griffin, Susan. 1978. *Woman and Nature: The Roaring Inside Her.* New York: Harper and Row.

Jahner, Elaine. "Heading 'Em Off At the Impasse: Native American Authors Meet the Poststructuralists." Unpublished essay, 1987.

Keene, Donald. 1955. *Japanese Literature: An Introduction for Western Readers.* New York: Grove Press.

Kroeber, Karl. 1979. "Deconstructionist Criticism and American Indian Literature." *boundary 2,* Spring 7:72–87.

Krupat, Arnold. 1987. "Post-Structuralism and Oral Tradition." In *Recovering the Word: Essays on Native American Literature,* edited by Brian Swann and Arnold Krupat, 113–128. Berkeley: University of California Press.

Lopez, Barry. 1989. "Landscape and Narrative." In *Crossing Open Ground.* New York: Vintage.

Rexroth, Kenneth. 1961. "American Indian Songs: The United States Bureau of Ethnology Collection." In *Literature of the American Indians: Views and Interpretations. A Gathering* of Indian Memories, Symbolic Contexts, and Literary Criticism, edited by Abraham Chapman. New York: New American Library.

Ruoff, A. LaVonne Brown. 1990. *American Indian Literatures: An Introduction, Bibliographic Review, and Selected Bibliography.* New York: Modern Language Association.

Ruppert, James. 1983. "Discovering America: Mary Austin and Imagism." In *Studies in American Indian Literature: Critical Essays and Course Designs*, edited by Paula Gunn Allen. New York: Modern Language Association.

Sandburg, Carl. 1917. "Review of *Chippewa Music.*" *Poetry: A Magazine of Verse* 9 (February).

Schubnell, Matthias. 1985. *N. Scott Momaday: The Cultural and Literary Background.* Norman: University of Oklahoma Press.

Simonson, Rick, and Scott Walker. 1988. "Introduction." *Graywolf Annual Five: Multi-Cultural Literacy.* St. Paul, Minn.: Graywolf Press.

Suzuki, Daisetz T. 1959. *Zen and Japanese Culture.* Princeton: Princeton University Press.

Swann, Brian. 1988. "Introduction." *Harper's Anthology of 20th Century Native American Poetry*, edited by Duane Niatum. San Francisco: Harper & Row.

Underhill, Ruth M. 1985 [1979]. *Papago Woman.* Prospect Heights, Ill.: Waveland Press.

Vizenor, Gerald. 1962. *Two Wings the Butterfly: Haiku Poems in English.* St. Cloud, Minn.: Privately published.

———. 1964a. *Seventeen Chirps: Haiku in English.* Minneapolis: Nodin Press.

———. 1964b. *Raising the Moonvines: Original Haiku in English.* Minneapolis: Nodin Press.

———. 1965. *Summer in the Spring: Lyric Poems of the Ojibway.* Minneapolis: Nodin Press.

———. 1966a. "The Ojibway." *Twin Citian*, May 8.10:18–19.

———. 1966b. *Slight Abrasions: A Dialogue in Haiku.* With Jerome Downes. Minneapolis: Nodin Press.

———. 1967. *Empty Swings: Haiku in English.* Minneapolis: Nodin Press.

———. 1970. *anishinabe nagomon: Songs of the People.* Minneapolis: Nodin Press. A revised edition of *Summer in the Spring* (1965).

———. 1972. "Tribal People and the Poetic Image: Visions of Eyes and Hands." *American Indian Art: Form and Tradition*, 15–22. Minneapolis: Walker Art Center.

———. 1978. *Darkness in St. Louis Bearheart.* St. Paul: Truck Press.

———. 1981. *Summer in the Spring: Ojibway Lyric Poems and Tribal Stories.* Minneapolis: Nodin Press. A revised edition of materials earlier published in *Summer in the Spring* (1965), *anishinabe adisokan* (1970), and *anishinabe nagamon* (1970).

———. 1984a. *Matsushima: Pine Islands.* Minneapolis: Nodin Press.

———. 1984b. *The People Named the Chippewa: Narrative Histories.* Minneapolis: University of Minnesota Press.

Yasuda, Kenneth. 1957. *The Japanese Haiku: Its Essential Nature, History, and Possibilities in English, with Selected Examples.* Rutland, Vt. and Tokyo: Charles E. Tuttle.

MYTH, HISTORY, AND IDENTITY IN SILKO AND YOUNG BEAR
Postcolonial Praxis

David L. Moore

"To believe otherwise,"
as my grandmother tells me,
"or to simply be ignorant,
Belief and what we were given
to take care of,
is on the verge
of ending . . . "

(4)

T he sense of historic tragedy in these lines by Ray Young Bear is complicated by their rhetorical ambiguity. Is Young Bear saying that "belief . . . is on the verge of ending" or that "to believe otherwise . . . is on the verge of ending"? As he forces the English language to follow the uneasy valences of his experience, where is this Iowa poet, a native speaker of Mesquakie, in relation to either the affirmative or the tragic option? We shall see how Young Bear uses the gap between a dominant history received as inevitable and a mythic history which transcends that inevitability to generate a key dynamic in the poems. He negotiates that gap largely by drawing on and extending the mythic histories of his own Mesquakie traditions.

In a similarly multidimensional positioning of the voice, Leslie Silko writes:

Thought-Woman, the spider,
    named things and

    as she named them
      they appeared.

She is sitting in her room
    thinking of a story now

I'm telling you the story
    she is thinking.
        (1)

Silko's voice in this text moves among vectors of agency between her Laguna Pueblo myth and her contemporary moment. Like Young Bear, she deconstructs divisions between historical possibilities and impossibilities of Native American experience, reopening doors of cultural identity. As we shall see, their works multiply the available positions of postcolonial subjects.

Silko's broadly popular novel *Ceremony* treats the concern for cultural and subjective survival through a mythopoetic stream of consciousness, drawing on the tradition of Laguna storytelling to enter the experiences of both persons and mythic powers and to make them mutual participants. Her fluid narrative of a Native American veteran of World War Two weaves, as numerous critics have shown, a psychological landscape of intense and tightly knit language and imagery. The novel achieves a nearly apocalyptic appeal.

Ray Young Bear's much quieter presence strangely achieves a linguistic power parallel to Silko's more dramatic one. As we shall see, a paradox in Young Bear's voice arcs that power as both formal and casual, discursive and colloquial, communal and intensely personal. His lines are unique in their forceful, eclectic blend of native Mesquakie tradition, of highly charged dream imagery, of the details of contemporary American popular culture. Out of this unusual voice, Young Bear's second collection, *The Invisible Musician,* generates insights into cultural struggle and subjectivity.

Two quandaries, subjectivity and agency (who am I, and what can I do about it?), shape the stakes of this study of Silko and Young Bear. These issues of nature, nurture, and free will divide Western modern from postcolonial postmodern thinkers, and these two writers offer creative voices to the discussion.[1] Such questions of subjectivity and agency may be rephrased, respectively, as issues of essentialism and of the imperial self, issues for which feminist theory has provided useful vocabularies. Linda Alcoff, in "Cultural Feminism Versus Post-Structuralism: The Identity Crisis in Feminist Theory," charts the theoretical drift:

Lacan uses psychoanalysis, Derrida uses grammar, and Foucault uses the history of discourses all to attack and "deconstruct" our concept of the subject as having an essential identity and an authentic core that has been repressed by society. (163)

If a modern bourgeois agenda is the humanist reconstruction of "the self-contained, authentic subject," of a "privileged, separate consciousness" (Alcoff 1988:163), then criticism of it may be said to be a postmodern bourgeois agenda. Much of the postmodern project among the various children of Marx and Freud tries to mount another Copernican revolution against this claim to an authentic subject. In various ways, it shows how social constructions in systems of dialectical materialism, and psychological constructions in systems of psychoanalysis have fractured humanist views of individuality. In the context of such deconstructions, the efforts of Silko and Young Bear to apply their mythic traditions to contemporary experiences, supply not another attack on but an alternative to both that humanist discourse and that postmodern critique. We shall see how their narratives and imagery deconstruct a humanist essentialist identity and the claim that there is an authentic core by modeling a dynamic identity.

When "autonomous" agency is added to the Western individualistic concept of subjectivity, the imperial self is born, with drastic consequences for native cultures operating with less of this psychological imperialism propelling their individuals. Where agency on the part of an autonomous subject assumes mastery or territorial dominance, imperial ambitions follow from this subject construction. Thus, bolstered by economic, political, and ideological constructions, the autonomous hero of modern culture, from Robinson Crusoe to the Lone Ranger to Rambo, tries not only to establish individual identity as autonomy, but also singlehandedly "to take on the world."

And that world, paradigmatically, is the "New World," the "Other" World of non-European natives who have certain political investments in describing a different paradigm. The stakes are clear, and Native American writers thus share the theoretical agenda for a new approach to subjectivity. In colonial history, the Euroamerican image of individual autonomy has made invisible various alternative Native American identity constructs, and the tasks that Native American writers have set themselves often include critiques of an ideology of transparent individualism, while affirming instead a more relational agency.

Meanwhile, the contemporary academy, driven by internal and external pressures, explores some parallel possibilities for redefinitions of subjectivity along the lines Alcoff described above. It is useful then for the analytic and the imaginative to read each other for parallels between academic theoretical discourses and discourses of contemporary Native American literatures, to find places where their vocabularies suggest intersecting projects.

Because the critical discussion of subjectivity and agency is vast, I must risk some generalizations. On the one hand, modernists after Descartes and Kant have tended to respond to these two ancient issues with a claim to self-constructed identity and existential agency, in an isolated and heroic model of individuality. Postmodernists after Marx and Freud, on the other hand, have tended to respond to these questions with the claim of a socially constructed nexus of identifications and exertions, in a model which may either frantically mourn or radically celebrate the end of individuality. While modernists struggle for a resurrection of the authorial voice in the original text, postmodernists announce the death and burial of the author in the text of culture.

This outline of differences summons not only the polarities of nature versus nurture, not only essence versus difference, but also of power versus powerlessness. By the ways in which the modernists versus postmodernists have built their battle lines, there appears to be little theoretical middle ground between the tragic modern imperial self and the tragicomic postmodern pawn. Such Western choices appear to be autonomy or dependency, subjectivity or subjection, with both sides claiming the positive term.

In their distinct ways, however, Young Bear and Silko are among those who conceive alternative choices. As Elaine Jahner points out, "the major American Indian creative writers, and most of their critics" give us new critical angles on "the conception of the subject as the organizer and sense-maker of lived experience, and the challenges posed to forms of Western thought by the liberation movements" (182) of the postcolonial period.[2]

By Jahner's reckoning the international tradition of theoretical analysis will deepen and expand in exchange with Native American literatures (which of course are also international). "Within this international context," Jahner writes,

American Indian literature encompasses a range of practices and responses that is, in and of itself, a testing of these critical discourses, and engaging in that testing can refine the possibilities of the critical enterprise as well as adding new dimensions to the reading of American Indian literatures. (182)

Such a cross-cultural reading begins with a recognition of the historical differences surrounding issues of the subject. The ontology within Euroamerican colonialism has been concerned with agency within subjectivity. Native Americans, on the receiving end of that colonial history, have become concerned since contact more directly with agency within subjection. Indeed, a definition of the "postcolonial" might consist precisely in that distinction between agency growing out of subjection and agency growing out of subjectivity. To elude the dialectical subjection of colonial subjectivity, which would merely mirror the oppression, postcolonial agents must find what I will call a relational rather than oppositional concept of identity. "Relational" suggests a multiplicity rather than a duality of directions for subjectivity. A postcolonial task of native discourse becomes then a redefining of the multiple possibilities of the subject to elude subjection to dualistic, self-other ideas of subjectivity. It is a task of native discourse that has compelling significance for non-native discourse.[3]

The summons on the part of Jahner and numerous other scholars[4] to juxtapose creative native texts with critical theory for cultural and critical insights is an assertion based on more than a hope of happy outcomes. There is a theoretical rationale here which we can review briefly through particular aspects of Michel Foucault's discourse analysis.

Foucault's concept of "visibility" provides a theoretical vocabulary to explain cross-cultural openings toward new notions of subjectivity (and another of Foucault's notions, that of "alterity," will close the circle of critical discussion as well).

Foucault's "visibility" concept suggests an unwritten history of cultural and in-stitutional tunnel vision. The term offers a way of critiquing views of American history, of American Indians in American history, of American identity, and of literary and critical treatments of these histories, as framed by such "visibility" which allows certain defini-tions and not others. John Rajchman, in "Foucault's Art of Seeing," explains:

> Foucault's hypothesis was that there exists a sort of "positive unconscious" of vision which deter-mines not what is seen, but what *can* be seen. . . . A period only lets some things be seen and not others. (71)

By revealing the dynamics of visibility, Foucault attempts, in his words, "not to show (*faire voir*) the invisible, but to show the extent to which the invisibility of the visible is invisible" (74) to the uncritical eye. Rajchman explains,

> Seeing is important in Foucault's work as philosopher and historian in this sense as an art of trying to see what is unthought in our seeing, and to open as yet unseen ways of seeing. (74)

This art of seeing may be generalized to include attempts to contrast various texts with various theories, or indeed to set any empirical event against any hypothesis, but as we may expect Foucault includes in this "aesthetics of seeing" certain political implications for power relations. Thus we return to agency. Precisely because "visibility" creates institutional perceptions (80–83), and because cultural power is so imbricated in institu-tions, the uncritical may fail to see resistance to institutions as possessing power.[5] Instead, institutions see resistances as "marginal," and thus may miss their significance. The role of chroniclers of those resistances is then to make visible the pockets of power, of agency, available to "marginal" subjects, in order to make more visible the operative power relations.

The term "visibility," when applied to literature, thus can articulate the ways in which Young Bear and Silko build new social and theoretical constructions, by making visible new "practices of the self," another Foucaultian term. Following such new pos-sibilities, Rajchman connects the concept of visibility with freedom. Certainly we are bound by the limits of cultural visibility,

> But it [Foucault's theory of visibility] also shows that we are much *more* free than we think, since the element of visibility is also something that opens seeing to historical change or transformation. (72)

When cultures clash, visibilities play against each other. Intercultural confrontation may offer constructive choices precisely because visibility can change through that battle, and then clarify the formerly invisible specificity of differences. Foucault's concept of visibility suggests that the collisions of differences which bring about change, collisions that come about due to the invisibility of visibilities and that characterize a postcolonial era, may simultaneously result in the creation of new visibilities, of transformations in ways of seeing and possibilities for agency. The freedom of visibility becomes, in Young Bear and Silko, one dynamic for a different sense of agency by changing the visible field, by writers' very act of making visible the cultural subjectivity of "difference."

Yet the historically specific, Foucaultian dynamics of visibility also suggest that "new ways of seeing" are not necessarily new laws of perception nor universal principles which translate to other historic moments and circumstances than those which produced those visibilities. This grounding in particularity and difference is the strength of the notion of visibility rather than its weakness, especially against a contrary notion of assimilation or cooptation of difference. That notion of assimilation posits a monolithic system of capitalistic culture which both generates and coopts its own oppositions. Visibility seeks out the cracks of specific differences in that monolith, and thus permits political contestation.

Such contestation faces a monolithic colonial mentality that continues to operate at the end of the twentieth century. Non-Indian governmental entities on the local, state, and federal levels deny tribal identity and nationhood by denying tribal sovereignty, by fighting tribal jurisdiction in reservation counties, by continuing erosions of treaty rights to natural resources, to education, to economic development. The literary efforts of Native American writers often turn on these issues and attitudes, and within these political concerns, the primary politics being those of cultural survival.

Such a cultural battle stirs up difficult questions of self and other, of subjectivity and agency. The historical pressure of centuries of stereotypes can translate psychologically into nostalgia for a past that was created by those stereotypes. It can translate politically for American Indians into policies of tribal enrollment based on blood quantum rather than on traditional kinship systems. Bureaucratic definitions of tribal membership, in turn, can inflict their own psychic wounds, splitting families by quantitative rather than culturally qualitative measures. The treatment of such afflictions is much of the subject of Native American artists.

Drawing on both "oral" and "literary" traditions, Young Bear and Silko find a reversed Northwest Passage around the colonial paradox of self and other by invoking relational identities. Because they do not put forward a "position" on these issues, in the sense of a polemical thesis, I will use the more fluid theoretical term, "positionality," to describe their views. Within their separate historical and cultural terms, I would call their constructions of identity "mythic positionalities."[6]

Reading Young Bear and Silko, one can see the cultural battle for mythic positionality, for identity, emerging along a circular line of three principles with particular significance to the work of modern theorists in this postcolonial setting: first, relationality without a center; second, agency without mastery; third, combining and locating the former two, positionality without language.

RELATIONALITY WITHOUT A CENTER

In Silko's novel *Ceremony,* Laguna myths weave allegorically through the personal and cultural healing of Tayo, a mixed-blood Laguna Pueblo veteran of the Second World War. Set in the Southwestern desert, in the aftermath of the bomb of 1945, near the actual spot by Laguna where the uranium was mined for the Manhattan Project, the stakes of Tayo's quest are to find an alternative to the destructive cosmology of dualism, represented by "the witchery," which sets white against Indian, contemporary against traditional culture, and thus Tayo against himself. Subordinate to the Thought Woman myth, Silko constructs a myth of "witchery" to dramatize the colonial antinomies of North American history and culture, in which power-driven witches feed on and manipulate the destructive oppositions between Indian and white. The texture of Silko's work, by mixing prose narrative and verse myths, reinforces a dynamic of contemporary identity within the traditional myth. Such mythic allegories echo the plot, casting historical and psychological moments of the narrative into mythic time.

Across time and culture, various relational[7] currents of Indian history rise to the surface through Betonie, the Navajo shaman, in whom races, cultures, and generations interact. Indeed, changing cultural terms becomes Betonie's explicit role in the narrative, as he speaks of a process of colonial adaptation:

"You see, in many ways, the ceremonies have always been changing. . . . At one time, the ceremonies as they had been performed were enough for the way the world was then. But after the white people came, elements in this world began to shift; and it became necessary to create new ceremonies. I have made changes in the rituals. The people mistrust this greatly, but only this growth keeps the ceremonies strong." (132–133)

By Betonie's description and prescription, which deny autonomous cultures and autonomous individuals, identities of individuals and communities survive by their very interaction.

That interaction is both material and mythical. In the narrative, Tayo's body is literally painted into the myth: "He sat in the center of the white corn sandpainting. The rainbows crossed were in the painting behind him" (148–149). And within that myth, as within the narrative, he has a particular, dramatic role to perform.

Echoing the sandpainting technique on the page, Silko inscribes Tayo's mythic positionality typographically in the novel, as well as through images and narrative, by her strategies of verse structure woven into the prose. For instance, she sets narrative passages of Tayo's healing ceremony into the same page-centered verse lines, which weave mythic passages throughout the prose. Thus she gives Tayo's experience both the musical mode of the healing song and the mythical mode of the traditional context:

> I have the dew,
> a sunray falls from me,
> I was born from the mountain
> I leave a path of wildflowers
> A raindrop falls from me
> I'm walking home
> I'm walking back to belonging
> I'm walking home to happiness
> I'm walking back to long life.
>
> When he passed through the last hoop
> it wasn't finished
> They spun him around sunwise
> and he recovered
> he stood up
> The rainbows returned him to his
> home, but it wasn't over.
> All kinds of evil were still on him.
>
> (151)

The verse form structures his ritual experience in a mythic discourse. Similar verse lines also contain discourse of a different sort, not heightened, but colloquial and vulgar, structurally reflecting the mythic dimensions of even quotidian events in the narrative as equally part of the mythic song, breaking boundaries of sacred and profane:

> We went into this bar on 4th Ave., see,
> me and O'Shay, this crazy Irishman.
> We had a few drinks, then I saw
> these two white women
> sitting all alone . . .
>
> (59)

Silko's technique of drawing material events in a mythic tone matches Tayo's own efforts to finish the ceremony by finding the mythic dimensions to his own experience, thus healing cultural antinomies within himself and within his world.

Relational identity is both the structure and the substance of his ceremonial role, whereby Tayo takes responsibility for the relational dynamics of his own will, the rain, the land, the people. This mythic ecology, which revives Tayo and which Tayo revives, is not a static structure. From Betonie's descriptions of necessary changes in the ceremonies, we can see it as a complex of changeable differences united merely by the mutual context which they form:

He cried the relief he felt at finally seeing the pattern, the way all the stories fit together—the old stories, the war stories, their stories—to become the story that was still being told. He was not crazy; he had never been crazy. He had only seen and heard the world as it always was: no boundaries, only transitions through all distances and time. (258)

Such relationality, being "only transitions," offers no center, as we shall see. Let's turn now to Young Bear for a sense of his invocations of relationality as both more comic and more sombre than Silko's.

Ray Young Bear's poems in *The Invisible Musician* echo against a traditional musical framework of three Tribal Celebration Songs and four Mesquakie Love Songs published among the poems. An effect is to personalize the Mesquakie tradition. The poems reveal a conflicted relationality between Young Bear's ironic persona and his land, his culture, his Mesquakie people, and his American nation. Precolonial and postcolonial images are woven throughout. Mesquakie traditions such as stories of O Ki Ma, The Sacred Chief, or the presence of a spirit in a whirlwind, or the wise ramblings of Old Man Bumblebee, arise beside images of the Vietnam War Memorial, a California campus, cartons of Marlboro cigarettes, scenes of highway driving. Within Young Bear's musical frame of Mesquakie songs, his poems leap associatively across his idiosyncratic imagination, across his traditional Mesquakie culture, and across the contemporary landscape. The poet's voice expands into Mesquakie myth as he draws myths into his experience.

Young Bear's strong first-person persona generates textual complexities particularly distinct from Silko's third-person fiction. His poetic persona is pained, contemplative, incisive, in a steady personal voice that swells with contained emotions. Paradoxically, Young Bear often employs an impersonal discursive tone to create ironies of formal, polysyllabic, Latinate discourse against his informal, intimate imagery. The effect is to compress and intensify the personal experience which passes through that discourse. For instance, in "Language of Weather," as he watches an oncoming storm across the Iowa landscape, and as he reels with sensations and feelings, he also discusses principles of "austerity" and his own "importunity" in the face of those powers, summoning such abstract language to counteract the concrete language of his experience. Similarly, many of his titles make a point to summon a certain academic discourse while setting it in a personal and cultural frame: for example, "The Significance of a Water Animal," "The First Dimension of Skunk," or "Emily Dickinson, Bismarck, and the Roadrunner's Inquiry." One general effect of this mixing of discourses is to blur the more common boundaries of culture, while enormously expanding the range of the poetic voice.

A further effect is to blur the boundaries of time, where mythic time associated with Mesquakie traditions interpenetrates the contemporary autobiographical elements. This stanza from the long poem "Emily Dickinson, Bismarck, and the Roadrunner's – Inquiry" spans history with a dreamlike intimacy:

> The day I heard from you,
> I accidentally fell down the steps
> of a steamboat and lost consciousness,
> which was befitting because
> there was little rationale
> for the play (I had just watched
> onboard) of a man who kept
> trying to roll a stone uphill,
> a stone which wanted to roll downhill.
> I found myself whispering
> "No business politicizing myth"
> the moment I woke up.
> Gradually, in the form of blood
> words began to spill from
> my injuries: Eagle feathers
> 1–2–3 & 4 on Pipestone.
>
> (23)

Young Bear's ironic link between Sisyphus's rolling a stone uphill and the "business" of "politicizing myth" raises many questions of postcolonial culture, where mythic traditions look for political leverage in the world, for agency in subjection. The final image of words in the form of blood spilling from his injuries focuses that mythic power, in the sacred number of four eagle feathers, into the political force of his poetry. As pipestone, red catlinite, alludes to the sacred pipe and its invocatory powers, he returns to that traditional symbol whose emptiness is its mythic strength.

These complex images arise in a poem which mixes a fragmentary narrative of a lost love, who has apparently returned to her drunken husband, with expressions of personal affection for and critical distance from Emily Dickinson. The poem ends in a flood of emotions and interrelations:

> Mesmerized, she can only regret
> and conform to the consequences
> of an inebriate's rage
> while I recede from her
> a listless river
> who would be glad
> to cleanse and touch
> the scar the third mutant flower
> made as it now burns and flourishes
> in her arms.

> I would go ahead and do this
> without hint or indication
> you would accept me,
>
> Dear Emily.
>
> (26)

In terms of this discussion, the passage's relationality across time and space entirely blurs the boundaries of subject and object, of humans and nature, of persons.

In "The Suit of Hand," describing the hospitalized death of a relative, he generates such a sense of relationality by layering traditional tales and surrealistic images of the Mysterious Rat of death, of the Negative Parrot, and of Gita, the Danish nurse, all moving violently around the death bed. For all its conflicted drama, the final stanza assumes a proliferation and mixing of worlds, spiritual and material, traditional and postmodern, breaking up dualistic boundaries and opening multiple directions for identity processes:

> I feel trapped: like The Incorporeal Hand
> which wears the suit of a human hand,
> punching out to us violently from inside
> an empty grocery bag. The abundance of food—
> fruits and meats—has no deterring effect.
> No regard for the holidays. The whole thing
> reminds me of an Alfred Hitchcock movie.
> I taste the wind with my antennaes
> and regress at the sound of a crow's
> masculine howl.
>
> (28)

Those antennae might refer to a key player in the collection, old man Bumblebee. Young Bear often presents us with the traditional figure of Bumblebee, a comic and authoritative player who speaks to and through, and thus amplifies, the poet's voice.

Like the shaman Betonie in *Ceremony,* Young Bear's Bumblebee is a figure who explicitly and ritually navigates issues of subjectivity and agency. He carries relationality into a postmodern mode. We are never certain whether he is human or insect, and that is the point. Bumblebee could be clothed in either denim overalls or an exoskeleton. Either way, he "confesses that he sleeps / with earphones attached to his apian body" (32). Like Betonie, he locates the claim to a symbiosis of a native present and a native past, of history and myth, of time and timelessness.

We see such double motion carefully navigated in a scene of Bumblebee from the poem "A Drive to Lone Ranger":

> As he lights the candle on the mirrored
> sconce, he translates our thoughts.

"Adjusting and manipulating
the strings and pulleys
of the exterior/interior masks
requires work at all levels.
The best test is the supernatural:
how to maintain calmness during its
manifestation; to witness and experience it
as it simply is, rather than camouflage it through
rational explanation."

(34)

This interplay "of the exterior/interior masks" is the paradigm of relationality which underlies Bumblebee's crosscultural confidence and attentions. Bumblebee's sophisticated, high-tech obsessions chart relational experience on a cosmological map.

Over pheasant omelettes and wine
he offers an explanation about his obsession
with technology.
"It may seem a contradiction
but those cassette tapes on the wall
are the intellectual foundation
of my progeny."

(33–34)

In a voracious, Whitmanesque gesture, Bumblebee recklessly embraces technology, surrounding it with his own tradition, affirming a relational selfhood that reverses colonial vectors of opposition. He would draw the full catalog of possibilities into his nearly-imperial self. A startling link stretches here between biology and technology, between Indian culture and consumer capitalism, between the body and the machine of postmodern culture.

Such a valorization of technological power and culture apparently does not subdue Bumblebee or his progeny, who can act, can take pleasure in omelettes and wine, can choose technology without negating native cultural identity, precisely because there appears to be no discrete essence either to the body or to the machine.[8] Young Bear breaks down, in Donna Haraway's terms,

the deepened dualisms of mind and body, animal and machine, idealism and materialism in the social practices, symbolic formulations, and physical artifacts associated with "high technology" and scientific culture. (71)

Although technological momentum is depicted elsewhere in the book as conflicted, especially when the poem "Race of Kingfishers" refers to our "impending nuclear demise," Young Bear's Bumblebee does predicate body, culture, and even technology as interrelational. As the voice of Bumblebee can combine past and present without erasure of either, so this subject "interfaces" biology and technology, myth and history.

Yet relationality in Young Bear, as in Silko, is not simply a celebration of interaction, not an affirmation of a primary harmony, but a complex sense of entangling interdependence and painful responsibility with inevitable loss and risk. In the poem "A Drive to Lone Ranger," old man Bumblebee voices an ambivalent prophecy:

> "In time we'll become prosperous,
> or else we'll become martyrs
> protecting the vast resources
> of the Well-Off Man Mountains . . .
> The force that placed us here
> cannot be trusted."
>
> (34)

Such assertions, while increasing the drama, decrease the nostalgia of myth in the poems. Like the apocalyptic ramifications of the witchery narrative in *Ceremony,* where The Bomb has emerged from the witches' ritual grounds, Young Bear's mythic relationality threatens even a nuclear confrontation, a sort of ultimately homogenizing, entropic relationality. Thus the overriding relationality which implicates Bumblebee and his progeny, while it unifies, also threatens. A nexus of mutual responsibility may either nourish or destroy.

These risks of relationality in the poems between natural and human, between past and present, extend in the poetic context to relationality of cultures and cultural identities. To reimagine the subject after colonial subjection, writers must find ways to elude ethnocentric models of colonial subjectivity by imaging a nonessential, relational subject. Such a subject would elude the mercantilism of colonial subjectivity, where the economic center subjects everything to itself. Because that colonial center has historical reality, any attempt to evade, ignore, or define it away becomes merely a dialectic reversal, a mirror image, a trap. The challenge is to reestablish identity in broader relations than merely to that center, to invoke other centers, to establish multiple definitions of power which multiply the concept of center, perhaps infinitely. By definition, attempts to reconceive identity as relational must necessarily be nonoppositional in order to be postcolonial, since colonial identities were oppositional and territorial.

James Clifford makes visible such a distinction in *The Predicament of Culture.* He contrasts conceptions of culture which I would call dichotomous with relational ones:

Stories of cultural contact and change have been structured by a pervasive dichotomy: absorption by the other *or* resistance to the other. A fear of lost identity, a Puritan taboo on mixing beliefs and bodies, hangs over the process. Yet what if identity is conceived not as a boundary to be maintained but as a nexus of relations and transactions actively engaging a subject? The story or stories of interaction must then be more complex, less linear and teleological. (343)

By this reckoning, cultures and identities do not move in a simple, dichotomous dialectic through some eventual synthesis or continuous antagonism, as in the dominant paradigm. Clifford sees an alternative from a different cultural angle, without oppositional identities claiming adversarial centers or margins. His alternative "nexus of relations and transactions" considers history "from the standpoint of groups in which exchange rather than identity is the fundamental value to be sustained" (343).

By such economies of exchange, Young Bear's and Silko's histories of contact and nonopposition call into question the assumed assimilation processes for non-Western subjects, as they multiply our conceptions of identity and culture. Foucault has described such a conceptual shift toward a diversity of structures as an event which yields new "visibilities." In parallel, Silko describes Tayo's discovery of "No boundaries, only transitions through all distances and time." Marking the risks of such relational structures, Young Bear relates his grandmother's words, "'To believe otherwise,' / as my grandmother tells me, / 'or to simply be ignorant, / Belief and what we were given / to take care of, / is on the verge / of ending.'"

The second half of this first term, "relationality *without a center,*" arises in the literature where Young Bear's persona and Silko's Tayo both negotiate the lack of a static cultural identity. Adding a psychological logic to these questions of relational subjectivity, we can find valuable parallels to native literary representations of centerlessness in Lacanian post-Freudian discussions of the "gaze" and the "look."

Kaja Silverman's discussion of Jacques Lacan's model of the gaze makes visible a subject not simply "without a center," but a dynamic subject continuously emptying into and being filled by a relational process. She suggests a sort of nexus of identity which fills in the internal specifics of Clifford's model of interactive cultural identities.

In an analysis of Lacanian theory, Silverman gives us a specific vocabulary for the dynamics of a postcolonial subjectivity where, to summarize her complex discussion, she differentiates between "the look and the gaze." Lacan's specialized definitions place the "gaze" as the received "look." The look is associated with a dominating subject, the gaze with a dominated object. The gaze is located in and thus locates the object, whereas the look is located in the subject. Thus the look projects the subject's desire onto an object, while the gaze receives that desire on behalf of the object.

By such a formulation, one might expect postcolonial identity to reside in that object. However, through a discussion of the interpenetration of each of these poles, Silverman finally locates identity between them on Lacan's notion of an interactive perceptual "screen." Rather than in any subjective or objective center, rather than in the object of the gaze or in the subject of the look, identity is suspended between them as a dynamic image on a screen, where the look and the gaze both empty onto that projected image. The image screen then becomes the identity, as the intersection on which subject and object can both project their respective gaze and look.

Now a colonial subjectivity claims for itself the subject position, and hence the "look" side of this equation, while it projects the object position onto the colonized, who hence receive the "gaze." It becomes the postcolonial project not only to reverse the look and the gaze, not only to reverse subject and object, but to generate a different dynamic, to elude that screen. Silverman identifies the political project which applies to a number of Native American writers: "The possibility of 'playing' with these images then assumes a critical importance, opening up as it does an arena for political contestation" (76). "Playing," in Foucault's and Lacan's terms, suggests creating literary events which open up new visibilities, new images and screens, often by reversing the power relations in the look and the gaze. Such cultural and artistic play with relationality without a center thus envisions a politics against the autonomous subject, a politics built around that very relational subject construction which is its trigger and its target. The emptying subject allows for play in the social and artistic performance of new visibilities by relational subjects without a center.

For Silko's Tayo, emptying subjectivity takes place through the performance of a ceremonial act. Gradually he discovers his relationality without a center as "no boundaries, only transitions through all distances and time." Like Betonie in his postmodern hogan, Tayo eventually finds agency in the discovery of centerlessness, of an emptying cultural subjectivity: "in many ways, the ceremonies have always been changing." A dynamic rather than static view of his own culture leaves him culturally free to contribute to that change in the ceremony.

Young Bear's short poem, "Debut of the Woodland Drum," where he explicitly addresses the startling juxtapositions of a decentered relationality across space and time, will serve as coda to this introductory discussion of relationality without a center. The poem's title refers to the first tour by Young Bear's Woodland Drum Group, his troupe of traditional drummers and singers who perform on the national powwow circuit.

> At the place
> where Midwestern glaciers
> supposedly came to a stop,
> having created the last
> buttes and stone cliffs
> along the Mississippi
> (which would one day remind
> extraterrestrials of home planet
> and thus establish a colony
> in the name of Scandinavia),
> we listened to Debra Harry
> of Blondie sing ATOMIC
> four hours from Oneida,
> Wisconsin.
>
> (60)

Young Bear claims these geologic, sci-fi, colonial, pop, and small-town-American images for himself and his traveling group of traditional Native musicians, and avoids explicit reference to images of what might be expected popularly to convey "Native American" experience. His voice and his silent self-reference carry the irony of his "look" at these images, while the weighted term "supposedly" hints at that underlying irony. By framing the scene in geologic time, he asserts the indigenous claim to the stage. By equating Scandinavian immigrants and settlers with extraterrestrials, he exaggerates their secondary claim. By juxtaposing Blondie with such geology and history, he summons the pastiche that places the whole scenario on the edge of uncertainty and meaninglessness. And by his ruminating tone, he gives it all a sense of import, if not meaning.

While Young Bear claims these images for the indigenous speaker, he does so not by a simple reversal of look and gaze, because he keeps the looking subject silent. He does not offer some representative "Native American judgment" of the scene which he describes. Neither does he describe the Indian observers in the car. He leaves that subjective experience blank and silent in the poem. He neither articulates the subjectivity of that look, nor posits a desiring center to which those relational elements might return, and thus he avoids the language trap of a dichotomous subject/other, an antinomial trap sprung by the absorptive pressures of history. He allows the speaker's subjectivity to remain empty, emptying onto the landscape of images which empty into the speaker's look. The connections thus can proliferate, but they do so, in directions perhaps both of hope and despair, on the basis of a relationality which proliferates without a center. Instead of individual autonomy, the poem elicits surprising interdependence.

Such a relational world may raise laughter through juxtaposition of apparent incongruities, midwestern glaciers, Blondie, a powwow drum. But Young Bear's jokes complicate even the laughter in his poems. A surreal sense of incongruity mixes laughter into his mythic persona, yet in the relational world he constructs that laughter becomes multiple, laughing at the idea that people would laugh, that readers would find his leaping associations incongruous. Because his relationality disavows standard disjunctions between categories such as geology and rock stars, or between rock music and powwow music, it is the opposite of incongruity, which operates by disjunction. The laughter plays on the irony that what he ultimately posits as relationality seems at first to posit incongruity, and he exercises his poetic will by transforming incongruities into relationalities, challenging his reader to follow him. His laughter is thus integral to his relationality.

Relationality without a center, then, is not the popular, sentimental, primeval harmony of "Hiawatha," nor of "pro-Indian" efforts in Hollywood, nor even of environmental nativism, which in fact tend to reflect mirror images of the noble savage. Silko and Young Bear evidently affirm a harmony and relationality in their respective worlds, but each is careful to confront the dangers of responsibility, and the ironies which follow that interlinking of lives. De facto responsibility is the foundation of another function of identity, agency.

AGENCY WITHOUT MASTERY

"*Un autre savoir, un autre pouvoir*" ("Another knowledge, another power"). Foucault adjusts the Eurocentricity of the Baconian proverb, "knowledge itself is power," by inserting otherness to fit a postcolonial politics. Those who know the "other" position in a relational, intercultural arena may find an "other power" in that very otherness, precisely via the visibility which otherness makes possible through political play between the gaze and the look. When the colonial object redefines its own subjectivity in a context not focused on the colonial subject, this redistribution of power is an engine of agency without mastery which we can trace in *Ceremony* and *The Invisible Musician*.

In the ceremonial narrative of Silko's novel, both Betonie and Tayo invoke agency in choosing at various stages to change the ceremony or to reenact it, and so to shape their relational world. "This has been going on for a long time now. It's up to you. Don't let them stop you. Don't let them finish off this world" (160).

This freedom of choice has a complex effect on the novel's cosmology as it qualifies any overarching determinism and amplifies the undecidability. By determining outcomes through Tayo's own ambivalent, grasping actions, Silko allows for a larger indeterminacy. Such an idea echoes the Derridean assertion that freedom requires undecidability. In a Derridean universe, which here overlaps with the universes of these Native American writers, because things are not predetermined, subjects can exercise a freedom in determining their own choices. At the climax (which is anticlimactic), Tayo's freedom not only determines the immediate victory, but simultaneously confirms a larger indeterminacy. A longstanding hostility toward the hateful Indian character named Emo, a clandestine witch, reaches an unexpected end:

It had been a close call. The witchery had almost ended the story according to its plan; Tayo had almost jammed the screwdriver into Emo's skull the way the witchery had wanted. . . . Their deadly ritual . . . would have been completed by him. He would have been another victim, a drunk Indian war veteran settling an old feud. (265)

That other outcome of opposition appears just as likely except for Tayo's choice. Yet his choice sets the world in a new visibility. Silko sets the social construction of his optional role as "a drunk Indian war veteran" within a mythic construction of witchery, personified by Emo, which feeds on antinomies of colonial dynamics, of Indian hating white hating Indian. The defeated myth of witchery incorporates historically destructive, dualistic dynamics of the Euroamerican invasion, whereas Tayo works freely against that history as a mythic event. Thus the plot, his healing, and the mythic momentum all pivot in the climax around his decision not to continue "fighting with the destroyers" (134). His is a choice not to act within or between the antinomies but to move outside the dichotomous metanarrative. He thus clarifies his relational, nondualistic will against the witches' own mythic antinomial structure which would dichotomize culture and identity, Indian against white. Within the web of his relationality without a center, he exercises his limited agency.

Yet there is no question of mastery on Tayo's part, any more than on Betonie's. Contingency and indeterminacy echo around their responsibility to the land. Offsetting his relative freedom, his nexus of choice against the witches' myth is contained within imagery of a greater myth in ever larger "concentric shadows" (125):

> He had arrived at a convergence of patterns; he could see them clearly now. The stars had always been with them, existing beyond memory, and they were all held together there. . . . Accordingly, the story goes on with these stars of the old war shield; they go on, lasting until the fifth world ends, then maybe beyond. The only thing is: it has never been easy. (266)

If it had been easy, it would have been determined, and mastered.

Young Bear's voice finds limited agency in a landscape with similar dominating forces, whether malevolent spirits or historical powers. "The force that placed us here / cannot be trusted" (34). Such a threatening field requires responsibility, choice, agency on the part of Bumblebee's protectors of the land.

The most immediate limit to subjective agency is marked in Young Bear by the colonial presence of an oppressive power. The middle section of his poem, "First Dimension of Skunk," evokes that presence:

> Whoever constructed
> the two railroad tracks
> and highways through Indian land
> must have planned and known
> that we would be reminded daily
> of what is certainty.
> (37–38)

The bitter twist in reducing certainty to invasive technologies pivots on the struggle for agency. On the one hand, the struggle is already lost if railroad tracks and highways are the only certain thing. On the other hand, the struggle has just begun if that one certain thing opens a dialectic field of collapsing binaries, of indeterminate outcomes that subjective agency can choose to effect. Such a suggestion plays again on the Derridean construction that freedom requires indeterminacy.

Another passage from "Emily Dickinson, Bismarck, and the Roadrunner's Inquiry" expresses the risky, sometimes hilarious balance of this strength without omnipotence, as Young Bear describes "the philosophy / of being Insignificant" (23) (his use of the capital "I" bears the significance of accepting such Insignificance):

> They tell me of your dissatisfaction
> in my society where traffic signs

overshadow the philosophy
of being Insignificant.

It is no different
than living under a bridge in Texas
beside the Rio Grande.

Please accept advice from the blind
pigmentless Salamander
who considers his past an inurement.
"Perplexity should be expected,
especially when such a voyage
is imminent."

(24)

This allusion to the focal creature of his first collection of poems, *Winter of the Salamander,* draws on that voice from the natural and mythic world. Expecting perplexity in a voyage assumes movement, a certain randomness to progress, a sense of agency to move without mastery, where traffic signs, which mark the potential for travel, also inhibit that momentum.

These passages invoke the relationality and that agency to permit a speech which we trace through the postcolonial junkyard of self and other. The lines ironically make visible in myth and material a different means to move across political uncertainties of self and other: to act, in other words, as a Mesquakie.

Agency without mastery then is the very movement of subjects within relationality, the exercise of choosing within the relational network itself. Tayo's choice not to kill Emo is a choice to be relational rather than oppositional, to "stop fighting the destroyers," as he thus finds his agency with no pretense to mastery. Similarly, Young Bear's persona is "reminded daily of what is certainty," that although there is no mastery of the colonial presence, he and his people have a responsibility to exercise their agency in "protecting the vast resources / of the Well-Off Man Mountains."

POSITIONALITY WITHOUT LANGUAGE

If relationality without a center is a sense of interactive responsibility, and if agency without mastery is action within that pattern of relationality, the question still remains, how do we conceive of the subject who acts within this web? By a dialectic synthesis of relationality and agency, the term "positionality" can help us visualize that agent. A formal definition might read thus: a fluid positionality, rather than a more static "position," points to a material presence which exercises agency by the phenomenological dynamics of its space and time in the relational world. A less formal definition: bodies carry de facto rights.

Elaine Scarry's discussion of "the grounding of consent in the body" (1990:867) is at the heart of this conception of positionality which operates in Young Bear and in Silko. In her analysis of the legal premises concerning the body in medical, political, and marital relations, Scarry establishes the function of the body as the primary political locus, where consent, liberty, will, volition all reside:

the body is here conceived of not simply as something to be brought in under the protection of civil rights, but as itself the primary ground of all subsequent rights. The substratum of all other political and civil rights is the relation of the person to her or his own embodied personhood. (869)

I take "personhood" to suggest the interaction of relationality and agency. Scarry shows us that the primary presence of the body at this intersection predicates all subsequent political and civil rights. While this is not an assertion of biodeterminism, the body becomes the de facto ethical and political position in a system of relationality and agency.

Scarry explains that "the will itself is couched in embodiment" (875), in the body that sustains agency in a relational system, whether natural, cultural, or legal. Laws protecting the rights of bodies are thus cultural codifications of relationality and agency based in those bodies. (Agency without mastery would be thus an enactment of a sort of democratic relationality.) This clarification of the body as the substratum of social or relational interaction and agency follows Foucault's project of material and historical specificity. The body becomes not an ultimate ground, but a necessary and primary one.

One particularly effective and subtle way to give the reader a sense of the body in a story or poem is by a structured silence. When other stylistic methods such as imagery, prosody, and pacing have suggested the bodily presence, the writer can open strategic gaps, elisions, tacit allusions—silences—to breathe life into that stylistic clay. As we will see, a crucial silence performs this function in Silko's novel and in a number of Young Bear's lines.

The climax of *Ceremony* involves just such a "mute disposition of the body" as Scarry describes. As we will see, Silko positions Tayo's agency in a body without language. The locus of meaning for the climactic scene in Silko's mythic context is not so much rational insight, nor a cognitive epiphany, as it is bodily action unmediated by language. In the horrific scene at the mine, Tayo observes Emo, but silently disengages himself from the oppositions which feed the witchery. His silence permeates even his mind, as active choices surface tacitly from Tayo's long-held cultural understandings, not from knowledge lost and rearticulated in his stream of consciousness. Only silence informs the action.

On the printed page, Silko places an extra blank space to shape this silence. I return to passages already partially quoted for a re-reading of this positionality in silence. Tayo, in horror and anger, has been watching the witches' ritual:

But Tayo stayed on his knees in the shadows. Leroy had a knee on Pinkie's throat, and he could hear raspy choking sounds. Emo was laughing loudly, pointing at the body hanging stiffly, swaying a little in the gusts of wind, then pointing at Leroy kneeling on Pinkie's throat.

The moon was lost in a cloud bank. He moved back into the boulders. It had been a close call. The witchery had almost ended the story according to its plan; Tayo had almost jammed the screwdriver into Emo's skull the way the witchery had wanted. (265)

In the silence between these two paragraphs we find that the healing of the land and Tayo's place within it are accomplished. It is a moment without articulation which exercises the elements of subjectivity that we can now identify as a mythic positionality: both within the urgent moment and within his Laguna myth, he affirms his relationality beyond antinomies without placing himself or an oppositional witchery at any center; he affirms his agency as a determining factor in the cosmos, but without any claim to mastery; and he affirms his own material presence, his positionality, in an ineffable gap of action, which is reflected in a silence of narration, as well as in a typographical gap on the page.

Here we can see the significance of Silko's use of silence to locate subjectivity for Tayo. By leaving language out of Tayo's most significant act, she lets him avoid the defeating dualities of linguistic structures of self and other, and she lets the significance of his nonoppositional act resonate through his body, where his possibilities for relationality and agency reside.

A similar dynamic silence positioning the body echoes through Young Bear's short poem "Debut for the Woodland Drum" which we looked at earlier in terms of relationality. Young Bear's manipulation of silence echoes Bumblebee's admonition: "to witness and experience it / as it simply is, rather than camouflage it through / rational explanation."

Although none of the identity claims of relationality and agency surfaces expressly in the language of "Woodland Drum," the entire scene posits a positionality built of relationality and agency analogous to Tayo's climactic choice. Young Bear's scene is in fact an extension of such a commitment as Tayo made to his own cultural identity. Where Tayo acts silently on behalf of his cultural ceremony of relationality in a way which avoids the anticultural antinomies of witchery, Young Bear's musical troupe is traveling on behalf of a similar cultural commitment to their music, and that action forms the silent foundation of the narrative in the poem. This drive to a powwow in Oneida, Wisconsin, is the debut of a cultural statement, a gift of music to a community of Native Americans who share a similar commitment. They are initiating the musical effort which will express their Mesquakie life, the Mesquakie songs which frame Young Bear's book of poetry. Yet after letting the title open that small but significant historic space around the drum group, the poem fills it with silence and relationality. Young Bear does not speak of that commitment, but of the screen of images which those who enact that commitment observe. "Debut of the Woodland Drum" is short enough to repeat here for this angle of analysis:

> At the place
> where Midwestern glaciers
> supposedly came to a stop,

having created the last
buttes and stone cliffs
along the Mississippi
(which would one day remind
extraterrestrials of home planet
and thus establish a colony
in the name of Scandinavia),
we listened to Debra Harry
of Blondie sing ATOMIC
four hours from Oneida,
Wisconsin.

(60)

The poem is filled, as we have seen, with images of multiplicity, of relationality: glaciers, pop music, and a powwow drum are woven into a network. What remains silent is any articulation of the singers' positional choice, of their cultural commitment and their subsequent agency, which places them in that relational landscape. Indeed, Young Bear avoids placing himself verbally at all, letting the silent presence of the singers' bodies in the car speak for that positionality. Precisely by silence, Young Bear avoids Clifford's "pervasive dichotomy: absorption by the other *or* resistance to the other." The poem does not say, "We are not these things we see." Nor does it say, "We become these things we see." He avoids that dichotomy by silence, by not using language to juxtapose his cultural choices against this postmodern scene. Such a dualistic expression would have invoked the discursive pressures of antinomial history, a history which absorbs the resistance of an articulated opposition.

Instead, the narrative expresses a sort of Lacanian "look" by a Native American subject as he reviews the objects of an American landscape on a trip to a powwow. The scene of the poem is in fact a Lacanian "screen" on which an image of identity projects itself silently. Young Bear and his fellow drummers, singers, and dancers have chosen to form this musical group, and their choice empties out of the silence at the heart of this poem onto the images of buttes and stone cliffs, of Scandinavian communities, of rock stars, and onto this page—onto the screen of their relational identity. That screen finds expression in the poem, indeed is the poem, but their steady commitment remains unspoken, hidden in the same silence behind the screen of language where Tayo's commitment enacted his climactic agency.

Young Bear and Silko thus redistribute power across the oppositional categories of speech and silence, of modern and traditional, of white and Indian, of civilized and savage, of present and past, of active and passive. They do so first by making visible not an articulated position, but an ineffable positionality in a body without language, where relationality and agency reside.

James Clifford explains the difficulty of seeing such relational flux as the basis for an identity position. He cites the pervasive habit in the West of sharply distinguishing synchronic from diachronic, structure from change. . . . These assumptions keep us from seeing how collective structures, tribal or cultural, reproduce themselves historically by risking themselves in novel conditions. Their wholeness is as much a matter of reinvention and encounter as it is of continuity and survival. (341)

Positionality may not only use uncertainty for action in a world of ambiguous identities and incontrovertible differences, but it may require such risk. Those risks predicate Tayo's drama and the complex tensions in Young Bear's voice.

Positionality thus can be a set of questions that sort through or stir up economic, political, philosophical, psychological issues, rather than a set of articulable answers. Allowing such an inarticulable step in the construction of meaning and agency assumes an element of silence, and thus positionality finds itself again in a mute but active body. Silence is not an ultimate expression of postcolonial subjectivity; it is in a sense one more question.

This positionality suggests a continually reconstructed response to questions of the essential, autonomous, and imperial subject of Euroamerican culture and history. This response is the reflective practice, the responsibility, operating in Silko and Young Bear. The buoyant consciousness behind Bumblebee's voice allows Young Bear to stake out a pragmatic redefinition of postcolonial self and other. The agonized struggle of Tayo to find a way not to fight against the witchery, but to let it destroy itself, dramatizes such a reflective process.

Their tack is not simply to claim difference, nor to retain the colonial position of "other" to reify the hegemonic "self." To avoid this pathos of self and other, the move which these writers make possible is akin to Foucault's "alterity." Linda Alcoff explains the efficacy of Foucault's concept:

Foucault . . . rejects all constructions of oppositional subjects—whether the "proletariat," "woman," or "the oppressed"—as mirror images that merely recreate and sustain the discourse of power. . . . It is not the point of an imagined absolute otherness, but an "alterity" which understands itself as an internal exclusion. (417–418)

The alterity Silko and Young Bear create is so built on the mythic traditions which populate their cultural worlds that the oppositional presence of a "dominant" culture is excluded from that subject position. Young Bear's work describes this sense of alterity in the intensity of his personal vision, devouring images of his postmodern world into the extremities of his mythic world, and making them not one, but multiple within a traditional, mythic context. Silko, in contrast, builds a subordinate myth of the witchery's having created the white man, and her fictional mythology, precisely because of its oppositional political ingenuity, tends to maintain the antinomial dynamics of colonialism by simply reversing the dominance in the Indian witches' creation of the whites. For both of these writers, however, their larger myths and the participants' positions in those myths offer the possibility of a continuing emergence out of those antinomies into a third term of reinvented difference. The nature of this third term, this emergence, is a literary moment, a daily event, and, as their narratives suggest, a livable question.

Relationality is thus a web; agency the tug on a strand or the casting out of a strand in that web; positionality, as an intersection of strands, is the de facto locus of that agency in that relationality. Silko's web is stories, each listener and teller enacting the tale. Young Bear's web is music in language, cultural songs, Mesquakie love songs, the language of weather, the invisible musician. Against a dominant mentality driven by dichotomies, Silko and Young Bear build relationality. Against cultural and historical determinisms, they express possibilities for agency. And against disempowering marginalities, they show their readers the dynamics of positionality for Native and other Americans.

NOTES

1. Rather than attempt to generalize cultural truths from the specifics of the literature, this critical reading can try to clarify an aesthetic and cultural context for more precise understanding of the operative processes both within the literature itself and within the reading process. Thus, rather than colonizing the literature, this approach is dialogic, listening for cultural dialogue, and even looking for approaches that are not as dichotomous as "dialogue" suggests.

2. *Postcolonial* is a term whose historical definitions carry cultural resonances. In the historical period after the dominance by Europe and the United States of the administration of world affairs, *postcolonial* describes the economic, political, and cultural processes of shifting authority from the former colonizers to the former colonized. Indeed the period is concurrent with the existence of the United Nations.

3. A fuller treatment would include more of an investigation into traditional Keres elements in Silko and into Mesquakie elements in Young Bear, amplifying the cultural aspects of their work in juxtaposition with the theoretical issues. From there the question would be sharper still: In terms of historical and tribal specificity, how translatable are specific native principles to theoretical questions about redefining identity?

4. Such as Karl Kroeber (1979); Arnold Krupat (1984); or A. LaVonne Brown Ruoff (1990).

5. I write this on the fiftieth anniversary of the bombing of Pearl Harbor. Today's CBS television documentary, "Remember Pearl Harbor," reaches a remarkable moment as newsman Charles Kuralt and his co-host General Norman Schwarzkopf agree to be explicit: That racism blinded the United States Pacific forces to underestimate the power of the Japanese, while a similar racism blinded the Japanese to the potential resolve of the United States. Pearl Harbor marks a postcolonial epitome of Foucault's principle of visibility.

6. The ritual and healing aspects of traditional ancient stories, myths, and elder-wisdom may seem to the postmodern eye to be nostalgic and irrelevant in the late twentieth century. A brief

context will be useful. According to Gerald Graff (1987:103–104), the modernist literary climate of mythic allusion reduced a sense of the social urgency of the critic's enterprise, and of literature itself. By Graff's reckoning, that "literary dictatorship" of high modernism saw literature in trans-historical terms, the embodiment either of timeless verbal symbols or of the eternal recurrences of archetypal myths. Such an invocation of timeless universals came through deconstruction to be seen as nostalgic.

However, the particular dynamics of different mythic contexts in the works of Silko and Young Bear defuse that very nostalgia. This defusion is possible because these writers use mythic allusion in exactly the opposite direction from that of high modernism, whose project was universalizing. Mythic positionality in these Native writers is neither universal nor retrospective but culturally and tribally specific.

Another assumption behind this question of nostalgia in myth is the notion that history writes reality precisely in contrast to the "romantic longings and attitudes" of myth (Philip Rahv's terms in *The Myth and the Powerhouse*). Yet more recent historians have admitted that mythic interpretations may not be separated discretely from history, nor from conflicted reality either. The binaries break down. As Arnold Krupat discusses Clifford Geertz's term "blurring of genres": "In both the social sciences and in the arts, [it] is actually only a return to that time when the line between history and myth was not very clearly marked" (1989:59)

7. I treat relationality more extensively than the other two terms, *agency* and *positionality,* in order to work at dispelling the romanticism and nostalgia so often associated by outsiders with notions of cosmic interdependence in American Indian ontologies.

8. Young Bear echoes Donna Haraway's "ironic political myth" in her "Manifesto for Cyborgs." Like Young Bear, she deconstructs the "leaky distinction . . . between animal-human (organism) and machine" (1985:69). Against transcendent dualism as the "ontology grounding 'Western' epistemology," Haraway's "alternative is not cynicism or faithlessness" (1985:70), but full of active questions. Young Bear's quizzical, elliptical tone is partly a strategy to evade such cynicism or faithlessness within his own conflicts.

REFERENCES

Alcoff, Linda. 1988. "Cultural Feminism Versus Post-Structuralism: The Identity Crisis in Feminist Theory." *Signs: Journal of Women in Culture and Society* 13.3:405–436.

Allen, Paula Gunn. 1979. "The Psychological Landscape of *Ceremony.*" *American Indian Quarterly* 5:7–12.

Clifford, James. 1988. *The Predicament of Culture.* Cambridge: Harvard University Press.

Graff, Gerald. 1987. "American Criticism Left and Right," chap. 5 of *Professing Literature: An Institutional History.* Chicago: University of Chicago Press.

Haraway, Donna. 1985. "Manifesto for Cyborgs: Science, Technology, and Socialist Feminism in the 1980s." *Socialist Review* 15:80:64–107.

Jahner, Elaine. 1989. "Metalanguages." In *Narrative Chance: Postmodern Discourse on Native American Indian Literatures,* edited by Gerald Vizenor, 155–186. Albuquerque: University of New Mexico Press.

Kroeber, Karl. 1979. "Deconstructionist Criticism and American Indian Literatures." *boundary* 2:7:73–89.

Krupat, Arnold. 1984. "Native American Literature and the Canon." In *Canons*, edited by Robert von Hallberg, 309–338. Chicago: University of Chicago Press.

———. 1989. "The Dialogic of Silko's *Storyteller*." In *Narrative Chance: Postmodern Discourse on Native American Indian Literatures*, edited by Gerald Vizenor, 55–68. Albuquerque: University of New Mexico Press.

Rajchman, John. 1991. *Philosophical Events: Essays of the '80s*. New York: Columbia University Press.

Ruoff, A. LaVonne Brown. 1990. *American Indian Literatures: An Introduction, Bibliographic Review, and Selected Bibliography*. New York: MLA.

Scarry, Elaine. 1990. "Consent and the Body: Injury, Departure, and Desire." *New Literary History* 21:867–896.

Self, Robert T. 1988. "Author, Text, and Self in *Buffalo Bill and the Indians*." In *Ambiguities in Literature and Film*, edited by Hans P. Braendlin, 104–116. Tallahassee: Florida State University Press.

Silko, Leslie Marmon. 1977. *Ceremony*. New York: New American Library.

Silverman, Kaja. "Masochism and Male Subjectivity." *Camera Obscura* 19:32–67.

Young Bear, Ray A. 1990. *The Invisible Musician*. Duluth, Minn.: Holy Cow! Press.

LITERATURE IN A "NATIONAL SACRIFICE AREA"
Leslie Silko's *Ceremony*

Shamoon Zamir

In *Ceremony* (1977) Betonie, the part-Mexican, part-Navajo medicine man, educated by whites at the Sherman Institute and now living on the edges of the Navajo community and the white town of Gallup, his hillside hut packed not only with medicine bundles but also with Coke bottles, telephone directories from various American cities, and advertising calenders, is the embodiment of a process of cultural transformation and innovation that sustains creative survival rather than the more familiar narratives of psychological and social disintegration of Native American cultures in the face of Western colonization. When the psychoanalysis at the army hospital and the traditional cures of the Laguna medicine men fail Tayo, Silko's hero is restored by Betonie. When Tayo comes to Betonie for help, Betonie explains to him that "at one time, the cermonies as they had been performed were enough for the way the world was then. But after the white people came, elements in this world began to shift; and it became necessary to create new ceremonies. . . . the people mistrust this greatly, but only this growth keeps the ceremonies strong." [1]

LOCAL AND GLOBAL: A CONTEST OF STORIES

Silko, like her character Betonie, is herself of mixed cultural and racial origins (being part Laguna, part Mexican, and part white) and Betonie's biography, the contents of his

396

hut, and his ceremonial transformations should be read not only literally but also as allegorical representations of Silko's effort to create a hybrid literary form, a novel in which Pueblo oral traditions and western literary forms and narratives are juxtaposed and intercut as part of a complex process of mutual transformation. It is, however, easier to conceptualize such metamorphoses theoretically as an idea than to grasp and analytically describe the actual practice and process of change in a work such as *Ceremony*. While critical studies of Silko's work have rightly celebrated her commitment to literary and cultural innovation they have failed too often to delineate in any precise detail the concrete form of her literary practice. I want in this essay to move toward such a descriptive analysis by examining the ways in which Silko deploys and changes various Pueblo and western narratives throughout her novel, particularly the way in which she either uses traditional oral stories in new contexts or changes these stories to meet new contexts, and the way in which these traditional stories are altered and mediated by being brought into alignment with western literary forms.

Both the juxtaposition of antithetical Native American narratives and the dialectical articulation of western and oral traditions in *Ceremony* constitute a contest of stories in which narratives are competing to describe and explain a Pueblo world radically dislocated by the penetrations of a capitalist political economy. If the cultural and political meanings of the narrativizations of cultural change and of the transformations of literary form in a work such as Silko's are to be understood properly, then minority literary criticism's preoccupations with the relationship of canon and margin and with the processes of intertextuality within this relationship must be shifted out of the Oedipal melodrama of an indigenous authenticity under the siege of "anxieties of influence." These textual relations must be seen instead as markers of a political history. I attempt, therefore, in this essay to articulate a literary (oral as well as textual) analysis with a model of anthropological analysis derived largely from political economy because it is political economy that has in recent years provided some of the most useful attempts to theorize and describe the political and cultural relationships of center and periphery, of local and global, as well as the transformation of the local under the penetration of the global.[2] It is in adapting the perspectives of political economy within its own localized ethnographic practice that anthropology has increasingly insisted since the seventies that "regional analysis should . . . involve not only geographic-economic mapping of what happens where, but also the relative power-linked articulation and conflict over ideologies, world views, moral codes, and the locally bounded conditions of knowledge and competence."[3] Within such a framework the contest of stories in *Ceremony* can be read as a complex dramatization of the intersections of the local and global in the modern American Southwest. The politics of Silko's literary practice emerge from such a reading as a paradoxical mixture of a newly emergent regionalist resistance and an internalization of global forms that simultaneously erases this resistance.

It is true, as Betonie explains, that in Native American cultures "the ceremonies have *always* been changing" and that this living tradition sanctions the changes that he himself makes (126, my emphasis). Such a view of traditional oral cultures is amply supported by contemporary ethnographic studies and Silko suggests toward the end of her novel that any attempt by "the old priests" to "cling to ritual without making new ceremonies" is only a kind of new fundamentalism born out of a fear that paralyses creative response (249). But nevertheless it is also true that the kind of changes Betonie makes in the ceremonies and Silko in the oral stories do constitute departures that are much more radical than those that occur during a process of change within a traditional environment. The reasons for and nature of this radical deviation can be understood only if they are seen as responses to a radically new social and political context for Navajo and Pueblo cultures in the Southwest. This new context is more than the history of contact between Native American and Western cultures; it is given above all by the unprecedented penetration and disruption of Native cultures by a capitalist political economy since the forties in the shape of uranium mining, atomic-power development, and an atomic-weapons testing program of grotesque proportions. In both *Ceremony* and *Storyteller* (1981) Silko herself is careful to map this form of colonization as an essential context for reading her work.

The climactic scene of *Ceremony,* the brutal and bloody torture of Harley by Emo, Leroy, and Pinkie, occurs in an old disused uranium mine. It is as he witnesses this scene that Tayo suddenly understands that his own mental disorder, the drought that plagues the land, the vision of the witchery explained by Betonie, the disruption of the social life of the Pueblos, and his own persisting confusion of Native American and Japanese faces during his service in the war in the Pacific all connect as part of a single historical schema when seen in the context of the atomic program:

He had been so close to it, caught up in it for so long that its simplicity struck deep inside his chest: Trinity site, where they exploded the first atomic bomb, was only three hundred miles to the southeast, at White Sands. And the top-secret laboratories where the bomb had been created were deep in the Jemez Mountains, on land the Government took from Cochiti Pueblo: Los Alamos, only a hundred miles northeast of him now. . . . There was no end to it; it knew no boundaries; and he had arrived at the point of convergence where the fate of all living things, and even the earth, had been laid. (245–246)

The mine becomes the point of convergence "in the middle of witchery's final ceremonial sandpainting," a "circle of death" that unites all human beings into "one clan" again (246). In the novel Tayo's grandmother, like some of the older people still living at Laguna when Silko was a child, remembers waking early one morning and mistaking the flash of the first atomic test for the dawn, a perverse inversion of the sunrise to which the Pueblo people offer prayers (*Ceremony* is dedicated to the sunrise at its close) (245).[4]

It is appropriate that the climactic scene of *Ceremony* takes place in a uranium mine, for Laguna Pueblo is the site of the largest open-pit uranium mine in the world.

From 1952 to 1981 the Anaconda Company leased seven thousand acres of Laguna land and operated a uranium-stripping operation there. When profitably extractable ore was exhausted, the company closed up operations, leaving behind them a massive crater and piles of highly radioactive slag. In *Storyteller* there is a photograph taken in the early sixties looking east from Paguate Village at this mine. The mine is a scar, but the familiar New Mexico landscape of hills and mesas still rises up around it. In a note added to this photograph in 1981 Silko points out that "the mesas and hills that appear in the background and foreground are now gone, swallowed by the mine."[5]

Congenital birth defects and early deaths from respiratory cancer and similar ailments have become more and more common in the area. The Laguna residents have discovered that the tribal council building, community center, and newly constructed jackpile housing are radioactive and that Anaconda had used low-grade uranium ore to "improve" the road system leading to the mine and the village. The Rio Paguate River, "which once provided the basis for a thriving tribal agriculture," is now contaminated. "With agriculture and cattle production withering under the glare of higher paying and more 'glamorous' work in the mine, the pueblo converted to ground water to meet all, rather than a portion of its potable needs," only to discover, in 1978, that *all* its available water sources were dangerously contaminated by radioactivity. Should this contaminated groundwater drain through a manmade fissure into the deep aquifers at Laguna and other pueblos, the survival of the Native American way of life for the Pueblo and Navajo cultures of the Southwest would be seriously threatened.[6]

In 1984 there were sixty-four "significant" uranium mines, thirty-five tailing piles, and eleven power plants ("present and projected") in the Four Corners region where most of the pueblos are located.[7] "It is estimated that about seventy-five percent of known uranium reserves in the United States are currently controlled by the seven major oil corporations (Kerr-McGee control more than half, mostly through leases on Indian lands)—hence the huge power of the uranium lobby to prevail over human welfare and common sense, not to speak of the law of the land."[8] In 1972, under the Nixon administration and "in conjunction with studies of US energy development need and planning undertaken by the Trilateral Commission, the feds sought to designate the Four Corners region and the impacted region of the Dakotas, Wyoming and Montana as '*National Sacrifice Areas*,' which means areas rendered literally uninhabitable through the deliberate elimination of the water supplies for industrial purposes (the aquifers are estimated to take from 5,000 to 50,000 years to effectively replenish themselves) and the proliferating nuclear contamination (much of which carries a lethal half-life from ¼ to ½ million years)."[9]

The effect of this global and sacrificial penetration in *Ceremony* is a state in which local cultural codes are either totally erased or radically dislocated and distorted.[10] The bright glare of the atomic explosion reveals to Tayo a world with "no boundaries, only transitions" (246). It is the nightmare vision of decoded flows in which Tayo finds himself adrift that constitutes the content of his psychic disorder: "he cried at how the world had come undone, how thousands of miles, high ocean waves and green jungles could not hold people in their place. Years and months had become weak, and people could push against them and wander back and forth in time" (18). The rupture of those codes that map the temporal and geographic dimensions of social existence entails a sense of placelessness, both literal and cultural: for Tayo the "fifth world" of the Pueblos has "become entangled with European names" (68) and he comes to believe that "there would be no peace and the people would have no rest until the entanglements had been unwound to the source" (69).

This desire to return to the source contains obvious dangers of a nostalgic and reactionary recoding, but Betonie's and Silko's insistence that all fundamentalist recrudescence be resisted seems to offer a guard against this kind of reinscription. I want to suggest, however, that *Ceremony* traces a precarious trajectory between a genuinely inventive local resistance and a deeply nostalgic recodification that aligns Silko's narratives not so much with their traditional sources of Pueblo oral culture as with Western high modernism's reactionary appropriation of a global mythology of sacrificial rejuvenation, an appropriation that in its mythification of historical crises adopts and internalizes the very logic of capitalist sacrifice Silko's work sets out to resist.

GIFT AND SACRIFICE: COMPETING NARRATIVE ECONOMIES

The witchery, Silko's diabolic myth for historical disruption and colonial violence, is a story told by a magician-witch, a story that becomes reality as it is being told (135). Against this Silko places the story being narrated by Grandmother Spider (a Pueblo deity representing creativity through thought rather than biology). At the start of *Ceremony* Silko suggests that she herself is re-telling Grandmother Spider's story and that this story in fact constitutes the novel as a whole (1). One aspect of what I have called the contest of stories in *Ceremony* is the attempt by Silko to manage and to contain the malign power of the witchery story within the larger narrative of Grandmother Spider's story. As Tayo realises at the end, the real contest is for the ending of the story and he must "keep the story out of the reach of the destroyers" if the ceremony is to be completed successfully. Throughout *Ceremony* the inner dynamic of this contest of narratives is presented as a conflict between competing economies, a conflict between an economy of reciprocity and small communities represented by gift exchange on the one hand, and on the other a sacrificial economy gone wild under the impact of the contemporary political economy of colonization.[11]

The story of Kaup'a'ta, the gambler, one of the many smaller narratives that makes up the larger narrative of drought and witchery in *Ceremony,* dramatises these two economies in struggle. Kaup'a'ta is a *ck'o'yo* magician who tricks people into gambling with him and gains power over his duped victims by feeding them blue cornmeal into which he has mixed human blood. All the victims eventually gamble away their lives and are themselves sacrificed to make the blue cornmeal mixture that will overpower other victims:

> He hung them upside down in his storeroom,
> side by side with other victims.
> He cut out their hearts
> and let their blood run down
> into the bins of blue cornmeal.
>
> (172)

When Kaup'a'ta captures the stormclouds, thus causing a drought, the Sun, their father, takes gifts of blue and yellow pollen, tobacco, and coral beads to Grandmother Spider in order to find a way of freeing the clouds. Spiderwoman advises him about the most useful strategy to use against Kaup'a'ta and the Sun succeeds in his mission (172–176). Gambling and the violence of witchery are, then, opposed to gift relationships and Silko directly links the freeing of the rainclouds with the curative ceremony undertaken by Tayo. As an act of triumph the Sun does not kill Kaup'a'ta but cuts out his eyes and throws them into the sky where they become "the horizon stars of autumn" (176). Immediately after this Tayo, in "late September," sees the stars drawn by Betonie to mark the final stage of Tayo's curative ceremony (178).

I have said that the story of Kaup'a'ta and the stormclouds is one of the smaller narratives that make up the larger narrative of the witchery in *Ceremony,* but this is not to suggest that Silko's myth of the witchery is simply an aggregate of smaller parts. What most distinguishes Silko's myth of malign magic is her transformation of local oral narratives into a comprehensive cosmological mapping of evil. Such a globalization, familiar in Christianity, is, in fact, not found in the Native American cultures of the Southwest. Although there is some belief in witchcraft at Laguna and in other Pueblo cultures, Silko has explained that the primary source of materials for her narrative of the witchery was the numerous stories of witchery and malign magic she heard on the Navajo reservation at Chinle, Arizona, where belief in witchcraft is much more widespread and much more a part of everyday life than at Laguna.[12] But while Silko has drawn upon these stories in *Ceremony,* the largest part of the witchery myth in the novel, the narrative of witchery's creation of white people and its manipulation of whites as the primary instruments of a horrific and global destruction (135–138), is almost entirely Silko's own creation.[13] Silko's globalization of the violent narrative patterns of Navajo stories reaches its cathartic climax in the brutal parody of Christian *sparagmos* at the end of the novel when Emo and the others tie Harley to the wire fence in the uranium mine and torture him, collecting pieces of his flesh in a brown paper bag (248–254).

Although Silko's expansion of the narratives of witchery departs significantly from her Navajo sources, her exacerbation or intensification of the violence of the oral stories in the context of an invasive colonial political economy reproduces the way in which Navajo stories and witchcraft practice have responded to similar historical crises. In his study of Navajo witchcraft Clyde Kluckhohn has noted that the practice and violence of witchcraft has significantly increased in those periods when Navajo society has experienced periods of radical destabilization. Kluckhohn comments on two periods in particular: the period between 1875 and 1890 when the nomadic Navajos were finally defeated and confined to a limited reservation area, and the period of the thirties and early forties in this century when Navajo society, by then largely integrated with the national economy, was deeply disrupted by the effects of the depression and the enforced stock-reduction program.[14] Witchcraft remains a potent form of aggression on the poverty stricken Navajo reservation today.[15]

The transformations of witchcraft in both Silko's novel and in Navajo culture can, then, be read as responses to contact with white political and economic institutions and controls.[16] But if the articulation of native socities and cultural forms with the national political economy suggests a major *cause* of these transformation, such an articulation does not in itself offer a critical understanding of the *effects* of such transformations. Kluckhohn's study is focused almost entirely on the functional role of witchcraft, stressing above all that it is an "adaptive and adjustive" strategy that seeks to return to and maintain social equilibrium, although Kluckhohn does acknowledge that such an emphasis "probably has the effect of insufficiently highlighting the disruptive effects which admittedly are important."[17] The problem with such a descriptive strategy is that it does not offer an interpretive framework within which it would be possible to reach any satisfactory political understanding of the cultural processes being described. In other words, it is difficult to decide, when reading Kluckhohn's presentation of data, whether the growth and intensification in witchcraft should be read as a resistance to political and economic colonization or be critically analyzed as either a reproduction and internalization of the violence of such colonization or a local and indigenous equivalent of this violence that is, at best, an ambivalent form of opposition. In a commentary on studies of cultural change in the Bolivian Andes Peter Gose has offered an analysis of the transformation of local sacrificial stories and practices under the impact of capitalist political economy that provides a more complex and critical model for understanding the meaning of changes in the traditional stories and practices in Navajo culture.[18] Only if we first understand the nature of change on this cultural level can we begin to understand the extent to which Silko's literary practice is identical to or different from the cultural ground upon which it draws for its materials.

Although Gose is dealing with Native American culture of the Bolivian Andes, there are striking parallels between this culture's experience of political economy and the experience of Native American cultures in the North American Southwest. Like the Pueblos and the Navajo the indigenous cultures of the Andes have experienced an intense and violent disruption of their cultures by corporate capitalist mining projects over many years. And as with Navajo witchcraft and Silko's myth of the witchery many of the Quechua myths of malign magic or threat and of sacrifice have become increasingly more exaggerated and violent as a response to this penetration. One Quechua story in particular offers a suggestive parallel with Silko's story of Kaup'a'ta the gambler. Gose describes how scary stories originally told to children to prevent them from wandering outside village bounds have become more and more violent and function now as part of a mythology of adult experience. These myths tell of a *ñakaq* (Quechua for "slaughterer" or "sacrificer"), imagined as a tall white man in white clothes and armed with a machete, who slits the throats of any adults wandering outside the village bounds, drags them off to caves or mineshafts, and hangs them upside down in order to drain out and collect their body fat. The theft of grease stands for the theft of human energy, and the Quechua believe that the grease is then sold on the international capitalist market as a valuable commodity.[19] (In Pueblo cultures blood, the substance drained by Silko's sacrificial gambler, is similarly associated with energy and with fertility.)[20]

In his analysis of myths such as that of the *ñakaq* as well as of sacrificial practice, Gose argues that there is, in fact, a complementary relationship between sacrifice and the commodity form in Andean culture. Sacrifice is used "as an image of social cohesion and power. Any relationship of tribute involves sacrifice because wealth is not alienable from the body, but a part of its vitality." This denial of alienability stands in opposition to commodity exchange inasmuch as it denies the mediation of individuals through things by its "annihilation of the mediating object." However, as Gose adds,

In this precise inversion of the commodity form, Andean culture does not resist capitalism, but expresses a profound historical experience of its dark side. . . . Although sacrifice is no longer an official part of the tribute owed by peasants to the state, as it was under the Inca empire, and despite the incorporation of the Andean region into the periphery of world capitalism, commodity exchange has not supplanted sacrifice as the dominant idiom of social synthesis. On the contrary, capitalist penetration has actually exacerbated the sacrificial logic of Andean culture. . . . Not only do the peasants view their own society through sacrifice, but they extend it to the innermost workings of capital, and their relation to it, by means of the *ñakaq,* an image of terror and power that constantly recreates itself in the Andean imagination.[21]

Gose concludes that "the *ñakaq* articulates an erotico-religious desire for transcendence in the face of power more than an economic analysis of it, or an ideology of political resistance to it."[22]

I want to suggest that the transformations of Navajo witchcraft and Silko's myth of the witchery can be read along lines similar to those of Gose's argument. The intensification of Southwestern witchcraft and its mythologies, like Andean sacrifice, expresses a deep "historical experience" of the "dark side of capitalism" and colonization by an exacerbation of the "sacrificial logic" already present in indigenous forms. But in juxtaposing the witchery narratives with gift narratives Silko at least dialogizes her representation of the sacrificial economy with an alternative economy. This dialectical engagement has the effect of exposing the politics of adaptive internalization implicit in the globalization of the mythologies of witchcraft while at the same time offering a local space of resistance to this politics. In this sense *Ceremony* offers a dramatization of sacrificial narratives that is, for want of a better way of putting it, more self-consciously critical than the folk practices of either the Navajo or the Quechua.

But, as I hinted earlier, the space of local resistance in *Ceremony* is constantly under threat, as much from Silko's particular form of literary hybridization as from the confrontation with a powerful counter-economy.[23] In order to see just what shape local resistance takes in the novel and the extent to which it does or does not survive the threats of dissipation it will be useful to take a closer look at Silko's narratives of gift exchange and their merger with non-Pueblo narratives.

Throughout *Ceremony* narratives of gift exchange are juxtaposed to the sacrificial narratives. In a story of the drought dissociated from the witchery stories, Corn Woman, angered by her sister Reed Woman, leaves this world and retires to the fourth world below. In order to bring her back Fly and Hummingbird have to take her gifts of pollen, turquoise beads, and prayer sticks (105). They also have to give similar gifts to Buzzard so that he will purify the town before Corn Woman returns (113). As Jarold Ramsey points out, such stories are not meant to be taken as etiological explanations but as illustrating certain moral values and "the properly reciprocal relationship" between the human world and nature.[24] Tayo is witness to the ritual enactment of such reciprocity in his childhood. Early in the novel he remembers that when as a young boy he went deer hunting with his uncles Josiah and Robert and his cousin Rocky, his uncles sprinkled pinches of cornmeal on the dead deer's nose in order to feed "the deer's spirit": "They had to show their love and respect, their appreciation; otherwise, the deer would be offended, and they would not come to die for them the following year" (51). This attitude stands in stark contrast to that of the white loggers who shoot bears and mountain lions around the Pueblo region "for sport" (186). In the very last stage of his ceremonial healing, when he is searching for his uncle's lost cattle, Tayo remembers the necessity for such a reciprocal offering and sprinkles pollen onto the tracks of a mountain lion, "the hunter's helper" in Pueblo mythology (196). It is the mountain lion who then saves Tayo's life by leading the white armed patrolmen away from him (202). Josiah, Robert, and Tayo all nourish the spirit of the gift, what the Maori call the *hau.*[25] The pollen is a return gift that ensures that the circle of reciprocity is not broken.[26] The "circle of gifts enters the cycles of nature and, in so doing, manages not to interrupt them and not to put man on the outside." Nature's "abundance is in fact a consequence of man's treating its wealth as a gift."[27]

Just as the violence of Emo and the others against Harley shifts the oral witchery narrative, presented throughout in verse form, into the main prose narrative of the novel, so the lesson of reciprocity taught by the oral gift narratives finds its fullest embodiment in the dramatization of the second half of Tayo's ceremonial healing. This second half, beginning after Tayo leaves Betonie's hut, dominates the last part of the novel. Tayo sets out on a quest to find his uncle's lost cattle, encounters and sleeps with the woman Ts'eh Montano (a mythically inscribed representative of a Pueblo goddess complex of Yellow Woman and a fertility-corn goddess[28]), relearns those structures of attention that place him in a balanced relationship with the land, and completes his cure by retrieving the cattle from the white ranchers and returning to Laguna.

By the end of the novel it is the stories of gift and reciprocity that seem to triumph. It is not blood sacrifice that regenerates the land (as it does in Silko's early story "Tony's Story" [1969]), at least not at first. The hero is cured and the rains come before the crucifixion of Harley (229, 234). Tayo is tempted to intervene in the final scene of *sparagmos,* to save Harley by killing Emo, but stops himself from doing so, believing that to meet violence with violence would be to abandon himself to the logic of the witchery (252–253). And while the scene in the uranium mine is the climactic moment of the novel, it is not the last. It is followed by the conclusion of the oral gift narrative where Corn Mother accepts the gifts brought her by Hummingbird and Fly and returns to the human world (255–256).

Silko's attempt to maintain a double resolution in her novel, to not make regeneration dependent upon sacrifice, appears at first as a resistance to the most common and pernicious form of the sacrificial-regenerative narrative patterns in western cultures, best known through the Grail Legend materials and particularly the dissemination of these and related materials through the highly influential *Golden Bough* of J. G. Frazer. Frazer's twelve volumes, which have had an incalculable impact on modern literature, constitute a monumental and ahistoric reduction of world mythology to a single monomythic structure of sacrificial regeneration and cyclical repetition, a failure to historicize mythology that acts, in effect, as a mythical alibi for the sacrifice of human energy within nineteenth-century capitalist production. What is problematic about Silko's apparent resistance to such a globalization of sacrificial mythology is that the overarching plot-form of her own novel, from the dislocations of the "wounded" hero in a drought-ridden land to the inevitable climax of sacrifice, regeneration, and healing, is (as one critic has already pointed out) nothing other than a Grail narrative.[29]

From this angle Tayo's refusal to participate in sacrifice, like Silko's attempt to dissociate the end of the drought from sacrifice, represents, at best, an "ambiguous compromise."[30] As one of Thomas Pynchon's characters accurately notes: "The basic problem has always been getting other people to die for you." These are "the terrible politics of the Grail."[31] Despite the apparent dissociation of the two economies in *Ceremony* the resolutions of both narratives do form a united or synchronized climax to the book where the sacrificial working-out of the witchery is placed as an integral part of the ongoing ceremony outlined by Betonie for Tayo. It is in this sense that the disconnection engineered by Silko is overridden by the utter predictability and inevitability of her instantly recognizable plot structure.[32] We know from "Tony's Story" that Silko is clearly attracted to the mythical simplification of historical complexities that is offered by sacrificial narratives in their crudest form. While *Ceremony* presents a more complex set of controls and adjustments than this earlier work, the novel remains a structure of contradictions that, in its most interesting moments, energizes itself by dramatizing these very contradictions, but at its weakest points unravels its precarious local critical practice into an ahistorical nostalgia for mythical transcendence.

If this conclusion about *Ceremony* has any validity at all, then, in order to understand the literary politics of the novel, we need to investigate not only the narrativization of the two competing economies of gift and sacrifice, but also the very nature of Silko's mythic perceptions, to watch those points of transition where a historical understanding of myth as a locally specific response to cultural process and change dissolves into an abandonment of the historicist literary imagination in favour of the transcendentalism T. S. Eliot termed the "mythical method."[33] In the end of course *Ceremony* aligns itself not so much with Arthurian romance or with Frazer's source materials as with the deployment of these materials as part of a strategy of negotiating historical crisis in modernist literary texts, most notably *The Waste Land* (1922).[34]

"WHAT THE THUNDER SAID": PUEBLO MODERNISM

Robert Bell points out that in many Native American curing rituals the patient's reenactments of mythological events, such as the hero's quest, are also an integral part of the ceremonies.[35] This should be a caution against a too-easy identification of the narratives of *Ceremony* with western mythical or literary narratives. But Silko's dramatization of the ceremonial healing of Tayo, like her version of the witchery myths, moves precisely toward such an identification in its radical departures from the Native American model that is its source.

The first part of the ceremony designed by Betonie and enacted in his hut is an almost exact reenactment of the Coyote Transformation section of the male branch of the Navajo Red Antway Evilway.[36] This section of what is a long ceremonial cure is specifically concerned with the correction of effects of witchcraft. The ceremony in which Tayo sits in the middle of a white sandpainting with crossed rainbows, while Betonie's mysterious helper, a bear child, buries ceremonial hoops in the ground and marks the earth with bear prints and Betonie himself paints four mountain ranges on the floor of the hut and then lightly makes a cut in Tayo's scalp (141–143) is in fact taken (often with direct quotation) from a version of the Red Antway told by the Son of Late Tall *Deshchini* to Father Berard Haile in 1933–34 and published by Leland C. Wyman in 1973.[37] Silko acknowledges her anthropological source in *Ceremony* by naming Betonie's grandfather, the originator of the the ongoing ceremony in which Betonie and Tayo participate, *Descheeny* (145).

The fact that Silko follows an anthropological report so closely may seem to contradict Betonie's insistence that the ceremonies must change (not to mention Silko's assertion that she never uses anthropological texts as sources for her stories[38]) but this is not really so. While there are several minor diferences between the version of the Coyote Transformation in *Ceremony* and that presented by Wyman, Silko's first major departure from her source is her isolation of the Coyote Transformation from the rest of the Red Antway Evilway. The immediate effect of this is to shift the focus from collective action to the individual hero. According to Wyman the myth of the Red Antway "departs from the standard Navajo pattern of the hero-quest" by centralizing the collective narrative of the Ant Peoples. A hero is provided only toward the end of the Coyote Transformation, itself only a part of the overall myth.[39]

The second half of Tayo's ceremonial healing (the solitary quest for the cattle and the encounters with Ts'eh Montano) only stresses further the individualist emphasis in Silko's narrative and constitutes Silko's second and certainly most significant departure from Native sources. As Betonie explains to Tayo, this second half is not separate from the ceremony of healing but constitutes the changes made in the ceremony in order to deal with Tayo's contemporary situation (152).

The foregrounding of the individual's centrality as well as of the quest narrative may be, in part, effects of Silko's transference of oral stories into the novel form and the inheritance of conventions of characterization and narrative teleology that such a transference can entail. The effect of such a foregrounding within the novel is, as I have suggested above, to align Silko's narrative with narratives of the Grail quest. Even if the narrative of the second half of Tayo's ceremony may have certain parallels with Native American hero-quests, the ritual conclusion of this narrative in the uranium mine, where "the lines of cultures and worlds" converge "in the middle of witchery's final ceremonial sand painting" (246), is based not on Native American sources but on the final section of Eliot's *The Waste Land*.

As Emo and the others torture Harley, Tayo hides among the dry boulders and watches the faces of the torturers lit by a fire around which they circle (248). This is the vision of "the torchlight on sweaty faces" and "the agony in stony places" (where there is "no water but only rock") that opens "What the Thunder Said."[40] The final section of Eliot's poem is based, in part, on the adventure of the Perilous Chapel, that part of the narratives of the Grail where the hero is tested for "initiation into the secrets of physical life" by "being brought into contact with the horrors of physical death," a test which could "end disastrously for the aspirant."[41] Eliot's chapel, a "decayed hole among the mountains,"[42] is transformed by Silko into the abandoned uranium mineshaft surrounded by the Southwest mountains, and Tayo, like Gawain, witnesses the horrors of physical death but survives the threat of disaster by refusing to participate in the violence. What differentiates Silko from Eliot is that where in Eliot the promise of "a damp gust / Bringing rain"[43] only haunts the wasted land, in *Ceremony* "clouds with round bellies [have] gathered for the dawn" (255) after Harley's crucifixion.

Like the incantation of "Shantih shantih shantih" from the Upanishads that closes Eliot's poem, *Ceremony* asserts of the witchery at its end

> It is dead for now.
> It is dead for now.
> It is dead for now.
> It is dead for now.
> (261)

and terminates the book by proferring it as an "offering" to the "Sunrise" (262), a redressing of the Pueblo world thrown into imbalance by the atomic perversion of the dawn. But while there is a sense of irony mixed in with the nostalgic longing in Eliot, there is no such qualification in Silko. Given the range of problematic contradictions and ruptures in Silko's work such self-confidence seems unstable in its assertion of a successful recuperation of centered cultural and individual wholeness. In the context of the novel's formal and ideological complexity such security can only constitute (to twist the meaning of Eliot's translation of the formal ending to an Upanishad) a "Peace which passeth understanding."[44]

For Eliot the modernist deployment of myth is "a way of controlling, of ordering, of giving shape and significance to the immense panorama of futility and anarchy which is contemporary history."[45] In aligning her literary procedures with Eliot's "mythical method" Silko finally retreats into an idea of myth as metaphysical security. This regression negates that other understanding of myth as a *poesis* attentive to the concrete particulars of localism that emerges only occasionally in *Ceremony* and which is articulated with precision to contra-Eliot by Charles Olson:

> a place as term in the order of creation
> & thus useful as a function of that equation
> example, that the "Place Where the Horse-Sacrificers Go"
> of the Brihadaranyaka Upanishad is worth more than
> a metropolis—or, for that matter, any moral
> concept, even a metaphysical one[46]

Writing of the inheritance of an Eliotic nostalgic romanticism in a good deal of Native American fiction, David Murray rightly argues that this writing "pushes back to a point which cannot be demythologised precisely because it is linked with *in illo tempore,* the time of myth rather than history."[47] As Tayo leaves Ts'eh's house, setting out for the final part of his ceremony, signs of primordial timelessness appear in the text. Tayo's horse stops grazing as the sun rises: "Maybe," writes Silko, "the dawn woke the instinct in the dim memory of the blood when horses had been wild as the deer and at sunrise went into the trees and thickets to hide" (183). Ts'eh's place is outside of history: "the house was like the mesas around it: years had little relation to it," (183) and looking out from it "there was no sign that white people had ever come to this land" (184). The association of history with the arrival of the Europeans here signals a sentimental nostalgia that reinscribes (or museumizes) Native Americans within the paralyzing stereotype of "a people without history."[48] In sacrificing its own localism to this kind of mythic regression and in sustaining this regression by means of a compulsive sacrificial teleology *Ceremony,* like the Quechua *ñakaq,* "articulates an erotico-religious desire for transcendence in the face of power more than an economic analysis of it, or an ideology of political resistance to it."[49]

NOTES

I would like to thank the John F. Kennedy Institute in Berlin for a generous research stipend that made much of the work for this study possible. My thanks also to Arnold Krupat and David Murray for their comments on and criticisms of an earlier draft. My special thanks to Katie Trumpener, international gift sender extrordinaire.

1. Leslie Silko, *Ceremony* (New York: Viking Press, 1977), 126. All further references are cited in the text.

2. The origins of political economy go back, of course, to the work of Adam Smith. There is a fine and simple description of the development of a world system and cosmopolitan world culture and literature within the colonial expansion of bourgeois capitalism in the first section of *The Manifesto of the Communist Party* (1848) that can still take the edge of most postmodernist theoretical novelties. Among the most influential modern works in political economy has been Immanuel Wallerstein's *The Modern World-System: Capitalist Agriculture and the Origins of the European World-Economy in the Sixteenth Century* (New York: Academic Press, 1974). I have also found the application of the political economy model and of Wallerstein's work to areas of ethnic culture and ethnic self-fashioning in Michael Hechter's *Internal Colonialism: The Celtic Fringe in British National Development, 1536–1966* (London: Routledge & Kegan Paul, 1975) particularly helpful. In anthropology two studies have been particularly stimulating: June Nash's *We Eat the Mines and the Mines Eat Us: Dependency and Exploitation in Bolivian Tin Mines* (New York: Columbia University Press, 1979), and Michael Taussig's *The Devil and Commodity Fetishism in South America* (Chapel Hill: University of North Carolina Press, 1980). I will return to the anthropological model later in the essay.

3. George E. Marcus and Michael M. J. Fischer, *Anthropology as Cultural Critique: An Experimental Moment in the Human Sciences* (Chicago: University of Chicago Press, 1986), 94.

The fourth chapter of this book provides a useful survey of the influence of political economy on contemporary anthropology. See also Sherry B. Ortner, "Theory in Anthropology since the Sixties," *Comparative Studies in Society and History,* 26 (1984):138–144. Jeanne Guillemin's *Urban Renegades: The Cultural Strategy of American Indians* (New York: Columbia University Press, 1975) is a particularly fine example in the area of Native American studies.

4. For Silko's recollections of being told about the event during her childhood, see Per Seyersted, "Two Interviews with Leslie Marmon Silko," *American Studies in Scandinavia,* 13:1 (1981):27.

5. Leslie Silko, *Storyteller* (New York: Seaver Books, 1981), 270.

6. Most of the information on the present state of Laguna here is taken from Winona LaDuke and Ward Churchill, "Native America: The Political Economy of Radioactive Colonialism," *The Journal of Ethnic Studies,* 13:3 (1985):123–126. LaDuke and Churchill also point out that "the Laguna people's experience is not unique. Dozens, scores, even hundreds of other similar stories can be told at Hopi, Zuni, Acoma, Isleta, Crow, Northern Cheyenne and elsewhere in the US, and at the Cree, Metis, Athabasca and other territories of Canada" (125). Another useful source of information for environmental conditions in the Pueblo region and on reservations throughout the United States is Peter Matthiessen's *Indian Country* (London: Fontana, 1986). Chapters 3, 11, and 12 deal with the Pueblo area. I am only looking at the impact of uranium mining and related industries here, but it is important to remember that there are many other forms of corporate presence on Native American territories (e.g., coal mining). Silko herself has co-authored an article on the problem of equitable sharing of water resources and on the environmental and human costs arising from an unfair distribution of these resources: see Helen M. Ingram, Lawrence A. Scaff, and Leslie Silko, "Replacing Confusion with Equity: Alternatives for Water Policy in the Colorado River Basin," in Gary D. Weatherford and F. Lee Brown, eds., *New Courses for the Colorado River: Major Issues for the Next Century* (Albuquerque: University of New Mexico Press, 1984), 177–199.

7. See the map of the region in LaDuke and Churchill, "Native America," 117.

8. Matthiessen, *Indian Country,* 294. Matthiessen also notes that "excepting the Great Wall of China, the smoke plume of the Four Corners plant near Farmington (just one component of 'the largest energy-generating power grid in the world,' transmitting electricity through an ugly web of lines and towers as far away as Texas and southern California) was the only man-made phenomenon observed by the astronauts in 1966. It has been called the greatest single source of pollution in the country, greater than the entire city of Los Angeles" (286–287).

9. LaDuke and Churchill, "Native America," 119–120, my emphasis.

10. This is the state that Gilles Deleuze and Félix Guattari refer to as a state of deterritorialization. For a fuller theoretical exposition of this idea, see their *Anti-Oedipus: Capitalism and Schizophrenia* (Minneapolis: University of Minnesota Press, 1983), and *Kafka: Towards a Minor Literature* (Minneapolis: University of Minnesota Press, 1987). While I have tried to avoid the abstracted vocabulary of these works they have nevertheless had a significant influence on the ideas in this essay.

11. The discussion of gift and sacrifice throughout this section is indebted to the two classic works in these areas, M. Mauss's *The Gift: Forms and Functions of Exchange in Archaic*

Societies (New York: Norton, 1967), and H. Hubert and M. Mauss's *Sacrifice: Its Nature and Function* (London: Cohen and West, 1964). The vast amount of anthropological work on sacrifice and gift exchange suggests that, in different cultures and in different historical contexts, there may not always be a clear or absolute separation between these economies. In the cultural and literary domain of Silko's novel, however, the structural relation of gift and sacrifice *is* represented, for the most part, relatively simply as an oppositional one. I have, accordingly, spoken of the competition between these two systems.

12. Larry Evers and Denny Carr, "A Conversation with Leslie Marmon Silko," *Suntracks* 3:1 (1976):31–32. Numerous examples of Navajo stories of witchcraft are given in detail in the appendices of Clyde Kluckhohn's *Navajo Witchcraft* (1944; reprint. Boston: Beacon Press, 1967).

13. See Carol Mitchell, "*Ceremony* as Ritual," *American Indian Quarterly*, 5:1 (1979): 29–30. Mitchell *does* note that "according to Laguna tradition *I'tcts'ity'i* is the mother of the white people while *Nau'ts'ity'i* is the mother of the Indian people, and *I'tcts'ity'i* is half witch. So there does seem to be a traditional connection between a witch and the creation of white people" (29–30). On the extent of Silko's invention in this narrative, see also Kathleen Sands and A. LaVonne Ruoff, eds., "A Discussion of *Ceremony*," *American Indian Quarterly* 5:1 (1979):70.

14. Kluckhohn, *Navajo Witchcraft*, 114–121.

15. An example given by Matthiessen suggests that it is, in fact, actively being used in support of the interests of profiteers and white corporations. The Navajo Council Chairman Peter MacDonald (also known as 'MacDollar,' appointed to Reagan's Energy Task Force and suspected by some of having sold out to corporate interests) lives a life of relative luxury and pays his council members more than twenty times the income of their fellow tribesmen "who are kept in line by threats of bad medicine and evil spells that would come their way from one or two male witches who were never very far from MacDonald's side . . . the Dineh [Navajo] are beset by witchcraft, reflecting a pervasive anxiety and frustration" (Matthiessen, *Indian Country*, 297–298). This reflects the conditions on the reservation in the mid-eighties.

16. Although in this study I am focusing on those cultural transformations that occur where white and native cultures meet, this is not to suggest that all transformations in native cultures are a result of contact with white culture. I have also left the issue of the origins of witchcraft in Pueblo and Navajo cultures to one side simply because, as far as I know, there is no definitive agreement on this point. Elsie Clews Parsons has suggested that, as far as Pueblo cultures are concerned, witchcraft is largely an importation from European (Spanish) culture (see Parsons, "Witchcraft among the Pueblos: Indian or Spanish?" *Man* 27:70 and 80 (1927):106–112, 125–128). Kluckhohn (*Navajo Witchcraft*, 71–72) argues that it is hard to sustain such a theory and that Native American witchcraft practices among the Pueblos and the Navajo are most probably a syncretic blend of Native American and European forms.

17. Kluckhohn, *Navajo Witchcraft*, 127.

18. Peter Gose, "Sacrifice and the Commodity Form in the Andes," *Man* 21:2 (1986):296–310. This article is, in part, a commentary on the work of June Nash and Michael Taussig (see note 2 above).

19. Gose, "Sacrifice and the Commodity Form," 296–297.

20. See Elsie Clews Parsons, *Pueblo Indian Religion* 2 vols. (Chicago: University of Chicago Press, 1939), 27, 397, 539, 760, 763–764. Kluckhohn also gives a Navajo witchery story of victims being decapitated and hung upside down and their blood being used to make malign medicine (Kluckhohn, *Navajo Witchcraft,* 133, 134).

21. Gose, "Sacrifice and the Commodity Form," 296.

22. Gose, "Sacrifice and the Commodity Form," 309.

23. As Lewis Hyde notes, "There are definite limits to the size of the feeling community. Gift exchange, as an economy of feeling life, is also the economy of the small group. When the commonwealth is too large to be based on emotional ties, the gift-feeling must be abandoned as the structuring element" (Hyde, *The Gift: Imagination and the Erotic Life of Property* [New York: Vintage Books, 1983], 267).

24. Jarold Ramsey, "From 'Mythic' to 'Fictive' in a Nez Perce Orpheus Myth," in Karl Kroeber, ed., *Traditional American Indian Literature: Texts and Interpretations* (University of Nebraska Press, 1981), 73.

25. Mauss, *The Gift,* 8–10.

26. As Elsie Clews Parsons notes, in Pueblo cultures cornmeal or pollen "represents growth or new life and so figures in all rites where new life or rebirth or renewal is in mind" (Parsons, *Pueblo Indian Religion,* 483).

27. Hyde, *The Gift,* 19. Silko also in passing nods toward a local Native American resistance to the economics of consumer society. At the Gallup Ceremonial, organized for the white tourists, the Indians "brought their things *to sell* to the tourists, and they brought things *to trade* with each other" (116, my emphasis). And when Tayo offers to pay Betonie for his ceremonial cure, the old man refuses to accept (152).

28. There is little space here to go into the figure of Ts'eh. For more detailed identifications of her, see Kenneth Lincoln, *Native American Renaissance* (Berkeley: University of California Press, 1985), 244–246, and Mitchell, *"Ceremony* as Ritual," 33.

29. The parallels between Silko's narrative and the Grail legends has been noted by Alan R. Velie, *Four American Indian Literary Masters: N. Scott Momaday, James Welch, Leslie Marmon Silko, and Gerald Vizenor* (Norman: University of Oklahoma Press, 1982), 121. Betonie as medicine man is seen as Gawain inasmuch as Gawain is also a healer. The heroic aspects of Gawain as questing knight are seen to be embodied in Tayo who is also seen as the wounded king. Ts'eh (and one could add Night Swan) is compared to the numerous women with supernatural powers in the Arthurian Grail romances. Velie's comparisons are by no means exhaustive but his basic identification seems accurate enough. For the classic outline of Grail legends, see Jessie L. Weston, *From Ritual to Romance* (Cambridge: Cambridge University Press, 1920), a book working within the interpretive framework provided by Frazer.

30. I have borrowed the phrase from Jacqueline Kaye and Abdelhamid's *The Ambiguous Compromise: Language, Literature, and National Identity in Algeria and Morocco* (London: Routledge, 1990).

31. Thomas Pynchon, *Gravity's Rainbow* (London: Picador, 1975), 701.

32. The plot of *Ceremony* is, of course, also strikingly similar to that of N. Scott Mom-

aday's *House Made of Dawn* (New York: Harper and Row, 1968), another novel of ritual regeneration.

33. See Eliot's essay on Joyce's *Ulysses,* "*Ulysses:* Order and Myth," in Eliot, *Selected Prose of T. S. Eliot,* ed. Frank Kermode (London: Faber and Faber, 1975).

34. According to Velie, Silko told him in a telephone conversation (on 3 February 1978) that she was not familiar with the Grail legend when she wrote *Ceremony* (Velie, *Four American Indian Literary Masters,* 108, 155 n. 7). But Silko, an English major who has taught in the Department of English at the University of New Mexico at Albuquerque, has acknowledged (in an interview recorded on 28 January 1977, the same year that her novel was published and a year before the conversation with Velie) that she used to read Eliot and "get irritated" with "all his Greek" (Dexter Fischer, "Stories and Their Tellers: A Conversation with Leslie Marmon Silko," in Fischer, ed., *The Third Woman: Minority Women Writers of the United States* [Boston: Houghton Mifflin, 1980], 21). If Silko read *The Waste Land,* even without reading its infamous annotations, she would have encountered the fragments of a Grail dramatization. As the next section of this essay attempts to demonstrate, there are strong parallels between Eliot's work and Silko's. Whether this is a direct result of Silko's reading of Eliot or not is not particularly important: the juxtaposition of the two texts allows the politics of Silko's mythical imagination to emerge more clearly.

35. Robert Bell, "Circular Design in *Ceremony,*" *American Indian Quarterly* 5:1 (1979):49–50.

36. The connection with the Coyote Transformation ceremony is noted in Bell, "Circular Design in *Ceremony,*" 62, but Bell offers no commentary or description.

37. Leland C. Wyman, *The Red Antway of the Navajo* (Santa Fe: Museum of Navajo Ceremonial Art, 1973), esp. 133–134. In *Ceremony* Betonie's ritual is interspersed with two ritual prayers (142, 143–144). These are part quotation and part adaptations of "Bear's Prayer" and "Thunder Prayers," both part of the Coyote Transformation (Wyman, *The Red Antway,* 134–135, 137–145), though Silko presents them in a different order to the one given in Wyman's text. The end of the Coyote Transformation is the freeing of the patient from the coyote skin in which he has been trapped by malign magic (Wyman, *The Red Antway,* 136). The same narrative is repeated toward the close of *Ceremony* (258).

38. See Evers and Carr, "A Conversation with Leslie Marmon Silko," 30.

39. Wyman, *The Red Antway,* 65.

40. T. S. Eliot, *The Waste Land and other Poems* (London: Faber, 1940), 39–40.

41. Jessie L. Weston, *The Quest of the Holy Grail* (New York: Haskell House, 1965), 90. For more on the Perilous Chapel, see chapter 13 of Weston's *From Ritual to Romance.*

42. Eliot, *The Waste Land,* 42.

43. Eliot, *The Waste Land,* 42.

44. Eliot, *The Waste Land,* 51.

45. Eliot, "*Ulysses:* Order and Myth," 177.

46. Charles Olson, *Muthologos: The Collected Lectures and Interviews* vol. 1, ed. George Buttrick (Bolinas: Four Seasons Foundation, 1978), 1.

47. David Murray, *Forked Tongues: Speech, Writing, and Representation in North American Indian Texts* (London: Pinter Publishers, 1991), 88.

48. The phrase is taken from Eric R. Wolf's *Europe and the People Without History* (Berkeley: University of California Press, 1982).

49. Gose, "Sacrifice and the Commodity Form," 309.

REFERENCES

Bell, Robert. 1979. "Circular Design in *Ceremony*," *American Indian Quarterly* (5(1):47–62.

Deleuze, Gilles, and Félix Guattari. 1983 [1972]. *Anti-Oedipus: Capitalism and Schizophrenia*. Minneapolis: University of Minnesota Press.

———. 1987 [1975]. *Kafka: Towards a Minor Literature*. Minneapolis: University of Minnesota Press.

Eliot, T. S. 1940 [1922]. *The Waste Land and Other Poems*. London: Faber and Faber.

———. 1975. *Selected Prose of T. S. Eliot*, edited by Frank Kermode. London: Faber and Faber.

Evers, Larry, and Denny Carr. 1976. "A Conversation with Leslie Marmon Silko." *Suntracks* 3(1):28–33.

Fisher, Dexter. 1980. "Stories and Their Tellers: A Conversation with Leslie Marmon Silko." In *The Third Woman: Minority Women Writers of the United States*, edited by Dexter Fischer, 18–23. Boston: Houghton Mifflin.

Frazer, Sir George. 1911–1915 [1890]. *The Golden Bough*. London.

Gose, Peter. 1986. "Sacrifice and the Commodity Form in the Andes." *Man* 21(2):296–310.

Guillemin, Jeanne. 1975. *Urban Renegades: The Cultural Strategy of American Indians*. New York: Columbia University Press.

Hechter, Michael. 1975. *Internal Colonialism: The Celtic Fringe in British National Development, 1536–1966*. London: Routledge and Kegan Paul.

Hubert, H., and M. Mauss. 1964 [1899]. *Sacrifice: Its Nature and Function*. London: Cohen and West.

Hyde, Lewis. 1983. *The Gift: Imagination and the Erotic Life of Property*. New York: Vintage Books.

Ingram, Helen M., Lawrence A. Scaff, and Leslie M. Silko. 1984. "Replacing Confusion with Equity: Alternatives for Water Policy in the Colorado River Basin." In *New Courses for the Colorado River: Major Issues for the Next Century*, edited by Gary D. Weatherford and F. Lee Brown, 177–199. Albuquerque: University of New Mexico Press.

Kaye, Jacqueline, and Abdelhamid Zoubir. 1990. *The Ambiguous Compromise: Language, Literature, and National Identity in Algeria and Morocco*. London: Routledge.

Kluckhohn, Clyde. 1967 [1944]. *Navaho Witchcraft*. Boston: Beacon Press.

LaDuke, Winona, and Ward Churchill. 1985. "Native America: The Political Economy of Radioactive Colonialism." *Journal of Ethnic Studies*, 13(3):107–132.

Lincoln, Kenneth. 1983. *Native American Renaissance*. Berkeley: University of California Press.

Marcus, George E., and Michael M. J. Fischer. 1986. *Anthropology as Cultural Critique: An Experimental Moment in the Human Sciences*. Chicago: University of Chicago Press.

Marx, Karl, and Freidrich Engels. 1848. *The Manifesto of the Communist Party*.

Matthiessen, Peter. 1986. *Indian Country.* London: Fontana.

Mauss, Marcel. 1967 [1925]. *The Gift: Forms and Functions of Exchange in Archaic Societies.* New York: Norton.

Mitchell, Carol. 1979. *"Ceremony* as Ritual." *American Indian Quarterly,* 5(1):27–35.

Momaday, N. Scott. 1968. *House Made of Dawn.* New York: Harper and Row.

Murray, David. 1991. *Forked Tongues: Speech, Writing, and Representation in North American Indian Texts.* London: Pinter Publishers.

Nash, June. 1979. *We Eat the Mines and the Mines Eat Us: Dependency and Exploitation in Bolivian Tin Mines.* New York: Columbia University Press.

Olson, Charles. 1978. *Muthologus: The Collected Lectures and Interviews.* Vol. I, ed. George Buttrick. Bolinas: Four Seasons Foundation.

Ortner, Sherry B. 1984. "Theory in Anthropology Since the Sixties." *Comparative Studies in Society and History,* 26:126–166.

Parsons, Elsie Clews. 1927. "Witchcraft among the Pueblos: Indian or Spanish?" *Man* 27(70 and 80):106–112, 125–128.

———. 1939. *Pueblo Indian Religion.* 2 vols. Chicago: University of Chicago Press.

Pynchon, Thomas. 1975. *Gravity's Rainbow.* London: Picador.

Ramsey, Jarold. 1981. "From 'Mythic' to 'Fictive' in a Nez Perce Orpheus Myth." In *Traditional American Indian Literatures: Texts and Interpretations,* edited by Karl Kroeber, 25–44. University of Nebraska Press.

Sands, Kathleen, and A. LaVonne Ruoff, eds. 1979. "A Discussion of *Ceremony.*" *American Indian Quarterly* 5(1):63–70.

Seyersted, Per. 1981. "Two Interviews with Leslie Marmon Silko." *American Studies in Scandinavia* 13(1):17–33.

Silko, Leslie. 1977. *Ceremony.* New York: Viking Press.

———. 1981. *Storyteller.* New York: Seaver Books.

Taussig, Michael. 1980. *The Devil and Commodity Fetishism in South America.* Chapel Hill: University of North Carolina Press.

Velie, Alan R. 1982. *Four American Indian Literary Masters: N. Scott Momaday, James Welch, Leslie Marmon Silko, and Gerald Vizenor.* Norman: University of Oklahoma Press.

Wallerstein, Immanuel. 1974. *The Modern World-System: Capitalist Agriculture and the Origins of the European World-Economy in the Sixteenth Century.* New York: Academic Press.

Weston, Jessie L. 1920. *From Ritual to Romance.* Cambridge: Cambridge University Press.

———. 1965. *The Quest of the Holy Grail.* New York: Haskell House.

Wolf, Eric R. 1982. *Europe and the People Without History.* Berkeley: University of California Press.

Wyman, Leland C. 1973. *The Red Antway of the Navajo.* Santa Fe: Museum of Navajo Ceremonial Art.

PART 3

Ethnocritiques

HEARING THE OLD ONES TALK

Reading Narrated American Indian Lives in
Elizabeth Colson's *Autobiographies of Three
Pomo Women*

Greg Sarris

One cold winter night some twenty-five years ago I listened to Great-Grandma Nettie tell the following story about her life.

Come that man what his name. That one, that old man come. Come there that time. Put hands on table, like that [gesturing with her hands turned down]. Give meat, first thing. That way know if poison man. Come to poison or what. Don't know. Watch. Listen.

Just girl that time. Ten, maybe twelve. but that man stranger man. Come looking for mother. Says that, come looking for mother. Saying that. Where mother? Says that. Not here. No mother here. Come in anyway, that man. Come in like that.

Me just girl that time. Ten years. Ten. Sitting alone. No mother. But start looking for meat. Only thing dry meat—*bishe*. Need live meat old rule way. Need live meat for poison people. But put dry meat out. Put there. Put like that.

Don't talk Indian, that man. Talk only Spanish. Look like Spanish, too. Light skin, that man. Still, half-Indian know something. Like old man Sensi. Done like that. Done old lady Mary other side creek like that. Done basket putting like that. He done like that, they say.

Don't touch meat, that man. Nothing. Talking Spanish. Talking, talking, talking. . . . Ten that time, 'bout that age. Only girl. Only know sí. Mean yes. Yes. I say sí [laughing]. Say that, that's all. Say sí. Say like that. Say sí.

Then happen man eat meat. Then happen never go again. Sitting there all day, that man. Sitting there hands on table, like that [gesturing with her hands turned down]. Hands like that, same. Maybe rape, do me like that. I start working roots. Start working basket roots, watching that man. Work, watching that man. Put food out sometime, acorn.

Nighttime mother come up. Come up road there. Later time mother say good thing keeping busy. Good watching that man. Fool that man. Fool that way. Trust no stranger people. No stranger people. Old man Sensi. Done old lady like that, they say.

Don't know what. Not poison me. What. Don't know. Don't know. Mother don't say. Just talking to that man. Just talking. Talking like that. Talking, talking, talking, talking. . . .

At the time Great-Grandma Nettie, as she was known to half our neighborhood, must have been ninety years old. She was small, wizened, with a shock of straight white hair. Yet Nettie was formidable. She commanded attention. You saw when she flicked her wrist, pointed with her extended chin and great downturned mouth. She sat leaning forward in an overstuffed chair opposite the television, her gnarled hands clutching the ends of the armrests, as if at any moment she would spring to her feet and set things straight.

That particular night Old Auntie Eleanor was visiting Great-Grandma Nettie.[1] Eleanor was a big boisterous woman who lived down the road. She was younger than Nettie, but not by much. She walked over a mile to visit and reminisce with Nettie. Sometimes they argued about this or that. They gossiped. They always conversed with one another in Indian, in their central Pomo language, and talked, whether or not anyone was listening, no matter how loud the television was. And that's what caught my attention: Great Grandma Nettie switched to English. And when she saw that I was listening, she cut a suspicious glance. I felt self-conscious, confused. Was she saying something *for* me or *about* me? Was I an *insider* or an *outsider?*

Unlike most of the children in the room just then, I was not a direct descendant of Nettie's, not one of her grandchildren or great-grandchildren. And I was a mixed-blood. I was living back and forth in Indian and white families. Nettie was telling a story from her life, but with her suspicious glances and all that talk in English about strangers, she called to mind my own life, that uncomfortable borderlands existence that I was reminded of at times like this.

I became Indian. I ignored her. Silence, the Indian's best weapon, an aunt of mine once said. Be an Indian, cut yourself off with silence any way you can. Don't talk. Don't give yourself away. My mother was white. My father was Filipino and Indian. He was of Coast Miwok and Kashaya Pomo ancestry. I had picked up a bit of the Kashaya, or southwestern Pomo, language. I knew certain words, phrases. The Kashaya Pomo language is different but similar to the central Pomo language Great-Grandma Nettie and Old Auntie Eleanor spoke. When Nettie finished her story, or at a given point in the story, she switched back to her Indian language. I was still listening, even with my eyes fixed on the television. She repeated the word *bishun,* or a word that sounded like *bishun,* which means stranger in Kashaya. Then she said something like *chu 'um gat 'to mul.* Don't forget this! And now, looking back, I imagine she said something that meant the same as this: *mi ge bake 'eh mau ama diche mu.* This story is for you.

Great-Grandma Nettie's story haunts me. Throw it out the back door and find it looking through the front-room window. I see it in a glance, the way someone is looking at me. I hear it in people's voices, in the words they use to talk to me. They don't say the exact words, but I hear the words all the same. Insider. Outsider. Indian. White.

I found it again as I read and thought about Elizabeth Colson's *Autobiographies of Three Pomo Women*.

Though Colson changed the three Pomo narrators' names as well as the place names of the area in which they lived, it is clear that the narrators, called respectively Sophie Martinez, Ellen Wood, and Jane Adams, were central Pomo.[2] And, like Nettie and Eleanor who were central Pomo, the narrators were born during the latter part of the nineteenth century. They probably spoke the same or a similar central Pomo language as Nettie and Eleanor. Each of the three Pomo women came from a different central Pomo group and spoke a different central Pomo dialect (Colson 1974:1). Nettie and Eleanor probably spoke one of these dialects. They probably would have been able to understand to some extent whatever language any one of these three Pomo narrators spoke. They shared the same history as the three Pomo narrators. They talked about some of the same things: people's names and how Indians name people; the poisoners and the medicine men and women and their stupendous deeds; the slave raids and the "raping time," first with the Spanish, and then with the Mexicans and the American squatters who followed the Spanish as invaders of Pomo territory.

My mother called me *tidai*. She would say that to me. She called me *mata* too. *Tidai* is just language. *Mata* means 'woman,' but not that way. In some different way, I think.

Sophie Martinez (40)

I was sick. I had lain in bed about five months. . . . Everybody doctored me that time. . . . That's why we have no beads. We paid those five people. They were all singing doctors.

Sophie Martinez (78)

Those days when first Mexicans came up here, they just grab the girls and take them in bushes. Have the pistol in one hand and do what they want and then let them go. My old aunt say they take her once. They put them in a house. One night she pried a board away and got away.

Ellen Wood (112–113)

Once I was sick for a long time. Something was wrong with my legs—somebody had poisoned me. They had taken my shoes and put them in a poison place.

Ellen Wood (169)

When I was a little girl, I used to go around with my mother digging basket roots. It wasn't so hard that time. We sneak around the river. But now [white landowners] won't let you. They make you get out of their place.

Jane Adams (202)

So I thought of Great-Grandma Nettie and Old Auntie Eleanor as I read. But when I gave the text a chance, when I looked at what I was reading, I found much that was different from what I remember hearing, especially in terms of language and narrative format and what was said or not said about certain things. I remember Nettie's English as different from that of the three Pomo narrators. Nettie repeated herself often. She seldom used pronouns and frequently began sentences with a verb which she repeated in successive sentences. Nettie rarely talked to strangers, especially about strangers. "Don't talk much with outside people," Nettie and Eleanor admonished. "Careful what you tell." When the professors visited each summer, Nettie became silent. Old Eleanor gave short, flat answers, told stories no one in the house had ever heard. Of course this just reminded me that the three Pomo narrators were talking to Colson. Anthropologist Colson not only went into the central Pomo community and collected the autobiographies, which has some-thing to do with what was said, but she also edited and wrote them, which has something to do with their language and narrative format.

But here I was also reminded of Nettie's story.

As I thought about the three Pomo narrators and Colson, I remembered hearing the old ones talking that winter night. I thought of Great-Grandma Nettie's story and her suspicious glances. I felt uncomfortable again. My impulse as a critic was to say what was truly Pomo, so that I could show what Colson missed, how ignorant she was as an outsider to Pomo culture. But who am I to speak for and define the central Pomo or any Pomo? To what extent would I be creating an Indian just as Colson had, albeit an Indian different from Colson's? Who am I as a spokesperson for either the Pomo or Colson? Who am I as a Pomo Indian? Who am I as a critic? I am caught on the borderlands again. Nettie's story once more. *Autobiographies of Three Pomo Women* is also a story for me. The text says to me: *mi ge bake 'eh mau ama diche mu.*

In this essay I want to read *Autobiographies* so that I might begin to understand it as a cross-cultural project. But, at the same time, I must begin to understand it as a story for me, not only as a story that positions me in certain ways, but also as a story that can inform me about that position. In light of the constitutive characteristics of narrated American Indian autobiography and critical work surrounding the genre, I will etch out a way to read the text so that I can see the text as well as myself as reader, so that I might inform the text and allow the text to inform me. Then I will come back to and further the discussion of myself and the text that I have started. Of course even in my discussion of the genre and an approach I will be talking about myself and the text, specifically in terms of the questions our relationship provokes. While much of this essay is narrow in focus, principally because it concerns one reader and one text, I hope that it raises questions and offers suggestions about reading narrated American Indian autobiography in general. And in doing as much, it might contribute to larger discussions of reading cross-cultural texts in various cultural contexts.

READING STORIES, READING STRANGERS

Naturally, not all American Indian autobiographies are narrated. Here I am distinguishing narrated autobiographies from those that are written. With narrated autobiographies, which I am discussing in this essay, a recorder-editor records and transcribes what was given orally by the Indian subject.[3] Written autobiographies, on the other hand, are written by the Indian subjects themselves with or without the assistance of editors.[4] Arnold Krupat, who refers to narrated Indian autobiographies as Indian autobiographies, as opposed to autobiographies (written) by Indians, notes: "the principle constituting the [narrated] Indian autobiography as a genre [is] that of *original bicultural composition*" (1985:31). This principle not only provides the key to the narrated autobiography's discursive type, but "provides as well the key to its discursive function, its purposive dimension as an act of power and will. [It is the] ground on which two cultures meet . . . the textual equivalent of the frontier" (31). Yet seldom is the story of that meeting apparent or revealed in the text. While there is a wide spectrum of editorial strategies for dealing with point of view in narrated Indian autobiography, the oldest and most common is what David Brumble calls the Absent Editor strategy, where the editor edits and presents the Indian's narrative "in such a way as to create the fiction that the narrative is all the Indian's own . . . that the Indians speak to us without mediation (Brumble 1988:75–76).[5]

The notion of autobiography as fiction, or interpretation, is nothing new. The autobiography, whether narrated or written, is not the life but an account, a story, of the life. A narrated American Indian autobiography then is in actuality an account of an account, a story of a story; the name of the self (Eakin 1974:214) is hardly the Indian's own. As Vincent Crapanzano observes "[the life history] is, as it were, doubly edited, during the encounter itself [between recorder-editor and narrator] and during the literary reencounter" (1974:4). In the encounter between non-Indian recorder-editor and Indian narrator it is important to remember that given the specific social contingencies of the exchange the Indian may be editing his or her oral narrative, let's say shaping the account, in certain ways. Think of Old Auntie Eleanor and the professors, how she gave them short, flat answers, told stories no one in the household ever heard. Then, after the Indian has presented his or her oral narrative, the recorder-editor translates and shapes the Indian's narrative in certain ways. The language and format in which the narrative was presented by the Indian are often altered significantly as they translated to English or to a more "standard" English and by the way they are shaped to meet the demands for linear chronology, human motivation, and so forth imposed by the genre of conventional autobiography. Yet, as mentioned, the extent to which the Indian's narrative was altered by the recorder-editor is often unclear, not discussed at great length, if at all, by the recorder-editor. The other problem has to do with the extent to which the recorder-editor can know the ways the Indian narrator may have edited his or her narrative for the recorder-editor.

In *Autobiographies* Elizabeth Colson provides introductory material about her collecting and editing the Pomo womens' autobiographies. She also offers "a considered sketch" (2), or brief ethnography, of Pomo culture as well as her analysis of the autobiographies. She notes in her introductory material that for each of the three Pomo narrators she provides a long autobiographical account and a brief autobiographical account.[6] She says that her method was to first collect this latter brief autobiography from the women and then to ask questions to have them enlarge on certain points, identify persons mentioned, and present material in chronological order (4). She then combined the brief autobiography with responses to these questions to produce the longer autobiography. She says the verbatim record of the brief autobiography can be found in an appendix after each long autobiography "since for some purposes it is essential to know just what was regarded as important by the narrator, or at least what she was willing to tell of her life given the time and circumstances" (2). Colson not only talks about the questions she asked and about how she combined them with the brief autobiographical narratives, but also about the changes she made in terms of the narrators' English (the interviews were conducted in English). But everything Colson says in her introductory material about her collecting and editing the narratives is from her point of view. What of her biases that she may not have been fully aware of? What of the ways her presuppositions about language and narrative format influenced her decisions regarding her editing the narratives? How much could she have known about the Pomo women's community and her position in it? What of the Pomo women's point of view about what Colson says? Or their point of view about the collaboration in general? Or about the written text? All that can be known from Colson's introductory material regarding these last three questions is that the Pomo women did not take part in the literary reencounter, that is, in the editing of what they had already said for Colson. They were not consulted in any way. Colson made decisions about editing the spoken text on her own.

It is not enough then just to study Colson's introductory material if I want to understand how *Autobiographies* was made, how both Colson and the three Pomo women participated in its production.[7] Except for including in the longer autobiographical accounts the questions she asked the narrators, Colson does not place herself in the texts of the narrators and functions as Absent Editor. She does not say in her introductory material how the questions she asked may have influenced the women's responses.[8] Granted, her introductory material regarding her collecting and editing the narratives is abundant, more extensive than that of many other recorder-editors. But fundamental questions about what each collaborator contributed to or took away from the text remain. How do I deal with those fundamental questions, specifically those I raised about Colson and her biases? About the Indian women's biases and how the Indian women may have edited their spoken narratives for Colson? I have come back to my original questions then. How do I begin to understand *Autobiographies* as a collaborative endeavor? How do I define, or make sense of, both Colson and the three Pomo women and what each contributed to or took away from the written text? What of my biases, my position as a reader? If I can inform the text in given ways, how might the text in turn inform me?

What is clear, at this point, is that in my approach to *Autobiographies* the cultural and historical background of both Colson and the Pomo narrators must be considered. This way I might not only be able to gain a sense of what each collaborator contributed to the text and the nature of the relationship between the collaborators, but I will also be able to gain a sense of myself as a reader. If I overlook or do not consider seriously one of the collaborator's roles in the production of the text, I am blinded to what that collaborator may have contributed to the composite text and hence to what makes for a fuller understanding of the relationship between collaborators. But, as important, I may be blinded to the ways I am reading, to my presence and the nature of my relationship with culturally diverse perspectives. When I consider both Colson and the Pomo women, I am reminded of my uncomfortable borderlands existence in the cultures of both Colson and the Pomo women and in the ways those cultures intersect in time and place. Those cultures intersect in *Autobiographies*. By using what I know from research and experience, I can *speculate* on what each collaborator brought to their meeting that resulted in the text at hand. Thus I can gain a wider picture of the relationship between Colson and the narrators and what constituted the relationship and the making of the text. What constituted the relationship, say patterns of avoidance or projection in the case of one or both parties, illuminates, and is located in, the history of Pomo and white interrelations. Because I am located in this same history and am positioned as a cultural human subject by it, I can now begin to see more clearly how these particular interrelations affect me and in turn how I might affect them. Reciprocity characterizes the approach: I inform text, which informs me, and so on.

I emphasized the word speculate for definite reasons. The objective here is not to frame *Autobiographies,* not to tell "the story" of the text's making, or of Colson or the Pomo women. Since in the text there are at least two parties present, and now a reader, there is no one story, nor can there ever be. And, again, as a reader I cannot assume knowledge and authority to speak for others and their relationships. Rather, the objective is to open a dialogue with the text such that I can continue to inform and be informed by the text. And this way my dialogue, my representation of my story with the text, can inform and be informed by other readers with other stories who read the text. Accordingly, the history, and what constitutes the history, of interrelations between the Pomo community and the white community is continually opened and explored. The text can be opened and explored in terms of other histories or a larger history of which the text may be a part. So much depends on the readers and what they bring to the text and my reading of the text and what the text and my reading can suggest to them.

The danger, and likely consequence, of assuming knowledge and power in my encounter with *Autobiographies,* specifically in the ways I might define Colson or the Pomo narrators, is that in losing sight of my presence as a reader I will not see how my critical work is tied historically and politically to a real world. Scholars of narrated American Indian autobiography sometimes position themselves in their encounters with the texts in such a way that they do not seem to see the limits of their work or its consequences in an historical and political realm. They may define the autobiographical works as bicultural and composite, but they do not consider each of the collaborator's histories and cultures on the respective collaborator's terms, at least not in a way that might enable the scholars to think about the nature of their work as scholars and its consequences.

Arnold Krupat, for example, argues for a historical approach in his principal study of the genre, *For Those Who Come After.* He examines various narrated autobiographies' relation to an historical period, to the discursive categories of history, science, and art (literature), and to Western modes of emplotment (xii) in order to answer questions regarding the text's production. But the historical period Krupat discusses in detail is, in point of view, distinctly Euroamerican. He observes that recorder-editor S. M. Barrett influenced by the objectivism of turn-of-the-century American social science and salvage anthropology, presents Geronimo, in *Geronimo's Story of His Life,* in a way that Geronimo is "denied the context of heroism [and] of individuality as well; for he is no different from 'any captive,' any 'prisoner of war,' no world-historical figure, but just another 'vanishing type'" (63). But what about Geronimo and Apache history, culture, and language? What about the ways Geronimo may have accommodated or resisted such a presentation of his life? Krupat does not see, or discuss, how he also has denied Geronimo context, in this case as a collaborator in the making of a composite text.

H. David Brumble in *American Indian Autobiography* may account for the Indian's part in the production of a particular narrated autobiography, but he invents "an Indian" as a way to make sense of him or her. He identifies anything unrecognizable or unfamiliar in a narrated American Indian autobiography, such as the presentation of seemingly disconnected deeds or actions, as authentic, as Indian, say, as opposed to Euroamerican, and from this deduces a tribal (Indian, nonliterate, unacculturated, ahistorical) sense of self distinguishable from an individual (Euroamerican, literate, cultured, historical) sense of self. Brumble concludes that Gregorio's sense of self in *Gregorio, The Hand Trembler* "was essentially tribal." "[For Red Crow, like Gregorio] we search in vain for any examination of his self, any self-definition, any sense that he might have been other than he was . . . we are allowed to see clearly just how a preliterate, unacculturated, tribal man conceives of his life and what it means to tell the story of a life" (111). The reality of the situation is that the self which is identifiable as Indian, and has come to signify Indian in the text, is Indian in contact with non-Indian. As Brumble points out, Gregorio listened while Alexander and Dorothea Leighton interviewed other Navajos in his neighborhood before he told them his story in 1940 (111). Gregorio probably ordered and presented an account of his life in a way he thought appropriate given the circumstances; he probably talked about things he figured the Leightons wanted to hear, things he heard other Indians discussing with the Leightons. Seemingly disconnected deeds or actions are likely to be indicative of Gregorio's unease with the genre and circumstances, rather than of his inability to examine and define his self. Of course Brumble was looking for the ways Gregorio, as he is presented textually, fit Brumble's definition of "Indian" and did not consider the ways Gregorio and the situation of the text's making may have qualified that definition.

In *American Indian Women: Telling Their Lives* feminist scholars Gretchen Bataille and Kathleen Sands examine "several autobiographies in terms of what they tell us about the reality of American Indian women's lives" (viii). They propose a "close examination of individual texts . . . to discern the thematic patterns [of tradition and culture contact, acculturation, and return to tradition]" (24). But Bataille and Sands seem to forget that these themes, or thematic patterns, not only may have been invented by them for the texts and understood in terms of their particular interests, but also may emerge in the written documents as a result of the particular interests of the recorder-editors. Bataille and Sands never question how their themes may or may not be relevant from the point of view of the Indian women narrators.[9]

Just as with Brumble and his invention of an "Indian self," Bataille and Sands use their themes and interests to frame or make sense of the Indian. The Indian has no voice of his or her own; the Indian is not considered in terms of his or her history, culture, and language. The scholars cited—Krupat, Brumble, and Bataille and Sands—have thus essentially positioned themselves so that questions of Indian history, culture, and language cannot inform the scholars' work. If Krupat, in his encounter with *Geronimo's Story of His Life,* had in fact considered Apache history, culture, and language, particularly if presented by Apache Indians orally or otherwise, he might have seen himself as present and gained a broader understanding of the text. He would have had to ask, or at least he would have had the opportunity to ask, questions that might have reminded him of his presence and bias. Can Apache stories, songs, and so forth be read (or heard) and thus understood in terms of Euroamerican-specific expectations of language and narrative? If not, why not? What is gained or lost when they are? What, from Krupat's perspective, or an Apache perspective, hinders Krupat's understanding of Geronimo? What might help Krupat understand? How might answers to these questions promote a better understanding of Barrett, or, say, that history, culture, and language in *Geronimo's Story of His Life* which may have seemed more familiar to Krupat? If Krupat knew more about himself as a reader and more about Geronimo, he might have been able to ask more questions about his reading of Barrett and, in turn, seen Barrett in new ways. Likewise, the Indian narrator's background might have helped Brumble and Bataille and Sands open a broader understanding of themselves and the texts they read. They might have seen the limits and consequences of their inventions and themes in their attempts to understand the Indian narrators. In any event, what these scholars—Krupat, Brumble, and Bataille and Sands—do not seem to see is that while purportedly defending Indians and enlightening others about them, they replicate in practice that which characterizes not only certain non-

Indian editors' manner of dealing with Indians, but that of an entire European and Euro-american populace of which these editors and scholars are a part. The Indians are absent or they are strategically removed from the territory, made safe, intelligible on the colonizer's terms.

The questions and issues raised in terms of these scholars' work should not be thought of as simply insider/outsider problems. It is important to note that regardless of the reader's cultural and historical affiliations he or she is not a perfect lens into the life and circumstances of either the non-Indian recorder-editor or the Indian narrator. A non-Indian scholar using an historical approach, for example, to understand a non-Indian recorder-editor's historical and cultural influences is neither the actual recorder-editor nor necessarily a member of the recorder-editor's community in place and time. S. M. Barrett worked at a time before Krupat was born. Differing subjectivities are at play within any tradition. An Indian, either as a scholar working in the university or as a non-university tribal scholar working as a consultant for a non-Indian's scholarly enterprise, is not an objective purveyor of the so-called truths of his or her culture. This is certainly the case among the Pomo where what constitutes, among other things, authentic cultural and reli-gious practices can vary in definition from group to group and even from family to family within a group. And what an Indian knows from his or her tribe may not apply to other tribes. In terms of their histories, cultures, and languages Indian people are different, sometimes radically different, from tribe to tribe.

Remember that in any narrated American Indian autobiography there are at least two parties present. And, just as in my case with *Autobiographies,* readers cannot assume knowledge and power to know and represent others and their relationships. If a reader is knowledgeable about a given historical period or a particular collaborator's culture, ques-tions remain regarding what constitutes the reader's knowing. What is the nature of the reader's knowledge? Specifically, how does the reader understand that knowledge and use it to frame or make sense of elements in a text? For me it is the presence of both a non-Indian and a Pomo Indian in the single text that provokes those questions that bring to light the nature and boundaries of my knowledge as a reader. For many non-Indian readers it might be their encounters with the Indian narrator's culture and language. Whatever it is, wherever the tensions felt, it is a place to start, a place for readers to open dialogue with both the non-Indian recorder-editor and the Indian narrator in a text. The dialogue that starts in one place opens the text and the readers' stories of their relationships with the text, stories that, in turn, inform other readers' stories, continually opening and ex-ploring the *original bicultural composition* at hand.

So much of what we do as readers of texts is unconscious. We aren't aware of all the cultural and personal influences that determine how we read; we aren't aware of our self-boundaries and how we work to tighten or widen them in our encounters with texts. The value of an approach as I have described it is that the reader can begin to unravel that which may be unspoken and unconscious in the making of a bicultural text as well as that which may be unspoken and unconscious in the reader's reading, in this case of two culturally diverse people as text. Readers can understand their encounter with the text as an instance of culture contact, where, as Gabriele Schwab notes, "[the reading] would not only consider our individual acts of reading as a form of culture contact, but also the processes by which we are socialized into our own reading habits. It could stress the social powers that control our reading inducing us to reduce the text's otherness as much as it could stress the subversive powers of the text that reside in its otherness" (112).[10] As Schwab suggests, the task is not to assimilate the text or any element of it to ourselves nor to assimilate ourselves to the text. It is not to reduce difference to sameness nor to exoticize or fetishize it. Rather, the task is to become aware of our tendencies to do any of these things. Maintaining a dialogue that works to validate and respect the subjectivities of text and reader is a way to accomplish the task (Schwab 1986:107–136). In terms of narrated American Indian autobiography beginning and maintaining that kind of dialogue makes for a way to begin to understand the interrelations between cultures within a text and, hence, between the reader and those interrelations within a text of which the reader has become a part.

It seems that I have been in the middle of Pomo and white interrelations for as long as I can remember. My uncomfortable existence within and between the two worlds has to do with the circumstances of my birth. It wasn't only that my mother was white and that my father was Indian. I was so-called illegitimate. My parents were not married. I was put up for adoption and first raised in a white family. I was darker than the other kids in the family. I was different. Before long I took up with some of my natural father's people—Indians. But I didn't know my father. I didn't have, or know of, my Indian brothers and sisters. And I am fair-skinned, obviously a mixed-blood. Too white-looking. As I have said, my life is made visible in a glance, the way someone is looking at me, and in the sound of a voice. It is made visible with stories, too.

Insider. Outsider. Indian. White.

Of course in many areas I am self-conscious, projecting my own insecurity. Great-Grandma Nettie's story may not have had anything to do with me. My insecurity and fear might have shaped the way I heard her voice and understood her glances that night. Certainly Colson and the three Pomo women did not have me in mind in their meeting together during the summers of 1939, 1940, and 1941. But *Autobiographies,* like Great-Grandma Nettie's story, provokes the same insecurities, the same tension. It is the glance, the sound of a voice again. It is the face looking through the front room window. I want to fit in. I want to belong. I don't want to be told I am a stranger.

When I was fourteen a mixed-blood Indian named Robert taught me to box. Actually, it was Robert and another guy named Manuel, who was Portuguese. Robert was part Portuguese. People whispered that both of them were really black. They were a few years older than me and the roughest guys in town. They said I had what it took to be a good fighter. "Hate in your eyes, brother," they said. "You got hate in your eyes." By the time I was sixteen I beat the hell out of people every chance I could, mostly white people. In the city park I beat hell out of a white boy just because I didn't like the way he was looking at me. Not many Indians I knew liked and trusted whites. I was a good Indian then. Any Indian could see I was.

Rejection. Distrust. Anger. Hatred.

These things seem to characterize so much of the history of Pomo and white interrelations. The Pomo Indians of what today are called Sonoma, Lake, and Mendocino counties in north-central California were first colonized by the Spanish and the Russians. The Spanish enslaved many Pomo, particularly those from the southern Pomo territories, in the San Rafael and Sonoma missions. The Russians established a colony called Fort Ross at Metini, the head village of the Kashaya Pomo on the coast. The Russians forced the Kashaya to work for the colony. Mexican and American "squatters" later occupied Pomo territory. They also enslaved the Pomo. Many Pomo groups resisted. The early Spanish chronicles characterized the Pomo as more intelligent, more savage and difficult to convert than other Indians. But by the mid-nineteenth century disease, slave raiding, and countless other forms of violence against the Pomo had reduced them to below ten percent of their precontact population. Some Pomo tribes, especially in the southern territories around Santa Rosa, were completely destroyed, annihilated.

In the winter of 1871–72 the revivalistic Bole Maru (Dream Dance) cult spread among the surviving Pomo like wildfire. Cult leaders preached Indian nationalism and isolationism. Interaction with non-Indians was restricted to work related activities, to the bare minimum necessary for Indian survival. The white world was considered taboo; excessive interaction with white people could cost an Indian his or her reward of everlasting life in the hereafter. A few Pomo tribes practiced the infanticide of mixed-blood children. This went on even as the landless Indians attended Christian churches and listened to the sermons of Catholic and Protestant clergy who provided the Indians food and shelter. The Indians feigned Christianity and the clergy and surrounding white community thought they finally had converted and civilized the Indians. The Indians attended separate "Indian" churches; they remained Indians, separate and not equal to the whites, but understandable, or seemingly understandable, on the whites' terms.

The Bole Maru cult lost its strength and influence in most Pomo communities by the 1930s. Among the Kashaya Pomo the cult movement lasted until 1979 when Essie Parrish, the last Bole Maru leader, died. Yet in the late 1940s Mrs. Parrish had dropped the intense nationalism and isolationism of her predecessors. But the absence or modification of the Bole Maru did not automatically pave the way for better relations between the Pomo and whites. Old patterns of domination, subjugation, and exclusion of Indians by whites continue, albeit in different and sometimes more subtle configurations. And the Indians react.

My father was heralded by his high school as one of its most valuable and cherished athletes. Yet when he went to date the town's fathers' daughters, the wealthy white girls, he was told at the door, "Sorry chief, we aren't hiring any gardeners. Get lost." My father got five of those white girls pregnant. My mother was one of them.

My father became a professional boxer. In the navy, where he started boxing, he was undefeated. His friends say he knocked down Floyd Patterson. When my father fought, he went crazy, his friends say. You could see it coming in his eyes. The same as when he drank.

My father married three times. Three white women. Two of them told me he beat them. He died of a massive heart attack at the age of fifty-two, after years of chronic alcoholism.

A cousin told me that my father's mother, my grandmother, used to tell my father, "Stay away from those white girls. You'll get in trouble and they'll have your ass strung up on a pole. They're like that."

My mother died ten days after she had me. She was sixteen. My father was twenty-one at the time and married to his first wife. My mother and father had been seeing one another for three years, since she was thirteen and he was eighteen. She never breathed a word, never said who the father of her baby was. She could have had his ass strung up on a pole.

"Don't marry no white woman," my cousin says to me. "Look, it was your father's downfall." Every time my cousin sees me she admonishes, "them whites are no good. White women are whores."

Rejection. Distrust. Anger. Hatred.

This history is not just mine. It is not just my story.

It informs *Autobiographies*. It informs the world in which Elizabeth Colson found herself the moment she stepped out of her car, or off the train, on that summer day in 1939. It was there, in Mendocino County, and she became a part of it.

Autobiographies can say something about this history. It can tell a story.

From the three Pomo women and from other sources, Colson learned that "the Pomo had a generalized hatred of whites and that they resent Pomo treatment at the hands of whites and feel them the source of much of their discomfort" (222). But what Colson could have known about this history or anything else, and how well she could have understood what she learned, depended on who she was at the time of her meeting with the three Pomo narrators. Here Colson's abundant commentary—her introductory material, overview of Pomo culture and history, analysis of the autobiographies—is useful, for in it she reveals, often inadvertently, much of who she was when she stepped into that world of the three Pomo women. Yet, as mentioned awhile back, as I begin to consider the text here, specifically in terms of what Colson says regarding who she was and her editing of the narratives, I must at the same time consider the narrators as Pomo speakers and thinkers. And, again, only that way can a broader picture of the relationship between Colson and the Pomo narrators and of the making of their collaborative text be discerned. Only that way can *Autobiographies* illuminate its history, my history, and tell a story.

When considering Colson as a collaborator with the three Pomo women, it is important to remember that she was an anthropologist in a given time and place. This of course had much to do with how she thought and positioned herself in the Pomo community and, subsequently, with what she did or did not see about herself and the Pomo women. As she notes in her introductory material, the autobiographies "were gathered during the summers of 1939, 1940, and 1941, when [Colson] was a member of the Social Science Field Laboratory under the direction of B. W. and E. G. Aginsky" (2). Specifically, she was interested in issues of acculturation and wanted to gain "insight into the life of Pomo women of a particular generation" (1). She worked at a time when the field of anthropology had become increasingly enmeshed with neighboring sciences, particularly psychology. Still, this newer anthropology, like its Boasian forerunner, maintained the split between fact and interpretation. When Colson writes that "this paper is the presentation and analysis of the life histories of the three Pomo women" (1), she is likely assuming that what is presented as a presentation, or actual life history, whether in a given narrator's long account or brief account (remember, Colson provides a long autobiographical account and a brief autobiographical account for each narrator), is something different from the analysis of the life history, in that the former exists for the reader as an artifact rendered independent of Colson's previous interpretive acts, that is, her editing of the narratives. She is likely assuming that her editing of the presentations has not affected them as "pure products" (Clifford 1988), as mirrors that reflect the Pomo women's lived lives.

What Colson notes about her transcriptions of the Pomo women's narratives makes questionable the extent "the presentation" is a fact or pure product. She says: "An attempt has been made to make the English more grammatical and at the same time to preserve some of the terms of speech which give the flavor of the original. Connectives have been placed where no connectives existed; identities have been made a little more secure by such devices as substituting the appropriate gender of pronouns; and occasionally whole sentences have been inverted and knocked into a more 'English' shape" (9). As Colson observes, the three Pomo women "speak habitually and think in this language" (1), and while the interviews were conducted in English, the Pomo English that Colson edited undoubtedly had features typical of, or associated with, the mother language. To see what Colson might have edited here, or to see what was at stake in terms of a pure product, it is important to explore, if only very briefly, features of the mother language that may have influenced the shape of the narrators' English.

In *Kashaya Texts* Robert Oswalt notes that Kashaya Pomo, which, again, is grammatically similar to the narrator's central Pomo, "has no articles and, although it does have a pronoun for 'he,' 'she,' and 'they,' such reference is customarily accomplished by verbal suffixes indicating the relative timing of the actions of the two verbs and whether there is a switch or combination of agent between the verbs. |ba|, for example, signifies that the verb to which it is attached is subordinated in an adverbial way to the main verb in time, and that both have the same agent" (18). It is no wonder, then, that English speakers who "speak Pomo habitually and think in this language" would have trouble with connectives and articles. Colson's adding connectives or appropriate genders of pronouns would not necessarily affect meaning, or sense of the text as the narrators presented it, per se.

But what might have happened when Colson "inverted and knocked whole sentences into a more 'English' shape"? Again Oswalt notes "a common feature of Kashaya Pomo narrative style . . . is the verb repeated in successive sentences with only one small new piece of information: He ran off. Having run off, he ran along. He ran like that. He arrived running" (19). In his translation Oswalt locates the pronoun "he" not only as the subject of the sentences, but in such a way that the subject is the salient feature of the sentences, indeed of the entire passage. Yet Oswalt infers—and he is correct—in his study of Kashaya grammar that the salient feature of the language is the verb. *Action,* and not *subject,* is thematized in Kashaya Pomo. The subject of a Kashaya sentence, whether a pronoun or not, is characteristically suffixed to, and subordinate to, the verb. The verb |mensi| "to do so" often begins the second sentence (i.e., of a narrative) serving only as a carrier for the suffix (Oswalt 19), which further stresses action. Note the same passage in Kashaya with a more literal translation:[11]

mobe	mensiba	mobe	menmobe	mensiba	bele	mo
run off	having run off he	run off	like that run off	having run off he	come	here

While Pomo English speakers from the narrators' generation—those Pomo born during the latter part of the nineteenth century—cannot replicate Pomo syntax in English, they often attempt, intentionally or otherwise, to thematize action when speaking English. You might hear something like: "Run off, way off, he did. Running like that. Running till he come here." Kathy O'Connor, a linguist who studied central and north-central Pomo languages, notes that here too the verb is the salient feature of the language as it is in Kashaya Pomo. Again, the languages are similar grammatically and sound somewhat alike. (The Kashaya are the southwestern tribe of Pomo, located approximately sixty miles west and south of the central Pomo tribes.) O'Connor suggests, however, that the central and northcentral Pomo speakers do not seem to use the verb |mensi| "to do so" as often as the Kashaya Pomo. Still, we can look back at Great-Grandma Nettie's central Pomo English as I remember it and see again how she repeated verbs in successive sentences and worked to thematize action, at least in terms of the topical features of her English. This must have had much to do with her dominant central Pomo language. Now examine the following passage from one of the central Pomo narrator's autobiographies, a narrator from the same generation and general locale as Nettie:

Those boys made that thing. They were singing, singing, singing; and they were making some kind of feather basket with red feathers. They put it on the top of their heads and they put a fish tail on it. Just like a fish they made it. Then they put marks on something on it, and they put it in the water. It was finished. They sang as they put in the water. It floated around there, and they called it back again. (51)

The copious use of verbs is apparent. But imagine a text where the verb, or action, is thematized:

Singing, singing, singing, making thing, them boys. Singing and same time putting red feathers on. Singing and putting red feathers. Making thing with fish tail on, them boys. They putting mark on later time. Putting mark, like that. Then singing more and putting in water. Putting fish tail thing in water. Putting so floating around there. Then calling back, them boys. Calling back later time. Calling back like that.

Of course, the passage quoted from *Autobiographies* may be quite close to the way it was presented by the narrator, Sophie Martinez. Perhaps Martinez, and the other Pomo narrators spoke a more "standard" English than Great-Grandma Nettie. Perhaps they altered their English for Colson, in a way they thought suitable for her, more in line with Colson's English. Unfortunately, there is no way of knowing. For, as Colson claims, she "no longer [has] any of the field notes used in preparing the accounts" (i). Yet Colson does say that "occasionally whole sentences have been inverted and knocked into a more 'English' shape." It is clear here that she edited the narrators' English, but it is not clear how often or to what extent. What does Colson mean by "occasionally"? Again, there is no way of knowing since there is no record of the narratives as they were presented by the narrators. But in light of my cursory study of Pomo linguistics and my experience with Pomo elders from the same generation as these Pomo narrators, it seems that when Colson "inverted" and "knocked" she is likely to have masked the narrators' efforts to stress action in a subject-oriented language. Or, if the narrators were not stressing action but adjusting their Pomo English for Colson, then what Colson was likely to have edited was the narrators' slips, or lapses, into their Pomo English. This also would be the case if the narrators regularly used an English close to what we find in Colson's transcription. Undoubtedly, there is more here to talk about than the thematization of action or subject; undoubtedly I have ignored many other factors regarding the narrators' grammar and Colson's transcription of it that may have affected the presentations as we see them. Suffice it to say that Colson's editing altered, perhaps in significant ways, the text's pureness as a so-called product from "Pomo women of a particular generation."

It is important to note here that linguistic features thematized in a language do not necessarily represent how the speaker thinks, or conceives, of his or her world. As Chester C. Christian, Jr., observes, "It is futile to create a science either of culture or of language through the use of language characteristics of any given culture" (149). Further, he cites in a footnote M. Edgarton, Jr., whose work, he suggests, "implies not only the limitations of language as an instrument of science, but also the persistence of culture and the relation of language to culture" (155). Violet Chappell, a fluent speaker of Kashaya

Pomo, says: "Yeah, us people of the [Kashaya] language think different, like our language is different [from English]. But it's more to it than just that." To suggest that linguistic features alone reveal how the narrators truly conceive of their world—that the narrators' emphasis on action rather than subject may have been more indicative of what they were saying about how they understood their lives—is to ignore the complex relation of language to culture and history and, consequently, important cultural issues related to the collaborative endeavor in question. To begin to understand the complex relation of language to culture and history it is imperative that scholars and other readers have an accurate sense of the speaker's language, of the language at hand.[12] If Colson or her readers take the Pomo narrators' textualized narratives as virtually pure presentations, or representations of those presentations, unaffected by Colson's editing, an understanding of that relation of language to culture and history is thus affected. It seems ironic given Colson's interest in issues of acculturation that she doesn't consider seriously the relation of the women's Pomo English to their Pomo language and culture and history. If she had, might her readers have found a different text, a different English used by the Pomo women?

Colson has edited not only the narrators' grammar but also certain features of their narrative formats, which again raises questions regarding the "factual" state of the presentations. Colson mentions in her introductory material that "in presenting the data, [she] has attempted to arrange them in chronological order, which has meant in general the sacrifice of the sequence of thought of the informant. The accounts given in the interviews have been cut and chopped to fit into the procrustean bed of chronological sequence. Also where several accounts of the same event are available, these have been combined and worked into one running description" (9). Older Pomo narrators, typical of speakers from many other traditionally oral cultures, move back and forth in time and place to use the past to comment on the present and vice versa. When Mabel McKay, a Cache Creek Pomo elder, tells me stories she moves in and out of given time frames. She might be talking about a man she knows and then in the next moment begin talking about her great-grandmother and then shift back to the man. For Mabel there is probably a clear connection between these time frames and the players in them, a connection I often do not readily discern, a connection that becomes intelligible to me in subsequent conversations and personal reflections or not at all. Speakers from traditionally oral cultures are not the only ones who repeat stories and details or disrupt the procrustean bed of chronological sequence. Imagine editing Faulkner's *Go Down, Moses, The Sound and the Fury,* or *Absalom, Absalom!* to fit into this bed and how meaning, as Faulkner understood and intended it, would be affected.

A Pomo narrator's mere mention of a place or name can work to set the scene or to thematize action in a story. The narrator might, for example, mention a taboo mountain, which will color events in a narrative in given ways for a Pomo listener familiar with the lore associated with the particular mountain.[13] The narrator will often repeat things—the name of a place or person, certain anecdotes—to underscore a theme or idea.

The name of the taboo mountain, or an anecdote associated with it, might be repeated over and over again by the narrator to achieve a certain effect or response from the listener. Or the narrator may repeat the name or anecdote simply because it is integral in some way to the story as the narrator understands and remembers it for himself or herself. I remember that Great-Grandma Nettie kept repeating her age when she told the story that winter night in Santa Rosa. She might have been reminding herself and Old Auntie Eleanor of how young she was at the time and how she nonetheless knew to behave in given ways around strangers. Or she may have had other reasons for repeating her age. She may have had many reasons. I don't know. But to edit out, or to "combine and work into one running description," Nettie's repetitions of her age or anything else is to overlook and make unavailable for readers these possibilities in Nettie's narrative.

In rereading my version of Sophie Martinez's passage (as presented by Colson) cited above, I note that I mention "red feathers" twice. In the passage quoted directly from the text Martinez mentions "red feathers" only once. For many Pomo the color red is associated with human blood, with evil, and is, hence, taboo. Red feathers—the red feathers of a woodpecker's top—are used in "sun baskets," baskets made for the purpose of poisoning people. Perhaps as a Pomo scholar I inadvertently repeated "red feathers" because of my own feelings and associations with them and the color red. Interestingly enough this passage was excerpted from a story about how a lake became taboo. Might Martinez also have repeated "red feathers" more than once? Again, there is no way of knowing.

Colson says, "since condensing many accounts into one leaves the reader with no indication as to the common motives or particular interests of the informant, the recurrence of themes or an eagerness to repeat a given event will be indicated in a footnote or dealt with in the final analysis" (9). Naturally, it is impossible for Colson who spent only three summers in the central Pomo community to fully comprehend the significance for the narrators of certain places, names, or anecdotes that are repeated unless perhaps Colson asked about the repetitions. But the reader cannot tell from anything Colson says in her introductory material and analysis or from the questions she poses (and inserts) in the narratives whether or not she asked about the repetitions.[14] All that can be known is that Colson made the decisions as to what constituted a "common theme" or a "recurrence of theme" and, as with the issues of grammar, Colson's biases are likely to have influenced her decisions.

Colson does mention that she is "fully aware of the disadvantage involved in thus extensively editing life history materials, especially in the drastic revisions necessary to humor the historical bias of our own culture" (9). And she concludes that she has "attempted to compromise somewhere halfway between the popularized life history and the truly scientific account" (10). If this is an admission regarding the extent the presentations are in fact interpretations, that she is present in the autobiographical accounts as an editor, then what she is saying is eclipsed by her additional material, particularly her overview, or brief ethnography, of Pomo culture "both past and present" (2), without which, in Colson's words, "the life histories lose much of their point" (2). This material frames the narratives in given ways and works to maintain that split between fact and interpretation, as if the ethnography, say, were a key that unlocks the raw presentations. Readers are provided an ethnography written by Colson that describes precontact and postcontact Pomo against which her readers can measure or place the women's "unedited" lives and see the extent to which the women are acculturated or whatever. The underlying assumption is that the ethnography is objective, a clear record of Pomo lifeways, just as the women's narratives are clear records of their lived lives. Both exist on the premise that Colson is fundamentally absent.

In all likelihood Colson's mention of her editing in terms of narrative format is in reference to her work on the longer autobiographical accounts. Remember, Colson notes that the brief autobiographical accounts that she provides for each narrator are "verbatim" (2) as opposed to the longer autobiographical accounts where Colson asked the narrators questions to have them enlarge on certain points and so forth and where she presented the material in chronological order. But given the issues of grammar discussed above, one wonders how verbatim even the brief autobiographical accounts are. Sophie Martinez, for whom "speaking in English was probably an effort" (6), uses the same English in both her long and brief narratives. Despite H. David Brumble's observation that "no interpreters were used" (1981:11), Colson notes that "on one occasion [Sophie Martinez] asked [her granddaughter] to act as an interpreter" (6). Colson continues: "The greatest amount of editing has been done on the account of Mrs. Martinez. That of Mrs. Wood and that of Mrs. Adams stand substantially in the language in which they were given" (9). Interestingly enough, the English of Wood and Adams, both in their long and brief accounts, is largely indistinguishable from that of Martinez.[15] Is this mere coincidence? Did Colson shape Martinez's English to look like that of Wood's and Adams's?

It is important to note that Colson influenced the direction of the "spontaneous" (5) brief autobiographical accounts even if it was merely to suggest that Sophie Martinez "start when she could first remember and tell as much as she could remember about her life" (4). With Ellen Wood, Colson asked specific questions (i.e., "What did children about that age do when you were young?") in several interviews before asking for a life history (4). Colson says, "The spontaneous, unquestioned, life history had already been obtained [by another fieldworker] from Mrs. Adams" (5). It is not clear then how spontaneous or unquestioned Mrs. Adams's account is since Colson either did not know or does not mention whether the fieldworker asked any questions or gave any suggestions regarding what to talk about to Mrs. Adams. But given the suggestion Colson gave Martinez and the questions Colson asked Wood, how can the autobiographical accounts of Martinez and Wood be considered spontaneous, unquestioned?

And this brings me directly to questions regarding Colson's presence in the Pomo women's community. Thus far I have talked only about language and narrative format, specifically about the ways Colson's editing may have affected the texts as mirrors from which Colson and her readers can see reflected the Pomo women's lived lives. Lest I talk about Colson's presence as a non-Indian recorder-editor in the Pomo community, it might be assumed that if Colson had left the women's narratives alone, if she had transcribed them exactly as they were spoken (if that were even possible), we might in fact have pure products. But, as Vincent Crapanzano pointed out, the spoken text is not only edited by the recorder-editor in the literary reencounter with the recorded text, but it is also edited by the narrator as she is speaking for the recorder-editor. While Colson edited what she recorded, the three Pomo women are likely to have edited *what* they told Colson. Perhaps Sophie Martinez did not repeat "red feathers" on purpose given the fact that she was talking to Colson. The point is that Colson's presence in the Pomo community surely positioned the narrators as speakers (and Colson as a recorder-editor) in certain ways. If an autobiographical account had been spontaneous, it was spontaneous for Colson, likely edited by the Pomo narrator for Colson.

As Colson learned from the three Pomo women and from other sources, "the Pomo had a generalized hatred of whites and that they resent Pomo treatment at the hands of whites and feel them the source of much of their discomfort" (222). Still, Colson claims her relationship with these women was good because Colson and other members of the Field Laboratory treated them "as equals" (8) and because Colson was "someone who was fairly neutral and who made no attempt to judge them" (8). The question remains whether these Pomo women treated Colson as an "equal," as one of them, that is, a non-white insider. Given Colson's appearance and her education, her obvious membership in the dominant white culture, and the Pomo Indians' "generalized hatred of whites," it is unlikely that the three narrators saw Colson as one of them. And it must be remembered that these particular narrators grew up at a time when the revivalistic Bole Maru movement, which preached Indian nationalism and isolationism, was at its peak among the Pomo. Speaking or interacting in any way with non-Indians unnecessarily was viewed by the Bole Maru advocates as sinful, as compromising the movement's resistance to white cultural and religious domination. To speak with a white person was to speak with the devil. As an Indian, you exercised extreme caution. You never said anymore to a white person than you had to.

The Pomo I know are generally very private, not given to open exchange with outsiders, particularly about personal and religious matters. From what I have been told by my Pomo elders this was the case even before contact with the European invaders. People from one village were cautious and respectful of those from another village, even a village just across the creek, or at the other end of the same valley. Furthermore, telling stories and long tales during the summer months—when Colson did all her interviewing—was considered taboo. Many elders still follow this ancient rule, insisting that they will speak of stories and such things only in winter. "[The ground] got to be clear of snakes, crawling lizards," Old Auntie Eleanor used to say. Mabel McKay said: "If you think about them things [tales and stories] during summer, you going to step on lizard, snake, or something. Not watching where you are going. Don't talk about to nobody then." So by approaching these women during the summer months, Colson may have invaded their privacy and asked them to break taboo. Colson notes how Sophie Martinez "would suddenly switch [topics of conversation] to a description of basket types or of food before [Colson] had realized that someone was approaching" (6). She received "some material regarding the women by other informants" (9), largely about topics the women did not discuss, such as one woman's involvement in a religious cult (99). In these instances it is clear the narrators edited their material for Colson.

The fact remains still that the Pomo women did speak, that they were willing to talk to Colson, to tell her stories. The question arises then as to what motivated these women to work with Colson. Certainly money had much to do with the women's willingness to speak. Colson relates that "almost every informant at some point argued that [twenty-five cents an hour] was insufficient and that they had been advised by other Pomo not to work unless they were paid more" (7). These Pomo women interacted with Colson at a time when virtually every Pomo community had had over thirty years of experience with ethnographers and others who were interested in various aspects of Pomo culture and willing to pay for information and material goods. Ethnographer S. M. Barrett had worked with the northern, central, and eastern groups of Pomo as early as 1906. Pomo women had been selling and trading their baskets to whites since the 1870s. Clearly, the Pomo saw in these interested whites the opportunity to make money, which usually was desperately needed. Just from what Colson notes about the narrators' mention of money, it seems these three Pomo women also saw the opportunity to make money, in this particular case by working with Colson.

Of course money does not guarantee so-called unedited information. I have watched Pomo informants, as they have been called, make an art of editing what they tell "them scientists." One Pomo woman calls it the "giving-them-a-piece work." She says: "I give them pieces of this and that. I tell them a few things. Even things we shouldn't talk about [to non-Indians]. They never get the whole picture, not with just pieces of this and that. Besides, they make up what they want anyway. They tell their own stories about whatever I tell them." Another Pomo elder refers to her experience with anthropologists as "money-storytelling-time." Speakers will often compare notes of their stories for anthropologists with one another. From these discussions comes raucous laughter. The so-called informants I know come from a long tradition of "giving-them-a-piece work" and "money-storytelling-time." At the time the three Pomo narrators worked with Colson "the tradition" was probably already over thirty years old, in existence for as long as Pomo speakers had been talking to anthropologists and other whites interested in learning about Pomo culture.

This is not to suggest that the three Pomo women were lying to Colson or that they were editing their accounts in the manner of these other Pomo speakers. As mentioned at the start of this essay, the three Pomo women—Sophie Martinez, Ellen Wood, Jane Adams—talked (to Colson) about some of the same things I remember hearing Great-Grandma Nettie and Old Auntie Eleanor talk about. But, as I also mentioned, Nettie and Eleanor were more guarded about some of these same things. When the professors visited each summer and asked about "charms" and "poisoning," Old Auntie Eleanor told stories no one in the house had ever heard. She certainly did not talk to the professors about these things in terms of people she knew or in reference to members of her own family. The three Pomo narrators did talk about these things and often in terms of people they knew or in reference to their own families. Sophie Martinez, for example, related the following about a snake charm:

My father's wife tried to get a baby that time. Some of them who want a baby would catch a bull snake. They catch it alive and put it around the woman's waist. I couldn't stand that bull snake around my body, but I saw them do that. She was crying and afraid of the bull snake. My grandfather did that [to her father's wife]. (Colson 43)

Martinez also mentions, as Colson notes, "ten deaths in her immediate family which she ascribes to poisoning" (223).

Given what these narrators did say, the question arises again regarding what motivated these women to work with Colson. Surely there may have been factors besides monetary payment. Perhaps the Pomo women saw in a recorded and written record of their lives the opportunity to clear up community rumors about them, to set the record straight about their lives and their families. Maybe in talking about the deaths of her family members Martinez saw the opportunity to convey her grief, or whatever, to others. In talking about her dreams Ellen Wood might have been using her situation with Colson to convey to others her power as a Pomo dreamer. Perhaps these narrators wanted to show other Indians in their community that in talking to Colson and earning money they could talk about certain "private" matters without giving away valuable tribal information. Perhaps they had their individual versions of "giving-them-a-piece work." Any combination of these possibilities and others I have not thought of or mentioned may have motivated the narrators to work with Colson.

Today a number of Pomo elders want to record life histories, songs, and tribal stories. Often they want a written record for the younger generations. They take pride in working with anthropologists, since in many ways the anthropologists' presence in their homes signals to others the elder's knowledge of tribal history and culture. I doubt, however, that the three Pomo narrators worked with Colson to pass down tribal information or to demonstrate to others how knowledgeable they were about their history or culture. They grew up at a time when talking about these things to outsiders was taboo. And apparently these narrators were still guarded about many subjects they talked to Colson about, particularly in front of other Indians. Remember that Sophie Martinez "would suddenly switch [topics of conversation] to a description of basket types or of food before

[Colson] had realized that someone was approaching." Finally, in thinking about what motivated the Pomo narrators to work with Colson, that is, in addition to monetary payment, I must consider the rumor that I have heard more than once about Colson having been forced by the narrators to change names and placenames because the narrators did not like what Colson had written. A Pomo elder told me: "One of them ladies [narrators] said to that white lady she was going to have her done in. Killed. Poison Indian way. Fix her for writing them things. She say to that white lady 'you better change my name, not say where this place is.'" Did one of the narrators talk about certain things and then change her mind about having them printed? Was she bending under community pressure? Was it a way for her to get paid and still be safe or unaccountable for anything she should not have talked about?

So much of any discussion at this point about what motivated the Pomo women to work with Colson is conjecture, as is any discussion about how the women edited their life stories for Colson and about the kind of English they spoke. More than space allows should be said, particularly from a Pomo perspective, about the intersecting cultures and histories of Colson and the Pomo women and the contingencies of exchange as they may have affected the production of the autobiographical narratives. More stories should be told, not to figure out "the story" or "truth" of the collaborators' relationship and the making of their composite text, but to further explore my discussion, say, about linguistic and cultural factors as they may have concerned the collaborators and their work together. My discussion, after all, is part of my story, the way I am constructing things so they might make sense to me. More should be said, certainly from a Pomo woman's perspective, about the relations between white women and Indian women in the central Pomo region. I know that white women in one town in the central Pomo region passed an ordinance near the turn of the century forbidding the hiring of Indian women as domestics. This came after the Pomo women had been working in the same white households for nearly two decades. It seems the white women became concerned about the "half-breed" children of the domestic help. This story is told among Indian women today. And given what my cousin said to me about white women and my father, it would seem that some Pomo women do not particularly care for white women. But the ways in which I can understand my cousin's remark and her anger are limited. What I can know and understand culturally and historically about the relations between Indian women and white women is shaped in gender specific ways. Pomo women and white women and women who are both Pomo and white and women who are neither Pomo nor white can tell stories, open the text in ways I cannot, ways that are relevant to them and that inform my own story of and with the text.

My discussion of Colson and the Pomo women serves only to suggest possibilities, possible factors and scenarios that may have been at work as Colson and the Pomo women made *Autobiographies*. It shows what may have constituted fundamental differences in language and culture between two cultures that may have affected how representatives from those cultures understood their own lives and were able to talk to others and understand others' lives. And, of course, there is a history of interrelations between these cultures that in some ways is associated with these differences and certainly affects inter- action between members of the respective cultures. What does seem clear from what I have suggested especially in terms of Pomo language and culture as they may have related to the situation at hand is that the autobiographical accounts are not pure products. Col- son's presence as a recorder in the Pomo women's community and her work as an editor of the women's spoken texts have affected the content, language, and shape of the wom- en's texts that are presented in *Autobiographies*. Her presence as a recorder and her work as an editor may have affected significantly the pictures readers get of the Pomo women's lived lives. The pictures are not mirrors that reflect the women's lives as the women necessarily see and understand their lives. They are not pictures the women might have drawn in other situations and for other listeners. The pictures here are composite pictures. But, again, this is the situation for any narrated American Indian autobiography.

A story that I discern in this particular case is that Colson did not see how her presence may have affected the women's accounts as representative of their lived lives. And Colson's introductory statement that "this paper is the presentation and analysis of the life histories of three Pomo women" helps me to understand what makes for the story. As suggested, Colson is likely assuming the presentation (of the life histories) is fact, raw data, as opposed to the analysis, which is interpretation. And, as also suggested, Colson's statement and assumption are probably predicated on her likely belief in and influence by an anthropology that maintained the split between fact and interpretation. This anthropol- ogy, like other social sciences at the time, stipulated that the social scientists could be and should be objective, that the social scientist's presence with its culture specific biases could be and should be put aside, transcended during the "scientific" undertaking. It becomes understandable, then, why Colson may have positioned her "self" as she did, as absent from her work, and why, as a result, she did not see how her presence affected "the presentation." If she did not see herself as present in the Pomo women's community, as someone sharing a history and associated with the Pomo women, how might she have seriously considered the ways the women might have been editing their accounts for her? If she did not see herself as present in her literary reencounter with the women's recorded texts, as someone influenced by certain linguistic and narrative biases, how might she have seen the ways her editing may have significantly altered the spoken texts? How might she have begun to understand the Pomo women (and herself) other than she did?

Remember, Colson does acknowledge that she edited the women's accounts. So in a sense she does see herself as present. But she does not discuss in any significant manner how her presence may have had an impact on the picture the accounts provide of the women's lives. As mentioned, any discussion, or admission, on the part of Colson regarding the extent the presentations are in fact interpretations, that her presence affected the pureness of the accounts, is undermined by her ethnography of Pomo culture, which frames the accounts in given ways, serving as a key to unlock the raw presentations. Also, in her "Analysis Of The Life Histories" she treats the autobiographical accounts as raw data. Her tone is detached, authoritative, conclusive. She writes, for example, "When one turns to in-group relationships the picture is entirely changed [from the Pomo's relationship with outsiders]. There is evidence from the life histories that aggressive feelings find an outlet in three forms: physical violence, poisoning, and gossip" (223). Another example: "This last fact [of Catholics underwriting Pomo subsistence] may account for the relatively little concern evinced in the life histories for subsistence" (225). This last observation appears ironic given Colson's earlier testimony that "almost every informant at some time argued that [twenty-five cents an hour] was insufficient and that they had been advised by other Pomo not to work unless they were paid more." Colson seems to be forgetting throughout her "Analysis" that she is looking at what she partly made.

In any event, had Colson seen her role and influence in the collaboration otherwise, she may have seen the Indians differently. She may have come to different conclusions about the Pomo women and their lives. Despite the fact that these three Pomo women lived in the midst of cultural flux and that they had many marriages, raised and lost several children, and moved from place to place, Colson concludes: "Pomo life, as portrayed in these three life histories, emerges as a fairly simple one from the point of view of its participants, for they live through much of the same events with little variation in happenings to distinguish their lives" (233). Colson's interest in the lives of these three Pomo women was in large part scientific. For, and to some extent with, the Pomo women she created a language that was flat and simple, a language which might have lead one to think that "Pomo life, as portrayed in these life histories, emerges as a fairly simple one from the point of view of its participants." Here, it seems, the text begs its interpretation.

The story I have drawn of Colson and the making of *Autobiographies* is not unusual, not surprising. Krupat points out that earlier in the century the objectivism of American social science influenced S. M. Barrett in his work with Geronimo in the making of *Geronimo's Story of His Life*. This objectivism not only influenced a host of recorder-editors working on Indian life histories, but also many others, most of whom were social scientists, working with American Indians (and other indigenous peoples) on other projects. The detached-observer mode was standard. Lately, some social scientists and various social critics have seen objectivism as a myth and pointed to its limits and dangers (Clifford 1983, 1988; Marcus and Fischer 1986; Rosaldo 1989). They have pointed to the limits of what "objective" observers can see and know about themselves and those they observe. They have pointed out that under the guise of objectivism these observers often assume authority to make sense and represent others (i.e., Clifford 1983). And they have illustrated how objectivism in this latter situation can be affiliated with hegemony and empire, particularly as it is used by members of a dominant group in their interactions with subordinate groups (i.e., Rosaldo 1989). These scholars are not suggesting that critical activity is impossible. Rather, they seem to be saying that critical activity is tied always to the subjectivity of observers and the relationships they establish with that with which they are observing or reading.

I have suggested what Colson may not have seen about herself and the Pomo women, particularly in terms of the women's language and culture, because of her objective stance, the way she positioned herself in relation to the women. And by positioning herself as objective, as fundamentally absent, in relation to the women, she likely did not have a good sense of the history she shared with these women nor of the ways her endeavors with them may have replicated and reinforced historical patterns of Pomo and white interrelations. It appears that to some degree Colson made the narratives sensible, or intelligible, on her terms so that she could make sense of (analyze) them, on her terms. Remember, the Pomo women did not take part in the editing of their spoken text in the literary reencounter. They were not consulted in any way. Colson made decisions about editing language and so forth on her own. Here historical patterns of Pomo and white interrelations are repeated, reconfigured in the encounter between Colson and the Pomo women and the making of *Autobiographies*. Pomo country is again cleaned up, made intelligible on white people's terms. Open, proactive intercultural communication collapses. Colson, like the nineteenth-century Catholic and Protestant clergy who provided the Pomo people "Indian" churches, could not see or imagine how the Indians were anything but what they seemed to her as an "impartial" observer. Just as the clergy did not see the Pomo in terms of their participation in the revivalistic Bole Maru cult, Colson did not see the Pomo in terms of what various aspects of Pomo language, culture, and history may have revealed about them (and her). For the Pomo certain attitudes about whites, especially those interested in learning about Indians, are reinforced. The Pomo elder who told me one of the narrators threatened to kill Colson said: "See, that's how them whites are. No respect. Do things, write anything they want. So don't tell them about us in the school. Don't trust them. They're like that white lady [Colson]. I tell all [Indian] young people about that."

I believe Colson was sincere when she said she was "someone who was fairly neutral and who made no attempt to judge [the women]" (8). I believe she treated the women "as equals" to the best of her ability and did not regard the Pomo Indians in the racist manner of the general local white community at the time. The discussion thus far is not meant simply to blame Colson, to place responsibility for problems regarding Pomo and white interrelations on her shoulders. The problems are not that simple. And Colson could not have fully understood the nature and consequences of her work. No one can fully understand the nature and consequences of his or her work. No one can see all of the ways he or she is not "fairly neutral." The story of Colson and the Pomo women and their making of *Autobiographies* teaches not only about the possible limits and dangers of objectivism, but also about the necessity for collaborators in any cross-cultural project to see themselves as present, as persons working in a given place at a given time. That way, they might begin to understand the nature and consequences of their work in the places they work and live.

The social scientists who discuss the limits and dangers of objectivism also stress the necessity for participants in a cross-cultural endeavor to see themselves as present. These scientists often speak of subjective knowledge and self-reflexivity and of poly-vocality both in one's encounter with others and in one's representation of the encounter. But all of this must also hold for the practice of reading texts, especially those where readers must negotiate differing cultural perspectives. Again, in narrated American Indian autobiographies readers must negotiate not only that in the texts which may be different or upsetting in terms of their own lives, but also that in the texts which may be different or upsetting between the parties that made the texts. Of course I am not the first to suggest readers think about, or historicize, their positions as readers (and critics). David Bleich (1986) and Edward W. Said (1989) have certainly sounded the trumpet. But these critics, like most others sounding the trumpet in various fields of study, present their arguments in conventional argumentative narratives, the forms of which usually undermine not only a record of the critic's interaction with the text, but in general the autobiography of the critic, a necessary component of the reading practice the critics are calling for.[16] The politics of reading (Boyarin 1991) are not seen in practice.

In this essay I hope to have documented in some degree my interaction with *Autobiographies*. Any story or lesson, any reading if you will, that I discern from the text, whether about objectivism or whatever, has to do with that interaction. Other readers can see, at least in terms of what I have revealed, what constitutes my reading; they have in this essay both my reading of the text, which opens and extends its story in certain ways, and my encounter with it, which calls up my influences and biases as a reader. They can see, to some extent, how my reading of *Autobiographies* is my own. The essay, then, exists as a document, whereby other readers can engage that which it contains, pointing out my limits and possibilities, failures and successes, replications and inven-tions, in terms of this text and history as well as other texts and other histories. The making of *Autobiographies* cannot be characterized solely by one story based on one reader's interaction with the text. The text itself provides the opportunity for many stories, many readings, a great deal of critical exchange. One story can start the talk, touch other stories, teach the reader. My one story is small and, as I noted, not so unusual in certain ways, but from it I see much of my history and understand, finally, how *Autobiographies* is a story for me.

HEARING THE OLD ONES TALK

For a long time I wanted to dismiss Colson. I wanted to show her as ignorant, arrogant, typically "white." I wanted to run her out of the territory.

I wanted my anger.

As an Indian that's what I know best. But that isn't exactly the case. My anger is also that of a mixed-blood caught in the middle.

Early on I learned to take sides. I chose the Indian side. Or I was quiet, never letting anyone know my predicament. I passed. Always I denied. I took a stand within myself. I took a stand against myself.

In the academy we are trained to take a stand and defend it. Perhaps that is why I have done so well and become a professor. All that early training. And in the academy scholars now want "an Indian point of view." And Indians want and need to talk, tell their stories. But what constitutes "an Indian point of view"? By what and whose definition is a point of view "Indian"? How might an Indian's story in turn define "Indian"? What of an Indian's story, then, that is not "Indian"?

I felt I had to take sides. As a scholar I had to be "Indian," a Pomo Indian who knows and discusses that which is "Pomo," that which, in turn, can be used to make sense of *Autobiographies* from a "Pomo point of view." I could say what was "Pomo" and what was "Colson." I kept looking at *Autobiographies* from an "Indian point of view." I kept thinking of how "Indians" really are. I didn't want to be reminded of my very real situation in two worlds. I didn't want personal experience to get in the way of my "Indian analysis and discussion" of the text. It would cloud a pure, authoritative reading from an "Indian" perspective. It would cloud a distanced academic stance that was now Indian. Indian and objective.

More denial. Rejection. Frustration and anger.

So I wanted to take my anger out on Colson. I could do it objectively, truthfully.

Objectivity, or what inheres in any supposed practice of it, namely the user's separation from his or her self and from whatever it is that is being viewed or studied, kept my anger alive. It also kept me blinded. By taking an "Indian stance," by keeping myself separate from both my larger personal experience and the text, I continue old patterns. My "Indian" objective truth versus Colson's objective truth. Either truth precludes us seeing the larger picture of the forces which position us as knowers of ourselves and others. Either truth precludes us seeing the limits and consequences of the truth we paint. In the case of Colson and the three Pomo women and myself we become a part of an old and vicious cycle. One says what the other is. The other gets defensive and says what the one is. No one sees what we do to ourselves and one another. No one sees beyond themselves. Personal and cultural boundaries are rigidified. We don't see how our worlds are interrelated. We don't see our very real situations in both worlds. There is nowhere to see, no way to talk to one another. Oppressive situations are internalized by individuals in given ways and played out again by the same individuals in given ways. The operation of a vicious cycle, a mean history.

Denial. Rejection. Frustration and anger.

Luckily, I kept hearing Great-Grandma Nettie. She wouldn't stay down. She and Old Auntie Eleanor were, after all, the only central Pomo I knew from the same generation as the three Pomo women. When I looked to Nettie and Eleanor for answers about what was "Pomo," they shot back those suspicious glances. Who was I? Was I Indian?

Was I a stranger? They didn't allow me to represent or define them for others. They reminded me of my story. And if I am reminded by them of my story, then I am taught by what I discerned in *Autobiographies* why I should not forget my story. And that's how *Autobiographies* is a story for me. It showed me the dangers of being absent, of attempting to separate myself from what I do, from my own life situation, as a scholar, as an Indian, as a human being in time and place. It showed me not only the importance of my stories, but also the importance of talking about them openly, honestly, so that I might, in whatever I do or read, see them anew. It brought me back to the old ones. It brought me back to their stories, to hearing the old ones talking, so I can see how something they say might be for me.

I am that man, that one at the table. With light skin. I am a quarter-breed man. But, like half-breed man, I know something, too. I know Indian poison. White poison, too. I know many ways to poison.

The old medicine people say a good medicine person must know about the poisons. Only that way can the medicine doctor know what to do to counteract them. What herbs to use. What songs to sing. The doctor has to know those poisons so well that the doctor could use them against other people. But a good doctor doesn't do that. That's not the purpose of learning about the poisons. Good medicine people know better.

What I have to say can work like good doctoring songs, good medicine.

Listen to my story.

So when I sit before you talking, talking, talking, talking you know who I am. Listen because I carry our history, yours and mine, ours. Some of it, anyway. Whoever you are.

Talk back. Tell stories. Put food out, meat. I will eat it. I'm not here to harm. I'm talking, telling stories. Watch. Listen.

Then you'll know I'm no stranger.[17]

NOTES

1. "Nettie" and "Eleanor" were not the women's real names. Neither woman is living now, and knowing the Pomo custom for privacy, I feel it appropriate to use fictitious names. At the time of the event I am describing both women were living in Santa Rosa, in the southern Pomo territory, which is approximately sixty miles south of Ukiah, the town in the central Pomo region close to where both women were born and raised.

2. It is impossible to know exactly which groups of Pomo in this region the three Pomo narrators come from. Colson notes that "Names and place names are disguised [by Colson]" (1974:14). It is only known, generally, that Colson worked somewhere in the central Pomo region, probably around Ukiah. Colson notes that "[she] sincerely hope[s] the material will cause no embarrassment to [the narrators], or to any other Pomo" (1974:14). She changed names "in order to

afford as much protection to all concerned as is possible" (1974:14). It is not clear if Colson was responding to the general Pomo concern for privacy, or if she was aware of it. She does not say.

3. R. D. Theisz refers to narrated Indian autobiographies as bi-autobiographies, distinguishing them from their two bordering relatives, biography and autobiography (1981:66). While Theisz's term is useful because it serves to remind the reader that at least two people were responsible for the production of the autobiographical text, Theisz's term might just as easily be used for written autobiographies where an editor helped write or edit, perhaps in significant ways, what the Indian had written. In this essay I wish to discuss only narrated autobiographies where one party (Indian) speaks and another party (non-Indian) writes. Eighty-three percent of the more that six hundred published American Indian texts that are autobiographical are narrated, forty-three percent collected and edited by anthropologists, the other forty percent collected and edited by non-Indians from many other walks of life (Brumble 1981:72).

4. Contemporary, and well-known written American Indian autobiographies include *The Names* and *The Way to Rainy Mountain* by N. Scott Momaday, *Storytell* by Leslie Silko, and *Interior Landscapes* by Gerald Vizenor. Earlier, Sarah Winnemucca Hopkins (*Life among the Piutes: Their Wrongs and Claims,* 1883) and others wrote autobiographies that were more extensive than the eighteenth- and early nineteenth-century apparently unmediated accounts of conversion to Christianity by Indians such as Samson Occom, William and Mary Apes, and George Copway.

5. It is well known, for example, that John G. Neihardt, editor of *Black Elk Speaks,* the best-known narrated American Indian autobiography, not only rearranged Black Elk's narratives in certain ways but added to them. The passage on the last page of the text about the death of a people's dream and Black Elk's conception of himself as "a pitiful old man who had done nothing" (1972:230), which lends the book its tragic sense, is not Black Elk's but Neihardt's. Neihardt wrote a preface about how he met Black Elk and eventually edited his autobiography, yet he allows the reader to believe that the actual autobiography is only Black Elk's.

At the other end of the spectrum of editorial strategies for dealing with point of view in narrated autobiography is the editor who self-consciously inserts himself or herself into the entire text. See, for example, Vincent Crapanzano's *The Fifth World of Enoch Maloney: Portrait of a Navaho* and *The Fifth World of Forster Bennett: A Portrait of a Navaho.* Extremely self-conscious editors often seem to wallow in self-reflexivity, forgetting the voice and presence of the Indian narrator. Brumble argues, and I would agree, that Crapanzano's texts mentioned here are not autobiographies, not of the Indians anyway. "Crapanzano's heroic extremes of subjectivity" result in a book about Crapanzano, his thoughts and ideas, and not so much about the Indian (Brumble 1988:88–93).

6. Colson refers in her table of contents to the longer accounts as life histories and to the briefer accounts as autobiographies. Here I see life history and autobiography as the same since, in varying degrees, both are bicultural texts, collaborative endeavors. Note the discussion of life histories in Crapanzano (1977) as "doubly edited" texts.

7. R. D. Theisz suggests that readers study recorder-editors' introductions to determine the manner of collaboration and the production of narrated American Indian autobiographies (1981:65–80). Here with the questions I have raised regarding Colson and the production of *Autobiographies* it is clear that studying recorder-editors' introductions is not enough.

8. Colson does say the narrators "seemed to have no objection to having what they told

written down as they spoke" (1974:6–7), and that sometimes "the informant indicated that a touchy spot had been hit" (1974:7). But she does not say what was or was not "touchy." She does mention that "Common questions dealt with the identification of persons mentioned in the account since these were rarely named or indeed identified further than 'that man' or 'that woman,' for the Pomo avoid the names of both living and dead." But, apparently, the narrators identified the persons when asked.

9. I must mention that not all of the Indian women's autobiographies that Bataille and Sands discuss are narrated. They provide lengthy discussions of Maria Campbell's *Halfbreed* and other autobiographies written by Indian women. Here my comments pertain only to their discussions regarding narrated autobiographies.

10. Here Schwab uses the term "culture contact" in the widest sense possible. She cites Gregory Bateson, who said: "I suggest that we should consider under the head of 'culture contact' not only those cases in which the contact occurs between two communities with different cultures . . . but also in cases within a single community. . . . I would even extend the idea of 'contact' so widely as to include those processes whereby a child is molded and trained to fit the culture into which he was born" (1986:64).

11. I am grateful to my aunt, Violet Chappell, for her help with the literal translation. Here I am assuming, quite arbitrarily that Pomo—or any traditionally non-written oral language—can be textualized as such. As Paul J. Hopper remarks, "Discourse with languages outside the Western tradition can only be fitted with great difficulty and obvious artificiality into Western-style written sentences" (1988:19). Even this "more literal translation" was difficult.

12. I am not implying here that it is always possible to have an exact transcription of a speaker's narrative. An exact transcription might not only be impossible given the limits of syntax, punctuation, and so forth, but might prove unreadable to many audiences. Rather, by an "accurate sense" I mean having an idea about what went into editing the speaker's spoken words, what might have been lost or gained in the transcription. In a very short space, I have attempted to provide an "accurate sense" of features of Pomo and types of Pomo English.

13. Renato Rosaldo illustrated with Ilongot storytelling how "people whose biographies significantly overlap can communicate rich understandings in telegraphic form. People who share a complex knowledge about their worlds can assume a common background and speak through allusion" (1986:107). Keith Basso observes that among the Western Apache "geographical features have served for centuries as mnemonic pegs on which to hang the moral teachings of their history" (1984:44) and that "narrative events are 'spatially anchored' at points on the land, and the evocative pictures presented by the Western Apache place-names become indispensable resources for the storyteller's craft" (1984:32). This familiarity with place is not unusual for a community that has shared over millennia the same landscape and various stories associated with the landscape, and often accounts for the paucity of description and human motivation typically found in the literature from such a community.

14. Colson does mention repetitions in her footnotes, but does not indicate whether she asked specific questions regarding the meaning of the repetitions for the narrators. She merely compares details and attempts to draw her own conclusions about the significance of the repetitions. "SM repeated this incident several times, and was always interested in speaking of it. Twice this account was substantially the way it is here. Once it was an abbreviated version which differed only

in the omission of certain details . . ." (1974:88). "The man was probably fixed for gambling, and had gone through certain rituals which assured luck but were also fatal to small children if they were brought in contact with the one who used them" (1974:88).

15. Martinez's English appears slightly more polished in terms of subject-verb agreement and so forth, which must be due to Colson's "amount of editing" of Martinez's accounts. This makes Martinez's unedited speech patterns all the more curious since she was, of the three narrators, the least comfortable with English, according to Colson. Again, there is no way to see Martinez's unedited speech since Colson "no longer [has] any of the field notes used in preparing the accounts" (1974:88).

16. In his essay, "Intersubjective Reading," David Bleich, for example, notes: "In very few instances does the critic actually study his or her own readings, much less the readings of others, while the great majority of discussions give all the attention to the texts" (1986:402). Bleich goes on to discuss the work, or ideas, of others (e.g., Gadamer, Barthes). The language, tone, and narrative format of the essay is typical of contemporary academic prose, specifically that of literary criticism and theory. Bleich is analytical and detached. Nowhere does he discuss his reading, historicize his position as the writer of this essay. He concludes the essay by commending that work which "lead[s] toward a rationality of multiple voices and common interests, toward readings 'responsible for the meaning of each other's inner lives'" (1986:420). Can he commend his own work?

I am not suggesting, nor do I think the scholars I have cited here—Clifford, Marcus and Fischer, Rosaldo, Bleich, Said—are suggesting, that the critic's subjectivism as it may be presented by him or her in a paper is alone the answer, or that it automatically conveys honesty or authenticity. After all, critics as writers can tell any kind of "personal" story they want, truthful or not. Rather, I am suggesting the critic's history can in the best circumstances help open the stories of the critic's relationship with a text, that which makes for the reader's reading. Again, in my work I am attempting to open a dialogue with the text I am reading such that my history and critical activity informs and is informed by the text, and my representation of that dialogue as a critical paper, is extended to other readers who can continue the dialogue in writing or otherwise.

17. I want to thank those who have helped me along the way, in writing this essay and otherwise, particularly Mary Sarris, Andrea Lerner, and three Pomo women—Mabel McKay, Violet Chappell, and Anita Silva.

REFERENCES

Apes, William. 1829. *A Son of the Forest: The Experience of William Apes, a Native of the Forest. Comprising a Notice of the Pequot Tribe of Indians. Written by Himself.* New York: published by the author.

Apess, Mary (variant of spelling of Apes above). 1837 [1833]. "Experience of the Missionary's Consort, Written by Herself." *Experience of Five Christian Indians of the Pequot Tribe,* 21–34. Boston: published by William Apess (variant spelling of Apes above).

Barrett, S. M., ed. 1906. *Geronimo's Story of His Life.* New York: Duffield.

Basso, Keith. 1984. "Stalking with Stories: Names, Places, and Moral Narratives among the Western Apache." *Text, Play, Story,* 19–55. Berkeley: University of California Press.

Bataille, Gretchen M., and Kathleen Sands. 1981. *American Indian Women: Telling Their Lives.* Lincoln: University of Nebraska Press.

Bateson, Gregory. 1972. "Culture Contact and Schismogenesis." *Steps to an Ecology of Mind,* 61–72. New York: Ballantine Books/Random House.

Bleich, David. "Intersubjective Reading." *New Literary History,* 17:3:401–421.

Boyarin, Jonathan. 1991. "Reading Exodus Into History." Unpublished paper.

Brumble, David H. III. 1981. *An Annotated Bibliography of American Indian and Eskimo Autobiographies.* Lincoln: University of Nebraska Press.

———. 1988. *American Indian Autobiography.* Berkeley: University of California Press.

Campbell, Maria. 1973. *Halfbreed.* Toronto: McCelland and Stewart-Bantam, Ltd.

Chappell, Violet. 1989. Personal communication. Kashaya Pomo Indian Reservation, Sonoma County, California.

Christian, Chester C., Jr. 1970. "The Analysis of Linguistic and Cultural Differences: A Proposed Model." *Report of the Twenty-First Annual Round Table Meeting on Linguistics and Language Studies,* 149–162. Washington, D.C.: Georgetown University Press.

Clifford, James. 1983. "On Ethnographic Authority." *Representations* 1:2:118–146.

Colson, Elizabeth, ed. 1974 [1956]. *Autobiographies of Three Pomo Women.* Berkeley: Archaeological Research Facility, Department of Anthropology, University of California.

Copway, George. 1847. *The Life History and Travels of Kah-ge-ga-gah-bowh.* Albany: Weed and Parsons.

Crapanzano, Vincent. 1969. *The Fifth World of Enoch Maloney: Portrait of a Navaho.* New York: Viking.

———. 1974. *The Fifth World of Forster Bennett: Portrait of a Navaho.* New York: Viking.

———. 1977. "The Life History in Anthropological Field Work." *Anthropology and Humanism Quarterly* 2:3–7.

Eakin, Paul John. 1974. *Fiction in Autobiography: Studies in the Art of Self-Invention.* Princeton: Princeton University Press.

Faulkner, William. 1954 [1929]. *The Sound and the Fury.* New York: Vintage Books.

———. 1972 [1936]. *Absalom, Absalom!* New York: Vintage Books.

———. 1973 [1942]. *Go Down, Moses.* New York: Vintage Books.

Great-Grandma Nettie (pseudonym). 1957–1962. Personal communication. Santa Rosa, California.

Hopkins, Sarah Winnemucca. 1883. *Life among the Piutes: Their Wrongs and Claims.* New York: G. P. Putman's Sons.

Hopper, Paul J. 1988. "Discourse Analysis: Grammar and Critical Theory in the 1980s." *Profession 88,* 18–24. New York: Modern Language Association.

Krupat, Arnold. 1985. *For Those Who Come After.* Berkeley: University of California Press.

Leighton, Alexander H., and Dorothea C., eds. 1949. "The Life Story." *Gregorio, The Hand-Trembler: A Psychobiological Personality Study of a Navaho Indian. Papers of the Peabody Museum of American Archaeology and Ethnography,* vol. 40, no. 1, 45–81. Cambridge: Harvard University.

Marcus, George E., and Michael M. J. Fischer. 1986. *Anthropology as Cultural Critique*. Chicago: University of Chicago Press.

McKay, Mabel. 1958–. Personal communication. Santa Rosa and vicinity.

Momaday, N. Scott. 1969. *The Way to Rainy Mountain*. Albuquerque: University of New Mexico Press.

———. 1976. *The Names*. New York: Harper and Row.

Neihardt, John G., ed. 1972 [1932]. *Black Elk Speaks*. New York: Washington Square Press.

Occom, Samson. 1982. "A Short Narrative of My Life." *The Elders Wrote: An Anthology of Early Prose by North American Indians, 1768–1931,* edited by Bernd Peyer, 12–18. Berlin: Dietrich Reimer Verlag.

O'Connor, Kathy. 1989. Personal communication. Berkeley, California.

Old Auntie Eleanor (pseudonym). 1957–1968. Personal communications. Santa Rosa, California.

Oswalt, Robert. 1964. *Kashaya Texts*. Berkeley: University of California Publications in Linguistics, vol. 36.

Pomo (unnamed Pomo friends and family members). 1957–. Personal communications. Santa Rosa, California and vicinity.

Rosaldo, Renato. 1986. "Ilongot Hunting as Story and Experience." *The Anthropology of Experience,* edited by Victor W. Turner and Edward M. Bruner, 97–138. Urbana: University of Illinois Press.

———. 1989. *Culture and Truth*. Boston: Beacon Press.

Said, Edward W. 1989. "Representing the Colonized: Anthropology's Interlocutors." *Critical Inquiry,* Winter 15:205–225.

Schwab, Gabriele. 1986. "Reader Response and the Aesthetic Experience of Otherness." *Stanford Literature Review,* Spring 107–136.

Silko, Leslie Marmon. 1981. *Storyteller*. New York: Seaver Books.

Theisz, R. D. 1981. "The Critical Collaboration: Introductions as a Gateway to the Study of Native American Bi-Autobiography." *American Indian Culture and Research Journal* 5:1:65–80.

Vizenor, Gerald. 1990. *Interior Landscapes*. Minneapolis: University of Minnesota Press.

■ ▪ ▬ ▪ ▬ ▪ ▬ ▪ ▬ ▪

HOW (!) IS AN INDIAN?
A Contest of Stories

■ ▪ ▬ ▪ ▬ ▪ ▬ ▪ ▬ ▪

Jana Sequoya

T he question of who and how is an Indian is an ongoing contest of stories in North America, a contest in many ways emblematic of global struggles to contain and control difference in modern societies. At stake are the social, political, and economic conditions of possibility for Indian identity within the encompassing national context. Who, what, where, and when can that Indian be, which the founding narratives of the North American nation construed as either absent—the empty land scenario—or inauthentic. Inauthentic, that is, by comparison with the imagined "original" Indian, whether of the Golden Age or demonic variety; inauthentic because rather than vanishing, American Indians in all our diversity are still here, alive and kicking against the odds.

Although the figure of the "authentic" Indian is a figment of the imagination—a symbolic identity invested with meanings of temporal inequality vis-à-vis the colonizing real(m)—it has real consequences for contemporary American Indian people. Among the most obvious of these is that we must respond to the question of Indian identity in terms of that figure. And because Native Americans must understand themselves in relation to conventional images of "Indianness," and therefore, in relation to the false question of authenticity—a "red-herring" discourse, one might say—even our own versions of who and how is an Indian are not so much the antithesis of the imaginary Indian, as its echo. The key paradox of Indian identity, then, is that it is when we least contradict the familiar images that Native American stories will seem most articulate and true. For in order to be perceived as speaking subjects American Indians must adopt categories of meaning and codes of representation that convey an implicit set of social goals in many ways contrary to those that articulate their own stories.

The grammar of identity, identification, and affiliation, presents a logical and ethical problem at the outset of this essay, as the shifting standpoint of the foregoing paragraph demonstrates. For in order to constitute ourselves as bicultural subjectivities, Indian-identified writers must negotiate a politics of position and of representation. And in order to do so adequately, we must sharpen our awareness of the multiple relationships out of and into which we write. Each subject position occupied in relation to Indian/non-Indian identity has its own story. Each perspective is critiqued by its other at the borders of its particular discourse along the social axis of "inside-outside." Thus the ambiguous positionality that complicates my own use of pronouns in speaking of Indian identification mirrors the subject-object under discussion—the relationship of narratives of identity and modes of identification as they respond to, accommodate, and resist the master narratives of national culture. For in contrast to the range of Euroamerican identities, self-evident to a degree in the dominant political and economic institutions, the discursive codes that constrain Native American interventions in the story of Indianness neither reflect traditional (resistant) Native American identities nor adequately mediate their responses to interpellation by those institutions.

Although the category "Indian" is a colonial one, having its roots in British expansion into Ireland as well as in the imaginary "Indios" of Spanish colonialism, because the name signified an elusive and threatening population "beyond the pale" of the colonizing system, Native Americans themselves adopted the name. As Roger Williams records in the early seventeenth century,

They have often asked me, why we call them Indians [. . . .] And understanding the reason, they will call themselves Indians, in opposition to English, &c. (Berkhofer 1979:15)

The imaginary Indian has its roots, of course, in material relationships, as well as in colonizing fantasies of timeless origins. When our bicultural forebears became obsolete as active intermediaries between the unmapped wilderness and the civilizing market, the fledgling economy of "manifest destiny" sold the concept of the Indian as Art before the product was on the streets, both figuratively and literally. In the earliest commodity form of the Vanishing Indian, tribal remnants of westward expansion were befeathered, furred, and frozen in attitudes of sorrowful nobility. The resulting iconograph, an image at once of land and soul, represented an ideal integral to the American self-image: all the wilderness that had been overcome, all the wildness waiting in the heart, ready to spring into action should the occasion demand (and occasions continue to demand: sporting occasions, occasions of warfare, confrontations between good and evil, right and wrong).

Although the displacement and control of that sorrowful wildness seemed to the young America a guarantee of its future, the contest with uncertainty was won at a certain cost. For freedom is not to be thought of as cheap; sacrifices must be made. As an iconograph of the cost, images of the Vanishing Indian (in contrast to narratives of democracy as an unending process of "becoming") constitute both the authenticating sign of "Indianness" and an alibi for usurpation of the territorial and cultural space indicated by that sign. Thus, essentialist images of Indianness fetishize that which would be preserved under the rubric of cultural revitalization. And the Indian who refuses that paradoxical legitimation—for whom, for example, tribal religion is vital practice rather than abstract belief—such an Indian is framed not as Art but as Outlaw.[1]

This is all to say that the problem indicated by questions of who and how is an Indian is that the material conditions of being Indian have changed over time, while the images of Indianness have not. The conditions of being Indian have changed, of course, for a variety of reasons, and many of those changes are directly related to differing degrees of access to land and resources among Native American peoples, as well as to corresponding restrictions on traditional religious and economic practices which depend on such access. Real, as distinct from imaginary, answers to the question of "how" is an Indian, then, must depend in part on whether one is Indian in the city or the country; whether in the ways of tradition or of modernization; whether drawing more on old or on new cultural influences.

But the question of "who" is an Indian is subject to other conditions as well, and these are indirectly related to federal restrictions on non-capital intensive access to the land. For it is one of the paradoxes of democratic government that without the appearance of a homogeneous political identity—an identity constituted in terms of the dominant system of representation—the issues crucial to Native American survival as regionally diverse peoples cannot be heard.

Thus under the auspices of legal, educational, esthetic, and popular representations, colonizing imperatives in many instances are not "post" but ongoing. Because each of those arenas is a site of struggle in the contesting stories of "who and how" is an Indian, the question entails a problem of disjunction between its rhetorical and material terms. Insofar as American Indians have been defined generically in terms of the past (but whose?) by tellers of tall and self-serving tales, whatever our own standpoints in the contest (and they will be many according to tribal and family histories), our presence in relationship to those terms must necessarily be equivocal. For our sense of who we are in relation to the majority society, as well as our judgment of other Indian-identified people, is conditioned by what continues to be at stake—the replacement of traditional Native American structures of identity with those of Euro-America. And because of the complexity of Indian identification in all its varied determinants and permutations, no matter how deeply bicultural Indians "know" who we are—as we are quick to avow when our identities are in question, the question of Indian identity itself is often a matter that goes with the territory. It is at this impasse then, that Native Americans must become particularly inventive.

The paradoxical situation of Native American discourse is evident in the emergent literary genre exemplified by the early work of N. Scott Momaday and Leslie Marmon Silko in the 1960s and 1970s. These syncretic works created great public and academic interest, to the extent that in the 1990s both authors are included in most standard American anthologies. Because the poetry, novels, and autobiographies of these two writers articulate perspectives that resonate with a growing movement in the schools and universities to reclaim the standpoints of those who continue to have much at stake but little say in North American culture and society, they continue to influence a new generation of writers and to encourage the development of critical commentary on all forms of Native American literature.

Although the works of Momaday and Silko are stylistically different, they share many similarities: both are concerned with the recuperation of indigenous sources of identity, and to this end both writers draw upon tribal oral stories. Most significantly for the focus of this essay, the first novels of both directly incorporate elements of traditional sacred story cycles—a practice constituting, along with an emergent literary form, an ethical question vis-à-vis the particular communities of which these authors write.[2] It is a question that arises out of the dual social contexts of these syncretic works, yet which tends to be answered in terms of academic interests. Because for the most part neither the university nor the mainstream reading public has regarded ethical considerations as relevant to the category of fiction, critical commentary has tended to follow the lead of the authors in effacing the communal sanctions that restrict the use of sacred oral stories in traditional tribal communities. This essay therefore is part of an ongoing project to include in discussions of contemporary Native American literature not only those canonical esthetics of the privileged imagination mediated by reified ethnographic material, but a sense of responsibility to the lived relationships in which culture functions as a connected way of life—connected, that is, to varied modes of continuity and emergence. For to many Indian-identified students it seems ironic at best that the literary incorporation of sacred story fragments is cited by critics of these novels as evidence of their particularly Native American character.

The problem, of course, is precisely one of context: what is misuse in relation to the sacred cultures of particular tribal communities evokes authentic atmosphere in relation to the secular humanist and popular cultures of the Euroamerican tradition. The prerogative of a cross-cultural preserve exempt from accountability to the tribal community whose worldviews it purports to represent is justified in the name of "fiction"; the category of esthetics is invoked to dismiss as impertinent any protest in the name of a politics of representation.

Perhaps one might consider such dismissive strategies as an institutional residue of the paradigm of the vanishing Indian by which traditional tribal communities are perceived less as subjects than as objects of knowledge, and hence as terminally up for grabs. But despite disciplinary pressures to dismiss the ethical issues attending academic and popular appropriations of Native American sacred cultures, those issues are slowly becoming a matter of public record as tribal spokespeople on behalf of traditional ethos are finding their voices in cross-cultural forums.

One example among many is an article published in the Northern Arizona University newspaper *The Lumberjack* (Feb. 1, 1991), in which Hopi tribal spokesman Vernon Masayesva protests that "[a]s people we have been studied as artifacts." Aside from documenting the elder's objections "to NAU's attempts to publish information concerning what [the Hopi] call their 'religious privacy'," the article illustrates a common editorial practice that tends to put into question the validity of the speaker within the representational space. Accordingly, Masayesva's claim for Hopi " 'religious privacy' " is framed by an ironic boundary within which the tribal elder's voice is contained and controlled by the normalizing gaze of the writer. The quotation marks function simultaneously to represent and to deny the Hopi elder's words, withholding the validity objections to a violation of Judeo-Christian proscriptions would be granted. Similarly, the marks setting off Masayesva's protest that there have been "too many instances where our elders have been betrayed" make his protest seem strange, even a bit paranoid. They signal an idiosyncratic space of difference that speaks to the mainstream imagination of a field of otherness—like the tribal lands set apart from the dominant modes of property. In consequence of the relations of power always in contention between dominant and subordinate groups, only a speaker authorized by the former can legitimate the Hopi elder's voice. Thus the director of cultural preservation for the tribe, Leigh Jenkins, is obliged to confirm and explain the elder's objection. And according to Jenkins, "The conflict arises when non-Indians want to preserve the Hopi culture by means of publishing their secrets [. . .] the tribe would prefer to lose its traditions." [3]

Although, in the context of the academy, such a position may be difficult to comprehend, self-destructive even, invoking as it does an ethic which is contrary to the prerogatives of the institution (i.e., the capitalization of knowledge), Hopi traditionalists may yet have some say in defense of tribal secrets; for Masayesva's protest on behalf of the tribe resulted, we are informed, in a "committee [that] will investigate guidelines on the limits and freedoms in Indian research." And to the extent that the committee sincerely questions the limits of academic freedom to interfere with ways of life based upon a different system of cultural values and practices, it is likely to become an arena of struggle in the contest of stories.

For all that Western narrative practices of displacement and distance have been internalized as convention and celebrated as style, they are nevertheless practices that deprecate contestatory points of view. They are not only the editorial practices of journalists, nor only the appropriative practices of anthropologists, but, more problematically, literary practices in defense of a corner on the market for local color and pedagogical practices converting knowledge of "others" to institutional power. A related issue was addressed by Vine Deloria (as cited by Ward Churchill in "A Little Matter of Genocide: Native American Spirituality & New Age Hucksterism," *The Bloomsbury Review;* Sept./ Oct. 1988). Deloria raises the question of non-Indian "experts" employed by the universities to train young Native Americans how to be Indian, and asserts that "[t]hese students are being trained to view themselves and their cultures in the terms prescribed by such 'experts' rather than in the traditional terms of the tribal elders." The Lakota scholar points to an important (but, of course, contestable) consequence of this aspect of the contest of stories:

The process automatically sets the members of Indian communities at odds with one another, while outsiders run around picking up the pieces for themselves. In this way the "experts" are perfecting a system of self-validation in which all semblance of honesty and accuracy are lost.

He concludes that this situation "is not only a travesty of scholarship but it is absolutely devastating to Indian societies." Similarly, Pam Colorado, an Oneida poet (cited by Churchill and in turn citing his article in a 1989 conference on Native American spirituality), warned the audience that "the process is ultimately intended to supplant Indians, even in areas of their own customs and spirituality."

The ontogeny of a mostly immigrant nation approves, perhaps, the displacement of indigenous systems of belief, of material culture, of political forms. But if you are the "host" in this relationship, you see the situation of culture different, as Colorado warns:

We are talking here about an absolute ideological/conceptual subordination of Indian people in addition to the total physical subordination they already experience. When this happens, the last vestiges of real Indian society and Indian rights will disappear. Non-Indians will then "own" our heritage and ideas as thoroughly as they now claim to own our land and resources.

The alarm sounded by these Native American social critics is easily dismissed by both non-Indian and Indian-identified academics according to postmodern perspectives that question claims to authenticity (or to reality, for that matter). Thus Colorado's invocation of "real Indian society" may be wrested from its communal context and repositioned in Anglo-American and other immigrant histories of diaspora, transgression of boundaries, and cultural assimilation of difference. From these standpoints, the ironic sense of "expert" in matters Indian implied by Churchill's gloss of both Deloria and Colorado is very much in question: do the ironizing marks imply that people most fully Indian by blood are automatically expert, or more expert than those with less genetic heritage? That is, to paraphrase more than one Indian "expert," does American Indian culture travel in the blood? This is unlikely to be the meaning since all three critics are of mixed racial as well as cultural heritage.

Instead the issue of these warnings is more likely to refer to the fact that since

Native American communities and traditions have in many instances been shattered, the young must reinvent viable conditions of being Indian. And because the process of reinvention entails recuperation of cultural fragments from many sources, including recourse to the alienated forms of archive material—often the purview of non-Indian "experts"—the dangers of "ideological/conceptual subordination" for young Indians in universities will be mitigated by a teacher whose knowledge is well grounded in a Native American community. Despite the often disrupted and interpellated condition of such communities, the preferred teacher of Indian students would be one who has internalized the perspectives of a Native American culture, as well as those of the dominant society. The best teacher for American Indian students, that is, would be fully bicultural. The problem of training young Indians in the critical issues of their own cultures thus becomes one of gaining informed perspectives on, in James Clifford's phrase, "the predicament of culture" (the title of his 1988 study of ethnography, literature, and art) from the standpoints of the more traditional American Indian social goals,[4] rather than from those of Euro-America.

Traditional Native American social goals are in many ways different from the general aims of the majority culture, and foremost among these differences is the function and meaning of culture itself. While experiences of diaspora, transgression of boundaries, and incorporation of difference inform both Indian and non-Indian societies, American Indians are more likely to designate culture as a system of alignment with the shifting forces of the environment—whether those forces be elemental or social—and that system is embodied in the living mediators of the ceremonial traditions. Rather than defining culture according to an evaluative set of binary oppositions to the geophysical surroundings, as is more characteristic of Judeo-Christian social systems, those raised in (or more influenced by) Native American traditions are more likely to point to the hill or river and say, "This is our culture." When the place which embodies the traditional culture is fenced off as "sacrifice" or "developed" for its material resources (for whom?), the social system that responded simultaneously to its symbolic and pragmatic value is effectively erased. And that is what is at stake in the predicament of American Indian culture.

A geocentric sense of identity may be understood from Western standpoints if it is considered in light of similar self-confirmation in reference to classical Greece, for example, or—as my French-Welsh grandmother avows—to Paris. Just as Western cultural traditions, embodied in its literature and art, located in museums and libraries, depend on access to those institutions, so indigenous cultural practices based on symbolic responses to the natural environment depend on physical access to those places in which tribal traditions are embodied. Contemporary Native American literature may be understood, in part, as a response to the threat of cultural extinction due to the capitalization of the environment—but it is a response that entails its own series of paradoxes as a function of the different social goals of Western and tribal story.

Literary forms of "cultural revitalization" are paradoxical forms in that they are necessarily not constituted in the cultural terms of the traditions which they would vitalize. "Necessarily not," that is, because in contrast to the centrifugal functions of displacement and substitution enacted by the print technologies attending stories in modern Western societies—a social practice underwriting the atomized individual in the interests of expanding the ground of dominant values—the social role of traditional tribal story is communally centripetal and integrative. In order to hear the stories that tell them who they are, that is to say, dispersed members of the tribal community must return to their elders; in order to receive the tribal knowledge encoded in the traditional stories, they must submit to the social terms of which the stories are a vital part. Thus, communal sanctions on the oral stories counter the disintegrative tendencies of the dominant society, encouraging the reintegration of acculturated (or deculturated) Indians with the community.

By contrast, the technologies of mechanical reproduction belong to the cultural logic of the colonial story—a logic of space rather than of place. As such, colonial technologies lend themselves to the *dis*placement of differently organized cultures. Moreover, because print literature reframes geocentric symbolic relationships in terms of commodity forms of culture, it enables the assimilation (and effective sacrifice) of traditional American Indian narrative and evaluative forms to those alien and alienating cultural modes.

Thus, in the same way that well-meaning academics may disparage as superstitious the objections of Native American traditionalists like Hopi elder Vernon Masayesva, or the warnings of social critics like Deloria, Churchill, and Colorado, authors and scholars of Native American literature may unwittingly denigrate or dispense with the specificity of tribal histories by assimilating the materiality of place and community to the representational esthetics of distance and displacement. Similarly, despite the best intentions, theories that are benevolent in the context of the academy may have negative consequences for those tribal people to whom the old ways of having stories are vital to the continuity of their social order. For according to the political climate in which theories of culture find their concrete expressions in state and federal policies, theoretical emphases on the provisional character of twentieth-century identities may be adapted to the ideology of "progress" through the self-evidence of "modernity" in support of the dominant mode of having stories. However, the dark side of those truths the U.S. Constitution holds to be self-evident is their justification of the continuing erasure of indigenous lifeways, a process that was nearly concluded in the United States in 1871 when Charles Darwin wrote, in *The Descent of Man*, "At some future period, not very distant as measured by centuries, the civilized races of man will almost certainly exterminate, and replace, the savage races throughout the world."

In pointing to the differences between ways of having stories (cultures), I intend a reminder that theoretical emphases on the expedient reinventions of culture in Western literary forms, for example, while functional for standpoints grounded in colonizing perspectives, override American Indian conceptions of identity with the landscape and the ancestors, conceptions every bit as determining for the cultures of indigenous people as Euroamerican institutions are for the people they serve.[5] And I hope to emphasize that the primary distinction between the indigenous and Western ethos turns on the divergent social aims of their different cultural institutions (without forgetting that the particularity of the former have been penetrated and altered by the economic dominance of the latter). Thus where the secular humanist definition of culture celebrates the creative capacities of the individual—and the development of the notion of the sovereign individual through the history of the European Enlightenment is itself a response to a particular set of political and economic circumstances—in contrast, traditional American Indian identities are not determined by the centrality of the ego. Instead, such identities include the interactive participation of sacred beings embodied in that geography, the plant and animal life of the region, its elemental characteristics, as well as ancestors and kin whose histories constitute a part of the place. In the words of Jack Forbes, the difference between Western and tribal identities consists fundamentally of the experience of our selves as "inside each other rather than outside." The goal-seeking drive of Native American systems of cultural organization, then, is different from that of European systems in its emphasis on preserving identification with ancestral events, customs, and values; and these are located as story and song, ritual, and memory in the members of living Indian communities, as well as in the territorial features of the homeplace. The system, therefore, is not fundamentally motivated by expansionist goals, but by conservative ones.

These differences have powerful consequences for the ways of having stories in both cultures. Therefore, this essay must engage (in a necessarily general way) the social realities of those Native American communities upon whose traditional stories Momaday's *House Made of Dawn* and Silko's *Ceremony* draw. While a common aim of tribal communities is to persist and to flourish as distinct national entities within the dominant economic and legal structures of American society, most are tenuously poised against assimilative pressures—whether they be the atomistic forces of economic necessity or of Western ideas of education; of changing federal policies and legal proscriptions on traditional practices or the multicorporate devastation of ancestral land bases. Indeed, the influences of global capitalism and its institutional expressions reach deeply into most tribal societies despite their often disproportionate poverty. Although the more conservative Pueblo communities are perhaps less internally divided by these influences than many others, there is nevertheless a tension along the lines of revitalizing tradition and selective modernization—imprecise terms that signify the divergent social goals I have attempted to clarify.

Those disparate influences and goals are differently engaged according to the relative material and social bases of regional tribal communities in general, altering customary values and practices, positioning some members at the center of traditional ways and others more at the margins of the community, nearer to mainstream culture. (The spatial metaphor of center–periphery understood from the tribal perspective refers to asymmetrical relationships to antithetical systems of power: traditionally based resources of power and knowledge, on the one hand, metaphysically encoded in ritual and oral traditions; the material technologies of the dominant society, on the other, transmitted through state or parochial education systems. Both entail problems of access to social resources: the former restricts specialized knowledge through clan and gender roles, the latter through evaluative criteria based on formal testing and informal "gatekeeping" relationships.)

In general, then, traditional or conservative forms of social organization are penetrated through economic, legal, and health-care systems, while the more permeable "modernizing" periphery enters the mainstream through the educational system. The latter prepares the way for increasing identification with the homogenizing influences of popular entertainment and advertising media. Institutions of capital define what it takes to be fully human in terms of those institutions—money and things—while the nostalgic soul of those global economic-cultural systems sees the Indian in terms of an imagined past. The elders have some say in all this, but again, conditions have changed and the situation is not all that clear. It is revealing of the problems for Native American identity in this contest of stories that Indian children who grew up with the genre of American frontier movies identified with the cowboy heroes rather than with the Indian bad guys; of course, Indians could not recognize themselves in the self-reflexive mirror held up by the popular media.

The emergence of syncretic cultures among American Indian peoples is related not only to federal pressures to replace tribal modes of social organization with dominant forms of representation, nor only to economic pressures to replace traditional evaluative narratives with those of modern capitalism, but also to the common practice of "mixed" marriage—a matter that itself reflects paradoxically on the idea of the racial basis of ethnicity. Most Native American communities define members on the basis of kinship affiliations and social acuity rather than blood quantum,[6] so that the key to being Native American in terms of a given community does not depend on the degree of Indian blood, but on the degree of incorporation into the social network of that community. Thus a full-blood may be thoroughly acculturated to the dominant society, while a mixed-blood may identify and function entirely as a member of a tribal group that has assimilated biological non-Indians over generations. However, the criterion of social incorporation may be a Catch-22 proposition, for the Pueblos depicted in *House Made of Dawn* and *Ceremony* tend to be conservatively organized communities, exclusive rather than inclusive, despite (or because of) centuries of Spanish and then U.S. colonialism and the corresponding religious and economic influences of each regime.[7]

The relationship of both Momaday and Silko to the tribal communities in which their first novels are set is similar, then, in that both write out of dual cultural contexts: dual in the sense that they are of mixed Native American and Euroamerican descent, and dual in that they did not grow up within the tribal traditions on which their early works draw. Rather, as their autobiographical writings indicate, both were raised in families with strong connections to the dominant society's educational and economic practices, and somewhat peripheral relationships with the tribal societies among whom they lived. Furthermore, while both writers identify with particular tribal traditions, that identification is conflicted in terms of their writing.[8] Although the syncretic and dual cultural influences to which their novels respond are in some respects complementary, in others they are at significant odds. Nevertheless, the works of both writers articulate the social forces contending for dominance within the tribal societies of which they write, as well as those of the mainstream reading public for whom they write.

Most importantly, the literary innovations of which Momaday's *House Made of Dawn* and Silko's *Ceremony* are exemplary attest at once to the assimilation of American Indian structures of identity to the mainstream[9] and to the "Indianization" of appropriated cultural forms. However, the apparent duality of social assimilation and resistance entails a metacommunication[10] at the cultural level of which James Clifford speaks as a moment of "hesitation" (*The Predicament of Culture*, 343). Similarly, but with an emphasis on Western—specifically Roman—notions of legendary moments of foundation, Hannah Arendt (*On Revolution*, 180–214), traces the political significance of "the hiatus between the end of the old order and the beginning of the new" (205), the relationship, that is, of narratives of exodus to the legitimation of the U.S. Constitution as an act of foundation that circumvents recourse to prior authority. The principle of revolutionary beginning, according to Arendt, is one of "a new event breaking into the continuous sequence of historical time" (205). She interprets these legends as indicating that "freedom is no more the automatic result of liberation than the new beginning is the automatic consequence of the end" (205). Rather, agents of change must undergo a period of transition prior to the inauguration of the new social order.

That transitional stage or—in Clifford's phrase, "hesitation"—preceding social change, is also theorized by Victor Turner (*The Ritual Process*, 94–130) as "liminality," an anti- or extrastructural phase characterized by disengagement with the social order. While hesitation marks a withdrawal that effectively places the subject outside of the system under consideration, it is a hiatus capable of fostering alternative standpoints in the contest of stories. That is, under conducive conditions, "hesitation" may enable conceptual reorganization preceding a new engagement, with more than a rhetorical difference, on the part of those who, like Momaday and Silko, are already positioned by existing educational and economic institutions to operate dominant forms for emergent class goals.

Although at the individual level innovations of dominant cultural forms in terms of American Indian narrative styles may be a means of negotiating mainstream bases of power under cover of currently valorized representations of difference, privileged bicultural mediators nevertheless reflect changing configurations of identity occurring simultaneously in mainstream and tribal cultures. Thus, to the extent that both Momaday and

Silko write out of and into these differently empowered social conditions, their works respond to the conflicted subject positions that are generated between traditional modes of social organization and adaptive tribal responses to the dominant society.

Yet because the tribally based aspects of their literary identities—as distinct from those aspects based in the esthetic values of mainstream society—are at odds with the more traditional tribal ethos, both *House Made of Dawn* and *Ceremony* might be considered not only as contemporary examples of Native American storytelling (as direct manifestations and transformations of the continuity of those traditions), but also in the more ambiguous light of the overlay of one set of social values by another.

In particular, they must be considered in relationship to the counterculture movement of the '60s and '70s when many white, middle-class Americans began looking for alternative modes of spirituality, since the popularity of these novels is more than incidental to that context. These works, therefore, may be more accurately understood as hybrid forms arising out of the general tendencies of North American culture to confrontation, alienation, and discontinuity. That is to say, the mixed-blood,[11] or "half-breed,"[12] authors of the syncretic literature exemplified by *House Made of Dawn* and *Ceremony* mediate cross-cultural traditions for the disaffected, at the same time that they engage in metacommunication about their own existential condition.

However, in so doing, they inevitably betray the "origins" (in the sense of communally sanctioned traditions) from which they derive their canonical status as representative Native American writers in the first place. Insofar, that is, as the traditional culture is not up for grabs, as Masayesva's objection witnesses, the bicultural author of North American Indian literature inscribes for the canonical record an ambiguous sign of Indianness—a fossilized trace of numinous passage, perhaps, though certainly not the mystic critter itself. The quite coopted analogy to the infamous Trickster suggests itself in this regard, as Gerald Vizenor and others have noted, though the Trickster is in no way constrained by analogies. (This essay got its title from one such Coyote who told his tale at a recent powwow: Two Mescalero Apaches were hanging out in a park, said Lorenzo Baca, when they were approached by a hippie speaking what he believed to be their native tongue. "How!" said the hippie to the Indians. Coyote looked at his friend, Ramon, and said "What?" Ramon looked back and said "Where?" Coyote asked "Who?" Ramon, "Why?" The hippie walked away muttering "Wow!" Lorenzo Baca, has included this tale in his collection *Songs, Poems And Lies.*

The syncretic works of Momaday and Silko articulate a paradoxical presence/absence in the general currency of representations: they invoke familiar images of the exotic, while giving the comfortable a peculiar twist. They may raise the art level a notch beyond our comfort zone, as—according to some tastes—in Momaday's early works; or may descend to tedium in their condensed or complicated syntax. Then again, fragments of the sacred may be recuperated from the already alienated context of anthropological archives—a sort of textual necrophilia. All this may comprise a double jeopardy, but whatever it is, it's not what it appears to be. In this forest of ambiguity the hermeneutical project of American literary criticism must contend with an unreadable sign like that legendary inscription carved into the tree in the abandoned Roanoke colony, composed only of the local Indian name designating a neighboring tribe, a sign that would seem to indicate distress, yet not punctuated by the agreed upon mark. That sign—of what if not of distress?—was perhaps the first move in such literature.

However, the category of Native American fiction may be clarified by placing it in the theoretical framework of colonial discourse, for aside from the phenotypal blending of formerly discrete gene pools characteristic of colonial societies, the "half-breed" protagonist articulates the range of emergent subjectivities generated by colonial dependence and postcolonial dissolution of those relationships. The biological offspring of that historical antinomy embodies a third term which, in some respects, mediates and, in others, negates the relation of opposition between colonizer and colonized. The mixed-blood in its ideal form (a form to be taken with a grain of salt) forges new openings in existing social relations, shifting the balance of power by constellating new categories of meaning out of the dissolution of the old. On the one hand, because the "half-breed" position is neither of the binaries constituting its condition of partiality, it may mark the site of a synchronic mediation of diachronic relationships of oppression and subordination;[13] yet insofar as it articulates simultaneously the excluded middle term of the historical antinomy *and,* as a function of its privileged relationship to hegemonic institutions, displaces that excluded position which would enter into representation, it writes itself over that along side which it would take its ethical and politicized stand. Consequently, if the privileged position of mediation is not to emerge as a new form of domination, bicultural mediators must explicitly critique both the ambivalence and the privilege of the positions we occupy.

In Mexico and the Americas to the south, and to varying degrees in Canada, the category of the mestizo or the métis refers to historically cohesive cultures. In North America, by contrast, pressures for assimilation tend to produce fragmentation and dispersal of identity and identification rather than cohesiveness. And though the Native American half-breed experience in the United States is an often painful one (cf. Paula Gunn Allen's essay in *The Sacred Hoop,* "A Stranger in My Own Life"), the tropological force of the mixed-blood position refers as much to contemporary resistance to nationalistic meltdown as to quantum of Indian "blood." In any case, the latter may be difficult to determine due to the powerful assimilative pressures exerted on our predecessors by federal policies. Racism, institutionalized as political and economic restrictions, and internalized as self-hatred, inclined our mixed-blood parents (speaking of my Chickasaw father, born in Oklahoma in 1914) more toward denial than to claiming what was generally considered to be a stigma. Unlike those to the north and south who are able to develop socially stable mixed identities, many of us embody a genealogical blank, filled with secondhand bits of information, partially uncovered tracks, fragments of photos in which we strain to recognize our own features and those of our children.

Our ancestors were ambivalent; caught between the lines of powerfully contending stories of origin and aim, they attempted to blend into the anonymous niches between, in Homi Bhabha's phrase, "almost, but not quite, (not white)." That legacy is as determining for mixed-bloods as was the more forthright horror of those who were rounded up and confined to reservations, or the resignation of others allotted eighty acres of poor land in exchange for a way of life that had long sustained and satisfied them.

Yet even moving nearer to the main currents of the dominant society, we will be hard pressed to find anyone who considers his or her identity to be an unproblematic unity appropriately integrated in available social structures. Without a doubt therefore, contemporary mixed-blood literature presents new paradigms of self-knowledge to the general public. At their best, instead of subject positions based on binary either/or oppositions, these works articulate relational subjectivities in the analogic mode of both-and, more-less, forging multiple sites of invention without collapsing the tension of difference back into a merely oppositional stance.[14]

Nevertheless, while these partial identifications may provide considerable flexibility in the context of mainstream society, such provisional strategies of self-constitution can be a problem from the point of view of the tribes on which syncretic novels are based. For to the extent that Native American fiction draws upon sacred oral traditions in order to satisfy the expectations of the reading public for local color—that is, insofar as it explicitly uses culturally proscribed narratives—it immediately becomes unrepresentative of the very communities it is taken to represent. However, at issue is not the colonial question of authenticity, but the ethical question of transgression of communal sanctions by cultural mediators.

Although the explicit incorporation of sacred oral stories in the novel form was initiated by N. Scott Momaday, Leslie Marmon Silko's *Ceremony* presents a network of issues immediately relevant to the conflicting ethos of tribal ceremonials and Western aesthetics at the conjunction of sacred and secular orientations. *Ceremony*'s thematic concern with mixed subjectivities, its motif of the spotted and the commingled, and its call for transcendence of boundaries—"no boundaries, only transitions through all distances and time" (258)—the complex relationships of these multiple subject positions are foreshadowed in the prologue's suggestion of a continuity between Silko's authorship of the novel and Thought-Woman's creation of the world: "Thought-Woman, the spider, named all things and as she named them they appeared," the clan-story begins. Shifting from the mediate to the immediate, the narrator adds, "She is sitting in her room thinking of a story now. I'm telling you the story she is thinking" (1).

From the standpoint of the outsider then, the narrator's identification with the Pueblo creatrix seems to authorize the novel's representation of that tradition. At the same time, the prologue's effacement of the contradictions between secular and sacred ways of having stories seems to legitimate the reader's access to the traditional narratives of the Pueblo. However, in the real terms of traditional communal functions, recourse to the clan stories presupposes conditions that are difficult to honor within the secular context of the novel. If, as according to Paula Gunn Allen, these clan stories are "not to be told outside of the clan," (1990:383) the narrator's shifting perspective from the communitarian context to that of the atomized writer defines the author's place as a site of transgression rather than of continuity between traditional tribal and Western storytelling traditions.

While the issue may be and probably is perceived differently among different Pueblo—Allen's standpoint is disputed by some (see note 2)—to the extent that it is generally upheld, as I have been told that it is, the prologue's admonishment (1) acquires a particular resonance:

> "They aren't just entertainment.
>   Don't be fooled,
> They are all we have, you see,
>   all we have to fight off illness and death."

For if the clan stories aren't "just entertainment," but have a survival function in sustaining the identity of the community—a function threatened by "they [who] try to destroy the stories / let the stories be confused or forgotten," then the problem introduced at the outset of the novel, that of defending the stories and hence their social relations against "the mighty evil," pivots on the paradox of their expropriation for the literary market by the cultural mediator. For by seeming to define an identity, the possessive "our" in reference to the clan stories effaces, but does not dispose of, the actual contradictions in ways of having stories—the different relations of production and distribution between tribal oral traditions and those of Native American novels. Thus the conflicted context in which we encounter the clan stories equivocally positions the reader in their defense.[15]

It is relevant to the present argument to observe that in the prologue's formulation of the threat to the clan stories as consisting in the possibility of their confusion, and its alternate (but related) threat to the stories constituted by the possibility of forgetting them, the narrator collapses distinct perspectives—those inside and outside the context of traditional sanctions—into an internally divided identity (a form which itself mirrors the bicultural subject). Thus, when we take on the subject position offered by the prologue in identification with traditional sanctions on the performative contexts of the clan stories—for "they are all we have"—and if the pronoun "we" and the possessive "our" refers to the *clan* whose stories these are and not to we readers who appropriate them in the context of the novel, we occupy a culturally familiar double-bind. For if the stories are confused, they will be forgotten. That is, if they lose significance for the lifeways of the Pueblo (as they may, for example, if they are disconnected from the ethical and symbolic contexts of traditional clan roles), they will cease to be told by those for whom they functioned to maintain those role allocations. And, on the other hand, if the stories are forgotten because of an ensuing confusion of their social function, the tribal identity which they once embodied and articulated will be lost. Underlying these related propositions is an irresolvable conflict in which *Ceremony* is caught up: that if the stories are told outside the sanctions of their communal context, as indeed they are in the commodity form of the novel, they will be confused in the terms of their communal context and hence forgotten because in the secular domain of the novel they *are* "just entertainment."

The ethical problem I am narrating in terms of a paradox would seem to have two possible solutions: either traditional sanctions are respected and the stories are entrusted to the internal vitality of those traditions, or they are assimilated as fragments of an exotic subculture into the dominant institutions which serve a different system of cultural values and social organization. The consequences of the latter transformation is that the clan stories cease to be what they were in their former context—the socially integrative means by which tribal communities maintain the structures of their identity—and the community itself will be ever more vulnerable to assimilation by the dominant society. And this is where agents of social change must become not only innovative but ethically accountable to the communities they purport to represent.

Because consideration of the ethical contexts of tribal cultures would call into question one of the presumed rights of the academy—that of pursuing knowledge for its own sake (for the sake, that is, of control and the legitimation of control), Silko's novel and its critical commentary reprise an historical dilemma: to the extent that authors and critics alike deny the real differences between the cultures in ways of having stories—differences in relations of production, in modes of circulation, in social functions—they silence crucial aspects of those tribal traditions they would reclaim. And insofar as the literary presence of bicultural Native Americans (as exemplified in its emergent phase) is predicated on an absence of the ethical context of the tribal communities on which they draw, that disjunctive space becomes the arena—at once place and space—of the contesting stories of who and how is an Indian.

The multiple perspectives brought to bear in this discussion attest to the material and ideological ambiguities alternately supporting and subverting my own critique of the misappropriation of communally proscribed traditions. They demonstrate, as well, that purist paradigms that impose either/or fictions on the question of "how" is an Indian unrealistically circumscribe lived narratives of "who" is an Indian. No single point of view can be said to be more valid than another; each reflects historically changing conditions constituting Indian (and in this case) specifically Pueblo identity. Each standpoint represents a particular set of relationships to the dominant order's narratives of individual freedom; each is differentially constituted in relation to the more traditional values of tribal community; and each perspective critiques the other along the social axis of "inside–outside."

Yet the bicultural arena is not only the permeable intersection of contesting narratives of identity and identification. What is at issue in the contest of stories entails far more than esthetic or rhetorical consequences. At stake is precisely the issue of viable material conditions for sustaining Indian identity. That the problem is critical is confirmed by the recent Greenpeace report informing the public of fifty-three proposals to locate incinerators, landfills, and nuclear waste repositories on Native American lands. It is well known among tribal people everywhere that their councils are being approached with financial "incentives" and employment "possibilities" that include lease agreements stipulating that the tribes waive their sovereign rights in relation to these sites of economic exploitation.[16] What is at stake in these devastating propositions compels the conclusion that the question of "how" is an Indian is increasingly crucial to the question of "who" is an Indian.[17]

NOTES

1. The 1990 Supreme Court decision in the case of Employment Division, Department of Human Resources of Oregon v. Alfred Smith states that it is an "unavoidable consequence of democratic government" that majority interests "must be preferred to a system in which each conscience is a law unto itself. . . ." That is, insofar as minority religious practices infringe on the laws of the majority society, those practices will be judged illegal by the superior rights of the latter. The decision reverses previous positions on religious freedom by saying that while we may believe whatever we wish, if we try to practice what we believe (in this case, using sacramental Peyote in the Native American church), we may not only lose our jobs, as did Al Smith, but can be thrown in jail. All this would sound quite familiar to the Pilgrims. In the words of Justice Scalia, "we cannot afford the luxury of deeming . . . invalid, as applied to the religious objector, every regulation of conduct that does not protect an interest of the highest order." The conflicting contexts in which this contest of stories is being fought out are reduced to the interests of dominant power, and the sense of ethical poverty expressed by the decision reflects badly on the status of democratic principles in the United States.

2. Paula Gunn Allen (1990). Critics of this article tend to consider the position Allen takes up against unsanctioned use of tribal stories problematic in view of her own appropriations of sacred material for the commercial market, a practice that she apparently did not forego following her critique of that practice. Despite her own contributions to the contradiction she critiques, the critique itself is valid to the extent that it does indeed reflect traditional sanctions on the use of sacred stories. But questions remain as to the status of the particular oral story fragments that Silko incorporates into *Ceremony*. According to the perspectives of two insiders, Tony and Wilma Purley of Mesita—the village to which the traditionals moved after Silko's great grandfather, Robert Marmon, became governor of Laguna, Silko's use of the oral stories is in no way transgressive because the stories she incorporates were always "like T.V.—just for entertainment." Moreover, they were already in the "public" domain thanks to their prior textualization by anthropologist, Elsie Clews Parsons. As an outsider I am not in a position to confirm or deny the syncretic cultural effects resulting from the particular Christian interventions (some say disruptions) in Laguna traditions instituted by Silko's paternal forebears, beyond offering a reminder of the distinction between the traditional *structures* of Pueblo social roles and the mediating symbolic *narratives* that those roles articulate in response to historically changing influences.

3. The article explains that "because the university supports many students' and profes-

sors' dissertations and research on the Indian reservation, the issue of disrespect for sacred Indian traditions has been a serious one in the past few years." NAU's confrontation was brought about "largely by a book written by NAU professor Ekkehart Malotki, *The Hopi Salt Journey,* [that] contains secrets the tribe does not want revealed," according to director of cultural preservation Jenkins. One might ask, If the Hopi are united in wishing to preserve their tribal secrets, how did Malotki get his information? Those possibilities include payments to a needy individual for his store of secrets and the mediation of an individual tribal member largely acculturated to the exchange value of knowledge.

4. I am using the term *traditional* in the way generally used by Native Americans to indicate a distinction between "modernizing" factions within tribal communities and those seeking to retain or revitalize cultural practices and values that sustained collective identity prior to conquest, relocation, and interpellation by dominant economic and social formations. For an analysis of "modernization" see Marshall Berman's *All That is Solid Melts Into Air,* as well as Raymond Rocco's essay in *Culture Studies* 4:3 (October 1991) "The Theoretical Construction of the 'Other' in Postmodern Thought," in which modernization "implies the progressive economic and administrative rationalization and differentiation of the social world: processes which brought into being the modern capitalist-industrial state" (1988:325). The distinction between Native American traditionalist and modernizing modes of social organization tends to become an opposition at the level of politics when the latter are closely associated with, or otherwise an ideological extension of, federal policies to capitalize tribal land bases. Conversely, although the more traditional enclaves within many tribal communities tend to be the most economically impoverished precisely because their priorities are survival to the seventh generation rather than economic exploitation of the land base, their cultural practices constitute an invaluable resource for assuring the continuity of perspectives able to counter the commodification of every value characteristic of global capitalism.

5. However, this is not to suggest that Native American identities constitute an 'Other' to contemporary social conditions. Rather, the various forms of colonization to which Native American societies were (and continue to be) subject, and our diverse histories of domination and subordination, are common to native as well as non-native populations. Both sides of the 'self-not-self' paradigm are thoroughly implicated in the paradoxical injunctions colonial histories entail. (I am thinking here of one of the first Native American authors—the early-seventeenth-century Andean, Guaman Poma's translation of his side of the story into the language and form of the colonizer in an effort to influence King Philip III of Spain on behalf of his community. Like Poma, North American Indians necessarily and regularly appropriate the technological and discursive forms, as well as the representational ideologies, of the dominant society, in order to negotiate the prevailing social conditions.) (See Adorno 1986.)

6. Because of generally resilient practices, and despite disruptive pressures on cohesive social formations, the influences of 'modernity' may disperse but do not entirely disrupt these traditionally centripetal communities. Tribal assimilation of the offspring of mixed marriages varies widely among Indian communities and even among the same tribe on a regional basis: for instance for one branch of the Lakota the word *Iyeska* in contemporary usage conveys a strongly pejorative attitude toward mixed bloods, while in others, its earlier sense of 'translator' continues to retain traces of the spiritual roots of precontact meanings. The particular communities of which both Momaday and Silko write traditionally denied full participation in community life to outsiders—a

condition defined by transgression of customary practices—including marriages outside the boundaries of sanctioned kinship affiliations. Particularly when these writers were growing up, the tribes of which they write tended to exclude outsiders from traditional tribal structures. The bias toward members of mixed descent is currently undergoing a transition to relative permeability of boundaries due to the tenacity of kinship ties. The ambiguous situation of mixed-blood children among these tribes is the topic of much of the writing by Allen (for example, "A Stranger in My Own Life," *The Sacred Hoop,* 1986 and "Special Problems in Teaching Leslie Marmon Silko's *Ceremony,* 1991, cited below).

7. The bicultural orientation of the Laguna Pueblo consequent on the influences of its multiply interpellated history is addressed by A. LaVonne Ruoff Brown in *MELUS* 5 (1978). Ruoff quotes Elsie Clews Parson's account of the history of Laguna: "Laguna was the first of the Pueblos to Americanize through intermarriage . . . and Silko's great grandfather, Robert Marmon, led the Americanization faction, resulting in the exodus of the traditional Laguna to Mesita and then to Isleta (2–3). However, Tony and Wilma Purley of Mesita, cited above, caution that it is a mistake to apply both the notion of relative "Americanization" and the counter-notion of "resistance" to the cultural situation of the main village at Laguna. They point out that all the villages partake of T.V. and other 'mainstream' cultural practices. They disagree, however, that such incorporation constitutes "Americanization." Because the national and global market economy has intervened in the symbolic meanings of Pueblo identity and identification, rather than resistance to national symbolic tropes and cultural practices, they emphasize that the Pueblos incorporate those structures of modernization into the old traditions. Nevertheless, the village "has its secrets" that outsiders should respect (but have notoriously betrayed).

8. Momaday, one might assume, identifies more particularly with the Kiowa of his paternal heritage than with the Jemez Pueblo and Navajo depicted in *House Made of Dawn,* and yet he also deeply identifies with the latter as he observes in *The Names* (New York: Harper Colophon Books, 1977). "My parents lived and taught at the Jemez Day School for more than a quarter of a century. It was my home from the time I was twelve until I ventured out to seek my fortune in the world. My most vivid and cherished boyhood memories are centered upon that place" (1977:117–118).

9. Arnold Krupat in Gerald Vizenor's *Narrative Chance* (1989). Speaking of a thematic movement in Native American autobiography from history and science to art, Krupat observes that "Native Americans have had to make a variety of accommodations to the dominant culture's forms, capitulating to them, assimilating them, sometimes dramatically transforming them, but never able to proceed independent of them" (1989:57).

10. My formulation of bicultural mediation extrapolates from the distinction between use and exchange value in Anthony Wilden (1980): "In the constitution of exchange value out of use value, the primary necessity is a 'point of contact' with the exterior." Similarly, the bicultural mediator, an exchange value of sorts, is constituted in relation to "external contact at a boundary which . . . brings about internal reorganization AFTER THE EVENT" (1980:252, glossed from Kojeve, 1947a:372ff). As such, the mediating subject articulates "a system of higher order complexity," than that on either side of the mediated boundary. The tension between assimilation and resistance consequently entails a third level metacommunication about the rearticulation of boundary relationships by representatives of some aspect of Native American culture in the terms

of some corresponding aspect of dominant culture. Although the representative dual subject functions as a translator between the two cultural systems, in so doing, he/she inevitably betrays some of the social rules of the former, just as does translation between languages. Thus the bicultural subject as translator for the dominant culture signals the paradoxical presence/absence of the temporal 'Other' imagined by that culture. The discourse of the bicultural mediator, then, refers to an aura of originary value in much the same way that economic exchange value functions in relationship to use value.

11. While I will use the term *mixed blood* in order to define a site of strategic articulation of both Western and indigenous perspectives, I wish to problematize the category. The category of blood is not an indigenous one, but circulates among the borrowings from Western ideologies, and like the appropriation of the horse or of firearms, functions to signify a resistant 'Indianness' that persists despite the encroachments of the colonizing cultures. Although the ideology of race derives from medieval Europe, constituting the self-affirmation of the nobility in its attempt to secure itself against gathering peasant and mercantile pressures, the same strategy is appropriated and transposed by indigenous peoples in order to affirm their resistance to the assimilative pressures of colonization. Thus the conceptual category of genealogy is reified in both European and indigenous contexts to describe a quality that travels in the blood: the notion of "blue blood" is adapted by post-"contact" Indian-identified peoples as the valorization of "red blood." (As an aside: the reader should be alert to the proliferation of tropes commonly resorted to in order to convey information concerning "red" and "white" relations. While the tropological basis of the notion of mixed blood must be foregrounded and the irony of its use registered, it is well to keep in mind the brute facts of colonization within which the signifier "mixed blood" functions.)

12. The term *half-breed* is commonly used by Native Americans of mixed descent both as affirmation of our sense of ambiguity and as a pejorative appelation (legitimating, by contrast, those whose identities are less ambiguously constituted). In its affirmative function, it belongs to the same category of resistance to assimilation as that earlier designation appropriated by indigenous peoples—Indian—to assert difference from their namers.

13. Anthony Wilden (1980:354) understands the synchronic perspective as "an overdetermined communication about some (overdetermined) relationship or other at another level." One can extrapolate the representative mixed-blood position, then, as consisting in a "metacommunication about a referent communication," that is, the crises of subjectivities generated by simultaneously identifying with contradictory systems of cultural organization and aim. The mixed-blood position can be understood as a communication, in a sense, about the double-bind experience consequent on internalizing conflicting messages regarding origins that form the underlying evaluative criteria of these systems. Yet the mixed-blood position, insofar as it presents itself as representative of the tribal community, can only speak with 'forked tongue,' and it is precisely that doubleness that is required by the multi-leveled contradictions, denials, and selective affirmations within the messages in circuit.

14. Anthony Wilden (1980:174).

15. I discuss the matter in detail in *Revising the Ethnic Canon*, (University of Minnesota Press, forthcoming 1994), edited by David Palumbo-Liu.

16. See, for example, an article in *The Amicus Journal* (Fall 1991) by Dick Russell, "Dances With Waste," which reports the efforts of Pine Ridge resident, Joann Tall, to organize resistance to this facet of "modernization."

17. Special thanks to my fellow graduate students at Stanford, Mike Morales, Arturo Heredia, and Heather Zwicker, for taking time out from their own work to offer editorial suggestions in the various stages of this essay.

REFERENCES

Adorno, Rolena. 1986. *Guaman Poma: Writing and Resistance in Colonial Peru.* Austin: University of Texas Press.

Allen, Paula Gunn. 1986. *The Sacred Hoop: Recovering the Feminine in American Indian Traditions.* Boston: Beacon Press.

———. 1990. "Special Problems in Teaching Leslie Marmon Silko's *Ceremony.*" Berkeley: *The American Indian Quarterly: Journal of American Indian Studies* 14:4:379–386.

Arendt, Hannah. 1963. *On Revolution.* London and New York: Penguin Books.

Bhabha, Homi. 1984. "Of Mimicry and Man: The Ambivalence of Colonial Discourse." *October,* number 28.

Clifford, James. 1988. *The Predicament of Culture: Twentieth Century Ethnography, Literature, and Art.* Cambridge Mass.: Harvard University Press.

Kojeve, Alexandre. 1947. *Introduction à la lecture de Hegel,* ed. Raymond Queneau, Paris: Gallimard.

Momaday, N. Scott. *House Made of Dawn.* New York: Harper and Row.

Silko, Leslie Marmon. 1977. *Ceremony.* New York: Viking Press.

Turner, Victor. 1969. *The Ritual Process: Structure and Anti-Structure.* Chicago: Aldine.

Vizenor, Gerald. 1989. *Narrative Chance: Postmodern Discourse on Native American Indian Literatures.* Albuquerque: University of New Mexico Press.

Wilden, Anthony. 1980. *System and Structure.* London and New York: Tavistock.

GRANDMOTHER, GRANDFATHER, AND
THE FIRST HISTORY OF THE AMERICAS

Clifford E. Trafzer

Humishuma, Mourning Dove, an Okanogan Indian, once wrote that Indian stories about the *chip-chap-tqut* or Animal People "are not myths nor fiction; they are real history, true accounts of what happened near the Beginning when the World was very young." Mourning Dove lived during a transitional period of American Indian history, between 1888 and 1936, when many Indians were adjusting to life on reservations and the forced educational system of the Bureau of Indian Affairs. Although she attended a Catholic mission school during her youth, Mourning Dove grew up in a fairly traditional manner in northern Washington state and southern British Columbia. Her parents and elders educated her in the old way, through the oral tradition of the historical texts or ancient Okanogan stories.[1]

Mourning Dove learned the old texts of her tribe from the native storytellers, the first of whom was her mother. "I recall with a heavy heart," she once stated, "a pen-picture in my mind of my dear Indian Mother who use[d] to put me asleep with tales of Indian lore and legends of my people." She remembered her mother in memories "dear and sacred to me," and she revered the "story tellers of the tribe [who] went from village to village telling legends and lore to the children, something in the form of our present day historians." The storytellers, she said, "preserve the history of their people." According to Native American elders, the ancient stories of the plants and animals, the rivers and rocks, are history in the native sense of the word. Elders say that the stories are "accurate representations of actual occurrences" but they are more.[2] The stories represent historical actions that provide a creative spark in life, offering significant meanings and interpretations of human action with each other and with the natural environment. The stories offer a dualistic understanding of history, of the past and present, positive and negative, and male and female. They provide knowledge and wisdom through the inter-action of the first inhabitants on earth. The stories are meant for all time and for all generations, and each time they are told, they offer a creative force that links today with yesterday. Thus, they are not linear like other historical texts, particularly those of Eu-roamericans. They are circular, carrying the participants in the stories, the storyteller, and the listeners to a time when the first creative activities emerged on earth.[3]

The first Native American historical texts were offered orally, and they link the earth-surface people with the plants and animals, the rivers and rocks, and all things believed significant in the life of America's first people. The texts tie Indian people to the earth and its life through a spiritual kinship with the living and dead relatives of Native Americans. Coyote, raven, fox, hawk, turtle, rabbit, and the other animal characters in the stories are considered by many Native Americans to be their relatives. The Animal People are believed by most tribes to have originated before humans and that the Animal People have physically changed over time. In the same way, the Plant People are related to Indian people. Oak, maple, pine, cedar, fir, spruce, and many other trees are viewed as relatives, and so are such plant foods as corn, squash, beans, berries, and roots. Ac-cording to traditional Native American scholars, the Animal People and Plant People participated in a history before and after the arrival of humans, and this history was kept through the spoken word.[4]

American Indian elders point out that the historical interaction between the plants and animals has never ended. However, humans are less sensitive to their relationship with plants and animals and modern society does not recognize the native view that this relationship over time can be considered history. Andrew George, a Palouse Indian holy man and storyteller, once stated, "You come from that university where they study plants and animals. But those people don't really know the plants and animals. I have heard things they have never heard, and I have seen things they have never seen." The tribal elder had not cut himself off from the Animal People and Plant People, and at the time, he continued his people's historical relationship with these elements of the world. He also explained that he had a similar relationship with the geographical features of the earth around him. Through the oral history of his people, he was a relative of the Palouse Hills, Palouse River, Snake River, Badger Mountain, Soap Lake, Blue Mountains, and others. He believed that Mount Saint Helens, Mount Rainier, Mount Adams, and the other moun-tains were alive and had a history that was known and understood by Native Americans of the Great Columbia Plain (George 1980).

This form of Native American history, derived from the oral tradition, has been passed down from one generation to the next since the beginning of the earth. Storytellers shared their ancient stories, and they were noted individuals within the tribes. They continue to offer their stories within the Indian communities today, and they are still considered powerful people who know their way around words. Storytellers captured the hearts and minds of the people, offering them an opportunity to reestablish their relationship with a creative historical past. Mourning Dove once wrote that the arrival of such a storyteller in her village elicited great excitement and anticipation. Whenever the elder teachers visited, Mourning Dove's mother anxiously awaited their arrival in the family's tipi and would joyously watch her children's eyes as the storyteller acted out an Animal Person by talking, singing, and dancing. "Sometimes the parents would join us in laughing at the clowned mimicing [*sic*] sight which gave us more interest in the story which was classed with us children as play instead of an Indian education of our ancestors history of their coming into this world" (Mourning Dove preface, n.d.). Children and adults alike delighted in the stories, and they relished the times they spent listening to storytellers and sharing their own stories with one another. The stories were far more than entertainment, for they offered a traditional education in many fields of study, including history.

Mourning Dove believed that the old stories about the Animal and Plant People constituted Native American history. She was not alone in her assessment of native history. Certainly Mourning Dove's mother as well as Old Narciss and Broken Nose Abraham—the storytellers who taught Mourning Dove her first stories—would have agreed that the ancient literature of the people was the tribe's original history (Mourning Dove preface, n.d.). For years, American Indian elders have argued that the old stories are not myths or fairy tales or, as one professional historian put it, "fish tales that grow with the telling." The stories form a body of knowledge that is the first history of America, and there is little understanding of Native American history, culture, or society without an appreciation of this viewpoint. American historians have long argued that they do not "uncover the absolute truth about the past," but rather historians interpret the past (Nash 1991:1). Native American would agree, but many would argue that non-Indian historians have failed to recognize that the old stories are a part of the historical past that deserves discussion and historical interpretation.

Most Native Americans would agree with Mourning Dove's views of American Indian history. Andrew George, the Palouse holy man and storyteller, was also an historian in the traditional sense of the word. George once recounted that when he was a child, his elders taught him numerous stories. His grandmother and grandfather instructed him to listen quietly and attentively to all of the stories. They wanted George and other children to overlearn the stories, so they repeated the tales again and again. George remembered that when he got older, the elders singled him out and asked him to retell particular stories. He had to recount the story correctly. Otherwise his teachers told him where he had committed an error and instructed him to start at the beginning of the story and retell it again. By the light of a small fire situated in a mat lodge located along the northern banks of the Snake River, Andrew George listened and learned the first history of his people. Most American Indian children learned in this fashion, including George.

Mourning Dove and Andrew George both once lived on the Columbia Plateau near the Snake and Columbia rivers. She spoke Salish, while he spoke Sahaptin. Some Salish and Sahaptin stories were unique to their people, but the two peoples shared other stories, although different versions of the same story contained slight variations in content, organization, and presentation. The Indians drew upon the stories as a source of information about life, and they were expected to learn from their traditional history. Through the positive and negative actions of the Animal People—particularly Coyote— the Indians were expected to grow intellectually, culturally, and socially. The people not only shared the stories orally as a form of comedy and tragedy, they discussed the stories and took meaning from the words. Throughout their lives, people interpreted the stories, explaining historical events in the context of their own time. This was particularly true of the storytellers but not limited to those persons. Stories were the domain of many people, not just the specialists. Everyone explained the stories, offering their own interpretation of their meanings. Understandably, different people interpreted the stories differently, drawing diverse conclusions from the same body of information. And undoubtedly, people interpreted the stories differently depending on the era in which they lived. Elders sometimes asked children to discuss the meaning of stories, using the historical lesson as a point of reference and expecting the child to be familiar with the details of the texts. Throughout their lives, Indians referred back to the stories, taking parts of these historical accounts and applying them to their everyday lives (Nash 1991:1; Trafzer and Scheuerman 1991:v–ix, 1–14).

One afternoon Andrew George discussed his life in the Palouse country at the beginning of the twentieth century. The old man with white hair hanging to the middle of his back took a moment to reflect before explaining how turtle created the Palouse Hills. Rather than begin the discussion with an account of his birth, parents, lineage, and childhood, George offered a discussion that tied his past with that of his people. His history began with a geographical overview of the Palouse country that tied the ancient and recent dead of his people—buried within the bosom of the earth and near the Snake and Palouse rivers—with the canyons, rivers, and hills of his home. George offered a unique creation story of the Palouse Hills that placed his life into a relationship with the earth and animals of the region. His perspective on history offers an understanding of his people and the world around him. According to his historical account, Speelyi, or Coyote, once spent a good amount of time boasting. He told all of the Animal People he had more power than anyone and that there was nothing he could not do. In particular, Coyote told the others that he could outrun anyone and would take on all challengers, including Deer, Antelope, or Rabbit. They were all fleet of foot, but weary of Coyote's power. It was possible, they thought, that they could lose a race against Speelyi. For this reason, they were slow in challenging Coyote. Turtle heard Coyote boasting but said nothing at first. Turtle was not a large person but had some power, especially power of the mind. After giving the situation some thought, Turtle told Coyote that he would race against the braggart.

Turtle's challenge surprised everyone, including Coyote who poked fun at the challenger and laughed until he was ill. Turtle remained unaffected by Coyote's insults. Instead, he began to seek a new vision of the world around him. Turtle prayed that the creative force would change the earth from a flat prairie to big, rolling hills. In his dream, Turtle saw undulating hills that appeared like waves of earth covered with bunchgrass. First came the vision, and then the reality. When Turtle awoke on the day of the race, the earth had been transformed into the hills he had envisioned. Coyote and the other Animal People did not understand this change, and Coyote was actually overconfident. He bragged that the hills meant nothing to him and that he would handily defeat Turtle without difficulty. At the start of the race, it appeared that Coyote was correct. He dashed off up the first hill and down the other side, but as he looked ahead toward the second hill, he saw Turtle just rounding the top of it.

Coyote raced forward and overtook Turtle, charging down the hill and up the next one. As he rounded the top of the hill, he saw Turtle moving over the top of hill in front of him. Confused by this, Coyote charged ahead to catch the challenger. This same situation occurred five times, until Coyote was out of breath and could not catch Turtle. The Animal Person with the hard shell crossed the finish line first and won the contest. Many years passed before Turtle told Coyote his secret. When the two were very old, Turtle explained that he had won the race by asking his family to cooperate with him. Members of the Turtle family positioned themselves on various hills to make it appear that Turtle was always in front of Coyote. Turtle reminded Coyote about the bragging and explained the vision of many hills. As a result, Impeish, the Creator, changed the earth and molded the hills in order to help Turtle. Pleased with this work, Impeish left the beautiful hills as a reminder of the time Turtle defeated Coyote, humbling the boastful one.

Andrew George also explained his life in terms of the relationship of the Palouse Indians to the Animal People and Plant People who lived on the earth before humans. However, in the early stages of human history, men, women, and children interacted with the Animals and Plants. Addressing the delicate balance between humans and fish, George told a story about a time when Indian people took too many salmon from the rivers. The elder introduced the issue because of the intense struggle between Native Americans in the Northwest and white fishing interests in the region. The point of his story was to inform us that he knew of a historical text that referred to the issue of taking too many salmon and the consequences of such human action. George maintained that there was a time in the far distant Palouse past when the Indians took too many fish, thus depleting the salmon. With spears, nets, seines, dip nets, weirs, hooks, and spears, the people soon depleted one of their central food sources. Salmon had no power to prevent the humans, so Salmon Chief sought the help of Rattlesnake. Salmon Chief moved his body onto the banks of the river where Rattlesnake sunned himself. Salmon asked Snake for some of his power, but Rattlesnake refused. The Chief responded by using his strong tail and beating Rattlesnake over the head. "Brother," said Salmon Chief, "may I have some of your power to combat the humans who are catching too many of my tribe?" Again, Rattlesnake refused and again Salmon Chief beat the snake over the head. Five times Salmon asked the same question. Finally, on the fifth request, Rattlesnake grudgingly shared a portion of his power with Salmon Chief. The chief obtained some of Rattlesnake's venom so that the fish could bite humans, infecting them but not killing them. More important, the gift of Rattlesnake helped reestablish the balance of power between humans and fish, a balance that must be maintained between two elements if they are to coexist over a period of time (George 1980).

The balance among different elements as depicted through characters is a common theme in the ancient history of America. In the Northwest, the cold Canadian wind has a prescribed relationship with the warm Pacific wind, and this relationship developed over time when the earth was young. Lalawish or Wolf brought a climatic change to the earth. According to a Wasco Indian storyteller, Five Wolf Brothers and one sister named Tahmattoxlee moved from the north onto the Columbia Plateau bringing cold northern winds.[5] They lived at Tamanttowla in a cave along the banks of the Chewana or Columbia River. The Five Wolf Brothers and their sister brought the Arctic winds, and they spread the cold by challenging all the Animal People to a wrestling match. Eagle's son lived across the river from Lalawish, and he had often heard the Five Wolf Brothers call out the challenge to fight. Each time he had refused, but with every victory, the earth became colder and colder until Young Eagle could take it no longer. He finally crossed the Columbia River to wrestle the Wolves.

Young Eagle fought to protect himself and his family from the bitter cold. He challenged the Five Wolf Brothers and wrestled the first Wolf. Before they engaged in mortal combat, Tahmattoxlee—the Wolf Sister—took five baskets of water and "poured water on the ground; making ice." Young Eagle "could not stand," stated storyteller Anawhoa (Black Bear) of the Wasco Indians. "He fell; and Coyote cut off his head. Cold-wind now boasted the more" (Anawhoa 1917). When the word reached the other Animal People that a Wolf Brother had killed Young Eagle, the people decided on war. Everyone chose sides, including the Five North Wind Brothers who allied with the Wolf Brothers. The Salmon Chief, his family, and the Five Chinook Wind Brothers joined forces against those who favored the cold weather. Salmon Chief challenged the Wolf Brothers to a wrestling match, but the North Wind Brothers decided on a plan. "We can wrestle with him and throw him down. Then there will be ice and cold over the Chewana, cold will be everywhere." The Wolf Brothers liked the plan. "When you throw Salmon Chief down," one Wolf Brother said, "we will fight and kill all of his children. We will make sure that none of them will survive" (McWhorter 1918).

Salmon Chief met the Five North Wind Brothers on the ice, but the chief told his people to beware of treachery. "I am afraid," he told his family. "I do not trust the North Wind or the Wolves. Be careful! If you see I am about to be beaten, you must run away quickly and hide!" The Five Wolf Brothers and Five North Wind Brothers called out for the match to begin. Tahmattoxlee poured five baskets of water on the ice covering the Chewana, making it very slippery. The Salmon Chief met and defeated the two oldest North Wind Brothers, but his victory was short-lived. He wrestled the third brother who was much stronger than his older brothers. The North Wind Brother easily threw Salmon Chief to the ice and angrily dragged him about before killing the chief. The Wolf Brothers, North Wind Brothers, and their allies sent up a victory cry: "*Ow-ow-ow-ow-ow-o-oo!*"

When Salmon Chief hit the ice, his family could not move swiftly enough to avoid disaster. Although they had been warned, the Wolf Brothers surprised them. The Five Wolf Brothers sprang on the Salmon People, and they were joined in a killing frenzy by Coyote and Fox families. Together they killed the children of Salmon Chief and then they killed his wife, splitting open her belly to find numerous eggs. They spread the eggs out over a flat rock and smashed each egg to ensure that none of them would survive. The Wolf Brothers and their allies destroyed all of the eggs except one that had lodged between two rocks and could not be reached. Although they worried about this egg, the Wolf Brothers began to sing, saying, "We have killed all of the Salmon! We have done a great thing! Now it will be cold all of the time!" (McWhorter 1918).

Chief Coyote had sided with the Wolf and North Wind Brothers until the slaughter of the Salmon People. At the height of the killing, Coyote declared, "I was wrong to help the Wolves." The North Wind Brothers and their allies had "killed a good man and destroyed a good people." He worried that their actions had changed the earth unnaturally, since "the warm wind will not blow, and we will be cold from now on." The Creator heard Coyote and had seen the battle between the Wolves and their allies and the Salmon. The Creator knew of the small egg slowly drying among the rocks along the Columbia River. At the conclusion of the fight, the Creator summoned the black clouds and had them gather over the Plateau. Rain poured down from the dark sky, washing the blood from the earth. Water ran in all directions cleansing the land and dislodging the tiny egg from between the rocks. The Creator nurtured this small egg and fertilized it, so that within five days, a small fish was born. On the sixth day it traveled downstream, always with its head pointing upstream. When it reached the mouth of the Columbia, Young Salmon met his grandmother, the mother of Salmon Chief.

According to one version of this historical text, Young Salmon's grandmother met her grandson so that she could train him to prepare for the great challenge of his life. "My grandson," Grandmother exclaimed, "your father was killed by the North Wind Brothers, as was his wife, and his children, and all of his followers. You are the only one who has survived, and I am glad that you have come to me." Grandmother Salmon took care of her kin, providing and teaching him how to live and survive. Young Salmon was quick to learn, since he listened well to his elders. One day Young Salmon asked his grandmother to tell him "how my father and mother were killed" and "how I was saved, and how I am alive today." Grandmother Salmon told the young one all that she knew and concluded her story by saying, "Grandson, I will help you grow fast and strong, so that one day you can stand against these brothers in the spring and beat them in a wrestling match as they beat your father!" True to her word, the elderly woman trained Young Salmon to be strong in mind, body, and spirit. He worked hard to develop himself, and he followed his grandmother's instructions. After months of training, Young Salmon was ready to face the North Wind Brothers. "I am happy," Grandmother Salmon announced one day. "You will be stronger than my son, your father. You will not fall before the cold North Wind" (McWhorter 1918).

When Spring arrived on the Northwest Plateau, the snow, wind, and ice refused to yield to the warm winds. Cold continued to grip the region, and the natural course of history could not progress in accordance with the creation. Most of the Salmon People could not travel up the Columbia River, but Grandmother Salmon told her grandson that he was ready and "can beat the five North Wind Brothers. Five baskets of oil to pour on the ice will give you secure footing on the smoothest of ice, and you will be able to stand firm and tall against each one of those brothers." Because Young Salmon was "going to face these brothers, the cold wind from the north," Grandmother gave her grandson a new name. "I will call you *Wenowyyi,* which means 'Young Chinook Wind.' You are the warm wind coming from the ocean, to drive away the cold." Grandmother Salmon explained to her family that her grandson would be aided in his fight with the North Wind Brothers by five baskets filled with oil that his supporters would spread on the slippery ice. The oil would provide better footing for Young Chinook Wind. With his family, Young Chinook began his journey up the Columbia River, bringing with him the warm winds off the Pacific Ocean.

The historical texts state that two women greatly aided Young Chinook in his quest of the North Wind Brothers. One was Grandmother and the other was his aunt. According to the story, he met his aunt near Celilo Falls on the Columbia River. Young Chinook Wind stopped at the falls to visit his elderly aunt. She lived in an A-frame mat lodge surrounded by ice, snow, and wind. When Aunt Salmon's nephew arrived, the icicles that hung from her hair melted away. "I knew it was you," she declared. "I knew the son of Salmon Chief would return one day to drive away the cold." The aunt explained that she was a prisoner of the cold and that she was beaten daily by the sister of the North Wind Brothers. Young Chinook Wind waited for the cruel sister to arrive, and when she did, he beat her with a thorny rose bush, driving her from the lodge and back to her family's cave farther up the Columbia River. She informed her brothers that Young Chinook Wind was on his way upstream. The warm wind had already reached their home, and the North Wind Brothers believed that the Salmon Chief had "come to life again" and was prepared to meet them "on the ice of the Columbia." The North Wind Brothers summoned their allies to watch the grand challenge, and when Young Chinook Wind arrived, they coyly asked, "Have you come to wrestle us, friend?" The challenger explained that he had come to fight, but the North Wind Brothers bragged among themselves. "We are strong, and there are five of us against one of him. It will be easy to kill this boasting Salmon boy" (McWhorter 1918).

At midday the Animal People met to watch Young Chinook Wind wrestle the five North Wind Brothers. Each time the young challenger faced his enemy, Aunt Salmon poured one of the five baskets of oil on the ice which provided better footing for Young Chinook Wind. With her help, and without great effort, the challenger defeated the three oldest North Wind Brothers, much to the delight of Coyote Chief who howled, *Ow-ow-ow-ow-ow-o-oo!*" The two youngest North Wind Brothers trembled with fear, but they faced the young salmon. The fourth brother fought harder than his older brothers, but in the end, he too lost. Young Chinook Wind was tired, but he had to face the last brother before claiming victory. The wrestling match proved to be a close contest, but in the end, Young Chinook Wind threw his opponent to the ice. "*Ow-ow-ow-ow-ow-o-oo!* Young Chinook, son of Salmon Chief, the Chief of the Chinooks, has won!" The sister of the North Wind Brother escaped while many of the Animal People celebrated, and she returns periodically to the Northwest to bring wind, snow, and ice. However, her power is not as great as that of her five brothers, and she cannot stand long against the warmth of Young Chinook Wind. The North Wind Brothers had altered the creation for a time, but in the end, the world was set right again with the help of Grandmother Salmon and Aunt Salmon as well as the dedication, courage, and strength of Young Chinook Wind (McWhorter 1918).

Tribal historians and storytellers offer a presentation of the past that does not fit the model commonly found in historical texts. When Emily Peone, an elder from the Colville Reservation, was asked to discuss her family's history she told of the origin story of her family from a Star Man. Peone provided an outline of this story, adding to it during several visits. Additional details of her family's origin story are found in an account given in December 1917 by William Poniah to Lucullus Virgil McWhorter. Poniah was a storyteller of mixed Chehalis and Yakima heritage. His story of the origin of the royal family of Chief Weowicht is more detailed than that given by Peone, but both are essentially alike in outline. Poniah or McWhorter entitled the story "The Two Sisters and Their Star Husbands," and McWhorter asserted correctly that the Klickitat Indians have their own version of the story with only slight variations.[6] According to Poniah's version of the story, two young girls named Tahpahlouh and Yaslumas left their village to dig roots for their mother (Poniah 1917). They dug roots all day, and when they made camp that evening, the two girls talked of many things. While they lay on the earth peering up at the bright sky, they talked about their future husbands. "I see two stars!" exclaimed Tahpahlouh, the oldest of the two. "They are not far apart. The smallest and red star, I wish would be your husband. The big bright star, I wish would be my husband." Unknown to the girls, the two stars heard this wish and transported them to a star land, although the girls awoke with "something like wax in their eyes" and did not know where they were. William Poniah did not identify the star in his narrative, but Emily Peone said that the girls had been transported to Venus, and that her family was related to the people on that planet.

"It was your wish," the Star Men told the two girls. "You wanted us," they explained. "You wished for him to be your husband! That is the reason we went down and brought you up here. Do not worry about anything any more. By your own wish; your own will, you became our wives." Without thought, the two girls became the wives of the Star Men, and soon after, Tahpahlouh gave birth to a baby boy (some say that the baby was Weowicht and others say that the boy was his father). Together, the band lived an idyllic life with an abundance of food. Each day the men hunted game and fished. Each day the women gathered roots and berries. The men warned the women not to dig a certain variety of root. "When you find a long root," they told Tahpahlouh and Yaslumas, "do not dig it up." They told the women this "law" five times, but the women became curious. One day Tahpahlouh found a long root and dug it completely out of the soil. "A big wind came up through the hole," and the women became conscious of their situation. By peering through the hole left by the root, they saw the earth and realized that they were in a star land. At this point, the women became fearful that the men would find out that they had broken the "law" and they became homesick. Immediately, they determined to return home to earth.[7]

When the men returned to their home, they noticed the wind. "Where did the wind come from? We have no wind up here!" The women claimed that they did not know the origin of the wind, and they succeeded in convincing the Star Men that the "wind just passed us." Satisfied, the men continued with their lives, but the women began braiding a lengthy rope of hazelnut bark that stretched from the star world to the earth. On the appointed day, the two women and the baby boy tied the rope to a tree and dug out the hole from which they had taken the forbidden root. All three of them escaped and returned to their people. "From the older sister and the star sprang the race [family] of Chief We-owitkt, the first root of the Yakimas" (Poniah 1917).

Weowicht's family is considered a royal family, filled with leaders well known in Northwestern Indian history. His daughter, Kamoshnite married Tsiyiyak, and their first child was Kamiakin, one of the great leaders of the Yakima and Palouse of the nineteenth century. Weowicht's sons, Owhi and Teias, and their children were also superb leaders. Descendents of this family consider themselves to be regal, the bearers of tribal leadership. To this day, the people of this family believe that they originated from the relationship between Tahpahlouh and the Star Man. This is the family's history and a factual presentation of their past. It is also part of the history of the Yakima and Palouse tribes, a story known to many Indians in the Northwest. The story offers an understanding of the Weowicht family and more. It presents a way of thinking that is very native to America and specific to the Plateau Indians. In the larger context, the text offers an historical understanding of Northwestern Indian history. As an historical account, the story of the Starman makes a great deal of sense to Indian people, presenting insights into the past of the tribes and family involved (Poniah 1917; Peone 1980; Trafzer and Scheuerman 1986:33).

The story of the Starman and the Yakima woman is a unique creation story that contains only a few lessons about appropriate or inappropriate behavior. Thus, proper behavior is not the major theme of the story. However, the issue of behavior is a central point of many traditional stories among Native Americans on the Columbia Plateau. Mourning Dove knew a number of such stories and recorded a few of them. Urged by several people to record the history of her people, Mourning Dove spent the last few years of her life writing different versions of Okanogan stories. Before her death on August 8, 1936, Mourning Dove composed an insightful essay about the Animal People that condemns incest. According to her account, Chief Coyote lived in a tipi overlooking Kettle Falls on the Columbia River with his large family, including a beautiful daughter. Young men from far and wide came to the tipi to court Coyote's daughter, but the chief sent each of them away. One day the girl grew tired of sitting in such a way as to hide her feet, "which was the custom of that day." She stretched out her cramped legs and exposed her shapely ankle. "Coyote fell in love with her, and he began to scheme how he was to get the girl." The chief designed a plan and put it to work immediately. Coyote told his wife that he felt ill, but asked her to watch for a friend of his whom he expected any day. The visitor was a Kutenai Indian, a warrior and medicine man who was very rich.[8]

According to Mourning Dove's version of this traditional text, Coyote continued to feel worse and told his wife he was about to die. "When I die, bury me on a high knoll overlooking the waters of where I was raised, just as if I could see the land of my birth. Bring me food each day, and do not bury my body, but put it on a high scaffold in the trees and leave it there." So Coyote faked his death, allowing his family to mourn, prepare his body, and lay it forever on a wooden scaffold high on the banks of Kettle Falls. His wife dutifully brought him food each day. Not long after his death, a stranger arrived in a canoe colored in many fine shades and loaded with expensive furs. He spoke in a strange language, but the People knew this was the Kutenai leader spoken of by Coyote before his death. Coyote's wife invited the stranger to her tipi and asked the Medicine Man to cure her daughter. Coyote had caused his own daughter to become ill so that the Kutenai Medicine Man could cure her. Without great effort the Medicine Man worked his wonders, and the girl recovered. Her elders forced her to marry the Medicine Man, but the girl did so against her will. A few days later she noticed something strange. While "bathing with the other women, the girl noticed that coyote hairs grew among her robes." It was then that she understood. She picked up dog excrement and threw it at the Medicine Man, whose features changed into those of Coyote. Stricken by the disclosure, the girl ran off Kettle Falls and killed herself rather than face the shame of her incestuous relationship with her father (Trafzer and Scheuerman 1991:51–57).

Mourning Dove's story came from a people concerned about teaching younger people the inappropriateness of incest. Here lies one of many basic distinctions between the culture and attitudes of the Native American tradition and those of the Judeo-Christian tradition. The story of Lot and his daughters in the book of Genesis is also an oral history on the subject of incest, but the point is somewhat different. The offspring of Lot and his daughters became the Moabites and Ammonites, neighbors of Abraham and his followers but not members of God's chosen people (Gen. 19:28). The story of Coyote's lust for his daughter served to instruct Indians of the impropriety of incest, setting an example of an impure life and the consequences of acting upon one's vile instincts. In contrast, the story of Lot reveals a preexisting aversion to incest, used to distinguish a group of people from its neighbors by associating an "unclean act" with the "foreigners."

Non-Indian historians, the newcomers to America, have often separated the first history of America from that of the "chosen" historical *truths* of Euroamericans. Some of them argue that the Indian history taught by Native American elders is unimportant because it is not based on fact. Some maintain that the traditional Indian stories have little or no bearing on the course of the "real" history of the Americas. Many professional historians ignore or discount the oral history of Native Americans. Some scholars have pushed aside the sacred teaching of Indian people, claiming that oral history taught by American Indian elders is mere myth, fable, and fairy tale. Some have summarily discounted the teaching of the oral tradition, conveniently labeling the first history only as literature without understanding that traditional historical teachings of Native Americans involve an interdisciplinary approach that encompasses literature, art, religion, government, society, medicine, history, and more.

Some American historians have perverted the oral history of American Indian tribes in North, South, and Central America and in some cases have tried to destroy this field of American history. Yet, like the revitalization of the small egg wedged in the rocks along the Columbia River and the Young Chinook Salmon that emerged from the egg, the first history of America has gained strength, credibility, and acceptance in some scholarly circles (Nashone 1988:11–29). Slowly, a few scholars have become increasingly aware that the first history of America did not begin with the arrival of Christopher Columbus in 1492. It began with the creation and the interaction of plants, animals, humans, and elements of the natural world when the earth was very young. Storytellers like Mourning Dove, Andrew George, Emily Peone, and William Poniah provided the historical texts of Native Americans that were intended for all time and for all generations. They offer timeless historical texts, and when they present the traditions orally or in writing, they offer a communal remembrance of the creation. Native American historical texts offer a literary communion with Indian origins and an understanding of a native interpretation of past and present. The presentation of the oral traditions is much like wrapping prayer feathers, placing in motion words that recreate the world and take the present and place it into the context of the past. The recreation of the act of storytelling and the remembrance of the first history, provides an understanding of Native American history that cannot be found in any written documents except those written by the first historians of the Americas.

NOTES

1. With the exception of the story about Rattlesnake and Salmon, none of the stories offered in the work above are found in the McWhorter Collection. Further, it is believed by the author that neither Dean Guie or L. V. McWhorter edited the stories offered by Mourning Dove in this work. The author has copied every story he could find in the McWhorter Collection and is preparing an edited work of these traditional historical accounts of the Plateau Indians. See Mourning Dove Preface, n.d.; Mourning Dove (1933); Trafzer and Scheuerman (1991:v–ix, 1–14).

2. Elders argue that the events described in the old stories are not only history, but they reflect actual incidents that occurred in world history. Thus, they are not myths that never took place in chronological time, but events that happened in accordance with the creation in order for humans to understand for all time the interrelationship of different forms of life.

3. The author expresses his thanks to Alanna Brown and the other outside reviewer for the Smithsonian Institution Press. He also wishes to thank Professor Robert Griffin for his insights into the issues of myth and history relative to Native Americans, Greeks, Romans, and early Christians.

4. The spirits within the earth, including those of dead humans, plants, and animals, have a great influence on the history of Native Americans. The remains of their people enrich the earth with bone, blood, and flesh. They mark the Americas as a place of Native Americans, and they tie Indians closely with their ancestral homes and the geographical features found there. Such beliefs are a common, sometimes subtle, theme found within the ancient historical texts.

5. Two versions of this story are found in the Lucullus Virgil McWhorter Collection, Manuscripts and Archives, Washington State University, Pullman. One is entitled, "Battle of the *Attiyiyi* and *Toqueenut*," 4 July, 1918 with an unknown storyteller. The other is by *Anawhoa* (Black Bear), a Wasco Indian, dated 1917, entitled "Battle of Cold Wind and Chinook Wind." McWhorter provided a note: "To be added to Legend of Battle of Cold Wind and Warm Wind, offering the Nez Perce version of the story. This was probably provided by Chief Joseph's nephew, Yellow Wolf. The three stories are similar with slight variations. The best version of "Battle of the *Attiyiyi* and *Toqueenut*" is found in Nashone, *Grandmother Stories of the Northwest* (Newcastle, Calif.: Sierra Oaks, 1988), 11–29. This version of the story is largely cited in this work unless otherwise noted.

6. Oral interviews by Richard D. Scheuerman with Emily Peone, January–June 1980, Colville Reservation, Nespelem, Washington, found at the Scheuerman home, Endicott, Washington. The details of the story presented here are taken from that version found in the McWhorter Collection provided by William Poniah, 1917.

7. On page 28 of the manuscript, McWhorter explained that different tribes have variations of this story. He also indicated where the petrified remains of the rope could be found today.

8. Mourning Dove, "Coyote the Medicine Man," Guie Collection, Yakima, Washington. In the same collection are two other stories addressing incest, including "How Disease Came to the People" and "Coyote Marries His Own Daughter." See also Trafzer and Scheuerman (1991:51–57).

REFERENCES

Anawhoa (Black Bear). 1917. "Battle of the *Attiyiyi* and *Toqueenut*." Manuscripts and Archives, Washington State University Library, Pullman, Washington.

George, Andrew. 1980. Interview by author, Richard D. Scheuerman, and Lee Ann Smith.

Griffin, Robert. 1991. Letter to author.

Mourning Dove, n.d. "Coyote Marries His Own Daughter." Geraldine Guie's Personal Collection, Yakima, Washington.

Mourning Dove. 1933. *Coyote Stories*. Caldwell, Id.: Caxton Printers.

Mourning Dove. n.d. "Coyote the Medicine Man." Geraldine Guie's Personal Collection, Yakima, Washington.

Mourning Dove. n.d. "How Disease Came to the People." Geraldine Guie's Personal Collection, Yakima, Washington.

Mourning Dove. n.d. "Preface." Geraldine Guie's Personal Collection, Yakima, Washington.

Hemene Moxmox (Yellow Wolf). n.d. "To be added to Legend of Cold Wind and Warm Wind." Manuscripts and Archives, Washington State University Library, Pullman, Washington.

Nash, Gary, ed. 1991. "Struggle Through Diversity: Multicultural Perspectives in Teaching United States and World History." *A Teacher's Guide to Multicultural Perspectives in Social Studies*. Boston: Houghton Mifflin.

Nashone. 1988. *Grandmother Stories of the Northwest*. Newcastle, Calif.: Sierra Oaks.

Peone, Emily. 1980. Multiple interviews by Richard D. Scheuerman.

Poniah, William. 1917. "The Two Sisters and Their Star Husbands." Manuscripts and Archives, Washington State University Library, Pullman, Washington.

Trafzer, Clifford E., and Richard D. Scheuerman. 1986. *Renegade Tribe: The Palouse Indians and the Invasion of the Inland Pacific Northwest*. Pullman: Washington State University Press.

Trafzer, Clifford E., and Richard D. Scheuerman, eds. 1991. *Mourning Dove's Stories*. San Diego: San Diego State University Press.

"THEN CAME THE TIME CROW SANG FOR THEM"

Some Ideas about Writing and Meaning in the Work of Peter Kalifornsky

Katherine McNamara

"But you know, grandson, this world is fragile."

The word he chose to express "fragile" was filled with the intricacies of a continuing process, and with a strength inherent in spider webs woven across paths through sand hills where early in the morning the sun becomes entangled in each filament of web. It took a long time to explain the fragility and intricacy because no word exists alone, and the reason for choosing each work had to be explained with a story about why it must be said that way. That was the responsibility that went with being human, old Ku'oosh said, the story behind each word must be told so there could be no mistake in the meaning of what had been said; and this demanded great patience and love.—Leslie Marmon Silko

You know when you're educated: when you know how to think. It's very important to think. But it's more important to think with your own words.—Peter Kalifornsky

CROW STORY GGUGGUYNI SUKT'A

By Peter Kalifornsky
English Version by Katherine McNamara and Peter Kalifornsky

Long ago, the Dena'ina did not have songs and stories. Then came the time that Crow sang for them. Till then, as they worked together and traveled, *di ya du hu* kept them in time.

And so, Crow was flying along the beach. Where a creek flowed out lay on old, rotten fish. Crow looked up the bank and spotted a village. He turned into a good-looking man and went to visit the people.

Only women were at home. "Where are the men?" he asked. "They're in the woods, hunting," the women said. "Have a bite to eat with us," they said.

"I never eat with strangers," he told them (he lived on fish washed up on the beach). He asked for the loan of a dipnet, and back down he went.

A cottonwood driftlog lay on the beach. He plucked out an eye and set it on the log. "If you see people, shout *Yu hu!*" he told it and tied a bandage across his head. He went down to his fish and began to eat.

The eye called, "Yu hu."

He ran to it. No one was there. He smacked the eye and set it back down. "If you see anyone, shout *Yu hu!*" he told it.

Once again, no one was there.

A third time the eye called "*Yu hu!*" But Crow stayed with the fish.

But soon he heard people talking. He walked up to meet them.

"What are you doing?" they asked him.

"Fishing. But no fish here. Only old ones lying around; some bird picked at them."

"What hurt your head?"

"Sand in my eye."

"Let's see," one of them said. "It might be bad."

"Oh no!" he said. "When I'm hurt I heal it myself."

They spotted the eye lying on the driftlog. "Ah. That looks like an eye," they said.

"No! Don't touch it! You'll do something wrong. It looks out for your good luck," he said. "I know what to do," he told them.

He picked up the eye. He tossed it into the air three times. Three times he sang:

"We found a wonder!
Ch'i'ushi ch'i'un!
Ch'i'ushi ch'i'un!
Ch'i'ushi ch'i'un!

He pulled the bandage from his head. The eye dropped back into its socket.

And again he sang:

"Ya la ya la ah hi ah hi hi yu!"

He sang three times:

"Good! Good!
I hoodwinked the people!
I hoodwinked the people!
And took back my eye!"

Now he turned back into Crow. Three times he crowed *"Gyugh!"*

And he flew away.

Then *di ya du hu* became a song with the Crow songs, and they sang them and danced to do away with bad things.

Then they sent a runner to the next village, to tell the neighbors what they had learned.

Now the neighbors were on the trail, coming to visit and celebrate the songs. It grew dark and they wanted to camp. The runner, cutting wood, began to say, "Lend me an ax!" His words became a song.

*"Du gu li
Sh ghu ni hish
Y ha li
Y li ma che ha
A ya ha a li*
Lend me an axe.
It will be fine!
We will have fire.
We will have game."

Now they had four songs.

The young runner had worn through his moccasin. An old woman, always prepared for emergencies, took a piece of skin and cut it. She poked holes along its edge and threaded a skin thong through them. He stepped into the skin, and she tied the thong around his ankle. After the Dena'inas had their new song, he had a new moccasin.

The people built a fire and had a celebration. They talked about this Crow and sang his song. Crow turned himself into a handsome young man and came to visit them, but did not speak.

"He doesn't speak our language," they said. "Welcome him anyhow."

He listened to their stories about clever, foolish Crow; then, when they weren't looking, he slipped away.

"He's gone!" they said.

Sometime later, Crow visited his friend Camprobber and told him the story. "I went to visit the Campfire People," he said. "They tell stories about me full of jokes and good times. When they go hunting I wish them good luck. Then they make a kill, and all of us Crows have a good dinner party!"

Long ago, the story begins, *the Dena'ina did not have songs and stories. Then came the time that Crow sang for them. Till then, as they worked together and traveled,* di ya du hu *kept them in time. . . .*

The story is called *Ggugguyni Sukt'a;* translated, it is *Crow Story.*

The word *sukt'a* in the title is from the words for "old" and "the broth of cooked meat," as the broth belongs to the meat. The word means, "That long-time-ago story belonging to some certain person." It refers to that person's right to tell the story—on old story, or a personal or family story—and also in his or her version or style. Crow Story as its author wrote it is a *sukt'a;* it is also a *sukdu,* one of the very old stories, from the words for "old" and "from our lips." The figuration of *sukt'a* has a pleasing double image: the broth is to the meat as the story is to the teller, and broth is nourishing. In former times, younger people were encouraged to drink broth rather than water, because of the benefits of the meat juices and the warmth of the liquid against the cold.

Now I write this word on the page, *dnelnish:* the pattern that we recognize. The word is in a language one old man speaks. His name is Peter Kalifornsky; his Dena'ina is an Athabaskan tongue, one of four of the same name: the other three spoken by friends, neighbors, but not his relatives. He is Alaskan; he is the writer of old stories, and the writer of Crow Story.

Dnelnish, he wrote, and evoked the way of life of the old Dena'ina.

Peter Kalifornsky is the first Dena'ina to write of a whole people, their dreams and beliefs, their laws and society, their history, their names and songs, their language come down to the memory and spirit of that one mind, and expressed in an act of the imagination. He writes from within a boundaried world, in a language that answers its ceaseless, regular movement.

For some years, I lived and traveled as a poet in the Interior of Alaska. In 1983 I read Crow Story, and it began to live with me. In time, I was able to visit him, to ask if I understood his story correctly.

Poetry is an ancient art. In all societies it is believed to be of a sacred origin. Crow Story also is of sacred origin, as it tells me; and as any great story does, it lets me understand things at once. It is the story of a gift, and of gift-giving.

The Dena'ina had no songs and stories; they chanted to keep in rhythm. Crow gave them a song: that is, he gave them words to go with the chanted sounds (they made the song from their rhythm and Crow's words). What made Crow give them their song? The women were exquisitely polite to him, a visitor and a stranger. They courteously answered his questions, they offered him food (he declined it; crows and people are supposed to eat separately), and they loaned him the tool he needed (which he told them he needed, as any of them would need it) to catch fish, that is, food: I am speaking of sustenance, which supports life.

Crow borrows the net (which he does not need: perhaps he is testing their generosity) and goes back to his fish. He leaves his eye to stand watch: but his eye, tricky as Crow, fools him, and when the Campfire People (the name the animals gave humans) show up, he is almost taken off guard. Artfully distracting them from his real business, he gives them a song.

And what do they do? They make it their own, taking his diversion and putting it to their rhythm. They are proud to be the first with this new delight, and gleefully pass on the news to their neighbors. Now their neighbors can make their own songs. Then the Campfire People devise more songs, to celebrate what happens in life.

Crow is greatly pleased by this and confides his pleasure to his partner, Camprobber: "I like that, so I wish them luck when they go hunting. Then they make a kill [that's Crow's luck working for them], and everybody gets to eat." The ambiguous gift has circled back in a proper form to Crow himself.

The song is a gift from a sacred source—from Crow, who is Raven, the great tricky actor of Athabaskan stories, believed by many (although not by the Dena'ina) to have made the world—gathering power as it moves. The Dena'ina receive the gift that has the power to please Crow. It becomes something by which they know themselves, in their rhythm, in the world; and they also can teach the how of it to their neighbors. The bonds between humans and animals are made stronger: they feed each other, with songs and with food, and the fish, who are living creatures, give themselves to humans if they are treated correctly.

If they are treated correctly. When Crow came to the women, they greeted him courteously, that is, ceremoniously: they offered him food and the dipnet, the tool he might need (according to their way) to catch his food. Everything that happened afterward began when, or because, the women acted in this way: thus, what seems like ordinary courtesy might well be ceremonial behavior. A ceremony may be described as a protocol of acts or events in which the sacred and the secular worlds become joined. The lesson is: Crow can show up at any time, in any guise; but whether he treats people well depends on how they treat him.

So I offered Mr. Kalifornsky a figure of his story as a gift-circle relating humans and animals; and said I took it as the figure of the ceremony of the hunt, which Alaska Native people call *subsistence,* and, *our way of life.* He smiled, obviously pleased that a reader had found meaning in his work.

"There *is* meaning behind the story," he agreed. "There is a compact between the humans and the animals. Crow and the humans made a bargain."

He went on to tell me more about Crow and his tricky behavior, how he zig-zagged through the stories ("Seems like the truth goes all the way back to Crow!"). He described a theory of story. He spoke at length about writing and meaning. Behind the stories, he said, was the "back story," their meanings, that explained and completed them. But first, he suggested, I ought to learn about the writing: for even his orthography, that is, the spelling he had adapted from a standard linguistic system, fit the Dena'ina logic, and that logic was "the pattern that we recognize." The pattern lay in the story.

Now we enter a world dense with story, dense with meaning, enclosed in a circle. We are in a small apartment in a home for old people. An aged man is seated on the sofa, a pillow close, to cushion his arthritic hip; his small dog is curled up at his feet. The young women has just poured tea for him. She half-turns, seats herself at the table, and picks up her pen. "Let's go to work," the old writer says. She smiles and asks her question; deferentially, she does not use his name. He calls her Little Girl.

He explains how writing came to the Dena'ina from the outside, and how he adapted it to fit their pattern. She wants to understand the pattern. She listens wholeheartedly; her mind is alert. Her past life falls away from her. She is lost and confused, she is frightened; but she trusts the canny old man, who is guiding her down the trail through the old stories; and in the end, she also recognizes the pattern. Their minds have met. Then, because she does not belong in that place, and because she cannot bear the weight of the pattern, she must leave.

I came away from him with respect and appreciation, but I write in wonder and profound sadness, for to step into the pattern was as easy as knocking on a door. But to leave it: I returned home altered in spirit. To have taken the risk of entering the pattern of the Dena'ina, one then might well understand what a Dena'ina must have faced when huge and various powers from the outside confronted him in his native country.

What I write here is an attempt to convey, briefly, the sense I made of the pattern. I will describe, as he told it to me, and as I understood it, how he translated—carried across—an ancient oral literature into writing. At a certain moment of our work (we were talking about the distinction between imagination and metaphor), our minds touched. He described that contact: "What we're doing: we're trying to put together these stories, and trying to do it so people could understand how we work. We're trying to put together things so they could be understood."

"I wrote the story, yes, in my native language," he said. "It's written; and all I was fighting for was to preserve my native language. But what we're getting into—how to read the background—gets complicated. From the beginning, the stories were put forward for a people to study, the nations and what-not."

For two days, we drank tea and talked. "I've been looking for somebody like you," he grinned. "I've been saying to them for a long time I needed a secretary."

I became his secretary; and as he talked, I wrote. Sometimes he joked about my "little hand making those chicken scratches." He did not care to be recorded on tape, fearing his stories would be transcribed without his permission, and I was more comfortable writing. We worked easily that way, in intervals, for nearly four years. He let me ask questions, a method good for both of us. Older Athabaskan people, it was said, generally did not like questions, particularly direct questions; but questions always exist among people, although they take their own form. I followed the etiquette of the Athabaskan form, using the indirect statement, turning the point upon myself ("I wonder if . . ."): it left him free to answer of not, as he wished. He noticed the effect, for he said to me, with what sounded like interest, "Your questions open my mind. They let me think."

In his autobiography, he recorded his friendship with a young linguist who came to him in the early 1970s, eager to study his language. The young linguist showed the old man how to write Dena'ina, and the old man began the work he seemed to have been intended to do.

For, as a young boy, he had been carefully instructed by his mother's relatives. From 1915 to 1921 (when he was ten), he stayed in camp with his maternal uncle, whom he went to after his mother's death; and the relatives, whom he knew only by kinship title, came down to camp to visit. They told stories as he tended their steam bath fires: he was the only youngster they kept with them then.

After he went back to his father, several of the old men also took him aside. "But they were taking steps into a new life already," he said. "And the kids didn't mind. But these old men: once in a while they would set a time for me, chase their kids away— 'Go to poolroom, play cards!'—and they told me a little bit.'

"And then, this old man, he was all by himself, and he took me like I was his own son. He told me stories, or put them into a joke. I don't know if he knew the background of them. He was the last person left from his village; they moved him here when he was small. He refreshed lots of these stories for me, in part.

"I'm still puzzled. Where did those Dena'inas get their stories from? I just sit back, puzzled. I can only write it down the way they told it to me. I didn't know what these old people were handing me, until now." He laughed, sounding a bit wondering and also wry. "'He's going to be preserved after we're gone.' What did they mean by it? To relay their language and their stories."

I asked how it was for him when he wrote rather than told the stories. Did he have people in mind when he worked on the page?

"No," he replied, "it is difficult enough getting the story straight and making sure the words are right. That's why I used the blackboard.

"There are some lost words. I had not heard them since I was a kid. They were in my head, but lost, even the sound. But I knew I heard them from the old people. I kept a blackboard there. Go to bed, think of nothing; in my dream I would pick up that sound, that word. I'd wake up, pick up the chalk. I'd test the word that way. I'd keep at it till it was right, and then I could write it down.

"There must be some reason for this I don't know. For myself, in the beginning,

I had no help with these stories. I had to sit and think and get them separated. A lot of words I missed; and I had to *think*. A lot of words I heard pronounced. I would be dreaming, and hear it pronounced, and get up and write it on the blackboard.

"I don't have too much believing in religion as the old Dena'inas said it, but I respect it. Why did I get that Potlatch Song? Maybe because I was left alone with no help.

"Human life is funny."

Writing a story and telling a story, even if they are the same story, remembered from generation to generation, are not the same way of preseving the story. The teller and the writer use different faculties of mind, and have different habits and disciplines of language, memory, tradition. Each has a different responsibility to his story, and to his listener or the page. The teller's relationship to his story and his listener, both at once, is so direct, in the warmth of breath and body. The writer wrestles with the page, with his story, in solitude.

The old man began to write because he feared his language would disappear, as his tribe no longer spoke it: the stories were to be its means of preservation. But as he went deeper, he uncovered layers of meaning; and this, combined with his education, and with some other, mysterious thing, made him a *writer*. As a writer, he enlarged his study of Dena'ina, finding patterns of sense that speaking had not told him, and comparing them with the memories of his boyhood, when he was made the reservoir of stories. He continued in the tradition of the stories, by using his mind to interpret meaning.

He discovered something about the spelling, as well: that it did not represent his language correctly. He was taught that in the standard system, Dena'ina words were spelled as the recording linguist heard them (roman letters represented individual sounds, or phonemes). The old man mastered the spelling and its rules, and then realized that speakers of the four Dena'ina languages pronounced words differently from each other, and even used the same words differently. How they were written, then, depended on which person the linguist chose as his standard voice, and how good his documenting ear was.

Mr. Kalifornsky recognized the crux of the issue as the vowels; there are four of them in his language: *i, e, a, u*. He saw that an unchanging meaning could be represented by each vowel, depending on its function in the word. And so, he saw, the letter, the vowel, ought to represent that *meaning,* that constant relationship with *what is* in the world; not sound, which varied among speakers. What he understoood, I believe, was precisely the connection between the letter and the spirit. In answer, he drew up a scheme for representing Dena'ina patterns of meaning using the graphic symbols, the "alphabets."

"You don't think my native language disappeared all that time?" he asked. We had been talking about how reliable the stories are as records of belief, law and regulation, history. "But I was afraid it would disappear now. And working this way gives me a different point of view. Now, even looking at the verbs opens a little more background.

"Where it really started was with those two words, *dghili* [mountain] and *dgheli* [he sang]. These are the two words I noticed were spelled wrong. I still don't know why I had that feeling that I wanted my native language in writing to be correct. So I took a study on it. And I had to learn it my own way and prove it with the vowels."

The difficulty was, the two words had become confused. They came together in the phrase that laid out an important regulation, or customary law: "The chief sang a mountain song," *duyeq dghili k'eli dgheli.* It was the "word of protection" sung by the chief when he called for a council meeting of the tribes: no retaliation could come back at him if any bad thing followed from his decision.

To show the difference between the words, the old man put them into the following pattern:

> dghili k'eli dgh*i*nli: *you* sang a mountain song
> dghili k'eli dgh*e*li: *he* sang a mountain song
> dghili k'eli dgh*a*li: *I* sang a mountain song

When he compared *dghili* and *dgheli,* they showed him a logic of association, a way of marking the relative positions of the speaker, the listener(s), and the object(s) referred to. Once he understood this, he devised lists of the "forms" of words. He wrote a number of such patterns to show his vowel relationships, his correlations of letter and meaning.

And, as was so often true, these patterns had another level of meaning, as well. For example, *duyeq dghili k'eli dgheli,* "The chief sang a mountain song," was one of the earliest Dena'ina regulations, or customary laws. He had conveyed a great deal of history and thought to me about law and regulation, not intending to write it. I asked if he knew a story to explain this rule, as he often knew stories for important words.

"No," he said. "It would be hard to explain. But by studying the writing, the spelling shows it. The . . . law words: they have their explanation in them. *Why the words are written that way is to study the meaning of them.* You break the word down to study what goes into it."

This he did by looking at the "parts" of any word, which come from other words. When he "broke words down," as he called it, he showed me how a word was a combination made from parts of other words and put into a pleasing and interesting form. There are rules by which the words divide and form anew, based on the intricate structure of Athabaskan languages, their systems of prefixes and suffixes and stems. He formed as well new words to let his language speak of new things. He kept a notebook of these word lists and coinages, which he intended to make into a dictionary of his language, where the meanings of words would be laid out in these associative patterns.

"English is a mixed-up language, they say," he pointed out kindly. "In that dictionary, it says there are all different sorts of languages in this English. My language is clearer, and the meanings go deep. In one word, I can say things clearly that I cannot say in English."

I asked if writing itself helped make this clearer.

"To me it does, in my own language," he replied. "We're talking. But by study-ing the writing, you see the movement behind the words. Then they go into higher words, too. I talk the language, and of course it's much easier for me to study it, why the words are put that way."

The linguists with whom he had worked were from the influential Alaska Native Language Center. Their goal was to standardize in writing what they called dialects of the various Athabaskan languages. (Thus, they considered Mr. Kalifornsky's Dena'ina to be one of four dialects of that language, and the least used.) Standardization was the method they chose to preserve the dominant dialect, because of their frustration at what they called the death of Native languages under the pressure of English. Their limited resources of money, and of persons able to document the tongues as they passed away, or to resus-citate versions of those still in use caused them to concentrate their energies. (Among the Dena'ina, one of the linguists told me, puzzled, their publications were greeted with polite lack of interest.)

But Mr. Kalifornsky's observation, as I understood it, was that their method was an arbitrary and erratic way of representing the meaning of words. What he inter-preted was the constant relationship between the graphic mark ("the alphabets") and the significance of the word, its sacramental connection to that person, or thing, or motion, or position it represented. He recognized how the vowels are associated with specific meanings, which must be expressed *as meaning,* not as sound. These meanings are not arbitrary or attributed, but are given in the language.

What this indicated to me was that the sounds those linguists heard are not related to writing in Dena'ina except by their (the lingusts') conventions of representation. An-other way to say it is that written phonomes, taken as pure sound units, are meaningless in Dena'ina; and so, any system or representation based on them is dangerous, because it distorts meaning.

The writer described to me his anguish at reading aloud his own texts as they had first been published. He could not read his language. The words came out of his mouth garbled. And so, in defense, he devised a corrected scheme for representing mean-ing in relation to the graphic symbols. He taught me that relationships between sign and meaning are, and must be, deduced from his language, not from an externally motivated writing system. They must be represented accurately and coherently, without variation. Phonemes, because they are represented as sound (heard by the linguist-listener), propose incoherence, disorderly variation.

Mr. Kalifornsky's understanding of meaning, I recognized, is that it is given, not socially constructed; that it can be represented and expressed, but not invented. He de-scribed minutely how the Dena'ina believed in—observed and recorded—powers greater than those of the human mind. He told me that the powers of the human mind are great, and must be used well, but that the mind is not compassed by the faculty of human intellect.

He had contemplated the spelling system, studying its purpose, and adapted it to fit the Dena'ina pattern, but no academic scholar would listen to his explanation of it. For a time, he gave the stories out to be published; but when they left his house, they were rewritten at the Native Language Center and brought out in print in their standard system for Athabaskan languages. There were two chapbooks and two books, in Dena'ina, with approximate English translations. These were distributed, in part, by Mr. Kalifornsky's tribal council. The writer was so disturbed by the misspellings that he asked that the books not be used to teach his language to tribal children or college students; and he requested that the tribal office insert a statement in the books, which said in part:

I want to spell my native language to what it means, not the sound. This is my native language that I wrote. I did not know how far off the spelling was until I was asked to read my book for radio.[1]

Because Mr. Kalifornsky has asked me to work with him, there remained for me to consider a question of principle, for a poet cannot lend her talents indiscriminately to another's purpose. I considered how the dutiful boy had been made the reserve of the stories of his elders; how their words had come back to the old man in memory and dreams; how he had thought about them and chosen them carefully. The written words had come from his hand. His control of them was a matter of authority, of the doubled authority of writer and storyteller. He was, I came to believe, the speaker and writer, the thinker and scholar, of his language.

The writer's text is crucial. His writing springs from his imagination, so strong and delicate and mysterious in its workings, so easily invaded by misunderstanding or ill-will, so often reduced by them to nonsense and child's play. In the house of literature, to respect the integrity of the writer's writing, his very words, is a matter of justice, which means precision, balance, the right measure. His words cannot be added to, or taken away from, without his willing agreement; otherwise, they are false, and no longer his.

The disagreement between the old man and the linguists about spelling raised questions that any poet, any writer, in such circumstance as mine would have had to answer to the satisfaction of her conscience. Whose reasoning should she trust? Whose language was Dena'ina?

"This is my language," the old man told me firmly. He made sense to me. His were the language and texts from which we worked.

It had been his practice to write the stories, then to make interlinear translations, word for word, from Dena'ina to English. But too much was lost in this method, he acknowledged: "Every word has two meanings, and sometimes three or four angles of meaning behind them." It was more useful for him to explain the Dena'ina, word by complex word; but I think that the opacity of the American English available to him affronted his sense of form. How to make the Dena'ina clear? There was too much of American English he felt he did not know, and too little of it that seemed to fit over his world. Athabaskan rhetorical style prefers terseness, an almost riddling quality, that can make a speaker's English sound flat to unknowing readers.

At some point during our work, he picked up his pen again, and more stories flooded from him. Some of them he had already told me; others he wrote, and then told me; and still others were texts revised and corrected. He told me all of the stories more than once, and the more important ones, more than twice. It was interesting to hear how a story might vary in the pitch of its emotion, or in its embellishment, without losing its essence, the without-which it would no longer be that story. I heard shadings between speaking and writing, for his written stories were marked by the formality of their tone and the kinds of details he put in or left out, compared to his spoken versions, which were looser. His spoken versions might also vary with his purpose: some stories he told me first and wrote afterward; others he told from his texts, with commentaries, in order to teach and explain as he went along. His interesting tellings danced the *pas de deux* of form and movement that always enlivens old stories.

He found phrases that pleased him with their precision and repeated them, so that I saw why they should not vary. He was wary of paraphrase. The stories themselves moved through his talk as quick references—a catch-phrase, a title, a character, an allusion—and I had to recognize them immediately in order to follow his thought and respond to it.

He told me how to put the stories in their proper order, in four "circles," that were an archeology of the old Dena'ina mind. He titled them

From the First Beginning, When the Animals Were Talking
From the Believing Time, When They Tested for the Truth
From the Time of Law or Regulation
From the Time When Things Have Been Happening to the People

To collect our discussions, to puzzle out a form of coherence for them, I followed the four circles of story, using their order as the good guide. The talks matched the stories, and ran parallel to them as commentaries, even concordances, of a sort. Reading them, I saw how the Dena'ina world had been coherent. What the old man had told bit by bit, in his elliptical way, came together in its whole. Reading, I understood the logic of association, the poetics, of the Dena'ina pattern.

The first principle of the Dena'ina world was: Nothing exists by itself; everything is in two parts. This principle recurs, manifesting itself through the stories, as the form taken by truth, by the theory of knowledge, by social relations, by the partnerships between the animals, by the stories themselves. It is not a dualistic or dialectical principle. True relations are of partnership and completion, distinction but not difference, and not separation.

The Campfire People learned this from the animals. From the First Beginning, the animals went in pairs: they chose each other as friends, or smaller animals chose a protector. The stories about them belong to the First Beginning, When the Animals Were Talking. They came to the dreamers, the men of power who prayed and fasted to dream the truth. These men dreamed, and then told their dream to the other men who gathered to talk over what had happened: the shaman, the chief, the herb doctor, the man who read the sky, the man whose word came true.

The shaman tested the dream for scent, to see if a human had sent it; but he would find no scent, no trace, and so the dream was marked and put into their memory, "like pages of a book," until "later along in human life," when it could be matched—literally and precisely—with experience. Only then, when dream and experience had been matched, did the story, the *sukdu,* come into being.

I've said that Mr. Kalifornsky's writing was an act of the imagination, and have proposed that his theory of spelling follows from the old Dena'ina logic. This is an immense topic; we spent many hours discussing it. My observation has been that his writing promises a continuation of the old knowledge formed in the hard discipline of the oral mind; and the linguists' conventions sound a dissonance between that mind and its representation in print. I would like to touch lightly, allusively, on the immense nature of the Dena'ina imagination, and to affirm that it also represents a continuity—always retaining its distinctive character—with other traditions of inspired knowledge. The genuine work of such an imagination is not an isolated or invented thing, but is connected to something larger than itself.

In the Dena'ina world, in the whole North, everything that lives has its own spirit, and it must be respected. The spirit cannot die, but returns in a new body; and truth occurs "like an electrical contact," when the spirit of a being touches a human mind, and the mind forms an image of that contact.

The Dena'ina lived with many kinds of beings, some more powerful than they were, some less. With their minds they explored and described that spiritual world, the "other half," the "added-on-to" of material life. "They lived life by imagination," Mr. Kalifornsky wrote, "the power of the mind."

"Something unusual appears in their mind," he explained. "They tried to find out what it was. It was not invented. They would talk about it with the people to figure out what value it might be. The shaman couldn't understand it, because it had no scent or trace. When they see something like that, they work on it with their imaginations; or, it may *happen.* 'In the stories there are things beyond explanation, that cannot be understood': maybe for people to realize there's something else besides what they already know, or what a human mind can do. If anything happened that they didn't know, they went out to look for it."

The Dena'ina knew through their bodies, their senses, with their intuitive spirit, and with reflective thought; these were not separate, but they were distinct. What they knew was the inner and outer faces of the world, the material and the supernatural, joined, if not always visible. Their minds and spirits were trained as well as their senses. "They were a competent people," he said. "They had strong minds: whatever they wanted to do, they stayed with it."

Imagination: the word for it is *eynik' delnish. Eynik'* is joined from the words for "in between" and "nose," to mean: Something works on the mind invisibly, contacting it; implying: breathing into it. *Delnish* is a jointed word meaning "it turns over," the motion of turning from side to side, regularly, cyclically, as the seasons turn; and is related both to "nose," and the *dnelnish,* the pattern that we recognize.

Between spirit and mind a connection is made. And some thing *acts,* to connect. *Eynik' delnish* implies motion: the evenness of invisible, regular movement, "the pattern that we recognize"; and it implies breathing. It implies a power, or being, acting from without the mind. "Then all at once, some inspiration, something like a picture, appears in the mind."

Inspiration refers to the spirit that breathes into us and quickens our mind. For the old Dena'ina, the breath was a mystery, a holiness. In the stories, he told me: "It says, 'There is something that gives us what we breathe: what is it?' "

"You could put that in front of all the stories," he added. "or below them: 'What is this story about—we cannot find what is behind it./The story lays a trail before us; we follow it to become human./Something gives us what we breathe: what is it?' "

The marvel of existence: of breathing, of having come into being from some source that we do not know. In the saying, 'Something gives us what we breathe,' the words in Dena'ina describe the motion: going toward something. They indicate, " 'Something we lost and we've found it back.' "

This is life, returning again and again to the sentient world.

"Where did this life come from?" the writer asked. "Some place, we don't know where. But we do come to life some way. 'What is it?' We weren't planted, like flowers. But we did come from some place, to be here. It expresses what we went through in order to breathe to begin with.—Of course, we know we have a mother, to be born from. But in this form, the beginning is unknown."

What is the great power that gave these truths to those humans? This is not known; it is something that those humans were not.

Similarly, but in another form, in Crow Story we are told that Crow gave the Dena'ina their first songs. This story contains two "halves," one answering the other: tricky Crow, singing his songs; and the Dena'ina, alone, without songs or stories. In the story, they touch and intermingle, and each half gains some large benefit from this.

"They claim everything is in pairs," Mr. Kalifornsky explained. "There's nothing in life that's only one; there's always two. Why is it that way? That I don't know. Whatever there is has two lives."

This logic, the Dena'ina pattern of it, was formed in poetic and religious minds. Having *imagined* contact between the mind and spirit ("there's always two"), a human re-presents his inspired image in artful words to his listeners. He gives them the figure of the spirit that touched his mind. Similarly, the first stories came to the dreamers, who gave them to the people: but they were not *sukdu* until they had been tested in experience. (And so also in the material world: places were named descriptively, for how they looked; people and animals were named for what they did, or how they moved.) The old Dena'ina were a realistic people, skeptical and exacting in their tests of reality, as their stories portray them.

The old Dena'ina presumed nothing to be meaningless, "for nothing." ("You hear us say that often, 'for nothing,'" a woman told me once. "It's *useless*. For us, what is useful is what lets us live. It's what brings us together.")

Mr. Kalifornsky said often that his stories were about a way of life that had ended. This made me curious. The world of the stories was not static: humans, he had said, unlike animals, grew as they studied the world and learned what it revealed to them. He had told me how the old Dena'ina tested what was new; they studied what they did not recognize or understand, even to their own cost. What outsiders called "change" in the lives of the Dena'ina, I thought, might have been interpreted as something else by their thinkers. They may have been waiting and watching, to see what the meaning was.

For instance, his language is full of what English calls nouns or naming words, but it forms them differently than this language does, and uses them diplomatically. And it represents in its complex verb structures aspects of time, movement, position of speaker and listener and what is being spoken of, and other markers of relationship among beings and things in time, space, mood, gender. Names of animals and of humans are given to describe what they do, how they move. The world is described as it looks to the intelligent speaker, in its depth and extension and texture; it is nuanced; it is always in motion.

By writing his language, Mr. Kalifornsky saw patterns of these relationships he had not noticed when he spoke it. Writing had its own delight. Meanings and forms of words played off one another, as figured speech. They wanted a quick mind to understand them, or they laughed at their hearer.

One day he wrote out a pattern of words, showing me how they were related, and, just as much, enjoying the pictures and sound that the words released in the mind.

"When an animal is killed," he said, "he 'swells up,' *dneldum,* from gasses.

"When an orchestra starts playing, the music 'swells up,' *k'neldum.* That sound 'bulges out.'

"That one point you can see, the other one you hear, in that form.

"Then you hear splashing water. You ever hear a beaver on a lake? When the beaver flaps his tail, it makes a splashing sound. *Tudałum:* his sound."

Some time later, we were speaking of pattern and change. When I asked if his language had a word for *change,* he expanded on this pattern.

Nałshtunen dnelnish, he wrote, " 'Our mind gets twisted around by something': either, it goes blank, or, something in it changes. What makes it do that? Words like that are complicated to break down. *Nałshtunen:* 'our mind goes blank.' 'I wonder . . .' *Dnelnish:* the pattern that we recognize.

"It's hard to break down," he said. "*Dnelnish* goes into *k'neldum,* the music form. 'He came to the end of his life.' Someone's sick; they're expecting him to die, no hope. When he passes away, 'he comes to the end,' they say, 'as music comes to the end.' Something that rings in our mind becomes blank.

"Music is a pattern. And in thinking, something appears in our mind: it's like that pattern."

I was enchanted by this. No wonder that Crow taught them how to sing! I laughed.

He let out a peal of laughter, too. "That old Crow, he's got his head full of *k'neldum.* Music playing in his ear all the time.

"So when a man gets into the form *nałshtunen dnelnish,* he can't recognize anything. He's lost.

"So the people who go to sleep and don't wake up anymore: *nishich'k'den'un:* the music stops playing."

NOTE

This essay and Crow Story are drawn from *From the First Beginning When the Animals Were Talking,* vols. 1 and 2. Volume 1 is "The Stories Have Always Been Happening," annotated English versions of Peter Kalifornsky's stories, written by me from his tellings and interlinear explanations. Volume 2 is "The Stories Lay a Trail Before Us," our conversations about their background and meaning, with notes. The research was supported, in part, by the Alaska Humanities Forum. Mr. Kalifornsky said that he did not take pay for working on his language. He agreed, however, to accept an honorarium offered to him as writer and teacher.

1. Mr. Kalifornsky's will to correct the misspellings was, by any measure, heroic. He stopped all taping and began to write his stories. He explained his theory of spelling to the linguist, who was also his publisher at ANLC, the Alaska Native Language Center. The linguist's public analysis was that the old man had developed an idiosyncratic, though brilliant, phonetic system; and that he was a stylist in his language. Alaska is a small place, and people know each other well. The linguist with whom Mr. Kalifornsky worked spoke of him warmly to visiting poets and writers; this man had first given me galleys of the book containing the Crow Story.

The writer continued to make his case. He explained his ideas to his visitors and asked them (as he asked me) to sign a petition requesting that his language be corrected in new editions of his books. He corrected the printed texts by retyping the misspelled words, reducing them by photocopying them onto self-stick correction tapes used by typists, and pasting them over the printed words. (Regular typeface wouldn't fit neatly over the print.) In each of the four books there were hundreds of these corrections. He wrote the statement (quoted in part above) explaining his spelling and asked that it be inserted in his last volume, in the copies distributed by his tribe.

He told me his first story had been published as a transcription of an audio tape; he had seen that the spelling was incorrect, but wanted publication and agreed to go along with it. He continued to explain his theory to the linguist, and he began to write, rather than tape, his stories. In time, there were enough stories for a book, and then another book. The linguist, to his credit, encouraged Mr. Kalifornsky to keep writing, but felt free to take any drafts he knew of. Before publication, he changed their spelling to conform to the ANLC standard. As far as I know, Kalifornsky did not see galleys, nor proofread them, nor have the chance to correct them.

In Athabaskan and Yup'ik villages, I had been told by respected speakers (with some urgency and distress) that ANLC's method seriously distorted their language in writing. Mr. Kalifornsky's method was the first I knew of that proposed a systematic alternative. When I asked linguists working in Athabaskan languages at ANLC why they thought he was incorrect, I was told: "It's bad linguistics." I was told that the only people who could read the language were linguists; and that, if his books were reprinted (they were out of print), his spelling would be used, with a disclaimer. "He's dear to us," I was told, "and we certainly don't want to hurt an old man by arguing about this any more." It astonished me to learn that the linguists, not the writer, assume control of the writer's texts.

The reader will wish to know how Mr. Kalifornsky, and then I, put the stories and conversations together. He had written successive drafts; he began again, and made a final draft of his new and revised, collected texts. He gave me a copy and, in 1988, deposited the manuscript and audio tapes of the stories (made at home by him), in the archives of the university library in Fairbanks. The linguist pressured him (I witnessed this) to give a copy to ANLC, when he had not intended to do it; he finally agreed, but asked me to write a note specifying that they could not publish the manuscript.

When I met Mr. Kalifornsky, perhaps half of his stories, as well as his thoughts on writing, still remained in his head (especially the extensive law material). We spoke English, he in the idiom of his generation; I, in an American literary English mingled with local usages I had learned. As for Dena'ina, in effect, he taught me to read and understand the texts and some spoken words; but out of respect for its complexity, I claim only to have begun to learn it. For personal reasons, relevant in another context, I did not attempt to speak his language.

When I finished my versions of the stories, I read each one of them aloud to him and corrected them as he suggested; gave him advance copies of any stories and articles I allowed to be published ("Get it out," he would say); and in early 1988, gave him a bound, photocopied first draft, in two volumes, stories and conversations, with annotations and notes. I followed up with a long list of questions. The new material enlarged the first draft considerably; I rewrote it entirely, finishing in autumn 1989. I checked it for mistakes and misspellings in Dena'ina.

In 1987, at his insistence, we made an oral agreement that none of his Dena'ina writings could be published without his permission, and none of my English versions could be published without mine. This follows Dena'ina rule of ownership of the stories, including my having learned them from him correctly; and follows *ne'ushchwat'en,* the "gentlemen's agreement," that is the basis of all Dena'ina law.

BECAUSE OF THIS I AM CALLED
THE FOOLISH ONE
Felix White, Sr.'s, Interpretations of
the Winnebago Trickster

Kathleen A. Danker

T rickster, like the adaptable coyote, whose name he shares in some tribal languages, is alive and flourishing in America. His tracks can be traced in those
Native American communities where oral stories are still performed, in contemporary Native American written literature, and in the pages of popular and
scholarly books and journals. However, few of the thousands of printed words explicating
the various Native American trickster figures can be attributed directly to traditional oral
storytellers. On the contrary, many of Trickster's most influential interpreters have explained his stories in terms of such non-Native analytical frameworks as psychoanalytic
theory, structuralist criticism, and comparative religion.

Other writers, both Native and non-Native, do reflect knowledge of traditional
Native American viewpoints in their creative and critical works. Contemporary Native
American poets, fiction writers, and critics including Simon Ortiz, Peter Blue Cloud, and
Leslie Marmon Silko keep Trickster alive in the medium of print as they retell traditional
stories and create new ones. They follow the lead of early Native authors and writers like
Zitkala-Ša (Gertrude Bonnin), who in 1901 included trickster stories in her collection of
Sioux narratives, *Old Indian Legends,* and Humishuma (Mourning Dove), who in 1933
published *Coyote Stories,* composed chiefly of tales about the Okanogan trickster. A
number of non-Native critics, collectors, or translators including Larry Evers, Lawrence
Hennigh, Arnold Krupat, Howard Norman, Dennis Tedlock, and Barre Toelken, to mention only a few contemporaries, either advocate or practice the publication of Native

interpretations of oral literature. Yet, even these writers often phrase these interpretations in their own words.

One reason for the scarcity of printed commentary from traditional Native American storytellers undoubtedly lies in the difficulties inherent in collecting it. Not all storytellers are both able and willing to discuss the meaning of their narrations in any depth. Many prefer to let the stories speak for themselves. And even the most articulate, knowledgeable, and generous of individuals is unlikely to share such information outside the context of a longstanding collaborative relationship. Indeed, a reasonably complete picture of a storyteller's understanding of stories usually emerges only over the course of many discussions and recording sessions. Once recorded, the storyteller's remarks often must be translated between radically different languages.

Translating between languages, however, is in some ways less difficult than translating from the oral to the written medium. When oral passages are transcribed, they typically contain more repetition and different kinds of organization, cohesion, transitions, and vocabulary than readers expect in written exposition. As a result, writers generally find it clearer and easier to paraphrase and summarize informant commentary than to quote it.

Even when writers are committed to the idea of conveying their informants's own concepts about their stories as closely as possible, they cannot do so entirely through quotations. One of the most outstanding examples of the publication of traditional native interpretation of trickster stories in recent decades appears in the 1981 essay "Poetic Retranslation and the Pretty Languages of Yellowman" by Barre Toelken and Tacheeni Scott. In this work, the authors rely on a combination of questions, quotations, and paraphrase to structure and focus their presentation of Yellowman's views:

> Does Yellowman consider these to be chiefly children's stories? Not at all, although he spends more time telling them to his own children than to anyone else. Adults in the audience do not remove themselves; they are as emotionally involved as the children. And, as Yellowman points out, stories of Coyote and his role in the creation, emergence and placement of stars, and in the continuing fortunes of men and animals, are told during the most serious of adult circumstances. . . . Why tell the stories? "If my children hear the stories, they will grow up to be good people; if they don't hear them, they will turn out to be bad." Why tell them to adults? "Through the stories everything is made possible."
>
> Why does Coyote do all those things, foolish on one occasion, good on another, terrible on another? "If he did not do all those things, then those things would not be possible in the world." Yellowman thus sees Coyote less as a Trickster per se and more as an enabler whose actions, good or bad, bring certain ideas and actions into the field of possibility, a model who symbolizes abstractions in terms of real entities. (80–81)

As with Toelken and Scott in their work with Yellowman, I hope to present in this essay an accurate and informative representation of the commentary of Felix White, Sr., concerning Wakjankaga, the Foolish One, the trickster of the Winnebago or Hochank tribe, a Siouan-speaking group with communities in central Wisconsin and northeastern Nebraska. In order to do this, I have selected certain representative statements and stories from recordings made of White, and I have ordered his comments and provided transitions between them in which I summarize and paraphrase his words. Thus, this essay is a collaborative work which, along with White's views, reflects my understandings of his ideas and my efforts to include as much of his wording as possible.

Felix White, Sr., is a man of many talents: a storyteller, a translator, and an explicator and transmitter of Winnebago culture, history, and law. In over twenty years of friendship, I have come to appreciate his knowledge of Winnebago oral traditions, his fine intellect, and his artistic command of oral style, both in English and in Hochangra, the Winnebago language. White's ideas about the meaning and purpose of Wakjankaga stories are traditionally Winnebago: he values the stories for their humor, their moral and intellectual instruction, and their religious context. As such, his interpretations differ in a number of significant ways from those of Western commentators like Paul Radin.

During his distinguished scholarly career, Radin published numerous books and articles on Winnebago culture, which remain the most extensive ethnographic record of the tribe. *The Trickster: A Study in American Indian Mythology* (1956/1972) is probably his most widely read work and the only readily available printed source of Winnebago Wakjankaga stories. Radin collected the Wakjankaga and Washjingega (Hare) story cycles which he published in *The Trickster* from a single storyteller living on the Nebraska Winnebago reservation in 1912. Unwilling to work directly with Radin, this anonymous storyteller told the stories to one of Radin's informants, who wrote them down using a syllabary that members of the tribe had developed in the 1880s in order to correspond with relatives in Wisconsin. Another informant translated this syllabary transcription into English, and Radin revised it again before publishing it with commentary and analyses, first in small private printings, then in an *International Journal of American Linguistics* Memoir in 1948, and finally under the present title of *The Trickster* in 1956 (1948: 630–631; 1972:111–112).

Radin made a point of recording verbatim material from his sources in his publications, and he encouraged one informant to write a book-length story of his life, *The Autobiography of a Winnebago Indian* (1920), which Radin republished with additions in 1926 as *Crashing Thunder: The Autobiography of an American Indian*. Radin even entitled one volume of transcriptions and translations of traditional stories which he had collected from Nebraska Winnebago storytellers, *The Culture of the Winnebago: As Described by Themselves* (1949).

Nonetheless, the major interpretive emphasis in *The Trickster* is not indigenous, but that of Western psychoanalytic theory. The volume includes "On the Psychology of the Trickster Figure" by Carl Jung, in which he equates Wakjankaga with the collective unconscious archetype of the Shadow, "an epitome of all the inferior character traits in individuals" (1972:209). Jung claims that the Wakjankaga tale cycle "was supposed to have a therapeutic effect" and that "because of its numinosity the myth has a direct effect on the unconscious, no matter whether it is understood or not" (1972:207). Radin also holds the Wakjankaga cycle to be "basically psychological" in import (1972:xxiv) and, in an earlier work, equates Wakjankaga with "the undifferentiated libido" and describes him as "a mechanism for expressing all the irritations, the dissatisfactions, the maladjustments, in short, the negativisms and frustrations of Winnebago society" (1948:8, 30).

The forty-nine Wakjankaga stories that Radin printed in *The Trickster* make up one of the longest Native American trickster cycles ever published. As such, it has attracted enduring attention from scholars interested in the overall structure and meaning of the trickster myth. One notable example of this interest is Barbara Babcock's 1975 article "'A Tolerated Margin of Mess': The Trickster and His Tales Reconsidered." She discusses the structure of Radin's Wakjankaga cycle at length, comparing it to the three-part form of the rite of passage: separation, limen, and reaggregation. Babcock finds Radin's psychological approach to these narratives reductive and unconvincing, and she draws on the structuralist theories of Claude Lévi-Strauss in describing Trickster as a mediating figure:

> Seeming undifferentiation and ambivalence are characteristic of mediating figures, and it may well be that the mediating figure of Trickster does not represent a regression to a primal, undifferentiated unity but is created in response to a present and constant perception of opposition, of differences essential to human constructs (viz. Lévi-Strauss). (166)

In "The North American Indian Trickster," Mac Linscott Ricketts also criticizes Radin's psychological interpretation of trickster tales. Viewing these stories from the perspective of comparative religion, Ricketts finds Radin's theory that Trickster develops in his stories from an undifferentiated psyche into a more conscious individual to be an assumption based too exclusively on the Winnebago cycle and not attested to in the trickster stories of other Native American tribes (1965). In spite of such criticism, however, Radin's work in *The Trickster* remains influential to the present day. Alan Velie includes thirty-two of Radin's Wakjankaga tales in his 1991 edition of *American Indian Literature: An Anthology,* and he follows the lead of Radin and Jung in suggesting that Trickster represents "the spirit of saturnalia, or licensed anarchy" (1991:45).

Non-native interpretive approaches, including psychoanalytic, comparative, structuralist, and other types of criticism, have provided valuable insights into the nature of trickster stories. It is not my intention to suggest that such intellectual efforts lack critical interest. I simply wish to add my voice to those who have been saying, since the days of Franz Boas and Melville Jacobs at least, that it is important to record and publish Native understandings of oral literatures as well.

Native perspectives may in some instances corroborate Euramerican theories and in others indicate new approaches to the literature. Informant commentary is especially central to an understanding of the role and significance of oral literature in Native culture. As such, it is the kind of information which is apt to be of most interest to future Native scholars and students. When Native American storytellers agree to being recorded, they often do so from a desire to pass on to their own communities traditions which otherwise might die out. White speaks of a fear that Winnebago stories and cultural knowledge will go down the *ho:jarara,* "the hollow of echoes"—"in the end, it's going to disappear and no one will hear it" (1972). For the purpose of handing down traditional Winnebago culture to future members of the tribe, it is as important to preserve and publish White's understandings of the stories he tells as it is to preserve and publish the stories themselves.

Publishing the interpretations of Native American storytellers in depth may also make it more likely that they will receive due recognition and credit for their contributions to knowledge. The names of the original informants who shared their insights with ethnographers and other researchers have too often been lost somewhere along the academic paper trail with the result that they are not cited in subsequent scholarship. Dell Hymes and others have pointed out the importance of gaining an appreciation for the individual voices of storytellers (1981, 1987). So, too, we have much to gain from hearing the individual voices of those, like Yellowman and Felix White, Sr., who are knowledgeable explicators of the stories they tell.

White narrates twelve Wakjankaga stories. As with the other *waikan,* or sacred stories, that he knows, he will tell them only during the winter months, when the snakes are below ground, roughly November through March. He learned these stories from his grandparents and other Winnebago storytellers on the Winnebago Reservation in Nebraska prior to 1918, when, at the age of eleven, he was sent to an off-reservation boarding school. He will not tell a story that he has read in a source such as *The Trickster* if he does not remember hearing it as a child or if he recalls it only partially or vaguely. He tells two Wakjankaga stories, one of which appears below, that were not published in Radin's volume.

White made the interpretive remarks quoted here over a number of different audio and video recording sessions between 1972 and 1991. Most sessions took place at his home in Winnebago, Nebraska, usually with only myself as audience. The majority of these recordings are in English, though some are in Hochangra. Some of the quotations come from video tapes made in 1975 at the Nebraska Educational Television Network studios in Lincoln where White described Winnebago culture and narrated stories to an audience of around twenty people.

The style of White's oral commentaries differs from written scholarly critical analysis as markedly as the style of oral storytelling differs from that of written literature. Although not couched in academic prose, the following introduction to a number of tales which White narrated in Hochangra in March of 1983 provides important perspectives on the nature of Wakjankaga. As with his stories, White and I collaborated on the translation of this introduction into English. We transcribed it together, and he provided the literal morphemic translation of content, which I wrote down. I then arranged an English version in which I attempted to reflect his oral style as closely as possible.

I am indebted in my translations to the groundbreaking work of Dell Hymes (1981, 1987) and Dennis Tedlock (1978, 1983a, 1983b) on the poetic and dramatic nature of Native American oral narrative, work that demonstrates the benefits of writing such narratives in the form of lines of verse divided into acts and scenes. I have found that verse presentation allows me to retain word order and words themselves that I had changed or omitted in my earlier prose translations, and that verse creates a closer approximation of the effect of White's oral performance.

I present White's narration in lines divided according to pauses and pitch changes in the oral original; for segmentation into stanzas, I also take into account the evidence of clause or sentence-ending verbal suffixes. I determined the segmentation into sections A–E in the introduction below on the basis of the same sort of pause, pitch, and morpho-syntactic data combined with the presence of certain clause-initial morphemes such as *a:* "ah" or *hā:,* "yes," and, sometimes, with greater speech intensity. This is the same basis on which I divide White's narratives into acts and scenes, with the addition that I also attempt to display in the acts and scenes what I perceive, at least, to be White's structuring of his stories into four-part segments. I assign titles and subtitles to the narratives to facilitate reading and indicate words spoken with intensity with bold type, and those spoken loudly with capital letters.

The sample of Ho:chungra transcription below corresponds to the first seven stanzas of the translation of White's introduction to Wakjankaga which follows it. In the transcription, an upward-pointing arrow at the end of a word indicates rising pitch and a downward-pointing arrow falling pitch. A double arrow following a word means that its last syllable is drawn out, and a number following an arrow indicates a pause measured in seconds. The letters "sp" stand for a short pause of a half second or less, and a colon indicates that the preceding vowel is approximately twice as long in duration as other vowels. Letters within parentheses have been elided in speech.

1. Transcription and literal translation

Felix White, Sr.'s, Introduction to Wakjankaga

A.
1. á: ↑ sp
   ah

   wakǰaká-ga ↑
   foolish -personal name suffix

   gi   **-ká(h)iňe**   **-(hihi)re**   **-šŭnū**   **-nǎ** ↑
   indirect object marker-to tell myths/3p pl-to do it/3p pl-customarily-declarative suffix

   že: ↑ .75
   that

   čo:ní ↑ 2.1
   to begin with

2. **á:** ↑ 2.4
   ah

(wa)-wi   -há'ū   -kǰenè-(nā) ↓ ²·⁰⁶
them-plural-to do/1p sg-future-declarative suffix

3. ǰo:b-čí ↑
four-intensifier

é:ǰaxǰì̃ ↓ ³·¹³
perhaps

4. ho:xčánā   té: ↑ ˢᴾ
evening   this

(hi)he: -kšéne-nā̀ ↓
to say it/1p sg-future-declarative suffix

B.

1. hā:-hā ↑ (with intensity)
yes-yes

e:gí ↑ ·⁸ (with intensity)
and

2. wakǰāká-ga ↑
foolish -personal name suffix

wakǰāká-ga ↑
foolish -personal name suffix

á(h)ire   -šūnū   -nā̀ ↓ ³·⁴
to say it/impersonal-customarily-declarative suffix

3. če:g xǰí   -ňā ↓ ²·³⁶
new   -intensifier-definite suffix

II. Translation

Felix White, Sr.'s, Introduction to Wakjankaga

A. Stories About Wakjankaga
   Ah—
   Wakjankaga,
   the stories they used to tell about him,
   those,
   to begin with—

   Ah—
   I will do them.

   About four,
   perhaps.

   This evening,
   I will tell them.

B. His Name

Yes, yes!
and—

Wakjankaga,
Wakjankaga,
they used to call him.

When It Was All New.

As I said in whiteman's talk,
this is how it was—
Ma'una (The Earthmaker)—

The sons he made,
that's who he was:
he was kununa (the first son).

People,
those who walk on two legs,
when, on earth,
they were going through difficulties—

That's what happened,
somehow, then,
that's what happened—

Bad things,
big things—

Because they were playing rough
with the people,
so it was—

Ma'una,
it was because he saw them—

He made for himself a person, and,
when he sent him to the earth,
that's what happened—

He was called Wakjankaga.

Until that time
he was called, then,
Kunuga (First Son),
he was called, though.

On arriving,
well,
something wakjanka (foolish),
because he did it—

So it was
Wakjankaga (the Foolish One) he was called.

He brought the name on himself.

C. His Duties

Yes,
When It Was All New—

When he arrived here,
it was in order to watch over this earth,
that's what, then, he should have done—

Those that were playing rough with people,
this is how it was—

He was supposed to kill them.

Then again—

Good—
if they would do anything at all good,
he was to teach them things, too.

Not teachable—
if they weren't,
well,
he was supposed to kill them;
that's how it was—

He came to do it, maybe.

D. His Folly and His Travels

Yes,
When It Was All New,
when he arrived here,
it happened like this—

The people,
because he saw them, then—

These who walk on two legs,
because he was fascinated by them, then,
he started to tease them, maybe.

Again,
because he acted like that,
well—

Whatever he was doing, too—

> He forgot about it, and
> then all over the earth
> he went traveling.

E. His Longing

> Yes,
> finally, he would arrive someplace, and
> then—
>
> Yes and
> then—
>
> The Winnebagoes,
> again it was to them
> he would start to go back, then—
>
> People,
> people,
> because he longed for them.

In this introduction, White establishes some basic facts about Wakjankaga. First of all, he is a supernatural being since he is the first (the *kunu*) of five sons created by Ma'una, the Earthmaker, the Winnebago creator deity. Wakjankaga's supernatural status and creative potential are underscored by his appearance on earth during the mythic time of creativity, *Che:gxjina*, "When It Was All New." Thus, stories about him are *waikan* or sacred.

Wakjankaga's reputation for and identification with foolishness are his own doing. He is foolish to allow himself to be distracted by human beings (in these stories always Winnebagoes). He forgets the duty for which Ma'una sent him to earth, that of destroying the evil beings which at that time were preying on people, and he begins to wander aimlessly about. Irresponsible though he may be, an emotional bond ties him to the Winnebagoes. Wherever he goes, his longing for people eventually impels him to return to them.

When White tells a traditional story in Hochangra, he almost always begins and ends it with a brief introduction and conclusion. These serve as transitions from the world he shares with his audience into the world of the story and back. In them, he will sometimes refer directly to himself or to a listener, something he does not do during the stories proper. He often refers in them to the last story he has told, making a link between the tales. And he sometimes includes in them interpretive or explanatory material relating to his narrative, as can be seen in the following story in which Wakjankaga mistakes windblown sumac bushes for a group of dancing Winnebagoes. I have italicized the introduction and conclusion here to set them off. White narrated this story in Ho:chungra in March 1983. It is not included in the Wakjankaga cycle published in *The Trickster*, although Radin mentions in that volume having heard a paraphrase of it from an informant (1972:148):

Wakjankaga Dances

Introduction

Yes,
one time, then,
around the earth
when he was patrolling, then—

People,
those who walk on two legs,
because he longed for them, then:
  "Yes,
  Well, I'll start back home,"
he said, so they say.

The Drumbeat

Ii

  So, then,
  for days,
  great heaps of them too, then,
  he traveled, so they say, then.

  The nights too, a great many of them,
  he slept and
  then—

  ONE TIME,
  the land, then,
  it became recognizable,
  that way.

  This is what happened,
  this Hochank land, then,
  when he started to get back close to it, then.

  The hills
  he saw and then
  trees—
  Sort of landmarks, then.

  So when he started seeing them,
  well—

  He didn't take it easy;
  well, he tried to get back in a hurry, so they say.

Iii

Yes,
that's how it was
while he was doing that—

Now then—

A bit farther on,
a hill,
a high one,
there—

It was sitting.

From Where the Wind Blows from the Pines (The North)
he was coming back, maybe, then.

So,
that's the way of it—

His climbing,
it was difficult.

Well,
as he did it, then—

One time, then,
nearly to the hilltop,
when he was about to step onto it,
then—

A drum being beaten, so they say,
he heard it, maybe.

Iiii

Yes, then,
he stopped.

He stopped and
then there
he listened, so they say.

And then,
well, it went like that—

Gum-gump.
    Gum-gump.
        Gum-gump.

   "Hey!

   "That's it—
   perhaps, because one of the scouts caught a glimpse of me,

"If he went back to tell the story, then,
right away, then—

"They're getting together for me, so they say.

"Well, right away, too,
well, they'll be celebrating."

Iiv

And again,
when he listened, then—

Sure enough, then,
he heard it, so they say, then—

Gum-gump.
     Gum-gump.
          Gum-gump.

"Hii!

"Well, they are together dancing," he said, so they say.

Well, again,
well, he climbed the hill—
well, he did it with all his might, maybe.

The Dancers

IIi

Finally,
the hilltop,
when he stepped onto it,
it was like this—
well, there,
sort of breezes were moving, so they say—
the wind.

Well,
hill,
on the other side of the hill, then—

A sort of hollow,
when he sent a glance at it,
this was the way of it—
sure enough,
well, there—

The people were together dancing.

Well, they were dressed up;
well, the feathers, then—

Part of them, they were **red** and also
well, **yellow,** they were;
well, there,
they were together **dancing.**

IIii

"**HEY-EY!**" he said, so they say.

And yet,
well,
no
attention there did they pay to him.

Still,
there,
when he listened,
sure enough, then—

Gum-gump.
    Gum-gump.
        Gum-gump.

IIiii

"Hey!"

Yet again
he hollared, so they say—

"**HEY-EY!**
   I'VE COME BACK!" he said, so they say, then.

Well,
they didn't look at him, so they say.

IIiv

"Haaaa!

"Koraa!
Perhaps
for best dancer,
because they're competing for it,
they are doing it," so they say.

"**HEY!**

"Well,
let them do it," he said, so they say.

"Well,
I'll show them a good dancer."

"Now, only I, myself,
know how to do it right."

Wakjankaga Dances

IIIi

So,
the sort of little backpacked things
which he was backpacking along,
that's what happened—
on the earth
he placed them and,
here—

That's it—
a raccoon skin,
they said.

Well, that's what it was—
a blanket which he would use,
really, a raccoon
which was a great big one, then,
that was it—

The hide
he used, so they say.

These things,
things which he sort of backpacked—

It was like that—
all of them,
on the earth
he placed them, and,
finally,
then—

IIIii

Again
he warwhooped, maybe.

"YIII YI!" he said, so they say.

IIIiii

Still, no
attention, there, did they pay to him, so they say.

"HA!
There'll be an end to that!"

Then there
he danced around, so they say.

Gum-gump.
　　Gum-gump.
　　　　Gum-gump.

IIIiv

From When The Day-Moon Is Standing Straight Up (noon),
is when he did it, then,
well, all afternoon long, maybe.

They never stopped, so they say.

The Sumac

IVi

Finally,
one time,
When the Day-Moon Prepares to Go Beyond (sunset),
too, then,
this was how it was—

Well,
he danced with all his might;
while he was doing it with all his might,
well,
he didn't watch **them over there** at all, so they say.

The wind, then,
when it came to an end, then—

Finally,
below the hill,
when he looked,
it was like this—
those who were together dancing,
well,
all of them had stopped.

IVii

"Yes!
at last.

"At last,
they see me," he said, so they say, then.

His own breast,
he beat on it and also, then,
he warwhooped, so they say.

"ʏɪ! ʏɪ-ʏᴀ!"

IViii

Well,
no one
said anything, so they say.

"Well, Kora Tee!
What's going on?"

IViv

So, then,
because they didn't reply, then,
the backpack, then,
he took it back up, and
the hill,
he went down, so they say.

This is what happened,
later,
at the place where they danced together—
there,
when he arrived,
that was it—

That was it—
sort of this **sumac,**
that's what it was, so they say.

Well,
when it's getting to be fall, then,
the leaves become red—

Some, **yellow.**

Some **very yellow,** and also
now,
now, a mixture.

"**Hii!**" he said, so they say.
"Because of this
I am called it, maybe—
Wakjankaga (the Foolish One),
they call me this," he said, so they say.

Conclusion

Yes,
well, that's how,
again, that's how it was, then.

He heard his own heartbeat, and
that was it—

when he thought it was a drum beating, so they say,
that's what happened.

That's how it was,
right away,
then, when he took it that way,
a drum beating, so they say,
because he thought it—

There, he fooled himself.
Hihaa!
and,
THAT'S IT*—*

There, I will leave it.

In his introduction to this story, White draws attention to Wakjankaga's characteristic travels and to the preoccupation and identification with people that motivates his actions. In the conclusion, he explains how the dance drum that Wakjankaga thought he heard was his own heartbeat, and he emphasizes that it is the Foolish One's own responsibility that he was fooled by this sound—he fooled himself. The didactic implications of this observation are far from accidental. White considers the teaching function of Wakjankaga narratives, combined with their humor, to be their most important characteristic. Shortly before narrating this story, he remarked to me (in English): "I guess we have quite a bit of fun telling them stories, huh? Well, that's what they're supposed to be like, you know. It's teaching in that kind of a mental mood" (1983).

Many times in the course of our discussions, White has stressed that he believes Wakjankaga stories teach moral lessons about the proper behavior of individuals in society. These lessons are taught primarily through the negative example of the stories' main character, and their value lies not only in what listeners learn, but how they learn it. In the process of figuring out the significance of stories, listeners learn how to solve problems and reach conclusions through conscious thought. This is one reason traditional storytellers would not usually explain the deeper meanings of stories to children or to adults. It was only through working out the meanings of stories themselves, individually or in peer-group discussions, that listeners would learn how to think and to control their behavior. White has put it like this (also in English):

The story character, he does so many unthought of things in there that it causes the listener to start thinking: "Why does he do that?" It's a process of making somebody exercise his mind to think, I believe. . . . Instead of coming right out and telling a person, '**Don't** ever do this. If you're doing something, **don't** do it this way,' [a storyteller would] build [it] up in the story and make the person, the listener, decide that "I guess it shouldn't be done that way." (1976a)

According to White, listening to stories about Wakjankaga would "promote curiosity, push you out to learn something, to observe and wonder and question" (1983).

[A story would] create some problems in a child's mind, and he [would] think, "The next time they tell a story, I'm going to listen closer to the point and get in with these guys and we'll talk about it." First thing you know . . . the peer group begin[s] to discuss certain things. . . . The more they talk about it, [the more] the story sticks. (1984)

White makes it clear that the lessons taught in these stories are intended not only for the good of individuals, but for that of society as a whole. This emphasis on conscious behavioral rules for the good of the group differs significantly from Radin's psychological interpretation of the stories and from Jung's idea that they primarily serve to unconsciously promote the mental health of individuals. That Radin was aware of the indigenous point of view is indicated in an aside he makes in *The Trickster.* He writes that early converts to the semi-Christian peyote religion used Wakjankaga stories "to point a moral," and adds, "It would be quite erroneous to imagine that this was an entirely new attitude; it existed long before the peyote rite came into existence" (1972:148). White shares this traditional Winnebago attitude, believing that the morals pointed to in Wakjankaga stories are important for the proper functioning of society:

And so, [Wakjankaga], in his actions and so forth, in the majority of times in those incidents he is showing somebody else what could happen to them. Supposing everybody became Wakjankaga, and really, actually, had no strings attached? This society would become a mess. . . . And so, his antics are kind of a teaching thing, although it's on the opposite side. Where they say, "No, you can't do that. You shouldn't do that"—well, that's where he travels. And he shows what the consequences are. (February 1991)

In spite of their function of social restraint, the stories allow for considerable freedom of individual interpretation, since the meanings derived from them are left up to the listeners:

After [a storyteller] goes through the whole stories, causing each individual to think, then your thinking mechanism is your own free will to think and how. And it does something for the individual to think about that. He receives an education which no one else directs but the person himself, if he wants to learn. (1983)

From a traditional Winnebago standpoint, the importance of these stories for individuals and society cannot be separated from their religious implications. The stories are sacred not only because Wakjankaga is Ma'una's son, but because human beings must train their minds to learn how to survive on the world Ma'una has created.

Ma'una, Earthmaker, had made his creation . . . and in it, he created everything that is in the earth, animals, birds, insects. And each one was given a task. . . . Each one has been doing this since the beginning of time. Offspring have offspring, old ones die off and they're food for another animal, and so forth. But what these creatures are doing is what he designated at the time that he created them that they should do. And of all his creation, the-one-that-walks-on-two-legs, he gave him a mind, but he was the poorest, or the lowest of all his creatures. And he gave him a free mind to do something with. And now, he's going to have to train his own mind to do things. Although he realized who his creator was, he was

still, you might say, the weakest, the least blessed of all creation. Because each one of these other creatures, they had certain duties to perform. And they do that in their seasons; they carry on their work as
it was designated for them—except the-one-that-walks-on-two-legs. . . .

And so, it saddened the Creator, Ma'una, that he looked on him and didn't give him any
specific things to do. He gave him a mind, a free will to do as he pleased. And so of all creation, he was
the lowest, where each one [of the others] had control of something, had duties to perform, and they did
that day by day, year after year. Except this one had to train his own mind to live, find out the ways of
Ma'una, to exist and continue. (1972)

What exactly are the lessons pointed to in Wakjankaga stories? According to White, they
revolve around always remembering who one is, one's powers, and one's responsibilities.
Wakjankaga is foolish to allow his fascination with human beings to distract him from his
responsibilities:

[Wakjankaga] had orders from his father, the Earthmaker, to get down here and get rid of the beasts and
monsters, say, giants, or whatever caused trouble among his little people. So, we didn't say where he
came from, but it is wherever Ma'una is. But, anyhow, we have the arrival of this number one son,
and he walked among the people and he looked at them. Of course, these people were Winnebagoes,
Hochangra, and nobody else.

So he looked at them and watched what they were doing, and he thought they were cute. . . .
And his attention came to rest on what they were doing. Now, he got to show his true colors. He was
forgetful, also. And he had instructions what to do when he came. And so his attentions turned to the
people. And he said, "I'll tease" (he talked to himself), "I'll tease this one and tease that one, and so
we'll have a little laughter." "Oh," he said, "They are cute. I'd like to see them laugh a little more."
And, so, he gets around and sets little traps here and there, little tricks to pull on the people, and
thought, "Well, they're going to have a lot of fun; I'm going to have a great time."

So this is where he began to forget his orders. Just like you send some kids down to the store
and say, "Don't go this way, don't stop to do this. . . . Don't tease the neighbor's dog behind that fence
there because he might jump over it and come get you." But going to the store, you have to stop and
tease that dog. And just like a child, so he was. And he—the more he involved himself with the people,
the more he forgot, the farther away he got from his instructions. (1975)

As a result of forgetting his responsibilities, Wakjankaga begins to forget his powers and
identity as a son of Ma'una. White believes this process can happen to people as well.

Now, after [Wakjankaga is] turned loose down here—why, I mean, he begins to forget who he is
because he isn't paying attention to what he's supposed to be doing. . . . See, that's the punishment for
not paying attention to what your duties are and so forth; you also are going to forget, and you're going
to get yourself in bad fixes. (July 1991)

It doesn't make any difference who we are—if we don't stick strictly to our walk in life, supposedly, the
duties that we are supposed to do . . . somehow we're going to get in trouble, and we look foolish to
other people. And we'll also almost forget who we are—we're having such a good time. (1983)

It is clear that White finds the idea of remembering one's identity to be of particular
importance to Winnebagoes today. Very few tribal members currently living on the Ne-

braska reservation can speak Hochangra, narrate traditional stories, or pass on knowledge of pre-reservation traditions. After generations of enforced boarding school and public school acculturation to white society, Winnebagoes face a difficult struggle to hold on to what remains of their original culture. White believes that much of it has been lost and will have to be reclaimed.

So pretty soon that which [a Winnebago] does know becomes a forgotten thing. And then he has to find out for himself again. He does not remember. So how can you remember? You remember things when you know of your beginning, your roots, and those things which you should honor, those things which you should [honor by] holding your desires and what you wish to do and so forth in abeyance to complying with the supernatural." (1983)

According to White, when Wakjankaga forgets who he is, he not only forgets his abilities and powers, but loses his sense of identity with his own body. In some stories, he even physically harms himself:

Now, he's supposed to be a supernatural being. He's got all kinds—he has the same supernatural powers that the old man had, that sent him down here, you know, to do all this stuff. But he's forgotten. He even forgets his hands are his—you know, part of him. He makes them fight. . . . He starts ordering different parts around, you know." (1983)

White uses the idea of Wakjankaga's decreasing awareness and increasing foolishness as the guiding principle, along with seasonal progression (ie. a story set in the fall before one set in the winter), for how he sequences the stories he tells. He indicates how he goes about this in the following remarks:

Have we got him to a place where he's really silly or foolish? . . . See, it was kind of a gradual thing. If you want to build this Wakjanka story up—well, you know, a whole, get a whole cycle, I mean the whole thing in there, you have to start off there when he shows some sane thoughts. (1983)

Thus, when asked to tell a number of trickster tales at one time, White will usually begin with that of Wakjankaga dancing with the sumac, since in this story Wakjankaga is not so dissociated from his body as to do himself physical injury. Nonetheless, Trickster's failure in this tale to recognize his own heartbeat hints at more serious alienation to come. Although White follows no strict order in narrating his stories, he will usually tell a number of them before the one in which Wakjankaga engages his hands in bloody rivalry over a buffalo knife or the one in which he punishes his anus by scorching it with a burning stick.

Trickster has occupied White's thoughts for many years and he has often expressed a preference for stories about him:

Of all these characters, because maybe I lean toward the humorous side of life . . . like the funny man, like the clowns in the circuses, I somewhat paid more attention to the stories about this character,

Wakjankaga. . . . I don't believe that he was really a mean person. He was a character that, just on the spur of the moment, he saw a chance to be funny, although maybe he wasn't funny at all. And he was setting himself up a trap to entrap himself many times. (1975)

When Paul Radin was collecting Winnebago stories in the period between 1908 and 1918, he interviewed converts to the peyote religion who equated Wakjankaga with Satan. More conservative Winnebagoes, however, looked on him with affection similar to White's. One such traditionalist told Radin that Wakjankaga "was created by Earthmaker, and he was a genial and good-natured person. . . . Wakdjunkaga roamed about this world and loved all things. He called them all brothers and yet they all abused him. Never could he get the better of anyone. Everyone played tricks on him" (1972:147).

White claims that familiarity with Wakjankaga has helped him to know himself, saying, "I can see where [these stories] helped me a lot because I liked this character. I see myself in it a lot of times, in afterthought, you know, checking over something" (1976a). Indeed, White believes that Wakjankaga, in his actions as well as in his physical appearance, constitutes a prototype of humankind:

He was a person that had a mind of his own, and you might say that he could be disobedient. There is a lot of things about this character that bring out what is in man—his, man's, way of doing things. At times he is rebellious against orders, disobedient against direction. . . . There is no end to these stories. If you observe closely your fellow man, you will see Wakjankaga also, portrayed by different ones of us, each one portraying something about the Trickster." (1975)

Many of the Native and non-Native thinkers who have enjoyed and puzzled over Trickster's antics have seen him as someone who encompasses human experience and human possibility. Ricketts finds Trickster to be the "embodiment of a certain mythic apprehension of the nature of man and his place in the cosmos" (336), while Radin describes him simply as "a figure foreshadowing the shape of man" (1972:xxiv). Babcock believes that Trickster "embodies all possibilities—the most positive and the most negative" (154), and Yellowman tells us that through his stories "everything is made possible" (Toelken and Scott 80). Perhaps White sums it up best when he says, "I guess, the Trickster, that's why I like him so much. He goes through everything—everything a human can do or has potential to do" (1976b).

REFERENCES

Babcock, Barbara. 1985. "'A Tolerated Margin of Mess': The Trickster and His Tales Reconsidered." In *Critical Essays on Native American Literature*, edited by Andrew Wiget, 153–185. Boston: G. K. Hall.

Blue Cloud, Peter. 1982. *Elderberry Flute Song: Contemporary Coyote Tales*. Trumansburg, N.Y.: Crossing Press.

Boas, Franz. 1940. *Race, Language, and Culture*. New York: Basic Books.

Evers, Lawrence J., and Felipe Molina. 1987. *Yaqui Deer Songs: Masa Bwikam, A Native American Poetry*. Tucson: Sun Tracks—University of Arizona Press.

Hennigh, Lawrence. 1966. "Control of Incest in Eskimo Folktales." *Journal of American Folklore*, April/June 312:356–359. Austin: University of Texas Press.

Hymes, Dell. 1981. *"In Vain I Tried to Tell You" : Essays in Native American Ethnopoetics*. Philadelphia: University of Pennsylvania Press.

———. 1987. "Anthologies and Narrators." In *Recovering the Word*, edited by Swann and Krupat, 41–84. Berkeley: University of California Press.

Jacobs, Melville. 1959. *The Content and Style of an Oral Literature: Clackamas Chinook Myths and Tales*. Chicago: University of Chicago Press.

Jung, C. G. 1972. "On the Psychology of the Trickster Figure." In *The Trickster*, edited by Paul Radin, 195–211. New York: Schocken Books.

Kroeber, Karl, ed. 1981. *Traditional American Indian Literatures: Texts and Interpretations*. Lincoln: University of Nebraska Press.

Krupat, Arnold. 1989. *The Voice in the Margin: Native American Literature and the Canon*. Berkeley: University of California Press.

Norman, Howard, ed. and trans. 1982a. *The Wishing Bone Cycle: Narrative Poems from the Swampy Cree Indians*. Santa Barbara: Ross-Erikson Publishing.

———, ed. and trans. 1982b. *Where the Chill Came From: Cree Windigo Tales and Journeys*. San Francisco: North Point Press.

———. 1987. "Wesucechak Becomes a Deer and Steals Language: An Anecdotal Linguistics Concerning the Swampy Cree Trickster." In *Recovering the Word*, edited by Swann and Krupat, 402–421. Berkeley: University of California Press.

Ortiz, Simon. 1977. *A Good Journey*. Berkeley: Turtle Island.

Radin, Paul. 1948. *Winnebago Hero Cycles: A Study in Aboriginal Literature*. Bloomington: Indiana Publications in Anthropology and Linguistics, Memoir 1.

———. 1949. *The Culture of the Winnebago: As Described by Themselves*. Bloomington: Indiana Publications in Anthropology and Linguistics, Memoir 2.

———. 1963 [1920]. *The Autobiography of a Winnebago Indian*. New York: Dover.

———. 1972 [1956]. *The Trickster: A Study in American Indian Mythology*. New York: Schocken Books.

———. 1983 [1926]. *Crashing Thunder: The Autobiography of a Winnebago Indian*. Lincoln: University of Nebraska Press.

Ricketts, Mac Linscott. 1965. "The North American Indian Trickster." *History of Religions* 5:327–350.

Silko, Leslie Marmon. 1981. *Storyteller*. New York: Seaver Books.

Swann, Brian, ed. 1983. *Smoothing the Ground: Essays on Native American Oral Literature*. Berkeley: University of California Press.

Swann, Brian, and Arnold Krupat, eds. 1987. *Recovering the Word: Essays on Native American Literature*. Berkeley: University of California Press.

Tedlock, Dennis. 1978 [1972]. *Finding the Center: Narrative Poetry of the Zuni Indians*. Lincoln: University of Nebraska Press.

———. 1983a. "On the Translation of Style in Oral Narrative." In *Smoothing the Ground*, edited by Brian Swann, 57–77. Berkeley: University of California Press.

———. 1983b. *The Spoken Word and the Work of Interpretation*. Philadelphia: University of Pennsylvania Press.

Toelken, Barre, and Tacheeni Scott. "Poetic Retranslation and the 'Pretty Languages' of Yellowman." In *Traditional American Indian Literatures*, edited by Karl Kroeber, 65–116. Lincoln: University of Nebraska Press.

Velie, Alan R., ed. 1991. *American Indian Literature: An Anthology*, rev. ed. Norman: University of Oklahoma Press.

White, Felix, Sr. 1972. Personal interview (audiotaped). Winnebago, Nebraska. 14 October.

———. 1975. Storytelling performance and interview (videotaped). Nebraska Educational Television Network, Lincoln, Nebraska.

———. 1976a. Personal interview (audiotaped). Winnebago, Nebraska. 29 September.

———. 1976b. Personal interview (audiotaped). Winnebago, Nebraska. 29 September.

———. 1983. Storytelling performance and personal interview (videotaped). Winnebago, Nebraska. March.

———. 1983. Personal interview (audiotaped). Winnebago, Nebraska. November.

———. 1984. Personal interview (audiotaped). Winnebago, Nebraska. March.

———. 1991. Personal interview (audiotaped). Winnebago, Nebraska. 18 February.

———. 1991. Personal interview (audiotaped). Winnebago, Nebraska. 27 July.

Wiget, Andrew, ed. 1985. *Critical Essays on Native American Literature*. Boston: G. K. Hall.

"POETIC FANCY"

A Glimpse at the Translative Commentary
of Martin J. Sampson

Crisca Bierwert

Martin Sampson was a singer, historian, political and civic leader of the Upper Skagit tribe of Western Washington; by profession he was a civil engineer. This essay introduces Martin Sampson as an exemplary interlocutor of Native American literature, a position that he self-consciously articulated with a keen sense of historical moment and purpose.

My writing is motivated from a passing acquaintance with the man and a deep involvement in the legacy of his work. I seek to demonstrate the exercise of rhetorical power in a figure who, despite playing a minor role in explicating his culture, can be acclaimed to a wider audience for his abilities in negotiating cultural difference. This work of reclamation is intended to inspire additional scholarly study not only of Martin Sampson but also of other Native American leaders who have persistently worked on cultural boundaries and whose historical presences should not be overlooked.

Martin Sampson was born in Skagit County, Washington, in 1888 and died there in 1981 at the age of ninety-three. As a child, he attended an Indian day school on his home Swinomish Reservation. He then went to boarding school in Oregon and to technical college in Virginia. As an engineer he worked in both the public and private sectors. He was a public figure, a respected public speaker, in both Native and non-Native organizations. A perceptive observer of cultural transformation among his people, Sampson was also a creative participant both as a singer and an interpretor of songs and oral texts.

Some of his insights have been recorded, not only in his own writing but also in tape recordings.

Sampson was called upon throughout his life to sing honoring songs for gatherings. At a naming of Vi Hilbert's children and grandchildren in 1978 I met and heard Martin Sampson myself. He was ninety years old then, tall, lean, and physically strong. His voice as he led the honoring songs was deeply resonant and fluid. I felt in him a warm and directing presence. His songs helped transform the Swinomish community gymnasium into the place of tradition it is for such gatherings, invoking ancestral presence for the benefit of an audience that included many non-Native guests as well as a large gathering of family and Native guests. Among the political allusions in witnessing speeches that afternoon were positive references to ongoing collaborations between Native and non-Natives in writing, fishing, and the adjusting to a recent federal court decision that allocated fifty percent of Washington's harvestable salmon catch to Native tribes.

THE DOCUMENTARY PROJECT: WRITTEN TEXT

Sampson was a familiar figure to Native and non-Native people from Skagit County. His publications include pamphlets and brochures explicating the cultural traditions of his people and the major work Indians of Skagit County, published in 1972 by the Skagit County Historical Society of Mount Vernon, Washington. Some features of Indians of Skagit County show us the command of images that Martin Sampson marshaled in his written work. Sampson knew that his readers would be primarily the residents of rural Skagit County some forty miles north of Seattle, Washington. I see Sampson's book as being intended for this specific audience, situated in time and place, but also rich with cultural significance that can be more widely appreciated. I present below a few examples of detail and organization from his book to illustrate, first, the diverse images of Indianness and traditional authority that Sampson layers in his work and, second, his use of juxtaposition to make cultural shifts and convey diversity.

Opening Pictures

The first two photographs of Indians of Skagit County introduce cultural representations that clearly mark historical time. Both present people dressed in ceremonial regalia who pose formally in the setting of a neutral, studio-like background. The first is captioned "Bill Jacobs and his wife, Mary, taken about 1912. They were Kik-i-allus,[1] and are in authentic Puget Sound headdress. Note the drum. Collection of Mrs. Martin Sampson." The elderly couple is pictured facing the photographer, composed as if ready to sing. Her hands make a quiet but ready gesture before her, open, and he holds a drum and drumstick ready also. They are outfitted in a distinctive Puget Sound style that is quite recognizable to people of their culture today, although headdresses have changed somewhat over the past eighty years. Her headdress is thick with overlapping feathers that crown forward, some arching beaklike over her face, and others rising in plumes on top. His headdress is a ribboned band and open framework that holds a few feathers in place and a few feathers set in "spinners" which would allow them to dart and twirl in motion.

These headdresses look anachronistic and exotic, but not "Indian" in a stereotypic sense. The caption is necessary to identify the Jacobs's dress as "authentic Puget Sound" style, for cultural outsiders would have had no opportunity to see such local ceremonial dress. In effect, this first photograph provides a representation that was probably quite surprising to most of Sampson's readers: what "old-time" traditional Indians look like to local Native people. The photograph and caption together establish at the opening of the book a locally specific culture whose antiquity is silently attested to by the date of the photograph and the evident age of Bill and Mary Jacobs.

The second photograph in the book is of the author. In it, Martin Sampson appears in profile, wearing a beaded buckskin jacket and a warrior bonnet; his self-representation conforms to public imagery. The caption to this photo reads, "The author, Chief Martin J. Sampson of the Swinomish, dressed as Chief Morning Cloud for a program over station KFVW. Collection of Martin Sampson." Martin Sampson smiles slightly in the photograph; the expression is, I think, bemused. His endearing sentiment transforms what might have been a conventionalized warrior portrait into that of (no less conventionalized) benevolent Chief. The picture appeals to an audience of interested others who are looking for recognizable signs of Indian identity, a Pan-Indian.

Chief Morning Cloud offers some familiarity to the outsider that the "authentic" Bill and Mary Jacobs do not. It seems clear that Martin Sampson willingly puts himself forward here as a conventionalized chiefly character to bridge a cultural gap, establishing himself as an authority, in others' terms, and possibly tongue-in-cheek. But another point is subtler. By putting his elders first in the book, he acknowledges their priority and precedence in a culturally appropriate way. And in deferring to their authority, he allows (I think) himself to play a different role, one more accessible to his audience. Thus, Martin Sampson subtly navigates time and cultural boundaries, beginning to lay the groundwork for the variety of written text and cultural perspectives included in his book.

The Written Project

In his preface, Sampson invokes his mother's authority for "much of the older Indian lore." His treatment of this material has a different voice than those he uses on other subjects. His published version of the Star Child story includes these words [the Star Child] gave them Mystic Words, a prayer, the means of mental communication between men, between man and all living creatures, between man and material things such as trees, mountains, etc., for all have life which makes them grow and move.

The name he gave Mystic Words is "Huch-had-ud," or "Se-wuw-ead." The name is used by public speakers as a prayer to mother earth or nature to sustain them and to gain the good will of their audiences and control their thinking.

The hunter uses Mystic Words to get close to game and to make his arrows fly straight to the mark. The word was used by people in all walks of life: the lover, the healer in applying medicine, the athlete, the singer and dancer, the warrior, and yes, it was even employed to hypnotize. (1972:54)

In this narrative aside, in the diction of romantic popular prose, Sampson defines "Mystic Words" with an intentionally haunting quality. While the voice may sound like that of a generic Morning Cloud, Sampson's text is not generically Indian; his words describe a particularly Upper Skagit (or more generally Coastal Salish) complex of ideas and their applications and are rooted in his language as well as his family's particular version of the Star Child story. The description of the power of words here strongly resembles Momaday's celebration of "a man made of words," which was contemporaneous although expressed in another world of discourse (1970). The relationships among thoughts, messages, prayers, and actions follow principles very much like those that underlie Silko's storytelling (1979). The indexical and analogical connections between words and arrows parallel Gerald Vizenor's "wordarrows" concepts (1979). Like these prominent Native American writers, Martin Sampson does not confine his praise of Mystic Words to the realm of the celestial or of the natural, for that matter. He speaks of the power both in terms of essentialist qualities and in terms of its deployment. And, for all the celebration of the efficacy and variety of charisma, this former radio announcer adds the caveat: "yes, it was even employed to hypnotize." If Sampson's words are spellbinding, at least he admits to the manipulative (not just creative) potential in his rhetorical power.

The rhetorical climax of this passage shifts cultural reference. For the first twist in his narrative aside, the suspense heightened even by undisguised device, Martin Sampson breaks through from the mysterious diction of "older Indian lore" to use the term "hypnosis." He plays on the audience's familiarity with hypnosis to validate in scientific terms the existence of one form of the power he has been describing. The shift in diction signals a shift from glamorizing to directness. The warning of possible manipulation which is contained here is sharpened by the word hypnosis. Like a snap of the fingers, the word returns the reader to his or her own reality.

Folklore is not Sampson's only vehicle of expression; he writes with different rhetoric on other matters. Some of his historical accounts, for example, are written in a terse, clear, and analytical style. He documents traditional village sites and differences between villages. He also traces political relations between those villages and the families which comprised them, and between Native people and the non-Natives who occupied

Skagit territory. The following passage illustrates his command of historical accounts and his complex treatment of intertribal and interracial influences.

The teachings of the Catholic doctrine were brought to the Flathead Tribe in Montana on the vaguely defined fringe of what later was Oregon Territory early in the 19th century by Iroquois Indians under the leadership of Chief Ignace. These Catholic Indians from eastern Canada were employed in considerable numbers by the Northwest Fur Company in the early 1800s. Later in 1813 when the Northwesters took over John Jacob Astor's Pacific Fur Company at Astor, Iroquois in the employ of the former company made contact with the coast Indians on the Columbia River.

These penetrations of the west by the Catholic Iroquois lend credibility to the belief that the sign of the Cross and some knowledge of Catholicism antedated the arrival of the first black-robed missionaries in the Northwest by a long period of time. (1972:14)

"The belief that signs . . . antedated the arrival of the first black-robed missionaries" refers to local oral tradition, as well as traditions articulated widely in North America that missionaries were foreseen or anticipated by Native people. As he did narrating the Star Child origin story, he writes of the historical relationships between the fur trade and Catholicism in a way that substantiates belief while demystifying its origins. Material signs and human agency are at the center of his analysis.

In addition to historical narrative, Sampson writes tribal histories which are anecdotal and snappy, with personal reminiscences of historic figures which are often sentimental. Martin Sampson also printed in his book a set of documents which were crucial to the political issues of his day: fishing and land rights and Indian education. This section of authoritative documents ranges from the text of the 1855 Treaty of Point Elliott to a 1972 memorandum on Indian education policy that Sampson sent to the local office of the BIA. These texts testify to the obligations of non-Native institutions to Native leaders; they serve as witnesses of commitments that Sampson implicitly asks his readership to honor. Finally, Sampson records several Indian jokes that pit the wits of stereotyped Indians and whites against one another. His style here is rather like Will Rogers's and typical of another generation. Reading from a contemporary urban perspective finds the caricatures anachronistic and sometimes uncomfortably self-abrogating, but a sympathetic reading locates the humor of another time and place. The jokes are a reminder of Martin Sampson's wish to convey realities of Indian humor with the best of intentions. Just as the image of Chief Morning Cloud conceals the adroit actor under an unfortunately cliched headdress, the hackneyed jokes are a form of signifying. In these jokes, local Native people express mutual recognition in the absence of external affirmation. Sampson was writing "out" for an audience of allies, letting them in on another perspective.

Writing on the cultural borders was for Martin Sampson, I believe, a political act. Just as Sampson addressed cultural and historical differences, he made rather explicit Indian peoples' perceptions of their Others: non-Natives. The jokes, the cliched images, are realities of discourse on the borders of cultures in a rural setting. By making explicit some Indian cultural boundary markers, he let others "in," at least to the point of sharing the textual lines of demarcation. The act of publication was also an act of trust and humanity that Sampson communicates not with egotistical pandering but with unmistakable sincerity.

In sum, Martin Sampson's writing demonstrates his self-conscious negotiation of cultural differences. His use of visual images plays in a relaxed manner with stereotypes and cultural authenticity. His rhetoric indulges in romanticism yet also intersects with common sense. His historical rendering deploys insight in the interest of factual accounting of events that are difficult to comprehend. He chronicles political and interpersonal discourse that are the backbones of local communities.

THE LITERARY PROJECT: ORAL TEXT

From this brief survey of Martin Sampson's rhetorical strategies in print, I can move to regard his work in more specifically literary analysis. My aim here is to illustrate his methods in some detail, suggesting that his shifting of language and cultural frameworks has the structure of careful negotiation of territory rather than a flickering between alternative cultural constructions, even though the clear acknowledgment of such constructions is part of his genius.

Martin Sampson analyzed the Upper Skagit oral literature of his mother, Susie Sampson Peter, in tape-recorded sessions with his cousin Vi Hilbert in the late 1970s and early 1980s. Vi Hilbert's work with Sampson was part of a larger project of reclaiming Lushootseed (Puget Salish) texts recorded by elders in the 1960s in separate enterprises of amateur collector Leon Metcalf and linguist Thom Hess. These texts were transcribed and analyzed by Hess and Hilbert. Some have by now been published in English translation (Hess and Hilbert 1978; Hilbert 1979, 1980, 1981, 1985) and a corpus of texts is nearing readiness for publication. I have been involved with Hilbert, Hess, and others in the translation project.

Susie Sampson Peter's texts posed particular difficulties for analysis and translation. She was no longer living when Hess began fieldwork, and her language was archaic and a dialect removed from that which Hess had analyzed. Hilbert, a native speaker of Skagit, took on the task of transcription as a labor of family love and she turned to her cousin Martin Sampson for help in explicating his mother's texts. She tape-recorded their sessions, which she structured to clarify transcriptions and glossing. Although Hilbert had intended at first to reuse the tapes after work sessions had served their immediate purpose, she saw that Sampson used the recording sessions as an opportunity to record his own cultural commentary and literary analysis. She kept the tapes then, and it is from these tapes that we have a record of Martin Sampson as interlocutor.

A particularly variegated fragment of Sampson's commentary, tape-recorded by Hilbert in 1979, illustrates his extemporaneous speaking style and the rhetorical devices he used to compare Lushootseed and English. In this fragment of near-monologue, Sampson juxtaposes a series of cultural frames. In the space of a few performative minutes, Martin Sampson's commentary moves about, convincing from a variety of perspectives. His personal rhetorical style is revealed as a cluster of expressive forms that work together almost like an interdisciplinary panel or intertribal council on the project of cross-cultural interpretation.

In the following passage, Sampson and Hilbert are talking about a story of Susie Sampson Peter called "Mink's Houseparty." Hilbert has been playing segments of that tape and then taping Sampson's comments in response. She is working in particular here to transcribe the words of songs in the story, and Hilbert has just played deer's song.

[I have transcribed the conversation to include Sampson's pauses as line end markers. At the end of one line, the → mark indicates the absence of a pause. I have laid out the text to reveal a bit of the parallelism in it. I have edited out only a few times that Vi Hilbert repeated Martin's words.]

> Vi: This is *sqigʷəc* [deer] now.
>
> Martin:
>> He says, "I'll be just—
>>> game for the coming generations.
>>
>> . . .
>>
>>> "I'll be game for the coming generations,
>>>> hunted you know,
>>>> *yəqʷəd.*
>>
>> . . .
>>
>> *yəyəqʷəwayadiʔ.*
>> That's speaking of the coming generations.
>> *yəqʷəd* is to get this game.
>> Referring to the coming: *yəyəqʷəwayadiʔ.*
>>> in the future.
>>
>> *yəqʷəd* is right here; *yəyəqʷəwayadiʔ* is the coming,→
>> → in the coming generations.
>> But the present time is *yeqʷəd.*
>> *yəqʷəd* is to get this game.
>
> Vi: Another new concept.
>
> Martin:
>> Yeah. Now *yəqʷəd*—
>>> You just—
>>> You just have to get this.
>>> *Do you have it on?*
>> So the people were coming along,
>> and here is the deer standing there.

They don't even have to hunt.
So the people were coming along →
and here is a deer standing:
yəqʷəd tiʔəʔ sqigʷəc.

[Sampson is referring to a cultural understanding that the deer "gives himself up" to the people for food, hence "here is the deer standing there." *yəqʷəd* signifies this kind of game: hunted but also offered food.]

Well, in order to make it plural: yəyəqʷəwayadiʔ,
which is what she wants to do: "for the coming →
generations."

Vi: yəyəqʷəwayadiʔ.
yəyəqʷəwayadiʔ is—

Martin:

—in the future.

Vi: . . . in the future.
That's a brand new word to me.

Martin:

Well, that's a—
See, the language we speak
is only about one quarter of the Indian language.

That's what the white man calls putting it in poetics.
in the poetic sense.
in poetic sense.
This is in the language of the *sqʷəlalitut* of the
sqigʷəc.

[The *sqʷəlalitut* is the spirit helper which a person may have: *sqigʷəc* is deer. The song they are discussing expresses the *sqʷəlalitut* of deer at the time when animals are persons.]

Yeah. Well, yeah. Now listen:
[italics here signal an emphatic tone of voice]
The young Indian brave woos his sweetheart with lovesong
As ardently as his white brother woos the paleface maiden
And all who now sing, "Love me and the world is fine"
To willing and credulous ears, as words express the admiration
And poetic fancy of lovers whatever their race or condition.

"*poetic fancy of lovers. . . .*"
Now,—
You can—
                Keep that on . . .
        just say the lovers and so on,
but you express it in the full language,
                        full expression.

> Now mother takes it and puts it in a full expression,
>> when she says all these other things onto it.

Vi: Beautiful.

Martin: →It's the language.

> I don't have to say,
> "poetic fancy of lovers whatever their race or condition".
> Keep the "poetic fancy" out of it.

> Just make it short and simple.
> But that's what mother does, in the Indian language.
> She puts all of these little extra meanings in it,
>> makes the language complete.

Vi: It's beautiful.

Martin Sampson's interweaving of commentary, control, recitation, and thematic development is accomplished. His statements "Do you have it on?" and "keep that on" show clearly his intent that his comments reach a wider audience. Sampson had to work a bit to keep Vi Hilbert's hand away from the "silencer" (the tape recorder's pause button) during his explicative diversion. I suggest that his impulse was not, in these moments, primarily to educate Vi Hilbert; his vocabulary lesson had fulfilled her immediate pragmatic need, and countless other unrecorded occasions conveyed to her his aesthetic philosophy. Whether Sampson had in mind that his spoken words might be published one day is not clear; what is clear is that he meant his words to be recorded precisely. That the structure of his speech changes cultural paradigms suggests to me that he intended this talk of his to move between cultural worlds. Martin Sampson was moved to express words he wanted to be kept on record, words which formulated his own sense of Lushootseed meaning and esthetics.

In Sampson's first two lines, he gives a straightforward translation of deer's song. His language is deferential to his mother's text and to the song therein: "He says," credits the words to deer; "I'll be just game for the coming generations" translates the song precisely. Sampson's next statements focus on the root word in question and begin to expand his glossing of that core word. Lushootseed, of which Skagit is a dialect, is a polysynthetic language. Complex meanings are built by affixing before and after root words, sometimes in lengthy sequences and by reduplicating elements of the core. There is a concentric structure to word and meaning formation, then, a pattern of building signification which Sampson follows in his explication of *yəyəqʷ‍ədayadiʔ*. He first repeats the summary translation, then offers an alternative diminished gloss, a gloss only for the core with "hunted (you know)," and then concludes with succinct Skagit to specify the root "*yəqʷ‍əd.*" In this sequence, different expressions of the core word are set in apposition to one another. This rhetorical structure—repetition, syntactic parallelism, and variations in augmentation or diminishing form—is one distinctive form of Sampson's speech.

Sampson's third and fourth set of statements emphasize contrasts and are structural inversions of one another. In both sets, he juxtaposes statements about the future reference of the expanded root with statements about the present reference of *yəqʷəd* itself. In the third set, two sets of statements about *yəyəqʷəwayadiʔ* frame a short statement about *yəqʷəd*. In the fourth set, two sets of statements about *yəyəqʷəwayadiʔ* frame a long statement about *yəyəqʷəwayadiʔ*. The center statement in the third set concludes the fourth set. (An alternative reading is to consider these two sets as one and see the contrastive statements as simply alternating.)

In the next, fifth set, Sampson returns to focus on the meaning of *yəyəqʷədwayadiʔ* itself. After announcing his focus, he ensures his words will be recorded, and then he follows with two parallel three-line statements:

> So the people were coming along,
> and here is the deer standing there.
>   They don't even have to hunt.
> So the people were coming along →
> and here is a deer standing:
>   *yəqʷəd tiʔəʔ sqigʷəc.*

What is most beautiful to me about the structure of this sequence is that it is a frequently occurring pattern in Lushootseed poetics. Toby Langen describes the structure as repetition with pendants (1989–90, 1992). I interpret the structure here as a rhetorical device that, like the appositions described above, gives logical equation to the pendants.

In this sequence, the two repeated lines describe action from the two perspectives involved (that of the people and that of the deer). These lines of narration "cause" the parties to "come together," creating or narrating a convergence or coincidence, if you will. The third line is a conclusion, a result, and in a more remote sense even a restatement of the convergence of the people on the deer. The third and sixth lines stand for one another. Interestingly, the glossing is not literal; "they don't even have to hunt" is not a translation of *yəqʷəd tiʔəʔ sqigʷəc*. The Skagit statement is affirmative: "they get this deer." These two contrasting lines, then, are negative and positive statements of the same condition: the fortuitous presentation of the deer before the people. The structure of Sampson's "explanation" interlocks in the same manner that the actors he describes interact.

At this point, I must expand on this important cultural formulation. The verb *yəqʷəd* reflects some Salish hunters' understanding of the "luck" they have in getting game. The "cause" of good fortune in hunting is expressed here more in terms of enacting the communicative idea which Sampson called "Mystic Words" than in terms familiar to a non-Native audience. Sampson is speaking in primarily English words but in Skagit logic. The hunter asks for food; the deer responds. The hunter must act, but the deer will be standing there. We have in this set of remarks a phenomenological explanation expressed in compressed Skagit poetic form.

In the next two lines, the sixth set, Sampson alternates statements of his mother's intent with the future form of *yəqʷəd*. Again the Skagit and English expressions are set in apposition, but this time the focus is on time and the sense of the core's expansion "for the coming generations." This set brings us to the conclusion of the direct explication of Susie Sampson Peter's text. Thus, when Hilbert begins to restate what *yəyəqʷədwayadiʔ* is, Sampson breaks in and reiterates the last component "in the future," his final point of explication at this level.[2]

The overall shape of his explication, by the way, starts with the affixes, then moves to define the root, and then returns to the affixes, creating another, larger concentric pattern.

The rest of what Sampson says is a moving commentary on poetics itself. I see him shifting cultural frames on the level of metacommentary, starting as he did in his translation discussion with some distance from his subject, leading into expressive depths (now in English), and then concluding with comments on his mother's intent.

In his first lines, Sampson speaks in an authoritative tone, using categorical and quantitative measurement to differentiate his mother's narrative speech (and the language of deer's song) from everyday speech. Next, he sets himself apart from "the white man" but still uses that cultural frame to define what he is discussing as "poetics." The next statement, "This is in the language of the *sqʷəlalitut*," although it relies on English, is fully within the Skagit cultural context.

Having established a triad of definitions, Sampson introduces a non-Native analogy to the *sqʷəlalitut* song. "Now listen:" Sampson announces (his own?) poetry. He simply springs into English poetics which he sees as being comparable in power to the deer's song. Here his voice is clearly from another time and place, revealing power, charm, and artifice quite distinct from those he has revealed earlier, but still invoking similar esthetic principles to "credulous ears."

Sampson focuses here on a compounded figure of speech that is comparable in complexity and texture to *yəyəqʷədayadiʔ*, although he makes no claims to a specific comparison. As before, he announces his focus: "poetic fancy of lovers." And then he makes his contrasts. He contrasts the everyday language "lovers" with the poetic. But he also compares your expression with his mother's expression.

> You can . . . just say the lovers and so on,
> but you express it in the full language,
>   full expression.
> Now mother takes it and puts it in a full expression.

In the first three of these lines, Sampson cultivates in the outside listener's mind the intentionality of "what the white man calls putting it in poetics." In the final line, he deftly shifts his focus and attributes the same esthetic intention and effort to his mother's words.

In his closing, Sampson uses simple language, retreating from his poetic and persuasive registers. His common sense tone suggests that the issues are settled. Invoking now "the language we speak," he concludes where he began. Still, two sequences are juxtaposed in his conclusion. The first four lines join his "I" with an implied "you"; the second three lines refer to his mother and distinguish her as a poet. To conclude, he shifts attention away from himself and the listener, summarizing what his analysis of her song has told us in other words: "She puts all of these little extra meanings in it, makes the language complete." And here Sampson surrenders his authority and returns to his deferential position as interlocutor of his mother's text.

As Sampson works the boundaries of cultural difference, why does he use his love poem to equal the poetic force of a Skagit hunting scene? Exploration of this comparison is beyond the limits of this essay, but a few points of cultural contrast can be introduced here. For example, there is no word for "love" in Skagit (although there is a word for desire). And while Lushootseed stories abound with dramas of attraction and convergence, "love" does not stand apart from the world in quite the sense it does in the romantic tradition. On the other hand, mythic traditions of non-Native Americans don't seem to include a place for a deeply emotive power in the phrase "food for the coming generations." The art of interpreting Native American texts may create a meeting place where voices of different traditions come together in order to know what they can teach us.

I began by asserting that Martin Sampson invoked numerous voices in his written and oral work in such a way that would be instructive to those studying and writing about Native American literatures. His oral text is certainly a polyphonic construct that is much more than a pastiche of styles. Not only are his voices varied and his cultural referents changing, but he uses a variety of logical structures. Interweaving these differences creates an interlocking of cultural frames. Skagit and English poetics are related by Sampson; Skagit thinking emerges in English; English and Skagit lines are paired to carry meaning cross-culturally. Just as important is the non-hierarchical structure in his arrangement of voices. What "tops" Sampson's rhetoric is a love poem that overflows in universalist sentiment without taking over, indeed by allowing the power of his rhetoric to enhance, his mother's words. The concentric patterning of referentiality, moreover, returns the final focus to his mother.

In 1981, Vi Hilbert wrote,

I am especially grateful . . . for . . . the stories told by my beloved aunt Susie Sampson Peter. Her stories embody the vocabulary and style which is no longer heard in Lushootseed country.

I was fortunate to have the generous, omniscient help and encouragement of her son the late Chief Martin J. Sampson, as I transcribed her stories. He cautioned me that I would find it extremely difficult to find anything in the English dictionary that would be adequate to the thoughts expressed in our language.[3]

Despite his sense of the limits of English vocabulary, Martin Sampson worked to translate ideas from his Native culture in the language which had come to dominate his land. His work is part of American intellectual history. He never occupied the position in non-Native intellectual circles that George Copway or Charles Alexander Eastman did, nor contest hegemony as conspicuously as Vine Deloria or N. Scott Momaday do or even as covertly as Warren did. His presence is not conspicuous in writing. Instead of seeking or achieving wide acclaim, he was well known in a local community during a rich life. He worked the outer limits of his political world, but the respect he achieved there was practical and not long-lasting. It is because of the focused nature of his work rather than despite it that a study of Martin Sampson's work and words is important today. Indeed, reclaiming his work may be an exceptional opportunity to look at the powerful undercurrents that keep local traditions vital. As a literary project, Sampson's mediation between cultures not only informs the present translation work of scholars, but more important, also charts some ways to negotiate the territories of cultural differences.

NOTES

1. Kik-i-allus was a village location and political group which Sampson documents as one of the Skagit tribes.

2. Sampson's etymology of yəyəqʷədwayadiʔ is not complete in itself. -adiʔ makes an addition as to a house, hence the "coming generations," and the reduplication makes the word plural. But such detailed parsing was unnecessary in the context. Given the glosses of yəqʷəd and yəyəqʷədwayadiʔ, Vi Hilbert could easily analyze the morphological structure on her own. By this time, she knew the linguistic rules of polysynthetic Lushootseed, and Sampson was well aware of this. This is not to diminish his contribution: there would be no telling what yəqʷəd or yəyəqʷəd-wayadiʔ was without him, even though the knowledge of this kind of hunt is still very current knowledge in Salish culture.

3. *Huboo*. Self-published in Seattle, Washington.

REFERENCES

Hilbert, Violet. 1979. "*yehaw*". *Lushootseed Literature in English*. Private publication.
———. 1980. *Huboo. Lushootseed Literature in English*. Private publication.
———. 1981. *Ways of the Lushootseed People*. Seattle: Daybreak Star Press.

————. 1985. *Haboo*. Seattle: University of Washington Press.

Hilbert, Violet, and Thom Hess. 1978. "Lushootseed: How Daylight Was Stolen." *International Journal of American Linguistics, Native American Text Series* 2:4–32.

Langen, Toby C. S. 1989–90. "The Organization of Thought in Lushootseed (Puget Salish) Literature: Martha Lamont's 'Mink and Changer.'" *MELUS* 16:1:77–94.

————. 1992. "Translating Form in Classical American Indian Literature." In *On the Translation of Native American Literature*, edited by Brian Swann. Washington, D.C.: The Smithsonian Institution Press.

Momaday, N. Scott. 1970. "The Man Made of Words." In *Indian Voices*. San Francisco: Indian Historian Press.

Sampson, Martin J. 1972. *Indians of Skagit County*. Mount Vernon, Wash.: Skagit County Historical Society.

Silko, Leslie Marmon. 1979. "Language and Literature from a Pueblo Indian Perspective." In *English Literature: Opening Up the Canon*, edited by Leslie A. Fiedler and Houston A. Baker, Jr. Baltimore: Johns Hopkins Press.

Vizenor, Gerald. 1979. *Wordarrows: Indians and White in the New Fur Trade*. Minneapolis: University of Minnesota Press.

INDEX

U

V

W